Management

Authors

John R. Schermerhorn • Daniel G. Bachrach

ISBN 9781119987888

10 9 8 7 6 5 4 3 2 1

List of Titles

Management, 14th edition
by John R. Schermerhorn and Daniel G. Bachrach
Copyright © 2019, ISBN: 978-1-119-49765-3

Table of Contents

CHAPTER 1

Management, Managers, and Careers

Everyone Needs Management Skills

Brad Swonetz/Redux

Zappos CEO Tony Hsieh believes in happiness. His goal is "to set up an environment where the personalities, creativities, and individuality of all different employees come out and shine."

Career Readiness – What to Look for Inside

Thought Leadership

Analysis > *Make Data Your Friend*
Multiple Generations Meet and Greet in the Workplace

Choices > *Think before You Act*
Want Vacation? No Problem, Take as much as You Want

Ethics > *Know Right from Wrong*
Social Media Searches Linked with Discrimination in Hiring

Insight > *Gain Self-Awareness*
Self-Awareness and the Johari Window

Skills Make You Valuable

- **Evaluate** *Career Situations:*
  What Would You Do?
- **Reflect** *On the Self-Assessment:*
  Career Readiness "Big 20"
- **Contribute** *To the Class Exercise:*
  My Best Manager
- **Manage** *A Critical Incident:*
  Team Leader Faces Test
- **Collaborate** *On the Team Project:*
  The Amazing Great Job Race
- **Analyze** *The Case Study:*
  Trader Joe's: Keeping a Cool Edge

Chapter Quick Start

Management is part of our everyday lives. We manage ourselves, relationships, teams, and co-workers. And as the world grows more and more complex, it has never been more important to study the fundamentals of management, understand your capabilities, and build critical skills for long-tem career success.

LEARNING OBJECTIVES

1.1 Summarize the challenges of developing and maintaining career readiness in the new economy.

1.2 Describe what organizations are like as work settings.

1.3 Discuss what it means to be a manager.

1.4 Explain the functions, roles, and activities of managers.

1.5 Summarize how we learn and use essential skills for career success.

1

Welcome to *Management Fourteenth edition*. The focus is on personal development for career success. We live and work in complex and changing times. Unemployment and job scarcities, financial turmoil and uncertainties, environmental challenges, and complex global economics and politics are regularly in the news. Today's organizations are rapidly changing, as are the economy and the nature of work itself. Talent and technology are core requirements for the most desired jobs. Learning, performance, and flexibility are key individual attributes, while habit, complacency, and free-riding are out. The best employers provide inspiring leadership and supportive work settings full of respect, involvement, teamwork, and rewards.[1] In return, they expect nothing but the best from those who work for them.

1.1 Career Readiness Today

LEARNING OBJECTIVE 1.1

Summarize the challenges of developing and maintaining career readiness in the new economy.

> **Learn More About**
> Talent • Technology • Globalization • Ethics • Diversity • Careers and connections

In her book *The Shift: The Future of Work Is Already Here,* scholar Lynda Gratton challenges us to navigate many dramatic and continuing changes in the world of work. "Technology shrinks the world but consumes all of our time," she says, "globalization means we can work anywhere, but must compete with people from everywhere."[2] What does this environment of change and challenge mean for you and your career? Do you realize there's no guarantee of long-term employment? Do you accept that the best jobs have to be earned and continually re-earned everyday through high performance? Do you understand that careers today are more and more defined by "flexibility," "free agency," "skill portfolios," and "entrepreneurship?"

There's no doubt that your success - in a career and in life - will require lots of initiative, self-awareness, resilience, and continuous learning. The question is: Are you ready? Whether your answer is strong "Yes" or a tentative "Maybe," this book and management course can help strengthen your **career readiness**. Think of this as a set of skills, competencies, aspirations, and goals that will advance your career success, even in a rapidly changing environment.

Career readiness is a set of skills, competencies, aspirations, and goals that will advance your career, even in a rapidly changing environment.

Talent

A study by management scholars Charles O'Reilly and Jeffrey Pfeffer found that high-performing companies are better at getting extraordinary results from employees. "These companies have won the war for talent," they argue, "not just by being great places to work—although they are that—but by figuring out how to get the best out of all of their people, every day."[3]

People and their talents—what they know, what they learn, and what they achieve—are the foundations of organizational performance. They are what managers call **intellectual capital**, the combined brainpower and shared knowledge of an organization's employees.[4] Intellectual capital is a strategic asset that organizations can use to transform human creativity, insight, and decision making into performance. Intellectual capital also is a personal asset, one to be nurtured and continually updated. It is the package of intellect, skills, and capabilities that sets us apart, and that makes us valuable to potential employers.

Consider the personal implications of this **intellectual capital equation**: Intellectual Capital = Competency × Commitment.[5] What are it's insights for career success? **Competency** represents your personal talents or job-related capabilities. Although important, by itself competency won't guarantee success. You have to be committed. **Commitment** represents how hard you work to apply your talents and capabilities to important tasks. Both are essential. It takes competency and commitment to generate intellectual capital.

Intellectual capital is the collective brainpower or shared knowledge of a workforce.

Intellectual capital equation Intellectual Capital = Competency × Commitment.

Competency represents your personal talents or job-related capabilities.

Commitment represents how hard you work to apply your talents and capabilities to important tasks.

Multiple Generations Meet and Greet in the New World of Work

Hero/Media Bakery

The changing and diverse mix of ages and attitudes in the workplace is putting pressure on traditional employment practices. Not only is the "9 to 5" job fast becoming a relic, job choices and expectations are bringing new dynamics to the workplace as well. Consider this set of data.

- 60% of new hires change their first jobs after three years and employers spend up to $25,000 and more recruiting replacements.
- The best predictor of job loyalty for millennials is "a good culture fit."

- 45% of millennials rate workplace flexibility higher than pay and 71% hope co-workers will become a "second family."
- 68% of millennials get high scores for being enthusiastic about work, 45% for being team players, and 39% for being hardworking.
- 73% of boomer managers get high scores for being hardworking, 55% for being team players, 21% for flexibility, and 16% for inclusive leadership.
- 72% of college students say they want "a job where I can make an impact."
- Gen Zers are entering the workforce as a new wave: 72% express desires to start their own businesses, 75% would like to make jobs out of hobbies, and 61% would like to be their own bosses.
- Gen Zers grew up with "native" tech skills but 53% express preferences for face-to-face communication versus e-mail or instant messaging.

What are the Implications?

How do these findings compare with your own career preferences or what you hear from people you know? What characteristics and practices define your ideal employer? What can employers do to attract and retain talented while keeping older generations happy? Is what's good for today's college graduates necessarily good for everyone? How can managers effectively integrate people with varying needs and interests so employees from different generations work together with respect and pride?

The information age—defined by technology and change—has been dominated by **knowledge workers** whose minds—their creativity and insight—are critical assets.[6] Futurist Daniel Pink says we are advancing to where the premium is focused on "whole mind" competencies. Those who have them will be both "high concept"—creative and good with ideas—and "high touch"—joyful and good with relationships.[7] Test yourself. Do you have the abilities to do well in a **smart workforce** whose members have both technical and human skills, and are good at working together in "communities of action" to solve ever changing problems?[8] Mastering these challenges requires ongoing development of multiple skill sets that will always keep your personal competencies aligned with emerging job trends.

A **knowledge worker** is someone whose mind is a critical asset to employers.

Members of a **smart workforce** have both technical and human skills, and work in "communities of action" to share tasks and solve problems.

Technology

Technology continuously tests our talents and enters into every aspect of our lives. And it's much more than Skype, Twitter, Instagram, Facebook, Whatsapp, Tumblr and the like. Sure we struggle to keep up with our social media, stay connected with messaging, and deal with inboxes full of e-mail. And sure, it is likely that you are reading this "book" in digital rather than in its traditional form. But the most important issue isn't what has already happened with how we use technology, it's what things will look like tomorrow. We are entering the **fourth industrial age**, one where the cloud, mobile Internet, automation and robotics, and artificial intelligence are driving forces of change.[9] Are you ready? Do you understand what all this means for your career readiness and future success?"

It is critical to build and to maintain a high **Tech IQ**—the ability to use current technologies at work and in your personal life, combined with the commitment to keep yourself updated as technology evolves. Whether you're checking inventory, making a sale, ordering supplies,

The **fourth industrial age** is unlocking the cloud, mobile Internet, automation and robotics, and artificial intelligence as driving forces of change.

Tech IQ is the ability to use technology and to stay updated as technology continues to evolve.

sourcing customers, prioritizing accounts, handling payrolls, recruiting new hires, or analyzing customer preferences, Tech IQ is essential. More and more people spend at least part of their workday "telecommuting" or "working from home" or in "mobile offices." Workplaces are full of "virtual teams" with members who meet, access common databases, share information and files, make plans and decisions, solve problems together, and complete tasks without ever meeting face to face.

Tech IQ is a baseline foundation for succeeding in today's smart workforce and it should be center stage in your career readiness. Even finding work and succeeding in the job selection process involves skilled use of technology. Poor communication, sloppy approaches, and under-researched attempts do not work in the world of electronic job search. Filling in your online profile with the right key words does work. Many employers use sophisticated software to scan online profiles for indicators of real job skills and experiences that fit their needs. Most recruiters today also check social media for negative indicators about applicants.

Globalization

National boundaries hardly count anymore in the world of business.[10] Over 6 million Americans work in the United States for foreign employers.[11] We buy cars from Toyota, Nissan, BMW, and Mercedes that are assembled in America. We buy appliances from the Chinese firm Haier and Eight O'Clock coffee from India's Tata Group. Top managers at Starbucks, IBM, Sony, Ford, and other global companies really don't use the words "overseas" or "international" in their vocabulary. They operate as global businesses serving customers around the globe. They source materials and talent wherever in the world it can be found at the lowest cost.

Globalization is the worldwide interdependence of resource flows, product markets, and business competition.

These are some of the consequences of **globalization**, which is the worldwide interdependence of resource flows, product markets, and business competition.[12] Under its influence, government leaders worry about national identities and the competitiveness of nations, just as corporate leaders worry about branding and competitiveness.[13] Today's global economy connects countries and people in labor markets, trade networks, and financial systems. We increasingly take it for granted that customer service calls may be answered in Ghana, CT scans read by a radiologist in India, and business records maintained by accountants in the Philippines.

Job migration occurs when firms shift jobs from a home country to foreign ones.

Of course, not everyone is happy about globalization. Take the issue of **job migration**, which is the shifting of jobs from one country to another. While the United States has been a net loser to job migration, countries like China, India, and the Philippines have been net gainers. Politicians and policymakers regularly debate the costs of globalization as local jobs disappear and communities lose economic vitality. One side pushes for protectionist government policies to stop job migration and strengthen local employers. The other side calls for patience, arguing that jobs will grow in the long run as the national economy readjusts to global realities.

Reshoring occurs when firms move jobs back home from foreign locations.

The flip side of job migration is **reshoring**, which is the shift of manufacturing and jobs back home from overseas. As global manufacturing and transportation costs rise along with worries about intellectual property protection in countries like China, manufacturing firms are doing more reshoring.[14] When Intel announced an expansion of its semiconductor plant in Arizona, an industry analyst said: "The huge advantage of keeping manufacturing in the U.S. is you don't have to worry about your intellectual property walking out the door every evening."[15]

Ethics

It's old news now that Bernard Madoff was sentenced to 150 years in jail for a Ponzi scheme costing investors billions of dollars. But the message is still timely and crystal clear: Commit white-collar crime and you will be punished.[16] Madoff's crime did terrible harm to numerous individuals who lost their life savings, charitable foundations that lost millions in gifts, and employees who lost their jobs. Society also paid a large price as investors' faith in the business system was damaged.

Although high profile, the Madoff scandal was neither a unique nor isolated case of bad behavior. Fresh scandals continue to make the news. And the issues extend beyond criminal behavior and into the broader realm of ethics—a code of moral principles that sets standards for conduct that is "good" and "right" versus "bad" and "wrong."[17] At the end of the day we depend on individuals, working at all organizational levels, to behave in ethical ways. Even though ethics failures get most of the publicity, you'll find many examples of managers who show good moral leadership and integrity. Believing that most CEOs are overpaid, the former CEO of Dial Corporation, Herb Baum, once gave his annual bonus to the firm's lowest-paid workers.[18] In his book *The Transparent Leader,* he argues that integrity is a key to leadership success and that an organization's ethical tone starts at the top.

> **Ethics** set moral standards of what is "good" and "right" in one's behavior.

A good indicator of ethics in organizations is the emphasis given to social responsibility and sustainability practices. Patagonia, for example, states its commitment to a *responsible economy* "that allows healthy communities, creates meaningful work, and takes from the earth only what it can replenish."[19] Another ethics indicator is the strength of corporate governance. Think of it as the oversight of top management decisions, corporate strategy, and financial reporting by a company's board of directors.

> **Corporate governance** is the active oversight of management decisions and performance by a company's board of directors.

Diversity

The term workforce diversity describes the composition of a workforce in terms of gender, age, race, ethnicity, religion, sexual orientation, and able-bodiedness.[20] Members of minority groups now constitute more than one-third of the U.S. population, and women may soon outnumber men in the U.S. workforce.[21] By the year 2050, African Americans, Native Americans, Asians, and Hispanics will be the new majority, and by 2050 the U.S. Census Bureau expects that more than 20% of the population will be at least 65 years old.

> **Workforce diversity** describes workers' differences in terms of gender, race, age, ethnicity, religion, sexual orientation, and able-bodiedness.

Despite these changes, the way we deal with diversity in the workplace remains complicated. Women now lead at least a dozen S&P 500 companies, but they still hold just a small

---

Ethics: Know Right from Wrong | Subtleties in social media postings can contribute to discrimination in the recruitment process.

Social Media Searches Linked with Discrimination in Hiring

Jakob Helbig/Cultura/Getty Images

It's no secret that many employers gather information and impressions about job candidates from their social media feeds. It is also well known that inappropriate postings can hurt you. So much so that its always wise to double-check and to edit the bad things out of public profiles. But research also suggests that subtleties in social media postings can contribute to discrimination in the recruitment process.

Researchers in one study distributed 4,000 résumés to job posting sites and associated the résumés with Facebook profiles offering subtle cues—background photos and quotes, for example, on the candidates' religion (Muslim or Christian) and sexuality (gay or straight). Results showed that Muslims (2%) were less likely to be called for follow-up interviews than Christians (17%). Sexuality cues made no significant difference in call-back rates.

It's against U.S. employment law to use religion or sexuality as hiring criteria, but discrimination based on social media investigations can be unconscious rather than intentional, with the employer showing the bias without realizing it. Other social media cues at risk of discriminatory behavior are photos of women showing pregnancies or children, and applicants with names often associated with ethnic, racial, or religious communities.

Where Do You Stand?

Privacy settings are intended to shield from public consumption information intended only for friends. But does this go far enough to protect individual privacy? Is it ethical for employers to use social media to "peek" at the personal lives of prospective candidates? Should there be strict laws preventing them from doing so? What about individual responsibility? Shouldn't job seekers already be informed enough to rigorously screen out potentially harmful and discriminatory information? Are job seekers at fault if negative consequences result when they don't? How about it, is it time for you to conduct a personal social media review and edit?

percentage of top jobs in large firms in the United States and worldwide.[22] People of color hold just 11% of executive jobs and African American women hold just 2% of middle management jobs in the Fortune 500.[23] Furthermore, a McKinsey & Co. survey shows that the proportion of management jobs held by women decreases with each step up the corporate hierarchy. This **leaking pipeline problem** occurs when otherwise qualified and high-performing women face obstacles that cause them to drop out of upward career paths.[24]

Why aren't there more women and people of color leading and moving up in organizations? To what extent does diversity bias influence recruitment, selection, and promotion decisions? Even though U.S. laws prevent such practices, the reality is that they still exist. Researchers, for example, have found that résumés with white-sounding first names like Brett receive 50% more responses from employers than equivalent résumés with black-sounding first names such as Kareem.[25] Researchers also note that white leaders are viewed as more successful than minority leaders, and that white leaders are perceived to succeed because of competence while non-white leaders are perceived to succeed despite incompetence.[26]

The stage for diversity bias is set by **prejudice**—which is the display of negative, irrational opinions and attitudes toward people who are different from us. An example is lingering prejudice against working mothers. The nonprofit Families and Work Institute reported that in 2008 67% of men and 80% of women believed that mothers can be good employees.[27] Would there be 100% support for working mothers today? If not, why?

Prejudice becomes active **discrimination** when minorities are unfairly treated and denied the full benefits of organizational membership. How, for example, do you account for a study that sent faux résumés to recruiters and found that the least desirable candidates were women with children?[28] What about a supervisor who refuses to promote a working mother for fear that parenting responsibilities will make it hard for her to do a good job? Such acts of discrimination give rise to the leaking pipeline problem and create the **glass ceiling effect**, an invisible barrier or ceiling that prevents the career advancement of women and minorities.

A troublesome source of workplace discrimination is **implicit bias**, also called **unconscious bias**. It is an embedded prejudice that is largely unconscious but still results in the discriminatory treatment of others. The Kirwan Institute for the Study of Race and Ethnicity says these biases "are activated involuntarily and without an individual's awareness or intentional control."[29] In other words, unconscious bias is something we aren't aware of and that affects our decisions and behaviors is ways that we don't realize. According to the Kirwan Institute, implicit biases "develop over the course of a lifetime beginning at a very early age through exposure to direct and indirect messages."[30]

Careers and Connections

When the economy is down and employment markets are tight, finding a career entry point can be very difficult. It always pays to remember the importance of online résumés and job searches, and the power of social networking with established professionals. In addition, job seekers should consider internships as pathways to first-job placements. But everything still depends on the mix of skills you can offer a potential employer and how well you communicate those skills. Picture yourself in a job interview. The recruiter asks this question: "What can you do for us?" How do you reply? Your answer can set the stage for your career success . . . or something less.

British scholar and consultant Charles Handy uses the analogy of the **shamrock organization** to highlight the challenges of developing skill portfolios that fit the new workplace.[31] The first leaf in the shamrock is a core group of permanent, full-time employees who follow standard career paths. The number of people in this first leaf is shrinking—and it's shrinking fast.[32] They are being replaced by a second leaf of "freelancers" and "independent contractors" who offer specialized skills and talents on a contract basis, then change employers when projects are completed.[33] Full-time employees are also being replaced by a third leaf of temporary part-timers. They often work without benefits and are the first to lose their jobs when an employer runs into economic difficulties.

The fact is that you will have to succeed in a **free-agent and on-demand economy**, where people change jobs often and take "gigs" on flexible contracts with a shifting mix of

---

The **leaking pipeline problem** occurs when women face obstacles that cause them to drop out of upward career paths.

Prejudice is the display of negative, irrational attitudes toward people who are different from us.

Discrimination actively denies minority members the full benefits of organizational membership.

The **glass ceiling effect** is an invisible barrier limiting career advancement of women and minorities.

Implicit bias or **unconscious bias** is an embedded prejudice that is largely unconscious and that results in the discriminatory treatment of others.

A **shamrock organization** operates with a core group of full-time long-term workers supported by others who work on contracts and part-time.

In a **free-agent and on-demand economy** people change jobs often and take "gigs" on flexible contracts with a shifting mix of employers.

employers over time. They must be carefully maintained and upgraded continuously. All this places a premium on your capacity for **self-management**—being able to assess yourself realistically, recognize strengths and weaknesses, make constructive changes, and manage your personal development. Take a moment to consider the early career survival skills listed here.[34]

Self-management is the ability to understand oneself, exercise initiative, accept responsibility, and learn from experience.

- *Mastery:* You need to be good at something; you need to be able to contribute real value to your employer.
- *Networking:* You need to know people and get connected; networking with others within and outside the organization is essential.
- *Entrepreneurship:* You must act as if you are running your own business, spotting ideas and opportunities and pursuing them.
- *Technology:* You have to embrace technology; you have to stay up-to-date and fully utilize all that is available.
- *Marketing:* You need to communicate your successes and progress—both yours personally and those of your work team.
- *Renewal:* You need to learn and change continuously, always improving yourself for the future.

Connections really count in the free-agent economy. They open doors to opportunities and resources that otherwise wouldn't be available. People with connections have access to valuable information about jobs and often get more interviews and better jobs than those without connections. While in the past the best connections may have been limited to people who had gone to the "right" kinds of schools or came from the "right" kinds of families, this is no longer the case. **Social networking** tools—such as LinkedIn, Facebook, and Reddit—that bring together users with similar interests have become a great equalizer. They make connecting much easier and more democratic than ever before. Importantly, they can help you make connections for job searches and career advancement.

Social networking is the use of dedicated websites and applications to connect people having similar interests.

Learning Check

LEARNING OBJECTIVE 1.1

Summarize the challenges of working in the new economy.

Be Sure You Can • describe how intellectual capital, ethics, diversity, globalization, technology, and the changing nature of careers influence working in the new economy • define *intellectual capital, workforce diversity,* and *globalization* • explain how prejudice, discrimination, and the glass ceiling can hurt people at work

1.2 | Organizations

LEARNING OBJECTIVE 1.2

Describe what organizations are like as work settings.

WileyPLUS

See Author Video

> **Learn More About**
>
> Organizational purpose • Organizations as systems • Organizational performance • Changing nature of organizations

As pointed out earlier, what happens from this point forward in your career is largely up to you. So, let's start with organizations. In order to make good employment choices and perform well in a career, you need to understand the nature of organizations and recognize how they work as complex systems.

Organizational Purpose

An **organization** is a collection of people working together to achieve a common purpose.

An **organization** is a collection of people working together to achieve a common purpose. It enables its members to perform tasks far beyond any single individual. This description applies to organizations of all sizes and types from large corporations to small businesses, as well as nonprofit organizations such as schools, government agencies, and community hospitals.

The broad purpose of any organization is to provide goods or services valued to customers and clients. A clear sense of purpose tied to "quality products and services," "customer satisfaction," and "social responsibility" can be an important source of organizational strength and performance advantage. IBM's former CEO, Samuel Palmisano, once said: "One simple way to assess the impact of any organization is to ask the question: How is the world different because it existed?"[35] Whole Foods founder John Mackey answers by saying: "I think that business has a noble purpose. It means that businesses serve society. They produce goods and services that make people's lives better." On the Whole Foods website this is stated as a commitment to "Whole Foods—Whole People—Whole Planet."[36]

Organizations as Systems

An **open system** transforms resource inputs from the environment into product outputs.

All organizations are **open systems** that interact with their environments. They do so in a continual process of obtaining resource inputs—people, information, resources, and capital—and transforming them into outputs in the form of finished goods and services for customers.[37]

As shown in **Figure 1.1**, feedback from the environment indicates how well an organization is doing and influences future actions. When Starbucks started a customer blog, for example, requests for speedier service popped up. The company quickly made changes that eliminated required signatures on credit card charges less than $25. Salesforce.com is another company that thrives on feedback. It set up a website called Idea Exchange to get customer suggestions, even asking them at one point to vote on a possible name change—the response was "No!"[38] Gathering and listening to customer feedback is important; without loyal customers, a business can't survive. When you hear or read about bankruptcies, they are stark testimonies to this fact of the marketplace.

Organizational Performance

Organizations create value when they use resources to produce good products and take care of their customers. When operations add value to the original cost of resource inputs, then a

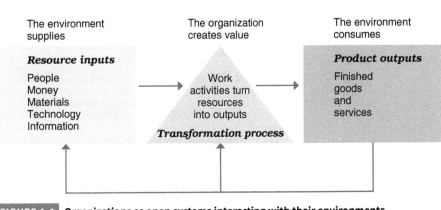

FIGURE 1.1 **Organizations as open systems interacting with their environments.**

business can earn a profit—selling a product for more than the costs of making it, and a non-profit organization can add wealth to society—providing a public service like fire protection that is worth more than its cost.

One of the most common ways to assess performance is **productivity**. It measures the quantity and quality of outputs relative to the cost of inputs. And as **Figure 1.2** shows, productivity involves both performance effectiveness and performance efficiency.

Productivity is the quantity and quality of work performance, with resource utilization considered.

Performance effectiveness is an output measure of task or goal accomplishment. If you are working as a software engineer for a computer game developer, performance effectiveness may mean that you meet a daily production target in terms of the quantity and quality of lines of code written. This productivity helps the company meet customer demands for timely delivery of high-quality gaming products.

Performance effectiveness is an output measure of task or goal accomplishment.

Performance efficiency is an input measure of the resource costs associated with goal accomplishment. Returning to the gaming example, the most efficient software production is accomplished at a minimum cost in materials and labor. If you produce fewer lines of code in a day than you are capable of, this amounts to inefficiency; if you make lots of mistakes that require extensive rewrites, this is also inefficient work. Inefficiencies drive up costs and reduce productivity.

Performance efficiency is an input measure of resource cost associated with goal accomplishment.

Changing Nature of Organizations

Change is a continuing theme in our society, and organizations are no exception. The following list shows some organizational trends and transitions relevant to the study of management.[39]

- *Focus on valuing human capital:* The premium is on high-involvement work settings that rally the knowledge, experience, and commitment of all members.
- *Demise of "command-and-control":* Traditional top-down "do as I say" bosses are giving way to participatory bosses who treat people with respect.
- *Emphasis on teamwork:* Organizations are becoming less hierarchical and more driven by teamwork that pools talents for creative problem solving.
- *Preeminence of technology:* Developments in computer and information technology keep changing the way organizations operate and how people work.
- *Importance of networking:* Organizations and their members are networked for intense, real-time communication and coordination.
- *New workforce expectations:* A new generation of workers is less tolerant of hierarchy, attentive to performance merit, more informal, and concerned for work–life balance.
- *Concern for sustainability:* Social values call for more attention on the preservation of natural resources for future generations and understanding how work affects human well-being.

Goal Attainment	Resource Utilization: Poor	Resource Utilization: Good
High	**Effective but not efficient** • Goals achieved • Resources wasted	**Effective and efficient** • Goals achieved • No wasted resources **High productivity**
Low	**Neither effective nor efficient** • Goals not achieved • Resources wasted	**Not effective but efficient** • Goals not achieved • No wasted resources

FIGURE 1.2 Productivity and the dimensions of organizational performance.

LEARNING OBJECTIVE 1.2

Describe what organizations are like as work settings.

Be Sure You Can • describe how organizations operate as open systems • explain productivity as a measure of organizational performance • distinguish between performance effectiveness and performance efficiency • list several ways in which organizations are changing today

1.3   Managers

LEARNING OBJECTIVE 1.3

Discuss what it means to be a manager.

> **Learn More About**
>
> What is a manager? • Levels of managers • Types of managers • Managerial performance • Changing nature of managerial work

In an article titled "Putting People First for Organizational Success," Jeffrey Pfeffer and John F. Veiga argue forcefully that organizations perform better when they treat their members better.[40] Managers in these high-performing organizations don't treat people as costs to be controlled; they treat them as valuable strategic assets to be carefully nurtured and developed. So, who are today's managers and just what do they do?

What Is a Manager?

A **manager** is a person who supports, activates, and is responsible for the work of others.

You find them in all organizations and with a wide variety of job titles—team leader, department head, supervisor, project manager, president, administrator, and more. We call them **managers**, people who directly support, supervise, and help activate the work efforts and performance accomplishments of others. Whether they are called direct reports, team members, work associates, or subordinates, these "other people" are the essential human resources whose contributions represent the real work of the organization. And as pointed out by management scholar Henry Mintzberg, being a manager remains an important and socially responsible job. "No job is more vital to our society than that of the manager," he says. "It is the manager who determines whether our social institutions serve us well or whether they squander our talents and resources."[41]

Levels of Managers

Members of a **board of directors** or board of trustees are supposed to make sure an organization is well run and managed in a lawful and ethical manner.

At the highest levels of organizations we find a **board of directors** whose members are elected by stockholders to represent their ownership interests. In nonprofit organizations such as a hospital or university, this is often called a *board of trustees,* and may be elected by local citizens, appointed by government bodies, or invited by existing members. The basic responsibilities of board members are the same in both business and the public sector—to make sure the organization is well run and managed in a lawful and ethical manner.[42]

Want Vacation? No Problem, Take as Much as You Want

Gareth Cattermole/Getty Images Entertainment/Getty Images

How about a job with "unlimited" vacation? Sounds unreal, doesn't it? But don't be too fast to dismiss the idea. Some fashion-forward employers are already doing it. Netflix is one. The firm prizes what CEO Reed Hastings calls its "freedom and responsibility culture." One of the things that brings this culture to life is how vacation time is handled. Hastings says this about the Netflix

culture and vacation policy: "We want responsible people who are self-motivating and self-disciplined, and we reward them with freedom. The best example is our vacation policy. It's simple and understandable: We don't have one. We focus on what people get done, not on how many days they worked."

Netflix used to follow what Hastings calls a "standard vacation model," but finally realized it was just "an industrial era habit." He wonders why employers should track vacation days when people don't keep track of the number of hours they work? And he sets the example. "I make sure to take lots of vacation . . . ," says Hastings, "and I do some of my creative thinking on vacation."

While not common yet, the employer review website Glassdoor identifies a number of "cool companies" that offer unlimited vacation days. The policies vary, but Hubspot, Dropbox, Github, Workday, and KeepTruckin are among the current examples where flexible vacation time is a valued job perk.

Your Take?

So, is this approach to vacation time something that more employers should be planning? Is it the next hot thing you're going to add to your employment "wish list'? What are the risks and limits for employers, if any? How about the "motivation" issues? Would this be a turn-on for you, something that would keep you productive and loyal? If unlimited vacation time is such a good idea, why aren't more employers doing it?

Common job titles just below the board level are chief executive officer (CEO), chief operating officer (COO), chief financial officer (CFO), chief information officer (CIO), chief diversity officer (CDO), president, and vice president. These **top managers** constitute an executive team that reports to the board and is responsible for the performance of an organization as a whole or for one of its larger parts. They are supposed to set strategy and lead the organization consistent with its purpose and mission. They must pay special attention to the external environment and stay alert to potential long-run problems and opportunities. The best top managers are strategic thinkers who make good decisions under highly competitive and uncertain conditions. A CEO at Procter & Gamble once said the job of top managers is to "link the external world with the internal organization . . . make sure the voice of the consumer is heard . . . shape values and standards."[43]

Top managers guide the performance of the organization as a whole or of one of its major parts.

Reporting to top managers are **middle managers**, who are in charge of relatively large departments or divisions consisting of several smaller work units. Examples include clinic directors in hospitals; deans in universities; and division managers, plant managers, and regional sales managers in businesses. Job descriptions for middle managers may include working with top managers, coordinating with peers, and supporting lower–level team members to develop and pursue action plans that implement organizational strategies.

Middle managers oversee the work of large departments or divisions.

A first job in management typically involves serving as a **team leader** or supervisor—someone in charge of a small work group composed of non managerial workers.[44] Typical job titles for first-line managers include department head, team leader, and supervisor. The leader of an auditing team, for example, is a first-line manager, as is the head of an academic department in a university. Even though most people enter the workforce as technical specialists such as engineer, market researcher, or systems analyst, at some point they probably advance to positions of initial managerial responsibility.

Team leaders report to middle managers and supervise groups of non-managerial workers.

Types of Managers

Line managers directly contribute to producing the organization's goods or services.

Staff managers use special technical expertise to advise and support line workers.

Functional managers are responsible for one area, such as finance, marketing, production, personnel, accounting, or sales.

General managers are responsible for complex, multifunctional units.

An **administrator** is a manager in a public or nonprofit organization.

Accountability is the requirement to show performance results to a supervisor.

An **effective manager** helps others achieve high performance and satisfaction at work.

Quality of work life is the overall quality of human experiences in the workplace.

Many types of managers comprise an organization. **Line managers** are responsible for work that directly contributes to the organization's outputs. For example, the president, retail manager, and department supervisors of a local department store all have line responsibilities. Their jobs in one way or another are directly related to the sales operations of the store. **Staff managers**, by contrast, use technical expertise to advise and support the efforts of line workers. In a department store chain like Nordstrom or Macy's, the corporate director of human resources and chief financial officer have staff responsibilities.

Functional managers have responsibility for a single area of activity such as finance, marketing, production, human resources, accounting, or sales. **General managers** cover many functional areas. An example is a retail store manager who oversees everything from purchasing to sales to human resources to finance and accounting. In public or nonprofit organizations managers may be called **administrators**. Examples include hospital administrators, public administrators, and city administrators.

Managerial Performance

All managers help people, working individually and in teams, to perform. They do this while being personally accountable for achieving results. Look at **Figure 1.3**. **Accountability** is the requirement of one person to answer to a higher authority for performance in their area of responsibility. As shown in the figure, accountability flows upward. The manager's or team leader's challenge is to fulfill this performance accountability while being dependent on others to do most of the work.

So, what defines excellence in managerial performance? When is a manager "effective"? A good answer is that **effective managers** help others achieve high performance and satisfaction in their work. This dual concern for performance and satisfaction introduces **quality of work life** (QWL) as an indicator of the overall quality of human experiences at work.

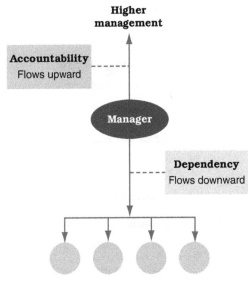

FIGURE 1.3 The Manager's Challenge – Fulfilling Performance Accountability while Dependent on Others to do the Work.

A "high-QWL" workplace offers respect, fair pay, safe conditions, opportunities to learn and use new skills, room to grow and progress in a career, and protection of individual rights and wellness.

Scholar Jeffrey Pfeffer considers QWL a high-priority issue of human sustainability. Why, he asks, don't we give more attention to human sustainability and "organizational effects on employee health and mortality"?[45] What do you think? Should managers be accountable for performance accomplishments and human sustainability? Shouldn't productivity and quality of working life go hand in hand?

Changing Nature of Managerial Work

When Cindy Zollinger was president and CEO of Cornerstone Research, she directly supervised and more than 20 people. But at the time she said: "I don't really manage them in a typical way; they largely run themselves. I help them deal with obstacles and making the most of opportunities."[46] These comments describe a workplace where the best managers are known more for "helping" and "supporting" than for "directing" and "order giving." The words *coordinator, coach,* and *team leader* are heard as often as *supervisor* or *boss.*

The concept of the **upside-down pyramid** shown in **Figure 1.4** fits well with the changing mind-set of managerial work today. Notice that the operating and frontline workers are at the top of the upside-down pyramid, just below the customers and clients they serve. They are supported in their work efforts by managers below them. These managers aren't just order-givers; they mobilize and deliver the support others need to do their jobs best and serve customer needs. Sitting at the bottom are top managers and C-suite executives; their jobs are to support everyone and everything above them. The upside-down pyramid view leaves no doubt that the entire organization is devoted to serving customers and that the job of managers is to support the workers who make this possible.

The **upside-down pyramid** view of organizations shows customers at the top being served by workers who are supported by managers.

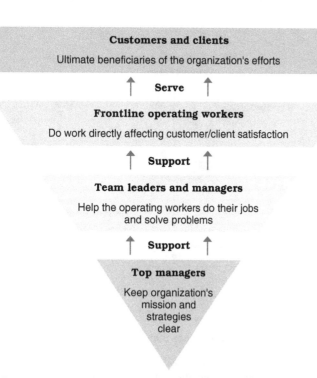

FIGURE 1.4 **The organization viewed as an upside-down pyramid.**

> **Learning Check**

LEARNING OBJECTIVE 1.3

Discuss what it means to be a manager.

Be Sure You Can • describe the various types and levels of managers • define *accountability* and *quality of work life,* and explain their importance to managerial performance • discuss how managerial work is changing today • explain the role of managers in the upside-down pyramid view of organizations

1.4 | The Management Process

LEARNING OBJECTIVE 1.4

Explain the functions, roles, and activities of managers.

> **Learn More About**
>
> Functions of management • Managerial roles and activities • Managerial agendas, networks, and social capital

The ultimate "bottom line" in every manager's job is to help an organization achieve high performance by best utilizing its human and material resources. This is accomplished through the four functions of management in what is called the **management process** of planning, organizing, leading, and controlling.

*The **management process** is planning, organizing, leading, and controlling the use of resources to accomplish performance goals.*

Functions of Management

All managers, regardless of title, level, type, and organizational setting, are responsible for the four management functions shown in **Figure 1.5**. These functions are continually engaged as a manager moves from task to task and opportunity to opportunity in his or her work.

Planning is the process of setting goals and objectives and making plans to accomplish them.

Planning   **Planning** is the process of setting performance objectives and determining what actions should be taken to accomplish them. Through planning, a manager identifies desired results—goals and objectives, and ways to achieve them—action plans.

There was a time, for example, when top management at EY became concerned about the firm's retention of female professionals.[47] Then-chairman Philip A. Laskawy launched a Diversity Task Force with the planning objective to reduce turnover rates for women. When the task force began its work, this turnover was running at 22% per year, and it cost the firm about 150% of a departing employee's annual salary to hire and train each replacement. Laskawy considered this unacceptable and put plans in place to improve it.

Organizing is the process of defining and assigning tasks, allocating resources, and providing resource support.

Organizing   Once plans are set, they must be implemented. This begins with **organizing,** the process of assigning tasks, allocating resources, and coordinating the activities of individuals and groups to accomplish plans. Organizing is how managers put plans into action by defining jobs and tasks, assigning them to responsible persons, and then providing support such as technology, time, and other resources.

At EY, Laskawy organized and chaired a Diversity Task Force to meet his planning objective. He also established a new Office of Retention and hired Deborah K. Holmes, as global director of corporate responsibility. Holmes's office was responsible for identifying retention

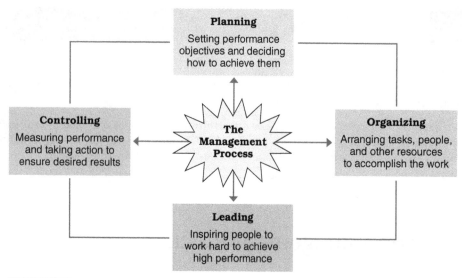

FIGURE 1.5 **Four functions of management—planning, organizing, leading, and controlling.**

problems, creating special task forces to tackle them, and recommend location-specific solutions to the Diversity Task Force.

Leading

Leading is the process of raising enthusiasm and inspiring people to work hard to fulfill plans and accomplish objectives. Managers lead by building commitments to a common vision, encouraging activities that support goals, and influencing others to do their best work on the organization's behalf.

Deborah K. Holmes actively pursued her leadership responsibilities at EY. She noticed that, in addition to stress caused by intense work at the firm, women often faced more stress because their spouses also worked. She became a champion for improved work–life balance and pursued it vigorously. She started "call-free holidays" where professionals did not check voice mail or e-mail on weekends and holidays (see the Choices feature for a new approach to vacation benefits adopted by some companies.) She started a "travel sanity" program that limited staffers' travel to four days a week so they could be home for weekends. And, she started a Woman's Access Program to provide mentoring and career development.

> **Leading** is the process of raising enthusiasm and inspiring efforts to achieve goals.

Controlling

The management function of **controlling** is the process of measuring work performance, comparing results to objectives, and taking corrective action as needed. Managers exercise control by staying in contact with people as they work, gathering and interpreting performance data and using this information to make positive changes. Control is critical to the management process. Things don't always go as anticipated, and plans must often be modified and redefined to fit new circumstances.

At EY, Laskawy and Holmes documented the firm's retention rates for women and this gave them a clear baseline so they could track progress. They regularly measured retention rates for women and compared them to the baseline. They were able to identify successes and pinpoint where they needed to further improve their programs. Their data showed that turnover rates for women were reduced at all levels.

> **Controlling** is the process of measuring performance and taking action to ensure desired results.

Managerial Roles and Activities

The management process and its responsibilities for planning, organizing, leading, and controlling are more complicated than they appear at first glance. They must be successfully accomplished during a workday that can be very challenging. In a classic book, *The Nature of Managerial Work,* Henry Mintzberg describes the daily work of CEOs as follows: "There was no break in the pace of activity during office hours. The mail . . . telephone calls . . . and meetings

Interpersonal roles	Informational roles	Decisional roles
How a manager interacts with other people • Figurehead • Leader • Liaison	How a manager exchanges and processes information • Monitor • Disseminator • Spokesperson	How a manager uses information in decision making • Entrepreneur • Disturbance handler • Resource allocator • Negotiator

FIGURE 1.6   Interpersonal, Informational, and Decisional Roles of Managers

. . . accounted for almost every minute from the moment these executives entered their offices in the morning until they departed in the evenings."[48] Today, with our smartphones in hand, we should add always available to "work anytime and anywhere."

In trying to better understand the complex nature of managerial work, Mintzberg identified a set of roles commonly filled by managers.[49] Shown in **Figure 1.6**, they describe how managers must be prepared to succeed in in a variety of interpersonal, informational, and decisional responsibilities.

A manager's interpersonal roles involve interactions with people inside and outside the work unit. A manager fulfilling these roles will be a *figurehead*, modeling and setting key principles and policies; a *leader*, providing direction and instilling enthusiasm; and a *liaison*, coordinating with others. A manager's informational roles involve the giving, receiving, and analyzing of information. A manager fulfilling these roles will be a *monitor*, scanning for information; a *disseminator*, sharing information; and a *spokesperson*, acting as official communicator. The decisional roles involve using information to make decisions to solve problems or address opportunities. A manager fulfilling these roles will be a *disturbance handler*, dealing with problems and conflicts; a *resource allocator*, handling budgets and distributing resources; a *negotiator*, making deals and forging agreements; and an *entrepreneur*, developing new initiatives.

Managers must not only master key roles, they must implement them in intense and complex work settings. Their work is busy, demanding, and stressful at all levels of responsibility. The managers Mintzberg studied had little free time to themselves. In fact, unexpected problems and continuing requests for meetings consumed almost all available time. Their workdays were hectic; the pressure for continuously improving performance was all-encompassing.[50] Mintzberg summarized his observations this way: "The manager can never be free to forget the job, and never has the pleasure of knowing, even temporarily, that there is nothing else to do. . . . Managers always carry the nagging suspicion that they might be able to contribute just a little bit more. Hence they assume an unrelenting pace in their work."[51]

Managerial Agendas, Networks, and Social Capital

Scene: On the way to a meeting, a general manager ran into a colleague from another department. In a two-minute conversation she used this opportunity to (a) ask two questions and receive the information she had been needing; (b) reinforce their good relationship by sincerely complimenting her colleague on something he had recently done; and (c) get a commitment for the colleague to do something else that the general manager needed done. *Analysis:* This incident provides a glimpse of an effective general manager in action. It also portrays two activities that consultant and scholar John Kotter considers critical to a manager's success—agenda setting and networking.[52]

Agenda setting develops action priorities for accomplishing goals and plans.

Through **agenda setting**, good managers develop action priorities that include goals and plans spanning long and short time frames. These agendas are usually incomplete and loosely connected in the beginning, but they become more specific as the manager utilizes information from many different sources. The agendas are always present in the manager's mind and are played out or pushed ahead whenever an opportunity arises.

Good managers implement their agendas by **networking**—building and maintaining positive relationships with people whose help they need to implement their agenda. Networking creates **social capital**—a capacity to attract support and help from others to get things done. In the earlier example, the general manager received help from a colleague who did not report directly to her. The manager's networks and social capital also include relationships she cultivates with other peers, higher-level executives, subordinates and members of their work teams, as well as with external customers, suppliers, and community representatives.

Networking is the process of creating positive relationships with people who can help advance agendas.

Social capital is a capacity to get things done with the support and help of others.

Learning Check

LEARNING OBJECTIVE 1.4

Explain the functions, roles, and activities of managers.

Be Sure You Can • define and give examples of each of the management functions—*planning, organizing, leading,* and *controlling* • explain Mintzberg's view of what managers do, including the 10 key managerial roles • explain Kotter's points on how managers use agendas and networks to fulfill their work responsibilities

1.5 | Skills for Career Success

LEARNING OBJECTIVE 1.5

Summarize how we learn and use essential skills for career success.

WileyPLUS

See Author Video

> **Learn More About**
> Lifelong learning and learning agility • Management skills • Career readiness skills

A **skill** is the ability to translate knowledge into action that results in desired performance.[53] And interestingly, a survey of corporate CEOs shows dissatisfaction with the skills they are seeing in business school students. Top criticisms include a lack of self-awareness, poor teamwork, weak critical thinking, and an absence of creativity.[54] While you might protest or disagree with the CEOs, their concerns are at least worth thinking about.

A **skill** is the ability to translate knowledge into action that results in desired performance.

Lifelong Learning and Learning Agility

There's no doubt that career success today depends greatly on **learning**—changing behavior through experience. Learning begins with **self-awareness**—having a real, unbiased understanding of your strengths and weaknesses. And when it comes to learning and self-awareness it's not just classroom learning that's important. There's a lot to be gained from making a sincere commitment to **lifelong learning**—continuous learning from daily experiences and opportunities.

Your everyday life—from full-time and part-time jobs to teamwork in school, sports, and leisure activities—contains wonderful learning opportunities. But they only count if you take full advantage of them. Is this a challenge you are confident in meeting? Do you have what the world's largest executive recruiting firm, Korn/Ferry International, calls **learning agility**, defined as the "willingness to grow, to learn, to have insatiable curiosity."[55]

Learning is a change in behavior that results from experience.

Self-awareness is having a real, unbiased understanding of our strength and weaknesses.

Lifelong learning is continuous learning from daily experiences.

Learning agility is a willingness to grow, to learn, and to have insatiable curiosity.

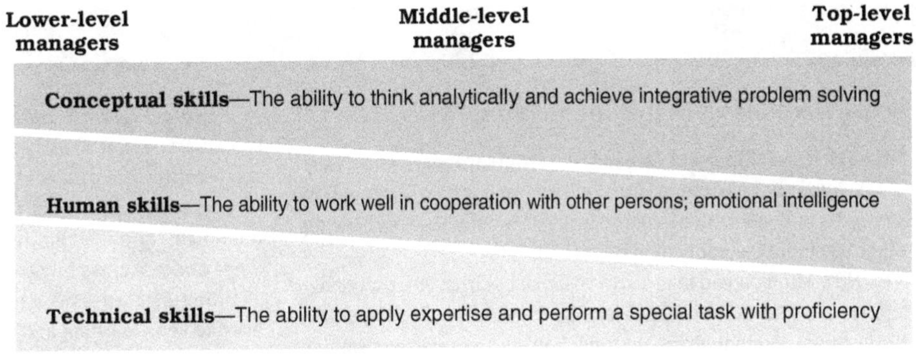

Lower-level managers	Middle-level managers	Top-level managers

Conceptual skills—The ability to think analytically and achieve integrative problem solving

Human skills—The ability to work well in cooperation with other persons; emotional intelligence

Technical skills—The ability to apply expertise and perform a special task with proficiency

FIGURE 1.7 Katz's essential managerial skills—technical, human, and conceptual.

Management Skills

Harvard scholar Robert L. Katz described the essential, or baseline, skills of managers in three categories: technical, human, and conceptual.[56] Although all three sets of skills are necessary for management success, their relative importance varies by level of managerial responsibility as shown in **Figure 1.7**.

Technical Skills

A **technical skill** is the ability to use expertise to perform a task with proficiency.

A **technical skill** is the ability to use a special proficiency or expertise to perform particular tasks. This is what someone can do that brings value to an employer. Accountants, engineers, market researchers, financial planners, and systems analysts, for example, have technical skills in their areas of expertise. Knowing how to write a business plan with a cash flow projection, use statistics to analyze data from a market survey, update software on a computer network, and deliver a persuasive oral presentation are also technical skills. Although initially gained through formal education, technical skills can become quickly outdated. It is important to nurture and develop them through ongoing learning that takes full advantage of training and job experiences.

Figure 1.7 shows that technical skills are essential at job entry and early career levels. As you look at this figure, take a quick inventory of your technical skills. They are things you must be able to tell a prospective employer when interviewing for a new job. Get prepared by asking this all-important self-assessment question: "What, exactly, can I do for a prospective employer?"

Human and Interpersonal Skills

A **human skill** or interpersonal skill is the ability to work well in cooperation with other people.

Emotional intelligence is the ability to manage ourselves and our relationships effectively.

Recruiters today put a lot of emphasis on a job candidate's "soft" skills—things like ability to communicate, collaborate, and network, to lead and contribute to teams, and to treat others with trust, enthusiasm, and positivity.[57] These are all part of what Katz called the ability to work well in cooperation with others, or **human skill**. As pointed out in Figure 1.6, the interpersonal nature of managerial work makes human skills consistently important across all levels of managerial responsibility.

A manager with good human skills will have a high degree of **emotional intelligence**, defined by scholar and consultant Daniel Goleman as the "ability to manage ourselves and our relationships effectively."[58] Strength or weakness in emotional intelligence shows up as the ability to recognize, understand, and manage feelings while interacting with others. Someone high in emotional intelligence will know when her or his emotions are about to become disruptive, and act to control them. This same person will sense when others' emotions are negatively influencing a relationship, and try to understand and better deal with them.[59] Check your interpersonal skills and emotional intelligence by asking and answering this self-assessment question: "Just how well do I relate to and work with others in team and interpersonal situations?"

Conceptual and Critical-Thinking Skills

A **conceptual skill** is the ability to think analytically to diagnose and solve complex problems.

The ability to think analytically is a **conceptual skill**. It involves the capacity to break problems into smaller parts, see relations between the parts, and recognize the implications of any one problem for others. We call this a critical-thinking skill, and it is a top priority when recruiters screen candidates.[60] Annmarie Neal, Vice President, Cisco Center for Collaborative Leadership within Human Resources, describes

---

Insight: **Gain Self-Awareness** | Self-awareness helps us avoid seeing ourselves more favorably than is justified.

Self-Awareness and the Johari Window

Although it's an important career skill, **self-awareness** can be easy to talk about but hard to master. Self-awareness helps us build on strengths and overcome weaknesses, and it helps us avoid seeing ourselves more favorably than is justified.

How often do you take a critical look at your attitudes, behaviors, skills, personal characteristics, and accomplishments? When was the last time you thought about them from a career perspective—as you see them and as others do?

	Unknown to you	Known to you
Known to others	**Blind Spot**	**Open Area**
Unknown to others	**The Unknown**	**Hidden Self**

Exploring your *Johari Window* is one way to gain more self-awareness. It's a way of comparing what we know about ourselves with what others know about us. The "open" areas known to ourselves and others are often small. The "blind spot," "the unknown," and the "hidden" areas can be quite large. They challenge our capacities for self-discovery.

Self-awareness is a pathway to adaptability, something we need to keep learning and growing in changing times. But remember the insights of the Johari Window. True self-awareness means not just knowing your idealized self—the person you want or hope to be. It also means knowing who you really are in the eyes of others and as defined by your actions.

Get To Know Yourself Better

Map your Johari Window. Make notes on your "Open Area" and "Hidden Self." Speculate about your "Unknown." Ask friends, family, and co-workers for insights to your "Blind Spot." Write a summary of what you learn about possible career strengths and weaknesses.

---

it as an ability to "approach problems as a learner as opposed to a knower" and "taking issues and situations and problems and going to root components . . . looking at it [a problem] from a systematic perspective and not accepting things at face value . . . being curious about why things are the way they are and being able to think about why something is important."[61]

Figure 1.7 shows that conceptual skills become more important moving from lower to higher levels of management. This is because the problems at higher levels of responsibility are often ambiguous and unstructured, full of complications and interconnections, and pose longer-term consequences. The end-of-chapter feature *Career Skills & Competencies—Make Yourself Valuable* offers ways to further develop your conceptual skills in management. And, the relevant self-assessment question to ask and honestly answer is: "Am I developing the strong critical-thinking and problem-solving capabilities I will need for long-term career success?"

Career Readiness Skills

This book is filled with future value. Virtually everything we discuss can be applied to managing yourself in daily living as well as in a career. Now is the best time to prioritize your career readiness and start thinking about the strategic management of your future. The goal is to put skills, competencies, and aspirations together with learning agility so that you can always move forward with confidence, even as things change around you.

Take a good look at **Figure 1.8**. It shows how a strategic management tool called **SWOT analysis** that can help you stay on track with career readiness. A good SWOT analysis identifies individual Strengths and Weaknesses, as well as environmental Opportunities and Threats. When applied to you and your career, it is a powerful way to self-assess and self-regulate to achieve your goals.

Spend some time with Figure 1.8 and think seriously about your personal strengths. Be realistic and don't overestimate them. Are you good at reading people? Are you good at solving complex problems? Are you a good communicator? Do you have a network of helpful connections? Are you good at teamwork? Can you lead? These are the kinds of "strengths" that might be included in your personal SWOT. Surely you can identify many others.

Although it's difficult to think about personal weaknesses, all great leaders have a well-developed sense of their weak points. You should too. With such awareness you can avoid

SWOT analysis identifies individual strengths and weaknesses, as well as environmental opportunities and threats.

FIGURE 1.8   Using a Personal SWOT Analysis for Strategic Career Planning

getting into jobs or special assignments where success relies heavily on areas outside your expertise and competence. Even more importantly, it's a launching pad for learning and personal growth. Once weakenesses are recognized and accepted we can start taking action to correct or lessen them. Could you, right now for example, begin addressing weaknesses and even turn some into strengths? Think about special classes you might take, internships you might apply for, and trusted mentors you might approach to answer questions and guide you in positive ways.

In addition to assessing "who you are" in respect to strengths and weaknesses, it's also essential to explore "what's out there" in respect to opportunities and threats in a competitive career environment. Opportunities might include internships that coincide with experiences you've longed for or that represent employment entry points, an offer of a scholarship for graduate school, or personal connections that can open career doors. Threats might include industry and economic changes that are shrinking jobs in certain areas, new technologies that are creating job obsolence in your fields of interest, and the presence of other students with the same or better qualifications applying for the same internships or full-time jobs.

The critical takeaway here is to take charge of your career readiness. The responsibility is yours, no one else's. You must spend time on self assessment, thinking in a systematic way about yourself within a specific career setting. You must continually update your understanding of personal strengths and weaknesses in relation to external opportunities and threats. And, you must be excited about becoming a manager and team leader. As scholar Henry Mintzberg says:[62]

> No job is more vital to our society than that of the manager. It is the manager who determines whether our social institutions serve us well or whether they squander our talents and resources.

Learning Check

LEARNING OBJECTIVE 1.5

Summarize how we learn and use essential skills for career success.

Be Sure You Can • discuss the career importance of learning and lifelong learning • define three essential managerial skills—*technical, human,* and *conceptual skills* • explain how these skills vary in importance across management levels • define *emotional intelligence* as an important human skill

Management Learning Review: Get Prepared for Quizzes and Exams

Summary

LEARNING OBJECTIVE 1.1 Summarize the challenges of developing and maintaining career readiness in the new economy.

- Work in the new economy is increasingly knowledge based, and intellectual capital is the foundation of organizational performance.
- Organizations must value the talents of a workforce whose members are increasingly diverse with respect to gender, age, race and ethnicity, able-bodiedness, and lifestyles.
- The forces of globalization are bringing increased interdependencies among nations and economies, as customer markets and resource flows create intense business competition.
- Ever-present developments in information technology are reshaping organizations, changing the nature of work, and increasing the value of knowledge workers.
- Society has high expectations for organizations and their members to perform with commitment to high ethical standards and in socially responsible ways.
- Careers in the new economy require great personal initiative to build and maintain skill "portfolios" that are always up-to-date and valuable in a free-agent economy.

For Discussion What career risks and opportunities is globalization creating for today's college graduates?

LEARNING OBJECTIVE 1.2 Describe what organizations are like as work settings.

- Organizations are collections of people working together to achieve a common purpose.
- As open systems, organizations interact with their environments in the process of transforming resource inputs into product and service outputs.
- Productivity is a measure of the quantity and quality of work performance, with resource costs taken into account.
- High-performing organizations achieve both performance effectiveness in terms of goal accomplishment, and performance efficiency in terms of resource utilization.

For Discussion When is it acceptable to sacrifice performance efficiency for performance effectiveness?

LEARNING OBJECTIVE 1.3 Describe what it means to be a manager.

- Managers directly support and facilitate the work efforts of other people in organizations.

- Top managers scan the environment, create strategies, and emphasize long-term goals; middle managers coordinate activities in large departments or divisions; team leaders and supervisors support performance of frontline workers at the team or work-unit level.
- Functional managers work in specific areas such as finance or marketing; general managers are responsible for larger multifunctional units; administrators are managers in public or nonprofit organizations.
- The upside-down pyramid view of organizations shows operating workers at the top, serving customer needs while being supported from below by various levels of management.
- The changing nature of managerial work emphasizes being good at "coaching" and "supporting" others, rather than simply "directing" and "order-giving."

For Discussion In what ways should the work of a top manager to differ from that of a team leader?

LEARNING OBJECTIVE 1.4 Describe the functions, roles, and activities of managers.

- The management process consists of the four functions of planning, organizing, leading, and controlling.
- Planning sets the direction; organizing assembles the human and material resources; leading provides the enthusiasm and direction; controlling ensures results.
- Managers implement the four functions in daily work that is often intense and stressful, involving long hours and continuous performance pressures.
- Managerial success requires the ability to perform well in interpersonal, informational, and decision-making roles.
- Managerial success also requires the ability to build interpersonal networks and use them to accomplish well-selected task agendas.

For Discussion How might the upside-down pyramid view of organizations affect a manager's approach to planning, organizing, leading, and controlling?

LEARNING OBJECTIVE 1.5 Summarize how we learn and use essential skills for career success.

- Careers in the new economy demand continual attention to lifelong learning from all aspects of daily experience and job opportunities.

- Skills considered essential for managers are broadly described as technical—ability to use expertise; human—ability to work well with other people, including emotional intelligence; and conceptual—ability to analyze and solve complex problems with critical thinking.

- Human skills are equally important for all management levels, whereas conceptual skills gain importance at higher levels and technical skills gain importance at lower levels.

For Discussion Which management skills and competencies do you consider the most difficult to develop, and why?

Self-Test 1

Multiple-Choice Questions

1. The process of management involves the functions of planning, _____, leading, and controlling.
   a. accounting
   b. creating
   c. innovating
   d. organizing

2. An effective manager achieves both high-performance results and high levels of _____ among people doing the required work.
   a. turnover
   b. effectiveness
   c. satisfaction
   d. stress

3. Performance efficiency is a measure of the _____ associated with task accomplishment.
   a. resource costs
   b. goal specificity
   c. product quality
   d. product quantity

4. The requirement that a manager answer to a higher-level boss for performance results achieved by a work team is called _____.
   a. dependency
   b. accountability
   c. authority
   d. empowerment

5. Productivity is a measure of the quantity and _____ of work produced, relative to the cost of inputs.
   a. quality   c. timeliness
   b. cost   d. value

6. _____ managers pay special attention to the external environment, looking for problems and opportunities and finding ways for the organization to best deal with them.
   a. Top   c. Lower
   b. Middle   d. First-line

7. The accounting manager for a local newspaper would be considered a _____ manager, whereas the editorial director for sports would be considered a _____ manager.
   a. general, functional   c. staff, line
   b. middle, top   d. senior, junior

8. When a team leader clarifies desired work targets and deadlines for members of a work team, they are fulfilling the management function of _____.
   a. planning
   b. delegating
   c. controlling
   d. supervising

9. The process of building and maintaining good relationships with others who may help implement a manager's work agendas is called _____.
   a. governance   c. authority
   b. networking   d. entrepreneurship

10. In Katz's framework, top managers tend to rely more on their _____ skills than do first-line managers.
    a. human
    b. conceptual
    c. decision-making
    d. technical

11. The research of Mintzberg and others concludes that managers _____.
    a. work at a leisurely pace
    b. have blocks of private time for planning
    c. are never free from the pressures of performance responsibility
    d. have the advantages of flexible work hours

12. When someone holds a negative attitude toward minorities, this is an example of _____. When a team leader with a negative attitude toward minorities makes a decision to deny advancement opportunities to a Hispanic team member, this is an example of _____.
    a. discrimination, prejudice
    b. emotional intelligence, social capital
    c. performance efficiency, performance effectiveness
    d. prejudice, discrimination

13. Trends in the new workplace include which of the following?
    a. More emphasis by managers on giving orders.
    b. More attention by organizations to valuing people as human assets.
    c. Less teamwork.
    d. Less concern for work–life balance among the new generation of workers.

14. The manager's role in the "upside-down pyramid" view of organizations is best described as providing _____ so that workers can directly serve _____.

   a. direction, top management

   b. leadership, organizational goals

   c. support, customers

   d. agendas, networking

15. The management function of _____ is being performed when a retail manager measures daily sales in the women's apparel department and compares them with daily sales targets.

   a. planning

   b. agenda setting

   c. controlling

   d. delegating

Short-Response Questions

16. Discuss the importance of ethics in the relationship between managers and the people they supervise.

17. Explain how "accountability" operates in the relationship between (a) a team leader and her team members, and (b) the same team leader and her boss.

18. Explain how the "glass ceiling effect" may disadvantage newly hired African American college graduates in a large corporation.

19. What is globalization, and what are its implications for working in the new economy?

Essay Question

20. You have just been hired as the new head of an audit team for a national accounting firm. With four years of experience, you feel technically well prepared for the assignment. However, this is your first formal appointment as a "manager." Things are complicated at the moment. The team has 12 members of diverse demographic and cultural backgrounds, as well as work experience. There is an intense workload and lots of performance pressure. How will this situation challenge you to develop and use essential managerial skills and related competencies to manage the team successfully to high levels of auditing performance?

Career Skills & Competencies: Make Yourself Valuable!

Evaluate Career Situations for New Managers

What Would You Do?

1. Opportunity with International Employer

One of the plus sides of globalization is new jobs created by international employers setting up operations in local communities. How about you: Does it make any difference if you receive a job offer from an international employer such as Honda or a domestic one such as Ford? Assume you just had an offer from Honda for a great job in Marysville, Ohio. Prepare a Job Hunter's Balance Sheet. On the left list the "pluses" and on the right the "minuses" of working at home for a international employer.

2. Interviewing for Dream Job

It's time to take your first interview for a "dream" job. The interviewer is sitting across the table from you. She smiles, looks you in the eye,

and says: "You have a very nice academic record and we're impressed with your extracurricular activities." But she then says: "Now tell me, just what can you do for us that will add value to the organization right from day one?" You're on the spot. How will you answer? What can you add to the conversation that clearly shows you have strong human and conceptual skills, not just technical ones?

3. Supervising Old Friends

When people are promoted into management, they sometimes end up supervising friends and colleagues they previously worked with. This could happen to you. When it does, how can you best deal with this situation right from the start? What will you do to earn the respect of everyone under your supervision and set the foundations for what will become a well-regarded and high-performing work team?

Reflect on the Self-Assessment

Career Readiness "Big 20"

Instructions

Use this scale to rate yourself on the following "Big 20" personal characteristics for management and career success.[63]

(S) Strong, I am very confident with this one.

(G) Good, but I still have room to grow.

(W) Weak, I really need work on this one.

(U) Unsure, I just don't know.

Big 20 Personal Characteristics

1. *Inner work standards*: The ability to personally set and work to high performance standards.

2. *Initiative*: The ability to actively tackle problems and take advantage of opportunities.

3. *Analytical thinking*: The ability to think systematically and identify cause–effect patterns in data and events.

4. *Creative thinking*: The ability to generate novel responses to problems and opportunities.

5. *Reflective thinking*: The ability to understand yourself and your actions in the context of society.

6. *Social objectivity*: The ability to act free of racial, ethnic, gender, and other prejudices or biases.

7. *Social intelligence*: The ability to understand another person's needs and feelings.

8. *Emotional intelligence*: The ability to recognize and manage emotions.

9. *Cultural intelligence*: The ability to respect other cultures and work well in diverse cultural settings.

10. *Interpersonal relations*: The ability to work well with others and in teams.

11. *Self-confidence*: The ability to be consistently decisive and willing to take action.

12. *Self-objectivity*: The ability to evaluate realistically personal strengths, weaknesses, motives, and skills.

13. *Tolerance for uncertainty*: The ability to work in ambiguous and uncertain conditions.

14. *Adaptability*: The ability to be flexible and adapt to changes.

15. *Stress management*: The ability to get work under stressful conditions.

16. *Stamina*: The ability to sustain long work hours.

17. *Communication*: The ability to communicate well orally and in writing.

18. *Impression management*: The ability to create and sustain a positive impression in the eyes of others.

19. *Introspection*: The ability to learn from experience, awareness, and self-study.

20. *Application*: The ability to apply learning and use knowledge to accomplish things.

Self-Assessment Scoring

Give yourself 1 point for each S, and 1/2 point for each G. Do not give yourself points for W and U responses. Total your points and enter the result here [_____].

Interpretation

This assessment is a good starting point for considering where and how you can further develop useful managerial skills and competencies. It offers a self-described profile of your personal management foundations—things that establish strong career readiness. The higher you score the better. Are you a perfect 10, or something less? There shouldn't be too many 10s around. Ask someone you know to assess you on this instrument as well. You may be surprised at the differences between your score and the one they come up with.

Contribute to the Class Exercise

My Best Manager

Preparation

Working alone, make a list of the *behavioral attributes* that describe the "best" manager you have ever had. This could be someone you worked for in a full-time or part-time job, summer job, volunteer job, student organization, or elsewhere. If you have trouble identifying an actual manager, make a list of behavioral attributes of the manager you would most like to work for in your next job.

1. Make of list of the behavioral attributes that describe the "worst" manager you have ever had.

2. Write a short synopsis of things that this bad manager actually did or said that would qualify for "Believe it or not, it's really true!" status.

3. If you also made a list of attributes for your "best" manager, write a quick summary of the most important differences that quickly sort out your best from your worst.

Activity

Form into groups as assigned by your instructor, or work with a nearby classmate. Share your list of attributes and listen to the lists of others. Be sure to ask questions and make comments on items of special interest.

Work together in the group to create a master list that combines the unique attributes of the "best" and/or "worst" managers experienced by members. Have a spokesperson share that list with the rest of the class for further discussion. Share the "Believe it or not!" stories provided by group members.

Manage a Critical Incident

Team Leader Faces Test

It's happened again for the second time in a week. Charles walked into your cubicle and started a rant about his not getting enough support from you as his team leader. Before you could say anything, he accused you of playing favorites in assigning projects and not giving him the respect he deserved for his seniority and expertise. Then he gave you an angry look, turned around, and stomped off. You let

it go the last time he exploded like this. And after cooling down, he came by later to apologize and give you a fist-bump of reconciliation. You've since learned, however, that the other team members have been on the receiving end of his outbursts and are starting to complain to one another about him. Charles is your top software engineer and has a lot of technical expertise to offer the team and you. He's a valuable talent, but his behavior has become intolerable. It's time for action.

Questions

How do you handle Charles and the full team in these circumstances? Does this call for direct confrontation between you and him? If so, how do you handle it? If not, how do you handle it? Is this something that the team as a whole needs to get involved with? If so, how do you proceed as team leader? How can you use each of the management functions to best deal with this situation? How can essential managerial skills help you succeed in this and similar situations?

Collaborate on a Team Project

The Amazing Great Job Race

The fantastic variety of jobs out there for the well-prepared candidate is almost unimaginable. But our lives have gotten busy—really complicated! We spend time with work, school work, meetings, friends, family, video games, listening to music, watching television, surfing the Internet, going to concerts, social engagements, and so on! It seems like our calendars are always full with activities, leaving less time available to figure out what we really want from a first "real" job and a career.

You might say or hear: "I haven't got time for that—I need a job now . . . !" It's easy to overestimate how much you can get done at the last minute. There may also be lots of uncertainty as to what kind of job you really want. Thinking about likes and dislikes, talents and areas of deficit, goals, aspirations, wants, needs, understanding yourself and what makes you happy—all take time. It also takes time spent in the right ways.

A job that looks really great to you might require a series of classes that you haven't taken, an internship that you haven't done, software that you don't know, or a foreign language you don't speak. If you spend time thinking about what you want, searching for what's out there, and figuring out now what you'll need in order to be prepared when you graduate, you just might find yourself running and winning the Amazing Great Job Race.

Instructions

1. *Reflect*: What classes have you enjoyed the most? What did you like most about them? How was your thinking challenged in these courses? What work experiences have been most satisfying for you? Why?

2. *Share*: Listen without criticism to how others in the group answered these reflection questions. Share your answers and listen to the comments of others. Turn group discussion into a brainstorming session about the kinds of jobs each member might like to do and the careers they might pursue.

3. *Debate*: Push each other to identify baseline requirements for jobs that might be good fits for them. Ask: What classes would you need to take to be in a position to compete for these jobs? What kinds of internships would you need to participate in order to gain experience and access? What tests and certifications might be necessary? How much time would these preparations take so that you are ready to compete for your best job with other candidates who might want it also?

Analyze a Case Study

Trader Joe's | Keeping a Cool Edge

Go to **Management Cases for Critical Thinking** at the end of the book to find this case.

CHAPTER 2

Management Learning Past to Present

Great Things Grow from Strong Foundations

Latitudestock/Gallo Images/Getty Images

Great management isn't new and it isn't all about new technology. People have created wonderful things for centuries, and management lessons are part of our history.

Chapter Quick Start

Ancestry.com is a hugely popular website. It helps people learn more about their roots—and by extension, themselves. The history of management thought offers similar insights. In order to develop career readiness for the ever-changing future, it is critical to understand the insights and lessons of the past. Knowing where you're going requires knowledge of where you've been. That is our focus in this chapter.

LEARNING OBJECTIVES

2.1 Describe the principal insights of classical management thinking.

2.2 Identify key insights of the behavioral management approaches.

2.3 Explain the core foundations of modern management theory and practice.

Career Readiness – What to Look for Inside

Thought Leadership

Analysis > *Make Data Your Friend*
When #MeToo Becomes Catch 22

Choices > *Think before You Act*
AI Offers Instant Insights on Employee Morale

Ethics > *Know Right from Wrong*
New Rules for Office Engagement

Insight > *Gain Self-Awareness*
Make Learning Style Work for You

Skills Make You Valuable

- **Evaluate** *Career Situations:*
  What Would You Do?
- **Reflect** *On the Self-Assessment:*
  Managerial Assumptions
- **Contribute** *To the Class Exercise:*
  Evidence-Based Management Quiz
- **Manage** *A Critical Incident:*
  Theory X versus Theory Y
- **Collaborate** *On the Team Project:*
  Management in Popular Culture
- **Analyze** *The Case Study:*
  Zara International: Fashion at the Speed of Light

In his book *The Evolution of Management Thought*, Daniel Wren traces management as far back as 5000 BC, when the ancient Sumerians used written records to improve government and business activities.[1] Management was crucial in the construction of the Egyptian pyramids, the spread of the Roman Empire across the globe, and the renowned commercial success of fourteenth-century Venice. By the time of the start of the Industrial Revolution in the late 1700s, great social changes helped stimulate major manufacturing advances in basic products and consumer goods. Adam Smith's revolutionary (at the time) concepts of division of labor and task specialization accelerated industrial development. With the turn of the twentieth century, Henry Ford had made mass production a core aspect of the emerging economy. Since then, both the science and practice of management have been on the fast track toward continued development.[2]

Today's managers face challenges from what many call "the new industrial revolution."[3] It's a time full of technological and social uncertainties and opportunities. Perhaps more than ever it's a time to reach back and remember the management learning that comes from the past. Many crucial insights can be taken from the history of management thought. It's a mistake to assume that our generation needs to invent best practices in management out of thin air. Instead, it is important to understand that we can learn a lot from history that can benefit us as we try to perfect new ideas and approaches to best match current business realities.

2.1 | Classical Management Approaches

LEARNING OBJECTIVE 2.1

Describe the principal insights of classical management thinking.

WileyPLUS

See Author Video

> **Learn More About**
>
> Scientific management • Administrative principles • Bureaucratic organization

Our study of management begins with a focus on the three major classical approaches: (1) scientific management, (2) administrative principles, and (3) bureaucratic organization.[4] **Figure 2.1** ties each of these classical approaches to a prominent historical figure—Taylor, Fayol, and Weber. What can be seen here is that the classical approaches share a common assumption: People rationally consider their opportunities and do whatever is necessary to achieve the greatest personal and monetary gain.[5]

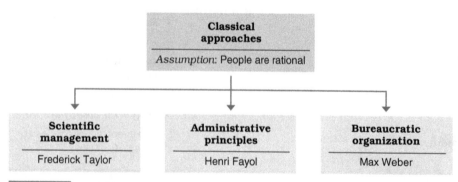

FIGURE 2.1   **Major branches in the classical approach to management.**

Scientific Management

In 1911, Frederick W. Taylor published *The Principles of Scientific Management*, where he stated: "The principal object of management should be to secure maximum prosperity for the employer, coupled with the maximum prosperity for the employee."[6] Taylor, often called the "father of scientific management," noticed that workers often did their jobs with wasted motions and without a consistent approach. This resulted in inefficiency and low performance. He believed that this problem could be fixed if workers were taught to do their jobs in the best ways and then were helped and guided by supervisors to always work this way.

Taylor's goal was to improve workers' productivity. He used the concept of "time study" to analyze the motions and tasks required to do a job, and to develop the most efficient ways to perform that job. He then linked these job requirements to both worker training and support from supervisors in the form of precise direction, work assistance, and monetary incentives. Taylor's approach, known as **scientific management**, includes four guiding principles.

> **Scientific management** emphasizes careful alignment of worker training, incentives, and supervisory support with job requirements.

1. Develop a "science" that includes rules of motion, standardized work implements, and proper working conditions for every job.
2. Carefully select workers with the right abilities for the job.
3. Carefully train workers to do the job and give them incentives to cooperate with the job "science."
4. Support workers by carefully planning their work and by smoothing the way as they do their work.

Although Taylor called his approach "scientific" management, contemporary scholars have questioned his truthfulness in reporting and the scientific rigor of his studies.[7] But Taylor's ideas still influence management thinking.[8] Consider these insights that still make sense today.

- Make results-based compensation a performance incentive.
- Carefully design jobs with efficient work methods.
- Carefully select workers with the abilities to do these jobs.
- Train workers to perform jobs to the best of their abilities.
- Train supervisors to support workers so they can perform to the best of their abilities.

An example is found with United Parcel Service (UPS), where workers are guided by carefully calibrated productivity standards. Sorters at regional hubs are timed according to strict task requirements and are expected to load vans at a set number of packages per hour. A GPS is used to plot the shortest delivery routes; delivery stops are registered in on-board computers that are studied to identify wasted time. Industrial engineers design explicit procedures for drivers—with delivery and pickup rules like avoid left turns in traffic, unbuckle seat belt with left hand, and walk at a "brisk" pace. Consistent with scientific management principles, efficiency is a top priority at UPS; saving a few seconds at each stop adds up to significant increases in productivity.[9]

One of the most enduring legacies of scientific management grew from Taylor's interest in **motion study**, the science of reducing a job or a task to its most basic physical aspects. Two of his contemporaries, Frank and Lillian Gilbreth, pioneered the use of motion studies as a management tool.[10] In one famous case, the Gilbreths cut down the number of motions used by bricklayers and tripled their productivity.

> **Motion study** is the science of reducing a task to its basic physical motions.

Administrative Principles

In 1916, after a career in French industry, Henri Fayol published *Administration Industrielle et Générale*[11] in which he outlines his views on the management of organizations and workers. Fayol identifies five "rules" or "duties" of management, which support the four functions of management—planning, organizing, leading, and controlling—that we talk about today:

1. *Foresight*—to complete a plan of action for the future.
2. *Organization*—to provide and mobilize resources to implement the plan.
3. *Command*—to lead, select, and evaluate workers to get the best work toward the plan.
4. *Coordination*—to fit diverse efforts together and to ensure information is shared and problems solved.
5. *Control*—to make sure things happen according to plan and to take necessary corrective action.

Fayol believed that management could be taught. He wanted to improve the quality of management and defined a number of "principles" to help managers. A number of these principles still guide managers today. They include the *scalar chain principle*—there should be a clear and unbroken line of communication from the top to the bottom of the organization; the *unity of command principle*—each person should receive orders from only one boss; and the *unity of direction principle*—one person should be in charge of all activities that have the same performance objective.

Bureaucratic Organization

Max Weber was a late-nineteenth-century German political economist who had a major impact in the fields of management and sociology. His ideas developed after noticing that organizations often performed poorly. Among other things, Weber noticed that employees often held positions of authority not because of their capabilities, but because of their "privileged" social status in German society. At the heart of Weber's thinking was an ideal; an intentionally rational, and very efficient form of organization called a **bureaucracy**.[12] It was founded on principles of logic, order, and legitimate authority. The defining characteristics of Weber's bureaucratic organization are:

A **bureaucracy** is a rational and efficient form of organization founded on logic, order, and legitimate authority.

- *Clear division of labor:* Jobs are well defined, and workers are highly skilled at performing them.
- *Clear hierarchy of authority:* Authority and responsibility are well defined for each position, and each position reports to a higher level.
- *Formal rules and procedures:* Written guidelines direct behavior and decisions in jobs, and written files are kept for historical record.
- *Impersonality:* Rules and procedures are impartially and uniformly applied, with no one receiving preferential treatment.
- *Careers based on merit:* Workers are selected and promoted on ability, competency, and performance, and managers are career employees of the organizations.

Weber believed that organizations structured as bureaucracies would use resources more efficiently and treat employees more fairly than other systems. He wrote:[13]

> The purely bureaucratic type of administrative organization . . . is, from a purely technical point of view, capable of attaining the highest degree of efficiency. . . . It is superior to any other form in precision, in stability, in the stringency of its discipline, and in its reliability. It thus makes possible a particularly high degree of calculability of results for the heads of the organization and for those acting in relation to it.

Today we recognize that bureaucracy works well sometimes, but not all of the time. In fact it's common to hear the terms *bureaucracy* and *bureaucrat* used with negative connotations. We picture bureaucracies as bogged down in excessive paperwork or "red tape," slow in handling problems, rigid in the face of shifting customer needs, and high in resistance to change and employee apathy.[14] These are disadvantages for organizations that have to be flexible and adaptive to the changing circumstances that are common today. A major management challenge is to know when bureaucratic features work well and what are the best alternatives when they don't. Later in the chapter we'll call this *contingency thinking*.

Learning Check

LEARNING OBJECTIVE 2.1

Describe the principal insights of classical management thinking.

Be Sure You Can • state the underlying assumption of the classical management approaches • list the principles of Taylor's scientific management • identify three of Fayol's principles for guiding managerial action • list the key characteristics of bureaucracy and explain why Weber considered it an ideal form of organization • identify possible disadvantages of bureaucracy in today's environment

2.2 | Behavioral Management Approaches

WileyPLUS

See Author Video

LEARNING OBJECTIVE 2.2

Identify key insights of the behavioral management approaches.

> **Learn More About**
>
> Organizations as communities • The Hawthorne studies • Maslow's theory of human needs • McGregor's Theory X and Theory Y • Argyris's theory of adult personality

During the 1920s an emphasis on the human side of the workplace began to influence management thinking. Major branches in the behavioral—or human resource—approaches to management are shown in **Figure 2.2**. These include Charles Spaulding's and Mary Parker Follett's ideas about organizations as communities, the Hawthorne studies, Maslow's theory

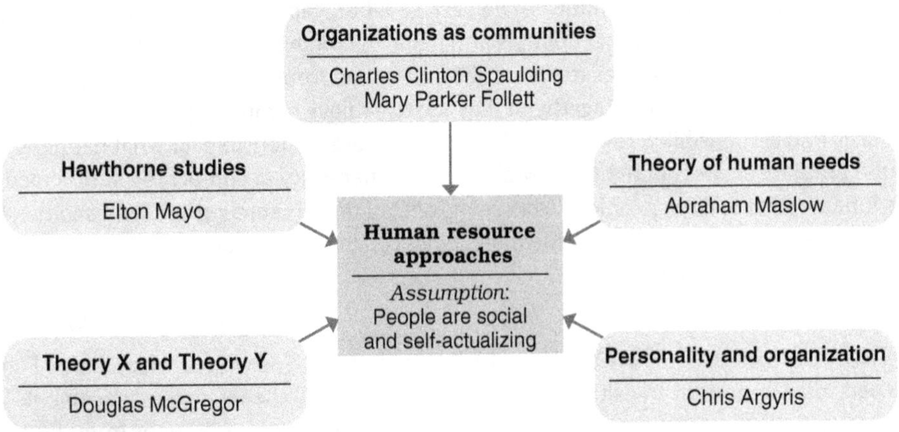

FIGURE 2.2 Foundations in the behavioral or human resource approaches to management.

of human needs, and related ideas of Douglas McGregor and Chris Argyris. The behavioral approaches assume that people enjoy social relationships, respond to group pressures, and search for personal fulfillment. These historical foundations set the stage for what is now known as the field of **organizational behavior**, the study of individuals and groups in organizations.

Organizational behavior is the study of individuals and groups in organizations.

Organizations as Communities

The field of management has benefited from executives and consultants that have written about their experiences and shared what they learned from them. Bookstores offer many contemporary examples and the selection keeps growing. But the lessons of experience-based management learning go back many years.[15] We'll pick them up early in the twentieth century with two examples that brought the human factor front and center into management thinking.

African American Insurance Executive
Recent work by scholars Leon Prieto and Simone Phipps highlights the insights of Charles Clinton Spaulding, whom they refer to as the "Father of African American Management."[16] Noting that the contributions of African Americans to the history of management has been overlooked, they studied Spaulding's experience as head of the North Carolina Mutual Life Insurance Company. What they found was an enlightened executive who started as a dishwasher and worked his way to the top of the largest African American business of his time.

Spaulding is described as a committed leader who helped people and communities, was always trying to understand the complexities of management and organizations, and was generous sharing his insights to help others become successful managers. He summarized his management learning in two articles published in 1927 in the *Pittsburgh Courier* and setting out what he called the "eight necessities" of management.[17]

1. Cooperation and teamwork
2. Authority and responsibility
3. Division of labor
4. Adequate manpower
5. Adequate capital
6. Feasibility analysis
7. Advertising budget
8. Conflict resolution

In addition to covering administrative basics—labor, capital, and budgets, Spaulding's eight necessities focus on respect people and belief in community. His necessity of cooperation and teamwork recognizes that contributions come from all levels of in organizations and that everyone must work together if they are to achieve common goals. His necessity of authority and responsibility reminds us that managers are responsible for what happens and are the ultimate arbiters of right and wrong. And, his necessity of conflict resolution focuses on a fundamental reality—people at work spend a lot of time interacting with one another, but not always successfully. Managers, therefore, must create a culture of cooperation "based on mutual goodwill and intelligence."[18]

Social Worker and Management Consultant
The work of Mary Parker Follett was part of an important transition from classical thinking into behavioral management. The book *Mary Parker Follett—Prophet of Management: A Celebration of Writings from the 1920s* offers an important reminder of the wisdom that can come from an understanding of history.

She taught respect for workers' experience and knowledge, warned against the dangers of too much hierarchy, and called for visionary leadership. Follett was eulogized upon her death in 1933 as "one of the most important women America has yet produced in the fields of civics and sociology."[19]

Follett thought of organizations as "communities" where managers and workers should labor in harmony without one party dominating the other, and with the freedom to talk over and truly reconcile conflicts and differences. Groups were a way for individuals to combine talents toward a greater good. The job of managers was to help workers cooperate with one another and to integrate their goals and interests. See the Analysis feature for a modern example.

Follett's emphasis on groups and her commitment to human cooperation are highly relevant themes today.[20] She believed that making every employee an owner in a business would create feelings of collective responsibility. Today, we address the same issues under such labels as *employee ownership*, *profit sharing*, and *gain-sharing plans*. She believed that business problems involve a wide variety of factors that must be considered in relationship to one another. Today, we talk about systems and "contingency thinking." Follett also believed that businesses were service organizations and that private profits should always be considered vis-à-vis the public good. Today, we pursue the same issues under the labels *managerial ethics*, *corporate social responsibility*, and *shared value.*

Analysis: Make Data Your Friend | "It's not surprising that so few people file formal complaints given the high cost of complaining."

When #MeToo Becomes Catch 22

Erik McGregor/Pacific Press/LightRocket/Getty Images

The #MeToo movement is no secret. But do you know the facts? Consider the following:

- 51% of women report being sexually harassed at work; 12% of men do so.
- 51% of women say they've seen sexual harassment at work; 38% of men say so.
- 24% of women say they are uncomfortable reporting sexual harassment; 12% of men say so.
- 43% of women say they believe more media attention will decrease sexual harassment in the workplace; 29% don't and 28% are not sure.

When it comes to the women who aren't reporting sexual harassment at work, the reasons vary.

- 52% don't want to create a "fuss."
- 34% don't believe it would make any difference.
- 28% are afraid of retribution.
- 19% feel shame or shared responsibility.

Consider data on sexual harassment claims filed with the Equal Employment Opportunity Commission. A study of four years worth of claims found that two-thirds of filers experienced retaliation—being transferred to different jobs or shifts, or being fired. Just 23% of complaints resulted in monetary awards, with the median compensation about $10,000. One analyst says: "It's not surprising that so few people file formal complaints given the high cost of complaining."

What are the Implications?

Where do we go from here? Is the glass on sexual-harassment progress half-empty or half-full? Why are some employers unable or unwilling to actively embrace policies that create harassment free work cultures? Is #MeToo capable of making a real difference in the everyday experiences of men and women at work? Will things change for the better as a new generation enters the workforce? What about you? Where in the #MeToo statistics are you, or will you be?

The Hawthorne Studies

The shift toward behavioral thinking in management gained momentum in 1924 when the Western Electric Company commissioned a research program to study worker productivity at the Hawthorne Works of the firm's Chicago plant.[21] A team led by Harvard's Elton Mayo set out to learn how economic incentives and workplace conditions affected workers' output. But they concluded that unforeseen "psychological factors" somehow interfered with their experiments.

Social Setting and Human Relations
One study focused on worker fatigue and output. Six assembly workers were isolated for intensive study in a special test room. Their production was measured as changes were made to the length of rest pauses, workdays, and workweeks. Results showed that productivity increased regardless of the changes. Researchers concluded that the new "social setting" in the test room made workers want to do a good job. They shared pleasant social interactions with one another and received special attention that made them feel important. They were given a lot of information and were frequently asked for their opinions. None of this was the case in their regular jobs. In other words, good "human relations" seemed to result in higher productivity (see the Ethics feature for insight into how employers can get this information).

Ethics: Know Right from Wrong | A Deloitte survey found that 40% of employers use artificial intelligence.

AI Offers Instant Insights on Employee Morale

Den Rise/Shutterstock.com

Human resource management used to be a face-to-face process. That's still there, but, artificial intelligence is starting to put the machine in many places where HR people used to be. A Deloitte survey found that 40% of employers now use artificial intelligence in HRM, and one of those areas is tracking employee morale.

Steel processor SPS in Manhattan, Kansas, conducts an annual survey to gauge how its 600 employees feel about management and their employer. That's old news. What's new is that AI software called Xander now analyzes the language used in answering open-ended questions to identify deep opinions and feelings, ones that are otherwise missed. Things like confusion, optimism, and anger are brought to light. One manager vowed

to make changes after learning that while team members viewed him as fair and honest, he was also prone to losing his temper when stressed.

First Horizon Bank in Memphis, Tennessee, puts AI to work as soon as data comes in from its annual employee survey. It used to take a six-person HR team up to three months to analyze and report back on 3,500 responses. Once reports were made and plans set for changes to be made, it was often time for the next survey. Since Xander now provides immediate insights, change plans—such as an update to the bank's training program—can be started right away.

Along with AI's opportunities to turn data into useful information come some controversies. By taking the person out of the equation, one worry—shared by the U.S. Equal Employment Opportunity Commission (EEOC)—is that AI's algorithm-based analyses of demographics can bias hiring, termination, and pay decisions. Also, some employees view the use of AI as a form of "tracking" that invades their privacy. In response, recommendations are to make sure there is a human review of all AI-generated decisions and that employees are well informed about the uses and limitation of AI in their workplaces.

What Do You Think?

New technology is bringing lots of changes to the workplace. Data is driving more and more decisions, and AI is driving more and more data analysis. How comfortable are you working for an employer that uses AI for hiring, firing, career development, and other HR decisions? What are the limits of bringing AI into more aspects of workplace decision making? Should AI be regulated, for example under the EEOC, to ensure that unintended biases don't creep into the employment process?

Further studies of employee attitudes, interpersonal relations, and group dynamics also led to "complex" and "baffling" results. Factors like work conditions or wages were found to increase satisfaction for some workers and dissatisfaction for others. Some workers were willing to restrict their output to avoid upsetting the group, even if it meant sacrificing pay that could otherwise be earned by increasing output.

Lessons of the Hawthorne Studies   Scholars now criticize the Hawthorne studies for poor research design and weak empirical support for the conclusions drawn.[22] Yet, despite these problems, the studies shifted managers' and researchers' attention toward social and human factors as drivers of productivity. They brought visibility to the idea that workers' feelings, attitudes, and relationships with co-workers affected their work, and that groups have important influences on individuals. They also identified the **Hawthorne effect**—the tendency of workers singled out for special attention to perform as well—or better than—anticipated because of expectations created by the situation.

The **Hawthorne effect** is the tendency of persons singled out for special attention to perform as expected.

Maslow's Theory of Human Needs

The work of psychologist Abraham Maslow, in the area of human "needs," also has had a major impact on the behavioral approach to management.[23] Maslow described a **need** as a physiological or psychological tension a person feels compelled to satisfy. These tensions that influence workers' attitudes and behaviors. Maslow placed needs into the hierarchy shown in **Figure 2.3**. From lowest to highest in order, they are physiological, safety, social, esteem, and self-actualization needs.

A **need** is a physiological or psychological deficiency that a person feels compelled to satisfy.

According to the **deficit principle** a satisfied need does not motivate behavior.

According to the **progression principle** a need is activated only when the next-lower-level need is satisfied.

Maslow's theory is based on two underlying principles—the **deficit principle** and the **progression principle**. The deficit principle is a satisfied need that does not motivate behavior. People try to satisfy "deprived" needs or those for which there is a "deficit" (e.g., when I'm hungry, I seek to satisfy my hunger by eating—when I'm done eating, hunger doesn't motivate me anymore). The progression principle is the five needs that exist in a hierarchy

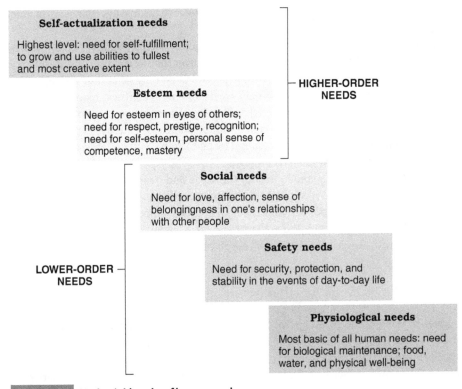

FIGURE 2.3 **Maslow's hierachy of human needs.**

of "prepotency." A need at any level becomes active only when the next-lower-level need is satisfied (e.g., I'm thirsty and lonely—but I won't be motivated to chat with my friends until I've had something to drink). Maslow argued that people try to satisfy these five needs in sequence. They progress, step by step, from the lowest level in the hierarchy up to the highest. Along the way, a deprived need dominates attention and determines behavior until it is satisfied. Then, the next-higher-level need is activated. At the level of self-actualization, the deficit and progression principles cease to operate. The more this need is satisfied, the stronger it grows.

Consistent with human relations thinking, Maslow's theory implies that managers who understand and help workers to satisfy their important needs at work will get more productivity out of their employees. Although scholars now recognize things are more complicated than this, Maslow's ideas are still relevant. Consider the case of volunteer workers at the local Red Cross, animal shelter, or other community organizations. What can be done to motivate workers who aren't paid? Maslow's ideas suggest linking volunteer work with opportunities to satisfy higher-order needs like esteem and self-actualization.

McGregor's Theory X and Theory Y

Douglas McGregor was heavily influenced by both the Hawthorne studies and Abraham Maslow. In his classic book, *The Human Side of Enterprise*, McGregor argued that managers should give more attention to workers' social and self-actualizing needs.[24] He called on managers to shift their view of human nature away from a set of assumptions he called Theory X and toward ones he called Theory Y. You can check your own managerial assumptions by completing the self-assessment at the end of the chapter.

According to McGregor, managers with **Theory X** assumptions believe that employees generally dislike work, have little ambition, are irresponsible and resistant to change, and prefer to be led rather than to lead. In contrast, managers with **Theory Y** assumptions believe employees are willing to work hard, accept responsibility, are capable of self-control and self-direction, and are imaginative and creative.

One important point regarding Theory X and Theory Y is that McGregor believed these assumptions create **self-fulfilling prophecies**. When managers behave consistent with the assumptions, he said, they end up encouraging employees to act in ways that confirm managers' original expectations.[25]

Managers with Theory X assumptions tend to act in a very directive, command-and-control, top-down way that gives employees little say over their work. These behaviors create passive, dependent, reluctant subordinates, who tend to do only what they are told to do or required to do, reinforcing the original Theory X viewpoint. In contrast, managers with Theory Y assumptions tend to behave in ways that engage workers, giving them more job involvement, freedom, and responsibility. This creates opportunities for employees to satisfy esteem and self-actualization needs, and they respond by performing with initiative and high performance, creating a positive self-fulfilling prophecy.[26]

Theory Y thinking is reflected in a lot of the ideas and developments discussed in this book, such as valuing diversity, employee engagement, self-managing teams, empowerment, and leadership. You need to ponder your Theory X and Y assumptions and think through their implications for how you behave as a manager and team leader. You also must be prepared to meet and work with others holding different assumptions.

> **Theory X** assumes people dislike work, lack ambition, act irresponsibly, and prefer to be led.
>
> **Theory Y** assumes people are willing to work, like responsibility, and are self-directed and creative.
>
> A **self-fulfilling prophecy** occurs when a person acts in ways that confirm another's expectations.

Argyris's Theory of Adult Personality

The ideas of Maslow and McGregor inspired the well-regarded scholar and business consultant Chris Argyris. In his book *Personality and Organization*, Argyris contrasts management practices found in traditional, bureaucratic organizations with the needs and capabilities of mature adults.[27] Argyris believed that problems, such as absenteeism, turnover, apathy, alienation, and low morale may be signs of a mismatch. He also argued that managers who treat employees as responsible adults will achieve the highest productivity. It's the self-fulfilling prophecy notion again: If you treat people as grown-ups, that's the way they'll behave.

Consider these examples of how Argyris's thinking differs from that of earlier management thinking. In scientific management, the principle of specialization assumes that people will work more efficiently as tasks become simpler and better defined. Argyris believed that this principle limits opportunities for self-actualization. In Weber's bureaucracy, people work in a clear hierarchy of authority, with higher levels directing and controlling lower levels. Argyris worried that this creates dependent, passive workers who feel they have little control over their work environments. In Fayol's administrative principles, the concept of unity of direction assumes that efficiency increases when work is planned and directed by supervisors. Argyris argued that this may create conditions for psychological failure; conversely, psychological success is more likely when employees are allowed to define their own goals.

Learning Check

LEARNING OBJECTIVE 2.2

Identify key insights of the behavioral management approaches.

Be Sure You Can • explain Follett's concept of organizations as communities • define the Hawthorne effect • explain how the Hawthorne findings influenced the development of management thought • explain how Maslow's hierarchy of needs operates in the workplace • distinguish between Theory X and Theory Y assumptions, and explain why McGregor favored Theory Y • explain Argyris's criticism that traditional organizational practices are inconsistent with mature adult personalities

---

2.3 | Modern Management Foundations

WileyPLUS

See Author Video

LEARNING OBJECTIVE 2.3

Explain the core foundations of modern management theory and practice.

> **Learn More About**
>
> Quantitative tools and data analytics • Organizations as systems • Contingency thinking • Quality management • Evidence-based management

The concepts, models, and ideas discussed so far helped set the stage for continuing developments in management thought. They ushered in modern management approaches that include the use of quantitative tools and data analytics, a systems view of organizations, contingency thinking, commitment to quality management, and the importance of evidence-based management.

Quantitative Tools and Data Analytics

The typical quantitative approach to management works like this: a problem is encountered, it is systematically analyzed, appropriate mathematical techniques are applied, and an optimum solution is identified. The following examples show this in action.

Problem: An oil exploration company is worried about future petroleum reserves in various parts of the world. *Quantitative tool—Mathematical forecasting* makes future projections for reserve sizes and depletion rates that are used in the planning process and oil prospecting strategies.

Problem: A "big box" retailer is trying to deal with decreasing profit margins by minimizing inventory costs, but must also avoid being "out of stock" for customers. *Quantitative tool—Inventory analysis* helps control inventories by mathematically determining how much inventory to automatically order and when to order it.

Problem: A grocery store is getting complaints from customers that wait times are too long for checkouts during certain times of the day. *Quantitative tool—Queuing theory* allocates service personnel and workstations based on alternative workload demands in a way that minimizes both customer wait time and personnel costs.

Problem: A manufacturer wants to maximize profits on the production of three different products on three different machines, each of which can be only be used at distinct periods of times and for runs at different costs. *Quantitative tool—Linear programming* calculates how best to allocate production across the three machines.

Problem: A real estate developer wants to control costs and finish building an apartment complex on schedule. *Quantitative tool—Network modeling* breaks large tasks into smaller components and diagrams them in step-by-step sequences. This allows project managers to analyze, plan, and control timetables for the completion of activity subsets.

Although quantitative analysis has always been useful in management, the availability of inexpensive, convenient, affordable computing is dramatically expanding its power. With the collection, storage, and analysis of data now easier than ever before, an area known as **data analytics** is becoming indispensable to organizations of all types. Think of data analytics as the systematic analysis of large databases—often called "big data"—to solve problems and make informed decisions.[28] Here are two examples.

Data analytics is the systematic analysis of large databases to solve problems and make informed decisions.

Problem—Sales were flat and inventories were high at the Schwan Food Company. Delivery drivers were using six-week-old lists of customers' prior orders to decide who to visit and what to offer them. *Analytics solution*—The situation improved substantially after Schwan installed a new analytics program. It churns vast amounts of historical data to predict customer preferences and sends daily sales recommendations directly to each driver's tablet.

Problem—Software engineering talent is in short supply for Google and other high-tech companies. Competition for new hires is intense and retention is difficult as experienced engineers become poaching targets for rival firms. *Analytics solution*—Google has an analytics tool that pools information from performance reviews, surveys, and pay and promotion histories. The data is mined with an algorithm that identifies engineers who might be open to offers from other firms. Managers use this information to develop plans for retaining these talented engineers and reduce the likelihood that they will find competing offers attractive.[29]

Organizations as Systems

Organizations have long been described as cooperative systems that achieve great things by focusing resources and the contributions of many individuals toward a common purpose. In reality, cooperation among people and different moving parts is imperfect and can be improved. That is why it's critical to understand the full complexity of organizations as a **system** of interrelated parts or **subsystems** that work together to achieve common goals.[30]

Organizations function as **open systems** that interact with their environment in a continual process of transforming inputs—people, technology, information, money, and supplies—into outputs—goods and services. **Figure 2.4** shows how an organization functions as an interacting network of subsystems. The activities of these subsystems individually and collectively support the larger system to make things happen. The operations and service management subsystems anchor the transformation process, while linking with other subsystems such as purchasing, accounting, and sales. Organizations can only perform well when each subsystem both performs its tasks well and cooperates with other subsystems.

A **system** is a collection of interrelated parts working together for a purpose.

A **subsystem** is a smaller component of a larger system.

An **open system** interacts with its environment and transforms resource inputs into outputs.

FIGURE 2.4 **Organizations as complex networks of interacting subsystems.**

Contingency Thinking

Contingency thinking tries to match management practices with situational demands.

Successful managers identify and implement practices that best fit with the unique demands of different situations. This requires **contingency thinking** that matches actions with problems and opportunities specific to different people and settings. From a contingency perspective there is no "one best way" to manage in all circumstances. The challenge is to understand situational differences and respond to them in ways that fit with their unique characteristics.[31] Can you think of situations at work or at school where you need to adjust your interpersonal behavior, for example, to succeed?

Contingency thinking is an important theme in this book, and its implications extend to all of the management functions—from planning and controlling for diverse environmental conditions, to organizing for different strategies, to leading in different performance situations. A good illustration takes us back once again to the concept of bureaucracy, which Weber offered as an ideal form of organization. But from a contingency perspective, bureaucracy is only one possible way of organizing. What turns out to be the "best" structure in any given situation will depend on a range of factors, including environmental uncertainty, an organization's primary technology, and the strategy being pursued. A tight bureaucracy works best when the environment is relatively stable and operations are predictable and uncomplicated. In complex and changing situations more flexible structures are needed.[32]

Quality Management

The work of W. Edwards Deming is a cornerstone of the quality movement in management.[33] His story began in 1951, when he was invited to Japan to explain quality control techniques that had been developed in the United States. "When Deming spoke," we might say, "the Japanese listened." The principles he taught the Japanese were straightforward and they worked: Tally defects, analyze and trace them to the source, make corrections, and keep a record of what happens afterward. Deming's approach emphasizes the use of statistical tools, commitment to quality assurance training, and constant innovation.[34]

Total quality management is an organization-wide commitment to continuous improvement, product quality, and customer needs.

These ideas contributed to the emergence of **total quality management**, or TQM, which incorporates quality principles in organizations' strategic objectives. TQM principles are applied to all aspects of operations with a focus on meeting customers' needs by doing things right the first time. Most TQM approaches begin with buy-in on a total quality commitment. This applies to all employees and every organizational subsystem—from resource acquisition and supply chain management, through production and into physical distribution of finished goods and services, and ultimately to customer relationships. The search for and commitment to quality

Make Learning Style Work for You

In light of all the complexities associated with modern management practice, it is important to know your own personal **learning style**. Think of learning style as how you like to learn through receiving, processing, and recalling new information.

Each of us tends to learn in slightly different ways. Look how some students do well in lecture classes, while others do not. But these others might excel in case study or project classes that

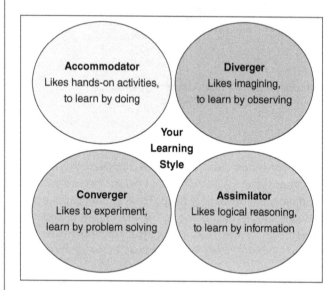

emphasize discussion and problem solving rather than digesting information.

There's no right or wrong learning style; however, it is critical to recognize and understand some underlying differences. Some people learn by watching. They observe others and model what they see. Others learn by doing. They act and experiment, learning as they go. Some people are feelers, for whom emotions and values are very important. Others are thinkers who emphasize reason and analysis.

It's a personal challenge to learn something new every day, and it's a managerial challenge to consistently help employees learn as well. One of our most significant challenges is to always embrace experiences at school, at work, and in everyday living and try our best to learn from these experiences. Every employee is unique, most problem situations are complex, and key performance factors are constantly changing. Professional success is much more likely for managers who are excited to learn, and also are excited to help others to learn.

Get To Know Yourself Better

Look at the diagram of learning styles and think about your own preferences. Shade in each circle to show the degree to which that description best fits with your preferences. This snapshot of your personal learning style is good food for thought. Ask: (1) "What are the implications of my learning style for how I perform academically and how well I perform at work?" (2) "How does my learning style influence my relationships with others in study groups and work teams?" (3) "How does my learning style influence the kinds of information I pay the most attention to and the kind of information I tend to overlook?"

---

reflects an emphasis on **continuous improvement**—always looking for new ways to improve on current practices. The key takeaway is that it is critical to never be satisfied; something always can and should be improved—whether it is machines, people, processes, or relationships (see Insight feature).

ISO certification by the International Standards Organization in Geneva, Switzerland, has become a global stamp of approval for quality management. Businesses and nonprofits that strive to be "world-class" are increasingly expected to have ISO certification. To obtain it, they undergo a rigorous assessment by independent auditors to determine whether ISO's strict quality requirements have been met.

Continuous improvement involves always searching for new ways to improve work quality and performance.

ISO certification indicates conformance with a rigorous set of international quality standards.

Evidence-Based Management

Managers are always searching for practical answers to questions dealing with day-to-day dilemmas and situations.[35] What is the best performance appraisal method? What selection method works best for high-performance teams? How should a merit pay system be designed and implemented? When does directive leadership work best? How do you structure organizations for innovation? Given the importance of the answers to such questions, it is critical to be cautious and a bit skeptical when separating fads from facts and assumptions from informed insight based on empirical data and analysis.

In light of the complexity of work and organizations today, a critical concern of management scholars is that we may be too quick to accept the results of studies based on poor science or questionable evidence. And if research may be flawed or preliminary in terms of drawing firm conclusions, extra care needs to be taken interpreting and applying results to management practice.[36]

New Rules for Office Engagement

laflor/E+/Getty Images

Things have changed in the workplace; one might say they've changed monumentally. The #MeToo movement is here and the facts on sexual harassment at work speak for themselves. If you missed it, just check the feature box on Ethics found earlier in the chapter. But let's be careful here being a man in the workplace isn't a bad thing. Perhaps it's a good time to take stock and offer men good advice on how to interact with women without crossing *the line*.

It isn't necessarily a good thing that more than half the men surveyed in a Pew Research poll expressed discomfort serving as mentors to female co-workers, being alone with them at work, and meeting them in work-sponsored social occasions. A lot of opportunities for coaching, networking, and career advancement for women may be missed as men withdraw from such situations and step back into their own safe spaces. After all, it may be better to watch your step as a man than to have an interaction misinterpreted.

Some men and employers are turning to training as a way out of the "to interact … or not to interact" dilemma. At a conference organized by AnitaB.org, men received advice on how to mentor and support female coworkers. The goal was to help attendees learn how to engage positively and not withdraw for fear of saying or doing something wrong. One female at the conference said: "I just want someone who has my back, listens to me communicate in my own way."

Your Take

Just what is *the line* that both men and women worry about being crossed in workplace interactions? Can you describe it in your own words? Could you, and are you willing to, describe this line to co-workers to create shared understandings of what is and is not okay for you? The workplace is a "team" place and organizations really can't afford to have men withdrawing any more than they can afford women being overlooked, degraded, or treated harmfully. So, what can we do? What are you looking for in an employer and organizational culture? Where does all this fit into your career aspirations and expectations?

Evidence-based management involves making decisions based on hard facts about what really works.

The notion of **evidence-based management** calls for management decisions to be made based on "hard facts"—that is, about what really works—rather than on "dangerous half-truths"—things that sound good but lack solid evidence.[37] The goal is for managers to be well informed and knowledgeable when making decisions. Evidence-based management is about managers "making decisions through the conscientious, explicit, and judicious use of four sources of information: practitioner expertise and judgment, evidence from the local context, a critical evaluation of the best available research evidence, and the perspectives of those people who might be affected by the decision."[38] You may recognize incidents in your personal affairs where you make decisions based on less-than-complete information, or even hearsay (see choices feature). When you do, are you prepared to learn from experience and rely more on evidence-based decision making in the future?

Management scholars support and inform evidence-based management by conducting solid and meaningful research using scientific methods, and by rigorously examining and reporting case studies and insights from managers' experiences.[39] Some research carves out new and innovative territory while other research refines and extends knowledge that has come down in building-block fashion over time. You'll notice that management research involves data collection and analysis in one form or another. But just because a research study uses data, doesn't make it solid and scientific. The following criteria are useful as a first step to determine whether or not good scientific methods have been used.

- A research question or problem is clearly identified.
- One or more hypotheses is stated to describe possible explanations.
- The research design provides a good test of the hypotheses.
- Data are rigorously gathered, analyzed, and interpreted.
- Hypotheses are accepted or rejected and conclusions made based on the evidence.

When research satisfies the scientific methods test, managers can be more confident accepting and applying results in actual practice. Gathering data from a sample of some 1,000 firms, for example, researchers examined the link between human resource management and organizational performance.[40] They found that firms using a mix of positive human resource management practices had more sales per employee and higher profits per employee than firms that did not. These positive practices included employment security, selective hiring, self-managed teams, high wages based on performance merit, training and skill development, minimal status differences, and shared information.[41]

Learning Check

LEARNING OBJECTIVE 2.3

Explain the core foundations of modern management theory and practice.

Be Sure You Can • define *system*, *subsystem*, and *open system* • apply these concepts to describe the operations of an organization in your community • define *contingency thinking* and give examples of how it is used by managers • describe evidence-based management and its link with scientific methods

Management Learning Review: Get Prepared for Quizzes and Exams

Summary

LEARNING OBJECTIVE 2.1 Describe the principal insights of classical management thinking.

- Frederick Taylor's four principles of scientific management focused on the need to carefully select, train, and support workers for individual task performance.
- Henri Fayol suggested that managers should learn what are now known as the management functions of planning, organizing, leading, and controlling.
- Max Weber described bureaucracy with its clear hierarchy, formal rules, and well-defined jobs as an ideal form of organization.

For Discussion Should Weber's notion of the ideal bureaucracy be scrapped altogether, or is it still relevant today?

LEARNING OBJECTIVE 2.2 Identify key insights of the behavioral management approaches.

- The behavioral approaches shifted management attention toward the human factor as a key element in organizational performance.

- Mary Parker Follett describes organizations as communities within which members combine talents to work for a greater good.
- The Hawthorne studies suggested that work behavior is influenced by social and psychological forces and that work performance may be improved by better "human relations."
- Abraham Maslow's hierarchy of human needs introduced the concept of self-actualization and the potential for people to experience self-fulfillment in their work.
- Douglas McGregor urged managers to shift away from Theory X and toward Theory Y thinking, which views people as independent, responsible, and capable of self-direction in their work.
- Chris Argyris pointed out that adults may react negatively when constrained by strict management practices and rigid organizational structures.

For Discussion How can a manager benefit by using insights from Maslow's hierarchy of needs theory?

LEARNING OBJECTIVE 2.3 Explain the core foundations of modern management theory and practice.

- Analytics that use advanced quantitative analysis techniques in decision sciences and operations management can help managers solve complex problems.
- Organizations are open systems that interact with their external environments, while consisting of many internal subsystems that must work together in a coordinated way to support the organization's overall success.
- Contingency thinking avoids "one best way" arguments, instead recognizing the need to understand situational differences and respond appropriately to them.

- Quality management focuses on making a total commitment to product and service quality throughout an organization, maintaining continuous improvement and meeting worldwide quality standards such as ISO certification.
- Evidence-based management uses findings from rigorous scientific research to identify management practices for high performance.

For Discussion Can system and subsystem dynamics help describe and explain performance problems for an organization in your community?

Self-Test 2

Multiple-Choice Questions

1. The assumption that people are complex with widely varying needs is most associated with the _____ management approaches.
   - a. classical
   - b. neoclassical
   - c. behavioral
   - d. modern

2. The father of scientific management is _____.
   - a. Weber
   - b. Taylor
   - c. Mintzberg
   - d. Katz

3. When the registrar of a university deals with students by an identification number rather than a name, which characteristic of bureaucracy is being displayed and what is its intended benefit?
   - a. division of labor, competency
   - b. merit-based careers, productivity
   - c. rules and procedures, efficiency
   - d. impersonality, fairness

4. If an organization was performing poorly and Henri Fayol was called in as a consultant, what would he most likely suggest to improve things?
   - a. Teach managers to better plan and control.
   - b. Teach workers more efficient job methods.
   - c. Promote to management only the most competent workers.
   - d. Find ways to increase corporate social responsibility.

5. One example of how scientific management principles are applied in organizations today would be:
   - a. conducting studies to increase efficiencies in job performance.
   - b. finding alternatives to a bureaucratic structure.
   - c. training managers to better understand worker attitudes.
   - d. focusing managers on teamwork rather than individual jobs.

6. The Hawthorne studies raised awareness of how _____ can be important influences on productivity.
   - a. structures
   - b. human factors
   - c. physical work conditions
   - d. pay and rewards

7. Advice to study a job, carefully train workers to do that job, and link financial incentives to job performance would most likely come from _____.
   - a. scientific management
   - b. contingency management
   - c. Henri Fayol
   - d. Abraham Maslow

8. The highest level in Maslow's hierarchy includes _____ needs.
   - a. safety
   - b. esteem
   - c. self-actualization
   - d. physiological

9. Which management theorist would most agree with the statement "If you treat people as grownups they will perform that way"?
   - a. Argyris
   - b. Deming
   - c. Weber
   - d. Fuller

10. When people perform in a situation as they are expected to, this is sometimes called the _____ effect.
    - a. Hawthorne
    - b. systems
    - c. contingency
    - d. open-systems

11. Resource acquisition and customer satisfaction are important when an organization is viewed as a(n) _____.
    - a. bureaucracy
    - b. closed system
    - c. open system
    - d. pyramid

12. The loan-processing department would be considered a _____ of your local bank or credit union.
    - a. subsystem
    - b. closed system
    - c. resource input
    - d. cost center

13. When a manager notices that Sheryl has strong social needs and assigns her a job in customer relations and gives Kwabena lots of praise because of his strong ego needs, the manager is displaying _____.

   a. systems thinking

   b. Theory X

   c. motion study

   d. contingency thinking

14. Which is the correct match?

   a. Follet–analytics

   b. McGregor–motion study

   c. Deming–quality management

   d. Maslow–Theory X and Y

15. When managers try to avoid hearsay and make decisions based on solid facts and information, this is known as _____.

   a. continuous improvement

   b. evidence-based management

   c. TQM

   d. Theory X management

Short-Response Questions

16. Explain how McGregor's Theory Y assumptions can create self-fulfilling prophecies consistent with the current emphasis on participation and involvement in the workplace.

17. How do the deficit and progression principles operate in Maslow's hierarchy-of-needs theory?

18. Define contingency thinking and give an example of how it might apply to management.

19. Explain why the external environment is so important in the open-systems view of organizations.

Essay Question

20. Enrique Temoltzin has just been appointed the new manager of your local college bookstore. Enrique would like to make sure the store operates according to Weber's bureaucracy. Describe the characteristics of bureaucracy and answer this question: Is the bureaucracy a good management approach for Enrique to follow? Discuss the possible limitations of bureaucracy and the implications for managing people as key assets of the store.

Career Skills & Competencies: Make Yourself Valuable!

Evaluate Career Situations

What Would You Do?

1. Paying a Summer Worker

It's summer job time and you've found something that just might work—handling technical support inquiries at a local Internet provider. The regular full-time employees are paid by the hour. Summer hires like you fill in when they go on vacation. However, you will be paid by the call for each customer that you handle. How will this pay plan affect your work behavior as a customer service representative? Is this summer pay plan a good choice by the management of the Internet provider?

2. Good Performance but No Pay Raises

As a manager in a small local firm you've been told that because of the poor economy workers can't be given any pay raises this year. You have some really hardworking and high-performing people on your team whom you were counting on giving solid raises to. Now what can you do? How can you use insights from Maslow's hierarchy of needs to solve this dilemma of finding suitable rewards for high performance?

3. I've Got This Great Idea

You've just come up with a great idea for improving productivity and morale in a shop that silk-screen T-shirts. You want to allow workers to work four 10-hour days if they want instead of the normal five day/40-hour week. With the added time off, you reason, they'll be happier and more productive while working. But your boss isn't so sure. "Show me some evidence," she says. Can you design a research study that can be done in the shop to show whether your proposal is a good one?

Reflect on the Self-Assessment

Managerial Assumptions

Instructions

Read the following statements. Use the space in the margins to write "Yes" if you agree with the statement, or "No" if you disagree with it. Force yourself to take a Yes or No position.

1. Is good pay and a secure job enough to satisfy most workers?

2. Should a manager help and coach subordinates in their work?

3. Do most people like real responsibility in their jobs?

4. Are most people afraid to learn new things in their jobs?

5. Should managers let subordinates control the quality of their work?

6. Do most people dislike work?

7. Are most people creative?

8. Should a manager closely supervise and direct the work of subordinates?

9. Do most people tend to resist change?

10. Do most people work only as hard as they have to?

11. Should workers be allowed to set their own job goals?

12. Are most people happiest off the job?

13. Do most workers really care about the organization they work for?

14. Should a manager help subordinates advance and grow in their jobs?

Scoring

Count the number of yes responses to items 1, 4, 6, 8, 9, 10, 12. Write that number here as [X = _____].

Count the number of yes responses to items 2, 3, 5, 7, 11, 13, 14. Write that score here as [Y = _____].

Interpretation

This assessment provides insight into your orientation toward Douglas McGregor's Theory X (your "X" score) and Theory Y (your "Y" score) assumptions as discussed earlier in the chapter. You should review the discussion of McGregor's thinking in this chapter and consider the ways you are likely to behave toward other people at work. Think, in particular, about the types of "self-fulfilling prophecies" your managerial assumptions are likely to create.

Contribute to the Class Exercise

Evidence-Based Management Quiz

Instructions

1. For each of the following questions answer "T" (true) if you believe the statement is backed by solid research evidence, or "F" (false) if you do not believe it is an evidence-based statement.[42]

   T F 1. Intelligence is a better predictor of job performance than having a conscientious personality.

   T F 2. Job candidates screened for values perform better than those screened for intelligence.

   T F 3. A highly intelligent person will have a hard time performing well in a low-skill job.

   T F 4. "Integrity tests" are good predictors of whether employees will steal, be absent, or take advantage of their employers in other ways.

   T F 5. Goal setting is more likely to result in improved performance than is participation in decision making.

   T F 6. Errors in performance appraisals can be reduced through proper training.

   T F 7. People behave in ways that show pay is more important to them than what they indicate on surveys.

   T F 8. People hired through employee referrals have better retention rates than those hired from other recruiting sources.

   T F 9. Workers who get training and development opportunities at work tend to have lower desires to change employers.

   T F 10. Being "realistic" in job interviews and telling prospective employees about both negative and positive job aspects improves employee retention.

2. Share your answers with others in your assigned group. Discuss the reasons members chose the answers they did; arrive at a final answer to each question for the group as a whole.

3. Compare your results with these answers "from the evidence."

4. Engage in a class discussion of how commonsense answers can sometimes differ from answers provided by evidence. Ask: What are the implications of this discussion for management practice?

Manage a Critical Incident

Theory X versus Theory Y

You've been at Magnetar Logistics Solutions for nine years and earned a reputation for leading a team that gets done what you say it will get done when you say it will be done. Now your sales team is close to landing a new 10-figure contract with an established client, Peterson Warehousing, Inc. You brought Peterson on board six years ago and have since grown and nurtured the relationship, and gotten to know this client in depth. One of the reasons you've achieved so much over the years is that you've always trusted your team members and given them the room and support they need to operate in their own way. They've repaid you by coming through time and time again with top quality solutions that always matched clients' needs. But Peterson is a different case—at least it seems that way to you—it's your baby and it's a big account. You know Peterson better than anyone else, and now you're facing a very hard deadline in only weeks, which will determine whether or not you get the new contract. At this point you're doing a lot of close supervision on this project and not giving team members very much space to operate. There are many complexities with Peterson that you're worried the team will overlook, but which you are on top of. The team as a whole is starting to feel the impact of your switch in management style.

Questions

(1) What are the consequences of your shifting management style midstream on this project . . . for success with the client? . . . for your team? . . . for your reputation as a successful manager? (2) Is a hands-on Theory X approach the best way to go here, or have you made a miscalculation? (3) Should you back off and return to the Theory Y assumptions that worked well in the past? (4) Is it too late to revert to your normal approach? (5) How can you infuse your Peterson expertise into the project while still keeping team members motivated and satisfied with your leadership?

Collaborate on the Team Project

Management in Popular Culture

Movies, television shows, and music display a lot about our popular culture. Many deal with work situations and themes—things like leadership, team dynamics, attitudes, personalities—that are topics of the management course. Management learning is readily available in popular culture. We just have to look for it.

Team Task

Choose one or more topics from this chapter or a previous chapter and discuss popular culture examples that offer insights into them. Select one to share with the class at large in a multimedia presentation. Be sure to include a strong justification for your choice.

Suggestions

- Listen to music. Pick out themes that reflect important management concepts and theories. Identify what their messages say about management and working today.
- Watch movies, YouTube videos, and television episodes and advertisements. Look for the workplace issues and management themes.
- Read the comics. Compare and contrast management and working themes in two or three popular comic strips.
- Create your own alternative to the above suggestions.

Analyze the Case Study

Zara International | Fashion at the Speed of Light

Go to **Management Cases for Critical Thinking** at the end of the book to find this case.

CHAPTER 3

Ethics and Social Responsibility

Character Doesn't Stay Home When We Go to Work

Alessia Pierdomenico/Reuters/Newscom

"Corporations are a legal fiction. You have to deter bad individual conduct within corporations. People who did the conduct are going to be held accountable."

Benjamin Lawsky, New York's Banking Regulator

Chapter Quick Start

From the classroom to the meeting room to the boardroom to the family room, we face complex, "gray area" issues all of the time. We live in a transparent world with free-flowing information, where our words and actions can be closely scrutinized. It's easy to get caught up in questionable situations that put values and ethics to the test. This chapter is an opportunity to think about ethics in our personal and work lives, as well as in the responsibilities organizations have to society.

LEARNING OBJECTIVES

3.1 Define ethics and describe the foundations of ethical behavior.

3.2 Discuss ethical dilemmas and common ethics issues in the workplace.

3.3 Describe approaches to maintaining high ethical standards.

3.4 Explain corporate social responsibility and corporate governance.

Career Readiness – What to Look for Inside

Thought Leadership

Analysis > *Make Data Your Friend* Manager Behavior Key to Ethical Workplace

Choices > *Think before You Act* Gender Quotas Add More Women to Corporate Boards

Ethics > *Know Right from Wrong* Child Labor is a Global Business Reality

Insight > *Learn about Yourself* Individual Character is a Confidence Builder

Skills Make You Valuable

- **Evaluate** *Career Situations:* What Would You Do?

- **Reflect** *On the Self-Assessment:* Terminal Values

- **Contribute** *To the Class Exercise:* Confronting Ethical Dilemmas

- **Manage** *A Critical Incident:* Dealing with a Global Supply Chain

- **Collaborate** *On the Team Project:* Stakeholder Maps

- **Analyze** *The Case Study:* Warby Parker: Disruption with a Conscience

46

Who doesn't want high ethics, social responsibility, and principled leadership in business, government, and all of the organizations of our society? But isn't it easy to become cynical when another scandal leads to photos of a big financial figure, corporate executive, or government official doing the "perp walk" into a police station? Why do some people and organizations do the wrong thing when given the chance, while others are positive ethical role models? In business, think of the good examples set by Ben and Jerry's, Burt's Bees, Patagonia, Tom's of Maine, and Whole Foods Markets. Surely there are others right in your local community.

The actions of organizations are driven by the people who run them. Principled—or ethical—behavior by leaders is the real difference between organizations that do good things and those that don't. When criticizing Toyota for misleading consumers about vehicle safety issues, for example, U.S. District Court Judge William H. Pauley declared that corporate misconduct is driven by people. He urged prosecutors "to hold those individuals responsible for making these decisions accountable."[1] There's no doubt that managers have special ethical responsibility. Consider this reminder from Desmond Tutu, archbishop of Capetown, South Africa, and winner of the Nobel Peace Prize.

You are powerful people. You can make this world a better place where business
decisions and methods take account of right and wrong as well as profitability. . . .
You must take a stand on important issues: the environment and ecology, affirmative
action, sexual harassment, racism and sexism, the arms race, poverty, the obligations
of the affluent West to its less-well-off sisters and brothers elsewhere.[2]

3.1 | Ethics

LEARNING OBJECTIVE 3.1

Define ethics and describe the foundations of ethical behavior.

WileyPLUS

See Author Video

> **Learn More About**
>
> Laws and values as influences on ethical behavior • Alternative views of ethics • Cultural issues and ethical behavior

How often do you ask this question: What should I do? How often do you consider "ethics" when deciding what to do? **Ethics** is defined as the moral code of principles that sets standards of good or bad, right and wrong.[3] An individual's moral code can be influenced by family, friends, local culture, religion, educational institutions, and individual experiences.[4] Importantly, ethics help people make moral choices and give us confidence in difficult situations. They encourage **ethical behavior** that is "good" and "right" in the context of the governing moral code.

Ethics establish standards of good or bad, or right or wrong, in one's conduct.

Ethical behavior is "good" or "right" in the context of a governing moral code.

Laws and Values as Influences on Ethical Behavior

People often assume that anything legal should be considered ethical. Slavery was once legal in the United States, and laws once permitted only men to vote.[5] But that doesn't mean these laws were ethical. Sometimes the law lags behind changes in a society's morals. The delay means that something that's technically legal can be morally wrong.[6] On the flip side, some things may be illegal when many or most people think they should be legal. Same-sex marriage was banned in some states until made legal by a U.S. Supreme Court decision in 2015. Marijuana use is still illegal in many states, while others are legalizing it for medical and recreational purposes.

Although the "law" is a broad-stroke benchmark, what is considered ethical becomes nuanced in times of social complexity and change. Just because something is not strictly illegal doesn't make it ethical.[7] Is it truly ethical, for example, for an employee to take longer than necessary to do a job? . . . to call in sick in order to take a day off work for leisure? . . . to fail to report rule violations or antisocial behavior by a co-worker? Although none of these acts is strictly illegal, many would consider them unethical.

Most ethical problems at work happen when people are asked to do something that violates their personal beliefs. As long as a request is technically legal or backed by authority some people will comply without worrying about it. For others, the request must pass an ethical test framed by personal **values**—the underlying beliefs and attitudes that influence behavior. The psychologist Milton Rokeach distinguishes between "terminal" and "instrumental" values.[8] **Terminal values** are preferences about desired ends or life goals. Examples include self-respect, family security, freedom, and happiness. **Instrumental values** are preferences about the means to accomplishing these ends. Among these are honesty, ambition, imagination, and self-discipline.

Although values tend to be stable over time, they also vary significantly from person to person. This can result in different interpretations of what is ethical or unethical behavior. After encountering cheating problems on an exam, a professor once told business school students they were emphasizing means over ends. "The academic values of integrity and honesty in your work," he said, "can seem to be less relevant than the instrumental goal of getting a good job."[9] And when about 10% of an MBA class was caught cheating on a take-home final, some argued this should be expected from students taught to value collaboration, teamwork, and mobile communications. Others argued that the instrumental values driving such behavior were totally unacceptable—it was an individual exam, honesty counted, the students cheated, and they should be penalized.[10]

Alternative Views of Ethics

Figure 3.1 shows four views of ethics—the utilitarian, individualism, moral rights, and justice views.[11] Each view offers a slightly different way to assess whether behavior is ethical or unethical, and each has its drawbacks. Examining issues through all four viewpoints provides a more complete picture of the ethics of a decision.

Utilitarian View The **utilitarian view** considers ethical behavior to be that which delivers the greatest good to the greatest number of people. Based on the work of nineteenth-century philosopher John Stuart Mill, this results-oriented view assesses the moral implications of actions in terms of their consequences. Managers, for example, tend to use profits, efficiency, and other performance criteria to judge what is best for the most people. An executive leading a firm facing hard financial times may decide to cut 30% of the workforce to keep the company profitable and save the jobs of remaining workers. She could justify this decision

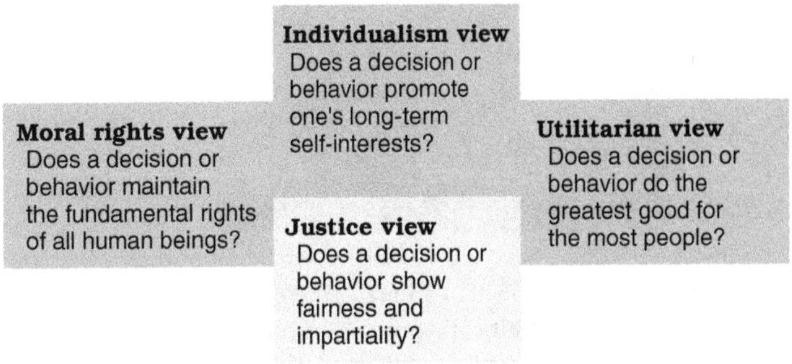

Values are broad beliefs about what is appropriate behavior.

Terminal values are preferences about desired end states.

Instrumental values are preferences regarding the means to desired ends.

In the **utilitarian view**, ethical behavior delivers the greatest good to the most people.

Individualism view
Does a decision or behavior promote one's long-term self-interests?

Moral rights view
Does a decision or behavior maintain the fundamental rights of all human beings?

Justice view
Does a decision or behavior show fairness and impartiality?

Utilitarian view
Does a decision or behavior do the greatest good for the most people?

FIGURE 3.1 **Four views of ethical behavior.**

based on a utilitarian sense of business ethics. But she can't know for sure if the economy gets better or worse, nor can she accurately measure the social and economic consequences for those losing their jobs.

Individualism View   The **individualism view** is based on the belief that one's primary commitment should be to advance long-term self-interests. The basic idea is that society will be best off if everyone maximizes their own utility or happiness. The faulty assumption is that people are self-regulating in the quest for long-term individual advantage. For example, lying and cheating for short-term gain should not be tolerated, because if everyone did this, then no one's long-term interests are served. The individualism view is supposed to promote honesty and integrity. But not everyone has the same level of self-control. If only a few individuals driven by greed take advantage of the freedom allowed by this approach, trust in the system dissolves. One executive described this as the tendency to "push the law to its outer limits" and "run roughshod over other individuals to achieve one's objectives."[12]

In the **individualism view** ethical behavior advances long-term self-interests.

Ethics: Know Right from Wrong | About 73 million children worldwide work in hazardous conditions.

Child Labor Controversies are a Global Business Reality

Thomas Cockrem/Alamy Stock Photo

The International Labour Organization (ILO) estimates there are 152 million child laborers worldwide. Half of them are 5–11 years old. About 73 million children work in hazardous conditions.

The ILO recognizes that labor can be good for kids when it "does not affect their health and personal development or interfere with their schooling." Examples include "helping their parents around the home, assisting in a family business or earning pocket money outside school hours and during school holidays." But, the ILO recognizes the bad side of child labor as well. It is work that "deprives children of their childhood, their potential and their dignity, and that is harmful to physical and mental development." Examples of child abuse through adverse working conditions include physically inappropriate work, outright slavery, forced labor or armed violence, prostitution, drug trafficking, and pornography.

It was once commonplace for children to work in factories in the United States. Some would say this contributed to the country's economic development. President Franklin D. Roosevelt signed the Fair Labor Standards Act of 1938, banning child labor in "oppressive" conditions. Today, a host of U.S. laws strictly govern the employment of children. Yet child labor is part of the economies of many countries and millions of families depend on the income children provide. Global businesses face differing laws and customs as they travel the world looking for resources, markets, and labor. Mining, food sourcing, and garment manufacturing are common targets of news exposes on child labor scandals.

What Do You Think?

Are you a "relativist" or an "absolutist" when it comes to child labor? Can you accept child labor in under certain conditions and in certain locations? Can you provide an example of when it is or could be acceptable? What is your take on the issue of economic development? If child labor did contribute to the economic development of America in the past, how do you answer those who argue that the practice should be allowed in countries struggling to achieve economic success today?

In the **moral rights view** ethical behavior respects and protects fundamental rights.

Moral Rights View

Behavior is ethical under a moral rights view when it respects and protects the fundamental rights of people. The teachings of John Locke and Thomas Jefferson uphold the rights of all people to life, liberty, and fair treatment under the law as sacred. In organizations today, this relates to employees' right to privacy, due process, free speech, health, safety, and freedom of conscience. This can be seen at the global level by the Universal Declaration of Human Rights, passed by the United Nations General Assembly in 1948 and highlighted here.[13]

- All human beings are born free and equal in dignity and rights.
- Everyone has the right to life, liberty, and security of person.
- No one shall be held in slavery or servitude.
- No one shall be subjected to torture or to cruel, inhuman, or degrading treatment or punishment.
- All are equal before the law and are entitled without any discrimination to equal protection of the law.

Although the moral rights view emphasizes individual rights, it does not address whether the outcomes associated with protecting those rights are beneficial to the majority of society. What happens, for example, when someone's right to free speech makes the workplace uncomfortable for others or offends a key customer or stakeholder of the organization?

In the **justice view** ethical behavior treats people impartially and fairly.

Justice View

The justice view maintains that behavior is ethical when people are treated equally according to the rules. This approach defines ethics based on whether outcomes are equitable.[14] Justice in organizations focuses on four dimensions—procedural, distributive, interactional, and commutative justice.[15]

Procedural justice is concerned that policies and rules are fairly applied.

Procedural justice is the degree that policies and rules are fairly applied to everyone. For example, is a sexual harassment charge against a senior executive treated the same as one against a first-level supervisor?

Distributive justice focuses on whether or not outcomes are distributed fairly.

Distributive justice is the degree that outcomes (i.e., rewards, vacation time, etc.) are fair across employees regardless of ethnicity, race, gender, age, or other individual characteristics. For example, are women and minorities treated fairly when promotions are made? Do universities an equal share of athletic scholarships to male and female students?

Interactional justice is the degree to which others are treated with dignity and respect.

Commutative justice is the degree to which an exchange or a transaction is fair to all parties.

Interactional justice is whether people treat one another with dignity and respect. For example, does a bank loan officer take time to fully explain why an applicant was turned down for a loan?[16]

Commutative justice focuses on the fairness of exchanges or transactions. Things are fair if all parties have access to relevant information and get some benefit.[17] Does a bank loan officer make it clear, for example, that an applicant may have difficulty repaying the loan if interest rates increase and the applicant's income does not?

Cultural Issues in Ethical Behavior

Situation: A 12-year-old boy is working in a garment factory in Bangladesh. He is the sole income earner for his family. He often works 12-hour days and was once burned badly by a hot iron. One day he is fired. His employer had been given an ultimatum by a major American customer: "No child workers if you want to keep our contracts." The boy says, "I don't understand. I do my job very well. My family and I need the money." *Question*: Should the boy be allowed to work?

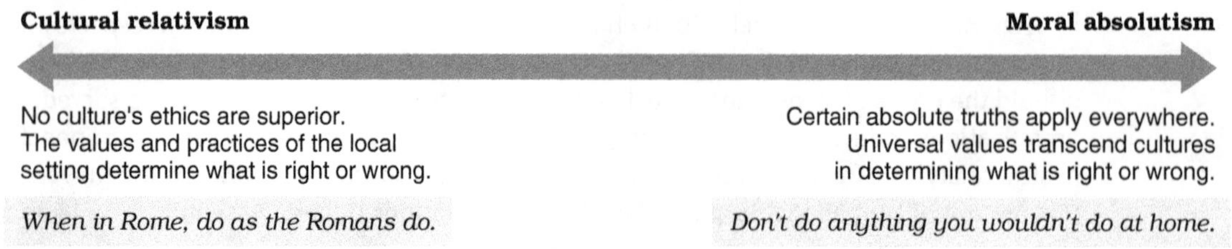

Cultural relativism   **Moral absolutism**

No culture's ethics are superior.   Certain absolute truths apply everywhere.
The values and practices of the local   Universal values transcend cultures
setting determine what is right or wrong.   in determining what is right or wrong.

When in Rome, do as the Romans do.   *Don't do anything you wouldn't do at home.*

FIGURE 3.2 **Cultural relativism and universalism in international business ethics.**
Source: Developed from Thomas Donaldson, "Values in Tension: Ethics Away from Home," *Harvard Business Review*,
vol. 74 (September–October 1996), pp. 48–62.

This complex situation is one example of the many ethics challenges faced in international business. Former Levi Strauss CEO Robert Haas once said that an ethical problem "becomes even more difficult when you overlay the complexities of different cultures and values systems that exist throughout the world."[18] Those who believe that behavior in foreign settings should be guided by the classic rule of "when in Rome, do as the Romans do" reflect an ethical position known as **cultural relativism**.[19] This is the belief that there is no one right way to behave and that ethics are determined by cultural context. An American business executive guided by cultural relativism, for example, would argue that child labor is acceptable in another country as long as it is consistent with local laws and customs (see Ethics feature).

> **Cultural relativism** suggests there is no one right way to behave; ethical behavior is determined by its cultural context.

Figure 3.2 contrasts cultural relativism with **moral absolutism**. This is the belief that if a behavior or practice is not ethical in one's home environment, it is not acceptable anywhere else. Moral absolutism maintains universal ethical standards which should apply across cultures and national boundaries. In the former example, the American executive would not do business where child labor was used since it is unacceptable at home. Critics of the absolutist approach argue it is a form of **ethical imperialism**, an attempt to impose one's ethical standards on others.

> **Moral absolutism** suggests ethical standards apply universally across all cultures.

> **Ethical imperialism** is an attempt to impose one's ethical standards on other cultures.

Business ethicist Thomas Donaldson finds fault with both cultural relativism and ethical imperialism. He argues instead that certain fundamental rights and ethical standards can be preserved at the same time that values and traditions of a given culture are respected.[20] Core values or "hyper-norms" that should transcend cultural boundaries include respect for human dignity, basic rights, and good citizenship. Donaldson believes international business practices can be modified for local and regional cultural contexts while maintaining core values. In the case of child labor, the American executive might take steps so that child laborers are provided daily scheduled schooling, as well as employment.[21]

Learning Check

LEARNING OBJECTIVE 3.1

Define ethics and describe the foundations of ethical behavior.

Be Sure You Can • define *ethics* • explain why obeying the law is not necessarily the same as behaving ethically • explain the difference between terminal and instrumental values • identify the four alternative views of ethics • contrast cultural relativism with moral relativism

3.2 Ethics in the Workplace

LEARNING OBJECTIVE 3.2

Discuss ethical dilemmas and common ethics issues in the workplace.

> **Learn More About**
> Ethical dilemmas • Influences on ethical decision making • Rationalizations for unethical behavior

The real test of ethics occurs when situations challenge personal values and standards. Often ambiguous and unexpected, these ethical challenges are inevitable. Everyone has to be prepared to deal with them, even students. A college student gets a job offer and accepts it, only to get a better offer two weeks later. Is it right to reject the first job to accept the second? A student knows his roommate submitted a paper that he bought on the Internet. Is it right for the student not to tell the instructor? One student confides to another that he purchased the answers to an upcoming exam from a student in another section of the class. Is it right for the confidant to inform the instructor's department head?

Ethical Dilemmas

An **ethical dilemma** is a situation that offers potential benefit or gain and that may also be considered unethical.

An **ethical dilemma** requires a choice that, although offering the potential for personal or organizational benefit, or both, may be unethical. It is often a situation where there is no clear "right" or "wrong." An engineering manager speaking from experience sums it up this way: "I define an unethical situation as one in which I have to do something I don't feel good about."[22] Here are some common examples of ethical dilemmas.[23]

- *Discrimination*—Your boss suggests that it would be a mistake to hire a qualified job candidate because she wears a headscarf for religious purposes. The boss believes your traditional customers might be uncomfortable with her appearance.

- *Sexual harassment*—A female subordinate asks you to discipline a co-worker whom she claims is making her feel uncomfortable with inappropriate sexual remarks. The co-worker, your friend, says that he was just kidding around and asks you not to do anything that would harm his career.

- *Conflicts of interest*—You are working in another country and are offered an expensive gift in return for making a decision favorable to the gift giver. You know that this is common practice in this culture and that several of your colleagues have accepted similar gifts in the past.

- *Product safety*—Your company is struggling financially and can make one of its major products more cheaply by purchasing lower-quality materials, although doing so would slightly increase the risk of consumer injury.

- Use of *organizational resources*—You bring an office laptop computer home so you can work after hours. Your wife likes the computer better than hers and asks if she can use it for her online business during the weekends.

It is almost too easy to confront ethical dilemmas from the safety of a textbook or a classroom discussion. In reality it is a lot harder to consistently make ethical decisions. We end up facing ethical dilemmas at unexpected and inconvenient times, in situations where events and facts are ambiguous, and when pressures to perform are intense. Is it any surprise, then, that 56% of U.S. workers in one survey reported feeling pressured to act unethically in their jobs? Or that 48% said they had committed questionable acts in the past year?[24]

Look at the six-step checklist for dealing with an ethical dilemma shown in **Figure 3.3**.[25] The checklist is a way to double-check the ethics of decisions before taking action. Pay special attention to Step 5 which addresses the risk of public disclosure. Asking and answering the *spotlight questions*

Guidelines for an ethics "quick check"

Step 1   Recognize the ethical dilemma.

Step 2   Get the facts and identify your options.

Step 3   Test each option: Is it legal? Is it right? Whom does it affect? Who benefits? Who gets hurt?

Step 4   Decide which option to follow.

Step 5   Double-check your ethics by asking these *spotlight questions:*

"How will I feel if my family finds out about my decision?"

"How will I feel about this if my decision is reported in the local newspaper or posted on the Internet?"

"What would the person I admire most for their character and ethical judgment say about my decision?"

Step 6   Take action.

FIGURE 3.3   **Quick Check for Dealing with Ethical Dilemmas.**

is a powerful way to test whether a decision is consistent with your personal ethical standards. Use them the next time you're making an uncomfortable decision. *Question:* "How will I feel if my family finds out, or if this gets posted on the Internet?" If the answer is "embarrassed," "mortified," or "anxious," the decision is probably not the one you should be making. *Question:* "What would the person I admire most for their character and ethical judgment say about my decision?" If the answer is "bad choice" or "I don't agree," the decision is probably not the one you should be making.

Influences on Ethical Decision Making

Standing up for what you believe is not always easy, especially in social situations. Consider these words from a commencement address delivered at a well-known school of business administration. "Greed is all right," the speaker said. "Greed is healthy. You can be greedy and still feel good about yourself." How would this speech be received today? Students at the time greeted the remarks with laughter and applause. The speaker was Ivan Boesky, once considered the "king of the arbitragers."[26] Not long after his commencement speech, however, Boesky was arrested, tried, convicted, and sentenced to prison for trading on inside information.

Personal Ethics   Values, family, religion, and personal needs all influence ethics. Managers without a strong, clear set of personal ethics will find their decisions varying from situation to situation. Those with a solid **ethical framework**, a set of personal rules or strategies for ethical decision making, will act more consistently and confidently. These frameworks are moral anchors that support ethical decisions in difficult circumstances. As shown in **Figure 3.4**, ethical frameworks

An **ethical framework** is a personal rule or strategy for making ethical decisions.

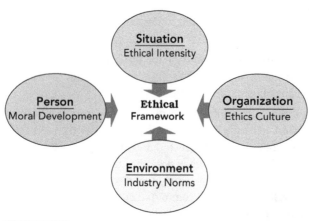

FIGURE 3.4   **Four Influences on Ethical Frameworks for Decision Making.**

for decision making are influenced by the moral development of a person, ethical intensity of the situation, ethics culture of the organization, and the environment of industry norms.

Stages of Moral Development

A person's moral foundations begin with individual character and personal values that emphasize virtues such as courage, honesty, fairness, integrity, andself-respect. Lawrence Kohlberg identified the three levels of moral development, shown in **Figure 3.5**—preconventional, conventional, and postconventional.[27] People at the different levels have different ethical approaches to situations. Very few of us consistently act at the postconventional level, and most operate at the preconventional or conventional levels.

People are self-centered at the *preconventional level* of moral development. Moral thinking focuses on punishment, obedience, and self-interest. Decisions are focused on personal gain or avoiding punishment, and following the rules. Behavior at the *conventional level* of moral development is more social-centered. Decisions follow social norms, to meet the expectations of group memberships, and to live up to agreed-on role obligations.

Moral development at the *postconventional level* is principle-centered and a strong ethics framework is evident. Individuals at this level are willing to break with norms and conventions, even laws, to make decisions consistent with universal principles. An example might be the student who doesn't cheat on a take-home test because he or she believes it's wrong. This belief holds even though other students will cheat, there is almost no chance of getting caught, and the consequence of not cheating is likely to be a lower grade.

Situational Context and Ethics Intensity

Ethical dilemmas sometimes catch us off guard and we struggle to respond morally. Other times, we might fail to see that an issue or a situation has an ethics component. This may happen with cheating, for example, when it becomes so common it results in an accepted standard of behavior. Scholars discuss this as an issue of **ethics intensity** or **issue intensity**, whether situations pose important ethics challenges.[28]

The greater the ethics intensity of the situation, the more attention people give to ethics issues and the more likely they are to be ethical. Ethics intensity rises when potential harm is great, likely, and imminent, when potential victims are visible and close by, and when there is more social agreement on what is good or bad about what is taking place. How do you see the ethics intensity of taking unprescribed Adderall to study for a test? Does low ethics intensity contribute to the likelihood of using unprescribed Adderall?

Ethics Culture of the Organization

The work and social settings of organizations have a strong influence on members' ethics. Many organizations try to set a high ethics bar by issuing

> **Ethics intensity** or **issue intensity** indicates the degree to which an issue or a situation is recognized to pose important ethical challenges.

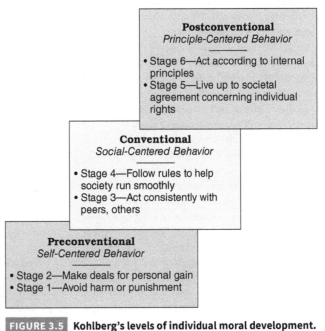

FIGURE 3.5 Kohlberg's levels of individual moral development.

formal policy statements and guidelines. But these ethics codes can have a limited impact—easy to write and post but much harder to really communicate and enforce. What does have high impact are the ways top managers, team leaders, and supervisors act, what they request, and what behaviors they reward or punish. The same holds true for the expectations of peers and group norms.[29] It's ultimately the character of the people in an organization that sets the ethics tone. In some cases, members find themselves shunned from a team when they don't do things that outsiders would consider unethical—for example, slacking off or abusing privileges. In other cases, high ethics standards may push employees to behave more ethically than they otherwise would.

Ethics Environment of Industry   Government laws and regulations can describe and encourage ethical behavior, but they can't guarantee it. Laws reflect social values and define appropriate behavior for employees. Regulations help governments monitor these behaviors and keep them within acceptable limits. After a number of high-profile corporate scandals hit the news, for example, the U.S. Congress passed the Sarbanes-Oxley Act of 2002 to make it easier for executives to be tried and sent to prison for financial misconduct.

The climate of competition in an industry also sets standards for what is considered ethical or unethical behavior. Two former presidents of airlines suffering from money-losing competition once had the telephone conversation that follows.[30]

Putnam: Do you have a suggestion for me?

Crandall: Yes . . . . Raise your fares 20 percent. I'll raise mine the next morning.

Putnam: Robert, we—

Crandall: You'll make more money and I will, too.

Putnam: We can't talk about pricing.

Crandall: Oh, Howard. We can talk about anything we want to talk about.

The U.S. Justice Department strongly disagreed with Crandall. It alleged that his suggestion of a coordinated fare increase amounted to an illegal attempt to monopolize airline routes.

Insight: Learn about Yourself | It's the character of the people making key decisions that determines whether our organizations act in socially responsible or irresponsible ways.

Individual Character Is a Confidence Builder

There is no doubt that **individual character** is evident in all we do. Persons with high character act consistently and confidently due to the self-respect it provides, even in difficult situations. Those with less character are more insecure. They act inconsistently and suffer in self-esteem and in the esteem of others.

Ethics and social responsibility issues facing organizations today can challenge individual character. We need to know ourselves well enough to make principled decisions we can be proud of and that others will respect. After all, it's the character of the people making key decisions that determines whether our organizations act in socially responsible or irresponsible ways.

Personal integrity is a foundation for individual character. It provides an ethical anchor shaping how we behave at work and in life. Think of it as demonstrated honesty, civility, caring, and sense of fair play. Your integrity and character should be more than occasional concerns. They deserve constant attention. Ethical dilemmas arise unexpectedly. Performance pressures—meeting deadlines, for example—can lead to unethical decisions. To deal with these situations we have to know ourselves well enough to make principled decisions we can be proud of and that others will respect.

One trait that can undermine individual character is hyper-competitiveness. You see it in people who think that winning—or getting ahead—is the only thing that matters. They

hate to lose. These types judge themselves more on their results than the methods used to get there. Moreover, they may be quick to put aside virtues to succeed in competitive situations.

Self-Check for Signs of Hyper-Competitiveness

- **Y or N** Winning makes me feel powerful.
- **Y or N** Winning increases my sense of self-worth.
- **Y or N** I hate to lose an argument.
- **Y or N** I turn everything into a contest.
- **Y or N** I am not satisfied unless I win a competition.
- **Y or N** If it helps me win, I am willing to obstruct my opponent.

Get To Know Yourself Better

Do a personal integrity and individual character self-check. Make notes on two situations that presented you with some ethical test. From the perspectives of a parent, loved one, or good friend, write a critique of how you handled each incident and what this shows about your individual character. Did you act with high integrity, or not? Watch yourself for signs of hyper-competitiveness in school and work situations. Ask: What are the ethical implications of my behavior?

Rationalizations for Unethical Behavior

Picture this: A college professor sends students an e-mail containing both the school's honor code and a link to answers from the prior year's final exam. The link is clicked by 41% of students. Why? *How about this situation?* An internal audit by Avon revealed that executives in its China operation made illegal payments to obtain local direct sales licenses for the firm.[31] Why?

The fact is that people rationalize unethical behavior with after-the-fact justifications like "*It's not really illegal.*"[32] This is a mistaken belief that behavior is acceptable in shady or borderline situations. When you are having trouble determining right from wrong, the advice is simple: Don't do it. "*It's in everyone's best interests.*" This excuse involves the mistaken belief that because someone benefits from the behavior, the behavior is also good for everyone. Overcoming this rationalization depends on looking beyond short-term results to address longer-term implications, and seeing how results are obtained. The best answer to the question "How far can I push it to accomplish this goal?" is probably "Don't try to find out."

Sometimes rationalizers tell themselves that "*no one will ever know about it.*" They mistakenly believe that questionable behavior is safe from discovery and won't be made public. And if no one knows, the argument goes, no crime was actually committed. Lack of accountability, unrealistic pressures to perform, and a supervisor who prefers "not to know" can reinforce this wrongful thinking. The best deterrent is for everyone to know that unethical behavior will be punished whenever it is discovered. Finally, rationalizers may mistakenly believe that "*the organization will stand behind me.*" This is misperceived loyalty. Believing that the organization benefits from their actions, the individual expects to be protected However, showing loyalty to the organization is not an excuse for misconduct. It shouldn't stand above the law and social morality (see the Analysis feature).

Analysis: Make Data Your Friend | The most common unethical acts by managers involve verbal, sexual, and racial harassment.

Manager Behavior Key to Ethical Workplace

Jon Feingersh Photography Inc/DigitalVision/Getty Images

There's no question that managers strongly influence ethical behavior at work. Whether you call them bosses, team leaders, or supervisors, people in management make decisions every day that set an ethics-tone affecting their co-workers. A survey conducted for Deloitte & Touche USA found the following.

- Most common unethical acts by managers and supervisors include verbal, sexual, and racial harassment, misuse of company property, and giving preferential treatment.

- 91% of workers are more likely to behave ethically when they have work–life balance; 30% say they suffer from poor work–life balance.

- Top reasons for unethical behavior are low personal integrity (80%) and poor job satisfaction (60%).

- Most workers consider it unacceptable to steal from an employer, cheat on expense reports, take credit for another's accomplishments, and lie on time sheets.

- Most workers consider it acceptable to ask a work colleague for a personal favor, take sick days when not ill, or use company technology for personal affairs.

What Does This Mean?

Are there any surprises in these data? Is this emphasis on manager and direct supervisor behavior justified as the key to an ethical workplace? What is your reaction to what the workers in this survey reported as acceptable and unacceptable work behaviors? Based on your experiences, what would you add to the list of unacceptable behaviors? Have you seen these kinds of behaviors where you work? What would your supervisor say if you reported these behaviors? Would you feel safe doing so? Why or why not?

LEARNING OBJECTIVE 3.2

Discuss ethical dilemmas and common ethics issues in the workplace.

Be Sure You Can • define *ethical dilemma* and give workplace examples • identify Kohlberg's stages of moral development • explain how ethics intensity influences ethical decision making • explain how ethics decisions are influenced by an organization's culture and the external environment • list four common rationalizations for unethical behavior

3.3 Maintaining High Ethical Standards

LEARNING OBJECTIVE 3.3

Describe approaches to maintaining high ethical standards.

WileyPLUS

See Author Video

> **Learn More About**
> Moral management • Ethics training • Codes of ethical conduct • Whistleblower protection

Headline–Bernard Madoff sentenced to 150 years in prison for masterminding the largest fraud in history by swindling billions of dollars from thousands of investors. *Headline*–H-P pays $108 million to settle a bribery case for corruption in Russia, Mexico, and Poland. *Headline*–U.S. safety regulators demand that General Motors answer 107 questions regarding the firm's handling of faulty ignition switches that resulted in thirteen deaths.[33]

There is rarely a shortage of bad news from the financial, corporate, and governmental worlds. And importantly, the stories behind the headlines demonstrate there is no substitute for staffing organizations with honest people and principled leaders who set positive examples and act as ethical role models.

Moral Management

Management scholar Archie Carroll distinguishes among immoral, amoral, and moral managers.[34] **Immoral managers** choose to behave unethically. They make choices for personal gain and knowingly disregard the ethics of their choice or the situation. **Amoral managers** also disregard the ethics of their choices and decisions, but do so unintentionally or unknowingly. These managers do not consider the ethical consequences of their actions, and typically use the law as a behavioral guideline. **Moral managers** pursue ethical behavior as a personal goal. They make decisions and choices in consideration of ethical issues.[35]

It may surprise you that Carroll believes that most managers act amorally. Although well intentioned, they remain mostly uninformed or undisciplined regarding ethical issues. They don't make unethical choices on purpose. They just don't think through the ethics issues. Moral managers, by contrast, always have ethics on their mind. They champion ethical behavior and role model for their co-workers.

An **immoral manager** chooses to behave unethically.

An **amoral manager** fails to consider the ethics of her or his behavior.

A **moral manager** makes ethical behavior a personal goal.

Ethics Training

Ethics training is one way to try to encourage ethical behavior. Structured programs help employees understand the ethical aspects of decision making and better integrate ethical

Ethics training seeks to help people understand the ethical aspects of decision making and to incorporate high ethical standards into their daily behavior.

standards into their actions. Look back to the six-step quick check for dealing with ethical dilemmas earlier in Figure 3.3. It's a sample from an ethics training session that provides a simple but powerful frameworks for double-checking the ethics of decisions. Other ethics training topics include ways to deal with conflicts of interest, gifts, client relationships, and bribery.

Colleges and universities also are strengthening ethics coverage in academic classes Do you think that you and your classmates benefit from these initiatives? Are coursework and discussions of ethics conducted in ways that keep cynicism from limiting their positive impact? Regardless of when, where, or how ethics training is conducted, it is important to recognize its limits: Training is no guarantee of ethical behavior. A banking executive once summed things up this way: "We aren't teaching people right from wrong—we assume they know that. We aren't giving people moral courage to do what is right—they should be able to do that anyhow. We focus on dilemmas."

Codes of Ethical Conduct

It is now common for most organizations to have **codes of ethics**. In fact, you may be asked to sign one as a condition of employment. These codes are formal statements of an organization's values and ethical principles that set expectations for behavior. Ethics codes typically address organizational citizenship, illegal or improper acts, and relationships with co-workers and customers. Specific guidelines are often set for bribes and kickbacks, political contributions, records-keeping honesty, and confidentiality of corporate information.

Ethics codes are very common in the world of International Business. For example, global manufacturing at Gap, Inc., is governed by a Code of Vendor Conduct that addresses issues like the following.[36]

Discrimination—"Factories shall employ workers on the basis of their ability to do the job, not on the basis of their personal characteristics or beliefs."

Forced labor—"Factories shall not use any prisoners, indentured servants or forced labor."

Working conditions—"Factories must treat all workers with respect and dignity and provide them with a safe and healthy environment."

Freedom of association—"Factories must not interfere with workers who wish to lawfully and peacefully associate, organize or bargain collectively."

But even as global firms like the Gap have ethics codes in place, it is hard to police practices when they have, potentially hundreds of suppliers from different parts of the world. In international business, as elsewhere, ethics codes are good at describing ethical expectations, but they cannot always guarantee ethical conduct.

Whistleblower Protection

- Agnes Connolly pressed her employer to report two toxic chemical accidents.
- Dave Jones reported that his company used unqualified suppliers in the construction of a nuclear power plant.
- Margaret Newsham revealed that her firm allowed workers to do personal business while on government contracts.
- Herman Cohen charged that the ASPCA in New York was mistreating animals.
- Barry Adams complained that his hospital followed unsafe practices.[37]

These five people come from different work settings and are linked to different issues. However, they share two important things in common. First, each was a **whistleblower** who exposed misconduct in and by their organizations while hoping to preserve ethical standards and protect against further wasteful, harmful, or illegal acts.[38] Second, each of these individuals was fired from their job.

At the same time that we can admire whistleblowers for taking a stand, there is no doubt they risk hurting their career and other forms of retaliation, up to and including getting fired. Although laws such as the Whistleblower Protection Act of 1989 offer some defense against "retaliatory discharge," legal protections for whistleblowers are continually being tested in court and many consider them inadequate.[39] Laws vary from state to state, and federal laws primarily protect government workers.

Research on whistleblowing shows that when ethical violations by co-workers, go unreported about half the time.[40] Top reasons why people don't report unethical behavior include lack of ethical leadership, unethical peers, lack of confidence that anything will be done and fear of being outed as the whistleblower.[41] Typical barriers to whistleblowing anything will be done include a strict chain of command that makes it hard to bypass immediate supervisors, strong work group identities that encourage loyalty and self-censorship, and ambiguous priorities that make it hard to distinguish right from wrong.[42]

Learning Check

LEARNING OBJECTIVE 3.3

Describe approaches to maintaining high ethical standards.

Be Sure You Can • compare and contrast ethics training and codes of ethical conduct as methods for encouraging ethical behavior in organizations • differentiate between amoral, immoral, and moral management • define *whistleblower* • identify common barriers to whistleblowing and the factors to consider when determining whether whistleblowing is appropriate

3.4 | Social Responsibility

LEARNING OBJECTIVE 3.4

Explain corporate social responsibility and corporate governance.

> **Learn More About**
>
> Social responsibility, stewardship, and the triple bottom line • Perspectives on corporate social responsibility • Evaluating corporate social performance • Corporate governance

WileyPLUS

See Author Video

All organizations have **stakeholders**, the persons, groups, and other organizations directly affected by the behavior of the organization and that hold a stake in its performance.[43] **Figure 3.6** shows a typical stakeholder network that includes owners or shareholders, employees, customers, suppliers, business partners, government representatives and regulators, community members, and future generations.

An organization's stakeholders can have different and conflicting interests that make it hard for all of them to be satisfied all the time. Customers typically want value prices and quality products; owners want profits and a strong return on their investment; suppliers want long-term business relationships; communities want good corporate citizenship and support for public services; employees want good wages, benefits, security, and satisfaction in their work; and future generations want a clean environment that isn't polluted by manufacturing

Stakeholders are the persons, groups, and other organizations that are directly affected by the behavior of the organization and that hold a stake in its performance.

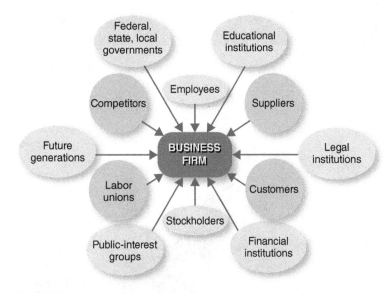

FIGURE 3.6 **The many stakeholders of organizations.**

by-products and industrial waste. When stakeholders' interests clash, an organization's leadership can face difficult challenges and controversial decisions.[44]

One way to deal with conflicting stakeholder interests is to assess the power of the stakeholder, the legitimacy of the demand, and the urgency of the issue.[45] **Stakeholder power** is the capacity of a stakeholder to affect the operations of an organization. **Demand legitimacy** reflects the stakeholder's demand is valid and the extent the demand comes from a party with a legitimate stake in the organization. **Issue urgency** is the extent the issues require immediate attention or action.

Social Responsibility, Stewardship, and the Triple Bottom Line

The way organizations behave in relation to their stakeholders is a good indication of their underlying ethics culture and moral character. When we talk about the "good" and the "bad" in business and society relationships, **corporate social responsibility**, or CSR, is center stage. CSR is the obligation of an organization to act in ways that serve the interests of multiple stakeholders, including society at large.

In a world where climate change and environmental justice are global concerns, CSR is entwined with the notion of **sustainability**-acting today in ways that protect the quality of life for future generations. The term **sustainable business** refers to firms that operate in ways that both meet the needs of customers and protect or advance the well-being of our natural environment.[46] A sustainable business operates in harmony with nature rather than by exploiting nature. Examples include producing less waste, avoiding toxic materials, and investing in renewable energy.

The good and the bad in CSR and sustainability practices come to life day-to-day as results of decisions made and actions taken by employees. When hazardous waste gets into landfills, people are doing the dumping. When a manufacturer fails to recall products with dangerous defects, one or more persons in authority are making the decision. The chapter opening photo caption states that you have to "deter bad individual conduct" to keep organizations from doing bad things. It also needs to be said that if organizations are to do the right things, their members—especially managers and leaders—must continually exercise good **stewardship**. This means taking personal responsibility to act in ethical ways that always respect and protect the interests of the full range of organizational stakeholders.

The tendency in the past was to focus business attention on the "bottom line" of profitability. Today, concerns for stewardship and sustainability have broadened attention

Stakeholder power refers to the capacity of the stakeholder to positively or negatively affect the operations of the organization.

Demand legitimacy indicates the validity and legitimacy of a stakeholder's interest in the organization.

Issue urgency indicates the extent to which a stakeholder's concerns need immediate attention.

Corporate social responsibility is the obligation of an organization to serve the interests of multiple stakeholders, including society at large.

Sustainability means acting in ways that support a high quality of life for present and future generations.

A **sustainable business** meets the needs of customers while protecting and advancing the well-being of our natural environment.

Stewardship means taking personal responsibility to always respect and protect the interests of organizational stakeholders.

Choices: Think before You Act | "Quotas are good, they're effective, but they're not enough."

Gender Quotas Add More Women to Corporate Boards

iStock.com/ImagesbyTrista

It's old news that women are underrepresented on corporate boards. Even though the situation is improving, there is still a lot of progress yet to be made. Consulting firm PwC reports that women now hold board seats at the majority of S&P 500 firms, but fill more than two seats at just 25% of them. Global data show women holding 15% of board seats. The number doubles to 34% for countries that set specific gender quotas and levy non-compliance penalties.

Gender quotas are being embraced as European countries tackle gender imbalance. Norwegian firms have to meet 40% targets or be dissolved. Belgium, France, and Italy have quotas with penalties. Germany has a 30% quota with no penalty, while the Netherlands asks companies to hit 30% and explain why if they don't. Legislation proposed to the European Commission would extend quotas to all EU countries if approved.

In the United States, only California has opted for gender quotas. Public companies with California headquarters must have at least one female. Those with five directors or more must fill 2–3 board seats with women by 2021 or face fines.

In respect to Europe, Dr. Anja Kirsch of Freie Universitat Berlin says: "There are definitely more women on boards that introduced legislation." But Dr. Florence Villeseche of the Copenhagen Business School says: "Quotas are good, they're effective, but they're not enough—they are the tip of the iceberg, if you will. There is no automatic trickle-down effect." In the United States, Professor Margarethe Wiersema at the University of California-Irvine comments: "I think we're way out of step with the rest of the world and it would be great if we could make more progress on it."

Your Take?

What is your view of quotas and penalties as a means of increasing female representation on corporate boards? Are quotas the best way to advance women into these roles? Can quotas work if they are not backed up by fines and penalties? What about the "trickle-down effect"? Can the imposition of quotas at the board level make a difference on diversity at all levels in the future? And how about the U.S? Is Europe setting the standard now or is there justification for U.S. hesitation to embrace board quotas for women?

---

to encompass the **triple bottom line** that measures organizational performance not only on financial criteria but also on social and environmental ones.[47] Many call this the **3 P's of organizational performance**—profit, people, and planet.[48] Triple bottom line outcomes are assessed by asking questions like these: *Profit*—Is the decision economically sound? *People*—Does the decision treat people with respect and dignity? *Planet*—Is the decision good for the environment?

> The **triple bottom line** evaluates organizational performance on economic, social, and environmental criteria.
>
> The **3 P's of organizational performance** are profit, people, and planet.

Perspectives on Corporate Social Responsibility

Chances are you'd like your employer to value social responsibility. But, would it surprise you to learn that CSR as a business priority has been a subject of considerable debate?[49]

Classical View   The **classical view of CSR** holds that management's only responsibility is to maximize profits. In other words, "the business of business is business" and the principal obligation of management is to owners and shareholders. This narrow stakeholder perspective is linked to the respected economist and Nobel Laureate, Milton Friedman, who once said: "Few trends could so thoroughly undermine the very foundations of our free society as the acceptance by corporate officials of social responsibility other than to make as much money for their stockholders as possible."[50]

Although not explicitly against CSR in its own right, the classical view maintains that society's interests are served in the long run by executives focused on maximizing profits. The belief is that society gains when business competition makes things like healthier foods and

> The **classical view of CSR** is that business should focus on profits.

energy-efficient products attractive to produce because they are profitable.[51] The fear is that pursuit of CSR as a separate business goal will reduce profits, raise costs, reduce competitiveness with foreign firms, and give business too much social power with too little accountability to the public.

Socioeconomic View   The **socioeconomic view of CSR** holds that managers should focus on the organization's effect on the broader social welfare and not just on profits. This broad stakeholder perspective puts the focus on the triple bottom line that emphasizes not just financial performance but also social and environmental performance as well. In its support, another distinguished economist and Nobel Laureate, Paul Samuelson, has said: "A large corporation these days not only may engage in social responsibility, it had damn well better try to do so."[52]

Proponents of the socioeconomic view argue that the pursuit of CSR will enhance long-run profits, improve public image, make organizations more attractive places to work, and help avoid government regulation (see the Choices feature for a discussion on government mandated quotas). They also believe that businesses should act responsibly because society provides them with the infrastructure they need to operate.

Shared Value View   Mark Kramer and Michael Porter advocate a **shared value view of CSR** where economic progress for the firm and social progress for the broader community are connected.[53] They believe that "the purpose of a corporation must be redefined as creating shared value, not just profit per se."[54] This creates a win-win situation for business and society by merging the interests of shareholders and other stakeholders. It also moves CSR and sustainability priorities away from serving mainly reputational and branding goals and up to the level of being strategic pillars of the core business model.

Organizations pursuing a shared value approach try to align strategies and practices with social issues like aging, illiteracy, nutrition, resource conservation, climate protection, and poverty. This ideally creates a **virtuous circle** where investments in CSR lead to improved financial performance, which, in turn, leads to more socially responsible actions.[55] Can you see where giving priority to reducing waste "can create cost savings?" Can you see, how support for local sourcing helps build communities while reducing distribution costs and ensuring supplies of high-quality products?

Evaluating Corporate Social Performance

If we are to get serious about social responsibility and shared value, we need to get serious about measuring social performance and holding leaders accountable for the results. It is increasingly common for organizations to take **social responsibility audits** at regular intervals and issue formal reports on their social performance. And, research finds that mandatory social reporting improves socially responsible behavior.[56] In other words, the more we measure CSR, the better it gets.

When social responsibility audits are taken, the performance of firms can be scored on behaviors that range from *compliance*—acting to avoid adverse consequences—to *conviction*—acting to create positive impact.[57] Compliance behaviors focus on being profitable and obeying the law, while conviction behaviors focus on doing what is right and contributing to society. **Figure 3.7** shows how different emphases on compliance and conviction result in alternative social responsibility strategies, ones you may recognize in news reports and current events.[58]

On the compliance side, an **obstructionist strategy** ("Fight social demands") focuses on economic priorities. Social demands outside the organization's self-interests are resisted. Cigarette manufacturers, for example, tried to minimize the negative health effects of smoking for decades until indisputable evidence became available. A **defensive strategy** ("Do minimum legally required") focuses on protecting the organization by meeting minimum legal requirements and responding to competitive market forces, perhaps even activist pressures. Mortgage lenders are required to provide certain information to customers concerning loans. But whereas some take time to carefully review everything with customers, others may rush the conversation in hopes the customer won't question details.

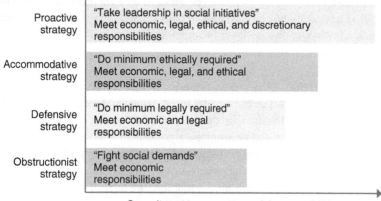

FIGURE 3.7 Four strategies of corporate social responsibility—from obstructionist to proactive behavior.

On the conviction side, an **accommodative strategy** ("Do minimum ethically required") focuses on satisfying society's ethics expectations. An oil firm may engage in appropriate cleanup activities following a spill and provide compensation to communities harmed by the spill. But the firm may be slow to invest in new technologies to prevent future spills. Following a more **proactive strategy** ("Take leadership in social initiatives"), the firm would invest in these technologies, and in the search for alternative energy sources, taking voluntary steps to making things better in the future.

An **accommodative strategy** accepts social responsibility and tries to satisfy society's basic ethical expectations.

A **proactive strategy** actively pursues social responsibility by taking discretionary actions to make things better in the future.

Corporate Governance

The term **corporate governance** refers to the active oversight of management decisions and company actions by boards of directors.[59] Businesses are required by law to have boards of directors elected by shareholders to represent their interests. Most public organizations, like state universities, have boards of trustees whose elected and appointed members serve the same purpose. The governance exercised by boards involves hiring, firing, and compensating top executives. It also involves verifying financial records, assessing strategies, and overall holding management accountable for high-performance leadership that is always ethical and socially responsible.

Corporate governance is the oversight of top management by a board of directors.

Ethics failures and CSR controversies by organizations are often blamed on *weak governance*—the failure of boards to control the actions of top managers. And, you will sometimes see government stepping in to fill this control gap by passing laws and setting regulations designed to reduce the likelihood of future failures. Hearings are held, bills are proposed and laws passed, and government agencies are directed or created to better regulate business practices. The **Sarbanes-Oxley Act of 2002** is a good example. It was passed by Congress in response to loud public outcries over major ethics and business scandals.

The **Sarbanes-Oxley Act of 2002**, SOX, is designed to hold top managers accountable for the financial conduct of the organizations they lead.

The goal of Sarbanes-Oxley, or SOX, is to protect investors and the public by making sure that top managers properly oversee and are held accountable for the financial conduct of the organizations they lead. Here are some SOX facts to remember.

- Saying "I didn't know" doesn't count—SOX "removes the defense of 'I wasn't aware of financial issues' from CEOs and CFOs, holding them accountable for the accuracy of financial statements."

- Violators can expect to be punished and penalties are tough—under SOX a "CEO or CFO who submits a wrong certification is subject to a fine up to $1 million and imprisonment for up to ten years. If the wrong certification was submitted 'willfully', the fine can be increased up to $5 million and the prison term can be increased up to twenty years."

- Whistleblowers are protected—SOX prohibits employers "from retaliating against employees who raise various protected concerns or provide protected information to the employer or the government."

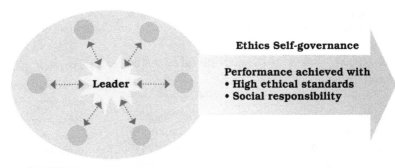

FIGURE 3.8 Ethics self-governance in leadership and the managerial role.

While the behavior and examples set by top-level executives have the longest reach, it is critical to recognize that all managers at all levels have personal responsibility for good stewardship of the organization. This includes setting and living up to its ethics culture, and making sure that everyone does the "right" things in their day-to-day work. **Figure 3.8** describes this as **ethics self-governance** and points out that it isn't enough to fulfill one's daily task responsibilities. They must be performed in ethical and socially responsible ways. Managers shoulder the full weight of this responsibility, and it holds in every organizational setting, from small to large, from private to nonprofit, and at every managerial level from team leader to chief executive. There is no escaping the ultimate reality—every manager is a steward of stakeholder interests and being a manager is an extremely socially responsible job.

Ethics self-governance is making sure day-to-day performance is achieved ethically and in socially responsible ways.

Learning Check

LEARNING OBJECTIVE 3.4

Explain corporate social responsibility and corporate governance.

Be Sure You Can • identify key organizational stakeholders and discuss stakeholder management • define *corporate social responsibility* • summarize arguments for and against CSR • define *shared value* and describe how it links business and society • explain the difference between compliance and commitment in social responsibility • identify four possible social responsibility strategies • define *corporate governance* and ethics self-governance, and discuss their importance to managers at all organizational levels

Management Learning Review: Get Prepared for Quizzes and Exams

Summary

LEARNING OBJECTIVE 3.1   Define ethics and describe the foundations of ethical behavior.

- Ethical behavior is behavior accepted as "good" or "right" as opposed to "bad" or "wrong."

- Because an action is not illegal does not necessarily make it ethical.

- Because values vary, the question "What is ethical behavior?" may be answered differently by different people.

- The utilitarian, individualism, moral-rights, and justice views offer alternative ways of thinking about ethical behavior.

- Cultural relativism argues that no culture is ethically superior to any other; universalism argues that certain ethical standards apply everywhere.

For Discussion Is there ever a justification for cultural relativism in international business ethics?

LEARNING OBJECTIVE 3.2   Discuss ethical dilemmas and common ethics issues in the workplace.

- An ethical dilemma occurs when someone must decide whether to pursue a course of action that, although offering the potential for personal or organizational benefit or both, may be unethical.
- Managers report that ethical dilemmas often involve conflicts with superiors, customers, and subordinates over issues such as dishonesty in advertising and communication, as well as pressure from supervisors to do unethical things.
- Common rationalizations for unethical behavior include believing the behavior is not illegal, is in everyone's best interests, will never be noticed, or will be supported by the organization.

For Discussion Are ethical dilemmas always problems, or can they also be opportunities?

LEARNING OBJECTIVE 3.3   Describe approaches to maintaining high ethical standards.

- Ethics training can help people better deal with ethical dilemmas in the workplace.
- Written codes of ethical conduct formally state what an organization expects of its employees regarding ethical behavior at work.
- Immoral managers intentionally choose to behave unethically; amoral managers do not really pay attention to or think through the ethics of their actions or decisions; moral managers consider ethical behavior a personal goal.
- Whistleblowers expose the unethical acts of others in organizations, even while facing career risks for doing so.

For Discussion Is it right for organizations to require employees to sign codes of conduct and undergo ethics training?

LEARNING OBJECTIVE 3.4   Explain corporate social responsibility and corporate governance.

- Social responsibility is an organizational obligation to act in ways that serve both its own interests and the interests of its stakeholders.
- The triple bottom line for assessing organizational performance reflects how well organizations achieve economic, social, and environmental performance outcomes.
- The argument against corporate social responsibility holds that businesses should focus on profit; the argument for corporate social responsibility holds that businesses should serve broader social concerns.
- The shared value concept links business and social goals with the idea that businesses can find economic value by pursuing opportunities and practices that advance societal well-being.
- An organization's social performance can be evaluated based on how well it meets economic, legal, ethical, and discretionary responsibilities.
- Corporate strategies in response to demands for socially responsible behavior include obstruction, defense, accommodation, and proactivity.
- Corporate governance is the responsibility of a board of directors to oversee the performance of C-suite executives.

For Discussion What questions would you include on a social audit for an organization in your community?

Self-Test 3

Multiple-Choice Questions

1. Values are personal beliefs that help determine whether a behavior is considered ethical or unethical. An example of a terminal value is _____.

   a. ambition
   b. self-respect
   c. courage
   d. imagination

2. Under the _____ view of ethical behavior, a business owner would be considered ethical if she reduced a plant's workforce by 10% in order to cut costs to keep the business from failing and thus save jobs for the other 90%.

   a. utilitarian
   b. individualism
   c. justice
   d. moral rights

3. A manager's failure to enforce a late-to-work policy the same way for employees on the day and night shifts is an ethical violation of _____ justice.

   a. ethical
   b. moral
   c. distributive
   d. procedural

4. The Sarbanes-Oxley Act of 2002 makes it easier for corporate executives to _____.

   a. protect themselves from shareholder lawsuits
   b. sue employees who commit illegal acts
   c. be tried and sentenced to jail for financial misconduct
   d. shift blame for wrongdoing to boards of directors

5. Two "spotlight" questions for conducting the ethics double-check of a decision are (a) "How would I feel if my family found out about this?" and (b) "How would I feel if _____?"

   a. my boss found out about this
   b. my subordinates found out about this
   c. this was published in the local newspaper
   d. this went into my personnel file

6. Research on ethical dilemmas indicates that _____ is/are often the cause of unethical behavior by people at work.

a. declining morals in society

b. lack of religious beliefs

c. the absence of whistleblowers

d. pressures from bosses and superiors

7. Customers, investors, employees, and regulators are examples of _____ that are important in the analysis of corporate social responsibility (CSR).

a. special-interest groups

b. stakeholders

c. ethics advocates

d. whistleblowers

8. A(n) _____ is someone who exposes the ethical misdeeds of others.

a. whistleblower

b. ethics advocate

c. ombudsman

d. stakeholder

9. A proponent of the classical view of corporate social responsibility would most likely agree with which of these statements?

a. Social responsibility improves the public image of business.

b. The primary responsibility of business is to maximize business profits.

c. By acting responsibly, businesses avoid government regulation.

d. Businesses can and should do "good" while doing business.

10. An amoral manager_____.

a. always acts in consideration of ethical issues

b. chooses to behave unethically

c. makes ethics a personal goal

d. acts without considering whether or not the behavior is ethical

11. An organization that takes the lead in addressing emerging social issues is being _____, showing the most progressive corporate social responsibility strategy.

a. accommodative

b. defensive

c. proactive

d. obstructionist

12. The criterion of _____ identifies the highest level of conviction by an organization to operate in a socially responsible manner.

a. economic justice

b. legal requirements

c. ethical commitment

d. discretionary responsibility

13. Which viewpoint emphasizes that business can find ways to profit by doing things that advance the well being of society?

a. classical

c. defensive

b. shared value

d. obstructionist

14. Managers show self-governance when they always try to achieve performance objectives in ways that are _____.

a. performance effective

b. cost efficient

c. quality oriented

d. ethical and socially responsible

15. The triple bottom line of organizational performance focuses on the "3 Ps" of profit, people, and _____.

a. principle

c. planet

b. procedure

d. progress

Short-Response Questions

16. Explain the difference between the individualism and justice views of ethical behavior.

17. List four common rationalizations for unethical managerial behavior.

18. What are the major arguments for and against corporate social responsibility?

19. What is the primary difference between immoral and amoral management?

Essay Question

20. A small outdoor clothing company has just received an attractive offer from a business in Bangladesh to manufacture its work gloves. The offer would allow for substantial cost savings over the current supplier. The company manager, however, has read reports that some Bangladeshi businesses break their own laws and operate with child labor. How would differences in the following corporate responsibility strategies affect the manager's decision regarding whether to accept the offer: obstruction, defense, accommodation, and proaction?

Career Skills & Competencies: Make Yourself Valuable!

Evaluate Career Situations

What Would You Do?

1. Window to the Future

You've just seen one of your classmates take a picture of an essay question on the exam everyone is taking. The instructor missed it and you're not sure if anyone else saw it. You know that the instructor is giving an exam to another section the next class period. Do you let it pass and pretend it isn't all that important? If you won't let it pass, what will you do?

2. Intern's Assignment

One of your first tasks as a summer intern is to design an ethics training program for the firm's new hires. Your supervisor says that the program should familiarize hires with the corporate code of ethics. But it should also go beyond this to help establish a solid foundation for handling a range of ethical dilemmas in a confident and moral way. What would your training program look like?

3. New Person at the Table

Your employer has a "roundtable" program that brings younger hires together with senior executives on a monthly basis. Each session tackles a topic. This month it's "CSR as a business priority." You've heard that some of the senior execs are skeptical of CSR, believing that business is business and the firm's priority should be on profits. What arguments might you make in support of CSR and the concept of "shared value"?

Reflect on the Self-Assessment

Terminal Values

Instructions

1. Read the following list of things people value. Think about each value in terms of its importance as a guiding principle in your life.

A comfortable life	Inner harmony
An exciting life	Mature love
A sense of accomplishment	National security
A world at peace	Pleasure
A world of beauty	Salvation
Equality	Self-respect
Family security	Social recognition
Freedom	True friendship
Happiness	Wisdom

2. Circle six of these 18 values to indicate that they are most important to you. If you can, rank-order these most important values by writing a number above them—with "1" being the most important value in your life, and so on through "6."

3. Underline the six of these 18 values that are least important to you.

Interpretation

Terminal values reflect a person's preferences concerning the ends to be achieved. They are the goals individuals would like to achieve in their lifetimes. As you look at the items you've selected as most and least important, what major differences are present in the items across the two sets? Think about this and then answer the following questions.

A. What does your selection of most and least important values say about you as a person?

B. What does your selection of most and least important values suggest about the type of work and career that might be best for you?

C. Which values among your most and least important selections might cause problems for you in the future—at work and/or in your personal life? What problems might they cause and why? How might you prepare now to best deal with these problems in the future?

D. How might your choices of most and least important values turn out to be major strengths or assets for you—at work and/or in your personal life, and why?

Contribute to the Class Exercise

Confronting Ethical Dilemmas

Preparation

Read and indicate your response to each of the following situations.

A. Ron Jones, vice president of a large construction firm, receives in the mail a large envelope marked "personal." It contains a competitor's cost data for a project that both firms will be bidding on shortly.

The data are accompanied by a note from one of Ron's subordinates. It says: "This is the real thing!"

Ron knows that the data could be a major advantage to his firm in preparing a bid that can win the contract. What should he do?

B. Kay Smith is one of your top-performing subordinates. She has shared with you her desire to apply for promotion to a new position just announced in a different division of the company. This will be tough on you since recent budget cuts mean you will be unable to replace anyone who leaves, at least for quite some time.

Kay knows all of this and, in all fairness, has asked your permission before she submits an application. It is rumored that the son of a good friend of your boss is going to apply for the job. Although his credentials are less impressive than Kay's, the likelihood is that he will get the job if she doesn't apply. What will you do?

C. Marty was pleased to represent her firm as head of the local community development committee. In fact, her supervisor's boss once held this position and told her in a hallway conversation, "Do your best and give them every support possible."

Going along with this advice, Marty agreed to pick up the bill (several hundred dollars) for a dinner meeting with local civic and business leaders. Shortly thereafter, her supervisor informed everyone that the entertainment budget was being eliminated in a cost-saving effort.

Not wanting to renege on supporting the community development committee, Marty charged the dinner bill to an advertising budget. An internal auditor discovered the charge and reported it to you, the firm's human resource manager.

Marty is scheduled to meet with you in a few minutes. What will you do?

Instructions

1. Working alone, make the requested decisions in each of these incidents. Think carefully about your justification for the decision.

2. Meet in a group assigned by your instructor. Share your decisions and justifications in each case with other group members. Listen to theirs.

3. Try to reach a group consensus on what to do in each situation and why.

4. Be prepared to share the group decisions, and any dissenting views, in general class discussion.

Manage a Critical Incident

Dealing with a Global Supply Chain

Situation

As the co-founder of a small outdoor clothing start-up, you have just received an attractive proposal from a business in Tanzania that wants to manufacture cotton textiles for your warm-up suits. Accepting the offer from the Tanzanian firm would allow for substantial cost savings compared to your current domestic supplier. At this point in your firm's life, every dollar you save really helps. The proposal is now being considered in a meeting that includes you and others in the executive group. Someone mentions that she had recently read reports that some companies in Tanzania use child labor. Her comment immediately broadens the discussion to issues of ethics and business opportunity. Everyone agrees that research on the Tanzanian firm is necessary before any decision can be made on the proposal. You agree and point out that now is a good time to consider not only what course of action is best in this case, but also what policy should be set for dealing with future situations involving how global suppliers treat their workforces. You stand up and say, "Let's assume the firm can meet all of our delivery times and quality standards," and then write these options on the whiteboard: (1) Accept the proposal. (2) Reject the proposal. (3) Reject the proposal if any laws in Tanzania are being violated. (4) Accept the proposal only if the head of the Tanzanian firm agrees not to employ children.

Questions

Does this list include all possible action alternatives? What others, if any, would you add? What alternative do you support and why? How could you defend your preference in the executive group meeting using concepts and ideas from this chapter?

Collaborate on the Team Project

Stakeholder Maps

Preparation

Review the discussion of organizational stakeholders in the textbook. (1) Make a list of the stakeholders that would apply to all organizations—for example, local communities, employees, and customers. What others would you add to this starter listing? (2) Choose one organization that you are familiar with from each list that follows. (3) Draw a map of key stakeholders for each organization. (4) For each stakeholder, indicate its major interest in the organization. (5) For each organization, make a list of possible conflicts among stakeholders that the top manager should recognize.

Nonprofit	University
Elementary school	United Way
Community hospital	Government
Church	Local mayor's office

State police	Convenience store
U.S. Senator	Movie theater
IRS	National retailer
Child Services	Local pizza shop
Business	Urgent care medical clinic

Instructions

In teams assigned by your instructor, choose one organization from each list. Create "master" stakeholder maps for each organization. These should include (1) statements of stakeholder interests and (2) lists of potential stakeholder conflicts. Assume the position of top manager for each organization. Prepare a "stakeholder management plan" that represents the high-priority issues the manager should address with respect to stakeholder interest. Make a presentation to the class for each of your organizations and discuss the importance and complexity of stakeholder analysis.

Analyze the Case Study

Warby Parker | Disruption with a Conscience

Go to *Management Cases for Critical Thinking* at the end of the book to find this case.

CHAPTER 4

Environment, Technology, and Sustainability

Carlos Caetano/Shutterstock.com

Less than 35% of America's 250 million tons of annual waste gets recycled . . . one ton of recycled paper saves 17 large pulp trees and 7,000 gallons of water . . . a TV runs for three hours on energy savings from one recycled aluminum can.

Career Readiness – What to Look for Inside

Thought Leadership

Analysis > *Make Data Your Friend*
Social Attitudes Shift on Women at Work, but Concerns for Equality Persist

Choices > *Think before You Act*
UN's Sustainable Development Goals and Business Action

Ethics > *Know Right from Wrong*
Offshore E-Waste Graveyards Bury a Problem

Insight > *Learn about Yourself*
Risk Taking Has Its Ups and Downs

Skills Make You Valuable

- **Evaluate** *Career Situations*
  What Would You Do?
- **Reflect** *On the Self-Assessment:*
  Tolerance for Ambiguity
- **Contribute** *To the Class Exercise:*
  The Future Workplace
- **Manage** *A Critical Incident:*
  It's Also about Respect
- **Collaborate** *On the Team Project:*
  Organizational Commitment to Sustainability Scorecard
- **Analyze** *The Case Study:*
  Patagonia: Leading a Green Revolution

Chapter Quick Start

We live in a complex and dynamic environment that presents a continual stream of problems and opportunities to us as individuals, to organizations, and to society. Managers need to understand the environment in order to help organizations and lead teams to create value for society, accomplish innovation, and contribute to sustainability.

LEARNING OBJECTIVES

4.1 Summarize key trends in the external environment of organizations.

4.2 Discuss value creation and competitive advantage in complex environments.

4.3 Describe how organizations embrace technology and pursue innovation.

4.4 Explain the challenges of sustainability as an environmental priority.

69

You've definitely seen them emblazoned with a futuristic "T" logo. Tesla vehicles stand out on the road, but they're not alone in the marketplace of electric-powered vehicles. Batteries power vehicles of all shapes, sizes, and purposes today—from cars to trucks to motorcycles to scooters, and more. What once was a disruptive and frame bending technological innovation funded by billionaires is now center stage in an intense competitive race. It's a race that challenges well-established old-economy corporate giants to innovate or face loss of market domination. And this is a loss they're not prepared to take.

Technology and ecology are now combining to propel through innovation an unprecedented, even revolutionary, market shift. It's a shift that appeals to both financial and sustainability values, and that extends across industries. Investments in cutting-edge technologies are helping businesses of all types create products and provide services in economic, practical, and ecologically sound ways. All this aligns well with growing recognition that extraordinary commitments must be made if we are to preserve our planet for future generations. Society is increasingly vocal in the message that businesses aren't just there to make money, but to also serve the common good. If a business is to compete today and be around to compete again tomorrow, it must innovate at the intersection of environment, technology, and sustainability.

4.1 The External Environment

WileyPLUS

See Author Video

LEARNING OBJECTIVE 4.1

Summarize key trends in the external environment of organizations.

> **Learn More About**
>
> Economic conditions • Legal-political conditions • Sociocultural conditions • Technological conditions • Natural environment conditions

The **general environment** consists of economic, legal-political, sociocultural, technological, and natural environment conditions in which the organization operates.

The **general environment** is made up of all external conditions that can play a part in managerial decision making. You might think of it as a broad set of dynamic forces that surround and influence an organization. **Figure 4.1** classifies these forces as economic, legal-political, sociocultural, technological, and natural environment conditions. Top managers and C-suite executives have special responsibility for monitoring these conditions and linking them with their

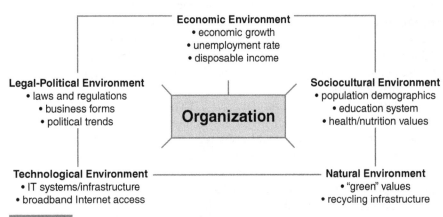

FIGURE 4.1 Sample elements in the general environments of organizations.

organization's mission, strategy, and activities. You can say that their job is to make sure that the voice of the environment gets heard within the organization. Cars like Ford's Focus Electric and Chevy's Bolt EV suggest that Ford Motor Company CEO James Hackett and General Motors' CEO Mary Barra may be listening.

Economic Conditions

Long-term joblessness • Income inequality • Falling middle-class incomes • Struggles to live on minimum wage • China's growing economic power

When economic conditions in the external environment begin to reflect extreme trends and imbalances, what does it mean for organizations and managers?[1] The overall health of an economy in terms of financial markets, inflation, income levels, unemployent, and job creation are powerful forces. They affect domestic and international business competitiveness, consumer spending and lifestyles, and even local and national government priorities. They must be assessed, forecasted, and considered when policymakers and executives make decisions.

Watch the news and you'll find states competing with one another while offering tax incentives to attract new investments from companies like Amazon and Apple, and even foreign manufacturers like Foxconn. The stakes are high, with businesses promising many new jobs and financial boosts for local economies. But such promises are a hot button issue as concerns are raised about benefits versus costs. "How many jobs are really created?" critics ask. "How much tax revenue is lost in the hope for economic gains?"

Jobs are center point in most economic debates of this sort. And for years American communities have suffered job losses as employers pursued **offshoring** by outsourcing work and jobs to lower-cost foreign locations. But economic conditions are becoming more favorable to **reshoring**, which moves jobs back home. Fueled by rising labor costs in foreign countries, higher transoceanic shipping costs, limited protection over intellectual property in some outsourcing destinations, public outcries over lost local jobs, and economic incentives for job creation offered by local communities, more companies are bringing jobs back home.[2]

Offshoring is the outsourcing of jobs to foreign locations.

Reshoring is the movement of jobs from foreign locations back to domestic ones.

Legal-Political Conditions

Immigration reform • Education reform • Tax reform • Health care reform

These issues were voted top priorities by 100 CEOs participating in a *Wall Street Journal* conference on business and public policy.[3] They are just a sample of legal-political conditions posing major implications for organizations and managers. The underlying issues are reflected in current and proposed laws and regulations, government policies, and the philosophy and objectives of political parties. As U.S. lawmakers debate over regulation of banks and the financial services industry, foreign trade agreements, protection of U.S. jobs and industries, the minimum wage, and more, corporate executives must stay informed. They have to follow the debates and monitor trends that can affect the regulation, oversight, and competitive direction of their businesses.

But the domestic scene is only part of the story. The legal-political conditions in the global business environment also vary significantly. Just as foreign firms have to deal with U.S. laws and politics, U.S. firms must adjust to the rules, regulations, and policies in other countries. The European Union fined Apple $14.5 billion for unpaid taxes in Ireland.[4] Uber has faced legal challenges in the United Kingdom, France, and Germany. Apple was sued by a Chinese company that had previously trademarked the name "iPad," and ended up paying $60 million for rights to use the iPad name in China.[5]

Not all countries support international copyright and intellectual property protection. Reports on intellectual property piracy regularly make the news, affecting companies

Internet censorship is the deliberate blockage and denial of public access to information posted on the Internet.

from SONY Pictures to Louis Vuitton to Microsoft. National policies also vary on **Internet censorship**—the deliberate blockage and denial of public access to information on the Internet. Global firms like Google, Facebook, and Twitter, for example, all face problems in China where laws restrict access to Internet content deemed off limits by the government.[6]

Sociocultural Conditions

Median household income for African Americans $38k, for Hispanics $46k, and for whites $63k • Workforce of U.S. technology companies 6.6% African American • Men outearn women by 23.5 cents per hour • Only 25 Fortune 500 CEOs are females and only 3 are African American • 1 in 4 women have experienced sexual harassment in the workplace and most don't file a complaint

These statistics reflect important social issues. Daily news is full of reports on economic justice, educational opportunity, diversity and aging, access to technology, sex and gender based harassment in the workplace, and more.[7] Think of sociocultural conditions in the general environment as demographics and norms of a society or region, as well as social values pertaining to such things as employment, gender roles, ethics, human rights, and lifestyles.

Generational cohorts consist of people born within a few years of one another and who experience somewhat similar life events during their formative years.

With respect to demographics and aging, for example, the workplace is a mix of **generational cohorts**—people born within a few years of one another and who experience somewhat similar life events during their formative years.[8] And, sometimes these generational subcultures

---

Analysis: Make Data Your Friend | 75% of women aged 18–32 believe more must be done to ensure workplace equality.

Social Attitudes Shift on Women at Work, but Concerns for Equality Persist

Blue Images/Corbis/Getty Images

Social attitudes toward women at work have moved in a positive direction. But polls and surveys show that a gender wage gap and bias toward working women remains.

- More women than men now receive college degrees and women comprise almost half the workforce.
- Women aged 25–34 earn 89 cents per dollar earned by young men, while women in general earn 82 cents per dollar earned by men.

- The 18 cent pay gap between men and women has narrowed from 36 cents in 1980, but has changed marginally since 2005.
- Women are three times as likely as men to take time off or quit working to care for a family member.
- 25% of women taking maternity leave believe it has hurt their careers; 13% of men taking paternity leave feel the same.
- One in four women report being paid less than men for the same work; one in 20 men report being paid less than women for the same work.
- The majority of men (63%) and women (77%) believe more must be done to improve gender equality at work.

What are the Implications?

What reasons—other than discrimination—can you give for the lingering wage gap between women and men? Do these explanations justify the gap? What are the implications of this wage gap for the economy, for families, for businesses, and for communities? How about the belief that women can't have it all—career and family—without making sacrifices? Is this your belief? What are the implications for society at large as well as for women and their families? Have you experienced or witnessed gender imbalance in compensation? How did it affect you and what, if anything, did you try to do about it?

clash. Whereas older generations are "digital immigrants" who have had to learn technology, "digital natives" have grown up in technology-enriched homes, schools, and friendship environments. These differing life experiences affect everything from how the generations shop, to how they learn, to how they like to work, socialize, date, and think about what's important in their lives. Characteristics often used to describe digital natives include ease of multitasking, the desire for immediate gratification, continuous contact with others, and less concern with knowing things than with knowing where to find out about things.[9]

Shifting currents and trends in social values affect how organizations deal with such things as reputation management, product development, advertising messages, human resource policies, and wage disparities. There was a time, for example, when the compensation of corporate CEOs wasn't a hot-button topic. No more. Public values are increasingly critical of high executive pay. A report by AFL-CIO Executive Paywatch, for example, showed CEOs at S&P 500 firms average $13.9 million per year, 361 times more than the average U.S. worker earns. The CEO at toy maker Mattel in one year earned 4,987 times the median pay of the company's workforce.[10] There was also a time when sexual harassment in the workplace was handled quietly or not at all. No more. The #MeToo movement has brought great visibility to the problem, forcing employers to review their sexual harassment policies and forcing employees to review and regulate their behavior toward coworkers.[11]

Technological Conditions

63% of smartphone owners say their employers expect more work availability • Teenagers spend less than 10 minutes per day reading off line • Worries grow about links between social media addiction and depression • When messaging apps are constantly open, people switch tasks 37 times per hour

No one doubts that continuing technological developments affect everything from the way we work to how we live our lives. It shouldn't be any surprise that businesses are spending tremendous amounts in social media for product promotions, reputation management, internal communication, and more.[12] A continuing wave of workplace apps ranges from new product development and advertising, to employee networking and data sharing, to virtual meetings.

Between fast-developing smart device technologies, increasing use of robotics and artifical intelligence, and ever-increasing bandwidth, technology continues to penetrate further and further into everyday life. Along with this come significant security and privacy problems. Cyber attacks with malware, ransomware, and cryptomining are commonplace. Individual and government concerns for the use of private data by suppliers of technology regularly make news headlines.

On the employee side, technology easily carries work responsibilities into non-work lives. How often do you hear people complaining that they "can't get away from the job" and that they are "always on" with work following them home, on vacation, and just about everywhere they go? How often do you hear warnings about career and reputation risk because of poorly chosen social media decisions? A CareerBuilder.com survey reports that 70% of employers screen social-network profiles of job candidates before deciding to hire the person.[13]

The employer side of ever-present and constantly-changing technology is full of potential problems as well as opportunities. It is a fact that many employees spend lots of personal time online. Some call this loss of productivity "social *not*working."[14] And, it's classroom issue as well. In one survey, 65% of business students said they sent at least one text message during each class, but only 49% felt guilty about it.[15] Recent airplane crashes have also raised questions about pilot training and technological dependency. The National Transportation Safety Board (NTSB) is concerned that overreliance on automation causes pilots to lose manual flight skills that are necessary cross-checks and last resorts in crisis situations.[16]

Natural Environment Conditions

Magnitude 9.0 earthquake and large tsunami hit Japan • 20,000 people killed • Fukushima Daiichi nuclear power station badly damaged • 80,000 residents evacuated • Nuclear radiation may prohibit return to some communities for decades

We tend to think most about the natural environment following a disaster—a nuclear plant failure, a major oil spill, or an enormous hurricane.[17] But concerns for the status and preservation of our natural environment are ever-present and global. Climate change is a major political theme in the U.S. and around the world. Calls for being "carbon neutral," "green," and "sustainable" are common on college campuses, in local communities, and in our everyday lives.

What are your top environmental concerns and priorities? How about for your community? Is it toxic waste that may be getting dumped in a regional landfill? Could it be global warming prompted by unusually high seasonal temperatures? Is it fossil fuel consumption and the search for reliable and affordable alternative sources of energy?[18] Just look around and you'll see people and organizations working harder to reduce water consumption, cut back waste and increase recycling, improve energy efficiency, buy more local produce, and eliminate pollution. As consumers we are asking for and getting more access to "green products and services." As job candidates, we increasingly seek "green job" opportunities. And as investors we can buy "green mutual funds" and "green bonds."[19]

It is important that society at large increasingly expects organizations and their managers to help preserve and respect the environment. When they don't, public criticism can be vocal, harsh, and expensive. Think about the world-wide marches and protests calling for more government action on climate change. Think about public debates over "fracking" in the search for oil and over the future of the coal industry. Think also about the outrage that quickly surfaces over disastrous oil spills. Incidents and controversies like these result in calls for stronger government oversight and control over corporate practices that put the natural world at risk.[20]

Ethics: Know Right from Wrong | It's a lot easier to send hazardous waste to another country than dispose of it at home.

Offshore E-Waste Graveyards Bury a Problem

ermingut/Getty Images

"Give me a plan," says the boss. "We need to get rid of this electronic waste."

This isn't an uncommon problem. Just think about all those old stereo components, televisions, out-of-date cell phones, used computers and monitors, and so on. Did you know that they often end up in e-waste graveyards in countries like Ghana, China, and Vietnam? The waste arrives by sea container or barge and ends up in huge dumps. Local laborers, often children, go to work disassembling the waste products to salvage valuable scrap metals, often burning the plastic and motherboards to access the sought-after scraps.

Those who work in and live around e-waste graveyards face real hazards to their health and welfare. That's the hidden problem behind the boss's directive; an offshore e-waste graveyard is an attractive low-cost option. But the price is paid in adverse environmental and health effects. What is the human and environmental price for the scrap materials being disassembled, recovered, and buried? It isn't a stretch to assume that the workers often inhale toxic fumes; nearby streams can get polluted with runoff waste; and even streets and living areas of the workers get cluttered with electronic debris.

What Do You Think?

Even as some countries become hosts for e-waste products, their governments may look the other way when it comes to the environmental and human costs. Whose responsibility is it to deal with the negative consequences of e-waste disposal? Does the originating country or consumer have any obligation to reduce waste creation and assist with safe waste disposal? If the "plan" given to the boss in this case is simply "ship it to Ghana," is that acceptable business practice? What are the long-term implications of this kind of approach? Do you see a world in the near future when it will be impossible for corporations to continue to function without addressing these issues?

4.2 | Environmental Uncertainty and Value Creation

LEARNING OBJECTIVE 4.2

List ways organizations pursue value creation and competitive advantage in complex environments.

WileyPLUS

See Author Video

> **Learn More About**
>
> Environmental uncertainty • Value creation and competitive advantage

The **specific environment** or **task environment** is composed of the organizations, groups, and persons with whom an organization interacts and conducts business. These **stakeholders** are the persons, groups, and institutions affected by the organization's performance.[21] Stakeholders are key players with an interest in how an organization operates. They are influenced by it, and they can influence it in return. For most organizations these include customers, suppliers, competitors, regulators, advocacy groups, investors/owners, employees, and society at large—including future generations.

> The **specific environment**, or **task environment**, includes the people and groups with whom an organization interacts.
>
> **Stakeholders** are the persons, groups, and institutions directly affected by an organization.

Environmental Uncertainty

As managers deal with stakeholders, create value, and gain competitive advantage, this can be complicated by **environmental uncertainty**—incomplete information about the environment. The more uncertain the environment, the harder it is to analyze the competitive landscape and make accurate predictions about the future. The greater the environmental uncertainty, the more risk taking is needed to act on problems and opportunities (see Insight feature).

> **Environmental uncertainty** is a lack of information regarding what exists in the environment and what developments may occur.

Two dimensions of environmental uncertainty are shown in **Figure 4.2**.[22] The first is the *degree of complexity*, the number of different factors in the environment. An environment is typically classified as relatively simple or complex. The second is the *rate of change* in and among these factors. An environment is typically classified as being stable or dynamic. The most challenging and uncertain situation is an environment that is both complex and dynamic. High-uncertainty environments require flexibility and adaptability in organizational designs and work practices, and decision makers comfortable with risk who can respond quickly as situations change.

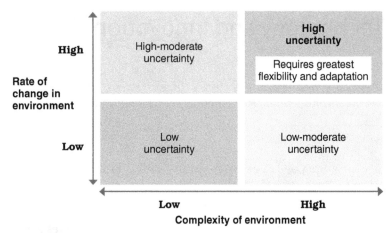

FIGURE 4.2 Dimensions of uncertainty in the external environments of organizations.

Value Creation and Competitive Advantage

Successful organizations contribute by creating value for—and satisfying the needs of—their stakeholders. Customers get quality products, owners can earn profits, suppliers and partners benefit from long-term relationships, employees benefit from wages and job satisfaction, communities benefit through corporate citizenship, and even competitors benefit through market stimulation and product/process innovations.

Organizations also strive for **competitive advantage**. This is something that they do extremely well, is difficult to copy, and gives them an advantage over competitors.[23] Think competitive advantage when you turn to Google for search, shop with "one-click" at Amazon, and stream movies from Netflix. The ultimate competitive advantage test is a good answer to this question: "What does my organization do better than any other?" Answers to this question can take many forms, including:[24]

Competitive advantage is something that an organization does extremely well, is difficult to copy, and that gives it an advantage over competitors in the marketplace.

- *Competitive advantage through cost*—finding ways and using technology to operate with lower costs than competitors earning profits with prices competitors can't match.
- *Competitive advantage through quality*—finding ways and using technology to create products and services of higher quality than competitors offer.
- *Competitive advantage through delivery*—finding ways and using technology to delivering products and services to customers faster, more consistently on time, and by developing timely new products.
- *Competitive advantage through flexibility*—finding ways and using technology to adjust and tailor products and services to fit customer needs in ways too difficult or expensive for competitors to match.

Learning Check

LEARNING OBJECTIVE 4.2

List ways organizations pursue value creation and competitive advantage in complex environments.

Be Sure You Can • describe how a business can create value for four key stakeholders • explain *competitive advantage* and give examples of how a business might achieve it • analyze the uncertainty of an organization's external environment using degree of complexity and rate of change

Technology and Innovation

LEARNING OBJECTIVE 4.3

Describe how organizations embrace technology and pursue innovation.

> **Learn More About**
>
> Technology, innovation, and careers • Types of innovations • The innovation process • Disruptive innovation

The uncertainty, complexity, and change in today's environment requires almost continuous **innovation**, the process of coming up with new ideas and putting them into practice. A major driver of competitive advantage, innovation is important for both organizations and for individuals.[25]

WileyPLUS

See Author Video

Innovation is the process of taking a new idea and putting it into practice.

Technology, Innovation, and Careers

Klaus Schwab, founder of the World Economic Forum, says we are in the midst of the Fourth Industrial Revolution. Previous ones were driven by coal and steam, followed by electricity and the automobile, and next by computing technologies. The fourth is being driven by mobile connectivity, artificial intelligence, and automation. These forces are having a major impact on the ways that businesses compete and the nature of the personal skills and competencies critical for career success today.

The impacts of technology and innovation are evident everywhere you look and, literally, everywhere you are—at work, at home, at play.[26] But whereas innovation used to be a remarkable, identifiable, and long-lasting event, technology is now moving so fast that the timeline of innovation is greatly compressed. The old adage of "here today, gone tomorrow" is a very accurate label. Just pick up your smartphone. It was once "the thing," now it's commonplace and the market is pretty much saturated. Consumers recognize technological changes and avidly await what comes next. But are job seekers similarly aware and thinking far enough ahead with their career readiness portolios?

Our economy is seeing an explosive growth in tech jobs, but employers often struggle to find enough well-trained workers to fill them. What changes in our education systems can help fill this gap? Are we innovating fast enough in those directions? We are on the front end of a tidal wave of efficiencies driven by artificial intelligence, robotics, automation, and smart machines. But there's also a decrease in human-centered jobs in everything from services to manufacturing. What can be done to restore gainful employment to those being displaced? What can be done to ensure that good jobs are available for all of us in the future? Are we innovating fast enough in those directions?

What about you? Are you not only on top of technology but also continuously learning and innovating around it to stay competitive with the brand called "You"? Do you accept that you are always "under construction" and that it's your responsibility to keep your skills set and career strategy market ready?[27] Do you understand not just the features and opportunities of new technologies, but also the costs and risks they pose? Are you building a tech mindset and developing learning agility so that you won't be caught flat-footed as technologies change ever more radically in the future?

Risk Taking Has Its Ups and Downs

Why is there so much interest in adventure sports like ice climbing, river running, base jumping, sky diving, and more? Some people assume it's for the adrenaline rush; others argue that the "thrill" is addictive. What is clear is that it's all about **risk taking**, and people differ in how comfortable they are taking risks in uncertain situations.

Risk taking is a way to step forward, stop "playing it safe," and try new things. But there's need for caution as well. There is a difference between a crazy gamble and calculated risk.

Research shows that executives in higher-performing organizations take risks while motivated by confidence. This helps them pursue opportunities and adapt to emergent problems. Executives in lower-performing organizations may take risks while motivated by desperation to escape difficulties. Because they lack confidence, they are likely to jump from one problem to the next without making sustainable gains.

Consider the nearby figure. On which side of the "risk line" do you most often fall—the positive side motivated by confidence, or the negative side motivated by desperation? It is interesting to note that research links high risk taking with boredom and dissatisfaction. Can this explain why some people are risk takers—because they're bored or dissatisfied?

It is important to understand tendencies toward risk taking. The figure identifies a "risk line" above which risk can be positive below which it can be negative. The former is driven by opportunity and confidence, the latter by fear and desperation. As you think about the complexities of organizations' external environment, including opportunities of innovation and sustainability, stop and ask: How do we individually, organizationally, and as a society deal with risk in our environments, and how can we do better?

Walking the Fine Line of Risk Taking

Positive Side of Risk-Taking Behavior
Risk taking from base of performance success; motivated by confidence in moving to even better situation; able to deal with problems as they arise; lots of staying power

Risk Line -------------------------- Risk Line

Negative Side of Risk-Taking Behavior
Risk taking from position of performance difficulty; motivated by desperation to get out of bad situation; hard time dealing with problems without losing focus; little staying power

---

Get To Know Yourself Better

Use the above figure to do a quick self-check of your risk-taking tendencies. Which side of the risk line are you most often on—positive or negative? Write short descriptions of risks you've taken at school, at work, and your personal life that were driven (a) by confidence and (b) by desperation. What do these descriptions suggest about how risk taking influences your behavior in professional and personal areas of your life?

Types of Innovations

Product innovations result in new or improved goods or services.

Process innovations result in better ways of doing things.

Business model innovations result in ways for firms to make money.

The innovations we experience every day sort into three broad forms: (1) **Product innovations** result in the creation of new or improved goods and services. (2) **Process innovations** result in better ways of doing things. (3) **Business model innovations** result in new ways of making money for the firm. Consider these examples:

Product Innovation—Groupon put coupons on the Web; Bluetooth earbuds took the wires out of listening to music. The "parking assist package" on many cars makes it easy to fit into tight spots.

Process Innovation—IKEA's "ready to assemble" furniture and fixtures transformed retail shopping; Amazon.com's "1-Click" ordering streamlined online shopping and Alexa made Amazon part of the home; Nike allows online customers to design their own shoes. Supermarket self-checkout decreases wait times and bottom-line costs.

Business Model Innovation—Netflix turned movie rental into a subscription business and Redbox put it into a vending machine; Zynga made "paying for extras" profitable in free online games.

Although there is a tendency is to view innovation as primarily focused on business issues, innovation also is essential for social problems—poverty, famine, literacy, disease—and the general conditions for economic and social development. **Social business innovation** uses business models to address important social problems. Think of it as business innovation with a focus on critical social issues.

Microcredit lending is an example of social business innovation. It was pioneered in Bangladesh, where economist Muhammad Yunus started the Grameen Bank. Recognizing that many of the country's citizens who are poor couldn't obtain regular bank loans because of insufficient collateral, Yunus introduced the "microcredit." He set up the Grameen Bank to lend small amounts of money to these citizens at very low interest rates, with the goal of promoting self-sufficiency through owning small enterprises. At one level this is a business model innovation—microcredit lending. But at another level it is a social business innovation—using microcredit lending to help tackle the ever-challenging issue of poverty.[28]

Social business innovation finds ways to use business models to address important social problems.

The Innovation Process

Whether the focus of innovation is a new product, an improved process, a unique business model, or social issues, the innovation process begins with *invention*—discovery—and ends with *application*—the act of use. Consultant Gary Hamel described innovation in the five-step *wheel of innovation* shown in **Figure 4.3**.[29] Step 1 is *imagining*—thinking about new possibilities. Step 2 is *designing*—building initial models, prototypes, or samples. Step 3 is *experimenting*—examining practicality and financial value through experiments and feasibility studies. Step 4 is *assessing*—identifying strengths and weaknesses, costs and benefits, and potential markets or applications. Step 5 is *scaling*—implementation and commercialization of new products or services, leading to new products, services, or processes that increase profits by improving sales or lowering costs.

The phenomenon called **reverse innovation** refers to innovation that comes from lower organizational levels and from diverse settings or locations.[30] The concept got its start as global firms realized that innovation wasn't just a "home market" activity that creates new products and services for distribution to "foreign markets." Instead, lots of innovations were found in environments where new products and services had to be created under income and pricing constraints. GE, for example, developed low-priced and portable electrocardiogram and ultrasound machines in India, where the prices of its existing lines were prohibitive. The firm brought the new machines through reverse innovation into U.S. markets, where their mobility and low prices made them popular with emergency units.

Reverse innovation is launched from lower organizational levels and diverse locations, including emerging markets.

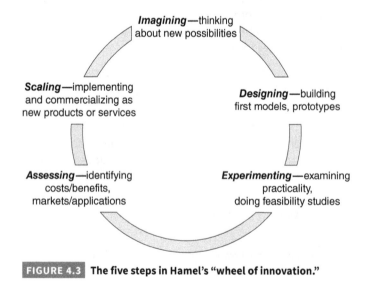

FIGURE 4.3 The five steps in Hamel's "wheel of innovation."

Disruptive Innovation

Disruptive innovation creates products or services that become so widely used that they largely replace prior practices and competitors.

The innovation process is sometimes so successful that it leads to **disruptive innovation**. Harvard scholar Clay Christensen defines it as the creation of an innovative product or service that starts out small scale and then moves "up market" to where it becomes so widely used that it displaces prior practices and competitors.[31] Historical examples include cellular phones that disrupted traditional landlines, MP3 digital music players that disrupted CDs and cassettes, and discount retailers that disrupted traditional department stores. Today we find online e-retailers disrupting fixed-place brick and mortar stores. Today we find online gaming and movie streaming disrupting "buy and own" models. Today we find electric vehicle technologies disrupting traditional internal combustion markets.

What's on your list for the next great disruptor of established products or business practices? What will come next as artificial intelligence and robotics continue to fundamentally disrupt the nature of work as we know it? Are we as a society and are you as a career builder really prepared for what the future might hold in job opportunities?

Learning Check

LEARNING OBJECTIVE 4.3

Describe how organizations embrace technology and pursue innovation.

Be sure you can • describe how technology drives innovation and career changes today • define *innovation* • contrast differences between process, product, business model, and social business innovations • list the five steps in the innovation process • explain how innovations get commercialized • define *reverse innovation* and *disruptive innovation* • give an example of a disruptive innovation that you use almost every day

4.4 | Sustainability and Social Issues

WileyPLUS

See Author Video

LEARNING OBJECTIVE 4.4

Explain the challenges of sustainability as an environmental priority.

> **Learn More About**
> Sustainable development • Sustainable business • Human sustainability

Sustainability is a commitment to protect the rights of present and future generations as co-stakeholders of the world's resources.

Think about climate change, carbon footprints, alternative energy, local foods, and broader links among people, organizations, and nature. They highlight issues of **sustainability**, a commitment to live and work in ways that protect the rights of both present and future generations as co-stakeholders of natural resources. It applies to everything from the air we breathe and the water we consume, to the spaces we inhabit, to the human labor that gives life to our best-loved foods, beverages, and electronic devices. Sustainability is so important that the United Nations is committed to the 17 Sustainable Development Goals shown in the Choices feature.

| Choices: **Think before You Act** | Goal accomplishment requires the partnership of governments, civil society organizations, businesses, and citizens |

UN's Sustainable Development Goals and Business Action

Justin Hession/Getty Images News/Getty Images

Described by the United Nations as "a universal call to action to end poverty, protect the planet and ensure that all people enjoy peace and prosperity," a set of 17 sustainable development goals (SDGs) has a target date for completion of 2030.

1. No poverty
2. Zero hunger
3. Good health and well-being
4. Quality education
5. Gender equality
6. Clean water and sanitation
7. Affordable and clean energy
8. Decent work and economic growth
9. Industry, innovation, infrastructure
10. Reduced inequalities
11. Sustainable cities and communities
12. Responsible consumption and production
13. Climate action
14. Life below water
15. Life on land
16. Peach, justice, strong institutions
17. Partnerships for the goals

The UN intends for these goals to drive sustainability accomplishments through the commitments of governments, civil society organizations, businesses, and citizens. In fact, the UN states that success in meeting the sustainability goals "requires" the partnership of all these players.

Your Take?

How much of the talk we hear about sustainability is just that—"talk"? Are pressing issues of sustainability getting the attention they deserve from businesses today? How important do you suspect the UN's 17 Sustainable Development Goals really rank on the list of top executive and small business owner priorities? Choose three of the SDGs on the list and jot down a few ideas of what a small business in your community could do to support them. How about big business, say on the scale of Google, BMW, Nike, or Delta Airlines? Choose another three SDGs and make suggestions for them to join in the "partnership" for action considered so important by the UN.

Sustainable Development

We live and work at a time when global consumption of fossil fuels is at an all-time high, water shortages are reaching critical proportions in many parts of the world, and air quality in major metropolitan areas around the globe is reaching all-time lows. It only makes sense that **sustainable development** is a major concern for governments, leaders, and the public. The term describes the use of environmental resources to support society's needs today, while also preserving and protecting them for use by future generations.[32]

"Renew," "recycle," "conserve," and "preserve" are all well-recognized sustainable development catchwords. They highlight preservation of **environmental capital** or **natural capital** as the world's supply of natural resources—atmosphere, land, water, and minerals—that sustain life on Earth.[33] But how do we balance our consumption of environmental capital to provide for everyday prosperity, convenience, comfort, and luxury, with its potential loss in the future? Former PepsiCo CEO Indra Nooyi said: "All corporations operate with a license from society. It's critically important that we take that responsibility very, very seriously; we have to make sure that what corporations do doesn't add costs to society."[34] Nooyi's point directs attention to a **triple bottom line** that measures economic performance as well as social and environmental performance.[35] You should recognize this is as the **3 P's of organizational performance**—profit, people, and planet.

Sustainable development uses environmental resources to support societal needs today while also preserving and protecting them for future generations.

Environmental capital or **natural capital** is the supply of natural resources—atmosphere, land, water, and minerals—that sustains life and produces goods and services for society.

The **triple bottom line** assesses the economic, social, and environmental performance of organizations.

The **3 P's of organizational performance** are profit, people, and planet.

Sustainable Business

A **sustainable business** operates in ways that meet the needs of customers while protecting or advancing the well-being of our natural environment.

Sustainable innovations or **green innovations** help reduce an organization's negative impact and enhance its positive impact on the natural environment.

Pursuit of the 3 P's is a hallmark of **sustainable businesses** that both meet the needs of customers and protect or advance the well-being of the natural environment.[36] They set goals for "recycling percentage," "carbon reduction," "energy efficiency," "ethical sourcing," and "food security," among others.[37] They have Corporate Sustainability Officers, Green Building Managers, Staff Ecologists, Sustainability Program Directors, and Sustainability Planners. They also pursue **sustainable innovation** or **green innovation** to create products and practices that reduce negative impact on the environment and work to achieve positive impact.[38]

A sustainable business model seeks win–win outcomes for the organization and the environment. Can you think of some good examples? Many firms approach their markets in this way. For example, Stonyfield Farm saved in energy costs after putting in a large solar photovoltaic array. Clif Bar cut shrink-wrapping and saved in plastic costs. Seventh Generation built a $40+ million business from green personal care and household products.[39] Subaru of Indiana Automotive saved millions by recycling plant waste, filtering and reusing paint solvents, and selling compost from food waste to local farmers.[40] Even basic changes in work practices can help with sustainability. Using virtual teams and conferences lowers travel costs. Offering work-at-home alternatives cuts commuting and energy consumption while also helping to attract and retain talent.[41]

Human Sustainability

Sustainability applies to more than the environment alone. Scholar Jeffrey Pfeffer offers a strong case for social and human sustainability—the "People" part of the 3 P's.[42] He says: "Just as there is concern for protecting natural resources, there could be a similar level of concern for protecting human resources. . . . Being a socially responsible business ought to encompass the effect of management practices on employee physical and psychological well-being."[43]

Pfeffer's concern for human sustainability highlights the importance of valuing employees as organizational stakeholders. An organization's commitment to human sustainability can be assessed by asking to what extent it supports human health and well-being by:[44]

- Offering health insurance for employees?
- Providing wellness programs?
- Avoiding job layoffs?
- Structuring work hours to reduce stress?
- Structuring work hours to reduce work–family conflict?
- Designing jobs to reduce stress and give people control over their work?
- Being transparent and fair in handling wage and status inequalities?

Learning Check

LEARNING OBJECTIVE 4.4

Explain the challenges of sustainability as an environmental priority.

Be Sure You Can • explain the triple bottom line and 3 P's of organizational performance • define the terms *sustainable development* and *environmental capital* • give examples of sustainability issues today • explain and give examples of *sustainable business practices* • discuss human sustainability as a management concern

Management Learning Review: Get Prepared for Quizzes and Exams

Summary

LEARNING OBJECTIVE 4.1 Summarize key trends in the external environment of organizations.

- The general environment includes background economic, sociocultural, legal-political, technological, and natural environment conditions.
- The economic environment influences organizations through the health of the local, domestic, and global economies in terms of such things as financial markets, inflation, income levels, unemployment, and job outlook.
- The legal-political environment influences organizations through existing and proposed laws and regulations, government policies, and the philosophy and objectives of political parties.
- The sociocultural environment influences organizations through the norms, customs, and demographics of a society or region, as well as social values on such matters as ethics, human rights, gender roles, and lifestyles.
- The technological environment influences organizations through continuing advancement of information and computer technologies that affect the way we work, how we live, and how we raise our children.
- The natural environment conditions influence organizations through the abundance of natural resources provided, and the need for organizational practices that both meet the needs of customers and protect future well-being.

For Discussion If the interests of a business firm's owners and investors conflict with those of the community, which stakeholder gets preference? What situational factors influence whose interests take precedence?

LEARNING OBJECTIVE 4.2 Discuss challenges of value creation and competitive advantage in complex environments.

- The specific environment or task environment consists of suppliers, customers, competitors, regulators, and other stakeholders with which an organization interacts.
- A competitive advantage is achieved when an organization does something very well that allows it to outperform its competitors.
- Environmental uncertainty is created by the rate of change of factors in the external environment and the complexity of this environment in terms of the number of factors that are relevant and important.

For Discussion Which of the two or three retail stores that you shop at weekly has the strongest competitive advantage and why?

LEARNING OBJECTIVE 4.3 Describe how organizations embrace technology and pursue innovation.

- Product innovations deliver new products and services to customers; process innovations improve operations; and business model innovations find new ways of creating value and making profits.
- Social business innovations use business models to help address social problems, things like poverty, famine, disease, and literacy.
- The innovation process involves moving from the stage of invention that involves discovery and idea creation all the way to final application that involves actual use of what has been created.
- Reverse innovation finds innovation opportunities in diverse locations, such as taking products and services developed in emerging markets and finding ways to utilize them elsewhere.
- Disruptive innovation, often involving technological advancements, is the creation of a new product or service that starts out small scale and then becomes so widely used that it displaces prior practices and competitors.

For Discussion Housing for the homeless is a problem in many communities. In what way might this problem be addressed through some form of social business innovation?

LEARNING OBJECTIVE 4.4 Explain the challenges of sustainability as an environmental priority.

- The concept of sustainability describes a commitment to recognize and protect the rights of both present and future generations as co-stakeholders of the world's natural resources.
- The triple bottom line evaluates how well organizations perform on economic, social, and environmental performance criteria; it is also called the 3 P's of organizational performance—profits, people, planet.
- Sustainable development uses environmental resources to support society today while also preserving and protecting those resources for use by future generations.
- Sustainable innovations pursue new ways for minimizing the negative impact and maximizing positive impact of organizations on the natural environment by reducing energy and natural resource consumption.

For Discussion When the costs of pursuing sustainability goals reduce business profits, which stakeholder interests should take priority, business owners or society at large? Where do you think the balance between profits and sustainability should naturally emerge?

Self-Test 4

Multiple-Choice Questions

1. The general environment of an organization would include _____.

    a. population demographics   **c.** competitors

    b. activist groups   **d.** customers

2. Internet censorship faced in foreign countries by firms such as Google is an example of how differences in _____ factors in the general environment can cause complications for global business executives.

    a. economic   **c.** natural environment

    b. legal-political   **d.** demographic

3. If the term *offshoring* describes outsourcing of work and jobs to foreign locations, what is it called when firms like Caterpillar move jobs back into the United States from foreign locations?

    a. protectionism   **c.** disrupting

    b. reshoring   **d.** upscaling

4. Work preferences of different generations and public values over things like high pay for corporate executives are examples of developments in the _____ environment of organizations.

    a. task   **c.** sociocultural

    b. specific   **d.** economic

5. A business that has found ways to use technology to outperform its rivals in the marketplace can be said to have gained _____.

    a. environmental capital   **c.** sustainable development

    b. competitive advantage   **d.** environmental certainty

6. Apps for an Apple iPhone or Google Android phone are examples of _____ innovations, whereas the use of robotics in performing manufacturing tasks previously done by humans is an example of _____ innovation.

    a. cost-benefit, process

    b. product, cost-benefit

    c. value-driven, service-driven

    d. product, process

7. Microcredit lending that makes it possible for poor people to get small loans so they can start small businesses is an example of a business model innovation that is also a _____ innovation.

    a. social business   **c.** disruptive

    b. technological   **d.** green

8. Two dimensions that determine the level of environmental uncertainty are the number of factors in the external environment and the _____ of these factors.

    a. location   **c.** importance

    b. rate of change   **d.** interdependence

9. One of the ways that corporations might better take into account their responsibility for being good environmental citizens is to redefine the notion of profit to: Profit = Revenue − Cost of Goods Sold − _____.

    a. operating expenses   **c.** costs to society

    b. dividends   **d.** loan interest

10. The three P's of organizational performance are Profit, People, and _____.

    a. Philanthropy   **c.** Potential

    b. Principle   **d.** Planet

11. What organizational stakeholder must be considered in any serious discussion about how a firm can better fulfill its obligations for sustainable development?

    a. owners or investors   **c.** suppliers

    b. customers   **d.** future generations

12. The first step in Hamel's wheel of innovation is _____.

    a. imagining   **c.** experimenting

    b. assessing   **d.** scaling

13. When a medical device is developed in India so that it can sell at a low price and still deliver high-quality results, and then that device is transferred for sale in the United States also at a low price, this is an example of _____.

    a. trickle-down innovation   **c.** reverse innovation

    b. disruptive innovation   **d.** sustainable innovation

14. What term is used to describe the world's supply of natural resources, things such as land, water, and minerals?

    a. sustainable development   **c.** climate justice

    b. global warming   **d.** environmental capital

15. Health insurance for employees, flexible work hours to balance work and family responsibilities, and programs to help employees deal with stress in their lives are ways organizations might try to improve their accomplishments in respect to _____.

    a. profits   **c.** innovation

    b. human sustainability   **d.** natural capital

Short-Response Questions

16. Who and/or what should be considered as key stakeholders by a business executive when mapping the task environment for her organization?

17. Exactly how should "sustainability" be best defined when making it part of a goal statement or strategic objective for a business or nonprofit organization?

18. How do product, process, and business model innovations differ from one another?

19. How does the process of reverse innovation work?

Essay Question

20. At a reunion of graduates from a business college at the local university, two former roommates engaged in a discussion about environment and sustainability. One is a senior executive with a global manufacturer, and the other owns a sandwich shop in the college town.

Global executive: "We include sustainability in our corporate mission and have a chief sustainability officer on the senior management team. The CSO is really good and makes sure that we don't do anything that could cause a lack of public confidence in our commitment to sustainability."

Sandwich shop owner: "That's all well and good, but what are you doing on the positive side in terms of environmental care. It sounds like you do just enough to avoid public scrutiny. Shouldn't the CSO be a real advocate for the environment rather than just a protector of the corporate reputation? We, for example, use only natural foods and ingredients, recycle everything that is recyclable, and compost all possible waste."

Question: If you were establishing a new position called *corporate sustainability officer,* what would you include in the job description as a way of both clarifying the responsibilities of the person hired and establishing clear accountability for what sustainability means to your organization?

Career Skills & Competencies: Make Yourself Valuable!

Evaluate Career Situations

What Would You Do?

1. Social Values on the Line

It is uncomfortable just to hear it. One of your friends brought his friend to lunch. When discussing a new female boss, he says: "It really irritates me not only that she gets the job just because she's a woman, but she's also Hispanic. No way that someone like me had a chance against her 'credentials.' Now she has the gall to act as if we're all one big happy team and the rest of us should accept her leadership. As for me, I'll do my best to make it difficult for her to succeed." Your friend looks dismayed but isn't saying anything. What will you say or do? How does this kind of exchange make you feel?

2. Innovation Isn't Everything

A member of your team comes into the office with a complaint. "You're a great boss," she says, "but. . . ." Well, it turns out the "but" has to do with an apparent bias on your part for praising in public only those members of the team who come up with new ideas. You seem to overlook or neglect the fact that other team members are working hard and producing good—albeit standard—work every day. Are you ready to accept the point that not all high performers are going to be great innovators? If so, what changes in your behavior might be made to reflect this belief? How can you balance great "conventional" work with efforts to innovate?

3. Humans Count, Too

Your boss is enthusiastic about making sustainability a top organizational priority. In a recent meeting he kept talking about "nature," "green practices," and "resource protection." You listened and finally said: "What about people—shouldn't they count when it comes to issues of sustainability?" After listening, perhaps after an initial thought to be critical of your response, he said in return: "Give me a proposal that we can discuss at the next staff meeting." What are you going to give him? How can you make sustainability part of the program at your place of work?

Reflect on the Self-Assessment

Tolerance for Ambiguity

Instructions

To determine your level of tolerance for ambiguity, rate each of the following items on this 7-point scale.[45]

strongly disagree		slightly disagree		slightly agree		strongly agree
1	2	3	4	5	6	7

_____ 1. An expert who doesn't come up with a definite answer probably doesn't know too much.

_____ 2. There is really no such thing as a problem that can't be solved.

_____ 3. I would like to live in a foreign country for a while.

_____ 4. People who fit their lives to a schedule probably miss the joy of living.

_____ 5. A good job is one where what is to be done and how it is to be done are always clear.

_____ 6. In the long run it is possible to get more done by tackling small, simple problems rather than large, complicated ones.

_____ 7. It is more fun to tackle a complicated problem than it is to solve a simple one.

_____ 8. Often the most interesting and stimulating people are those who don't mind being different and original.

_____ 9. What we are used to is always preferable to what is unfamiliar.

_____ 10. A person who leads an even, regular life in which few surprises or unexpected happenings arise really has a lot to be grateful for.

_____ 11. People who insist upon a yes or no answer just don't know how complicated things really are.

_____ 12. Many of our most important decisions are based on insufficient information.

_____ 13. I like parties where I know most of the people more than ones where most of the people are complete strangers.

_____ 14. The sooner we all acquire ideals, the better.

_____ 15. Teachers or supervisors who hand out vague assignments give a chance for one to show initiative and originality.

_____ 16. A good teacher is one who makes you wonder about your way of looking at things

_____ Total Score

Scoring

To obtain a score, first *reverse* the scale score for the eight "reverse" items, 3, 4, 7, 8, 11, 12, 15, and 16 (i.e., a rating of 1 5 7, 2 5 6, 3 5 5, etc.), then add up the rating scores for all 16 items.

Interpretation

Individuals with a *greater* tolerance for ambiguity are more likely to be able to function effectively in organizations and contexts with high turbulence, a high rate of change, and less certainty about expectations, performance standards, what needs to be done, and so on. They are likely to "roll with the punches" as organizations, environmental conditions, and demands change rapidly.

Individuals with a *lower* tolerance for ambiguity are more likely to be unable to adapt or adjust quickly in turbulence, uncertainty, and change. These individuals are likely to become rigid, angry, stressed, and frustrated when there is a high level of uncertainty and ambiguity in the environment.

Contribute to the Class Exercise

The Future Workplace

Instructions

Form teams as assigned by the instructor.

1. Brainstorm to develop a master list of the major characteristics you expect to find in the workplace in the year 2025. Use this list as background for completing the following tasks:

2. Write a one-paragraph description of what the typical "Workplace 2025" manager's workday will be like.

3. Draw a "picture" representing what the "Workplace 2025" organization will look like.

4. Summarize in list form what you consider to be the personal implications of your future workplace scenario for management students today. That is, explain what this means in terms of using academic and extracurricular activities to best prepare for success in this future scenario.

5. Choose a spokesperson to share your results with the class as a whole and explain their implications for the class members.

Manage a Critical Incident

It's Also about Respect

Situation

For three years you have worked in a small retail store selling gifts and party goods in a college town. This year the owner appointed you as manager and you've run into a perplexing situation. Of the store's eight employees, the only full-timer is a single mother who struggles financially to make ends meet. She lives in public housing, receives food stamps, and overall finds it almost impossible to survive on the minimum wage all employees receive. She just came to you and said that the national debate on raising the minimum wage prompted her to (finally) ask for an increase at least up to the level of the minimum wage ($15 per hour) being advocated by fast-food workers who are threatening strikes. Her point is not just that the wage she receives isn't a "livable" wage, but that "it's also about respect." You have listened to her story and find her case troubling. But you've also got seven part-timers to consider, as well as the owner's needs. At this point you arrange for a meeting with the owner to discuss what you call "wage and motivation issues" at the store. You want to have some concrete ideas ready to drive your discussion with the owner.

Questions

How will you frame your assessment of the situation for the store owner? What alternative courses of action can you suggest? What alternative do you prefer in this situation, and why? How does the preferred alternative handle wage and motivation issues for . . . the full-timer? the part-timers? yourself?

Collaborate on the Team Project

Organizational Commitment to Sustainability Scorecard

Instructions

In your assigned teams do the following:

1. Agree on a definition of "sustainability" that should fit the operations of any organization.

2. Brainstorm and agree on criteria for an Organizational Commitment to Sustainability Scorecard (OCSS) that can be used to audit an organization's sustainability practices. Be sure that an organization being audited would not only receive scores on individual dimensions or categories of sustainability performance, but also receive a total overall "Sustainability Score" for comparison with other organizations.

3. Present and defend your OCSS publically to the whole class.

4. Use feedback received from the class presentation to revise your OCSS so that it can be used to conduct an actual organizational sustainability audit.

5. Use your OCSS to complete a sustainability audit for a local organization.

6. Present the results of your audit to the instructor and the whole class. Include in the presentation not only the audit scores, but also: (a) recommendations for how this organization could improve its sustainability practices in the future, and (b) any benchmarks from this organization that might be considered sustainability "best practices" for other organizations to follow.

Analyze the Case Study

Patagonia | Leading a Green Revolution

Go to *Management Cases for Critical Thinking* at the back of the book to find this case.

CHAPTER 5

Global Management and Cultural Diversity

There Are Many Faces in the Neighborhood

UniversalImagesGroup/Getty Images

International travel is rich with cultural diversity. But even a day out shopping or a walk across a college campus can be a trip around the world . . . if you are willing to take it.

Career Readiness – What to Look for Inside

Thought Leadership

Analysis > *Make Data Your Friend*
Corruption and Bribes Haunt Global Business

Choices > *Think before You Act*
Reshoring Offers Alternative to Chinese Manufacturing

Ethics > *Know Right from Wrong*
Nationalism and Protectionism are a Potent Mix

Insight > *Learn about Yourself*
Cultural Intelligence Opens Doors to Opportunity

Skills Make You Valuable

- **Evaluate** *Career Situations:*
  What Would You Do?
- **Reflect** *On the Self-Assessment:*
  Global Intelligence
- **Contribute** *To the Class Exercise:*
  American Football
- **Manage** *A Critical Incident:*
  16 Hours to J-burg
- **Collaborate** *On the Team Project:*
  Globalization Pros and Cons
- **Analyze** *The Case Study:*
  Harley-Davidson: Style and Strategy with a Global Reach

Chapter Quick Start

Complexity and change in the world at large make it critical to understand the implications of globalization for managers, organizations, and everyday living. Global companies offer benefits and create controversies. Cultural differences are a source of both enrichment and misunderstandings for travelers, business executives, and government leaders. This chapter discusses the essentials of global management and cultural diversity with a focus on global learning.

LEARNING OBJECTIVES

5.1 Discuss the implications of globalization for management and organizations.

5.2 Describe global corporations and the issues they both face and create.

5.3 Define culture and identify ways to describe diversity in global cultures.

5.4 Identify the benefits of global learning for management and organizations.

87

Our dynamic global community is rich with information, opportunities, controversies, and complications. Continuous updates with real-time news give us the ability to be true global citizens. When crises occur, information and news reach around the world almost instantaneously. Social media keep us informed about North Korea's nuclear programs, famine in Yemen and Somalia, economic and political implosion in Venezuela, trade and tarrif wars, and much more on a daily basis. At the same time we play online games like *Fortnite* or *Dota 2* in global communities, while colleges and universities offer a stimulating range of study-abroad programs.

As for international businesses, "complexity" and "global reach" are ever present even when we don't realize it. IBM has more employees in India than in the United States[1] An heuser-Busch is owned by the Belgian firm InBev. Ben & Jerry's is owned by the British-Dutch firm Unilever. India's Tata Group owns Jaguar, Land Rover, Tetley, and Eight O'Clock. China's Geely Auto Group owns Volvo. Japan's Honda, Nissan, and Toyota receive a majority of their profits from sales in the United States.[2] Components for Boeing planes come from suppliers located in 40 countries.[3]

5.1 | Management and Globalization

WileyPLUS

See Author Video

LEARNING OBJECTIVE 5.1

Discuss the implications of globalization for management and organizations.

> **Learn More About**
> Global management • Why companies go global • How companies go global • Global business environments

In the **global economy**, resources, markets, and competition are worldwide in scope.

Globalization is the growing interdependence among elements of the global economy.

We live and work in a **global economy** in which resources, supplies, product markets, and business competition have a worldwide scope. We are heavily influenced by **globalization**, defined as the growing interdependence among the components in the global economy. Some see globalization as a "borderless world" where economic integration becomes so extreme that nation-states hardly matter anymore.[4] Others view it as a threat to national cultures, identities, and economic well-beings. In the midst of it all, government leaders try to balance economic impacts from global integration with local needs and priorities.[5]

There's no better way to illustrate the global economy than with the example of the clothes we wear. For example, where did you buy your favorite T-shirt? Where was it made? Where will it end up? In a fascinating book, *The Travels of a T-Shirt in the Global Economy*, economist Pietra Rivoli tracks the life of a T-shirt that she bought on vacation in Florida.[6]

As can be seen in **Figure 5.1**, Rivoli's T-shirt lived a very complicated global life before she bought it. That life began with cotton grown in Texas. It then moved on to China where the cotton was processed and the T-shirt was manufactured. The T-shirt was then sold to a firm in the United States that silk-screened and sold these T-shirts to retail shops for resale to American customers. These customers eventually donated the used T-shirts to a charity that sold them to a recycler. The recycler sold them to a vendor in Africa, who then distributed the T-shirts to local markets to be sold yet again to local customers.

It's quite a global story as this T-shirt travels the global commercial highways and byways of the world. To what is this referring? It's the first mention of "Limited Brands" in this chapter—is it referring to a story in another chapter? Does it help explain why Harvard scholar and consultant Rosabeth Moss Kanter described globalization as "one of the most powerful and pervasive influences on nations, businesses, workplaces, communities, and lives?"[7]

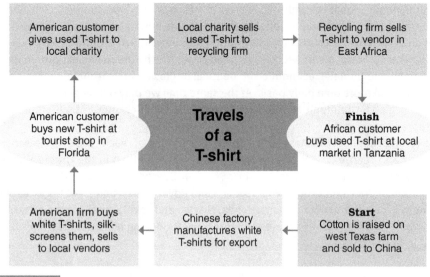

FIGURE 5.1   **Travels of a T-Shirt in the Global Economy.**

Global Management

The term **global management** describes management in organizations with interests in more than one country. For many firms, global management is a way of life. Procter & Gamble, for example, pursues a global strategy with customers in over 180 countries. The majority of McDonald's sales come from outside the United States. Toyota has 14 plants in North America. Their success depends on attracting and hiring truly **global managers** with a strong global perspective, who are culturally aware and informed about current international issues and events.

Global management involves managing business and organizations with interests in more than one country.

A truly **global manager** is culturally aware and informed on international affairs.

Why Companies Go Global

John Chambers, former chairman and CEO of Cisco Systems Inc., once said: "I will put my jobs anywhere in the world where the right infrastructure is, with the right educated workforce, with the right supportive government."[8] Cisco, Apple, Nike, and other firms like them are classic **international businesses** that conduct for-profit transactions of goods and services across national boundaries. They do so in the quest for benefits such as these:

Profits—Gain profits through expanded operations.

Customers—Enter new markets to gain new customers.

Suppliers—Get access to materials, products, and services.

Labor—Get access to lower-cost, talented workers.

Capital—Tap into a larger pool of financial resources.

Risk—Spread assets among multiple countries.

An **international business** conducts for-profit transactions of goods and services across national boundaries.

By the way, did you know that Nike has no domestic manufacturing infrastructure? All of its products are sourced internationally, including 100+ factories in China alone. Its competitor, New Balance, takes a different approach. Although extensively leveraging global suppliers and licensing its products internationally, New Balance proudly declares: "We're proud to be the only major company to make or assemble more than 4 million pairs of athletic footwear per year in the USA".[9] The two firms follow different strategies, but each is actively global. Both firms seek these benefits of international business.

Today you can add another benefit to this list, *economic development*—where a global firm does business in foreign countries and acts in ways that directly help the local economy and social structure. Coffee giant Starbucks, for example, helps local farmers in places like Nicaragua and Rwanda to improve production and marketing methods while also investing in community education and services. This creates a win–win scenario: The global firm gets a quality product at a good price; the local farmers gain skills and market opportunities, their families benefit, and the domestic economy improves.[10] Such a development-focused approach to international business energizes a virtuous circle, where all parties keep getting stronger as they work with one another.

How Companies Go Global

The ways of pursuing international business are shown in **Figure 5.2**. When a business is becoming international, global sourcing, exporting/importing, licensing, and franchising are typically the most common ways to begin. These are *market-entry strategies* that involve the sale of goods or services to foreign markets that don't require an expensive investment. Strategic alliances, joint ventures, and wholly-owned subsidiaries are *direct investment strategies*. These do require a major capital commitment, but also create rights of ownership and control over operations in the foreign country.

Global Sourcing

In **global sourcing**, materials or services are purchased around the world for local use.

Global Sourcing   The first step taken into international business by many firms is **global sourcing**—purchasing materials, manufacturing components, or locating business services around the world. It is an international division of labor in which activities are performed in countries at low cost. Global sourcing at Boeing means that aircraft parts and components flow in from a complex global supply chain for final assembly into 787 Dreamliners at American plants—center fuselage from Italy, landing gear from France, flight deck interiors from Japan, and more. In the service sector, it may mean setting up toll-free customer support call centers in the Philippines, locating research and development centers in Brazil, or hiring physicians in India to read digitized medical X-rays.[11]

Most manufacturers today—of toys, shoes, electronics, furniture, clothing, aircraft—make extensive use of global sourcing. China remains a major outsourcing destination. Even with controversies over unfair local laws, questionable business practices, and inadequate intellectual property protection diminishing its appeal, China is still pretty much the factory for the world. But things are changing in the world of global sourcing.

Reshoring shifts foreign manufacturing and jobs back to domestic locations.

Privacy and intellectual property concerns, rising labor rates, and higher costs for transportation in international supply chains are among the reasons why some firms have started to reduce their outsourcing and do more **reshoring**—moving foreign manufacturing and jobs back home. Reshoring brings attractive opportunities to access predictable government, cheaper energy, stable wage rates, better quality control, and good public relations by starting or expanding domestic operations. A survey of large U.S.-based manufacturers by the Boston Consulting Group (BCG) found that over half of U.S. firms had either started reshoring or were likely to do so in the future. The report concluded that "Companies are realizing that the economics of manufacturing are swinging in favor of the U.S."[12]

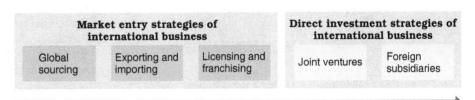

Depth of involvement in international business grows as businesses
move from market entry strategies into direct investment strategies

FIGURE 5.2 **Companies go global with international business strategies that range from market entry initiatives to direct investments in foreign operations.**

Exporting and Importing

A second form of international business involves **exporting**—selling locally made products in foreign markets. The flipside of exporting is **importing**—buying foreign-made products and selling them in domestic markets. Because the growth of export industries creates local jobs, governments often offer special advice and assistance to businesses seeking to develop or expand export markets.

After visiting a U.S. government–sponsored trade fair in China, Bruce Boxerman, president of a then small Cincinnati firm, Richards Industries, decided to take advantage of the growing market for precision valves. The decision doubled export sales one of his employees said: "It wasn't long ago that guys looked at globalization like it is going to cause all of us to lose our jobs. Now it's probably going to save our jobs."[13] And it certainly did. Richards is now the parent company to six product lines and has sales representatives around the world.

> In **exporting**, local products are sold abroad to foreign customers.
>
> **Importing** involves the selling in domestic markets of products acquired abroad.

Licensing and Franchising

International business also takes place through the **licensing agreement**, where foreign firms pay a fee for rights to make or sell another company's products in a specified region. The license typically grants access to a unique manufacturing technology, special patent, or trademark. Such licensing, however, involves potential risk.[14] New Balance, for example, licensed a Chinese supplier to produce one of its brands. Even after New Balance revoked the license, the supplier continued to produce and distribute the shoes around Asia. It was only through expensive, drawn-out litigation in China's courts that New Balance was able to deal with the problem.[15]

Franchising is a form of licensing where a firm buys the rights to use another's name and operating methods. The international version operates in a similar way to domestic franchising. McDonald's, Wendy's, and Subway, for example, sell facility designs, equipment, product ingredients, recipes, and management systems to foreign investors, while retaining brand,

> In a **licensing agreement** a local firm pays a fee to a foreign firm for rights to make or sell its products.
>
> In **franchising**, a fee is paid to a foreign business for rights to locally operate using its name, branding, and methods.

Choices: Think before You Act | "It's probably 30 percent cheaper to manufacture in China. But factor in shipping and all the other B.S. that you have to endure."

Reshoring Offers Alternative to Chinese Manufacturing

iStock.com/Pgiam

Over the past 15 to 20 years, if you were a manufacturer you went to China, at least as a first stop on your global scouting trip. However, things have and some firms are moving back home.

Why?

LightSaver Technologies tried for two years to get things done in China and then moved back to California. CEO Jerry Anderson said China lost its allure: "It's probably 30 percent cheaper to manufacture in China. But factor in shipping and all the other B.S. that you have to endure." Transportation costs are rising for goods moved from China to the United States and other world markets. Labor costs are up. Business risks, including new and changing regulations, are increasing. Theft of intellectual property is a problem. One small manufacturer says: "They're infamous over there for knocking [products] off." Another complains: "Now prices are escalating, quality is dropping, and deliveries are being delayed."

Your Take?

With super-efficient plants and supply chain infrastructure China remains a manufacturing superpower. But past practices, politics, competition from other nations, and global economics are dimming its attraction somewhat. When it comes to China today, are you on the reshoring side or the offshoring side of the issue? What facts are available to support or undermine your position? Consider this issue from a consumer's perspective. If you can buy a child's toy made in China for $8, would you be willing to pay $12 so that it could be labeled "Made in America"? Should more of America's businesses, large and small, say, "Not worth the trouble!" when Chinese manufacturers come calling with offers?

product, and operating controls. One of the challenges they face with international franchising is the creation of locally popular menu items while meeting broader branding goals.

Joint Ventures and Strategic Alliances

Foreign direct investment, or FDI, involves setting up and buying all or part of a business. For many countries, the ability to attract foreign business investors has been a key to succeeding in the global economy. The term **insourcing** is often used to describe foreign direct investment, or FDI, that results in local job creation. FDI in the United States totals over $4 trillion, for example, and creates just under 7 million local jobs.[16]

When foreign firms do invest in another country, a common way to start is with a **joint venture**. This is a co-ownership arrangement in which foreign and local partners pool resources, share risks, and jointly operate the new business. Sometimes the joint venture is formed when a foreign partner buys part ownership in an existing local firm. In other cases it is formed as an entirely new operation that the foreign and local partners start up together.

International joint ventures are types of **global strategic alliances** where foreign and domestic firms work together for mutual benefit. For the local partner, an alliance may bring access to technology and opportunities to learn new skills. For the foreign partner, an alliance may bring access to new markets and the expert assistance of locals who understand domestic markets and the local business context. But, over time partners' goals don't always match—for example, when the foreign firm seeks profits and cost efficiencies while the local firm seeks maximum employment and acquisition of new technology.[17] To minimize this risk, experienced global executives suggest the following guidelines on how to choose a join venture partner.[18]

- Familiar with firm's major business
- Employs a strong local workforce
- Values its customers
- Has potential for future expansion
- Has strong local market
- Has good profit potential
- Has sound financial standing

Foreign Subsidiaries

One way around the uncertainties and problems with joint ventures and strategic alliances is full ownership of the foreign operation. A **foreign subsidiary** is a local operation completely owned and controlled by a foreign firm. These subsidiaries may be built from the ground up as a **greenfield venture**. They also can be established by acquisition, where the outside firm purchases an entire local operation.

Although a foreign subsidiary represents the highest level of involvement in international operations, it can be very profitable to approach an international venture in this way. When Nissan opened a plant in Canton, Mississippi, an auto analyst said: "It's a smart strategy . . . building more in their regional markets, as well as being able to meet consumers' needs more quickly."[19] The analyst could also have pointed out that this plant allowed Nissan to claim reputational benefits by dealing with American customers as a "local" employer rather than a "foreign" company.

Global Business Environments

When Nissan comes to America or GM goes to China, a lot of what takes place in the foreign business environment is very different from what is common at home. Not only must global managers master the demands of operating with worldwide suppliers, distributors, customers, and competitors, they must also deal with many unique local challenges.

Legal and Political Systems

Some of the most substantial risks in international business come from differences in legal and political systems. Global firms are expected to abide

---

Insourcing is job creation through foreign direct investment.

A **joint venture** operates in a foreign country through co-ownership by foreign and local partners.

A **global strategic alliance** is a partnership in which foreign and domestic firms share resources and knowledge for mutual gains.

A **foreign subsidiary** is a local operation completely owned by a foreign firm.

A **greenfield venture** is a foreign subsidiary built from the ground up by the foreign owner.

by local laws, many of which may be unfamiliar. The more home-country and host-country laws differ, the harder it is for international businesses to adapt to local rules, regulations, and customs. Check out the legal complications faced by Amazon, Apple, Facebook, and Google with tax enforcement and privacy protection rulings from the European Competition Commission. The commission's head Margrethe Vestager says: "Being based in many countries, of course you have obligations wherever you go, with the rules made in those democracies where you do business. It's not about where you come from. It's about what you do when outside."[20]

Common legal problems in international business involve tax rules, incorporation practices, and business ownership; negotiation and implementation of contracts with foreign parties; handling of foreign exchange; and intellectual property rights—patents, trademarks, and copyrights. You may be most familiar with the intellectual property issue as it relates to movie and music downloads, sale of fake designer fashions, or software pirating. Companies like Microsoft, Sony, and Louis Vuitton face this issue in terms of lost profits due to their products or designs being copied and sold as imitations by foreign firms. After a lengthy and complex legal battle, for example, Starbucks won a major intellectual property case it had taken to the Chinese courts. A local firm was using Starbucks' Chinese name, "Xingbake" (*Xing* means "star" and *bake* is pronounced "bah kuh"), and was also copying its café designs.[21]

Political turmoil, violence, and government changes constitute another area of concern known as **political risk**—the potential loss in value of an investment in or managerial control over assets because of instability and political changes in the host country. The major threats associated with political risk come from terrorism, civil wars, armed conflicts, and new government systems and policies. Although these threats can't be prevented, they can be anticipated. Most global firms use a planning technique called **political-risk analysis** to forecast the probability of disruptive events that can threaten the security of foreign investments.

> **Political risk** is the potential loss in value of a foreign investment due to instability and political changes in the host country.
>
> **Political-risk analysis** tries to forecast political disruptions that can threaten the value of a foreign investment.

Ethics: Know Right from Wrong

| Bolivia's president announced that his government was nationalizing "all natural resources, what our ancestors fought for."

Nationalism and Protectionism are a Potent Mix

Aizar Raldes/AFP/Getty Images

The headline read "Bolivia Seizes Control of Oil and Gas Fields." Although oil industry executives couldn't say that this wasn't anticipated, it still must have been shocking when Bolivia's government announced that it was taking control of the country's oil and gas fields.

The announcement said: "We are beginning by nationalizing oil and gas; tomorrow we will add mining, forestry, and all natural resources, what our ancestors fought for."

Immediately following the announcement, Bolivia's armed forces secured all of the country's oil and gas fields. President Evo Morales set forth new terms that gave a state-owned firm 82% of all revenues, leaving 18% for the foreign firms. He said: "Only those firms that respect these new terms will be allowed to operate in the country." The implicit threat was that any firms not willing to sign new contracts would be sent home.

While foreign governments described this nationalization as an "unfriendly move," Morales considered it patriotic. His position was that any existing contracts with the state were in violation of the constitution, and that Bolivia's natural resources belonged to its people.

What Do You Think?

If you were the CEO of one of the global oil firms operating in Bolivia, how would you react to this nationalization? Would you resist and raise the ethics issue of honoring existing contracts with the Bolivian government? Or would you comply and accept the new terms being offered? As an everyday citizen of the world, do you agree or disagree with the argument that Bolivia's natural resources are national treasures that belong to the people, not foreign investors? What ethical issues inform the decision to nationalize Bolivia's oil and gas industry?

Trade Agreements and Trade Barriers

When international businesses believe they are being mistreated in foreign countries, or when local companies believe foreign competitors are disadvantaging them, their respective governments can take these cases to the **World Trade Organization (WTO)**. The WTO is a global organization established to promote free trade and open markets around the world. Its member nations, presently 151 of them, agree to negotiate and resolve disputes about tariffs and trade restrictions.[22]

WTO members are supposed to give one another **most favored nation status**—the most favorable treatment for imports and exports. Yet trade barriers are still common. They include outright **tariffs**, which constitute taxes that governments impose on imports. They also include **nontariff barriers** that discourage imports in nontax ways. These include quotas, import restrictions, and other forms of **protectionism** that give favorable treatment to domestic businesses. Foreign firms complain, for example, that the Chinese government creates barriers that make it hard for them to succeed when doing business in the country. A spokesperson for the U.S. Chamber of Commerce says that American multinationals like Caterpillar, Boeing, Motorola, and others have been hurt by "systematic efforts by China to develop policies that build their domestic enterprises at the expense of U.S. firms."[23]

One goal of most tariffs and protectionism is to protect local firms from foreign competition and save local jobs. You'll see these issues in political campaigns and election-year debates. These aren't easy to solve. Government leaders face conflicting goals of seeking freer international trade for their global firms while still protecting domestic industries from foreign competitors. Such political dilemmas create controversies for the WTO in its role as a global arbiter of trade issues. In one claim filed with the WTO, the United States complained that China's "legal structure for protecting and enforcing copyright and trademark protections" was "deficient" and not in compliance with WTO rules. China's response was that the suit was out of line with WTO rules and that "we strongly oppose the U.S. attempt to impose on developing members through this case."[24]

Regional Economic Alliances

Although forces of nationalism and economic populism are rallying cries for "go it alone" and "bring it home" approaches to the global economy, there are many **regional economic alliances** where nations work together for economic gains. NAFTA, the North American Free Trade Agreement, was formed in 1994 by the United States, Canada, and Mexico. It created a trade zone that frees the flow of goods and services, workers, and investment among the three countries.

The NAFTA alliance generated both pros and cons and remains controversial. Arguments in its favor include economic growth through more cross-border trade, greater manufacturing productivity, and improvements in the Mexican business environment. Arguments against include complaints about job losses to Mexico and lower wages for American workers.[25] NAFTA was renegotiated as the United States-Mexico-Canada Agreement, or **USMCA**. It will go into effect once ratified by the three governments.

The **European Union** (EU) is a regional economic and political alliance of global importance. The financial health of the EU is regularly in the news, as upswings and downswings in its economy affect the entire world. Until the United Kingdom voted to leave, the EU comprised 28 member countries that agreed to support mutual interests by integrating themselves politically—there is now a European Parliament, and economically—member countries have removed barriers to cross-border trade and business development. Seventeen EU members also are part of a common currency, the **Euro**, which has become a major competitor to the U.S. dollar in the global economy.

In Asia and the Pacific Rim, 21 member nations established the **Asia Pacific Economic Cooperation** (APEC) to promote free trade and investment in the Pacific region. Businesses from APEC countries have access to a some of the world's fastest growing economies, such as China, Republic of Korea, Indonesia, Russia, and Australia. The market potential of member countries, close to 3 billion consumers, far exceeding the reach of NAFTA/USMCA and the EU. Also in Asia, the 10 nations of the Association of Southeast Asian Nations (ASEAN) cooperate with a stated goal of promoting shared economic growth and progress.

World Trade Organization member nations agree to negotiate and resolve disputes about tariffs and trade restrictions.

Most favored nation status gives a trading partner most favorable treatment for imports and exports.

Tariffs are taxes governments levy on imports from abroad.

Nontariff barriers to trade discourage imports in nontax ways such as quotas and government import restrictions.

Protectionism is a call for tariffs and favorable treatments to protect domestic firms from foreign competition.

Regional economic alliances link member countries in agreements to work together for economic gains.

USMCA is the United Mexici States Canada Agreement linking Canada, the United States, and Mexico in an economic alliance.

The **European Union** is a political and economic alliance of European countries.

The **Euro** is now the common European currency.

The **Asia Pacific Economic Cooperation** (APEC) links 21 countries to promote free trade and investment in the Pacific region.

Africa is increasingly center stage in world business headlines.[26] The region's economies are growing, the middle class is expanding, and there is a promising rise in entrepreneurship.[27] Companies like Harley-Davidson, Walmart, Caterpillar, and Google are making their presence—and continental ambitions—known as they set up offices, invest in dealerships, and buy local companies.[28] The **Southern Africa Development Community** (SADC) links 14 countries in southern Africa in trade and economic development efforts. Its website posts this vision: "a future in a regional community that will ensure economic well-being, improvement of the standards of living and quality of life, freedom and social justice, and peace and security for the peoples of Southern Africa."[29]

> The **Southern Africa Development Community** (SADC) links 14 countries of southern Africa in trade and economic development efforts.

Learning Check

LEARNING OBJECTIVE 5.1

Discuss the implications of globalization for management and organizations.

Be Sure You Can • define *globalization* and discuss its implications for international management • list five reasons companies pursue international business opportunities • describe and give examples of global sourcing, exporting/importing, franchising/licensing, joint ventures, and foreign subsidiaries • discuss how differences in legal environments can affect businesses operating internationally • explain the goals of the WTO • discuss the significance of regional economic alliances such as USMCA, the EU, APEC, and SADC

5.2 | Global Businesses

LEARNING OBJECTIVE 5.2

Describe global corporations and the issues they both face and create.

> **WileyPLUS**
>
> See Author Video

> **Learn More About**
>
> Types of global businesses • Pros and cons of global businesses • Ethics challenges for global businesses

If you travel abroad, many of your favorite brands and products will travel with you. You can have McDonald's in over 100 countries, follow it with Häagen-Daz ice cream in 50, and then brush up with Crest toothpaste in 180. Economists even use the "Big Mac" index, which compares the U.S. dollar price of the McDonald's sandwich around the world, to track purchasing power parity among the world's currencies. A recent example showed a Big Mac costing $5.51 in the U.S. compared with $6.54 in Switzerland, $4.52 in Australia, and $2.57 in Mexico.[30]

Types of Global Businesses

Global corporations, also called *multinational enterprises* (MNEs) and *multinational corporations* (MNCs), are businesses with extensive international operations in many foreign countries. The largest global corporations are identified in annual listings such as *Fortune* magazine's Global 500 and the *Financial Times*'s FT Global 500. They include Walmart, BP, Toyota, Nestlé, BMW, Caterpillar, Sony, and Samsung, as well as others you may not recognize, such as the big oil and gas producers PetroChina (China), Gazprom (Russia), and Total (France).

There is likely no doubt in your mind that IBM and General Motors are American firms, while Sony and Honda are Japanese. But, this may not be how executives at these companies

> A **global corporation** is a multinational enterprise (MNE) or multinational corporation (MNC) that conducts commercial transactions across national boundaries.

A **transnational corporation** is a global corporation or MNE that operates worldwide on a borderless basis.

want their firms to be viewed. Many global firms now try to act as **transnational corporations** that do business around the world without being identified with one national home.[31] Executives of transnational firms view the entire world as their domain for acquiring resources, locating production facilities, marketing goods and services, and communicating brand images. The goal is described by a global executive as "source everywhere, manufacture everywhere, sell everywhere."[32]

Pros and Cons of Global Businesses

What difference does a company's nationality make? Does it really matter to an American whether local jobs come from a domestic giant like IBM or a foreign firm like Honda? How about size? Does it matter that Exxon/Mobil's revenues are larger than Sweden's gross domestic product (GDP)?[33] What about wealth? Is what some call the **globalization gap**—large multinationals and industrialized nations gaining disproportionately from globalization, a matter for social and personal concern?[34]

The **globalization gap** is where large multinational corporations and industrialized nations gain disproportionately from the benefits of globalization.

Host-Country Issues   Ideally, global corporations and the countries that host them should get benefits. But things can go right and wrong in these relationships.[35] Potential host-country benefits shown in **Figure 5.3** include a larger tax base, increased employment opportunities, technology transfers, introduction of new industries, and development of local resources. Potential host-country costs include complaints that global corporations extract excessive profits, dominate the local economy, interfere with the local governments, fail to respect local customs and laws, fail to help domestic firms develop, hire the most talented local personnel away from domestic firms, and fail to transfer their most advanced technologies to the host country.

Home-Country Issues   Global corporations also can get into trouble at home in the countries where they were founded and where their headquarters are located. Even as many global firms try to operate as transnationals, home-country governments and citizens still tend to identify them with local and national interests. They also expect global firms to act as good domestic citizens.[36]

When a global business cuts back home-country jobs, or closes a domestic operation in order to source work to lower-cost international providers, the loss is controversial. Corporate decision makers are likely to be called on by government and community leaders to reconsider and give priority to domestic social responsibilities. Other home-country criticisms of global firms include sending investment capital abroad and corruption. American lawmakers are concerned about corporate **tax inversion**, where a U.S.-based MNC buys a firm in a low-tax country in order to shield foreign earnings from U.S. taxes.

Tax inversion is where a U.S.-based MNC buys a firm in a low-tax country in order to shield foreign earnings from U.S. taxes.

What should go right in MNC host-country relationships	What can go wrong in MNC host-country relationships	
Mutual benefits	**Host-country complaints about MNCs**	**MNC complaints about host countries**
Shared opportunities with potential for • Growth • Income • Learning • Development	• Excessive profits • Economic domination • Interference with government • Hire best local talent • Limited technology transfer • Disrespect for local customs	• Profit limitations • Overpriced resources • Exploitative rules • Foreign exchange restrictions • Failure to uphold contracts

FIGURE 5.3 **What should go right and what can go wrong in global corporations and host-country relationships.**

Ethics Challenges for Global Businesses

Dateline Bangladesh: The collapse of eight-story Rana Plaza, an industrial building for garment factories, resulted in 1,129 deaths and 2,215 injuries. Although warnings had been issued about cracks in the building, employees faced loss of pay if they refused to work. Rana Plaza factories are connected to a global supply chain producing apparel for brands including Benetton, Cato Fashions, the Children's Place, and Walmart.[37]

We live at a time of global democratization of information and communication and the ready availability of reports on ethics-tied outcomes from business activity. Customers, governments, other stakeholders, and the public at large have access to more information about what is happening with MNCs and their complex supply chains than ever before. The consequences of business actions—the good and the bad, and anywhere in the world—have never been more visible and impactful. Although bad decisions will continue to be made, it's harder to hide them from intense public scrutiny and significant public relations and financial backlash.[38]

Corruption

Corruption occurs when people engage in illegal practices for their personal business interests. It's a source of continuing controversy and often makes headline news in the international business context.[39] The civil society organization Transparency International is devoted to eliminating corruption. Its annual reports and publications track corruption and are a source of insight for both executives and policymakers.[40] But corruption isn't always neat or clear-cut. An American executive, for example, says that payoffs are needed to get shipments through customs in some countries even though all legal taxes and tariffs are already paid. Local customs brokers build these payments into their invoices.[41]

What do you think? Should the act of paying extra for what you already deserve to receive be considered a bribe? Should U.S. firms facing such situations be allowed to do whatever is locally acceptable? How do you sort right from wrong when considering how to negotiate local customs and business expectations?

The **Foreign Corrupt Practices Act (FCPA)** makes it illegal for U.S. firms and their representatives to engage in corrupt practices.[42] U.S. companies are not supposed to pay or offer bribes or excessive commissions—including nonmonetary gifts—to foreign officials in return for business favors. Critics claim that the FCPA fails to recognize the realities in many foreign nations. Critics believe the FCPA puts U.S. companies at a competitive disadvantage because they can't offer the same "deals" or "perks" as businesses from other nations, deals locals may regard as standard business practice. Other nations, such as the United Kingdom with its Bribery Act, have begun to pass similar laws and the U.S. Department of Justice isn't backing down. FCPA penalties are now running over $1 billion per year.[43]

Child Labor and Sweatshops

The numbers are startling: 152 million child laborers worldwide, 73 million of them working in hazardous conditions.[44] **Child labor**—the employment of children to perform work otherwise performed by adults—is a major ethics issue that haunts global businesses as they follow the world's low-cost manufacturing from country to country. More than likely, you've heard about child labor used in the manufacture of handmade carpets, but what about your favorite electronic devices and sports items that are largely made by foreign suppliers?[45] How many are really child labor free? Companies find it difficult to always know for certain just who is employed in a foreign factory. After an Apple audit identified 106 underage workers used by 11 of its 400 suppliers, Apple required the firms to return children to their homes, pay for their enrollment in local schools, and pay their families what the children would have earned in annual income.[46]

Sweatshops—business operations that employ workers at low wages for long hours in poor working conditions—are another key ethical issue. The Bangladesh garment industry, for example, depends on workers, often female and illiterate, who are trying to escape lives of poverty. Their complaints include blocked elevators, filthy tap water, and unclean overflowing toilets in the factories.[47] When Walmart audited some 200 factories in its Bangladesh supply chains, 15% failed safety inspections. Walmart now claims it has a "zero tolerance policy"

Corruption involves illegal practices to further one's business interests.

The **Foreign Corrupt Practices Act (FCPA)** makes it illegal for U.S. firms and their representatives to engage in corrupt practices overseas.

Child labor is the employment of children for work otherwise done by adults.

Sweatshops employ workers at very low wages for long hours in poor working conditions.

Corruption and Bribes Haunt Global Business

ROBERTO SCHMIDT/AFP/Getty Images

If you want a world free of corruption and bribes, you share a lot in common with the global civil society organization Transparency International (TI). TI's mission is to "create change for a world free of corruption." The organization publishes regular surveys and reports on corruption and bribery around the world. Some recent

data reflecting on country-specific patterns of corruption can be seen below:

Corruption: Best and worst out of 180 countries in perceived public sector corruption.

Best—Denmark, New Zealand, Finland, Singapore, Sweden, Switzerland.

Worst—Somalia, Syria, South Sudan, Yemen, North Korea

On the decrease—Australia, Chile, Malta, Hungary, Turkey.

Bribery: Best and worst of 20 countries in likelihood of home country firms' willingness to pay bribes abroad.

Best—Netherlands, Switzerland, Belgium, Germany, Japan

Worst—Russia, China, Mexico, Indonesia

In Betweens—Canada, United States, Brazil, Turkey

Your Thoughts?

Are there any patterns evident in these data? Does it surprise you that the United States didn't make the "best" lists? How could TI's website be used by global business executives? Is there a meaningful difference between "corruption" and "bribery" in international business? What does the absence of a set of standardized global practices mean for an even international business playing field?

when its standards are violated and says it will cancel business contracts with any supplier that subcontracts work to others without informing Walmart.[48]

Conflict Minerals   It's no secret that the sale of scarce minerals helps support warlords and perpetuates strife in places such as the Democratic Republic of Congo and the surrounding region. Called **conflict minerals** because wealth gained from their sale helps pay for armed violence, they also are indispensable to many—if not all—the electrical devices we depend on.[49] It just isn't possible to make a phone, tablet, or other smart device, without components that use minerals like tin, tungsten, gold, and tantalum, each of which might be mined in conflict areas.[50]

> **Conflict minerals** are ones sourced in the Democratic Republic of Congo and surrounding region and whose sale finances armed groups that perpetuate violence.

Identifying the source of the minerals used in electronics manufacturing is extremely difficult in the murky world of global sourcing. Who knows, for example, how many times a supply of tungsten may have been passed from hand to hand and where its original source might be located? The Dodd-Frank Act of 2010 required U.S. companies to certify sourced minerals as "conflict free". But the law was appealed and firms now only have to report that they have "investigated" their supply chains for conflict minerals.[51] Whether you prefer the original Dodd-Frank requirement for certification or accept the alternative of investigation as sufficient, the fact is that companies have a lot to gain in reputation and moral standing by tracing the minerals used in their products and rejecting those sourced in conflict areas.

Learning Check

LEARNING OBJECTIVE 5.2

Describe global corporations and the issues they both face and create.

Be Sure You Can • differentiate a multinational corporation from a transnational corporation • list at least three host-country complaints and three home-country complaints about global business operations • give examples of corruption, sweatshops, and child labor in international businesses

5.3 | Cultures and Global Diversity

WileyPLUS

See Author Video

LEARNING OBJECTIVE 5.3

Define culture and identify ways to describe diversity in global cultures.

> **Learn More About**
>
> Cultural intelligence • Silent languages of culture • Tight and loose cultures • Values and national cultures

Situation: A U.S. executive goes to meet a business contact in Saudi Arabia. He sits in the office with crossed legs and the sole of his shoe exposed. Both are unintentional signs of disrespect in the local culture. He passes documents to the host using his left hand, which Muslims in Saudi Arabia generally consider to be unclean. He declines when coffee is offered, which suggests criticism of the Saudi's hospitality. *Outcome:* A $10 million contract is lost to a Korean executive better versed in the local culture.[52]

"Culture" matters, and cultural miscues can be costly in international business and politics. **Culture** is the shared set of beliefs, values, and patterns of behavior common to a group of people.[53] **Culture shock** is the confusion and discomfort a person experiences when in an unfamiliar culture. The box on stages in adjusting to a new culture is a reminder that these feelings must be mastered to travel comfortably and do business around the world. Have you ever had a surprising cross-cultural experience? Have you personally experienced culture shock?

> **Culture** is a shared set of beliefs, values, and patterns of behavior common to a group of people.
>
> **Culture shock** is the confusion and discomfort a person experiences when in an unfamiliar culture.

Cultural Intelligence

The American's behavior in Saudi Arabia was self-centered. He ignored and showed no concern for the culture of his Arab host. This displayed **ethnocentrism**, a tendency to view one's culture as superior to that of others. Some might excuse him as suffering from culture shock. Perhaps he was exhausted after a long international flight. Maybe he was so uncomfortable upon arrival that all he could think about was making a deal and leaving Saudi Arabia as quickly as possible. Still others might give him the benefit of the doubt as being well intentioned but not having time to learn enough about Saudi culture before making the trip.

> **Ethnocentrism** is the tendency to consider one's culture superior to others.

Regardless of possible reasons for the executive's cultural mistakes, they still worked to his disadvantage. They also showed a lack of **cultural intelligence**. Often called "CQ" for "cultural quotient," cultural intelligence is the ability to adapt, adjust, and work well across cultures.[54]

> **Cultural intelligence** is the ability to adapt, adjust, and work well across cultures.

Where do you stand when it comes to cultural intelligence? The Insight feature will help you determine your cultural intelligence. People with cultural intelligence are flexible in dealing with cultural differences and willing to learn from what is unfamiliar. They use that learning to self-regulate and modify their behaviors to act with sensitivity toward another culture's ways. In other words, someone high in cultural intelligence views cultural differences not as a threat but as an opportunity to learn.[55] You can do a quick test of your CQ by asking and answering these questions:[56]

1. Am I aware of the cultural knowledge I use in cross-cultural situations?
2. Do I know about the cultural values, practices, and religious beliefs of other cultures?
3. Do I enjoy interacting with people from diverse cultures?
4. Do I change my behavior when a cross-cultural situation requires it?

Silent Languages of Culture

The capacities to listen, observe, and learn are key building blocks of cultural intelligence. These skills and competencies can be developed by better understanding what the

Insight: Learn about Yourself

Cultural Intelligence Opens Doors to Opportunity

The complications and drama of global events are constant reminders that the ability to work and communicate well across cultures is one of the great challenges of our time. It is hard to pass a day, for example, without encountering Asia's influence on global politics and economics. When our business and government leaders venture into Asia, we want them to be successful. They must have high **cultural intelligence**, including an awareness of Confucian values such as those shown in the box.

Confucian Values in Asian Cultures

- **Harmony**—works well in a group, doesn't disrupt group order, puts group before self-interests
- **Hierarchy**—accepts authority and hierarchical nature of society; doesn't challenge superiors
- **Benevolence**—acts kindly and understandingly toward others; paternalistic, willing to teach and help subordinates
- **Loyalty**—loyal to organization and supervisor, dedicated to job, grateful for job and supportive of superiors
- **Learning**—eager for new knowledge, works hard to learn new job skills, strives for high performance

---

Cultural differences can be frustrating and even feel threatening. Our ways of doing things may seem strange or even offensive to others, and vice-versa. Consultant Richard Lewis warns of "cultural spectacles" that limit our vision, causing us to see and interpret things with the biases of our own culture. Cultural intelligence, by contrast, helps us to adapt to new cultures and work well in culturally diverse situations. It helps us break the habits of our culture and engage the ways of others with interest, respect, and learning. Importantly, it is a must-have competency in our global marketplace.

Get To Know Yourself Better

The cultural diversity of a college campus offers a trip around the world . . . if we're willing to reach out, learn, and embrace it. Take advantage of global diversity in your community. Observe and criticize yourself as you meet, interact with, and otherwise come into contact with persons from other cultures. Take notes on what you perceive as cultural differences and on your "first tendencies" in reacting to these differences. Assess what this suggests about your cultural intelligence. Make a list of what could be your strengths and weaknesses as a global manager. Write down personal reflections on your capacity to work well across cultural boundaries.

---

anthropologist Edward T. Hall calls the "silent" languages of culture.[57] He believes that these silent languages are found in a culture's approach to context, time, and space.

Context If we look and listen carefully, Hall says we'll recognize how cultures differ in their use of language.[58] Most communication in **low-context cultures** takes place via the written or spoken word. This is common in the United States, Canada, and Germany, for example. Americans in particular tend to say or write what they mean and mean what they say. Things aren't this way in many parts of the world.

Low-context cultures emphasize communication via spoken or written words.

In **high-context cultures** what is actually said or written may convey only part, and sometimes a very small part, of the real message. The rest must be interpreted from the situation, body language, physical setting, and even past relationships among the people involved. Dinner parties, social gatherings, and golf outings in high-context cultures such as Thailand and Malaysia, for example, are ways for potential business partners to get to know one another. Only after social relationships are established and a context for communication is developed does it become possible to begin making business deals.

High-context cultures rely on nonverbal and situational cues as well as on spoken or written words in communication.

Time Hall describes differences in how cultures deal with time. People in **monochronic cultures** often do one thing at a time. It is common in the United States, for example, to schedule meetings with specific people and focus on a specific agenda for an allotted period of time.[59] If someone is late to a meeting or brings an uninvited guest, this is viewed unfavorably.

In **monochronic cultures** people tend to do one thing at a time.

Members of **polychronic cultures** are more flexible in their views of time. They often try to work on many different things at once, perhaps not in any particular order, and give in to distractions and interruptions. A monochronic American visitor to the office of a polychronic

In **polychronic cultures** time is used to accomplish many different things at once.

Egyptian client may be frustrated. He may not get dedicated attention as the client greets and deals with a continuous stream of people flowing in and out of his office.

Space   The use of space is also one of the silent languages of culture. Hall describes these cultural tendencies in terms of **proxemics**, the study of how people use space to communicate.[60] Americans tend to like and value their own space, perhaps as much space as they can get. We like big offices, big cars, big homes, and big yards. We tend to get uncomfortable in tight spaces and when others stand too close to us in lines. When someone "talks right in our face," we don't like it; the behavior may even be interpreted as an expression of anger.

Members of some cultures are quite comfortable surrounded by smaller spaces and closer physical distances. If you visit Japan you are likely to notice very quickly that space is precious. Small homes, offices, and shops are the norm; gardens are tiny, but immaculate; public spaces are carefully organized for most efficient use; privacy is highly valued and protected. In many Latin cultures the *abrazzo*, or strong embrace, is a common greeting. In Vietnam, men often hold hands or link arms as a sign of friendship when talking with one another.

> **Proxemics** is how people use space to communicate.

Tight and Loose Cultures

The nail that sticks up will be hammered down.
Asian Proverb

The squeaky wheel gets the grease.
American Idiom

These two sayings are representative of two very different cultural settings. What are the implications of these two different ways of viewing outliers? Try to picture young children listening to their parents or elders as they offer these words of wisdom. One child grows up being careful to not speak out, stand out, or attract attention. The other grows up trying to speak up and stand out in order to get attention.

The contrast in childhoods just described introduces the concept of *cultural tightness-looseness*. Scholars Michele J. Gelfand, Lisa H. Nishii, and Jana L. Raver describe this as "the strength of social norms and degree of sanctioning within societies."[61] Two things are at issue in this definition: (1) the strength of norms that govern social behavior and (2) the tolerance for deviations from norms. Empirical studies have classified 33 societal cultures around the world on their tightness and looseness.[62]

In a **tight culture**, such as in Korea, Japan, or Malaysia, social norms are strong and clear. Members are expected to know the prevailing norms and let them guide their behavior. They tend to self-govern and conform, understanding that deviations are likely to be noticed, discouraged, and sanctioned. The goal in tight cultures, as suggested in the Asian proverb, is to fit in with society's expectations and not stand out.

> A **tight culture** has rigid social norms expects members to conform with them.

In a **loose culture**, such as in Australia, Brazil, or Hungary, social norms are relaxed and less clear-cut. Members may be more or less concerned with them, and conformity varies a good deal. Deviations from norms tend to be tolerated unless they take the form of criminal behavior or test the extremes of morality. It is acceptable for individuals to show unique identities and express themselves independently of the masses.

> A **loose culture** has relaxed social norms and allows conformity by members to vary a good deal.

Think about a class group or work team whose members come from different cultures. You've probably been there. What did you see and experience, and what might you expect the next time? Members from tight cultures may be slow to volunteer, criticize, show emotion, or seek praise. They may look toward formal authority for direction while trying to be on time and prepared. Members from loose cultures may be quick to voice opinions, criticize others, display emotions, and look for recognition. They may not bow to authority, and punctuality may be inconsistent. It takes a lot of cultural awareness for a team leader and team members to identify these culturally derived behaviors. It takes a lot of skill to create a team environment where everyone gets a chance to contribute and experience satisfaction.

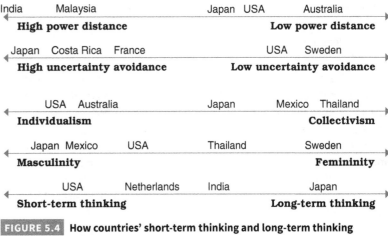

FIGURE 5.4   **How countries' short-term thinking and long-term thinking compare on Hofstede's dimensions of national culture.**

Values and National Cultures

The ideas of Geert Hofstede on value differences in national cultures are another useful way for considering how cultural differences influence management and organizational practices. After studying employees of a global corporation operating in 40 countries, Hofstede identified four cultural dimensions: power distance, uncertainty avoidance, individualism–collectivism, and masculinity–femininity.[63] Later studies added a fifth called time orientation.[64]

    Figure 5.4 shows how national cultures can vary on these dimensions. Try to imagine what these cultural differences might mean when executives try to work and make deals around the world, or when representatives of national governments meet to seek agreements or resolve problems. Remember that Hofstede warns against falling prey to the ecological fallacy. This is acting with the mistaken assumption that a generalized cultural value, such as individualism in American culture or masculinity in Japanese culture, applies equally to all members of the culture.[65]

> The **ecological fallacy** assumes that a generalized cultural value applies equally well to all members of the culture.

> **Power distance** is the degree to which a society accepts unequal distribution of power.

Power Distance   Power distance is the degree society accepts or rejects unequal distribution of power among people in organizations and society. In high power-distance cultures we expect to find great respect for age, status, and titles. People in these cultures tend to be tolerant of power and are prone to follow orders and accept differences in rank. Picture a businesswoman from low-moderate power-distance America visiting her firm's joint venture partner in high power-distance Malaysia. Could her tendencies toward informality, for example, using first names to address superiors and dressing casually in the office, create discomfort for local executives less accustomed to social egalitarianism?

> **Individualism–collectivism** is the degree to which a society emphasizes individuals and their self-interests.

Individualism–Collectivism   Individualism–collectivism is the degree a society emphasizes individual accomplishments and self-interests versus the collective accomplishments and interests of groups.[66] The United States had the highest individualism score of any country in Hofstede's data. Do you find the "I" and "me" words used a lot in conversations and meetings, or even when students are making team presentations? Such self-referential expressions reflect a cultural tendency toward individualism. This contrasts with the importance placed on group harmony in the Confucian and more collectivist cultures of Asia, as pointed out in the chapter opener. What might go wrong when team members from individualistic cultures try to work with those from more collectivist ones?

> **Uncertainty avoidance** is the degree to which a society tolerates risk and uncertainty.

Uncertainty Avoidance   Uncertainty avoidance is the degree a society is uncomfortable with risk, change, and situational uncertainty, versus having tolerance for them. Members of low uncertainty-avoidance cultures often display openness to change and innovation. In high uncertainty-avoidance cultures, by contrast, preferences for structure, order, and predictability are more likely. Persons in these cultures may have difficulty dealing with ambiguity and tend to follow rules, preferring more structure in their lives. Do you think that high uncertainty avoidance is one of the reasons why Europeans seem to favor employment practices that provide job security?

Masculinity–Femininity

Masculinity–femininity is the degree a society values assertiveness and materialism versus feelings, relationships, and quality of life.[67] You might think of it as a tendency for members of a culture to show stereotypically masculine versus feminine traits that reflect different attitudes toward gender roles. Visitors to Japan, with the highest masculinity score in Hofstede's research, may be surprised at how restricted career opportunities can still be for women. The *Wall Street Journal* has pointed out that "In Japan, professional women face a set of socially complex issues—from overt sexism to deep-seated attitudes about the division of labor." One female Japanese manager says: "Men tend to have very fixed ideas about what women are like."[68]

> **Masculinity–femininity** is the degree to which a society values assertiveness and materialism.

Time Orientation

Time orientation is the degree a society emphasizes short-term versus long-term goals and gratifications.[69] American tendencies toward impatience and desire for quick, even instantaneous, gratification show short-term thinking. Even our companies are expected to achieve short-term results; those failing to meet quarterly financial targets often suffer immediate stock price declines. Many Asian cultures are the opposite, displaying Confucian values of persistence, thrift, patience, and a willingness to work for long-term success. This might help explain why Japan's auto executives were more willing than their American counterparts to invest years ago in hybrid engine technologies even though market demand was very low and any return on the investments were likely to take a long time to materialize.

> **Time orientation** is the degree to which a society emphasizes short-term or long-term goals.

Learning Check

LEARNING OBJECTIVE 5.3

Define culture and identify ways to describe diversity in global cultures.

Be Sure You Can • define *culture* and *culture shock* • explain how ethnocentrism can create difficulties for people working across cultures • differentiate between low-context and high-context cultures, and monochronic and polychronic cultures • explain the differences between tight and loose cultures • list and illustrate Hofstede's five dimensions of value differences among national cultures

5.4 | Global Management Learning

LEARNING OBJECTIVE 5.4

Identify the benefits of global learning for management and organizations.

WileyPLUS

See Author Video

> **Learn More About**
>
> Are management theories universal? • Intercultural competencies • Global career readiness goals

Scholars in the area of **comparative management** study how management perspectives and practices systematically differ among countries and cultures.[70] They use cultural models like those described for Hall, Gelfand, et al., and Hofstede, to search for meaningful insights on management around the globe.[71]

> **Comparative management** studies how management practices differ among countries and cultures.

Are Management Theories Universal?

You might think that the management theories in this book and your course apply universally from one country and culture to the next. The fact is that the world is a complex place and management scholars understand this. They agree that there is lots left to understand and learn about global management.[72]

Geert Hofstede, whose framework for understanding national cultures was just discussed, urges caution when transferring practices across cultures. He points out that many management theories are really ethnocentric because they come from a single cultural context—often North American.[73] By way of example, he says that the American emphasis on participation in leadership reflects the culture's moderate stance on power distance. But, Americans must be ready to understand and respect the tolerance for hierarchy and authority found in countries like France and Malaysia that have higher power-distance scores. Hofstede also notes that the American cultural value of individualism is prominent in management theories on individual performance, rewards, and job design. These theories may be less applicable in countries where cultural values are more collectivist. Sweden, for example, has a history of designing jobs for groups of workers rather than for individuals.

Intercultural Competencies

Intercultural competencies are skills and personal characteristics that help us be successful in cross-cultural situations.

Even though management theories are not always universal, it may be that **intercultural competencies** are. These are skills and personal characteristics that help us function in cross-cultural situations. Intercultural competencies are "must haves" for anyone seeking career and life success in a diverse society.

It's not just global managers that cross cultural boundaries, we cross them everyday in our workplaces and communities. The intercultural competencies we all need begin with the notion of cultural awareness that introduced this chapter. But it's not enough to have an interest in and generalized openness to learning about different cultural ways. The real test is whether or not we act with sensitivity and confidence when working in another culture or interacting with others in culturally mixed settings. What scholars know in this regard is summarized in three pillars of intercultural competency—perception management, relationship management, and self-management.[74]

1. In *perception management*, a person must be inquisitive and curious about cultural differences. Being flexible and nonjudgmental are important when interpreting and dealing with situations in which differences are present.

2. In *relationship management*, a person must be genuinely interested in others, be sensitive to one's own emotions and feelings, and be able to make personal adjustments.

3. In *self-management*, a person must have a strong sense of personal identity and understand his or her own emotions and values. One must also stay self-confident even in situations that call for personal adaptations because of cultural differences.

Global Career Readiness Goals

In order to maintain career readiness for diverse workplaces and a global economy, it's essential to continually strengthen our intercultural competencies. They are particularly important if the goal is to have a successful career that involves international travel and global assignments. A truly global manager will look everywhere and anywhere in the world for new ideas, and will reject the view the home country and culture have monopolies on the best practices. In order to work effectively around the world it's important to engage in critical thinking about the ways people and organizations in other cultures do things and about the insights they offer for doing things better at home. As you explore global management learning, however, remember to hesitate before accepting any idea or practice as universally applicable. Culture and cultural differences always have to be considered. According to Hofstede, "Disregard of other cultures is a luxury only the strong can afford . . . increase in cultural awareness represents an intellectual and spiritual gain."[75]

Learning Check

LEARNING OBJECTIVE 5.4

Identify the benefits of global learning for management and organizations.

Be Sure You Can • describe the concept of global organizational learning • define *intercultural competency* and identify three of its major components • answer this question: "Do management theories apply universally around the world?"

Management Learning Review: Get Prepared for Quizzes and Exams

Summary

LEARNING OBJECTIVE 5.1   Discuss the implications of globalization for management and organizations.

- Global managers are informed about world developments and are competent in working with people from different cultures.

- The forces of globalization create international business opportunities to pursue profits, customers, capital, and low-cost suppliers and labor in different countries.

- Market-entry strategies for international business include global sourcing, exporting and importing, and licensing and franchising.

- Direct investment strategies of international business establish joint ventures or wholly owned subsidiaries in foreign countries.

- General environment differences, including legal and political systems, often complicate international business activities.

- Regional economic alliances such as USMCA, the EU, and SADC link nations of the world with the goals of promoting economic development.

- The World Trade Organization is a global institution that promotes free trade and open markets around the world.

For Discussion What aspects of the U.S. legal-political environment could prove difficult for a Chinese firm setting up a factory in America?

LEARNING OBJECTIVE 5.2   Describe global corporations and the issues they both face and create.

- A global corporation is a multinational enterprise or multinational corporation with extensive operations in multiple foreign countries.

- A transnational corporation tries to operate globally without a strong national identity and with a worldwide mission and strategies.

- Global corporations can benefit host countries by offering broader tax bases, new technologies, and employment opportunities.

- Global corporations can cause problems for host countries if they interfere in local government, extract excessive profits, and dominate the local economy.

- The U.S. Foreign Corrupt Practices Act prohibits American multinational corporations from engaging in bribery and corrupt practices abroad.

For Discussion Is the Foreign Corrupt Practices Act unfair to American firms trying to compete for business around the world?

LEARNING OBJECTIVE 5.3   Define culture and identify ways to describe diversity in global cultures.

- Culture is a shared set of beliefs, values, and behavior patterns common to a group of people.

- Culture shock is the discomfort people sometimes experience when interacting with persons from cultures different from their own.

- Cultural intelligence is an individual capacity to understand, respect, and adapt to cultural differences.

- Hall's "silent" languages of culture include the use of context, time, and interpersonal space.

- Hofstede's five dimensions of value differences in national cultures are power distance, uncertainty avoidance, individualism–collectivism, masculinity–femininity, and time orientation.

For Discussion Should religion be included on Hall's list of the silent languages of culture?

LEARNING OBJECTIVE 5.4   Identify the benefits of global learning for management and organizations.

- The field of comparative management studies how management is practiced around the world and how management ideas are transferred from one country or culture to the next.

- The foundations for intercultural competency are perception management, relationship management, and self-management.
- Global management learning must recognize that successful practices in one culture may work less well in others.

For Discussion   Even though cultural differences are readily apparent, is the tendency today for the world's cultures to converge and become more alike?

Self-Test 5

Multiple-Choice Questions

1. The reasons why businesses go international include gaining new markets, finding investment capital, and reducing _____.
    a. political risk
    b. protectionism
    c. labor costs
    d. most favored nation status

2. When shoe maker Rocky Brands decided to buy full ownership of a manufacturing company in the Dominican Republic, Rocky was engaging in which form of international business?
    a. import/export
    b. licensing
    c. foreign subsidiary
    d. joint venture

3. A form of international business that falls into the category of a direct investment strategy is _____.
    a. exporting
    b. joint venture
    c. licensing
    d. global sourcing

4. The World Trade Organization would most likely become involved in disputes between countries over _____.
    a. exchange rates
    b. ethnocentrism
    c. nationalization
    d. tariffs

5. Business complaints about copyright protection and intellectual property rights in some countries illustrate how differences in _____ can impact international operations.
    a. legal environments
    b. political stability
    c. sustainable development
    d. economic systems

6. In _____ cultures, members tend to do one thing at a time; in _____ cultures, members tend to do many things at once.
    a. monochronic, polychronic
    b. polycentric, geocentric
    c. collectivist, individualist
    d. neutral, affective

7. A culture that places great value on expressing meaning in the written or spoken word is described as _____ by Hall.
    a. monochromic
    b. proxemic
    c. collectivist
    d. low-context

8. It is common in Malaysian culture for people to value teamwork and to display great respect for authority. Hofstede would describe this culture as high in both _____.
    a. uncertainty avoidance and feminism
    b. universalism and particularism
    c. collectivism and power distance
    d. long-term orientation and masculinity

9. In Hofstede's study of national cultures, America was found to be the most _____ compared with other countries in his sample.
    a. individualistic
    b. collectivist
    c. feminine
    d. long-term oriented

10. It is _____ when a foreign visitor takes offense at a local custom such as dining with one's fingers, considering it inferior to practices of his or her own culture.
    a. universalist
    b. prescriptive
    c. monochromic
    d. enthnocentric

11. When Limited Brands buys cotton in Egypt, has tops sewn from it in Sri Lanka according to designs made in Italy, and then offers the garments for sale in the United States, this form of international business is known as _____.
    a. licensing
    b. importing
    c. joint venturing
    d. global sourcing

12. The difference between an international business and a transnational corporation is that the transnational _____.
    a. tries to operate around the world without a strong national identity
    b. does business in only one or two foreign countries
    c. is led by ethnocentric managers
    d. is based outside North America

13. The Foreign Corrupt Practices Act makes it illegal for _____.

  a. Americans to engage in joint ventures abroad

  b. foreign businesses to pay bribes to U.S. government officials

  c. U.S. businesses to make payoffs abroad to gain international business contracts

  d. foreign businesses to steal intellectual property from U.S. firms operating in their countries

14. When a member of a cross-cultural team is hesitant to speak up and offer ideas, defers to the team leader, and avoids accepting praise for individual work, the person is displaying characteristics consistent with a _____ culture.

  a. monochromic

  b. low-context

  c. tight

  d. loose

15. Hofstede would describe a culture whose members respect age and authority and whose workers defer to the preferences of their supervisors as _____.

  a. low masculinity

  b. high particularism

  c. high power distance

  d. monochronic

Short-Response Questions

16. Why do host countries sometimes complain about how global corporations operate within their borders?

17. Why is the "power-distance" dimension of national culture important in management?

18. What is the difference between a culture that is tight and one that is loose?

19. How do regional economic alliances impact the global economy?

Essay Question

20. Kim has just returned from her first business trip to Japan. While there, she was impressed with the intense use of work teams. Now back in Iowa, she would like to totally reorganize the workflows and processes of her canoe manufacturing company and its 75 employees around teams. There has been very little emphasis on teamwork, and she now believes this is "the way to go." Based on the discussion of culture and management in this chapter, what advice would you offer Kim?

Career Skills & Competencies: Make Yourself Valuable!

Evaluate Career Situations

What Would You Do?

1. To Buy or Not to Buy

You've just read in the newspaper that the maker of one of your favorite brands of sports shoes is being investigated for using sweatshop factories in Asia. It really disturbs you, but the shoes are great! One of your friends says it's time to boycott the brand. You're not sure. Do you engage in a personal boycott or not, and why?

2. China Beckons

Your new design for a revolutionary golf putter is a big hit with friends at the local golf course. You decide to have clubs with your design manufactured in China so that you can sell them to pro shops around the country. How can you make sure that your design won't be copied by the Chinese manufacturer and then used to make low-price knock-offs? What should you do in this situation?

3. Cross-Cultural Teamwork

You've just been asked to join a team being sent to Poland for 10 days to discuss a new software development project with your firm's Polish engineers. It is your first business trip out of the country. In fact, you've only been to Europe once, as part of a study-abroad semester in college. How will you prepare for the trip and for work with your Polish colleagues there? What worries you the most under the circumstances? After all, if you do well here more international assignments are likely to come your way.

Reflect on the Self-Assessment

Global Intelligence

Instructions

Use the following scale to rate yourself on each of these 10 items:[76]

  1 Very Poor

  2 Poor

  3 Acceptable

  4 Good

  5 Very Good

_____ 1. I understand my own culture in terms of its expectations, values, and influence on communication and relationships.

_____ 2. When someone presents me with a different point of view, I try to understand it rather than attack it.

_____ 3. I am comfortable dealing with situations where the available information is incomplete and the outcomes are unpredictable.

_____ 4. I am open to new situations and am always looking for new information and learning opportunities.

_____ **5.** I have a good understanding of the attitudes and perceptions toward my culture as they are held by people from other cultures.

_____ **6.** I am always gathering information about other countries and cultures and trying to learn from them.

_____ **7.** I am well informed regarding the major differences in the government, political, and economic systems around the world.

_____ **8.** I work hard to increase my understanding of people from other cultures.

_____ **9.** I am able to adjust my communication style to work effectively with people from different cultures.

_____ **10.** I can recognize when cultural differences are influencing working relationships, and I adjust my attitudes and behavior accordingly.

Interpretation

In order to be successful in the global economy, you must be comfortable with cultural diversity. This requires a global mind-set that is receptive to and respectful of cultural differences, global knowledge that includes the continuing quest to know and learn more about other nations and cultures, and global work skills that allow you to work effectively across cultures.

Scoring

The goal is to score as close to a perfect "5" as possible on each of the three dimensions of global intelligence. Develop your scores as follows:

1. Items (1 + 2 + 3 + 4)/4 = _Global Mind-Set Score_
2. Items (5 + 6 + 7)/3 = _Global Knowledge Score_
3. Items (8 + 9 + 10)/3 = _Global Work Skills Score_

Contribute to the Class Exercise

American Football

Instructions

Form into groups as assigned by the instructor. In the group do the following:[77]

1. Discuss "American Football"—the rules, the way the game is played, the way players and coaches behave, and the roles of owners and fans.

2. Use "American Football" as a metaphor to explain the way U.S. corporations run and how they tend to behave in terms of strategies and goals.

3. Prepare a class presentation for a group of visiting Japanese business executives. In this presentation, use the metaphor of "American Football" to (1) explain American business strategies and practices to the Japanese and (2) critique the potential strengths and weaknesses of the American business approach in terms of success in the global marketplace.

Manage a Critical Incident

16 Hours to J-burg

Just sit back and relax—the flight is underway, and you are sitting in business class on South African Airways flight 204 from JFK to Johannesburg. It's your first overseas assignment as an auditor for Deloitte, and you've been rushing to prepare.

You're flying in alone but will be met by four team members from Deloitte's local office in what they call "J-burg." You expect to be in country about a week. But it all happened so fast. One day you're in the office finishing a local audit, that afternoon the boss calls and says he's sending you to Johannesburg, and three days later you're on the plane. It's taken all your interim time to finish the last project, pack, and talk with family.

It turns out that your mother isn't very happy—she's not sure a single woman should be sent alone on this job. From your standpoint, though, an international assignment is a real statement that the company believes in your abilities. You even think this might be something you'd like to do more of and that you might make "being good at international" a strong part of your promotion portfolio.

Other than a short "meet-and-greet" video conference with the J-burg team and a description of the project from your boss, you haven't received any other preparation. Now that you're onboard SA204, the question is: Do you have what it takes to succeed with this assignment in a new country and culture?

Questions

The flight is 16 hours long, and you've decided to make some notes on "things I should do and not do." What's on your list, and why? As a good auditor, you also decide to self-assess on your readiness for cross-cultural teamwork in South Africa. So, you make a balance sheet of "personal assets and liabilities." What are the first five on your list of assets? How about the first five liabilities? What are the implications for your visit and for your career development?

Collaborate on the Team Project

Globalization Pros and Cons

Question

"Globalization" is frequently in the news. You can easily read or listen to both advocates and opponents. What is the bottom line? Is globalization good or bad, and for whom? What are the important issues to consider as the world becomes even more connected?

Instructions

1. Agree on a good definition for the term "globalization." Review various definitions and find the common ground.

2. Read current events relating to globalization. Summarize the issues and arguments. What is the positive side of globalization? What are the negatives that some might call its "dark" side?

3. Read what scholars say about globalization. Summarize their views on the forces and consequences of globalization for small and large companies, for countries, for people and society at large.

4. Consider globalization from the perspective of your local community and its major employers. Is globalization a threat or an opportunity in this context, and why?

5. Take a position on globalization pros and cons, and share it with the class. Justify your position.

Analyze the Case Study

Harley-Davidson | Style and Strategy with a Global Reach

Go to **Management Cases for Critical Thinking** at the end of the book to find this case.

CHAPTER 6

Entrepreneurship and New Ventures
Taking Risks Can Make Dreams Come True

Bloomberg/Getty Images

Nick D'Aloisio—17 years old . . . writes Summly app while in high school . . . puts $30 million in the bank. He says: "My parents at first were a bit concerned. . . . You shouldn't be keeping these hours."

Chapter Quick Start

Entrepreneurship is enticing more and more college students and experienced workers alike. Many of us have good ideas for business and social entrepreneurship that go unfulfilled. Understanding the nature of entrepreneurs, the challenges of running small businesses, and alternative ways of setting up and funding new ventures can help open the doors to this career pathway.

LEARNING OBJECTIVES

6.1 Define entrepreneurship and identify characteristics of entrepreneurs.

6.2 Describe how small businesses get started and the common problems they face.

6.3 Explain how entrepreneurs plan, legally structure, and fund new business ventures.

Career Readiness – What to Look for Inside

Thought Leadership

Analysis > *Make Data Your Friend* Minority Entrepreneurs Lead The Way

Choices > *Think Before You Act* Students Are Crowdfunding Their Human Capital

Ethics > *Know Right from Wrong* Grad-School Startup with Social Mission Takes on Global Competitors

Insight > *Learn About Yourself* Self-Management Keeps You Growing

Skills Make You Valuable

- **Evaluate** *Career Situations:* What Would You Do?

- **Reflect** *On the Self-Assessment:* Entrepreneurial Orientation

- **Contribute** *To the Class Exercise:* Entrepreneurs among Us

- **Manage** *A Critical Incident:* Craft Brewery In—or Out—of the Money?

- **Collaborate** *On the Team Project:* Community Entrepreneurs

- **Analyze** *The Case Study:* In-N-Out Burger: Building Them Better

Just out of the military and starting your civilian life? Why not create your own job? John Raftery did. After a four-year tour in the U.S. Marines—including two years of deployment—he earned an accounting degree through the GI Bill. But after being disappointed with slow advancement at an accounting firm, he answered an e-mail about a free Entrepreneurship Bootcamp for Veterans with Disabilities at Syracuse University. Raftery went to the camp and ended up with a business plan to start his own firm, Patriot Contractors, in Waxahachie, Texas.[1]

Struggling with work–life balance as a mother? Why not find flexibility and opportunity in entrepreneurship? Denise Devine did just that. Once a financial executive with Campbell Soup Co., she now has her own line of fiber-rich juice drinks for kids. Called **mompreneurs**, women like Devine find opportunity in niche markets for safe, useful, and healthy products they spot as a result of their child rearing. Says Devine: "As entrepreneurs we're working harder than we did, but we're doing it on our own schedules."[2]

Mompreneurs pursue business opportunities they spot as mothers.

Thinking about starting a female-owned business but in need of advice and role models? Check out the stories of the following companies and their founders including Bumble (Whitney Wolfe Heard), BentoBox (Krystle Mobayeni), Zola (Shan-Lyn Ma), and Landit (Lisa Skeete Tatum and Sheila Marcelo). The companies are not only entrepreneurial success stories, their founders are also committed to helping other women succeed. Wolfe Heard started Bumble Fund which offers $5,000 to $250,000 grants to help women launch startups. Ma, Mobayeni, Tatum, and Marcelo are part of the Female Founders Fund dedicated to "investing in the exponential power of exceptional female talent."[3]

These examples are hopefully inspiring. In fact, this is really a chapter of examples. The goal is not only to inform you, but also to get you thinking about starting your own business, becoming your own boss, and making your own special contribution to society as a whole. How does that sound? Could you get excited to join the world of entrepreneurship and small business management?

6.1   The Nature of Entrepreneurship

LEARNING OBJECTIVE 6.1

Define entrepreneurship and identify characteristics of entrepreneurs?

WileyPLUS

See Author Video

> **Learn More About**
>
> Who are the entrepreneurs? • Characteristics of entrepreneurs • Women and minority entrepreneurs • Social entrepreneurship

The term **entrepreneurship** describes strategic thinking and risk-taking that results in the creation of new opportunities. The late H. Wayne Huizenga started Waste Management with just $5,000 and once owned the Miami Dolphins. He advised: "An important part of being an entrepreneur is a gut instinct that allows you to believe in your heart that something will work even though everyone else says it will not."[4] Have you had experiences in your own life where you've continued along a path and succeeded, despite the advice of friends or family not to?

Entrepreneurship is risk-taking behavior that results in new opportunities.

Who Are the Entrepreneurs?

A **classic entrepreneur** is a risk-taker who pursues opportunities others fail to recognize, or even view as problems or threats. Who, for example, would consider starting a bookstore in Nashville, Tennessee, where both Borders and Barnes & Noble had already closed shop?

A **classic entrepreneur** is someone willing to pursue opportunities in situations others view as problems or threats.

Against the advice of family and friends, Ann Patchett did. She reasoned that a place that had previously supported 60,000 square feet of bookstore space still had enough customer potential to support a small center-city store. "Why can't I open 2,500 square feet of bookstore?" she reasoned. That confidence gave birth to Parnassus Books and a sales record that went on to exceed expectations.[5]

A **serial entrepreneur** starts and runs businesses and nonprofits over and over again, moving from one interest and opportunity to the next.

Some people become **serial entrepreneurs** that start and run new ventures over and over again, moving from one interest and opportunity to the next. Serial entrepreneurs can be found both in business and nonprofit settings. H. Wayne Huizenga, mentioned earlier, is a great example. He made his fortune founding and selling businesses like Blockbuster Entertainment, Waste Management, and AutoNation. A member of the Entrepreneurs' Hall of Fame, he described being an entrepreneur this way: "We're looking for something where we can make something happen: an industry where the competition is asleep, hasn't taken advantage."[6]

A **first-mover advantage** comes from being first to exploit a niche or enter a market.

A common pattern among successful entrepreneurs is **first-mover advantage**. They move quickly to spot, exploit, and deliver a product or service to a new market or an unrecognized niche. Consider some other brief examples of entrepreneurs who were willing to take risks and sharp enough to pursue first-mover advantage.[7]

Sara Blakely   "Like so many women, I bought clothes that looked amazing in a magazine or on the hanger, but in reality…" These words are Sara Blakely's, and her concerns led to innovation, entrepreneurship, and today a great business—Spanx. She started with $5,000 and a "new idea" to cut the feet out of a pair of pantyhose and create body-shaping underwear. Early attempts to convince manufacturers to make samples met with resistance. Some even called it a "stupid idea." But Blakely

Dia Dipasupil/Getty Images Entertainment/Getty Images

persisted and finally convinced a Neiman Marcus buyer to try her product in stores. Sales took off after she sent samples to Oprah Winfrey, who called them "one of her favorite things." Confidence, optimism, and resilience paid off for Blakely. She created a $400+ million business, achieved a net worth of over $1 billion, received a National Entrepreneur of the Year Award, and started the Spanx by Sara Blakely Foundation with the goal of "supporting and empowering women around the world."[8]

Shawn Corey Carter   You probably know him as Jay Z, and there's an entrepreneurial story behind the name. Carter began rapping on the streets of Brooklyn New York, where he lived with his single mom and three brothers. Hip-hop turned into his ticket to travel. "When I left the block," he told an interviewer, "everyone was saying I was crazy, I was doing well for myself on the streets, and cats around me were like, these rappers . . . just record, tour, and get separated from their families, while some white person takes all their money. I was determined to do it differently."[9] He did. Carter used his music millions to found the media firm Roc Nation, co-found the apparel firm Rocawear, and become part owner of the New Jersey Nets.

Kevin Mazur/Getty Images Entertainment/Getty Images

Earl Graves   With a vision and a $175,000 loan, Earl G. Graves Sr. started *Black Enterprise* magazine. That success grew into Earl G. Graves Ltd.—a multimedia company covering television, radio, and digital media including Black-Enterprise.com. Named by Fortune magazine as one of the 50 most powerful and influential African Americans in corporate America, he wrote the best-selling book *How To Succeed in Business Without Being White* and is a member of many business and non-profit boards. Graves says, "I feel that a large part of my role as publisher of Black Enterprise is to be a catalyst for black economic development in this country."[10]

Louis Johnny/SIpa/Sipa press/Miami Florida United States/Newscom

Anita Roddick   In 1973, Anita Roddick was a 33-year-old housewife looking for a way to support herself and her two children. She spotted a niche for natural skin and health care products, and started mixing and selling them from a small shop in Brighton, England. It became The Body Shop, a global retailer selling a product every half-second around the world. Known for her commitment to human rights, the environment, and economic development, Roddick was an early advocate of "profits with principles" and business social responsibility. She once said: "If you think you're too small to have an impact, try going to bed with a mosquito."[11]

Justin Man/BizOne News/EPN Photos/ Hong Kong Hong Kong/Newscom

Characteristics of Entrepreneurs

Is there something in your experience that could be a pathway to entrepreneurship? Have you thought about better ways to do something that perplexes you and a lot of others? Have you an idea for a new product or service?

There are lots of entrepreneurs in every community. Just look at those individuals who take the risk of buying a McDonald's or Papa John's franchise, open a retail shop selling vintage clothing or bicycles, start a self-employed service business such as financial planning or management consulting, or establish a nonprofit organization to provide housing for the homeless or deliver hot meals to house-bound senior citizens. All of them are entrepreneurs.[12]

Attitudes and Personal Interests   Researchers point out that entrepreneurs tend to share certain attitudes and personal characteristics. The general entrepreneurial profile is of an individual who is self-confident, determined, resilient, adaptable, and driven by excellence.[13] They also share personality traits and characteristics like those described here.[14]

- *Internal locus of control:* Entrepreneurs believe that they are in control of their own destiny; they are self-directing and like autonomy.
- *High energy level:* Entrepreneurs are persistent, hardworking, and willing to exert extraordinary efforts to succeed.
- *Self-confidence:* Entrepreneurs feel competent, believe in themselves, and are willing to make decisions.
- *Tolerance for ambiguity:* Entrepreneurs are risk takers; they tolerate situations with high degrees of uncertainty.

- *Self-reliance and desire for independence:* Entrepreneurs want independence; they are self-reliant; they want to be their own bosses, not work for others.
- *High need for achievement:* Entrepreneurs are motivated to accomplish challenging goals; they thrive on performance feedback.
- *Flexibility:* Entrepreneurs are willing to admit problems and errors, and are willing to change a course of action when plans aren't working.
- *Passion and action orientation:* Entrepreneurs try to act ahead of problems; they want to get things done and not waste valuable time.

Background, Experiences, and Interests   In addition to the personality traits and characteristics shown in **Figure 6.1**, entrepreneurs tend to have unique backgrounds and personal experiences.[15] Childhood *experiences and family environment* make a difference. Evidence links entrepreneurship with parents who were entrepreneurial and self-employed. Entrepreneurs often are raised in families that encourage responsibility, initiative, and independence. Another issue is *career or work history.* Entrepreneurs often go on to pursue numerous ventures. Prior work experience in the business area or the industry being entered also helps.

A report in the *Harvard Business Review* suggests that entrepreneurs have unique and *deeply embedded life interests.*[16] The article describes entrepreneurs as having strong interests in starting things. They enjoy creative production—things like project initiation, working with the unknown, and finding unconventional solutions. Entrepreneurs also have strong interests in running things. They enjoy enterprise control—being in charge, being accountable, and making decisions and moving others toward a goal. Are these characteristics that describe you?

Entrepreneurs also tend to emerge during certain *windows of career opportunity.* Most start their businesses between the ages of 22 and 45, an age spread associated with risk taking. However, being older in age shouldn't be viewed as a barrier. When Tony DeSio was 50, he founded the Mail Boxes Etc. chain. He sold it for $300 million when he was 67 and suffering heart problems. Within a year he launched PixArts, another franchise chain based on photography and art. When asked by a reporter what he liked most about entrepreneurship, DeSio replied: "Being able to make decisions without having to go through layers of corporate hierarchy—just being a master of your own destiny."[17]

Female and Minority Entrepreneurs

Necessity-based entrepreneurship takes place because other employment options don't exist.

When economists speak about entrepreneurs, they differentiate between entrepreneurs driven by new opportunities and those driven by need. Entrepreneurs in the latter category pursue **necessity-based entrepreneurship**, meaning that they start new ventures

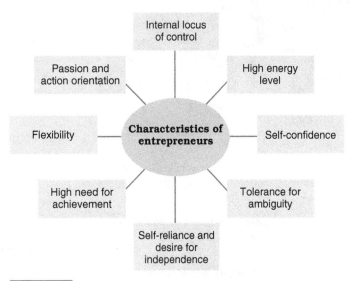

FIGURE 6.1   **Personality traits and characteristics of entrepreneurs.**

because they lack career options. This was the case for Anita Roddick, founder of The Body Shop. She said her entrepreneurship began because she needed "to create a livelihood for myself and my two daughters, while my husband, Gordon, was trekking across the Americas."[18]

Necessity-driven entrepreneurship is one way for women and minorities who have hit the "glass ceiling" in their careers or are otherwise cut off from mainstream employment opportunities to gain economic independence. One survey reported that 33% of women who left private-sector employment believed they were not being taken seriously by their employer, while 29% had experienced glass ceiling issues.[19] As to entrepreneurship by women of color, the report *Women Business Owners of Color: Challenges and Accomplishments* identifies glass ceiling issues that include not being recognized or valued by their employers, not being taken seriously, and seeing others promoted ahead of them.[20]

Female-owned small businesses are on the move. In a five year period the number grew 21% overall, 43% for businesses owned by women of color, and 50% for those owned by black women.[21] Nonetheless, the National Foundation for Women Business Owners (NFWBO) states that women "seem to be encountering 'glass walls' that keep their businesses from expanding" with the major obstacle being "raising capital."[22] *Forbes* reports that startups led by women receive just 3% of venture capital, while women hold only 7% of partnerships in the top venture capital firms. This gender gap exists even though researchers find that startups with female founders on the team out perform all-male startups by 63%.[23]

Obstacles to minority entrepreneurship—as with female entrepreneurship—are real and shouldn't be underestimated. Less than 1% of the available venture capital in the United States goes to minority entrepreneurs. High unemployment and declining wealth among minority households also make it hard to find startup financing. In an effort to address such issues, the U.S. Minority Business Development Agency of the Department of Commerce set up a nationwide network of 40 business development centers with the goal of helping minority-owned businesses grow in "size, scale, and capacity."[24]

Analysis: Make Data Your Friend | Minority entrepreneurs provide 6 million jobs but attract less than 1% of venture capital.

Minority Entrepreneurs Lead the Way

iStock.com/Jacob Wackerhausen

Economic necessity and career difficulties may help to explain the growth of minority entrepreneurship in the United States. Consider these facts and trends.

- The U.S. economy includes more than 4 million minority-owned firms that create over 4.7 million jobs.
- 45% of small business owners in the U.S. are African Americans; 14% are Hispanics; 8% are Asians; 4% are Native Americans.

- The growth rate of Hispanic-owned businesses is more than double that of all businesses.
- Minority entrepreneurs are less successful than majority entrepreneurs when making pitches to angel investors—15% versus 22% success rate.
- African American women own over 2.4 million small businesses, more that those owned by African American men.
- "Lack of capital/cash flow" was cited by 80% of African American women as the biggest challenge faced in their business. 63% of Hispanic business owners say the same.
- Immigrants are twice as likely as native-born Americans to start new businesses.

Your Thoughts?

What factors can help or hinder the growth of minority-owned businesses? Should we invest more in minority entrepreneurship as a way to fight economic disparities in our society? What can be done to reduce or eliminate obstacles minorities and women face on their pathway toward entrepreneurship? Why aren't minorities more successful in pitches to angel investors? Why are minorities and women underrepresented in the ranks of angel investors?

Social Entrepreneurship

Social entrepreneurship is a unique form of ethical entrepreneurship that seeks novel ways to solve pressing social problems.

Social enterprises have a social mission to help make lives better for underserved populations.

Entrepreneurship also plays a critical social role in society. For example, it addresses social issues such as housing and job training for the homeless, bringing technology to poor families, improving literacy among disadvantaged youth, reducing poverty, and improving nutrition. These and other social issues are targets for **social entrepreneurship**, a form of ethical entrepreneurship that seeks ways to solve pressing social problems. Social entrepreneurs take risks and create **social enterprises** to help make lives better for underserved populations.[25]

Social entrepreneurs and their enterprises, both nonprofit and for-profit, devise ways to meet needs that are not being served by government or the private sector.[26] *Fast Company* magazine tries to spot and honor social entrepreneurs that run their organizations with "innovative thinking that can transform lives and change the world." Consider these examples of those who strive to live up to these expectations.[27]

- Chip Ransler and Manoj Sinha—tackled the lack of power in many of India's poor villages. As University of Virginia business students, they realized that 350 million people lived in India's rice-growing regions without reliable electricity. After discovering that tons of rice husks were being discarded with every harvest, Ransler and Sinha started Husk Power Systems. It creates biogas from the husks and uses the gas to fuel small power plants.

- Rose Donna and Joel Selanikio—tackled public health problems in sub-Saharan Africa. After realizing that public health services in developing nations often are bogged down in

---

Ethics: Know Right from Wrong | Founded with a rebellious spirit and a lofty objective: to create boutique-quality, classically crafted eyewear at a revolutionary price point.

Grad-School Startup with Social Mission Takes On Global Competitors

AP Images/Kathy Willens

When four MBA students at Wharton asked that question they found an oligopoly industry where supply was controlled by just a few firms who had a disproportionate influence on prices. Spotting both a business opportunity and a social calling, they started a company to do what they felt was the right thing to do—make eyeglasses available to people at a reasonable price. Their creation, Warby Parker, was "founded with a rebellious spirit and a lofty objective: to create boutique-quality, classically crafted eyewear at a revolutionary price point."

The founders—David Gilboa, Neil Blumenthal, Andrew Hunt, and Jeffrey Raider—wrote a Web-driven business plan that many questioned at first. Could eyeglasses be sold over the Internet? The Warby Parker answer was: "Of course!" If you're in doubt, and

especially if you wear glasses, check out the offerings on warbyparker.com. You can buy stylish glasses for as low as $95—frames with Rx lenses and free shipping. All this is made possible by the founders' careful analysis of the industry and its supply chains. They source directly from manufacturers and then sell direct to customers, cutting out a lot of costs and profit-taking in the middle of the chain.

Warby Parker is e-commerce and customer friendly—letting you have free home try-ons of up to five "loaner" pairs. On the social side of the business model, if you end up buying from Warby Parker, you're also helping someone else who can't afford to buy new glasses for themselves. Warby Parker donates one pair of glasses to someone in need for every pair of glasses it sells. That adds up quickly when you consider that they sell more than 250,000 pairs a year.

The company's website announces: "Let's do good. We're building a company to do good in the world. . . . We think it's good business to do good." They call their business model "eyewear with a purpose." Over a billion people in the world don't have the eyeglasses they need for school, work, or everyday living. This is a pervasive social problem that Warby Parker aims to help solve through business.

What Do You Think?

Warby Parker's founders discovered that prescription eyeglasses could be sold for less than the current market. By selling for less they created more value for both customers and for society at large. Instead of buying glasses at a boutique for $695 you can buy a stylish pair online from Warby Parker for $95. Central to the founders' purpose, each purchase sends a free pair of eyeglasses to someone in need. Why aren't there more businesses like Warby Parker? Why aren't there more entrepreneurs who try to match social problems and business opportunities? How about you? Do you have any good ideas matching business opportunity with social need?

paperwork, they created software to make the process quicker and more efficient while increasing the reliability of databases. The UN, the World Health Organization, and the Vodafone Foundation are now helping their firm, DataDyne, move the program into 22 other African nations.

- Nissan Bahar and Franky Imbesi—tackled the lack of computers for African children living in poverty. They created Keepod, which puts an Android operating system on a USB drive that can be used in old PCs. This "operating system on a stick" makes each child an "owner" of a PC even when sharing machines with others. Bahar and Imbesi are testing the model in Nairobi, Kenya. Local workers buy flash drives for about $7, install the Keepod operating system, resell the drives for $9, and use the profit to pay themselves and fuel further expansion.

Lots of social entrepreneurship takes place without much notice, as most attention goes to business entrepreneurs making lots of money. However, you can find social entrepreneurs right in your own community. Lewisville, Texas, for example, is the home of the housekeeping service Buckets & Bows, owned by Debbie Sardone. She became alarmed after noticing that many of her clients with cancer struggled hard with everyday household chores. Her response was to start Cleaning for a Reason. It's a nonprofit that builds networks of linkages with cleaning firms around the country and owners willing to offer free home cleaning to cancer patients.[28]

Learning Check

LEARNING OBJECTIVE 6.1

Define entrepreneurship and identify characteristics of entrepreneurs.

Be Sure You Can • define *entrepreneurship* and differentiate between classic and serial entrepreneurs • list key personal characteristics of entrepreneurs • explain the influence of background and experience on entrepreneurs • discuss motivations for entrepreneurship by women and minorities • define *social entrepreneurship* and *social enterprises*

6.2 Entrepreneurship and Small Business

LEARNING OBJECTIVE 6.2

Describe how small businesses get started and common problems they face.

WileyPLUS

See Author Video

> **Learn More About**
> Why and how small businesses get started • Why small businesses fail • Family-owned small businesses

The U.S. Small Business Administration (SBA) defines a **small business** as a company that has 500 or fewer employees, is independently owned and operated, and does not dominate its industry. Over 99% of American businesses meet this definition.[29] They provide employment for 47.5% of private-sector workers.[30] Small businesses employ 43% of high-tech workers such as scientists, engineers, and computer programmers. They produce more patents-per-employee than large firms, receive 35% of federal government contract dollars, and export more than $400 billion of goods and services annually.[31] The most common small business areas are restaurants, skilled professions such as craftspeople and doctors, general services such as hairdressers and repair shops, and independent retailers.[32] The vast majority of small businesses employ fewer than 20 workers, and over half of small businesses are home-based.

A **small business** has fewer than 500 employees, is independently owned and operated, and does not dominate its industry.

How Small Businesses Get Started

There are many reasons why people start their own businesses—from necessity, as discussed earlier as a stimulus to entrepreneurship, to wanting to be your own boss, control your future, and fulfill a dream.[33] Would you be surprised to learn that the Gallup-Healthways Well-Being Index points to high satisfaction among small business owners? Self-employed business owners outrank working adults in 10 other occupations—including professional, manager/executive, and sales—on job satisfaction and emotional and physical health.[34]

Once a decision is made to go the small business route, the most common ways entrepreneurs get involved are to start a small business, buy an existing one, or buy and run a **franchise**—where a business owner sells the right to operate the same business in another location. A franchise such as Jimmy John's, Quiznos, or Domino's Pizza runs under the original owner's business name and guidance. In return, the franchise parent receives a specified share of income or a flat fee from the franchisee.

Any business—large or small, franchise or startup, needs a solid underlying **business model**. Think of a business model as a plan for making a profit by generating revenues that are greater than the costs of doing business. Serial entrepreneur Steven Blank calls business **startups** temporary organizations that are trying "to discover a profitable, scalable business model."[35] A startup is just that—a "start"; it's a new venture the entrepreneur is hoping will take shape and prove successful as the business develops and matures.

Blank's advice for those starting up a new venture is to move fast and create a "minimum viable product" that will attract customers, and that can be further developed and made more sophisticated over time. An example is Facebook, which started with simple message sharing and quickly grew into the complex social media operation we know today. Blank also favors something called a **lean startup**. It takes maximum advantage of resources like open-source software and free Web services to save on costs, while staying small and keeping operations as simple as possible.[36]

Why Small Businesses Fail

Small businesses have a high failure rate—one high enough to be intimidating. The SBA reports that about 50% of new small businesses fail in their first five years of operation, and only one-third survive for 10 years or more.[37] Part of this daunting statistic is a "counting" issue. The government counts as a "failure" any business that closes, whether it is because of the death or retirement of an owner, sale to someone else, or inability to earn a profit.[38] Nevertheless, the fact is that a lot of small business startups don't make it for reasons shown in **Figure 6.2**.[39]

A **franchise** is when one business owner sells to another the right to operate the same business in another location.

A **business model** is a plan for making a profit by generating revenues that are greater than costs.

A **startup** is a new and temporary venture that is trying to discover a profitable business model for future success.

Lean startups use resources like open-source software, while containing costs, staying small, and keeping operations as simple as possible.

FIGURE 6.2 Eight reasons why many small businesses fail.

When considering a small business start up, make plans to avoid these common reasons for failure.

- *Insufficient financing*—not having enough money to maintain operations while still building the business and gaining access to customers and markets.
- *Lack of experience*—not having sufficient know-how to run a business in the chosen market or geographic area.
- *Lack of commitment*—not devoting enough time to the requirements of running a competitive business.
- *Lack of strategy and strategic leadership*—not taking the time to craft a vision and mission, or formulate and properly implement a strategy.
- *Ethical failure*—falling prey to the temptations of fraud, deception, and embezzlement.
- *Lack of expertise*—not having expertise in the essentials of business operations, including finance, purchasing, selling, and production.
- *Growing too fast*—not taking the time to consolidate a position, fine-tune the organization, and systematically meet the challenges of growth.
- *Poor financial control*—not keeping track of the numbers, and failure to control business finances and use money to best advantage.

Family-Owned Small Businesses

In the little town of Utica, Ohio, there is a small child's desk in the corner of the president's office at Velvet Ice Cream Company. Its purpose is to help grow the next generation of leadership for the firm. "That's the way Dad did it," says Luconda Dager, president of the firm. "He exposed us all to the business at an early age." When Joseph Dager retired, he said: "It is very special for me to pass the baton to my oldest daughter . . . there is no one better suited for this position."[40]

Velvet Ice Cream is the classic **family business**, owned and financially controlled by family members. The Family Firm Institute reports that family businesses account for 78% of new jobs created in the United States and provide 60% of the nation's employment.[41] Family businesses must solve the same problems of other small or large businesses—strategy, competitive advantage, and operational excellence. When everything goes right the family firm is an ideal situation—everyone working together, sharing values and goals, and knowing that what they do benefits the family. But it doesn't always work out this way or stay this way.

"Okay, Dad, so he's your brother. But does that mean we have to put up with inferior work and an erratic schedule that we would never tolerate from anyone else in the business?"[42] This complaint introduces a problem that can all too often set the stage for failure in a family business—the **family business feud**. Here, family members get into disagreements about work responsibilities, business strategy, operating approaches, finances, or other matters. Frequent and unresolved family disagreements can make it hard to survive in a highly competitive environment.

Family businesses also can suffer from the **succession problem**—transferring leadership from one generation to the next. A survey of small and midsized family businesses showed that 66% of these firms planned to keep the business within the family.[43] But the key management questions are: How will the assets be distributed, and who will run the business when the current head leaves? Ideally, both business momentum and financial wealth are maintained in the succession process. But data on succession show that only about 30% of family firms survive to the second generation; 12% survive to the third; and only 3% are expected to survive beyond that.[44]

Business advisers recommend having a **succession plan**—a formal statement that describes how transition and financial issues will be handled. A succession plan should include procedures for choosing the firm's new leadership, legal aspects of ownership transfer, and financial and estate plans relating to the transfer. This should be shared and understood by all employees affected by it. The successor should be prepared through experience and training to perform in the new role when the time comes to take over.

A **family business** is owned and controlled by members of a family.

A **family business feud** occurs when family members have major disagreements over how the business should be run.

The **succession problem** is the issue of who will run the business when the current head leaves.

A **succession plan** describes how the leadership transition and related financial matters will be handled.

Small Business Development

Business incubators offer space, shared services, and advice to help get small businesses started.

One way that startup difficulties can be managed is for business owners to join a **business incubator**. Sometimes called *business accelerators*, these are facilities that offer space, shared administrative services, special equipment, and management advice at reduced costs. The goal is to help new businesses become healthy enough to survive on their own. Some incubators are focused on specific business areas, such as technology, light manufacturing, or professional services; some provide access to equipment like laser cutters and 3-D printing; some are located in rural areas, while others are based in urban centers; some focus only on socially responsible businesses.

Regardless of their focus or location, business incubators seek to increase the survival rates for new startups. Their goal is to help build businesses that will create new jobs and expand economic opportunities. An example is Y Combinator, an incubator located in Mountain View, California. It was founded by Paul Graham with a focus on Web businesses. Member entrepreneurs get offices, regular meetings with Graham and other business experts, and access to an investors. They also receive grants in exchange for the incubator taking small ownership stake. Y Combinator's 1,300+ graduates are found in over 50 countries. Prominent alumni include Airbnb and Dropbox.[45]

Small Business Development Centers founded with support from the U.S. Small Business Administration provide advice to new and existing small businesses.

Another resource for small business development is the U.S. Small Business Administration. Because small business plays such a significant role in the economy, the SBA works with state and local agencies and the private sector to support a network of over 1,100 **Small Business Development Centers** (SBDCs) nationwide.[46] These SBDCs offer guidance to entrepreneurs and small business owners (both actual and prospective) on how to set up and manage business operations. These centers are often associated with colleges and universities, and give students a chance to work as consultants with small businesses at the same time that they pursue their academic programs.

Learning Check

LEARNING OBJECTIVE 6.2

Describe how small businesses get started and common problems they face.

Be Sure You Can • give the SBA definition of *small business* • discuss the succession problem in family-owned businesses and possible ways to deal with it • list several reasons why many small businesses fail • explain how business incubators work and how both they and SBDCs can help new small businesses

6.3 | New Venture Creation

WileyPLUS

See Author Video

LEARNING OBJECTIVE 6.3

Explain how entrepreneurs plan, legally structure, and fund new business ventures.

> **Learn More About**
>
> Life cycles of entrepreneurial firms • Writing a business plan • Choosing the form of ownership • Financing the new venture

Whether your interest is low-tech or high-tech, online or bricks and mortar, opportunities for new ventures are always there for true entrepreneurs. Entrepreneurs start with good ideas and the courage to give them a chance. But to succeed, entrepreneurs must master the test of

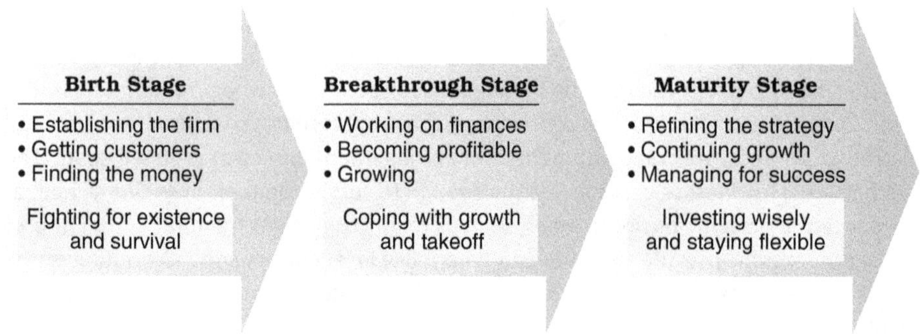

Birth Stage	Breakthrough Stage	Maturity Stage
• Establishing the firm • Getting customers • Finding the money	• Working on finances • Becoming profitable • Growing	• Refining the strategy • Continuing growth • Managing for success
Fighting for existence and survival	Coping with growth and takeoff	Investing wisely and staying flexible

FIGURE 6.3   **Stages in the life cycle of an entrepreneurial firm.**

strategy and competitive advantage. Can you identify a market niche or a new market that is being missed by other established firms? Can you generate a first-mover advantage by exploiting a niche or entering a market before other competitors establish themselves? Do you have a viable business model, or a plan, for your business? These are among the questions that entrepreneurs must ask and answer when beginning a new venture.

Life Cycles of Entrepreneurial Firms

Figure 6.3 describes the stages common to the life cycles of entrepreneurial companies. It shows the relatively typical progression from birth to breakthrough to maturity. The firm begins with the *birth stage*—where the entrepreneur struggles to get the new venture established and to survive long enough to test the viability of the underlying business model in the marketplace. The firm then passes into the *breakthrough stage*—where the business model begins to work well, the firm grows, and the complexity of managing the business expands. Finally, the firm enters the *maturity stage*—where the venture market success and financial stability, while also facing the continuing management challenges associated with remaining competitive in a changing environment.

Entrepreneurs often face control problems and other management dilemmas when their firms start to grow rapidly. The problems often involve the different skills needed for entrepreneurial leadership in the early life cycle stages versus strategic leadership in the later stages of maturity. Entrepreneurial leadership helps to bring ventures into being and steers them through the early stages of life. Strategic leadership requires managing and leading the venture into maturity as an ever-evolving and still-growing enterprise. If the founding entrepreneur doesn't have the skills or interests required to meet the firm's strategic leadership needs, its continued success may depend on selling to other owners or passing day-to-day management to professionals with these skills.

Writing a Business Plan

When people start new businesses or launch new units within existing businesses, they can benefit from a good **business plan**. This plan describes the details needed to obtain startup financing and operate a new business.[47] Banks and other sources of finance want to see a business plan before they loan money or invest in a new venture. Senior managers want to see a business plan before they allocate scarce organizational resources to support a new entrepreneurial project. There's good reason for this.

The detailed thinking required to prepare a business plan can contribute to the success of the new initiative. As shown in **Figure 6.4**, it forces the entrepreneur to be clear about the business model and think through important issues and challenges—financial, competitive, and managerial—before starting out. Ed Federkeil, who founded a small business called California Custom Sport Trucks, says: "It gives you direction instead of haphazardly sticking your key in the door every day and saying, 'What are we going to do?'"[48] More thoughts on why you need a business plan are presented in the nearby box.[49]

A **business plan** describes the direction for a new business and the financing needed to operate it.

Why You Need a Business Plan

- It forces you to be clear about your business model—how your business will make money.
- It makes you identify and confront the potential strengths and weaknesses of your proposed business.
- It makes you examine the market potential for your business's products or services.
- It makes you examine the strengths and weaknesses of the competitors for your proposed business.
- It helps you clarify the mission and key directions for the business, helping you to stay focused.
- It helps you determine how much money will be needed to launch and operate the business.
- It helps you communicate more confidently and credibly with potential lenders and investors.

FIGURE 6.4 **The benefits of a good business plan.**

Although there is no single template, it is generally agreed that a good business plan includes an executive summary, covers certain business fundamentals, is well-organized with headings, is easy to read, and runs no more than about 20 pages in length. Here is a sample business plan outline.[50]

- *Executive summary*—overview of the business purpose and the business model for making money.
- *Industry analysis*—nature of the industry, including economic trends, important legal or regulatory issues, and potential risks.
- *Company description*—mission, owners, and legal form.
- *Products and services description*—major goods or services, with competitive uniqueness.
- *Market description*—size of market, competitor strengths and weaknesses, and five-year sales goals.
- *Marketing strategy*—product characteristics, distribution, promotion, pricing, and market research.
- *Operations description*—manufacturing or service methods, supplies and suppliers, and control procedures.
- *Staffing description*—management and staffing skills needed and available, compensation, and human resource systems.
- *Financial projection*—cash flow projections for one to five years, break-even points, and phased investment capital.
- *Capital needs*—amount of funds needed to run the business, amount available, and amount requested from new sources.
- *Milestones*—a timetable of dates showing when key stages of the new venture will be completed.

Choosing a Form of Ownership

One of the important choices that must be made in starting a new venture is the legal form of ownership. A number of ownership alternatives are most common, and making the choice among these alternatives requires careful consideration of their respective advantages and disadvantages in light of the proposed business.

A **sole proprietorship** is simply an individual or a married couple pursuing business for a profit. This does not involve incorporation. One does business, for example, under a personal name—such as "Tiaña Lopez Designs." A sole proprietorship is simple to start, run, and terminate, and it is the most common form of small business ownership in the United States. However, the business owner is personally liable for business debts and claims.

A **partnership** is formed when two or more people agree to start and operate a business together. It is usually backed by a legal and written partnership agreement. Business partners agree on the relative contribution of resources and skills to the new venture, and

A **sole proprietorship** is an individual pursuing business for a profit.

A **partnership** is when two or more people agree to contribute resources to start and operate a business together.

on the sharing of profits and losses. The simplest and most common form is a *general partnership* where the partners share management responsibilities. A *limited partnership* consists of a general partner and one or more "limited" partners who do not participate in day-to-day business management. They share in the profits, but their losses are limited to the amount of their investment. A *limited liability partnership*, common among professionals such as accountants and attorneys, limits the liability of one partner for the negligence of another.

A **corporation**, commonly identified by the "Inc." designation in a company name, is a legal entity that is chartered by the state and exists separately from its owners. The corporation can be for-profit, such as Microsoft, Inc., or nonprofit, such as Count-Me-In, Inc.—a firm featured early in the chapter for helping female entrepreneurs get started with small loans. The corporate form offers two major advantages: (1) It grants the organization certain legal rights (e.g., to engage in contracts), and (2) the corporation becomes responsible for its own liabilities. This separates the owners from personal liability and gives the firm a life of its own that can extend beyond the life of its owners. The disadvantage of incorporation rests largely with the cost of incorporating and the complexity of required documentation.

> A **corporation** is a legal entity that exists separately from its owners.

The **benefit corporation** is a new corporate form for businesses with stated goals to benefit society while making a profit.[51] Businesses that choose this ownership type formally adopt the goals of social entrepreneurship and social enterprises to help solve social and environmental problems. Often called "B Corps" for short, these goals must be stated in the firm's bylaws or rules of incorporation. Each B Corp is required to file an annual "benefit report" as well as an annual financial report so that both social and financial performance can be

> A **benefit corporation**, or B Corp, is a corporate form for businesses whose stated goals are to combine making a profit with benefiting society and the environment.

Insight: Learn about Yourself | To be strong in self-management, you need lots of self-awareness plus the ability to self-regulate.

Self-Management Keeps You Growing

Entrepreneurship involves risk, confidence, insight, and more. But for those who have both the desire to attempt new things and **self-management** skills, it's a course with the potential for great personal and financial reward. Self-management skills reflect the ability to be objective in understanding personal strengths and weaknesses, and the capacity to make personal changes to continue improving and growing—both personally and professionally.

Being strong in self-management requires self-awareness in addition to the ability to self-regulate. Self-management requires self-knowledge as a person and in relationships with others, the exercise of initiative, acceptance of responsibility for good and bad behavior and accomplishments, and continuing adaptation for self-improvement. Self-management skills are critical for anyone seeking a successful career or wanting to do well in school, at work, and in everyday life. We are operating in challenging times full of uncertainty, change, and increasing complexity. The skills that serve us professionally and personally today may not serve well tomorrow as the relationships and technologies that define our lives continue to evolve.

Look at the self-management tips in the nearby box. These and other foundational tools for career success are available and can be grown and developed. But the motivation and the effort required to succeed through self-management must come from within. Only you can make the commitment to take charge of your personal and professional destiny and become a self-manager.

Self-Management Tips for Career Success

- *Perform to your best.* No matter what the assignment, you must work hard to quickly establish your credibility and work value.

- *Be and stay flexible.* Don't hide from ambiguity. Don't wait for structure. You must always adapt to new work demands, new situations, and new people.

- *Keep the focus.* You can't go forward without talent. Be a talent builder—always adding to and refining your talents to make them valuable to an employer.

- *Do the work.* Practice makes perfect. Like a professional golfer, you have to hit lots and lots of practice balls in order to make perfect shots during the match.

- *Don't give up.* Certainly never give up too soon. You have to stick with it, even during tough times. Remember—resilience counts. If you have talent and know what you love, go for it. Self-management is a way to realize your dreams.

Get To Know Yourself Better

One of the best ways to check your capacity for self-management is to examine how you approach college, your academic courses, and the rich variety of development opportunities available on and off campus. Ask: What activities am I involved in currently? How well do I balance these activities with academic and personal responsibilities? Do I miss deadlines or turn in assignments pulled together at the last minute? Do I accept poor or mediocre performance? Do I learn from my mistakes?

properly assessed against stated goals. The adoption of this form by a number of larger and well-recognized businesses—Ben & Jerry's, Patagonia, and Etsy, for example—have given the B Corp form growing public visibility.[52]

A **limited liability corporation** (LLC) is a hybrid business form combining the advantages of the sole proprietorship, partnership, and corporation.

The **limited liability corporation**, or LLC, has gained popularity because it combines the advantages of the other forms—sole proprietorship, partnership, and corporation. For liability purposes, LLCs function like a corporation and protect owners' assets against claims made against the company. For tax purposes, an LLC functions as a partnership in the case of multiple owners and as a sole proprietorship in the case of a single owner.

Financing a New Venture

Check out the photo feature on the reality TV show, *Shark Tank*. While being part of a reality TV show isn't common, Brian Duggan's situation is characteristic of that faced by entrepreneurs. Starting a new venture takes money, and that money must often be raised. The cost of setting up a new business or expanding an existing business can easily exceed the amount a would-be entrepreneur has available from personal sources. Initial startup financing might come from personal bank accounts and credit cards. Very soon, however, the chances are that much more money will be needed to sustain and grow the business. There are two major ways an entrepreneur can obtain such outside financing for a new venture.

Debt financing involves borrowing money that must be repaid over time, with interest.

Debt financing involves going into debt by borrowing money from another person, bank, or financial institution. This loan must be paid back over time, with interest. It also requires collateral that is pledged against business assets or personal assets, such as a home, to secure the loan in case of default. The lack of availability of debt financing became a big issue during the recent financial crisis, and the problem hit entrepreneurs and small business owners especially hard.

Choices: Think before You Act | Undergraduate student gets $38,500 upfront from investors in return for a portion of what he earns in the future.

Students Are Crowdfunding Their Human Capital

Kevork Djansezian/Reuters

Situation: An undergraduate student at an art and design school needs money to pay back student loans and fund ideas for a startup company. He goes online at Upstart.com and finds investors willing to give him upfront money in return for a portion of what he earns in the future. He signs on and takes in $38,500.

The idea here is to sell equity stakes in your human capital. In other words, get money now from people willing to invest in you while hoping for a good return from rights to a percentage of your future pre-tax earnings. Terms used to describe this form of crowdfunding are "human-capital contracts" or "social financial agreements."

Those in favor of students' crowdfunding their human capital are likely to say that it helps students get the education or resources they need to succeed. It's also a way to avoiding interest on debt. If the student fails to earn enough or the project fails, the investor loses his/her money. The investors may turn out to be good mentors and motivators that help the student to achieve higher levels of accomplishment. *Those against students' crowdfunding their human capital* are likely to say that it's a form of servitude. It's not right for one person to indenture themselves to another in this way. Young students, furthermore, may not be mature or insightful enough to make good decisions that commit them to long-term financial contracts. If the student's "back is to the wall," she or he is vulnerable to making a really bad personal decision.

Your Take?

What do you think? Is crowdfunding human capital something that sounds attractive to you? What are the possible risks and returns associated with crowdfunding as you see them? If you were a parent, would you let your child sell shares in his/her future? If you were an investor, would you consider this a legitimate way to earn a return on your money? Why or why not?

Equity financing is an alternative to debt financing. It involves giving ownership shares in the business to outside investors in return for their investment. This money does not need to be paid back. It is an investment, and the investor assumes the risk for potential gains and losses. The equity investor gains some proportionate ownership control in return for taking a risk on the venture.

Equity financing is usually obtained from **venture capitalists**, companies and individuals that make investments in new ventures in return for an equity stake in the business. Most venture capitalists tend to focus on relatively large investments of $1 million or more, and they usually take a management role, such as a seat on the board of directors, in order to oversee business growth. The hope is that a fast-growing firm will gain a solid market base and be either sold at a profit to another firm or become a candidate for an **initial public offering**, or IPO. An IPO is where shares of stock in the business are first sold to the public and begin trading on a public stock exchange. When an IPO is successful and the share prices are bid up by the market, the original investment made by a venture capitalist and entrepreneur rise in value. The quest for such returns on investment is the business model of the venture capitalist.

When large amounts of venture capital aren't available to the entrepreneur, another financing option is the **angel investor**. An angel investor is a wealthy individual willing to make a personal investment in return for equity in a new venture. Angel investors are especially common and helpful in the very early stages of a startup. Their presence can serve as a positive market signal, raise investor confidence, and help to attract additional venture funding that would otherwise not be available.

The rise of social media has given birth to **crowdfunding**, where entrepreneurs go online to obtain startup financing from a "crowd" of willing providers. Kickstarter, for example, focuses on fund-raising for innovative and imaginative projects from software to literature to films and more. Founder Yancey Strickler describes it as "a place of opportunity for anyone to make things happen."[53] Investors don't get ownership rights, but they do get the satisfaction of sponsorship and in some cases early access to the results. Ownership rights are part of the deal at AngelList, a crowdfunding site that offers equity participation and bills itself as the place "Where startups meet investors." AngelList matches entrepreneurs with pools of potential investors—called syndicates—willing to put up as little as $1,000 to back a new venture. All investors are vetted for financial background and legitimacy.[54]

The JOBS Act—Jumpstart Our Business Startups—made it easier for small U.S. companies to sell equity on the Internet. President Obama called crowdfunding a "game changer" when he signed the act in 2012.[55] The U.S. Securities and Exchange Commission, which oversees the practice, has implemented strict guidelines for both investors and the startup entrepreneurs.[56] As you might expect, crowdfunding has both advocates and skeptics. Advocates claim it spurs entrepreneurship by giving small startups a better shot at raising investment capital and helps small investors join in the venture capital area. Skeptics worry that small investors in a crowd may be easy prey for fraudsters because they won't do enough analysis or have the financial expertise to ensure they are making a good investment.[57]

Equity financing involves exchanging ownership shares for outside investment monies.

Venture capitalists make large investments in new ventures in return for an equity stake in the business.

An **initial public offering**, or IPO, is an initial selling of shares of stock to the public at large.

An **angel investor** is a wealthy individual willing to invest in a new venture in return for an equity stake.

In **crowdfunding**, entrepreneurs starting new ventures go online to get startup financing from crowds of investors.

Learning Check

LEARNING OBJECTIVE 6.3

Explain how entrepreneurs plan, legally structure, and fund new business ventures.

Be Sure You Can • explain the concept of first-mover advantage • illustrate the life cycle of an entrepreneurial firm • identify the major elements in a business plan • differentiate sole proprietorship, partnership, corporation, and limited liability corporation (LLC) • differentiate debt financing and equity financing • explain the roles of venture capitalists and angel investors in new venture financing

Management Learning Review: Get Prepared for Quizzes and Exams

Summary

LEARNING OBJECTIVE 6.1   Define entrepreneurship and identify characteristics of entrepreneurs.

- Entrepreneurship is risk-taking behavior that results in the creation of new opportunities.
- A classic entrepreneur is someone who takes risks to pursue opportunities in situations that others may view as problems or threats.
- A serial entrepreneur is someone who starts and runs businesses and other organizations one after another.
- Entrepreneurs tend to be creative, self-confident people who are determined, resilient, adaptable, and driven to excel; they like to be the master of their own destinies.
- Females and minorities are well represented among entrepreneurs, with some being driven by necessity or the lack of alternative, mainstream career options.
- Social entrepreneurs set up social enterprises to pursue novel ways to help solve social problems.

For Discussion If "necessity is the mother of invention," will a poor economy result in lots of entrepreneurship and new small business startups?

LEARNING OBJECTIVE 6.2   Describe how small businesses get started and common problems they face.

- Entrepreneurship results in the founding of many small businesses that offer new jobs and other benefits to local economies.
- The Internet has opened a whole new array of entrepreneurial possibilities for small businesses.
- Family businesses, which are owned and financially controlled by family members, represent the largest percentage of businesses operating worldwide; they sometimes suffer from succession problems.

- Small businesses have a high failure rate, with as many as 60% to 80% failing within five years; many failures result from poor management.
- Entrepreneurs and small business owners can often get help in the startup stages of their venture by working with business incubators and Small Business Development Centers in their local communities.

For Discussion Given that so many small businesses fail due to poor management practices, what type of advice and assistance should a Small Business Development Center offer to boost its success rate?

LEARNING OBJECTIVE 6.3   Explain how entrepreneurs plan, legally structure, and fund new business ventures.

- Entrepreneurial firms tend to follow the life-cycle stages of birth, breakthrough, and maturity, with each stage offering new and different management challenges.
- A new startup should be guided by a good business plan that describes the intended nature of the business, how it will operate, and how financing will be obtained.
- An important choice is the form of business ownership for a new venture, with the proprietorship, corporate, and limited liability forms offering different advantages and disadvantages.
- Two basic ways of financing a new venture are through debt financing—by taking loans, and equity financing—exchanging ownership shares in return for outside investment in the venture.
- Venture capitalists pool capital and make investments in new ventures in return for an equity stake in the business; an angel investor is a wealthy individual who is willing to invest money in return for equity in a new venture.

For Discussion If an entrepreneur has a good idea and his or her startup is beginning to take off, is it better to get money for growth by taking an offer of equity financing from an angel investor or taking a business loan from a bank?

Self-Test 6

Multiple-Choice Questions

1. _____ is among the personality characteristics commonly found among entrepreneurs.
    a. External locus of control
    b. Inflexibility
    c. Self-confidence
    d. Low self-reliance

2. When an entrepreneur is comfortable with uncertainty and willing to take risks, these are indicators of someone with a(n) _____.
    a. high tolerance for ambiguity
    b. internal locus of control
    c. need for achievement
    d. action orientation

3. Somewhere around _____ % of American businesses meet the definition of "small business" used by the Small Business Administration.

a. 40   c. 75

b. 99   d. 81

4. When a business owner sells to another person the right to operate that business in another location, this is a business form known as a _____.

a. conglomerate

b. franchise

c. joint venture

d. limited partnership

5. A small business owner who is concerned about passing the business on to heirs after retirement or death should prepare a formal _____ plan.

a. retirement   c. franchising

b. succession   d. liquidation

6. What is one of the most common reasons why new small business startups often fail?

a. The founders lack business expertise.

b. The founders are too strict with financial controls.

c. The founders don't want fast growth.

d. The founders have high ethical standards.

7. When a new business is quick to act and captures a market niche before competitors, this is called _____.

a. intrapreneurship

b. an initial public offering

c. succession planning

d. first-mover advantage

8. When a small business is just starting up, the business owner is typically most focused on _____.

a. gaining acceptance in the marketplace

b. finding partners for expansion

c. preparing an initial public offering

d. bringing professional skills into the management team

9. At which stage in the life cycle of an entrepreneurial firm does the underlying business model begin to work well and growth starts to occur?

a. birth

b. early childhood

c. maturity

d. breakthrough

10. A venture capitalist who receives an ownership share in return for investing in a new business is providing _____ financing.

a. debt   c corporate

b. equity   d. partnership

11. In _____ financing, a business owner borrows money as a loan that must eventually be repaid to the lender along with agreed-upon interest.

a. debt   c. partnership

b. equity   d. limited

12. The people who take ownership shares in new ventures in return for providing the entrepreneurs with critical startup funds are called _____.

a. business incubators

b. angel investors

c. SBDCs

d. intrapreneurs

13. The _____ form of small business ownership protects owners from any personal losses greater than their original investments; while the _____ form separates them completely from any personal liabilities.

a. sole proprietorship, partnership

b. general partnership, sole proprietorship

c. limited partnership, corporation

d. corporation, general partnership

14. The first component of a good business plan is usually a/an _____.

a. industry analysis

b. marketing strategy

c. executive summary of mission and business model

d. set of financial milestones

15. If a new venture has reached the point where it is pursuing an IPO, the firm is most likely _____.

a. going into bankruptcy

b. trying to find an angel investor

c. filing legal documents to become a LLC

d. successful enough that the public at large will want to buy its shares

Short-Response Questions

16. What is the relationship between diversity and entrepreneurship?

17. What are the major stages in the life cycle of an entrepreneurial firm, and what are the management challenges at each stage?

18. What are the advantages of a limited partnership form of small business ownership?

19. What is the difference, if any, between a venture capitalist and an angel investor?

Essay Question

20. Assume for the moment that you have a great idea for a potential Internet-based startup business. In discussing the idea with a friend, she advises you to be very careful to tie your business idea to potential customers and then describe it well in a business plan. "After all," she says, "you won't succeed without customers, and you'll never get a chance to succeed if you can't attract financial backers through a good business plan." With these words to the wise, you proceed. What questions will you ask and answer to ensure that you are customer-focused in this business? What are the major areas that you should address in writing your initial business plan?

Career Skills & Competencies: Make Yourself Valuable!

Evaluate Career Situations

What Would You Do?

1. Becoming Your Own Boss

It could be very nice to be your own boss, do your own thing, and make a decent living in the process. What are your three top choices for potential business entrepreneurship? How would you rank them on potential for personal satisfaction and long-term financial success?

2. Becoming a Social Entrepreneur

Make a list of social problems present in your local community. Choose one that might be addressed through social entrepreneurship.

Explain the basic plan or business model you would recommend. How will you or another social entrepreneur earn a living wage from this venture while doing good things for the community?

3. Making Your Startup Legal

Your small startup textbook-rating website is attracting followers. One angel investor is willing to put up $150,000 to help move things to the next level. But, you and your two co-founders haven't done anything to legally structure the business. You've managed so far on personal resources and a "handshake" agreement among friends. What is the best choice of ownership to prepare the company for future growth and outside investors?

Reflect on the Self-Assessment

Entrepreneurial Orientation

Instructions

Distribute five points between each pair of statements to indicate the extent to which you agree with "a" and "b."[58]

1. _____ (a) Success as an entrepreneur depends on many factors. Personal capabilities may have very little to do with one's success.

   _____ (b) A capable entrepreneur can always shape his or her own destiny.

2. _____ (a) Entrepreneurs are born, not made.

   _____ (b) People can learn to be more enterprising even if they do not start out that way.

3. _____ (a) Whether or not a salesperson will be able to sell his or her product depends on how effective the competitors are.

   _____ (b) No matter how good the competitors are, an effective salesperson always will be able to sell his or her product.

4. _____ (a) Capable entrepreneurs believe in planning their activities in advance.

   _____ (b) There is no need for advance planning, because no matter how enterprising one is there always will be chance factors that influence success.

5. _____ (a) A person's success as an entrepreneur depends on social and economic conditions.

   _____ (b) Real entrepreneurs can always be successful irrespective of social and economic conditions.

6. _____ (a) Entrepreneurs fail because of their own lack of ability and perceptiveness.

   _____ (b) Entrepreneurs often fail because of factors beyond their control.

7. _____ (a) Entrepreneurs are often victims of forces that they can neither understand nor control.

   _____ (b) By taking an active part in economic, social, and political affairs, entrepreneurs can control events that affect their businesses.

8. _____ (a) Whether or not you get a business loan depends on how fair the bank officer you deal with is.

   _____ (b) Whether or not you get a business loan depends on how good your project plan is.

9. _____ (a) When purchasing something, it is wise to collect as much information as possible and then make a final choice.

   _____ (b) There is no point in collecting a lot of information; in the long run, the more you pay the better the product is.

10. _____ (a) Whether or not you make a profit in business depends on how lucky you are.

    _____ (b) Whether or not you make a profit in business depends on how capable you are as an entrepreneur.

11. _____ (a) Some types of people can never be successful entrepreneurs.

    _____ (b) Entrepreneurial ability can be developed in different types of people.

12. _____ (a) Whether or not you will be a successful entrepreneur depends on the social environment into which you were born.

    _____ (b) People can become successful entrepreneurs with effort and capability irrespective of the social strata from which they originated.

13. _____ (a) These days business and personal success depends on the actions of government, banks, and other outside institutions.

    _____ (b) It is possible to succeed without depending too much outside institutions. What is required is insight and a knack for dealing with people.

14. _____ (a) Even perceptive entrepreneurs falter quite often because the market situation is very unpredictable.

    _____ (b) When an entrepreneur's prediction of the market situation is wrong, he or she is to blame for failing to read things correctly.

15. _____ (a) With effort, people can determine their own destinies.

    _____ (b) There is no point in spending time planning. What is going to happen will happen.

16. _____ (a) There are many events beyond the control of entrepreneurs.

   _____ (b) Entrepreneurs are the creators of their own experiences.

17. _____ (a) No matter how hard a person works, he or she will achieve only what is destined.

   _____ (b) The rewards one achieves depend solely on the effort one makes.

18. _____ (a) Organizational success can be achieved by employing competent and effective people.

   _____ (b) No matter how competent the employees are, the organization will have problems if socioeconomic conditions are not good.

19. _____ (a) Leaving things to chance and letting time take care of them helps a person to relax and enjoy life.

   _____ (b) Working for things always turns out better than leaving things to chance.

20. _____ (a) The work of competent people will always be rewarded.

   _____ (b) No matter how competent one is, it is hard to succeed without contacts.

Scoring

_____ *External Orientation Score.* Total your points for the following items: 1a, 2a, 3a, 4b, 5a, 6b, 7a, 8a, 9b, 10a, 11a, 12a, 13a, 14a, 15b, 16a, 17a, 18b, 19a, 20b.

_____ *Internal Orientation Score.* Total your points for the following items: 1b, 2b, 3b, 4a, 5b, 6a, 7b, 8b, 9a, 10b, 11b, 12b, 13b, 14b, 15a, 16b, 17b, 18a, 19b, 20a.

Interpretation

This Inventory measures the extent to which a person is internally or externally oriented in entrepreneurial activities. Scores greater than 50 indicate more of that orientation. Those who score high on entrepreneurial internality tend to believe that entrepreneurs can shape their own destinies through their own capabilities and efforts. Those who score high on entrepreneurial externality believe that the success of entrepreneurs depends on factors such as chance, political climate, community conditions, and economic environment—factors beyond their own capabilities and control.

Contribute to the Class Exercise

Entrepreneurs Among Us

Question

Who are the entrepreneurs or potential entrepreneurs in your class? What kinds of businesses are they involved in?

Instructions

Interview one another to find out who is already an entrepreneur and who would like to be one. Discuss your classmates' entrepreneurial examples and aspirations. Make an inventory of entrepreneurship insights and lessons available within the class. Critique them in terms of successes and failures, both real and potential. Choose one or two to share with the class as a whole. What challenges have these entrepreneurs faced? What funding directions have they pursued? What kinds of relationships have they developed in the process?

Manage a Critical Incident

Craft Brewery In—or Out—of the Money?

As the loan officer of a small community bank, you've just been approached for a commercial business loan. A group of three entrepreneurs are asking for $250,000 to start a craft brewery producing beers with a local flavor. There is already one micro-brewery in your town of 20,000 full-timers and another 20,000 university students. It has been linked with a popular tavern and music venue for several years, and recently expanded its brewing capacity to allow distribution into regional markets. The entrepreneurs proposing the new craft brewery include a brewer who learned his trade in Portland, Oregon, and won a national award for a strong, vanilla-mint specialty brew. The plan is to take his expertise and create spin-off brews that will be both national award-winners and local favorites. They want the bank financing to purchase and equip a brewing facility on the outskirts of town.

Questions

What will you look for as positive and negative signals in the business plan? When you meet with the would-be entrepreneurs, what will be the first five questions you will ask and what answers will you want to receive before deciding whether to lend them the funds? Overall, what are the major risks associated with this proposal and what is the probability of it being successful enough to justify a startup loan?

Collaborate on the Team Project

Community Entrepreneurs

Entrepreneurs are everywhere. Some might live next door to you, many own and operate the small businesses in and around your community, and you might even be one of them—or aspiring to be.

Question

Who are the entrepreneurs in your community and what are they accomplishing?

Instructions

1. Read the local news, talk to your friends and other locals, and think about where you shop. Make a list of the businesses and other organizations that have an entrepreneurial character. Be as complete as possible—look at both commercial businesses and nonprofits.

2. For each of the organizations, do further research to identify the people who are the entrepreneurs responsible for them.

3. Contact as many of the entrepreneurs as possible and interview them. Try to learn how they got started, why, what obstacles or problems they encountered, and what they learned about entrepreneurship that could be passed along to others. Ask for their "founding stories" and ask for advice they might give to aspiring entrepreneurs.

4. Analyze your results for class presentation and discussion. Look for patterns and differences in terms of the entrepreneurs as people, their entrepreneurial experiences, and potential insights into business versus social entrepreneurship.

5. Consider writing short cases of the entrepreneurs you find especially interesting. What kinds of stories would you tell? How would these stories probably end?

Analyze the Case Study

In-n-Out Burger | Building Them Better

Go to Management Cases for Critical Thinking at the end of the book to find this case.

CHAPTER 7

Hugo Infante/Government Of Chile/Shutterstock.com

Data and Decision Making
Nothing Beats a Great Decision

"Estamos bien en el réfugio–los 33." **For 69 days shift leader Luis Urzúa kept the trapped men in the Chilean mine organized and hopeful. On the 70th day, he was the last man safely out.**

Career Readiness – What to Look for Inside

Thought Leadership

Analysis > *Make Data Your Friend*
Intelligent Enterprises Know How to Win with Analytics

Choices > *Think before You Act*
Risks of Performance Reviews and Performance Boxes

Ethics > *Know Right from Wrong*
Climber Left to Die on Mt. Everest

Insight > *Learn about Yourself*
Self-Confidence Builds Better Decisions

Skills Make You Valuable

- **Evaluate** *Career Situations:*
  What Would You Do?
- **Reflect** *On the Self-Assessment:*
  Cognitive Style
- **Contribute** *To the Class Exercise:*
  Lost at Sea
- **Manage** *A Critical Incident:*
  Asking for a Raise
- **Collaborate** *On the Team Project:*
  Crisis Management Realities
- **Analyze** *The Case Study:*
  Target: Missing the Bull's Eye

Chapter Quick Start

"Big data" increasingly defines the decision-making landscape and plays a crucial role in how organizations process information. We all need the skills to gather and use data—big or otherwise—to make good decisions that solve problems and explore potential opportunities. It's essential to understand the decision-making process, know how to avoid pitfalls while making decisions in an ethical and timely manner, and be good at gaining the support of others whose help is needed for implementation.

LEARNING OBJECTIVES

7.1 Discuss the role of information, data, and analytics in management.

7.2 Identify different ways managers approach and deal with problems.

7.3 Explain the six steps in the decision-making process.

7.4 Describe the potential pitfalls and sources of creativity in managerial decision making.

131

When the San José copper and gold mine collapsed in Chile, 32 miners and their shift leader, Luis Urzúa, were trapped inside.[1] "The most difficult moment was when the air cleared and we saw the rock," said Urzúa. "I had thought maybe it was going to be a day or two days, but not when I saw the rock. . . ." In fact, the miners were trapped 2,300 feet below the surface for 69 days. Getting them out alive was a problem that captured the attention of the entire world.

After the rescue shaft was completed, Urzúa was the last man out. "The job was hard," he said. "They were days of great pain and sorrow." But the decisions Urzúa made as shift leader—organizing the miners into work shifts, keeping them busy, studying mine diagrams, making escape plans, raising morale—all contributed to the successful rescue of the miners. After embracing Urzúa when he arrived at the surface, Chile's President Sebastian Pinera said, "He was a shift boss who made us proud."

Most managers will never have to face such an extreme crisis, but decision making and problem solving are a critical aspect of every manager's job. Not all decisions are going to be easy; some will have to be made under tough conditions; and not all decisions will turn out well. But as with the case of Luis Urzúa trapped in the Chilean mine with 32 other miners, the goal is to always do the best you can under the circumstances.

7.1 | Information, Data, and Analytics

WileyPLUS

See Author Video

LEARNING OBJECTIVE 7.1

Discuss the role of information, data, and analytics in management.

> **Learn More About**
>
> Data, information, and information systems • Data mining big data, and analytics • Business intelligence and data visualization

Technological competency is the ability to understand new technologies and to use them to their best advantage.

Information competency is the ability to locate, gather, and organize information for use in decision making.

Analytical competency is the ability to evaluate and analyze information to make actual decisions and solve real problems.

Data are raw facts and observations.

Information is data made useful for decision making.

Our decision-making skills are tested everyday in both crisis and noncrisis situations, and the results have real consequences for ourselves and others. Society is now highly information-driven, digital, socially networked, transparent, and continuously evolving. Three "must-have" competencies are essential if we are to thrive in this context. **Technological competency** is the ability to understand new technologies and to use them to their best advantage. **Information competency** is the ability to locate, gather, organize, and display information. **Analytical competency** is the ability to evaluate and analyze information to make decisions and solve problems.[2] How about it—are you ready?

Data, Information, and Information Systems

This sign should be on every manager's desk—*Warning: Data ≠ Information!* **Data** are raw facts and observations. In contrast, **information** is data made useful and meaningful for decision making. We all have lots of access to data, but we don't always use it in ways that create useful information that meets the test of these five criteria:

1. *Timely*—The information is available when needed; it meets deadlines for decision making and action.

2. *High quality*—The information is accurate, and it is reliable; it can be used with confidence.

3. *Complete*—The information is complete and sufficient for the task at hand; it is as current and up to date as possible.

4. *Relevant*—The information is appropriate for the task at hand; it is free from extraneous or irrelevant material.

5. *Understandable*—The information is clear and easily understood by the user; it is free from unnecessary detail.

Organizations are at their best when they have the right information at the right time and in the right place. When the right people apply the right tools to data, that's when information can start to flow. This is can be done using **management information systems** serve a critical function in organizations to collect, organize, and distribute data. Information technology (IT) departments serve a critical function in organizations, and the CIO (chief information officer), CKO (chief knowledge officer), CTO (chief technology officer), or CDO (chief digital officer) are key members of the C-suite.

Information systems serve the needs described in **Figure 7.1**. Managers need vast amounts of *internal information* to make decisions and solve problems. They need information from their immediate work setting and from other parts of the organization. Internal information flows downward in the form of goals, instructions, and feedback. It flows horizontally to assist in cross-functional coordination and problem solving. And, it flows upward as performance reports, suggestions for improvement, and policy and personnel disputes.

Managers use *intelligence information* gathered from the environment to deal with customers, competitors, and other stakeholders such as government agencies, creditors, suppliers, shareholders, and community members. Organizations also send vast amounts of *public information* to stakeholders and the external environment. This often takes the form of advertising, public relations campaigns, social media posts, and financial reports.

> **Management information systems** collect, organize, and distribute data for use in decision making.

Data Mining, Big Data, and Analytics

Data mining is the process of analyzing data to produce useful information for decision makers. The goal is to explore data to reveal patterns, support predictions, and offer insights for decision makers.[3] There is now so much computing power that we talk in terms of **big data** which is collected in huge quantities and is difficult to mine without using sophisticated mathematical and analytical techniques.

Success in data mining, especially when mining Big data, requires strong **analytics**. Sometimes called *business analytics* or *management analytics*, this is the systematic evaluation and analysis of data to make informed decisions. Think of the vast amounts of data collected by the websites you browse and the social media that you use. The companies behind them mine the data for their own uses and to sell to others. Would you be surprised

> **Data mining** is the process of analyzing data for patterns, predictions, insights useful for decision makers.
>
> **Big data** exists in huge quantities and is difficult to process without sophisticated mathematical and computing techniques.
>
> Management with **analytics** involves systematic gathering and processing of data to make informed decisions.

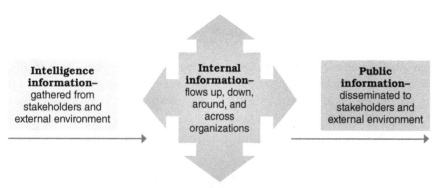

Internal and external information flows are essential to problem solving and decision making in organizations

FIGURE 7.1 Internal and external information needs in organizations.

that the United Nations buys social data from Twitter? It does, and it mines it for insights into social unrest around the world.[4]

Organizations of all types are investing heavily in big data initiatives, hiring people with strong analytics skills, and setting up analytics units and teams. Businesses use big data and analytics to reduce costs, predict market trends, guide marketing efforts, and improve hiring and career development, among many other possibilities. In education, big data might lead to e-solutions and active learner interfaces. In health care, it might be the prediction of epidemics. In communities, it might be predicting adverse weather patterns or redesigning road systems to meet future traffic demands.

Just because data exists in large quantities doesn't make it useful to decision makers. And just because analytics are solid doesn't mean that decision makers are working from the right data base or coming up with the right insights. In order for big data to become really useful in helping to solve critical problems and pursue attractive opportunities, it should satisfy the *Five "Vs" of Big-Data*.[5]

1. *Volume*—The first V of big data is volume. The data has to exist in large—think super large—quantities. At a time when Google searches total more than 40,000 per second, fortunately, today's technologies make that number very doable.[6] Just like our personal devices carry more and more on-board storage capacity, so too do cloud services and the servers used by organizations. With the right software in place, it's increasingly easy to collect and handle data in large volumes.

2. *Variety*—The second V of big data is variety. Technology makes it easy to collect and take advantage of data from many different sources. Social media content is one major provider, and it's a controversial one in respect to privacy concerns. Depending on the organizational setting, data also is there for the taking from many other sources—information provided by the National Weather Service, stories produced by the local news, global industrial manufacturing data, government statistics, and so on. The variety of data available to decision makers is really only limited by the creativity of those who architect the data pools.

3. *Veracity*—The third V of big data is veracity. This is just a complex way of saying that "believability counts." But it counts big. Before it's used for decision making, data must be tested for veracity. Just as with Internet searches, a lot of what's out there can be fabricated, misleading, and/or, harmful. You know this when pondering supposed reviews posted on travel sites like TripAdvisor, retailers like Amazon, and even career portals like Glassdoor.[7] The question challenging big data is always: "Can the data be trusted as representative or indicative of what's actually happening in the real world?"

4. *Velocity*—The fourth V of big data is velocity. The data in the big data sets don't or shouldn't represent just single snapshots of reality. Big data has to reflect what is currently happening in the world, in real time. And, the real world is complex, dynamic, and ever-changing. To be useful, big data has to keep up the pace. Again, technology can generate velocity by keeping the data flowing.

5. *Value*—The fifth and final V of big data is value. Even with the first four Vs satisfied, big data have to be worth the time, effort, and resources that go into its collection. Many organizations sit on huge and ever-increasing data sets. But being "huge" doesn't make them valuable. What's in a data set and how it's processed must pass the cost-benefit test to offer real value. Simply put, big data is worthy only when it helps decision makers solve critical problems and explore attractive opportunities.

Business Intelligence and Data Visualization

Business intelligence taps information to extract and report data in organized ways that are helpful to decision makers.

Business intelligence is the process of tapping or mining information to extract useful data. Its goal is to help decision makers identify, digest, and deal with trends and patterns with important implications. Some data provides *competitive information*. Among retailers, for example,

Analysis: Make Data Your Friend | Analytics-driven managers "know how to get the data to tell them the things that matter (and not the things that don't.)"

Intelligent Enterprises Know How to Win with Analytics

Monty Rakusen/Alamy Stock Photo

A survey on "The New Intelligent Enterprise" conducted by the *Sloan Management Review* asked 3,000 executives from around the world to report on how their organizations use and deal with data for business intelligence. Results included the following:

- 60% of executives said their organizations were "overwhelmed" by data and have difficulty making it useful for performance results.

- Organizations outperforming competitors were three times better at managing and acting on data.

- Top performers were two times more likely than low performers to say they needed to get even better with analytics.

- Top performers use analytics most often in finance, strategy, operations, and sales and marketing.

- Most frequent obstacles to adopting better analytics are lack of understanding, competing management priorities, and lack of skills.

- Analytic techniques expected to grow most in importance are data visualization, use of simulations and scenarios development, and use of analytics within business processes.

Your Thoughts?

What are the implications for your career planning and development? Recruiters say they have trouble finding enough managers who have the skills to "use data to shape business decisions." Are you prepared to compete for jobs and promotions in career situations where analytics count? How could your local schools, small businesses, and even government agencies gain by better harnessing the power of information and analytics?

---

competitive intelligence teams buy products from other retailers to check on their quality, speed, and customer service. Data on their purchases is analyzed and presented to top management to keep them ahead of the competition.[8] Some data provides *big picture information*. An example tracking financial results across different levels in the organization and doing historical comparisons in order to detect patterns indicating possible fraud. Other data provides *function-specific information*. An example is ensuring that manufacturing workers are aware of costs, marketing people are aware of sales expenses relative to sales revenues, and customer service employees know cost per service contact.[9]

Business intelligence is only useful when it is effectively communicated. It is one thing to have data and to have it well analyzed. It is quite another to communicate the results in ways that help others—perhaps those lacking strong mathematical and statistical skills—to understand what it means and how it might be used. This is where **data visualization** and the use of **executive dashboards** come into play. They communicate through easy-to-understand graphs, charts, and scorecards that can include real-time streaming of key performance indicators.

"If numbers are the language of business," says one chief financial officer, "then dashboards are the way we drive the business forward." He adds that they "take the daily temperature of a business."[10] Picture a sales manager whose office wall has a large flat-panel computer display much like the one you might use for TV at home. But this display calls up one or more dashboards filled with a wide range of real-time information about sales by product, salesperson, and territory, as well as tracking comparisons with past performance and current sales targets. Can you see how a manager armed with this efficient visualization of information might make more timely and better decisions?

Data visualization and **executive dashboards** present clear and efficient visualizations of key performance indicators on a real-time basis.

Learning Check

LEARNING OBJECTIVE 7.1

Discuss the role of data, information, and analytics in management.

Be Sure You Can • define and give examples of *technological competency*, *information competency*, and *analytical competency* • differentiate data and information • list the criteria of useful information • explain the importance of big data, analytics, business intelligence, and data visualization

7.2 Problem Solving and Managerial Decisions

WileyPLUS

See Author Video

LEARNING OBJECTIVE 7.2

Identify different ways managers approach and deal with problems.

> **Learn More About**
>
> Managers as problem solvers • Problem-solving approaches and styles • Structured and unstructured problems • Crisis problems • Problem-solving environments

Information is the anchor point for effective decision making. It helps managers sense the need for a decision, frame an approach, and discuss the decision with others.[11] An essential part of a manager's job, as depicted in **Figure 7.2**, is to serve as a nerve center for the flow

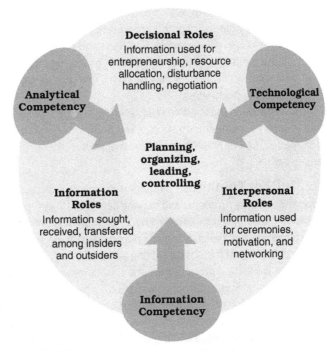

FIGURE 7.2 **The manager as an information processor and nerve center for planning, organizing, leading, and controlling.**

of information.[12] Managers are information processors who use analytical, technological, and information competencies to fulfill their roles in the management process.

Managers as Problem Solvers

Sometimes they are big things—how a small local retailer can compete with the big chains. Other times they're smaller but still consequential—how to handle the Fourth of July holiday staffing when everyone on the team wants the day off. Sometimes it's being able to recognize and correct an outright mistake—such as when the wrong item has been shipped to an important customer. What we are talking about in these situations is **problem solving**, identifying a discrepancy between an actual and a desired situation, and then taking action to resolve the problem.

Success depends on information to make good **decisions**—choices among alternatives. Managers make decisions while facing a continuous stream of daily problems. The most obvious situation is a **performance threat** where something is already wrong or has the potential to go wrong. This happens when actual performance is down or is moving in an unfavorable direction. Examples are when turnover or absenteeism suddenly increases, when a team member falls behind, or when a customer complains about service. Another important situation emerges as a **performance opportunity** with the chance for better performance if the right steps are taken. This happens when an actual situation either turns out better than expected or has the potential to exceed expectations.

> **Problem solving** involves identifying and taking action to resolve problems.
>
> A **decision** is a choice among possible alternative courses of action.
>
> A **performance threat** is a situation in which something is obviously wrong or has the potential to go wrong.
>
> A **performance opportunity** is a situation that offers the chance for a better future if the right steps are taken.

Problem-Solving Approaches and Styles

Problem: Airline aisles are clogged during boarding with frustrated passengers. Airline executives know that minutes saved in boarding can mean money saved.

Analysis: A study by astrophysicist Jason Steffen shows that boarding alternating rows back to front and boarding window–middle–aisle for each row beats other methods.

Result: Airline executives may be as stuck in their thinking as their passengers are in the aisles. Most have no plans to change current boarding systems.[13]

Openness to Problem Solving
Even with good information, managers often differ in their openness to problem solving. Some are more willing to accept the responsibilities associated with solving a problem. **Problem avoiders** ignore information signalling a performance opportunity or threat. They passively gather information, not wanting to make decisions or deal with problems. **Problem solvers** make decisions and try to solve problems, but only when forced into it by the situation. They are reactive in gathering information to solve problems after, but not before, they occur. They may deal well with performance threats, but they also are likely to miss many opportunities.

There is quite a contrast between the last two styles and **problem seekers** who constantly process information and look for problems to solve, even before they occur. True problem seekers are forward thinking. They anticipate threats and opportunities, and they take preemptive action to generate wins.

> **Problem avoiders** ignore information indicating a performance opportunity or threat.
>
> **Problem solvers** try to solve problems when they occur.
>
> **Problem seekers** constantly process information looking for problems to solve, even before they occur.

Systematic and Intuitive Thinking
Managers differ in their use of "systematic" and "intuitive" thinking when solving problems and making decisions. In **systematic thinking**, individuals approach problems using a rational, step-by-step, analytical process. The process is slow and methodical. Managers will typically make a plan before taking action and carefully search for information for a step-by-step problem-solving approach.

Someone using **intuitive thinking** is more flexible and spontaneous.[14] This involves a quick and broad evaluation of the situation and alternative courses of action. Managers who are intuitive will generally deal with many aspects of a problem at once, jumping from one issue to another, and consider "hunches" based on experience or spontaneous ideas. This approach is imaginative and tends to work best where facts are limited and there are few decision precedents.[15]

Amazon.com's Jeff Bezos recognizes that it's not always possible to make systematic fact-based decisions. There are times, he says, when "you have to rely on experienced executives

> **Systematic thinking** approaches problems in a rational and analytical fashion.
>
> **Intuitive thinking** approaches problems in a flexible and spontaneous fashion.

who've honed their instincts" and are able to make good judgments.[16] There's clearly a place for both systematic and intuitive decision making in management. Intuition balanced by support from good solid analysis, experience, and effort can be a great combination.[17]

Multidimensional Thinking

Multidimensional thinking is an ability to address many problems at once.

Managers often deal with portfolios of problems with multiple and interrelated issues. This requires **multidimensional thinking**—an ability to view many problems simultaneously, in relationship to one another and across both long and short time horizons.[18] The best managers "map" multiple problems into a network that can be actively managed over time as priorities, events, and demands change. They make decisions and take actions in the short run that benefit longer-run objectives. And, they also avoid being sidetracked while sorting through a shifting mix of daily problems. Harvard scholar Daniel Isenberg calls this **strategic opportunism**—the ability to remain focused on long-term objectives while being flexible enough to resolve short-term problems and opportunities in a timely way.[19]

Strategic opportunism focuses on long-term objectives while being flexible in dealing with short-term problems.

Cognitive Styles

When US Airways Flight 1549 was in trouble and pilot Chesley ("Sully") Sullenberger decided to land in the Hudson River, he had both a clear head and a clear sense of what he had been trained to do. The landing was successful and all of the 155 passengers and crew aboard survived. Called a "hero" for his efforts, Sullenberger described his thinking this way:[20]

> I needed to touch down with the wings exactly level . . . with the nose slightly up. I needed to touch down at . . . a descent rate that was survivable. And I needed to touch down just above our minimum flying speed but not below it. . . . I needed to make all these things happen simultaneously.

Cognitive styles are shown by the ways individuals deal with information while making decisions.

This example raises the issue of **cognitive styles**, or the way individuals deal with information while making decisions. People with the different cognitive styles shown in **Figure 7.3** are likely to approach problems and make decisions in very different ways. The figure contrasts tendencies toward information gathering—*sensation versus intuition,* and information evaluation—*feeling versus thinking.* Sully Sullenberger would probably score high in both sensation and thinking. But how about you? It is helpful to understand the following four styles and be able to recognize their characteristics in both yourself and others.[21]

- *Sensation Thinkers*—STs tend to emphasize the impersonal rather than the personal and take a realistic approach to problem solving. They like hard "facts," clear goals, certainty, and situations characterized by high levels of control.
- *Intuitive Thinkers*—ITs are comfortable with abstraction and unstructured situations. They tend to be idealistic, prone to intellectual and theoretical positions; they are logical and impersonal but also tend to avoid details.

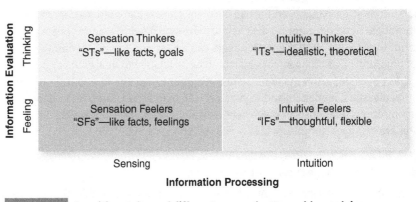

FIGURE 7.3 Cognitive styles and different approaches to problem solving.

- *Intuitive Feelers*—IFs prefer broad and global issues. They are insightful and also tend to avoid details, being comfortable with intangibles; they value flexibility and human relationships.
- *Sensation Feelers*—SFs tend to emphasize both analysis and human relations. They primarily have a realistic approach and prefer facts to speculation; they are open communicators and sensitive to feelings and values.

Structured and Unstructured Problems

Managers sometimes face **structured problems** that are familiar, straightforward, and clear with respect to information needs. Because these problems are routine and occur over and over again, they can be dealt with through **programmed decisions** that use solutions or decision rules available from past experience. Although not always predictable, routine problems can be anticipated. This allows for decisions to be programmed in advance and then executed as needed. In human resource management, for example, problems are common whenever decisions are made about pay raises and promotions, vacation requests, committee assignments, etc. Forward-looking managers use this understanding to decide in advance how to handle complaints and conflicts standardizing their approach.

Managers also deal with **unstructured problems** that are new or unusual situations characterized by ambiguities and information deficiencies. These problems require **nonprogrammed decisions** where novel solutions are crafted to meet the demands of unique situations. Many, if not most, problems faced by higher-level managers are unstructured, often involving the choice among different strategies and objectives in uncertain situations.

> **Structured problems** are straightforward and clear with respect to information needs.
>
> A **programmed decision** applies a solution from past experience to a routine problem.

> **Unstructured problems** have ambiguities and information deficiencies.
>
> A **nonprogrammed decision** applies a specific solution crafted for a unique problem.

Crisis Problems

One of the most challenging of all decision situations is a **crisis decision**. This appears as an unexpected problem that can lead to disaster if not resolved quickly and appropriately. The ability to handle a crisis could be the ultimate test of any manager's decision-making capabilities.[22] Luis Urzúa, who helped save the lives of his employees in the Chilean mine disaster, certainly passed this test with flying colors. Not everyone does as well in crisis situations. In fact, we sometimes react to a crisis by doing exactly the wrong things.

Researchers tell us that managers often err in crisis situations by isolating themselves and trying to solve the problem alone or as part of a small closed group.[23] But, this tendency to close ranks limits access to crucial information when it is most needed. And it not only sets things up for poor decisions—it may create even more problems as the situation escalates. When Toyota recalled over 5 million vehicles for quality defects—a disaster for the brand—one observer said: "Crisis management does not get any more woeful than this."[24] The poor crisis management was blamed on a corporate culture that discouraged transparency and public disclosure of quality problems. Toyota's CEO Akio Toyoda and the firm were criticized for "initially denying, minimizing and mitigating the problems."[25]

Good information systems and active problem seeking can help managers get on top of crisis situations. Good preparation also helps; there's no need to wait for crises to hit before figuring out how to deal with them. Managers can be assigned to crisis management teams ahead of time, and crisis management plans can be developed to deal with various contingencies. Just as police departments and community groups plan ahead and train to handle civil and natural disasters, managers and work teams can plan ahead and train to deal with crises. Many organizations offer crisis management workshops that offer suggestions like the following to prepare managers for unexpected and threatening events.

> A **crisis decision** occurs when an unexpected problem arises that can lead to disaster if not resolved quickly and appropriately.

1. *Figure out what is going on*—Take the time to understand what's happening and the conditions under which the crisis must be resolved.

2. *Remember that speed matters*—Attack the crisis as quickly as possible, trying to catch it when it is as small as possible.

3. *Remember that slow counts, too*—Know when to back off and wait for a better opportunity to make progress with the crisis.

4. *Respect the danger of the unfamiliar*—Understand the danger of all-new territory where you and others have never been before.

5. *Value the skeptic*—Don't look for and get too comfortable with agreement; appreciate skeptics and let them help you see things differently.

6. *Be ready to "fight fire with fire"*—When things are going wrong and no one seems to care, you may have to start a crisis to get their attention.

Problem-Solving Environments

Figure 7.4 shows that problems must be solved in three different environments—certainty, risk, and uncertainty. Although managers have to make decisions in all of these environments, the conditions of risk and uncertainty are common at higher levels of management where problems are more complex and unstructured.

A **certain environment** offers complete information on possible action alternatives and their consequences.

Certain Environment   The most favorable decision situation is a **certain environment**. This is an ideal decision-making situation because full and complete factual information is available about alternatives and their outcomes. The task is simple: Study the alternatives and choose the best solution. Certain environments are nice, neat, and comfortable for decision makers. However, very few managerial problems are like this.

A **risk environment** lacks complete information but offers "probabilities" of the likely outcomes for possible action alternatives.

Risk Environment   A basic fact of managerial decision making is that many, if not most, problems emerge in **risk environments** where facts and information on alternatives and their consequences are incomplete. Decision making in risk environments requires *probabilities* to estimate the likelihood a particular outcome will occur (e.g., 4 chances out of 10). Because probabilities are only possibilities, people vary in how they act under risk conditions. Some of us are risk takers and some are risk avoiders; some of us gain from taking risks and others lose.

Domino's Pizza former CEO J. Patrick Doyle was a risk taker. When deciding to change the firm's pizza recipe, he ran a television ad admitting that customers really disliked the old one because it was "totally devoid of flavor" and had a crust "like cardboard." Whereas some executives might want to hide or downplay such customer reviews, Doyle used them to help launch the new recipe. He said it was a "calculated risk" and that "we're proving to our customers that we are listening to them by brutally accepting the criticism that's out there."[26]

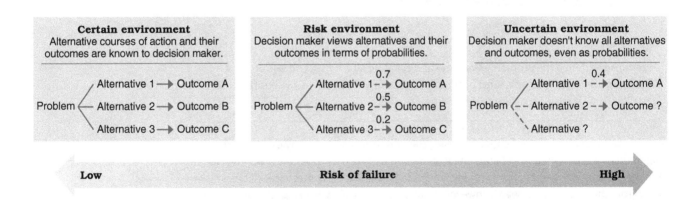

FIGURE 7.4   **Three environments for problem solving and decision making.**

General Motors' former Vice Chairman of Global Product Development, Bob Lutz, wasn't a risk taker. He once said: "GM had the technology to do hybrids back when Toyota was launching the first Prius, but we opted not to ask the board to approve a product program that'd be destined to lose hundreds of millions of dollars."[27] He and other GM executives either miscalculated the payoffs from hybrid vehicles or didn't believe the probabilities were high enough to justify the risk. Their Japanese competitors, facing the same risk environment, decided differently and gained the early mover advantage.

Uncertain Environment   When facts are few and information is so poor that managers are unable to even assign probabilities to the likely outcomes of alternatives, an **uncertain environment** exists. This is the most difficult decision-making condition. The high level of uncertainty forces managers to rely heavily on intuition, judgment, informed guessing, and hunches—all of which leave room for error. Perhaps there is no better example of the challenges of uncertainty than the situation faced by government and business leaders as they struggle to deal with global economic turmoil. Even as they struggle to find the right paths forward, great political, social, and economic uncertainties make their tasks difficult and the outcomes of their decisions hard to predict.

> An **uncertain environment** lacks so much information that it is difficult to assign probabilities to the likely outcomes of alternatives.

Learning Check

LEARNING OBJECTIVE 7.2

Identify different ways managers approach and deal with problems.

Be Sure You Can • describe how information influences the four functions of management • define *problem solving* and *decision making* • explain systematic and intuitive thinking • list four cognitive styles in decision making • differentiate programmed and nonprogrammed decisions • describe the challenges of crisis decision making • explain decision making in certain, risk, and uncertain environments

7.3 | The Decision-Making Process

LEARNING OBJECTIVE 7.3

Explain the six steps in the decision-making process.

> **WileyPLUS**
> See Author Video

> **Learn More About**
> Identify and define the problem • Generate and evaluate alternative courses of action • Choose a preferred course of action • Implement the decision • Evaluate results • At all steps—check ethical reasoning

All of those case studies, experiential exercises, class discussions, and essay exam questions in your courses are intended to get students to experience some of the complexities involved in managerial decision making, the problems and pitfalls, and even the pressures of crisis situations. From the classroom forward, however, it's all up to you. Only you can determine whether you step up and make the best out of very difficult problems, or collapse under pressure.

Figure 7.5 describes the five steps in the **decision-making process:** (1) Identify and define the problem, (2) generate and evaluate alternative solutions, (3) choose a preferred course of action, (4) implement the decision, and (5) evaluate results.[28] Importantly, ethical reasoning

> The **decision-making process** begins with identification of a problem and ends with evaluation of results.

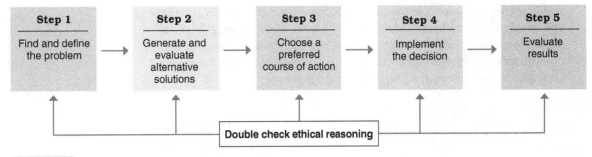

FIGURE 7.5 **Steps in the decision-making process.**

should be double-checked in all five steps. The decision-making process can be understood within the context of the following short case.

> *The Ajax Case.* On December 31, the Ajax Company decided to close down its Murphysboro plant. Market conditions were forcing layoffs, and the company could not find a buyer for the plant. Some of the 172 employees had been with the company as long as 18 years; others as little as 6 months. All were to be terminated. Under company policy, they would be given severance pay equal to one week's pay per year of service.

This case reflects how competition, changing times, and the forces of globalization can take their toll on organizations, the people who work for them, and the communities in which they operate. Think about how you would feel as one of the affected employees. Think about how you would feel as the mayor of this small town in Illinois. Think about how you would feel as a corporate executive forced to make the difficult business decision to close the plant down.

Step 1—Identify and Define the Problem

The first step in decision making is to find and define the problem. Information gathering and deliberation are critical in this stage. The way a problem is defined can impact how it is resolved, and it is critical here to clarify exactly what a decision should accomplish. The more specific the goals, the easier it is to evaluate results after the decision is implemented. But, three common mistakes can occur in this critical first step in decision making.[29]

Mistake number one is defining the problem too broadly or too narrowly. To take a classic example, the problem stated as "build a better mousetrap" might be better defined as "get rid of the mice." Managers should define problems in ways that give them the best possible range of problem-solving options.

Mistake number two is focusing on symptoms instead of causes. Symptoms are indicators that problems may exist, but they shouldn't be mistaken for the problems themselves. Although managers should be alert to spot problem symptoms (e.g., a drop in performance), they must also dig deeper to address root causes (such as discovering that workers need training in the use of a new IT system).

Mistake number three is choosing the wrong problem to deal with. For example, which of these three problems would you address first on a busy workday? 1—An e-mail message from your boss requesting a proposal "as soon as possible" on how to handle employees' complaints about lack of flexibility in their work schedules. 2—One of your best team members has just angered another by loudly criticizing her work performance. 3—Your working spouse has left you a voice mail that your daughter is sick at school and the nurse would like her to go home for the day. Choices like this are not easy. We have to set priorities and deal with the most important problems first. Perhaps the boss can wait while you telephone the school to learn more about your daughter's illness and then spend some time with the employee who seems to be having "a bad day."

> *Back to the Ajax Case.* Closing the Ajax plant put a substantial number of people from the small community of Murphysboro out of work. The unemployment will have a

significant negative impact on individuals, their families, and the town as a whole. The loss of the Ajax tax base will further hurt the community. The local financial implications of the plant closure will be great, and potentially devastating. The problem for Ajax management is how to minimize the adverse impact of the plant closing on the employees, their families, and the community.

Step 2—Generate and Evaluate Alternative Courses of Action

Once a problem is defined, it is time to assemble the facts and information to solve it. This is where we clarify exactly what is known and what needs to be known. Extensive information gathering should identify alternatives as well as their potential consequences. Key stakeholders in the problem should be identified, and the effects of possible courses of action on each of these should be considered. Importantly, a course of action can only be as good as the quality of the alternatives. The better the pool of alternatives and the more that is known about them, the more likely it is a good decision will be made.

It is important at this stage to avoid a very common decision-making error—*abandoning the search for alternatives and evaluation of their consequences too quickly*. This happens due to impatience, time pressure, and lack of commitment. But just because an alternative is convenient doesn't make it the best. It may have less potential than others discovered with the right approach (see the Insights feature) and adequate time commitment.

Decisions often have **unintended consequences** in the form of unanticipated positive or negative side effects. If alternatives are given proper attention, some of these could be

Unintended consequences are unanticipated positive or negative side effects that result from a decision.

Self-Confidence Builds Better Decisions

Does confidence put a smile on your face? It's a powerful force, something to be nurtured and protected. Managers need **self-confidence** not only to make decisions but to implement them. Once decisions are made, managers are expected to rally people and take effective action. This is how problems actually get solved and opportunities get explored. But lacking in confidence, procrastination becomes easy. Too many of us have difficulty deciding, and we have difficulty acting.

How would you proceed with the situation in the box—option A, or B, or C?

Jeff McCracken was the team leader who actually had to deal with this situation. He acted deliberately, with confidence, and in a collaborative fashion. After extensive consultations with the team, he decided to salvage the old track. The team worked 24 hours a day and finished in less than a week. McCracken called it a "colossal job" and said the satisfaction came from "working with people from all parts of the company and getting the job done without anyone getting hurt."

Self-confidence doesn't have to mean acting alone, but it does mean being willing to act. Management consultant Ram Charan calls self-confidence a willingness to "listen to your own voice" and "speak your mind and act decisively." It is, he says, an "emotional fortitude" that counteracts "emotional insecurities."

Decision Time

Situation: A massive hurricane has damaged a railroad bridge over a large lake. The bridge is critical for relief efforts to aid a devastated city. You are leading a repair team of 100. Two alternatives are on the table: Rebuild using new tracks, or rebuild with old track salvaged from the lake.

Question: How do you proceed?

A. Decide to rebuild with new tracks; move quickly to implement.

B. Decide to rebuild with old tracks; move quickly to implement.

C. Consult with team; make decision; move quickly to implement.

Get To Know Yourself Better

Opportunities to improve your self-confidence are everywhere, but you have to act in order to take advantage of them. What about your involvement in student organizations, recreational groups, intramural sports teams, and community activities? Do a self-check: Make a list of things you are already doing that offer ways to build your self-confidence. What are you gaining from these experiences? Make another list that describes what you could do to gain more experience and add more self-confidence to your skills portfolio between now and graduation. Becoming an officer in a club where you are a member? Starting a new student organization? Organizing a community service project for you and your friends? Becoming a tutor for a class where you did well? Volunteering at a local food bank or homeless shelter?

identified ahead of time and their implications used to modify and strengthen a decision. A growing number of states and localities, for example, are passing minimum wage laws higher than federal standards. Although the intent is to help low-wage workers fight poverty and cope with living costs, unintended consequences have appeared as affected employers struggle to maintain profits in face of higher labor costs. On the positive side, the higher wages have sometimes driven innovation—for example, a Carl's Jr. owner in California now filters shortening more frequently to extend its life and save costs. On the negative side, the higher wages have sometimes caused layoffs and reduced work hours—for example, a White Castle owner in Illinois eliminated two jobs to protect profit margins without raising prices.[30]

One way to strengthen the search for alternatives is to seek consultation and the involvement of others. Adding more people to the process brings new perspectives and information to a problem, generates more alternatives, reveals more about possible consequences, and can result in a better outcomes for those affected by the decision. Another way to strengthen the search for alternatives is to put each through a rigorous **cost-benefit analysis**. This compares what an alternative will cost in relation to what it will return in respect to expected benefits. At a minimum, the benefits of an alternative should be greater than its costs. And, it should also be ethically sound.

> *Back to the Ajax Case.* The Ajax plant is going to be closed. Given that, the possible alternative approaches that can be considered are (1) close the plant on schedule and be done with it; (2) delay the plant closing until all efforts have been made to sell it to another firm; (3) offer to sell the plant to the employees and/or local interests; (4) close the plant and offer transfers to other Ajax plant locations; or (5) close the plant, offer transfers, and help the employees find new jobs in and around the town of Murphysboro.

Cost-benefit analysis involves comparing the costs and benefits of each potential course of action.

Step 3—Choose a Preferred Course of Action

This is the point where an actual decision is made to select a preferred course of action. Just how this choice occurs and who makes it must be successfully resolved in each problem situation. Management theory recognizes substantial differences between the classical and behavioral models of decision making as shown in **Figure 7.6**.

The **classical decision model** describes decision making with complete information.

An **optimizing decision** chooses the alternative giving the absolute best solution to a problem.

Classical Decision Model
The **classical decision model** views the manager as acting rationally in a certain world. The assumption is that a rational choice of the preferred course of action will be made by a decision maker who is fully informed about all possible alternatives. Here, managers face a clearly defined problem and know all possible alternatives, as well as their consequences. As a result, managers make an **optimizing decision** that gives the best solution to the problem.

Behavioral Decision Model
Behavioral scientists question the assumptions of perfect information underlying the classical model of decision making. Perhaps best represented by the work of scholar Herbert Simon, behavioral decision making instead recognizes

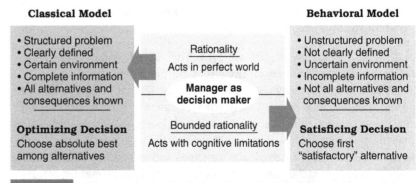

Classical Model
- Structured problem
- Clearly defined
- Certain environment
- Complete information
- All alternatives and consequences known

Optimizing Decision
Choose absolute best among alternatives

Rationality
Acts in perfect world

Manager as decision maker

Bounded rationality
Acts with cognitive limitations

Behavioral Model
- Unstructured problem
- Not clearly defined
- Uncertain environment
- Incomplete information
- Not all alternatives and consequences known

Satisficing Decision
Choose first "satisfactory" alternative

FIGURE 7.6 **Differences in the classical and behavioral decision-making models.**

that there are *cognitive limitations* on our information-processing capabilities.[31] These make it hard for managers to become fully informed and make optimizing decisions. They create a **bounded rationality**, such that managerial decisions are rational only within the boundaries set by the available information and known alternatives, both of which are incomplete.

Because of cognitive limitations and bounded rationalities, the **behavioral decision model** assumes that people act with partial knowledge about available alternatives and their consequences. As a result the first alternative that offers a satisfactory resolution is likely to be chosen. Simon, who won a Nobel Prize for his work, calls this the tendency to make **satisficing decisions**—choosing the first satisfactory alternative. The behavioral model describes how many decisions get made in ambiguous and fast-paced problem situations.

> *Back to the Ajax Case.* Ajax executives decided to close the plant, offer transfers to company plants in another state, and offered to help displaced employees find new jobs in and around Murphysboro.

Bounded rationality describes making decisions within the constraints of limited information and alternatives.

The **behavioral decision model** describes decision making with limited information and bounded rationality.

A **satisficing decision** is the choice of the first satisfactory alternative that comes to one's attention.

Step 4—Implement the Decision

Once a decision is made, actions must be taken to implement it. Nothing new can or will happen unless action is taken to solve the problem. Managers not only need the determination and creativity to arrive at a decision, they also need the ability and willingness to implement it.

Difficulties encountered when decisions get implemented may trace to **lack-of-participation error**. This is a failure to adequately involve individuals whose support is necessary to put the decision into action. Managers who use participation wisely get the right people involved in problem solving from the beginning. When they do, implementation typically follows quickly, smoothly, and to the satisfaction of all stakeholders. Closely related to this is **false participation error**. This occurs when people are asked to voice their opinions or ideas about a decision, but, in reality, nobody with authority is listening. Commentary in the *Wall Street Journal* once called this "the biggest mistake bosses make in decision making." Due to the "deception and pretense" involved, the end result is "discouraging and demotivating." Of course, this is just the opposite of what a manager really wants.

Lack-of-participation error is failure to involve in a decision the persons whose support is needed to implement it.

False participation error occurs when people are told they have a voice in decision making but no one in authority listens to their inputs.

> *Back to the Ajax Case.* Ajax ran ads in the local and regional newspapers. The ad called attention to an "Ajax skill bank" composed of "qualified, dedicated, and well-motivated employees with a variety of skills and experiences." Interested employers were urged to contact Ajax for further information.

Step 5—Evaluate Results

The decision-making process is not complete until results are evaluated. If the desired outcomes are not achieved or if undesired side effects result, corrective action should be taken. Evaluation is a form of managerial control. It involves gathering data to measure performance and compare these results against goals. If results are less than what was desired, it is time to reassess and return to earlier steps. In this way, problem solving becomes a dynamic and ongoing activity. Evaluation is always easier when clear goals, measurable targets, and timetables are established at the beginning of the process.

> *Back to the Ajax Case.* How effective were Ajax's decisions? We don't know for sure. But after the advertisement ran for two weeks, the plant's industrial relations manager said: "I've been very pleased with the results." That's all we know, and more information would certainly be needed for a good evaluation of how well management handled this situation. Wouldn't you like to know how many of the displaced employees got new jobs locally and how the local economy held up? You can look back on the case as it was described and judge for yourself. Perhaps you would have approached the situation and the five decision making steps somewhat differently.

Ethics: Know Right from Wrong | "Human life is far more important than just getting to the top of a mountain."

Climber Left to Die on Mount Everest

Bobby Model/National Geographic

Some 40 climbers are winding their ways to the top of Mount Everest. About 1,000 feet below the summit sits a British mountain climber in trouble, collapsed in a shallow snow cave. Most of those on the way up just look while continuing their climbs. Sherpas from one passing team pause to give him oxygen before moving on. Within hours David Sharp, 34, is dead of oxygen deficiency on the mountain.

A climber who passed by says: "At 28,000 feet it's hard to stay alive yourself . . . he was in very poor condition . . . , it was a very hard decision . . . he wasn't a member of our team."

Someone who made the summit in the past says: "If you're going to go to Everest . . . I think you have to accept responsibility that you may end up doing something that's not ethically nice . . . you have to realize that you're in a different world."

After hearing about this case, the late Sir Edmund Hillary, who reached the top in 1953, said: "Human life is far more important than just getting to the top of a mountain."

What Do You Think?

Who's right and who's wrong here? Should the climbers have ignored Sharp and continued on their way to the top of Mount Everest? Does this situation happen in real life—not on mountains but in our workplaces? How often do we meet people who are struggling or in trouble, but just pass them by as we pursue our own career interests and personal goals? When we encounter others who are having difficulties, what are our ethical or moral obligations to them? How do we make choices between what is best for us versus what is best for others?

At All Steps—Check Ethical Reasoning

Each step in the decision-making process can and should be linked with ethical reasoning.[32] Choices often have moral dimensions that might easily be overlooked (see the Ethics feature). For example, job eliminations in the prior Ajax case might not be sufficiently considered for their implications on all stakeholders, including the affected persons, their families, and the local community. We sometimes have to take care to stay tuned into *virtues*—things like fairness, kindness, compassion, and generosity—and guard against *vices*—things like greed, anger, ignorance, and lust.[33]

One way to check ethical reasoning in decision making is to ask and answer questions that bring critical thinking into the process. Gerald Cavanagh and his associates, for example, suggest that a decision should test positive on these four ethics criteria.[34]

1. *Utility*—Does the decision satisfy all constituents or stakeholders?
2. *Rights*—Does the decision respect the rights and duties of everyone?
3. *Justice*—Is the decision consistent with the canons of justice?
4. *Caring*—Is the decision consistent with my responsibilities to care?

The **spotlight questions** test the ethics of a decision by exposing it to scrutiny through the eyes of family, community members, and ethical role models.

Another way to test ethical reasoning is to consider a decision in the context of full transparency and the prospect of shame.[35] Asking and answering these **spotlight questions** can be a powerful ethics checkpoint. *Ask:* "How would I feel if my family found out about this decision?" *Ask:* "How would I feel if this decision were published in the local newspaper or posted on the Internet?" *Ask:* "What would the person you know or know of who has the strongest character and best ethical judgment do in this situation?"

It also is helpful to check decisions against the hazards of undue rationalizations. Caution is called for when you hear yourself saying, "It's just part of the job" . . . "We're fighting fire with fire" . . . "Everyone is doing it" . . . "I've got it coming" . . . "It's legal and permissible" . . . "I'm doing it just for you." These are warning signs which, if heeded, can prompt a review of the decision being made and lead to a more ethical outcome.

LEARNING OBJECTIVE 7.3

Explain the six steps in the decision-making process.

Be Sure You Can • list the steps in the decision-making process • apply these steps to a sample decision-making situation • explain cost-benefit analysis in decision making • discuss differences between the classical and behavioral decision models • define *optimizing* and *satisficing* • explain how lack-of-participation error can hurt decision making • list useful questions for double-checking the ethical reasoning of a decision

7.4 Decision-Making Pitfalls and Creativity

LEARNING OBJECTIVE 7.4

Describe the potential pitfalls and sources of creativity in managerial decision making.

WileyPLUS

See Author Video

> **Learn More About**
> Decision errors and traps • Creativity in decision making

Once we accept that we are likely to make imperfect decisions at least some of the time, it makes sense to try to understand why. Two common mistakes are falling prey to decision errors and traps, and not taking full advantage of creativity. Both can be avoided.

Decision Errors and Traps

Test: Would you undergo heart surgery if the physician tells you the survival rate is 90%? Chances are you would. But if the physician tells you the mortality rate is 10%, the chances of you opting for surgery are likely to be substantially lower!

What is happening here? We often rely on simplifying strategies when making decisions with limited information, time pressures, and even insufficient energy. Psychologist Daniel Kahneman describes this as a triumph of *System 1 thinking*—automatic, effortless, quick, and associative—over *System 2 thinking*—conscious, slow, deliberate, and evaluative.[36] In the above test, the simplification of System 1 thinking is called "framing" because the decision to have surgery or not varies whether the information is presented as a survival rate—encouraging, or a mortality rate—threatening.[37] This and other simplifying strategies or rules of thumb are known as **heuristics**.[38] Although heuristics can be helpful in dealing with complex and ambiguous situations, they also lead to common decision-making errors.[39]

Heuristics are strategies for simplifying decision making.

Framing Error   Managers sometimes suffer from **framing error** that occurs when a problem is evaluated and resolved in the context in which it is perceived—either positively or negatively. Suppose, for example, data show that a particular product has a 40% market share. A negative frame views the product as deficient because it is missing 60% of the market. The likely discussion would focus on: "What are we doing wrong?" Alternatively, the frame could be a positive one, looking at the 40% share as a strong market foothold. In this case the discussion is more likely to proceed with "How can we do things better?" Sometimes people use framing as a tactic for presenting information in a way that gets other people to think within the desired frame. In politics, this is often referred to as "spinning" the data.

Framing error is trying to solve a problem in the context in which it is perceived.

The **availability bias** bases a decision on recent information or events.

Availability Bias

The **availability bias** occurs when people assess a current event or situation by using information that is "readily available" from memory. An example is deciding not to invest in a new product based on your recollection of a recent product failure. The potential bias is that the readily available information is fallible and irrelevant. For example, the product that recently failed may have been a good idea that was released to market at the wrong time of year, or it may have belonged to an entirely different product category.

The **representativeness bias** bases a decision on similarity to other situations.

Representativeness Bias

The **representativeness bias** occurs when people assess the likelihood of something happening based on its similarity to a stereotyped set of occurrences. An example is deciding to hire someone for a job vacancy simply because he or she graduated from the same school attended by your last and most successful new hire. The potential bias is that the representative stereotype masks factors important and relevant to the decision. For instance, the abilities and career expectations of the job candidate may not fit the job requirements; the school attended may be beside the point.

The **anchoring and adjustment bias** bases a decision on incremental adjustments from a prior decision point.

Anchoring and Adjustment Bias

Anchoring and adjustment bias occurs when decisions are influenced by inappropriate importance given to a previous value or starting point. An example is a manager who sets a new salary level for an employee by simply raising her prior year's salary by a small percentage. Although the increase may appear reasonable to

---

Choices: Think before You Act | "We hired all-their-lives A students, and they felt they were getting a C."

Risks of Performance Reviews and Performance Boxes

iofoto/Deposit Photos

There are two things that are pretty much facts of life in organizations. One, people get reviews on their performance. Two, people put other people into performance categories. Both are being reconsidered as a new generation takes its place in the workforce.

Let's start with performance reviews. The traditional model is an annual or semi-annual review that gets documented and placed in the record. It's likely tied to things like merit raises and possible promotions. But research is raising questions. One study found that at least half of workers are often surprised by the ratings they get and 90% of them are disappointed because they expected higher ratings. Of them, almost a quarter report a decline in their job engagement.

Now, let's talk about performance categories. Most reviews "score" employees for their performance—something as simple as "A" for top performer, "B" for average performer, and "C" for poor performer. This is great if you're an A, but how do the Bs and Cs

react to this feedback? Their first thought might be to question the basis for the rating. Why? How come? Explain it to me? The second thought might be more extreme: "I'm out of here." At Microsoft, for example, ratings under the old performance review system caused problems. Lisa Dodge, as director of global performance programs, said: "We hired all-their-lives A students, and they felt they were getting a C."

In light of research and pushback, some employers are shifting their approaches. At Cigna, ratings are out and frequent performance chats with managers are in. The goal is effective coaching rather than scoring. And, results are positive. One employee says: "This is the first honest conversation I've had with my manager about me, about what I should do, instead of these goals that aren't really related to me." Microsoft has also downplayed ratings and switched to the frequent conversation model. According to Dodge: "The lack of rating … mitigates the threat, the distraction, and internal competition."

Not everyone agrees that the shift to no ratings or rankings is the best move. One consultant argues: "You can still have good numerical rankings that motivate people if you put as much effort into the quality of the conversation."

Your Take?

As the person doing the job, does the frequent conversation with a manager rather than an annual formal performance review approach appeal to you? Or, do you feel the need for a more definitive rating that clearly puts you into a performance category? How about as a team leader? Are you comfortable engaging in frequent performance chats and communicating about development goals with team members, rather than handing out ratings to team members? Might the approach to performance reviews be something that makes a difference in your choice of employer? Are you prepared to raise this issue while interviewing, and put your views and hopes on the table?

the manager, the decision actually undervalues the employee relative to the job market. The small incremental salary adjustment, reflecting anchoring and adjustment bias, may end up prompting her to look for another, higher-paying job.

Confirmation Error   One of our tendencies after making a decision is to try and find ways to justify it. In the case of unethical acts, for example, we try to "rationalize" them after the fact. This is called **confirmation error**. It means that we notice, accept, and even seek out only information that confirms or is consistent with a decision we have made. Contrary information that suggests what we are doing is incorrect or unethical is downplayed or denied.

A **confirmation error** occurs when focusing only on information that confirms a decision already made.

Escalating Commitment   Another decision-making trap is **escalating commitment**. This occurs as a decision to increase effort and perhaps apply more resources to pursue a course of action that is not working.[40] Managers prone to escalation let the momentum of a situation and personal ego overwhelm them. They are unwilling to admit they were wrong and unable to "call it quits," even when the facts indicate this is the best alternative. This is a common decision error, perhaps one you are personally familiar with. It is sometimes called the *sunk-cost fallacy*. The following advice can help you to avoid the escalation trap in decision making.[41]

Escalating commitment is the continuation of a course of action even though it is not working.

- Set advance limits on your involvement and commitment to a particular course of action; stick with these limits.
- Make your own decisions; don't follow the leads of others, since they are also prone to escalation.
- Carefully assess why you are continuing a course of action; if there are no good reasons to continue, don't.
- Remind yourself of what a course of action is costing; consider saving these costs as a reason to discontinue.
- Watch for escalation tendencies in your behaviors and those of others.

Creativity in Decision Making

Situation—Elevator riders in a new high-rise building are complaining about long waiting times.

Building engineers' advice—Upgrade the entire system at substantial cost. Why? He assumed that any solutions to a slow elevator problem had to be mechanical ones.

Creativity consultant's advice—Place floor-to-ceiling mirrors by the elevators. Why? People, he assumed, would not notice waiting times because they were distracted by their and others' reflections.

Outcome—the creativity consultant was right.[42]

Creativity in decision making shows up as a novel idea or unique approach to solving problems or exploiting opportunities.[43] The potential for creativity is one of our greatest personal assets, although we often let it go unrecognized. One reason is that we focus too much on what researchers call **Big-C creativity**—when extraordinary things are done by exceptional people.[44] Think Big-C creativity when you use an iPhone or iPad—Steve Jobs's creativity, or buy something on Amazon, Jeff Bezos's creativity.

Don't get sidetracked by Big-C creativity alone. There is lots of **Little-C creativity** around also. It occurs when people come up with unique ways to deal with daily events and situations. Think Little-C creativity, for example, the next time you solve relationship problems at home, or find ways to pack too many items into a small suitcase.

Just imagine what can be accomplished with all the creative potential—Big-C and Little-C—in an organization. How do you turn that potential into creative decisions? David Kelley, founder of the design firm IDEO, believes that a lot, perhaps most, of us start to lose our creativity skills in elementary school.[45] It's something about being taught to look

Creativity is the generation of a novel idea or unique approach that solves a problem or crafts an opportunity.

Big-C creativity occurs when extraordinary things are done by exceptional people.

Little-C creativity occurs when average people come up with unique ways to deal with daily events and situations.

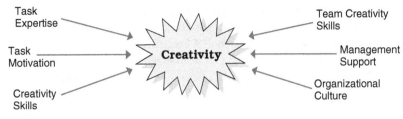

Design thinking unlocks creativity in decision making through a process of experiencing, ideation, and prototyping.

for answers to assigned problems and fearing failure when taking standardized tests. But, he also believes our creativity can be reenergized when we stop fearing failure and commit to **design thinking**. First comes *experiencing*—defining problems by research and observation; not simply accepting the parameters of a problem or issue as delivered. Second comes *ideation*—visualizing and brainstorming potential solutions in collaboration with others. Third comes *prototyping*—testing and modifying the potential solution over and over to achieve the best outcome.

Personal Creativity Drivers

Figure 7.7 shows a combination of personal and situational creativity drivers, things that can increase the likelihood of creativity by individuals, teams, and organizations. Let's start with the personal creativity drivers of task expertise, task motivation, and creativity skills.[46] Creative decisions are more likely when an individual has a lot of *task expertise*. Creativity grows from something one is good at or knows about, while extending it in new directions. And, creative decisions are more likely when someone is highly *task-motivated*. Creativity often happens when people work exceptionally hard to resolve a problem or exploit an opportunity.

Creative decisions also emerge when people have strong personal *creativity skills*. Creative people tend to work with high energy, hold their ground in the face of criticism, and respond in a resourceful way in difficult situations. They are good at making connections among seemingly unrelated facts or events. Creative people also are good at questioning, observing, networking, and experimenting.[47] They are good at synthesizing information to find correct answers (convergent thinking), looking at diverse ways to solve problems (lateral thinking), and thinking "outside of the box" (divergent thinking).[48]

Situational Creativity Drivers

Look again at Figure 7.7. If you mix creative people and traditional organization and management practices, what will you get? You may not get much. It takes more than individual creativity alone to make innovation a way of life in organizations. Situational creativity drivers are important too.

Managers should staff their organizations and teams with creative members. But they should also realize these *team creativity skills* are most likely to blossom when buoyed by *management support* and the right *organizational culture*. This means having a team leader with the patience to allow for creative processes to work themselves through a decision situation. It means having top management be willing to accept and even celebrate failure, and to provide the resources—time, technology, and space—to help the creative process. It also means making creativity a top organizational priority and a core value of the organizational culture.

Think creativity gained the next time you see a young child playing with a really neat toy. It may be from Fisher-Price Toys—part of Mattel, Inc. In the firm's headquarters you'll find a special place called the "Cave," and it's not your typical office space. Picture bean-bag chairs, soft lighting, and casual couches. It's a place for brainstorming, where designers, marketers, engineers, and others can work together without any strings attached to come up with the next great toy for preschoolers. Consultants recommend that such innovation spaces be separated from the normal workplace and be large enough for no more than 15 to 20 people.[49]

Think creativity wasted the next time you watch TV on a flat-screen TV. In 1964, George H. Heilmeier showed his employers at RCA Labs his new discovery—a liquid-crystal display, or LCD. They played with it until 1968 when RCA executives decided the firm was so heavily invested in color TV tubes that they weren't really interested. Today the market is dominated by Japanese, Korean, and Taiwanese producers, with not a single U.S. maker in the market. Ironically, Heilmeier received the Kyoto Prize, considered the Nobel Prize of Japan, for his pioneering innovation.[50]

Learning Check

LEARNING OBJECTIVE 7.4

Describe the potential pitfalls and sources of creativity in managerial decision making.

Be Sure You Can • explain the availability, representativeness, anchoring, and adjustment heuristics • illustrate framing error, confirmation error, and escalating commitment in decision making • identify key personal and situational creativity drivers

Management Learning Review: Get Prepared for Quizzes and Exams

Summary

LEARNING OBJECTIVE 7.1 Discuss the roles of information, data, and analytics in management.

- Technological, information, and analytical competencies are all needed to take advantage of information technology in decision making.
- Data are raw facts and figures; information is data made useful for decision making; useful information is timely, high quality, complete, relevant, and understandable.
- Management information systems collect, organize, store, and distribute data to meet the information needs of managers.
- Analytics is the systematic evaluation and analysis of information for decision making. Data mining analyzes data to identify patterns, support predictions, and offer insights for decision makers. Big data is collected in huge quantities and is difficult to mine without using sophisticated mathematical and analytical techniques.
- Business intelligence systems organize and communicate data, often in the form of data visualization and executive dashboards, so that patterns and trends are evident to decision makers.

For Discussion What are the potential downsides to the ways IT is changing organizations?

LEARNING OBJECTIVE 7.2 Identify different ways managers approach and deal with problems.

- Managers serve as information nerve centers in the process of planning, organizing, leading, and controlling activities in organizations.
- Managers can display problem avoidance, problem solving, and problem seeking in facing problems.
- Managers vary in the use of systematic and intuitive thinking, and in tendencies toward multidimensional thinking.
- Managers must understand the different cognitive styles people use in decision making.
- Programmed decisions are routine solutions to recurring and structured problems; nonprogrammed decisions are unique solutions to novel and unstructured problems.
- Crisis problems occur unexpectedly and can lead to disaster if not handled quickly and properly.
- Managers face problems and make decisions under conditions of certainty, risk, and uncertainty.

For Discussion When would a manager be justified in acting as a problem avoider?

LEARNING OBJECTIVE 7.3 Explain the six steps in the decision-making process.

- The steps in the decision-making process are (1) find and define the problem, (2) generate and evaluate alternatives, (3) decide on the preferred course of action, (4) implement the decision, and (5) evaluate the results.
- An optimizing decision, following the classical model, chooses the absolute best solution from a known set of alternatives.
- A satisficing decision, following the behavioral model, chooses the first satisfactory alternative to come to attention.
- To check the ethical reasoning of a decision at any step in the decision-making process, it is helpful to ask the ethics criteria questions of utility, rights, justice, and caring.
- To check the ethical reasoning of a decision at any step in the decision-making process, it is helpful to ask the spotlight questions that expose the decision to transparency in the eyes of family, community members, and ethical role models.

For Discussion Do the steps in the decision-making process have to be followed in order?

LEARNING OBJECTIVE 7.4 Describe the potential pitfalls and sources of creativity in managerial decision making.

- Common decision errors and traps include the availability, representation, and anchoring and adjustment biases, as well as framing error, confirmation error, and escalating commitment.
- Creativity in decision making can be enhanced by the personal creativity drivers of individual creativity skills, task expertise, and motivation.
- Creativity in decision making can be enhanced by the situational creativity drivers of group creativity skills, management support, and organizational culture.

For Discussion Which decision trap seems most evident as an influence on bad choices made by business CEOs today?

Self-Test 7

Multiple-Choice Questions

1. Among the ways information technology is changing organizations today, _____ is one of its most noteworthy characteristics.
   a. eliminating need for top managers
   b. reducing information available for decision making
   c. breaking down barriers internally and externally
   d. decreasing need for environmental awareness

2. Whereas management information systems use the latest technologies to collect, organize, and distribute data, _____ involves tapping the available data to extract and report it in organized ways that are most useful to decision makers.
   a. analytics
   b. business intelligence
   c. anchoring and adjustment
   d. optimizing

3. A manager who is reactive and works hard to address problems after they occur is known as a _____.
   a. problem seeker
   b. problem avoider
   c. problem solver
   d. problem manager

4. A(n) _____ thinker approaches problems in a rational and an analytic fashion.
   a. systematic   c. internal
   b. intuitive   d. external

5. A person likes to deal with hard facts and clear goals in a decision situation; she also likes to be in control and keep things impersonal. This person's cognitive style tends toward _____.
   a. sensation thinking   c. sensation feeling
   b. intuitive thinking   d. intuitive feeling

6. The assigning of probabilities for action alternatives and their consequences indicates the presence of _____ in the decision environment.
   a. certainty   c. risk
   b. optimizing   d. satisficing

7. The first step in the decision-making process is to _____.
   a. identify alternatives
   b. evaluate results
   c. find and define the problem
   d. choose a solution

8. Being asked to develop a plan to increase international sales of a product is an example of the types of _____ problems that managers must be prepared to deal with.
   a. routine   c. crisis
   b. unstructured   d. structured

9. Costs, timeliness, and _____ are among the recommended criteria for evaluating alternative courses of action.
   a. ethical soundness   c. availability
   b. competitiveness   d. simplicity

10. A common mistake made by managers in crisis situations is that they _____.
   a. try to get too much information before responding
   b. rely too much on group decision making
   c. isolate themselves to make the decision alone
   d. forget to use their crisis management plan

11. The _____ decision model views managers as making optimizing decisions, whereas the _____ decision model views them as making satisficing decisions.
   a. behavioral, human relations   c. heuristic, humanistic
   b. classical, behavioral   d. quantitative, behavioral

12. When a manager makes a decision about someone's annual pay raise only after looking at his or her current salary, the risk is that the decision will be biased because of _____.

   a. a framing error

   b. escalating commitment

   c. anchoring and adjustment

   d. strategic opportunism

13. When a problem is addressed according to the positive or negative context in which it is presented, this is an example of _____.

   a. framing error

   b. escalating commitment

   c. availability and adjustment

   d. strategic opportunism

14. When a manager decides to continue pursuing a course of action that facts otherwise indicate is failing to deliver desired results, this is called _____.

   a. strategic opportunism

   b. escalating commitment

   c. confirmation error

   d. the risky shift

15. Personal creativity drivers include creativity skills, task expertise, and _____.

   a. emotional intelligence   **c.** organizational culture

   b. management support   **d.** task motivation

Short-Response Questions

16. What is the difference between an optimizing decision and a satisficing decision?

17. How can a manager double-check the ethics of a decision?

18. How would a manager use systematic thinking and intuitive thinking in problem solving?

19. How can the members of an organization be trained in crisis management?

Essay Question

20. As a participant in a new mentoring program between your university and a local high school, you have volunteered to give a presentation to a class of sophomores on the challenges in the new "electronic office." The goal is to sensitize these high school students to developments in information technology and motivate them to take the best advantage of their high school academics so as to prepare themselves for the workplace of the future. What will you say to them?

Career Skills & Competencies: Make Yourself Valuable!

Evaluate Career Situations

What Would You Do?

1. Tired of Excuses

Little problems are popping up at the most inconvenient times. They make your work as team leader sometimes difficult and even aggravating. Today it's happened again. Trevor just called in "sick," saying his doctor advised him yesterday that it was better to stay home than to come to work and infect others with the flu. It makes sense, but it's also a hardship for you and the team. What can you do to best manage this type of situation since it's sure to happen again?

2. Social Loafing Problem

You are under a lot of pressure because your team is having performance problems. They trace, in part at least, to persistent social loafing by one team member in particular. You have come up with a reason to remove her from the team. But, the decision you are about to make fails all three of the ethics spotlight questions. As team leader, what will you do now?

3. Task Force Selection

You have finally caught the attention of senior management. Top executives asked you to chair a task force to develop a creative new product that can breathe fresh life into an existing product line. To begin, you need to select the members of the task force. What criteria will you use to choose members who are most likely to bring high levels of creativity to this team?

Reflect on the Self-Assessment

Cognitive Style

Instructions

This assessment is designed to get an impression of your cognitive style based on the work of psychologist Carl Jung. For each of the following 12 pairs, place a "1" next to the statement that best describes you. Do this for each pair, even though the description you choose may not be perfect.[51]

1. (a) I prefer to learn from experience.

   (b) I prefer to find meanings in facts and how they fit together.

2. (a) I prefer to use my eyes, ears, and other senses to find out what is going on.

   (b) I prefer to use imagination to come up with new ways to do things.

3. (a) I prefer to use standard ways to deal with routine problems.

   (b) I prefer to use novel ways to deal with new problems.

4. (a) I prefer ideas and imagination.

   (b) I prefer methods and techniques.

5. (a) I am patient with details, but get impatient when they get complicated.

   (b) I am impatient and jump to conclusions, but I am also creative, imaginative, and inventive.

6. (a) I enjoy using skills already mastered more than learning new ones.

   (b) I like learning new skills more than practicing old ones.

7. (a) I prefer to decide things logically.

   (b) I prefer to decide things based on feelings and values.

8. (a) I like to be treated with justice and fairness.

   (b) I like to be praised and to please other people.

9. (a) I sometimes neglect or hurt other people's feelings without realizing it.

   (b) I am aware of other people's feelings.

10. (a) I give more attention to ideas and things than to human relationships.

    (b) I can predict how others will feel.

11. (a) I do not need harmony; arguments and conflicts don't bother me.

    (b) I value harmony and get upset by arguments and conflicts.

12. (a) I am often described as analytical, impersonal, unemotional, objective, critical, hardnosed, and rational.

    (b) I am often described as sympathetic, people-oriented, unorganized, uncritical, understanding, and ethical.

Self-Assessment Scoring

Sum your scores as follows, and record them in the parentheses. (Note that the *Sensing* and *Feeling* scores will be recorded as negatives.)

(–   ) *Sensing* (*S Type*) 5 1a 1 2a 1 3a 1 4a 1 5a 1 6a

(   ) *Intuitive* (*N Type*) 5 1b 1 2b 1 3b 1 4b 1 5b 1 6b

(   ) *Thinking* (*T Type*) 5 7a 1 8a 1 9a 1 10a 1 11a 1 12a

(–   ) *Feeling* (*F Type*) 5 7b 1 8b 1 9b 1 10b 1 11b 1 12b

Interpretation

This assessment contrasts personal tendencies toward information gathering (sensation vs. intuition) and information evaluation (feeling vs. thinking) in one's approach to problem solving. The result is a classification of four cognitive styles and their characteristics. Read the descriptions provided in the chapter text and consider the implications of your suggested style, including how well you might work with people whose styles are very different.

Contribute to the Team Exercise

Lost at Sea

Situation

You are sailing on a private yacht in the South Pacific when a fire of unknown origin destroys the yacht and most of its contents. You and a small group of survivors are now in a large raft with oars. Your location is unclear, but you estimate that you are about 1,000 miles south-southwest of the nearest land. One person has just found in her pockets five $1 bills and a packet of matches. Everyone else's pockets are empty. The items below are available to you on the raft.[52]

	Individual ranking	Team ranking	Expert ranking
Sextant			
Shaving mirror			
5 gallons water			
Mosquito netting			
1 survival meal			
Maps of Pacific Ocean			
Floatable seat cushion			

(*Continued*)

	Individual ranking	Team ranking	Expert ranking
2 gallons oil-gas mix			
Small transistor radio			
Shark repellent			
20 square feet black plastic			
1 quart 20-proof rum			
15 feet nylon rope			
24 chocolate bars			
Fishing kit			

Instructions

1. *Working alone,* rank the 15 items in order of their importance to your survival ("1" is most important and "15" is least important).

2. *Working in an assigned group,* arrive at a "team" ranking of the 15 items. Appoint one person as team spokesperson to report your team ranking to the class.

3. *Do not write in Column C* until your instructor provides the "expert" ranking.

Manage a Critical Incident

Asking for a Raise

Situation: You want a raise.[53]

Problem: The question is: How do you get your boss to decide that you deserve one?

Insight: Researchers tell us that when negotiating a raise it's better to not use a round number as a target—such as "about $65,000," and better to use a precise number—such as "$63,750." The round number suggests a person has only a general idea of the market for their skills, whereas the precise number gives the impression that they've done the research and know their facts.

Task: Describe what you will say and do to get your boss to agree that you deserve a raise. Prepare a narrative that presents the exact words, justifications, and dollar target you would use to ask for a raise in your current job. Alternatively, assume you have been working in your chosen career field for five years, have developed lots of expertise and earned high performance reports, and now want a raise.

Collaborate on the Team Project

Crisis Management Realities

Questions: What types of crises do business leaders face, and how do they deal with them?

Instructions

- Identify three crisis events from the recent local, national, and international business news.
- Read at least three different news reports on each crisis, trying to learn as much as possible about its specifics, how it was dealt with, what the results were, and the aftermath of the crisis.

- For each crisis, use a balance sheet approach to list sources or causes of the conflict and management responses to it. Analyze the lists to see if there are any differences based on the nature of the crisis faced in each situation. Also look for any patterns in the responses to them by the business executives.

- Score each crisis (from 1 = low to 5 = high) in terms of how successfully it was handled. Be sure to identify the criteria that you use to describe "success" in handling a crisis situation. Make a list of "Done Rights" and "Done Wrongs" in crisis management.

- Summarize the results of your study in a report on "Realities of Crisis Management."

Analyze the Case Study

Target | **Missing the Bull's Eye**

Go to **Management Cases for Critical Thinking** at the end of the book to find this case.

CHAPTER **8**

Planning Processes and Techniques

Get There Faster with Objectives

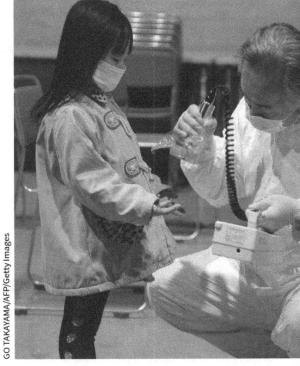

GO TAKAYAMA/AFP/Getty Images

"Considering the future of our children and young people . . . we have no choice but to go ahead with the village-wide evacuation."

Mayor Noro Kanno of Kawamata-cho town, after a 9.0 earthquake and monster tsunami destroyed nuclear power facilities in Fukushima, Japan.

Chapter Quick Start

Most of our days are full of time pressure, numerous tasks, and multiple activities—expected and unexpected. A good plan can help us to stay focused and get a reasonable number of things accomplished. Managers need plans, too, but the planning environment can be complicated. Now more than ever it important to understand the essential planning processes and techniques.

LEARNING OBJECTIVES

8.1 Identify the importance of planning and the steps in the planning process.

8.2 List and give examples of the types of plans used by managers.

8.3 Discuss useful planning tools and techniques.

8.4 Explain how goals and participation influence planning success.

Career Readiness – What to Look for **Inside**	
Thought Leadership	**Skills Make You Valuable**
Analysis > *Make Data Your Friend* Policies on Office Romances Vary Widely	• **Evaluate** *Career Situations:* What Would You Do?
Choices > *Think before You Act* Keep Your Career Plan Tight and Focused . . . or Loosen Up?	• **Reflect** *On the Self-Assessment:* Time Management Profile
Ethics > *Know Right from Wrong* What Really Works When Fighting World Poverty?	• **Contribute** *To the Team Exercise:* Personal Career Planning
Insight > *Learn about Yourself* Time Management Unlocks Performance Capacity	• **Manage** *A Critical Incident:* Policy on Paternity Leave for New Dads
	• **Collaborate** *On a Team Project:* The Future Workplace
	• **Analyze** *The Case Study:* Uber: Riding the Gig Economy

No one can know what the future holds, but no one doubts its likely complications. Each year the meeting of the World Economic Forum in Davos, Switzerland, for example, identifies key risks for the world at large. Recent concerns highlight political instability in countries around the world, extreme weather events, climate change, cyber-attacks, rising unemployment and underemployment, and growing income disparities.[1] What are the implications for small and large companies, or for our hospitals, schools and governments? What might they mean to you?

Like all of us, managers need to look ahead, make good plans, and help themselves and others meet future challenges. But it can be easy to get so caught up in the everyday details of work and life that we forget to think about or plan for what happens next. Other times a rush to get to the next thing can go off track because we don't account for uncertainties or an unfamiliar playing field. Even the best of plans—organizational and personal—have to be adjusted or modified to new circumstances. This requires the insight and courage to be flexible, and the discipline to stay focused on goals even as events change and problems arise.

8.1 | Why and How Managers Plan

LEARNING OBJECTIVE 8.1

WileyPLUS

See Author Video

Identify the importance of planning and list the five steps in the planning process.

> **Learn More About**
>
> Importance of planning • The planning process • Benefits of planning • Planning and time management

The management process involves planning, organizing, leading, and controlling resources to achieve performance objectives. The first of these, **planning**, sets the stage for the others by providing a sense of direction. It involves setting objectives and determining how to accomplish them. At its core, planning involves deciding what needs to be accomplished and how to go about it.

Planning is the process of setting objectives and determining how to accomplish them.

Importance of Planning

When planning is done well it creates a platform for the other management functions. It helps with *organizing*—allocating and arranging resources to accomplish tasks, *leading*—guiding and inspiring others to achieve high levels of accomplishment, and *controlling*—monitoring accomplishments and taking corrective action when needed.

The centrality of planning is shown in **Figure 8.1**. Good planning helps us become better at what we are doing and to stay action-oriented. An Eaton Corporation annual report, for example, once stated: "Planning at Eaton means making the hard decisions before events force them upon you, and anticipating the future needs of the market before the demand asserts itself."[2]

We're going to talk about planning from a managerial perspective. But you should remember—everything we discuss applies to you, your career, and your personal affairs. Consider, for example, the choice of academic major. Many students take out large loans to pay for their studies, but different majors command different starting salaries. How many students have a good plan for turning their choice of major into future career opportunities . . . and quickly paying off their loans? One expert advises students to carefully consider these planning questions: "Will your major and career choice allow you to meet your family obligations? Will the ratio of your earnings to debt be something you can manage? Will your major selection make you competitive in your career?"[3]

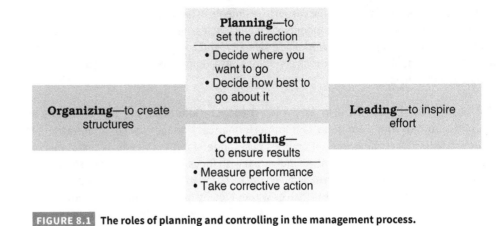

Planning—to
set the direction

• Decide where you
  want to go
• Decide how best to
  go about it

Organizing—to create
structures

Leading—to inspire
effort

Controlling—
to ensure results

• Measure performance
• Take corrective action

FIGURE 8.1   **The roles of planning and controlling in the management process.**

The Planning Process

The five basic steps in the planning process are:

1. *Define your objectives*—Identify desired outcomes or results in very specific ways. Know where you want to go; be specific enough that you will know you have arrived when you get there, or know how far off the mark you are at various points along the way.

2. *Determine where you stand vis-à-vis objectives*—Evaluate current accomplishments relative to the desired results. Know where you stand in reaching the objectives; know what strengths work in your favor and what weaknesses may hold you back.

3. *Develop premises regarding future conditions*—Anticipate future events. Generate alternative "scenarios" for what may happen; identify for each scenario things that may help or hinder progress toward your objectives.

4. *Analyze alternatives and make a plan*—List and evaluate possible actions. Choose the alternative most likely to accomplish your objectives; describe what must be done to follow the best course of action.

5. *Implement the plan and evaluate results*—Take action and carefully measure your progress toward objectives. Follow through by doing what the plan requires; evaluate results, take corrective action, and revise plans as needed.

Objectives and **goals** are specific results that one wishes to achieve.

Stretch goals are performance targets that one must work extra hard and stretch to reach.

A **plan** is a statement of intended means for accomplishing objectives.

Planning should focus attention on **objectives** and **goals** that are specific results or desired outcomes. But the objectives and goals should push you to achieve substantial accomplishments. It's common now to talk about what are called **stretch goals**—performance targets that we have to work extra hard and really stretch to reach. Do you agree that stretch goals can add real strength to the planning process for both organizations and individuals?

It's important to remember the action side of planning. The process should always create a realistic and concrete **plan**, a statement of action steps to accomplish objectives and goals. These steps must be clear and compelling, so that the all-important follow-through takes place. Plans alone don't deliver results; implemented plans do. Like other decision making in organizations, the best planning includes the active participation of those whose work efforts will eventually determine whether or not the plans get put into action.

It's also important to remember that planning is not something managers do only on occasion or while working alone in quiet rooms, free from distractions, and at scheduled times. It is an ongoing process, enacted continuously while dealing with a busy work setting filled with distractions, interpersonal dynamics, and constant performance pressures.

Benefits of Planning

The pressures organizations face come from many sources. Externally, these include changing social norms and ethical expectations, government regulations, uncertainties of a global economy, new technologies, and the cost of investments in labor, capital, and other resources. Internally, they include the quest for operating efficiencies, new structures and technologies, alternative work arrangements, workplace diversity, and concerns for work–life balance. As you would expect, planning under such conditions has a number of benefits for both organizations and individuals.

Planning Improves Focus and Flexibility

Good planning improves focus and flexibility, both of which are important for performance. Managers in an organization with focus recognize what the organization does best, understand the needs of customers, and know how to serve customers well. An individual with focus knows where he or she wants to go in a situation, career, and life in general. An organization with flexibility is willing and able to change and adapt to shifting circumstances without losing focus, and operates with an orientation toward the future rather than the past. An individual with flexibility adjusts career plans to fit new opportunities and constraints

Planning Improves Action Orientation

Planning focuses attention on priorities and helps avoid the **complacency trap**—simply being carried along by the flow of events. It is a way for people and organizations to stay ahead of the competition and become better at what they are doing. Planning keeps the future visible as a performance target and reminds us that the best decisions are often those made before events force problems on us.

The **complacency trap** is being carried along by the flow of events.

Management consultant Stephen R. Covey once pointed out that the most successful executives "zero in on what they do that 'adds value' to an organization."[4] Instead of working on too many things, they work on the things that really count. Covey said that good planning makes managers more: (1) results oriented—creating a performance-oriented sense of direction; (2) priority oriented—making sure the most important things get first attention; (3) advantage oriented—ensuring that all resources are used to best advantage; and (4) change oriented—anticipating problems and opportunities so they can be dealt with most effectively.

Planning Improves Coordination and Control

Planning improves coordination.[5] Individuals, groups, and subsystems in organizations are all engaged in multiple tasks and activities simultaneously. But their efforts must also be combined into meaningful contributions to the organization as a whole. Good plans promote coordination of employees' activities and organizational subsystems so that their accomplishments advance critical performance initiatives.

Planning that is done well facilitates control. The link between planning and controlling begins when objectives and standards are set. They make it easier to measure results and take action to improve things as necessary. After launching a costly IT upgrade, for example, executives at McDonald's realized that the system couldn't deliver on its promises. They stopped the project, took a loss of $170 million, and refocused the firm's plans and resources on projects with more direct impact on customers.[6]

This is how planning and controlling work closely together in the management process. Without planning, control lacks objectives and standards for measuring how things are going and identifying what could be done to make them go better. Without control, planning lacks the follow-through necessary to ensure that things work out as planned. With both good planning and good control, it's a lot easier to spot when things aren't going well and make the necessary adjustments.

Planning and Time Management

As president of Fidelity Personal Investing, Kathleen Murphy is calendar-bound. Her conferences and travel are booked well ahead. Meetings are scheduled at half-hour intervals and workdays can last 12 hours. She spends lots of time traveling, but tries to make good use of her time on planes. "No one can reach me by phone," she says, "and I can get reading and thinking done."[7]

Kathleens's is a common executive story—tight schedules, little time alone, lots of meetings and phone calls, and not much room for spontaneity. The keys to success in such classic management scenarios rest, in part at least, with another benefit of good planning—time management. Review these useful tips on personal time management skills.

- *Do* say "No" to requests that divert you from what you really should be doing.
- *Don't* get bogged down in details that you can address later or leave for others.
- *Do* have a system for screening telephone calls, e-mails, and requests for meetings.
- *Don't* let drop-in visitors or instant messages use too much of your time.
- *Do* prioritize what you will work on in terms of importance and urgency.
- *Don't* become calendar-bound by letting others control your schedule.
- *Do* follow priorities and work on the most important and urgent tasks first.

Most of us have experienced the difficulties of balancing available time with our many commitments and opportunities. As suggested in the chapter opener, it is easy to lose track of time and get caught by what consultants identify as "time wasters." All too often we allow our time to be dominated by other people or to be misspent on nonessential activities.[8] To-do lists can help, but they have to contain the right things. In daily living and in management situations, it is important to distinguish between things that you must do (top priority), should do (high priority), would be nice to do (low priority), and really don't need to do (no priority).

Insight: Learn about Yourself | It isn't a waste of time to occasionally relax . . . it is a waste to let friends dominate your time.

Time Management Unlocks Performance Capacity

When it comes to planning, one of the first things that comes to mind is time. It is one of our most precious resources, and **time management** is an essential career skill.

Some 77% of managers in one survey said that the digital age has increased the number of decisions they have to make. Forty-three percent said there was less time available to make these decisions. Who hasn't complained or heard others complain, "There are just not enough hours in the day to get everything done"?

Don't you wonder about the time you waste every day?—instant messages, voice and text messages, drop-in visitors, wasting time online and more? Of course, you have to be careful defining what "waste" means to you. It isn't a waste of time to occasionally relax, take a break from work or school or just day-to-day activities, and find pleasure in socializing. But it is a waste to let friends dominate your time so you don't work on a paper until it's too late to write a really good one, or delay a decision to apply for an internship until the deadline has passed.

Time management is a form of planning that is consistently rated one of the top "must-have" skills for new graduates entering fast-paced and complicated careers in business and management. Many of us, perhaps most of us, keep to-do lists. But it's the rare person who is consistently successful living up to their list. Planning can suffer the same fate as to-do lists—it starts with the best of intentions, but may end up with little or nothing to show as to real results.

Can the "Checkup" shown here help you keep time management on your side?

Time Management Checkup

List 1—What I have to do tomorrow
- (A) Most important, top priority—these are things you *must* do.
- (B) Important, not top priority—these are things you *should* do.
- (C) Least important, low priority—these are things you *might* do.
- (D) Not important, no priority—these are things you *should not* do.

Ask: Do my actions match the priorities?

List 2—Time wasters
- (A) Things I can control—they won't happen if I don't let them.
- (B) Things I can't control—they happen and I can't do anything about it.

Ask: Are you taking control where you can?

Get To Know Yourself Better

Now is a good time to improve your planning capabilities. It's a key management function and a critical life skill. Start by getting in touch with how you manage and use your time. *Task 1*—Keep a daily time log for at least two days, listing what you do and how long it takes. Then write up an analysis of where you seem to be wasting time and where you are using it well. *Task 2*—Complete the lists requested in the Time Management Checkup. Double-check List 1 "B" items and reclassify any that are really "As" or "Cs." Look at your "As" and reclassify any that are really "Bs" or "Cs." Write a priority to-do list for your day tomorrow. Also check your time wasters in List 2. Write down a plan to take charge of things that are controllable.

Types of Plans Used by Managers   **161**

Learning Check

LEARNING OBJECTIVE 8.1

Identify the importance of planning and the steps in the planning process.

Be Sure You Can • explain the importance of planning as the first of four management functions • list the steps in the formal planning process • illustrate the benefits of planning for an organization familiar to you • illustrate the benefits of planning for your personal career development • list at least three things you can do now to improve your time management

8.2 | Types of Plans Used by Managers

LEARNING OBJECTIVE 8.2

List and give examples of the types of plans used by managers.

WileyPLUS

See Author Video

> **Learn More About**
>
> Long-range and short-range plans • Strategic and tactical plans • Operational plans

"I am the master of my fate: I am the captain of my soul." How often have you heard this phrase? The lines are from "Invictus," written by British poet William Earnest Henley in 1875. He was sending a message, one of confidence and control, as he moved forward into the future. That notion, however, worries a scholar by the name of Richard Levin. His response to Henley is: "Not without a plan you're not."[9]

Managers use a variety of plans as they face different kinds of challenges in organizations. In some cases, the planning environment is stable and predictable; in others, it is more dynamic and uncertain. Different situations call for different types of plans.

Long-Range and Short-Range Plans

In the not-too-distant past, **long-term plans** looked three or more years into the future, while **short-term plans** covered one year or less. But, the increasing environmental complexity and dynamism of recent years has severely tested the concept of "long-term" planning. Most executives would likely agree that these complexities and uncertainties challenge how we actually go about planning and how far ahead we can really plan. There is a lot less permanency to long-term plans today and they are subject to frequent revisions.

Even though the time frames of planning may be shrinking, top management is still responsible for setting longer-term plans and directions for the organization as a whole. They set the context for lower-level management to work on useful short-terms plans. Unless everyone understands an organization's long-term plans and objectives, there is always risk that the pressures of daily challenges will divert attention from "important tasks." Without a sense of long-term direction, employees can end up working hard and not achieve significant—or mission-critical—results.

Management researcher Elliot Jaques believed that people vary in their capability to think with different time horizons.[10] As shown in **Figure 8.2**, he suggested that most people work comfortably with only three-month time spans; a smaller group works well with a one-year span; and only the very rare person can handle a 20-year time frame. These are provocative and personally challenging ideas. Although a team leader's planning may fall primarily in the

Long-term plans typically look three or more years into the future.

Short-term plans typically cover one year or less.

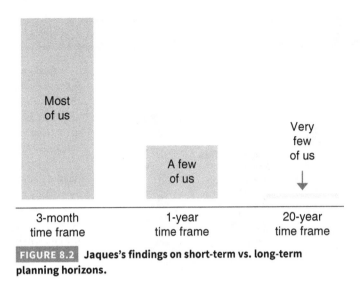

FIGURE 8.2 **Jaques's findings on short-term vs. long-term planning horizons.**

weekly or monthly range, a chief executive is expected to have a vision extending years into the future. Career progress to higher levels of management requires the conceptual skills to work well with longer-range time frames.

Strategic and Tactical Plans

When a sports team enters a game, it typically does so with a "strategy" in hand. Most often this strategy is set by the head coach in conjunction with assistant and position coaches. The goal is clear: Win the game. As the game unfolds, however, situations arise that require actions to solve problems or exploit opportunities. They call for "tactics" that deal with a current situation in ways that advance the overall strategy for winning. The same logic holds true for organizations. Plans at the top of the traditional organizational pyramid tend to have a strategic focus. Those at the middle and lower levels of the organization are more tactical.

Strategic plans are focused on the organization as a whole or a major component. They are longer-term plans that set broad action directions and create a frame of reference for allocating resources for maximum performance impact. Strategic plans ideally set forth the goals and objectives needed to accomplish the organization's **vision** in terms of mission or purpose and what it hopes to be in the future.

Tactical plans are developed and used to implement strategic plans. They specify how resources can be used to put strategies into action. In the sports context you might think of tactical plans as having "special teams" or as "special plays" ready to meet a particular threat or opportunity. Tactical plans in business often take the form of **functional plans** that indicate how different components of the firm will contribute to the overall strategy. Such functional plans might include:

- *Production plans*—dealing with work methods and technologies.
- *Financial plans*—dealing with money and capital investments.
- *Facilities plans*—dealing with physical space and work layouts.
- *Logistics plans*—dealing with suppliers and acquiring resource inputs.
- *Marketing plans*—dealing with selling and distributing goods or services.
- *Human resource plans*—dealing with and building a talented workforce.

Operational Plans

Operational plans guide behavior and describe what needs to be done in the short term to support strategic and tactical plans. They include both *standing plans* like policies and procedures that are used over and over again, and *single-use plans* like budgets that apply to one specific task or time period.

A **strategic plan** identifies long-term directions for the organization.

A **vision** clarifies the purpose of the organization and expresses what it hopes to be in the future.

A **tactical plan** helps to implement all or parts of a strategic plan.

Functional plans indicate how different operations within the organization will help advance the overall strategy.

An **operational plan** identifies short-term activities to implement strategic plans.

Keep Your Career Plan Tight and Focused . . . or Loosen Up?

sirtravelalot/Shutterstock.com

Executive 1. "Career planning is more art than science. . . . Nonetheless, some form of plan can greatly enhance the evaluation of various opportunities and enable you to make better career decisions. A career plan allows you to identify how to use your basic strengths to maximum advantage, set major career objectives, and establish immediate milestones to measure personal development and advancement."

Executive 2. "A career . . . is a series of accidental changes of job and shifts of scenery on which you look back later, weaving through the story retroactively some thread of logic that was not visible at the time. If you try to carefully plan your life, the danger is that you will succeed—succeed in narrowing your options and closing off avenues of adventure that cannot now be imagined."

Those in favor of tight career planning are likely to say: "You need a plan to give yourself a sense of direction." . . . "Having a career objective is highly motivating." . . . "Without a plan you'll wander and not accomplish much of anything." *Those against tight career planning are likely to say:* "How can you know today what the future might offer?" . . . "If you are too tightly focused you won't spot unique opportunities." . . . "We grow and change over time, our career plans should too."

Your Take?

Both executives are talking from experience and personal success. Is executive 1's advice right for most people—careers should be carefully planned and then implemented step-by-step to achieve a long-term goal? Or is executive 2's advice right for most people—careers are best built with flexibility and spontaneity to take advantage of opportunities that pop up along the way? How do these perspectives fit with what we know about job markets and career directions today? Which position do you favor? Would you prefer to blend both perspectives to carve out your career pathway?

Policies and Procedures
A **policy** communicates broad guidelines for making decisions and taking action in specific circumstances. Organizations operate with lots of policies that set expectations for many aspects of employee behavior. Typical human resource policies cover things like employee hiring, termination, performance appraisals, pay increases, promotions, and discipline (see the Analysis feature). For example, Judith Nitsch made sexual harassment a top priority when starting her engineering-consulting business.[11] Nitsch defined a sexual harassment policy, took a hard line on its enforcement, and appointed a male and a female employee for others to talk with about sexual harassment concerns.

> A **policy** is a standing plan that communicates broad guidelines for decisions and action.

Procedures describe specific rules for what actions are to be taken in various situations. They are stated in employee handbooks and often called SOPs—standard operating procedures. Whereas a policy sets a broad guideline, procedures define precise actions to be taken. In the prior example, Judith Nitsch was right to establish a sexual harassment policy for her firm. But, she should also put into place procedures that ensure everyone receives fair, equal, and nondiscriminatory treatment under the policy. Everyone in the firm should know both how to file a sexual harassment complaint and just how that complaint will be handled.

> A **procedure** is a rule describing actions that are to be taken in specific situations.

Budgets
Budgets are single-use plans that commit resources for specific time periods to activities, projects, or programs. Managers typically spend a fair amount of time bargaining with higher levels to get adequate budgets to support the needs of their work units or teams. They are also expected to achieve work objectives while keeping within allocated budgets. Being "over budget" is generally bad, while coming in "under budget" is generally good.

> A **budget** is a plan that commits resources to projects or activities.

Managers deal with and use a variety of budgets. *Financial budgets* project cash flows and expenditures; *operating budgets* plot anticipated sales or revenues against expenses; *nonmonetary budgets* allocate resources like labor, equipment, and space. A *fixed budget* allocates an established amount of resources for a specific purpose, such as $50,000 for equipment purchases in a given year. A *flexible budget* allows resources to vary in proportion with emergent

Analysis: Make Data Your Friend | Some employees sign "love contracts" saying office relationships won't interfere with their work.

Policies on Office Romances Vary Widely

Allison Michael Orenstein/The Image Bank/Getty Images

The press is quick to report when a top executive or public figure runs into trouble over an office affair. But the fact is that work is still a common place for romance to bloom. Twenty percent of respondents to one survey said they met their spouses in the workplace. Yet, with the rise of #MeToo, things are becoming very sensitive. It's important to understand the rules, even as employer policies on office relationships vary. One survey puts the issues in perspective:

- 24%—prohibit relationships among employees in the same department.
- 13%—prohibit relationships among employees who have the same supervisor.
- 80%—prohibit relationships between supervisors and subordinates.
- 5%—have no restrictions on office romances.
- New trend—"love contracts," where employees pledge that their romantic relationships in the office won't interfere with their work.
- Small business caveat—it's hard to separate dating and married couples in small business settings. The CEO of a 30-person e-commerce firm says, "At one point, exactly one third of the whole workforce was married to or dating a co-worker."

Your Take?

Do you know anyone who has been involved in an office relationship? What is your thinking on this issue? Is this an area that employers should be regulating? Or should office romances be left to the best judgments of those involved? After all, it's their private business—isn't it?

---

levels of activity, such as having extra money available to hire temporary workers when workloads exceed certain levels.

Because budgets link planned activities with the resources needed to accomplish them, they are useful for activating and tracking performance. But budgets can get out of control, creeping higher and higher without getting sufficient critical reviews. In fact, one of the most common budgeting problems is that resource allocations get "rolled over" from one time period to the next without rigorous scrutiny; the new budget is simply an incremental adjustment over the previous one. In a major division of Campbell Soups, for example, managers once discovered that 10% of the marketing budget was going to sales promotions no longer relevant to current product lines.

A **zero-based budget** allocates resources as if each budget were brand new.

A **zero-based budget** deals with this rollover budget problem by approaching each new budget period as it if were brand new. In zero-based budgeting there is no guarantee that any past funding will be renewed; all proposals, old and new, must compete for available funds at the start of each new budget cycle. What do you think? Does zero-based budgeting make sense in government and other organizations that struggle to balance goals and available resources?

Learning Check

LEARNING OBJECTIVE 8.2

List and give examples of the types of plans used by managers.

Be Sure You Can • differentiate between short-range and long-range plans • differentiate between strategic and operational plans and explain how they relate to one another • define *policy* and *procedure* and give examples of each in a university setting • define *budget* and explain how zero-based budgeting works

8.3   Planning Tools and Techniques

LEARNING OBJECTIVE 8.3

Discuss useful planning tools and techniques.

WileyPLUS

See Author Video

> **Learn More About**
> Forecasting • Contingency planning • Scenario planning • Benchmarking • Staff planning

Planning delivers the most benefits when its foundations are strong. Useful planning tools and techniques include forecasting, contingency planning, scenario planning, benchmarking, and staff planning.

Forecasting

What are top executives around the world thinking about as they make plans for the future? Are they on top of the right trends? How about you and your career plans? Things are moving fast today in the world of work. Are you looking ahead, spotting trends, and making good decisions now to set yourself up well in the future?

Planning in business and our personal lives often involves **forecasting**, predicting what will happen in the future.[12] Periodicals such as *Business Week*, *Fortune*, and *The Economist* regularly report forecasts of industry conditions, interest rates, unemployment trends, and national economies, among other issues. Some are based on *qualitative forecasting*, which uses expert opinions to predict the future. Others involve *quantitative forecasting*, which uses mathematical models and statistical analyses of historical data and surveys to predict future events.

Although useful, all forecasts should be treated cautiously. They are planning aids, not substitutes. Forecasts rely on human judgment—and can be wrong. It is said that a music agent once told Elvis Presley: "You ought to go back to driving a truck, because you ain't going nowhere." And when it came time to make the second pick in the 1984 NBA draft, the Portland Trail Blazers chose Sam Bowie. The next-in-line Chicago Bulls used the third pick to choose Michael Jordan.

Forecasting attempts to predict the future.

Contingency Planning

Picture the scene: A professional golfer is striding down the golf course with an iron in each hand. The one in her right hand is "the plan"; the one in her left is the "backup plan." Which club she uses will depend on how the ball lies on the fairway. One of her greatest strengths is being able to adjust to the situation by putting the right club to work in the circumstances she encounters.

Planning is often like that. By definition it involves thinking ahead. The more uncertain the planning environment, the more likely it is that an original forecast or intention will turn out to be inadequate or wrong. The golfer deals with uncertainty by having backup clubs available. This amounts to **contingency planning**—identifying alternative courses of action that can be implemented if circumstances change. A really good contingency plan will even contain "trigger points" to indicate when to activate preselected alternatives. In the face of uncertainties, this can be an indispensable tool for managerial and personal planning.

Poor contingency planning was center stage when debates raged over how BP managed the disastrous Deepwater Horizon oil spill in the Gulf of Mexico. Everyone from the public at large to U.S. lawmakers to oil industry experts criticized BP not only for failing to contain the spill quickly, but also for failing to anticipate and have contingency plans in place to handle such an ecological crisis.[13]

Contingency planning identifies alternative courses of action to take when things go wrong.

What Really Works When Fighting World Poverty?

Diptendu Dutta/AFP/Getty Images

Developing countries send $100+ billion in aid to poor countries; private foundations and charities spend $70+ billion more fighting poverty and its effects around the world. Their plans and goals are praiseworthy, but not all of it is being well spent, that's for sure. That's one of the problems being tackled by the

Poverty Action Lab at the Massachusetts Institute of Technology. The director, Abhijit Banerjee, a development economist, says: "We aren't really interested in the more-aid-less-aid debate. We're interested in seeing what works and what doesn't." The lab criticizes "feel-good" approaches and pushes for rigorous evaluations of poverty-fighting programs using scientific methods. Here's an example.

The Indian antipoverty group Seva Mandir was concerned about teacher absenteeism and low performance by rural school children. Its original plan was to pay extra tutors to assist teachers in 120 rural schools. The Poverty Lab Plan suggested paying extra tutors in 60 schools, making no changes in the other 60, and then comparing outcomes to see if the plan worked. An evaluation of results showed no difference in children's performance, even with the higher costs of extra tutors.

A new plan was made to buy cameras for 60 teachers, have them take time/date-stamped photos with children at the start and end of each school day, and have the photos analyzed each month. Teachers would receive bonuses or fines based on their absenteeism and student performance. Again, no changes were made in the other 60 schools. Evaluation revealed that teacher absenteeism was 20% lower and student performance was significantly higher in the camera schools. With the Poverty Lab's help, Seva Mandir concluded that investing in closely monitored pay incentives could improve teacher attendance in rural schools.

What do you think?

Look around your organization and at cases reported in the news. How often do we draw conclusions that "plans are working" based on feel-good evaluations or anecdotal reports rather than solid scientific evaluations? What are the consequences at work and in society when plans are implemented at great cost, but without systematic, defensible systems for evaluation? Even if the objectives of a project are honorable, what ethical issues arise in situations where it isn't clear that the project is having the intended benefit?

A BP spokesperson initially said—"You have here an unprecedented event . . . the unthinkable has become thinkable and the whole industry will be asking questions of itself."

An oil industry expert responded—"There should be a technology that is preexisting and ready to deploy at the drop of a hat. . . . It shouldn't have to be designed and fabricated now, from scratch."

Former BP CEO Tony Hayward finally admitted—"There are some capabilities that we could have available to deploy instantly, rather than creating as we go."

The lesson in the BP case is crystal clear. Contingency planning is essential. It can't prevent crises from occurring. But when things do go wrong, there's nothing better to have in place than good contingency plans.

Scenario Planning

Scenario planning is a long-term version of contingency planning. It involves identifying several possible future scenarios or states of affairs and then making plans to deal with each scenario should it actually occur.[14] In this sense, scenario planning forces us to think ahead and to be open to a wide range of possibilities.

Scenario planning can be used to tackle such issues as climate change and sustainable development. Most typically it involves descriptions of "worst cases" and "best cases." For example, a worst-case scenario might be that global conflict and devastating effects on the natural environment occur as nations compete to secure increasingly scarce supplies of oil and other natural resources. A best-case scenario might be that governments work together to find pathways that take care of present needs while making real commitments to alternative energy and making investments to ensure long-term sustainability of global resources.

> **Scenario planning** identifies alternative future scenarios and makes plans to deal with each.

Benchmarking

Planners sometimes become too comfortable with the ways things are going and become overconfident that the past is a good indicator of the future. It is often better to keep challenging the status quo and not simply to accept things as they are. One way to do this is through **benchmarking**—which is the use of external and internal comparisons to better evaluate current performance and identify possible ways to improve for the future.[15]

The purpose of benchmarking is to determine what other people and organizations are doing very well, and then plan how to incorporate these ideas into one's own operations. It is basically a way of learning from others. One benchmarking technique is to search for **best practices**—things people and organizations to achieve superior performance.

Well-run organizations emphasize *internal benchmarking* that encourages members and work units to learn and improve by sharing best practices. They also use *external benchmarking* to learn from competitors and non-competitors alike. Xerox, for example, has benchmarked L.L. Bean's warehousing and distribution methods, Ford's plant layouts, and American Express's billing and collections. Ford benchmarked BMW's 3 series.[16] And in the apparel industry, the Spanish retailer Zara has become a benchmark for excellence in "fast fashion."[17]

> **Benchmarking** uses external and internal comparisons to plan for future improvements.

> **Best practices** are things people and organizations do that lead to superior performance.

Staff Planning

As organizations grow, so do their planning challenges and so does the use of planners. These specialists are experts in all steps of the planning process, as well as in the use of planning tools and techniques. They can help bring focus and expertise to a wide variety of planning tasks. But one risk is a tendency for a communication gap to develop between the staff planners and line managers. Unless everyone works together, resulting plans may be based on poor information. Also, an organization's employees may end up with little commitment to implement the plans made by the staff, no matter how good they are.

Learning Check

LEARNING OBJECTIVE 8.3

Discuss useful planning tools and techniques.

Be sure you can • define *forecasting, contingency planning, scenario planning,* and *benchmarking* • explain the benefits of contingency planning and scenario planning • describe pros and cons of using staff planners

8.4 | Implementing Plans to Achieve Results

LEARNING OBJECTIVE 8.4

Explain how goals and participation influence planning success.

> **Learn More About**
> Goal setting • Goal management • Goal alignment • Participation and involvement

Plans are, we might say, words with promises attached. These promises are only fulfilled when plans are implemented and their purposes are achieved. And the foundations for successful implementation are set with the planning processes of goal setting, goal alignment, and participation and involvement.

Goal Setting

Although most of us are aware of the importance of goal setting in management, we may mistakenly think that goal setting is easy to accomplish. The reality is that how goals are set can have a big impact on how well they function as performance targets and motivators. There's a significant difference between having "no goals" or even just everyday run-of-the-mill "average goals," and having really "great goals" that inspire effort and result in plans being successfully implemented. **Figure 8.3** shows that great goals—think SMART goals—have five characteristics.

1. *specific*—clearly targeted key results and outcomes to be accomplished.
2. *measurable*—described so results can be measured without ambiguity.
3. *attainable*—include a challenging stretch factor while still being realistic and possible to achieve.
4. *relevant*—focused on important results, not just on activities or effort expended.
5. *timely*—linked to specific timetables and "due dates."

One of the more difficult aspects of goal setting is making performance objectives as measurable as possible. It's best to achieve agreement on a *measurable end product*—for example, "to reduce travel expenses by 5% by the end of the fiscal year." But performance in some jobs, particularly managerial positions, can be hard to quantify. Rather than abandon the quest for a good objective in such cases, it is often possible to agree on *verifiable work activities*. Their accomplishment serves as an indicator of performance progress. An example is "to improve

FIGURE 8.3 **Five characteristics of SMART goals.**

communications with my team in the next three months by holding weekly team meetings." Whereas it can be difficult to measure "improved communications," it is much easier to document whether the "weekly team meetings" have been held.

Goal Management

Scandal—The state auditor in Ohio charged that teachers and principals in one school district were pressured to change student test scores and attendance rosters to improve the district's performance scorecard on goals that affected state funding. Failing grades were changed to passing for at least 7,000 students.[18]

Scandal—An internal audit of the U.S. Department of Veterans Affairs system charged that managers covered up long appointment waiting times and used bogus lists to meet tight scheduling goals and receive personal bonuses. More than 120,000 veterans failed to get care, and at least 23 died waiting for treatment.[19]

It isn't enough to set smart goals—the goals and the quests for their accomplishment must also be well managed. Look again at the scandals just reported. The ethics and performance failures involved unrealistic goals that were linked to performance rewards. In the Ohio school district, the teachers and principals pursuing the goals—not the students—became the cheaters. In the VA scandal, auditors claimed that unrealistic goals for patient waiting times were imposed "before ascertaining the resources required." They also said that schedulers—feeling pressured—engaged in "inappropriate practices in order to make waiting times appear more favorable."[20]

The fact is that goals can have a "dark" as well as positive side.[21] Negative consequences are likely when goals are set unrealistically high, when individuals are expected to meet high goals over and over again, and when people striving to meet high goals aren't given the support they need to accomplish them.[22] The downsides of poorly managed stretch goals include excessive stress for the goal seeker, poor performance results, fabricated performance reports, and possible unethical or illegal behavior.

Good management of goal setting can help to avoid downside problems. Scholars Gary Latham and Gerard Seijts advise paying attention to both **learning goals** that create the knowledge and skills required for performance, and **outcome goals** that set targets for actual performance results. If outcome goals are emphasized while learning goals are minimized or ignored, undesirable outcomes are likely. Latham and Seijts say: "It is foolish and even immoral for organizations to assign employees stretch goals without equipping them with the resources to succeed—and still punish them when they fail to reach those goals. This lack of guidance often leads to stress, burnout, and in some instances, unethical behavior."[23]

> **Learning goals** set targets to create the knowledge and skills required for performance.
>
> **Outcome goals** set targets for actual performance results.

Goal Alignment

It is one thing to set great goals, make them part of a plan, and then manage and support them well. It is an entirely different thing to make sure goals and plans are well integrated across many people, work teams, and levels of an organization as a whole. The process of **goal alignment** makes sure that goals everywhere in the organization are linkend together to advance its overall mission or purpose.

Figure 8.4 shows that goal alignment begins at the team level when team leaders and team members engage in regular goal-oriented conversations. These conversations should be

> **Goal alignment** makes sure that goals throughout an organization are linked together to advance the mission.

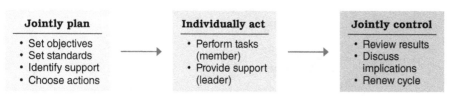

Jointly plan		**Individually act**		**Jointly control**
• Set objectives	→	• Perform tasks (member)	→	• Review results
• Set standards		• Provide support (leader)		• Discuss implications
• Identify support				• Renew cycle
• Choose actions				

FIGURE 8.4   **MBO as a process of goal alignment between team leader and team member.**

two-way discussions that result in all parties agreeing on: (1) performance objectives for a given time period, (2) plans through which objectives will be accomplished and what support will be provided, (3) standards for measuring whether objectives have been accomplished, and (4) procedures for reviewing performance results. This process is sometimes called *management by objectives* or MBO for short.[24]

As goal alignment moves up to an organization-wide level, the focus is on building a well-defined **hierarchy of goals** or **hierarchy of objectives**. It links lower-level goals and objectives in clear means-end fashion with the accomplishment of higher-level ones.

Participation and Involvement

Planning is a process, not an event. And "participation" and "involvement" are two of its core components. **Participatory planning** includes all planning steps, the people who will be affected by the plans and those who are asked to help implement them. One of the things that research is most clear about is that when people participate in setting goals, they gain motivation to work hard to accomplish them.[25] This power of participation is unlocked in planning when people who are involved in the process gain commitment to work hard and support the implementation of plans.

Figure 8.5 shows the role of participation and involvement in the planning process. Notice that participation can and should be engaged in all planning steps. Think of it using the metaphor of a big kitchen table. Everyone from family members to guests sits around the table and enjoys the meal while joining in the conversation. The same can happen with planning, if the manager invites others to the table. When he or she does, the conversation focuses on defining objectives, assessing the present and potential future state of affairs, identifying action alternatives, and discussing implementation successes and failures.

There are many benefits when and if this participatory planning approach is followed. Participation can increase the creativity and information available for planning. It can also increase the understanding and acceptance of plans, as well as commitment to their success. Even though participatory planning takes more time, it can improve performance results by improving both the quality of the plans that are made and the effectiveness of their implementation.

In a **hierarchy of goals** or **hierarchy of objectives**, lower-level goals and objectives support accomplishment of higher-level goals and objectives.

Participatory planning includes the persons who will be affected by plans and/or those who will implement them.

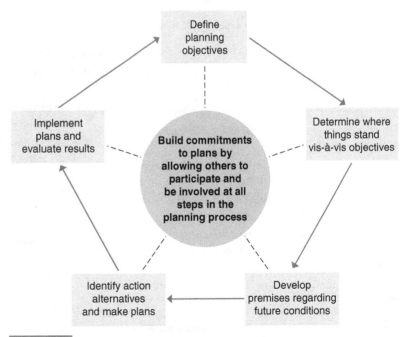

FIGURE 8.5 How participation and involvement help build commitment to plans.

Learning Check

LEARNING OBJECTIVE 8.4

Explain how goals and participation influence planning success.

Be Sure You Can • list the criteria of great goals • describe the value of a hierarchy of objectives • give examples of improvement and personal development objectives • explain how goal alignment can take place between a team leader and team members

Management Learning Review: Get Prepared for Quizzes and Exams

Summary

LEARNING OBJECTIVE 8.1 Identify the importance of planning and the steps in the planning process.

- Planning is the process of setting performance objectives and determining what should be done to accomplish them.
- A plan is a set of intended actions for accomplishing important goals and objectives.
- Five steps in the planning process are: (1) Define your objectives, (2) determine where you stand vis-à-vis your objectives, (3) develop your premises regarding future conditions, (4) identify and choose among alternative ways of accomplishing objectives, and (5) implement action plans and evaluate results.
- The benefits of planning include better focus and flexibility, action orientation, coordination, control, and time management.

For Discussion Which step in the planning process is likely to cause the most difficulties for managers?

LEARNING OBJECTIVE 8.2 List and give examples of the types of plans used by managers.

- Short-range plans tend to cover a year or less; long-range plans extend up to three years or more.
- Strategic plans set critical long-range directions; operational plans are designed to implement strategic plans.
- Policies, such as a sexual harassment policy, are plans that set guidelines for the behavior of organizational members.
- Procedures and rules are plans that describe actions to be taken in specific situations, such as the steps to be taken when persons believe they have been subjected to sexual harassment.
- Budgets are plans that allocate resources to activities or projects.

For Discussion Is there any real value to long-term planning in today's rapidly changing environment?

LEARNING OBJECTIVE 8.3 Discuss useful planning tools and techniques.

- Forecasting, which attempts to predict what might happen in the future, is a planning aid but not a planning substitute.
- Contingency planning identifies alternative courses of action that can be implemented if and when circumstances change.
- Scenario planning analyzes the implications of alternative versions of the future.
- Planning through benchmarking utilizes external and internal comparisons to identify best practices for possible adoption.
- Staff planners with special expertise are often used to assist in the planning process, but the risk is a lack of involvement by managers and others who must implement the plans.

For Discussion Shouldn't all plans be supported by contingency plans?

LEARNING OBJECTIVE 8.4 Explain how goals and participation influence planning success.

- Great or SMART goals are specific, measurable, attainable, relevant, and timely.
- Goals can have negative consequences, including unethical or illegal behavior, when they are poorly managed and set unrealistically high.
- A hierarchy of objectives helps to align goals from top to bottom in organizations.
- Goal alignment is facilitated by a participative process that clarifies performance objectives for individuals and teams and identifies support that can and should be provided by managers.
- Participation and involvement open the planning process to valuable inputs from people whose efforts are essential to the effective implementation of plans.

For Discussion Given its potential advantages, why isn't goal alignment a characteristic of all organizations?

Self-Test 8

Multiple-Choice Questions

1. Planning is the process of _____ and _____.
   a. developing premises about the future, evaluating them
   b. measuring results, taking corrective action
   c. measuring past performance, targeting future performance
   d. setting objectives, deciding how to accomplish them

2. The benefits of planning include _____.
   a. improved focus
   b. lower labor costs
   c. more accurate forecasts
   d. higher profits

3. In order to help implement its corporate strategy, a business firm would likely develop a _____ plan for the marketing department.
   a. functional
   b. single-use
   c. production
   d. zero-based

4. _____ planning identifies alternative courses of action that can be taken if and when certain situations arise.
   a. Zero-based
   b. Participative
   c. Strategic
   d. Contingency

5. The first step in the control process is to _____.
   a. measure actual performance
   b. establish objectives and standards
   c. compare results with objectives
   d. take corrective action

6. A sexual harassment policy is an example of _____ plans used by organizations.
   a. long-range
   b. single-use
   c. standing-use
   d. operational

7. When a manager is asked to justify a new budget proposal on the basis of projected activities rather than past practices, this is an example of _____ budgeting.
   a. zero-based
   b. variable
   c. fixed
   d. contingency

8. One of the benefits of participatory planning is _____.
   a. reduced time for planning
   b. less need for forecasting
   c. greater attention to contingencies
   d. more commitment to implementation

9. The ideal situation in a hierarchy of objectives is that lower-level plans become the _____ for accomplishing higher-level plans.
   a. means
   b. ends
   c. scenarios
   d. benchmarks

10. When managers use the benchmarking approach to planning, they _____.
    a. use flexible budgets
    b. identify best practices used by others
    c. are seeking the most accurate forecasts that are available
    d. focus more on the short term than the long term

11. One of the problems in relying too much on staff planners is _____.
    a. a communication gap between planners and implementers
    b. lack of expertise in the planning process
    c. short-term rather than long-term focus
    d. neglect of budgets as links between resources and activities

12. The planning process isn't complete until _____.
    a. future conditions have been identified
    b. stretch goals have been set
    c. plans are implemented and results evaluated
    d. budgets commit resources to plans

13. When a team leader is trying to follow an approach known as management by objectives, who should set a team member's performance objectives?
    a. the team member
    b. the team leader
    c. the team leader and team member
    d. the team member, the team leader, and a lawyer

14. A good performance objective is written in such a way that it _____.
    a. has no precise timetable
    b. is general and not too specific
    c. is almost impossible to accomplish
    d. can be easily measured

15. Which type of plan is used to guide resource allocations for long-term advancement of the organization's mission or purpose?
    a. tactical
    b. operational
    c. strategic
    d. functional

Short-Response Questions

16. List five steps in the planning process and give examples of each.

17. How might planning through benchmarking be used by the owner of a local bookstore?

18. How does planning help to improve focus?

19. Why does participatory planning facilitate implementation?

Essay Question

20. Put yourself in the position of a management trainer. You have been asked to make a short presentation to the local Small Business Enterprise Association at its biweekly luncheon. The topic you are to speak on is "How Each of You Can Use Objectives to Achieve Better Planning and Control." What will you tell them and why?

Career Skills & Competencies: Make Yourself Valuable!

Evaluate Career Situations

What Would You Do?

1. The Planning Retreat

It's been a bit over two years since your promotion to division manager. You're now accountable for delivering about 10% of your firm's total revenues, and you oversee more than 100 people working in five different departments. This year you'd like to make the annual planning retreat really valuable to everyone. All managers, from team leaders to functional heads, will be present. You will have them off site for a full day. What goals will you state for the retreat in the e-mail you send out with the retreat agenda? Knowing the steps in the planning process, what will the retreat agenda look like, and why?

2. Sexual Harassment

One of the persons under your supervision has a "possible" sexual harassment complaint about the behavior of a co-worker. She says that she understands the organization's sexual harassment policy, but the procedures are not clear. You're not clear, either, and take the matter to your boss. She tells you to draft a set of procedures that can be taken to top management for approval. What procedures will you recommend so that sexual harassment complaints like this one can be dealt with in a fair way?

3. Getting "Buy In"

A consulting firm has been hired to help write a strategic plan for your organization. The plan would be helpful, but you are worried about getting buy-in from all members, not just those at the top. What conditions can you set for the consultants so that they not only provide a solid strategic plan, but also create strong commitments to implementing it from members of your organization?

Reflect on the Self-Assessment

Time Management Profile

Instructions

Complete the following questionnaire by indicating "Y" (yes) or "N" (no) for each item. Be frank and allow your responses to create an accurate picture of how you tend to respond to these kinds of situations.

1. When confronted with several items of urgency and importance, I tend to do the easiest first.

2. I do the most important things during that part of the day when I know I perform best.

3. Most of the time I don't do things someone else can do; I delegate this type of work to others.

4. Even though meetings without a clear and useful purpose upset me, I put up with them.

5. I skim documents before reading and don't finish any that offer little value for my time.

6. I don't worry much if I don't accomplish at least one significant task each day.

7. I save the most trivial tasks for that time of day when my creative energy is lowest.

8. My workspace is neat and organized.

9. My office door is always "open"; I never work in complete privacy.

10. I schedule my time completely from start to finish every workday.

11. I don't like to-do lists, preferring to respond to daily events as they occur.

12. I block out a certain amount of time each day or week that is dedicated to high-priority activities.

Scoring

Count the number of "Y" responses to items 2, 3, 5, 7, 8, 12. Enter that score here [ ]. Count the number of "N" responses to items 1, 4, 6, 9, 10, 11. Enter that score here [ ]. Add the two scores together here [ ].

Self-Assessment Interpretation

The higher the total score, the more closely your behavior matches recommended time management guidelines. Reread those items where your response did not match the desired response. Why don't they match? Do you have reasons why your behavior in this instance should be different from the recommended time management guideline? Think about what you can do to adjust your behavior to be more consistent with these guidelines.

Contribute to the Team Project

Personal Career Planning

Instructions

Part 1—Complete the following activities as an individual assignment. Part 2—Share your results with your team. Part 3—Prepare a team summary of member's career plans and present it for discussion with the class and instructor.

Activity 1 Strengths and Weaknesses Inventory Different occupations require special talents, abilities, and skills. Each of us, you included, has a repertoire of existing strengths and weaknesses that are "raw materials" we presently offer a potential employer. Actions can (and should!) be taken over time to further develop current strengths and to turn weaknesses into strengths. Make a list identifying your most important strengths and weaknesses in relation to the career direction you are likely to pursue after graduation. Place a * next to each item you consider most important to focus on for continued personal development.

Activity 2 Five-Year Career Objectives Make a list of three career objectives that you hope to accomplish within five years of graduation. Be sure they are appropriate given your list of personal strengths and weaknesses.

Activity 3 Five-Year Career Action Plans Write a specific action plan for accomplishing each objective. State exactly what you will do, and by when, in order to meet these objectives. If you will need special support or assistance, identify it and state how you will obtain it. An outside observer should be able to read your action plan for each objective and end up feeling confident that he or she knows exactly what you are going to do and why.

Manage a Critical Incident

Policy on Paternity Leave for New Dads

As the Human Resource Director for a medium-sized business with 800 employees, you've been asked by the CEO to draft a paternity leave policy. At present new moms get up to eight weeks off with pay and an option for another four without pay. New dads are informally allowed to take up to a week off. After doing some research, you find that about 85% of new dads take one or two weeks off with the birth of a new child. But few new dads take more than that, even when it's available, because of a variety of worries about their careers and job security.[26]

Questions

What is your plan for drafting this new paternity leave policy? How will you go about getting good information and making sure the new policy is a good fit with your organization and its employees? What is your plan for making sure that new dads take full advantage of the new policy and aren't afraid to use it because of job and career concerns? In short, you need to not only develop the new policy but make sure it is accepted by all of the stakeholders affected by the policy.

Collaborate on a Team Activity

The Future Workplace

Instructions

Form groups as assigned by the instructor. Brainstorm to develop a master list of the major characteristics you expect to find in the workplace in the year 2025. Use this list as background for completing the following tasks:

1. Write a one-paragraph description of what the typical "Workplace 2025" manager's workday will be like.

2. Draw a "picture" representing what the "Workplace 2025" organization will look like.

3. Summarize in list form what you consider to be the major planning implications of your future workplace scenario for management students today. That is, explain what this means in terms of using academic and extracurricular activities to best prepare for success in this future scenario.

4. Choose a spokesperson to share your results with the class as a whole and explain their implications for the decisions most likely to lead to professional success for the members of the class.

Analyze the Case Study

Uber | Riding the Gig Economy

Go to **Management Cases for Critical Thinking** at the end of the book to find this case.

CHAPTER 9

MikeDotta/Shutterstock.com

Control Processes and Systems
What Gets Measured Happens

"Our managers weren't trained, our people weren't supported."

Quote from Harvard Professor Frances Frei after Uber hired her to restore control and change "a rotten culture."

Chapter Quick Start

Facts are important and measurement keeps us on target. Why, then, are we so often late to the party when it comes to exercising good control in our jobs and personal lives? We miss deadlines, we default on commitments, and we disappoint ourselves and others. There is a lot to learn about making control a personal asset, one that helps improve our performance as well as the performance of our teams and organizations.

LEARNING OBJECTIVES

9.1 Identify the types of controls used by managers and the reasons for them.

9.2 List and describe the steps in the control process.

9.3 Explain how to use common control tools and techniques.

Career Readiness – What to Look for **Inside**

Thought Leadership

Analysis > *Make Data Your Friend* Small Distractions Can Be Goal Killers

Choices > *Think before You Act* Some Parents Pay Their Kids for Good Grades

Ethics > *Know Right from Wrong* France to Fine Firms with Gender Pay Gaps

Insight > *Learn about Yourself* Resiliency Offers Strength from Within

Skills Make You Valuable

- **Evaluate** *Career Situations:* What Would You Do?

- **Reflect** *On the Self-Assessment:* Internal/External Control

- **Contribute** *To the Class Exercise:* After Meeting/Project Remorse

- **Manage** *A Critical Incident:* High Performer but Late for Work

- **Collaborate** *On the Team Project:* Building a Balanced Scorecard

- **Analyze** *The Case Study:* Electronic Arts: Inside Fantasy Sports

175

Keeping in touch . . . staying informed . . . being in control: These are important responsibilities for every manager. But "control" is a word like "power." If you aren't careful when and how it's used, just the thought of it carries a negative connotation. Yet, control plays a positive and necessary role in everyday living and in the management process. Having things "under control" helps to get things done; when things are "out of control" it is generally more difficult.

Nike and Uber are high-profile companies with different control stories. At Nike the story is positive. The firm's stylish shoes are made by innovative micro-level precision engineering that is great for controlling costs of materials, time, and labor.[1] At Uber the story is negative, at least it was for a time. Under co-founder and former CEO Travis Kalanick, the company was described as growing fast but "out of control and pretty chaotic." Employees were subjected to bullying and sexual harassment, and lacked protections from basic human resource policies.[2] What lies behind these different control stories?

9.1 Why and How Managers Control

LEARNING OBJECTIVE 9.1

Identify the types of controls used by managers and the reasons for them.

> **Learn More About**
> Importance of controlling • Types of controls • Internal and external control

Control is important for organization success, and we practice a lot of control quite naturally. Think of the things you do for fun—playing golf or tennis or Frisbee, reading, dancing, driving a car, or riding a bike. Through activities like these you've already become an expert in the control process. How? Most probably by having an objective in mind, always checking to see how well you are doing, and making continuous adjustments to get it right.

Importance of Controlling

Controlling is the process of measuring performance and taking action to ensure desired results.

The management function of planning involves setting goals and making plans. It is closely linked with **controlling**, the process of measuring performance and making sure that plans turn out as intended. Information is the foundation of control and facts are friendly. An experienced CEO once said: "Facts that reinforce what you are doing are nice, because they help in terms of psychic reward. Facts that raise alarms are equally friendly, because they give you clues about how to respond, how to change, where to spend the resources."[3]

Figure 9.1 shows how controlling fits in with the other management functions. *Planning* sets the direction and the parameters for resource allocation. *Organizing* brings people and

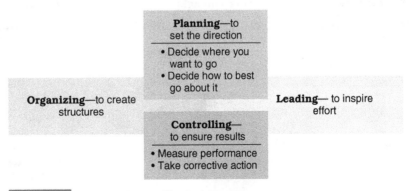

FIGURE 9.1 **The role of controlling in the management process.**

material resources together in working combinations. *Leading* inspires people to best utilize these resources. *Controlling* makes sure that the right things happen, in the right way, and at the right time. It's a way to ensure that performance is consistent with plans and that the accomplishments of a team or organization are coordinated.

One of the great benefits of effective control is learning. Consider, for example, the program of **after-action review** pioneered by the U.S. Army and now used in numerous organizations. It is a process for a structured review of lessons learned and results in a completed project, task force assignment, or special operation. Participants answer questions like: "What was the intent?" "What actually happened?" "What did we learn?"[4] The after-action review helps make continuous improvement a shared norm. It encourages participants to take responsibility for their actions, what they achieved, and how they can be more effective in the future. The end-of-chapter team exercise is modeled on this approach.

> An **after-action review** is a systematic assessment of lessons learned and results accomplished in a completed project.

Types of Controls

The open-systems perspective shown in **Figure 9.2** is one of the best ways to understand control. It shows how feedforward, concurrent, and feedback controls are linked with different phases of the input–throughput–output cycle.[5] The use of these control types increases the likelihood of high performance.

Feedforward Controls

Feedforward controls, also called *preliminary controls*, take place before a work activity begins. They ensure that objectives are clear, that directions are established, and that the right resources are available to accomplish the objectives. The goal is to solve problems before they occur by asking an important but often neglected question: "What needs to be done before we begin?"

Feedforward controls are preventive. Managers using them take a forward-thinking and proactive approach. At McDonald's, for example, preliminary control of food ingredients plays an important role in the firm's quality program. The company requires that suppliers of its hamburger buns produce them to exact specifications, covering everything from texture to uniformity of color. Even in overseas markets, the firm works hard to develop local suppliers that can offer dependable quality.[6]

> **Feedforward control** ensures that directions and resources are right before the work begins.

Concurrent Controls

Concurrent controls focus on what happens during the work process. Sometimes called *steering controls,* they make sure that plans are being followed and the right things are being done in the workflow. You can also think of this as control through direct supervision. In today's increasingly complex virtual world, that supervision can be computer driven and virtual as well as face-to-face.

The goal of concurrent controls is to solve problems as they happen. The key question is, "What can we do to improve things right now?" Picture this scene at the Hyundai Motors headquarters in Seoul, South Korea, in what the firm calls its Global Command and Control Center.[7]

> **Concurrent control** focuses on what happens during the work process.

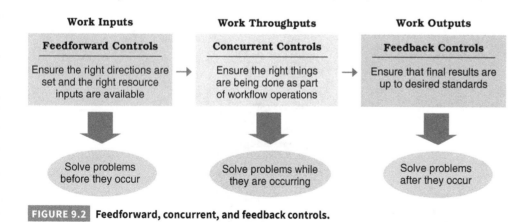

FIGURE 9.2 **Feedforward, concurrent, and feedback controls.**

With dozens of computer screens relaying video and data, it [the Global Command and Control Center] monitors Hyundai operations around the world. Parts shipments are traced from the time they leave the supplier until they reach a plant. Cameras cover assembly lines from Beijing to Montgomery and keep a close watch on Hyundai's giant Ulsan, Korea, plant, the world's largest integrated auto factory.

In the Hyundai example, computers monitor operations and gather business intelligence in real time. Using sophisticated information systems, managers are able to spot and immediately correct problems in the manufacturing cycle. The same kind of process intervention also happens at McDonald's, but there, the concurrent control is face to face. Ever-present shift leaders constantly observe the unit as a whole, while helping with the work necessary to keep the unit running. They are trained to intervene as needed to correct things on the spot.

Feedback Controls   **Feedback controls**, also called *post-action controls,* take place after work is done. They focus on the quality of end results rather than on inputs and activities. Feedback controls are largely reactive; the goals are to solve problems after they occur and prevent future problems. They ask the question: "Now that we are finished, how well did we do?"

We are all familiar with feedback controls and probably recognize their weak points from a customer service perspective. Restaurants often ask how you liked a meal after it is eaten; course evaluations tell instructors how well they performed after the course is over; a budget summary identifies cost overruns after a project is completed. Feedback about mistakes may not enable their immediate correction, but can help to improve performance in the future.

> **Feedback control** takes place after an action is completed.

Internal and External Control

Managers have two broad options with respect to control systems. First, they can trust and expect people to control their own behavior. This puts priority on internal or self-control. Second, they can exercise external control by structuring situations to increase the likelihood that

---

Choices: Think before You Act | *"If there's more than one child in the family, it's unfair if they don't all get rewards."*

Some Parents Pay Their Kids for Good Grades

Tetra Images/Alamy Stock Photo

Managing is a lot like parenting, and allocating rewards isn't easy in either situation. What about children and their school grades? How often have you heard someone say: "We pay for As"? Perhaps you've heard or said it yourself, or plan to do it when you've got kids in school. But is this the correct thing to do? Can paying for grades improve parental control over children's study habits and academic performance?

Those in favor of paying for grades are likely to say: "It gets the kid's attention" . . . "It motivates them to study more" . . . "It gets them ready for work where pay and performance go together." Those against the practice are likely to say: "Once they get paid for As, they'll be studying for financial gain, not real learning" . . . "It hurts those who work hard but still can't get the high grades" . . . "If there's more than one child in the family, it's unfair if they don't all get rewards."

Your Take?

Is paying for grades a good way to control kids' school performance? As a parent, will you pay for grades or not? How can you justify your position? The pros and cons of this approach as you see them? Were you, or are you, paid for good grades? What is your experience? By the way, what can parenting teach us about managing people at work?

things will happen as planned.[8] The alternatives here include bureaucratic or administrative control, clan or normative control, and market or regulatory control. The most effective control typically involves a mix of these options.

Self-Control

We all exercise internal control in our daily lives. We manage our money, our relationships, our eating and drinking, our health behaviors, our study habits, and more. Managers can take advantage of this capacity for **self-control** by unlocking, allowing, and supporting it. This means helping people to be good at self-management, giving them freedom, and encouraging them to exercise self-discipline in performing their jobs. Any workplace that emphasizes participation, empowerment, and involvement will rely heavily on self-control.

Managers can gain a lot by assuming that people are ready and willing to exercise self-control in work.[9] But, an internal control strategy requires trust. When people are willing to work on their own and exercise self-control, managers have to have the confidence to give them the freedom to do so. Self-control is most likely when the process used to set objectives and standards is participative. The potential for self-control also increases when capable people have a clear sense of the organization's mission and the resources to do their jobs. The potential for self-control is also greater in inclusive organizational cultures in which everyone treats everyone else with respect and consideration.

It's important to think about self-control as a capacity, even a life skill. How good are you at taking control of your time and maintaining a healthy work–life balance? Do you ever wonder who's in control, you or your phone? It used to be that we sometimes took work home, did a bit, put it away, and took it back to work the next day. Now work is always there, on the computer and in our e-mails and messaging apps. All this is habit forming, and some of us handle this intrusion into our non-work lives better than others.[10]

> **Self-control** is internal control that occurs through self-management and self-discipline in fulfilling work and personal responsibilities.

Insight: Learn about Yourself | "Resilient people are like trees bending in the wind. . . . They bounce back."

Resiliency Offers Strength from Within

Managerial control is all about how to increase the probability that things go right for organizations even as they deal with an increasing number of operational complexities. It's the same for us—every day, in our work and personal lives. We need to spot and understand where things are going according to plan or going off course. We need to have the courage and confidence to change approaches that aren't working well. Our success, simply put, depends a lot on **resiliency**—the ability to call on inner strength and keep moving forward even when things are tough.

Think of resiliency in personal terms—caring for an aging parent with a terrible disease or single parenthood with small children. Think of it in career terms—juggling personal and work responsibilities, continuously attending to e-mails, voice mails, instant messages, and rushing to many scheduled and unscheduled meetings. We need to be managed, we need to exercise control, and we need staying power to perform over the long term. Resiliency helps us hold on and keep things moving forward even in the face of personal and professional adversity.

Resilient people face up to challenges; they don't hide or back away from them. They develop strategies, make plans, and find opportunity even in challenging situations. Dr. Steven M. Southwick, professor of psychiatry at Yale University, says "Resilient people are like trees bending in the wind. . . . They bounce back." Does this description fit you . . . or not? Why?

Resiliency Quick Test

Score yourself from 1 = don't at all agree, to 5 = totally agree, on the following items:

- I am an upbeat person for the most part.
- Uncertainty and ambiguity don't much bother me.
- I tend to adapt quickly as things change.
- I can see positives even when things go wrong.
- I am good at learning from experience.
- I am good at problem solving.
- I am strong and hold up well when times are tough.
- I have been able to turn bad situations into positive gains.

Get to Know Yourself Better

Take the Resiliency Quick Test. A score of 35 or better suggests you are highly resilient; with any lower score you should question how well you hold up under pressure. Double-check the test results by looking at your behavior. Write notes on how you handle situations like a poor grade at school, a put-down from a friend, a denial letter from a job application, or criticism from a supervisor or co-worker on your job. Summarize what you've learned in a memo to yourself about how you might benefit from showing more resiliency in difficult situations.

Bureaucratic Control

One form of external control uses authority, policies, procedures, job descriptions, budgets, and day-to-day supervision to encourage people to work toward organizational interests. It's called **bureaucratic control**, control that flows through the organization's hierarchy of authority. Organizations typically have policies and procedures regarding sexual harassment, for example. Their goal is encourage members to behave respectfully and with no suggestion of sexual pressure or impropriety. Organizations also use budgets for personnel, equipment, travel expenses to keep behavior targeted within set limits.

Another level of bureaucratic control comes from laws and regulations. An example is the Sarbanes-Oxley Act of 2002 (SOX), which establishes procedures to regulate financial reporting and governance in publicly traded corporations.[11] SOX was passed in response to major corporate scandals over inaccurate financial reports. Under SOX, chief executives and chief financial officers must personally sign off on financial reports and certify their accuracy. Those who misstate financial records can go to jail and face substantial personal fines. Many firms now appoint chief compliance officers (CCOs) and set up compliance departments. They are most effective when the CCO reports directly to the chief executive or to the board of directors.[12] Actions are also being taken to strengthen governance by boards. Stricter management oversight is evident in moves for directors to become more actively involved in leadership and to separate the CEO and board chairman roles.[13]

> **Bureaucratic control** influences behavior through authority, policies, procedures, job descriptions, budgets, and day-to-day supervision.

Clan Control

Whereas bureaucratic control emphasizes hierarchy and authority, **clan control** influences behavior through norms and expectations set by the organization's culture. Sometimes called *normative control,* it harnesses the power of cohesiveness and collective identity to influence behavior in teams and organizations.

> **Clan control** influences behavior through norms and expectations set by the organizational culture.

Analysis: Make Data Your Friend | Office workers get distracted as often as once every 3 minutes; it can take 23 minutes to refocus after a major interruption.

Small Distractions Can Be Goal Killers

Hiya Images/Corbis/Getty Images

Most of us work with good intentions. But when distractions hit, focus gets lost, plans fall by the wayside, and progress suffers. Whether it's chatting with co-workers, following social media, or tackling electronic in-boxes, interruptions are more plentiful than we might admit.

- Office workers get distracted as often as once every 3 minutes and it takes an average of 23 minutes to refocus after a major interruption.
- Handling up to 100 electronic messages can kill up to one-half of a workday.

- Facilitators of disruptions include open-plan office spaces, use of multiple electronic devices, and constant checking of social media and messaging windows.

Lacy Roberson, eBay's director of learning and organization development, calls the situation "an epidemic" and says it's hard for people to get their work done with all the interruptions and the strain that they cause. The fight against disruptions causes some employees to start their day very early or to stay late to get their jobs done. Employers are starting to fight back and to try to protect "real work" time.

"No devices" is a rule at some eBay meetings. Intel is experimenting with allowing workers blocks of "think time" where they don't answer messages or attend meetings. Abbot Laboratories is retraining workers to use the telephone rather than e-mail for many internal office communications.

Your Thoughts?

How prone are you to letting distractions consume your time? Does this problem apply to your personal affairs and relationships, not just work? It's interesting that some employers are trying to step in and set policies that might minimize the negative impact of distractions, particularly electronic ones. Where's the self-control? Aren't there things we can all do to protect our time and keep our work and goals on track?

Clan control happens as people who share values and identify strongly with one another behave in consistent ways. Just look around the typical college classroom and campus. You'll see clan control reflected in how students dress, use language, and act in class and during leisure time. People typically behave according to the expectations of peers and the groups with whom they identify. The same holds true in organizations, where clan control influences the members of teams and work groups to display common behavior patterns.

Market Control   Market control is essentially the influence of customers and competition on the behavior of organizations and their members. Business firms show the influence of market control in the way that they adjust products, pricing, promotions, and other practices in response to consumer feedback and what competitors are doing. A good example is the growing emphasis on green products and sustainability practices. When a firm like Walmart starts to get positive publicity from setting goals linked to climate change and sustainability, for example, the effect is felt by competitors.[14] They have to adjust their practices to avoid losing the public relations advantage. In this sense the time-worn phrase "keeping up with the competition" is really another way of expressing the dynamics of market controls in action.

> **Market control** is essentially the influence of market competition on the behavior of organizations and their members.

Learning Check

LEARNING OBJECTIVE 9.1

Identify the types of controls used by managers and the reasons for them.

Be Sure You Can • define *controlling* as a management function • explain benefits of after-action reviews • illustrate how a fast-food restaurant uses feedforward, concurrent, and feedback controls • discuss internal control and external control systems • give examples of bureaucratic, clan, and market controls

---

9.2 The Control Process

LEARNING OBJECTIVE 9.2

List and describe the steps in the control process.

WileyPLUS

See Author Video

> **Learn More About**
>
> Establish objectives and standards • Measure actual results • Comparing results with objectives and standards • Taking corrective action

The control process involves the four steps shown in **Figure 9.3**: 1—establish performance objectives and standards, 2—measure actual performance, 3—compare actual performance with objectives and standards, and 4—take corrective action as needed. Although essential to management, these steps apply equally well to personal and career decisions as well. Consider this—without career objectives, how do you know where you really want to go? How can you allocate your time and other resources to take advantage of available opportunities? Without measurement, how can you assess whether any progress has been made? How can you adjust your current behavior to improve the prospects for positive future results?

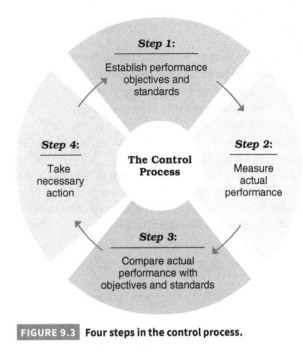

FIGURE 9.3 Four steps in the control process.

Step 1—Establish Objectives and Standards

The control process begins with planning, when performance objectives and measurement standards are set. The objectives are standards that define what one wants to accomplish in terms of key results. However, the word *key* deserves special emphasis. The focus when setting objectives and standards should be on "critical" or "essential" results that make a real performance difference. Unfortunately we often expend too much time and effort on things that aren't important, and we let the really important things slip. To stay on focus, productivity experts suggest remembering the **Pareto Principle** that 80% of consequences (think—real impact) come from 20% of causes (think—work accomplished).[15]

The **Pareto Principle** states that 80% of consequences come from 20% of causes.

An **output standard** measures performance results in terms of quantity, quality, cost, or time.

Output Standards   The control process uses **output standards** that measure actual outcomes or work results. Businesses use many output standards, such as earnings per share, return on investment, sales growth, and market share. Others include quantity and quality of production, costs incurred, service or delivery time, and error rates. Based on your experience at work and as a consumer, you can probably come up with many examples of relevant output standards.

When Allstate Corporation launched a new diversity initiative, creating "diversity index" quantified performance across a range of diversity issues. The standards included how well employees met the goals of bias-free customer service and how well managers met the firm's diversity expectations.[16] How about output standards for other types of organizations, such as a symphony orchestra? When the Cleveland Orchestra wrestled with performance standards, the members weren't willing to rely on vague generalities like "we played well" or "the audience seemed happy" or "not too many mistakes were made." Rather, they decided to track standing ovations, invitations to perform in other countries, and how often other orchestras copied their performance style.[17]

An **input standard** measures work efforts that go into a performance task.

Input Standards   The control process also uses **input standards** that measure work efforts. These are common in situations where outputs are difficult or expensive to measure. Examples quantified for a college professor might be an orderly course syllabus, meeting all class sessions, and returning exams and assignments in a timely way. Of course, as this example might suggest, measuring inputs doesn't mean that outputs such as high-quality teaching and learning are necessarily achieved. Other examples of input standards at work include conforming to rules, efficient use of resources, and work attendance.

Step 2—Measure Actual Performance

The second step in the control process is to measure actual performance. It is the point where output standards and input standards are used to document results. Linda Sanford, a senior vice president at IBM, has had a high-performance career with the company. She grew up on a family farm where measuring results was a way of life. Sanford says: "At the end of the day, you saw what you did, knew how many rows of strawberries you picked." In one of her manager roles at IBM she was known for walking around the factory, just to see "at the end of the day how many machines were going out of the back dock."[18]

Performance measurement in the control process must be accurate enough to identify differences between what is really taking place and what was originally planned. Without measurement, effective control is impossible. With measurement tied to key results, however, an old adage often holds true: "What gets measured happens."

Step 3—Compare Results with Objectives and Standards

Step 3 in the control process is to compare objectives with results. You can remember its implications by this **control equation**:

> Need for Action = Desired Performance – Actual Performance

The question of what constitutes "desired" performance plays an important role in the control equation. Some organizations use *engineering comparisons.* United Parcel Service (UPS), for example, carefully measures drivers' routes and routines to establish the times expected for each delivery. When a delivery manifest is scanned as completed, the driver's time is registered in a performance log that is monitored by supervisors. Organizations also use *historical comparisons*, where past experience becomes the baseline for evaluating current performance. They also use *relative comparisons* that benchmark performance against that being achieved by other people, work units, or organizations.

The **control equation** states: Need for Action = Desired Performance – Actual Performance.

Ethics: Know Right from Wrong | By focusing on enforcement, France aims to create an "obligation for results."

France to Fine Firms with Gender Pay Gaps

Miguel Medina/AFP/Getty Images

French companies are going to get fined if they underpay women relative to men. A new law requires companies to use government metrics and to report how much they pay their male and female employees. Any pay gaps must be corrected within three years or a firm will be fined 1% of its annual payroll.

Whereas U.S. laws allow women to file lawsuits for pay discrimination, the French approach is one of enforcement. The *Wall Street Journal* reports that "By focusing on enforcement, France aims to create 'an obligation for results.'"

French women overall suffer a 9% pay gap, while top female earners suffer a 15% gap. These data are substantially worse than those for neighboring Belgium and Italy. The French government demands change and intends to hold firms accountable through measurement. Firms will be scored on metrics like pay comparisons between women and men doing the same job, data on pay raises and promotions for women and men, pay raises for women coming back from maternity leaves, and how many women are in a firm's top 10 wage earners. If the metrics look bad, employers will pay a steep price for noncompliance.

What Do You Think?

Is measurement and enforcement the way to finally get a grip on pay discrimination faced by women? Are firms in France more likely to take concrete action to close pay gaps now that they face fines, as opposed to firms in the U.S., where they don't? Is this approach to measurement and enforcement the way to go? What are the ethics involved? Is it correct to force firms to take such actions, or should this be left to the marketplace where consumer support—or its absence—is the ultimate control lever?

Step 4—Take Corrective Action

The final step in the control process is to take actions to correct problems or make improvements. **Management by exception** is the practice of giving attention to situations that show the greatest need for action. It saves time, energy, and other resources by helping managers focus their attention on high-priority areas.

Managers should be alert to two types of exceptions. The first is where actual performance is less than desired. This *problem situation* must be understood so that corrective action can restore performance. The second is where actual performance turns out higher than what was desired. This *opportunity situation* must be understood with the goal of continuing or increasing these high levels in the future.

> **Management by exception** focuses attention on substantial differences between actual and desired performance.

Learning Check

LEARNING OBJECTIVE 9.2

List and describe the steps in the control process.

Be Sure You Can • list the steps in the control process • explain why planning is important to controlling • differentiate between output and input standards • state the control equation • define *management by exception*

9.3 Control Tools and Techniques

WileyPLUS

See Author Video

LEARNING OBJECTIVE 9.3

Explain how to use common control tools and techniques.

> **Learn More About**
> Project management and control • Inventory control • Breakeven analysis • Financial controls • Balanced scorecards

Managers in most organizations use a variety of control systems and techniques. Some of the most common include special techniques of project management, inventory control, breakeven analysis, and financial controls, as well as the use of balanced scorecards.

Project Management and Control

It might be something personal, like an anniversary party for your parents or grandparents; a fundraiser for a homeless shelter; or the launch of a new product or service at your work. It might be the completion of a new student activities building on campus, or a new advertising campaign. What these examples and others like them share in common is that they encompass relatively complicated sets of interrelated tasks with multiple components that have to happen in a certain sequence, and that must be completed by a specified date. We call them **projects**, complex one-time events with unique components and an objective that must be met within a set time frame.

> **Projects** are one-time activities with many component tasks that must be completed in proper order and according to budget.

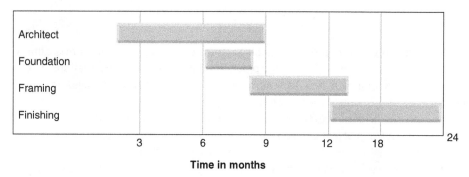

FIGURE 9.4 **Gantt chart showing tasks to be scheduled for a building project.**

Project management takes responsibility for overall planning, supervision, and control of projects. A project manager's job is to ensure that a project is well planned and then completed according to plan—on time, within budget, and consistent with objectives. Two useful techniques for project management and control are Gantt charts and CPM/PERT.

A **Gantt chart** like the one shown in **Figure 9.4** graphically displays the scheduling of tasks that go into completing a project. As developed in the early twentieth century by Henry Gantt, an industrial engineer, this tool has become a core element of project management.

The visual overview a Gantt chart provides of what needs to be done on a project allows for easy progress checks to be made at different time intervals. It also helps with event or activity sequencing to make sure key aspects of a project get accomplished in time for later work to build on them. One of the biggest problems with projects, for example, is when delays in early activities create problems for later activities. Something as simple as preparing and using a Gantt chart can go a long way to overcoming such situations.

A more advanced use of the Gantt chart is a technique known as **CPM/PERT**—a combination of the *critical path method* and the *program evaluation and review technique*. Project planning based on CPM/PERT uses a network chart like the one shown in **Figure 9.5**.

A CPM/PERT network chart moves a step beyond the Gantt chart in details and planning insights. It breaks a project into a series of smaller subactivities that have clear beginning and end points. These points become "nodes" in the chart, and the arrows between nodes show in what order the activities must be completed. The full diagram shows all the interrelationships that must be coordinated for the project to be successfully completed.

Use of CPM/PERT helps project managers track activities to make sure they happen in the right sequence and on time. If you look at the network in Figure 9.5, you should notice that the time required for each activity can be easily computed and tracked. The longest pathway from start to conclusion in a CPM/PERT network is called the **critical path**. It represents the quickest time in which the entire project can be finished, assuming everything goes according to schedule and established project plans. In the example, the critical path is 38 days.

Project management is the responsibility for overall planning, supervision, and control of projects.

A **Gantt chart** graphically displays the scheduling of tasks required to complete a project.

CPM/PERT is a combination of the critical path method and the program evaluation and review technique.

The **critical path** is the longest pathway in a CPM/PERT network.

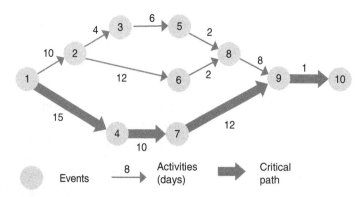

FIGURE 9.5 **CPM/PERT network chart showing critical path for project planning.**

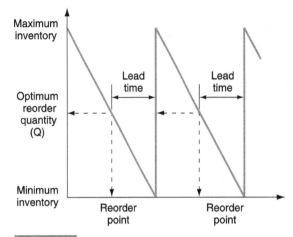

FIGURE 9.6 Reorder points in the economic order quantity form of inventory control.

Inventory Control

Inventory control ensures that inventory is only big enough to meet immediate needs.

The **economic order quantity** method places new orders when inventory levels fall to predetermined points.

Just-in-time scheduling (JIT) routes materials to workstations just in time for use.

Cost control is always an important performance concern. And a very good place to start is with inventory. The goal of **inventory control** is to make sure that any inventory is only big enough to meet immediate needs, so that carrying costs are minimized.

The **economic order quantity** form of inventory control, shown in **Figure 9.6**, automatically orders a fixed number of items every time inventory falls to a predetermined point. The order sizes are mathematically calculated to minimize inventory costs. A good example is your local supermarket. It routinely makes hundreds of daily orders on an economic order quantity basis.

Another popular approach to inventory control is **just-in-time scheduling (JIT)**. These systems reduce costs and improve workflow by scheduling materials to arrive at a workstation or facility just in time for use. Because JIT nearly eliminates the carrying costs of inventories, it is an important business productivity tool.

Breakeven Analysis

The **breakeven point** occurs where revenues just equal costs.

A frequent control question asked by business executives is: "What is the **breakeven point**?" In **Figure 9.7** you'll see that breakeven occurs at the point where revenues are just equal to costs. You can also think of the breakeven point as where losses end and profit begins. A breakeven point is computed using this formula:

$$\text{Breakeven Point} = \text{Fixed Costs} \div (\text{Price} - \text{Variable Costs})$$

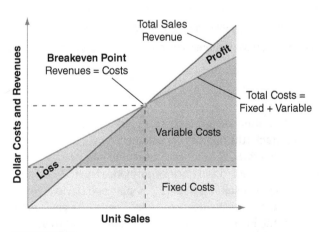

FIGURE 9.7 Use of breakeven analysis to make informed "what-if" decisions.

Managers using **breakeven analysis** perform what-if calculations under different projected cost and revenue conditions. *Question*—Suppose the proposed target price for a new product is $8 per unit, fixed costs are $10,000, and variable costs are $4 per unit. What sales volume is required to break even? (*Answer*: breakeven at 2,500 units.) *Question*—What happens if you can keep variable costs to $3 per unit? (*Answer*: breakeven at 2,000 units.) *Question*—If you can produce only 1,000 units in the beginning and at the original costs, at what price must you sell them to break even? (Answer: $14.) Business executives perform these types of cost control analyses every day.

Breakeven analysis performs what-if calculations under different revenue and cost conditions.

Financial Controls

The foundation for measuring financial performance rests with a firm's balance sheet and income statement. Each looks at finances in slightly different ways, and together they provide a good picture of financial health. The **balance sheet** shows assets and liabilities at a point in time. It will be displayed in an Assets = Liabilities format. The **income statement** shows profits or losses at a point in time. It is displayed in a Sales − Expenses = Net Income format. You are likely to remember both from an accounting course.

A **balance sheet** shows assets and liabilities at one point in time.

An **income statement** shows profits or losses at one point in time.

Financial ratios help managers use information from balance sheets and income statements for control purposes. They indicate *liquidity*—the ability to generate cash to pay bills; *leverage*—the ability to earn more in returns than the cost of debt; *asset management*—the ability to use resources efficiently and operate at minimum cost; and *profitability*—the ability to earn revenues greater than costs.

Profitability—measures ability to earn revenues greater than costs

- *Net Margin* = Net Income/Sales
- *Return on Assets* (ROA) = Net Income/Total Assets
- *Return on Equity* (ROE) = Net Income/Owner's Equity

   Higher is better: You want higher net income relative to sales, assets, and equity.

Liquidity—measures ability to meet short-term obligations

- *Current Ratio* = Current Assets/Current Liabilities
- *Quick Ratio or Acid Test* = Current Assets − Inventories/Current Liabilities

   Higher is better: You want more assets and fewer liabilities.

Leverage—measures use of debt

- *Debt Ratio* = Total Debts/Total Assets

   Lower is better: You want fewer debts and more assets.

Asset Management—measures asset and inventory efficiency

- *Asset Turnover* = Sales/Total Assets
- *Inventory Turnover* = Sales/Average Inventory

   Higher is better: You want more sales relative to assets and inventory.

Balanced Scorecards

If an instructor takes class attendance and assigns grades based on it, students tend to come to class. If an employer tracks the number of customers employees serve per day, employees tend to serve more customers. So if "what gets measured happens," shouldn't managers take advantage of "scorecards" to record and track performance results?

Strategic management consultants Robert S. Kaplan and David P. Norton advocate using the **balanced scorecard** for management control.[19] They say it gives managers "a fast, but comprehensive view of the business." The basic principle is that to do well and to win, you have to keep score. Like sports teams, organizations tend to perform better when their members always know the score.

A **balanced scorecard** tallies organizational performance in financial, customer service, internal process, and innovation and learning areas.

Developing a balanced scorecard begins with clarification of the organization's mission and vision—what it wants to be and how it wants to be perceived by key stakeholders. Next, the following questions are used to develop scorecard goals and measures:

- *Financial Performance*—"How well do our actions directly contribute to improved financial performance? To improve financially, how should we appear to our shareholders?" Sample goals: survive, succeed, and prosper. *Sample measures:* cash flow, sales growth and operating income, increased market share, and return on equity.
- *Customer Satisfaction*—"How well do we serve our customers and clients? To achieve our vision, how should we appear to our customers?" Sample goals: new products, responsive supply. *Sample measures:* percentage sales from new products, percentage on-time deliveries.
- *Internal Process Improvement*—"How well do our activities and processes directly increase the value we provide our customers and clients? To satisfy our customers and shareholders, at what internal business processes should we excel?" Sample goals: manufacturing excellence, design productivity, new product introduction. *Sample measures:* cycle times, engineering efficiency, new product time.
- *Innovation and Learning*—"How well are we learning, changing, and improving things over time? To achieve our vision, how will we sustain our ability to change and improve?" Sample goals: technology leadership, time to market. *Sample measures:* time to develop new technologies, new product introduction time versus competition.

When balanced scorecard measures are taken and routinely recorded for critical managerial review, Kaplan and Norton expect managers to make better decisions and organizations to perform better in these four performance areas. Like the financial ratios discussed earlier, the balanced scorecard is a good fit for executive dashboards and visual displays of business intelligence. Again, what gets measured happens.

Think about the possibilities for balanced scorecards in all types of organizations. How can this approach be used, for example, by an elementary school, a hospital, a community library, a mayor's office, or a fast-food restaurant? How might the performance dimensions and indicators vary among these different organizations? And if balanced scorecards make sense, why don't more organizations use them?

Learning Check

LEARNING OBJECTIVE 9.3

Explain how to use common control tools and techniques.

Be Sure You Can • define project management • explain how Gantt charts and CPM/PERT analysis can assist in project management • explain how inventory controls and breakeven analysis can assist in cost control • list and explain common ratios used in financial control • identify the four main balanced scorecard components and give examples of how they might be used in organizations of various types

Management Learning Review: Get Prepared for Quizzes and Exams

Summary

LEARNING OBJECTIVE 9.1   Identify the types of controls used by managers and the reasons for them.

- Controlling is the process of measuring performance and taking corrective action as needed.

- Feedforward controls are accomplished before a work activity begins; they ensure that directions are clear and that the right resources are available to accomplish them.

- Concurrent controls make sure that things are being done correctly; they allow corrective actions to be taken while the work is being done.

- Feedback controls take place after an action is completed; they address the question "Now that we are finished, how well did we do, and what did we learn for the future?"
- Internal control is self-control and occurs as people take personal responsibility for their work.
- External control is based on the use of bureaucratic, clan, and market control systems.

For Discussion Can strong input and output controls make up for poor concurrent controls?

LEARNING OBJECTIVE 9.2   List and describe the steps in the control process.

- The first step in the control process is to establish performance objectives and standards that create targets against which later performance can be evaluated.
- The second step in the control process is to measure actual performance and specifically identify what results are being achieved.
- The third step in the control process is to compare performance results with objectives to determine if things are going according to plans.
- The fourth step in the control process is to take action to resolve problems or explore opportunities that are identified when results are compared with objectives.

For Discussion What are the potential downsides to management by exception?

LEARNING OBJECTIVE 9.3   Explain how to use common control tools and techniques.

- A project is a unique event that must be completed by a specified date; project management is the process of ensuring that projects are completed on time, on budget, and according to objectives.
- Gantt charts assist in project management and control by displaying how various tasks must be scheduled in order to complete a project on time.
- CPM/PERT analysis assists in project management and control by describing the complex networks of activities that must be completed in sequence for a project to be completed successfully.
- Economic order quantities and just-in-time deliveries are common approaches to inventory cost control.
- The breakeven equation is: Breakeven Point = Fixed Costs ÷ (Price − Variable Costs).
- Breakeven analysis identifies the points where revenues will equal costs under different pricing and cost conditions.
- Financial control of business performance is facilitated by a variety of financial ratios, such as those dealing with liquidity, leverage, assets, and profitability.
- The balanced scorecard measures overall organizational performance in four areas: financial, customers, internal processes, and innovation.

For Discussion Should all employees of a business be regularly informed of the firm's overall financial performance?

Self-Test 9

Multiple-Choice Questions

1. After objectives and standards are set, what step comes next in the control process?
    a. Measure results.
    b. Take corrective action.
    c. Compare results with objectives.
    d. Modify standards to fit circumstances.

2. When a soccer coach tells her players at the end of a game, "I'm pleased you stayed with the game plan," she is using a/an _____ to a measure performance, even though in terms of outcomes her team lost.
    a. input standard
    b. output standard
    c. historical comparison
    d. relative comparison

3. When an automobile manufacturer is careful to purchase only the highest-quality components for use in production, this is an example of an attempt to ensure high performance through _____ control.
    a. concurrent
    b. statistical
    c. inventory
    d. feedforward

4. Management by exception means _____.
    a. managing only when necessary
    b. focusing attention where the need for action is greatest
    c. the same thing as concurrent control
    d. the same thing as just-in-time delivery

5. When a supervisor working alongside an employee corrects him or her when a mistake is made, this is an example of _____ control.
    a. feedforward
    b. concurrent
    c. internal
    d. clan

6. If an organization's top management visits a firm in another industry to learn more about its excellent record in hiring and promoting minority and female candidates, this is an example of using _____ for control purposes.
    a. a balanced scorecard
    b. relative comparison
    c. management by exception
    d. progressive discipline

7. The control equation states: _____ = Desired Performance − Actual Performance.
    a. Problem Magnitude
    b. Management Opportunity
    c. Planning Objective
    d. Need for Action

8. When a UPS manager compares the amount of time a driver takes to make certain deliveries against standards set through a quantitative analysis of her delivery route, this is known as _____.

   a. a historical comparison

   b. an engineering comparison

   c. relative benchmarking

   d. concurrent control

9. Projects are unique one-time events that _____.

   a. have unclear objectives

   b. must be completed by a specific time

   c. have unlimited budgets

   d. are largely self-managing

10. The _____ chart graphically displays the scheduling of tasks required to complete a project.

   a. exception   c. Gantt

   b. Taylor   d. after-action

11. When one team member advises another team member that "your behavior is crossing the line in terms of our expectations for workplace civility," she is exercising a form of _____ control over the other's inappropriate behaviors.

   a. clan   c. internal

   b. market   d. preliminary

12. In a CPM/PERT analysis the focus is on _____ and the event that link them together with the finished project.

   a. costs, budgets

   b. activities, sequences

   c. timetables, budgets

   d. goals, costs

13. If fixed costs are $10,000, variable costs are $4 per unit, and the target selling price per unit is $8, what is the breakeven point?

   a. 2   c. 2,500

   b. 500   d. 4,800

14. Among the financial ratios used for control, Current Assets/Current Liabilities is known as the _____.

   a. debt ratio

   b. net margin

   c. current ratio

   d. inventory turnover ratio

15. With respect to return on assets (ROA) and the debt ratio, the preferred directions when analyzing them from a control standpoint are _____.

   a. decrease ROA, increase debt

   b. increase ROA, increase debt

   c. increase ROA, decrease debt

   d. decrease ROA, decrease debt

Short-Response Questions

16. List the four steps in the controlling process and give examples of each.

17. How might feedforward control be used by the owner/manager of a local bookstore?

18. How does Douglas McGregor's Theory Y relate to the concept of internal control?

19. What four questions could be used to organize the presentation of a real-time balanced scorecard in the executive dashboard for a small business?

Essay Question

20. Assume that you are given the job of project manager for building a new student center on your campus. List just five of the major activities that would need to be accomplished to complete the new building in two years. Draw a CPM/PERT network diagram that links the activities together in required event scheduling and sequencing. Make an estimate for the time required for each sequence to be completed and identify the critical path.

Career Skills & Competencies: Make Yourself Valuable!

Evaluate Career Situations

What Would You Do?

1. Adrift in Career

A work colleague comes to you and confides that she feels "adrift in her career" and "just can't get enthused about what she's doing anymore." You think this might be a problem of self-management and personal control. How can you respond most helpfully? How might she use the steps in the management control process to better understand and improve her situation?

2. Too Much Socializing

You have a highly talented work team whose past performance has been outstanding. You've recently noticed team members starting to act like the workday is mainly a social occasion. Getting the work done too often seems less important than having a good time. Recent data show that performance is on the decline. How can you use controls in a positive way to restore performance to high levels in this team?

3. Yes or No to Graduate School

You've had three years of solid work experience after earning your undergraduate degree. A lot of your friends are talking about going to graduate school, and the likely target for you would be an MBA degree. Given all the potential costs and benefits of getting an MBA, how can breakeven analysis help you make the decision: (a) to go or not go, (b) to go full time or part time, and (c) even where to go?

Reflect on the Self-Assessment

Internal/External Control

Instructions

Circle either "a" or "b" to indicate the item you most agree with in each pair of the following statements.[20]

1. (a) Promotions are earned through hard work and persistence.
   (b) Making a lot of money is largely a matter of breaks.
2. (a) Many times the reactions of teachers seem haphazard to me.
   (b) In my experience I have noticed that there is usually a direct connection between how hard I study and the grades I get.
3. (a) The number of divorces indicates that more and more people are not trying to make their marriages work.
   (b) Marriage is largely a gamble.
4. (a) It is silly to think that one can really change another person's basic attitudes.
   (b) When I am right, I can convince others.
5. (a) Getting promoted is really a matter of being a little luckier than the next guy.
   (b) In our society, an individual's future earning power is dependent on his or her ability.
6. (a) If one knows how to deal with people, they are really quite easily led.
   (b) I have little influence over the way other people behave.
7. (a) In my case, the grades I make are the results of my own efforts; luck has little or nothing to do with it.
   (b) Sometimes I feel that I have little to do with the grades I get.
8. (a) People such as I can change the course of world affairs if we make ourselves heard.
   (b) It is only wishful thinking to believe that one can really influence what happens in society at large.
9. (a) Much of what happens to me is probably a matter of chance.
   (b) I am the master of my fate.
10. (a) Getting along with people is a skill that must be practiced.
    (b) It is almost impossible to figure out how to please some people.

Scoring

Give yourself 1 point for 1a, 2b, 3a, 4b, 5b, 6a, 7a, 8a, 9b, 10a. Total scores of: 8–10 = high *internal* locus of control, 6–7 = moderate *internal* locus of control, 5 = *mixed* locus of control, 3–4 = moderate *external* locus of control, 0–2 = high *external* locus of control.

Interpretation

This instrument offers an impression of your tendency toward an *internal locus of control* or *external locus of control*. Persons with a high internal locus of control tend to believe they have control over their own destinies. They may be most responsive to opportunities for greater self-control in the workplace. Persons with a high external locus of control tend to believe that what happens to them is largely in the hands of external forces or other people. They may be less comfortable with self-control and more responsive to external controls in the workplace.

Contribute to the Class Exercise

After-Meeting/Project Remorse

Instructions

A. Everyone on the team should complete the following assessment after participating in a meeting or a group project.[21]

1. How satisfied are you with the outcome of the meeting project?

   Not at all satisfied   1 2 3 4 5 6 7   Totally satisfied

2. How would the other members of the meeting/project group rate your influence on what took place?

   No influence   1 2 3 4 5 6 7   Very high influence

3. In your opinion, how ethical was any decision that was reached?

   Highly unethical   1 2 3 4 5 6 7   Highly ethical

4. To what extent did you feel *pushed into* going along with the decision?

   Not pushed into   1 2 3 4 5 6 7   Very pushed
   it at all   into it

5. How committed are you to the agreements reached?

   Not at all   1 2 3 4 5 6 7   Highly
   Committed   committed

6. Did you understand what was expected of you as a member of the meeting or project group?

   Not at all clear   1 2 3 4 5 6 7   Perfectly clear

7. Were participants in the meeting/project group discussions listening to each other?

   Never   1 2 3 4 5 6 7   Always

8. Were participants in the meeting/project group discussions honest and open in communicating with one another?

   Never   1 2 3 4 5 6 7   Always

9. Was the meeting/project completed efficiently?

   Not at all   1 2 3 4 5 6 7   Very much

10. Was the outcome of the meeting/project something that you felt proud to be a part of?

    Not at all   1 2 3 4 5 6 7   Very much

B. Share results with all team members and discuss their meaning.

C. Summarize and share with the instructor and class the implications of this exercise for: (a) the future success of this team if it was to work on another project, and (b) each individual team member as he or she goes forward to work in other teams and on other group projects in the future.

Manage a Critical Incident

High Performer but Late for Work

You are an elementary school principal. One of your best teachers—perhaps the best—is causing a bit of an uproar. She is in her second year on staff after graduating from college and is doing a wonderful job with the second graders. They're happy, the parents are happy, and you're happy. The other teachers aren't happy, at least some of them aren't. Two of the more outspoken and senior teachers came to you today with a request. "Do something about her," they said. "She is consistently late in the mornings. You know our policy is for the teacher to be in the classroom at least 30 minutes before school starts." You are aware of her tardiness, but you also know that she consistently stays late and is most often the last teacher out of the building at the end of the day. She isn't aware that her co-workers have complained about her. You can't put this off because the grumbling is starting to spread.

Questions

What do you do, and why? How can you turn this into an opportunity to develop an approach that accommodates a range of personal work styles and different classroom approaches, all while holding up high performance standards?

Collaborate on the Team Project

Building a Balanced Scorecard

Instructions

In your assigned teams do the following.

1. Choose a local organization of interest to team members and about which you collectively have some information and insights.

2. Build a Balanced Scorecard that can be used for control purposes by this organization's top management. Make sure your scorecard covers these four areas—financial performance, customer satisfaction, internal process improvement, and innovation and learning.

3. For each of the four scorecard performance areas, be very specific in identifying what you recommend as possible performance goals and areas of performance measurement.

4. Design a scorecard format that makes analysis easy and informative. If possible demonstrate how your proposed scorecard might fit into an Executive Dashboard.

5. Present your proposed Balanced Scorecard to the entire class, along with justification for all suggested goals and measures. Explain in your presentation why you believe this scorecard could help the organization perform better in the future.

Analyze the Case Study

Electronic Arts | Inside Fantasy Sports

Go to **Management Cases for Critical Thinking** at the end of the book to find this case.

CHAPTER 10

Strategy and Strategic Management

Insight and Hard Work Deliver Results

AP Images/CLAYTON DE SOUZA

"There is often a disconnect between the providers of for-profit education and what students need . . . At Khan Academy, we're 100% focused on the learners and teachers."

Career Readiness – What to Look for Inside

Thought Leadership

Analysis > *Make Data Your Friend*
Disposable Workers Becoming Indispensable to Business Profits

Choices > *Think before You Act*
Today's Graduates Must "Jump Right In"

Ethics > *Know Right from Wrong*
Can the Sharing Economy Create Good Jobs?

Insight > *Learn about Yourself*
Get and Stay Ahead with Critical Thinking

Skills Make You Valuable

- **Evaluate** *Career Situations:*
  What Would You Do?
- **Reflect** *On the Self-Assessment:*
  Intuitive Ability
- **Contribute** *To the Class Exercise:*
  Strategic Scenarios
- **Manage** *A Critical Incident:*
  Kickstarting a Friend's Business Idea
- **Collaborate** *On the Team Project:*
  Contrasting Strategies
- **Analyze** *The Case Study:*
  Dunkin' Donuts: Betting Dollars on Donuts

Chapter Quick Start

Strategic management is a most significant planning challenge. All organizations face a complex array of forces. Uncertainties of many types—market, economic, political, social, and more—must be understood and analyzed while leaders craft strategies for competitive success. As with organizations, each of us faces personal life and career challenges that test our abilities with strategic management. We too need to make and implement strategies to achieve our goals.

LEARNING OBJECTIVES

10.1 Discuss the process and importance of strategic management.

10.2 Identify the essential elements in strategic analysis.

10.3 Compare alternative corporate strategies.

10.4 Explain alternative business-level strategies.

10.5 Describe the foundations for strategy implementation.

193

Don't take the opening photo of Sal Khan too lightly. His innovative online Khan academy has the goal of "changing education for the better by providing a free world-class education for anyone anywhere."[1] The success of Kahn helped spur the development of MOOCs—massive open online courses—as "disrupters" of the traditional university model of face-to-face delivery of pay-per-credit courses.

Our institutions of higher education are facing strategic challenges—online learning is a game changer, politicians are attacking college costs, graduates worry about paying off student loans, and opportunities for "technical" certification in areas like software development are even raising questions about the value of "the degree." Leaders in organizations of all types and sizes and in all settings are being similarly challenged in this time of changing expectations, tastes, and technologies. And as *Fast Company* magazine states: "If you want to make a difference as a leader, you've got to make time for strategy."[2]

There was a time when Henry Ford could say: "The customer can have any color he wants as long as it's black." Those days are long gone. They're gone for businesses large and small, they're gone for hospitals and local governments, and they're gone for universities as well. A senior IBM executive described this shift in strategic landscape as the "difference between a bus which follows a set route, and a taxi which goes where customers tell it to go."[3]

There are a lot of strategy and strategic management ideas and insights in this chapter. As you think about them, remember that everything applies equally well to you and your career. What's your personal strategy for career and life success? Are you acting like a bus following a set route, a taxi following opportunities, or some combination of both?

10.1 | Strategic Management

WileyPLUS

See Author Video

LEARNING OBJECTIVE 10.1

Discuss the process and importance of strategic management.

> **Learn More About**
>
> Competitive advantage • Strategy and strategic intent • Levels of strategy • Strategic management process

The many forces and constant changes in today's environment confront all organizations and industries. This complexity places a great premium on "competitive advantage" and how it is achieved—or not—through "strategy" and "strategic management."[4]

Competitive Advantage

Competitive advantage is the ability to do something so well that one outperforms competitors.

The term **competitive advantage** describes an organization's ability to use resources so well that it performs better than the competition. Typical sources of competitive advantage are:[5]

- *Technology*—using technology to gain operating efficiencies, market exposure, and customer loyalty.
- *Cost and quality*—operating with greater efficiency and product or service quality.
- *Knowledge and speed*—doing better at innovation and speed of delivery to market for new ideas.
- *Barriers to entry*—creating a market stronghold that is protected from entry by others.
- *Financial resources*—having better investments or loss absorption potential than competitors.

Achieving and retaining competitive advantage is a difficult goal to master. Whenever organizations do things very well, rivals try to duplicate and copy their approach. The ideal achievement is **sustainable competitive advantage**—competitive advantage that is durable over time and difficult or costly for others to copy or imitate. Think, for example, about Apple's iPhone. It was first to market as an innovative product linking design, technology, and customer appeal. It was also backed by Apple's super-efficient supply chain, which made it a high-margin product. The iPhone is still a top seller, but consumers can now choose from an array of competing products offering many similar features. Apple's experience shows that the timeline for "sustainability" of competitive advantage keeps getting shorter. Yes, competitive advantage is the goal. Yes, it's achievable. But, the reality is that competitive advantage has to be re-earned almost every day.

> **Sustainable competitive advantage** is the ability to outperform rivals in ways that are difficult or costly to imitate.

Strategy and Strategic Intent

If sustainable competitive advantage is the goal, "strategy" is the means to achieve it.[6] A **strategy** is a comprehensive action plan that identifies the long-term direction for an organization and that guides resource utilization to achieve sustainable competitive advantage. It is a "best guess" about what must be done for future success in the face of competition and changing market conditions. And, it involves risk taking.

> A **strategy** is a comprehensive plan guiding resource allocation to achieve long-term organization goals.

Speaking about risk, things like time, money, and people get wasted when they are invested in ways that don't result in real accomplishments. The presence of a strategy helps ensure that such resources are used with consistent **strategic intent**—that is, with all energies directed toward accomplishing a long-term target or goal. When Patagonia states that "We're in business to save our home planet," its strategic intent is clear. And it's backed by a pledge to ". . . use the resources we have—our business, our investments, our voice and our imaginations—to do something about it." Can you see how clear strategic intent can keep organizations focused on doing things that really count and avoid investing in those that don't?

> **Strategic intent** focuses and applies organizational energies on a unifying and compelling goal.

Levels of Strategy

> *CVS Health buys Aetna for $69 billion . . . Panera Revamps 122 Ingredients in a New "Clean" Menu . . . AI-enabled robots to steal 75 million jobs*

These headlines display the three levels of strategy shown in **Figure 10.1**. At the corporate level of strategy, CVS expands its reach in health care by acquiring the insurer Aetna. At the business level of strategy, Panera Bread Co. invested lots of time and money to remove "man-made preservatives, sweeteners, colors and flavors" and offer customers a "clean" menu. At the functional level of strategy, executives in a wide variety of settings are investing in the task

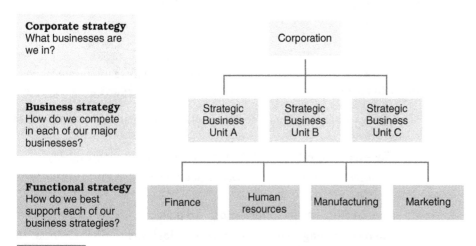

FIGURE 10.1   Corporate-level strategy, business-level strategy, and functional strategy.

efficiencies of robotics and artificial intelligence. They are doing so to the point where the World Economic Forum warns that millions of human jobs are at risk.[7] In order to really understand the stories behind such headlines, you need to understand the strategy at play and how it fits with the business purpose, current competitive conditions, and society at large.

A **corporate strategy** sets long-term direction for the total enterprise.

Corporate-Level Strategy

At the highest level, **corporate strategy** directs the organization as a whole toward sustainable competitive advantage. It answers this *corporate-level strategic question*: "In what industries and markets should we compete?" The purpose of corporate strategy is to set direction and guide resource allocations for an entire company. It identifies how large and complex organizations can compete across multiple industries and markets.

You may think of CVS as a pharmacy, but after buying Aetna it's a health insurer as well. You know Google as a search company. But it's parent company Alphabet owns technology businesses in life sciences, driverless cars, and business incubation. And what about Disney? In addition to theme parks it's into movies, music, television, and more. These complex businesses are called *conglomerates* and their leaders have to make corporate-level strategic decisions allocating resources across many different business opportunities.

A **business strategy** identifies how a division or strategic business unit will compete in its product or service domain.

Business-Level Strategy

Business strategy sets the direction for a single business unit or product line. It involves asking and answering this *business-level strategic question*: "How are we going to compete for customers in this industry and market?" Typical business strategy decisions include choices about product and service mix, facilities locations, and new technologies. Panera's move to a "clean" menu is a business strategy shift with a clear social message.

The term *strategic business unit* (SBU) is often used to describe a business that operates as one part of a larger and complex enterprise. While the organization as a whole will have a corporate strategy, each SBU will have its own business-level strategy. Porsche for example, is owned by Volkswagen. Historically a two-door sports car company, Porsche adjusted its business strategy and successfully marketed a sport utility vehicle, the Cayenne. This was followed by another success—a four-door sedan, the Panamera.[8]

A **functional strategy** guides activities within one specific area of operations.

Functional Strategy

Functional strategy guides the use of organizational resources within a specific area such as marketing, manufacturing, finance, or human resources. The *functional-level strategic question* is: "How can we best utilize resources within a function to implement our business strategy?" Answers to this question might focus on ways to better advertise products, gain distribution efficiencies, improve employee retention, and enhance customer service.

When Starbucks teamed with Arizona State University to provide online educational opportunities for it's employees, this was a functional-level commitment to talent development. Starbuck's CEO Howard Schulz and ASU's Pesident Michael Crow said: "We hope more employers will join us by making an investment in tomorrow's workforce by increasing access to a college degree." And if you notice a robot cleaning the aisles in Walmart, you're witnessing a functional strategy shift toward what CEO Doug McMillon calls "tech-empowered stores."[9]

Strategic Management Process

Developing strategy for an organization may seem like a simple task: Find out what products and services customers want, provide these at the best possible price, and make sure competitors can't easily copy what you are doing. In practice, this can get very complicated.[10]

The reality is that strategies don't just happen; they must be developed and then implemented effectively. At the same time that managers in one organization are doing all of this, their competitors are trying to do the exact same thing—only better. Succeeding in this mix of competitive pressures depends on **strategic management**, the process of formulating and implementing strategies to accomplish long-term goals and sustain competitive advantage.

Strategic management is the process of formulating and implementing strategies.

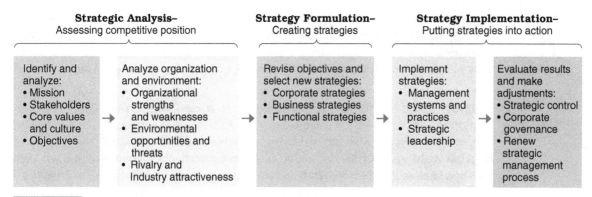

FIGURE 10.2 **Major elements in the strategic management process.**

As shown in **Figure 10.2**, the strategic management process begins with **strategic analysis** to assess the organization, its environment, its competitive positioning, and its current strategies. Next in the process is **strategy formulation**, developing a new or revised strategy at the corporate, business, or functional levels. The final phase is **strategy implementation**, using resources to put strategies into action, and then evaluating results so that the implementation can be improved or the strategy changed. As the late management consultant and guru Peter Drucker once said: "The future will not just happen if one wishes hard enough. It requires decision—now. It imposes risk—now. It requires action—now. It demands allocation of resources, and above all, it requires work—now."[11]

Strategic analysis is the process of analyzing the organization, the environment, and the organization's competitive position and current strategies.

Strategy formulation is the process of crafting strategies to guide the allocation of resources.

Strategy implementation is the process of putting strategies into action.

Learning Check

LEARNING OBJECTIVE 10.1

Discuss the process and importance of strategic management.

Be Sure You Can • define *competitive advantage, strategy*, and *strategic intent* • explain the concept of sustainable competitive advantage • differentiate corporate, business, and functional strategies • differentiate strategy formulation from strategy implementation • list the major phases in the strategic management process

10.2 Essentials of Strategic Analysis

LEARNING OBJECTIVE 10.2

Identify the essential elements in strategic analysis.

WileyPLUS

See Author Video

> **Learn More About**
>
> Analysis of mission, values, and objectives • SWOT analysis of organization and environment • Five forces analysis of industry attractiveness

When it comes to the essentials of strategic analysis, there is a core set of strategic questions that any top manager should be prepared to answer. What is our business mission? Who are our customers? What do our customers value? What have been our results? What is our plan?[12]

Analysis of Mission, Values, and Objectives

The strategic management process begins with an analysis of mission, values, and objectives. This sets the stage for assessing the organization's resources and capabilities, as well as opportunities and threats in its external environment.

A **mission** statement expresses the organization's reason for existence in society.

Mission and Stakeholders

The **mission** or purpose of an organization describes its reason for existence in society.[13] Strategy consultant Michael Hammer believes that a mission should represent what the strategy or underlying business model is trying to accomplish. In order to clarify mission he suggests asking: "What are we moving to?" "What is our dream?" "What kind of a difference do we want to make in the world?" "What do we want to be known for?"[14]

How do the following mission statements stack up to Hammer's advice? Patagonia—"Build the best product, cause no unnecessary harm, use business to inspire and implement solutions to the environmental crisis." REI—"We inspire, educate and outfit for a lifetime of outdoor adventure and stewardship." Life is Good—"To spread the power of optimism." Can you see how these mission statements give each firm a unique identity while competing with rivals?

Stakeholders are individuals and groups directly affected by the organization and its strategic accomplishments.

A clear and compelling mission helps inspire the support, loyalty, and respect of an organization's **stakeholders**. These are individuals and groups—employees, customers, shareholders, suppliers, creditors, community groups, future generations, and others—who are directly affected by the organization and its accomplishments. **Figure 10.3** gives an example of how stakeholder interests can be linked with an organization's mission.

Core values are broad beliefs about what is or is not appropriate behavior.

Core Values and Culture

The strategic management process should clarify organizational values and culture to make sure they are well aligned with the mission.[15] **Core values** are broad beliefs about what is or is not appropriate behavior. Patagonia founder and chairman Yvon Chouinard says: "Most people want to do good things, but don't. At Patagonia it's an essential part of your life."[16] Patagonia operates with a commitment to sustainability founded in these core values— "build the best product . . . cause no unnecessary harm . . . use business to protect nature . . . not bound by convention."[17]

Organizational culture is the predominant value system for the organization as a whole.

Core values help build a clear organizational identity. They give the organization a sense of character as seen through the eyes of employees and external stakeholders. This character is part of **organizational culture** or the predominant value system of the organization as a whole.[18] A clear and strong organizational culture helps guide members in ways that are consistent with the organization's mission and values. When browsing Patagonia's website for job openings, for example, the message about hiring to fit the corporate culture is clear: "We're especially interested in people who share our love of the outdoors, our passion for quality, and our desire to make a difference."[19]

Employees
We respect the individuality of each employee . . . creativity and productivity are encouraged, valued, and rewarded.

Communities
We are committed to being caring and supportive corporate citizens within the worldwide communities in which we operate.

Mission

Shareholders
We are dedicated to . . . performing in a manner that will enhance returns on investments.

Customers
We are committed to providing superior value in our products and services.

Suppliers
We think of our suppliers as partners who share our goal of . . . highest quality.

FIGURE 10.3 **External stakeholders as strategic constituencies in an organization's mission statement.**

Objectives

Objectives   Whereas a mission statement lays out an organization's purpose and core values set standards for accomplishing it, **operating objectives** direct activities toward key performance areas. Typical operating objectives for a business include the following:[20]

> **Operating objectives** are specific results that organizations try to accomplish.

- *Profitability*—operating with a net profit.
- *Sustainability*—helping to preserve, not exploit, the environment.
- *Social responsibility*—acting as a good community citizen.
- *Financial health*—acquiring capital; earning positive returns.
- *Cost efficiency*—using resources well to operate at low cost.
- *Customer service*—meeting customer needs and maintaining loyalty.
- *Product quality*—producing high-quality goods or services.
- *Market share*—gaining a specific share of possible customers.
- *Human talent*—recruiting and maintaining a high-quality workforce.
- *Innovation*—developing new products and processes.

Well-chosen operating objectives can turn a broad mission into specific performance targets. In the case of Patagonia, mission, values, and operating objectives fit together as a coherent whole. Chouinard says that he wants to run Patagonia "so that it's here 100 years from now and always makes the best-quality stuff." Although one of the firm's objectives is revenue growth, this doesn't mean growth at any cost. Chouinard's objective is modest growth, not extreme or uncontrolled growth.[21]

SWOT Analysis of Organization and Environment

A technique known as **SWOT analysis** is a useful first step in analyzing the organization and its environment. As **Figure 10.4** describes, it is an internal analysis of *organizational strengths and weaknesses* as well as an external analysis of *environmental opportunities and threats*. Although the following examples and discussion apply SWOT to organizations, you can also apply it in your own career and life planning.

> A **SWOT analysis** examines organizational strengths and weaknesses and environmental opportunities and threats.

A SWOT analysis begins with a systematic evaluation of the organization's resources and capabilities—its basic strengths and weaknesses. You can think of this as an analysis of organizational capacity to achieve its objectives. Strategies should ideally build on strengths and minimize the negative impact of weaknesses.

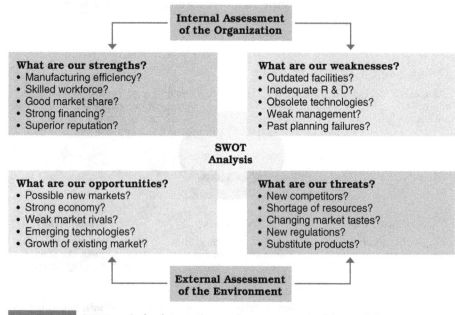

FIGURE 10.4   **SWOT analysis of strengths, weaknesses, opportunities, and threats.**

A **core competency** is a special strength that gives an organization a competitive advantage.

A major goal in SWOT analysis is to identify **core competencies**—things the organization does exceptionally well in comparison with competitors. They are capabilities that—by virtue of being rare, costly to imitate, and not substitutable—become potential sources of competitive advantage.[22] An organization's core competencies may be found in special knowledge or expertise, superior technologies, efficient supply chains, or unique distribution systems, among many other possibilities. As an individual, core competencies may include your unique combination of intelligence, knowledge, experience, personality, and enthusiasm.

Organizational weaknesses represent the other end of the competency spectrum. The goal here is to identify things that inhibit performance and hold the organization back from fully accomplishing its objectives. Examples might be outdated products, lack of financial capital, shortage of talented workers, and outdated technology. At the individual level, weaknesses may include limited work experience, poor interpersonal and communication skills, or a lack of technical expertise. Once weaknesses are identified, plans can be set to eliminate or reduce them, or turn them into strengths. Even if some weaknesses cannot be corrected, it is important that they be understood.

No SWOT analysis is complete until opportunities and threats in the external environment also are assessed. As shown in Figure 10.4, opportunities may be present as possible new markets, a strong economy, weaknesses in competitors, and emerging technologies. Environmental threats may include the emergence of new competitors, resource scarcities, changing customer tastes, new government regulations, and a weak economy. It's important here to remember the career implications. After all, your career environment holds also both opportunities and

---

Choices: Think before You Act | "You and your classmates will likely be expected to operate on a more sophisticated level than graduates of past decades."

Today's Graduates Must "Jump Right In"

Daxus/iStock/Getty Images

When you hear the term "sunrise industry," you think upbeat, on the move, one to watch. When you hear the term "sunset industry," you think on the decline, past prime, watch out. Now, think strategically. Picture yourself as an industry. Are you "sunrise" or "sunset"? And, what can you do now to make sure that you are on the right side when answering this question?

A *Wall Street Journal* survey of employers confirms that technical skills are changing fast. It's a bit like the popular TV show *Project Runway*: One day you're in and the next day you're out. The report goes on to say that employers want "fast learners who can quickly evolve and have exceptional soft skills—the ability to write, listen and communicate effectively." In other words, when the sun

is setting it's time to muster all of your learning capacities and face the sunrise ready to conquer a new day.

Here's a summary of career advice from top CEOs in a variety of industries:

- "People sniff out BS. ... No one likes a phony. Don't be a different person at work." *Mandy Ginzberg, Match Group Inc.*
- "Having the capacity to engage with people and understand their perspectives is really critical." *Mark Hoplamazian, Hyatt Hotels Corp.*
- "Before taking a new role, ask: 'What if I didn't take that job? What if I tried something else?'" *Gary Erickson and Kit Crawford, Clif Bar & Co.*
- "The boss makes all the difference. ... Pick you early bosses wisely. A good test: Do you even like them?" *Barbara Corcoran, Barbara Corcoran Inc.*
- "Dig in. Don't treat your job as a temporary stop. ... Too many people are always thinking about the next job." *Laura Alber, Williams Sonoma*

Your Take?

How would you turn the advice just given into a set of "guidelines" for your behavior in a new job? What do you self-assess as personal strengths and weaknesses based on this list? Make a list of your "hard skills"—the technical ones. Then list your "soft skills"—the ones the *WSJ* survey suggests are most likely to help you in the long term. What are the implications of these lists? Perhaps most important of all: Are you a "fast learner" prepared to continuously update and improve yourself to stay a step ahead of the changes taking place in our fast-paced environment?

threats–present and future. What does a SWOT analysis of your strategic readiness for career entry or advancement look like? What actions does it suggest to best prepare for the future you want? What classes should you take? What internships should you apply for?

Five Forces Analysis of Industry Attractiveness

The ideal strategic setting for any firm is to operate in *monopoly conditions* as the only player in an industry—to have no rivals to compete with for resources or customers. But this is rare except in highly regulated settings. The reality for most businesses is intense rivalry either under conditions of *oligopoly*—facing just a few competitors such as in airlines, or *hypercompetition*—facing several direct competitors such as in the fast-food industry.[23]

Both oligopoly and hypercompetition are strategically challenging. Harvard scholar and consultant Michael Porter offers a "five forces" framework for understanding competition within an industry and developing strategies to deal with it.[24] Porter's five forces of "industry structure" are:

1. *Industry competition*—the intensity of rivalry among firms in the industry and the ways they behave competitively toward one another.

2. *New entrants*—the threat of new competitors entering the market, based on the presence or absence of barriers to entry.

3. *Substitute products or services*—the threat of substitute products or services, or the ability of customers to get what they want from other sellers.

4. *Bargaining power of suppliers*—the ability of resource suppliers to influence the price that a firm has to pay for their products or services.

5. *Bargaining power of customers*—the ability of customers to influence the price that they will pay for the firm's products or services.

As shown in **Figure 10.5**, Porter suggests that the status of the five forces determines an industry's attractiveness or potential to generate long-term business returns. The less attractive

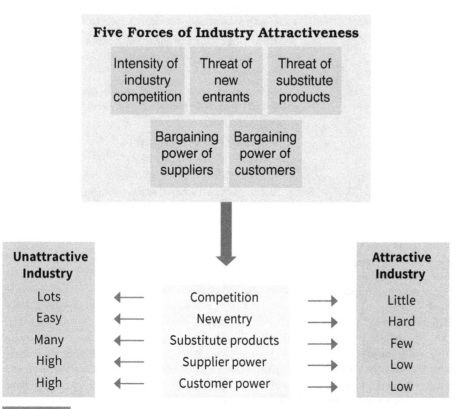

FIGURE 10.5 **Porter's model of five strategic forces affecting industry attractiveness.**

the industry structure, the harder it is to generate sustained competitive advantage. According to a five forces analysis, an *unattractive industry* has intense rivalry among competitors, faces substantial threats from new entrants and substitute products, and deals with suppliers and buyers having bargaining power over price and quality. An *attractive industry*, by contrast, has less competition, fewer threats from new entrants or substitutes, and lower supplier and buyer bargaining power.

Learning Check

LEARNING OBJECTIVE 10.2

Identify the essential elements in strategic analysis.

Be Sure You Can • explain how a good mission statement helps organizations relate to stake-holders • define *core values* and *organizational culture* • List several operating objectives for organizations • define *core competency* • explain SWOT analysis • use Porter's five forces model to assess the attractiveness of an industry

---

10.3 | Corporate-Level Strategy Formulation

WileyPLUS

See Author Video

LEARNING OBJECTIVE 10.3

Explain alternative corporate strategies.

> **Learn More About**
>
> Portfolio planning model • Growth and diversification strategies • Retrenchment and restructuring strategies • Global strategies • Cooperative strategies

It's easy to find examples of organizations choosing and changing courses of action in search of the best strategy—one that keeps them moving forward in a complex and ever-changing competitive environment. Think of this the next time you want to watch a movie or TV show at home. This is a fast-moving and highly competitive landscape where Netflix, Apple, Amazon, and the cable and entertainment companies battle to capture and retain your attention. They have to constantly worry about and deal with one another, as well as with startups that offer alternatives to their products.

Portfolio Planning Model

Alphabet's CEO Sundar Pichai faces a difficult strategic question all the time: How should he allocate resources across the firm's diverse mix of businesses, each with it's own goals, problems, and opportunities? Heading what started out as a search engine and software company, Pichai now has to manage everything from Google search to YouTube to robotics to smart homes to wind farms to self-driving cars, and more.[25] That's his strategic leadership challenge.

If you think about it, Pichai's strategic issues are similar to those we face in our own lives. How, for example, do you create a good mix of cash, stocks, bonds, and real estate investments? What do you buy more of, what do you sell, and what do you hold? Executives ask and try to answer such questions all the time. They are *portfolio-planning* questions, and they have major strategic implications. Shouldn't they be made systematically rather than randomly?[26]

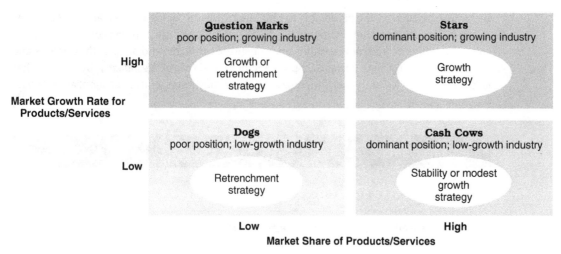

FIGURE 10.6 The BCG Matrix approach for portfolio planning in corporate-level strategy formulation.

The Boston Consulting Group became quite famous for developing a strategic planning approach known as the **BCG Matrix** and shown in **Figure 10.6**. Although more complicated models are available, the BCG Matrix is a good foundation for understanding the portfolio planning approach to making resource allocation decisions. It focuses strategic analysis on two major questions: (1) What is the market growth rate for the industry? (2) What market share is held by the firm?[27] Answers to these questions sort businesses or products into four strategic types: Dogs, Stars, Question Marks, and Cash Cows. Each type comes with a recommended core or master strategy.[28]

BCG Matrix analyzes business opportunities according to market growth rate and market share.

- *Grow the Stars*. Businesses or products with high market shares in high-growth markets are "Stars" in the BCG Matrix. They produce large profits through substantial penetration of expanding markets. The preferred strategy for Stars is growth, and the BCG Matrix recommends making further resource investments in them. Not only are Stars high performers in the present—they offer similar potential for the future.

- *Milk the Cash Cows*. Businesses or products with high-market shares in low-growth markets are "Cash Cows" in the BCG Matrix. They produce good profits and a strong cash flow, but with little upside potential. Because the markets offer limited growth opportunity, the preferred strategy for Cash Cows is stability or modest growth. Like real dairy cows, the BCG Matrix advises firms to "milk" these businesses. They should invest just enough to keep them stable or growing just a bit. This keeps them generating cash that can be reinvested in other more promising areas.

- *Grow or Retrench the Question Marks*. Businesses or products with low-market shares in high-growth markets are "Question Marks" in the BCG Matrix. Although they may not generate much profit at the moment, the upside potential is there because of the growing markets. But nothing is guaranteed. Question Marks make for difficult strategic decision making. The BCG Matrix recommends targeting only the most promising Question Marks for growth, while retrenching those that are less promising.

- *Retrench the Dogs*. Businesses or products with low-market shares in low-growth markets are "Dogs" in the BCG Matrix. They produce little if any profit, and they have low potential for future improvement. The preferred strategy for Dogs in the BCG Matrix is retrenchment.

Growth and Diversification Strategies

Among the core or master strategies just illustrated in the BCG Matrix, **growth strategies** expand the size and scope of operations. The goal is to increase total revenue, product or service lines, and operating locations. When you hear terms like "acquisition," "merger," and "global

A **growth strategy** involves expansion of the organization's current operations.

Get and Stay Ahead with Critical Thinking

Managers face significant challenges as they try to move their organizations forward with success in increasingly complex and ever-changing environments. When the environment is complex and uncertain, **critical thinking** skills are especially important. They help us to gather, organize, analyze, and interpret information to make good decisions in situations that range from difficult to totally perplexing.

The case studies and problem-solving projects in your courses help to develop your critical thinking skills. But beware—a lot of information in circulation on and off the Internet is anecdotal, superficial, irrelevant, and often just plain inaccurate. You have to be disciplined, cautious, and discerning when interpreting the credibility and usefulness of available information. In other words, you must be good at critical thinking.

The same critical thinking that is part of a rigorous class discussion or case study in your course is what helps managers create strategies that result in competitive advantage. But managers rarely have the luxury of full information boxed up for analysis in a nice, neat case format. Many life and career events are a lot like puzzles—everything looks pretty easy until you sit down and try to put all the pieces together. Are your critical thinking skills up to the challenges of the constantly changing competitive landscape? How good are you at making critical connections in unusual situations? For starters, take a stab at the two puzzles shown here.

Puzzle 1
Divide this shape into four shapes that are exactly the same size as one another.

Puzzle 2
Draw no more than four lines that cross all nine dots; don't lift your pencil while drawing.

Get To Know Yourself Better

Is your personal career strategy well attuned to the future job market, and not just the present one? Are you showing strong critical thinking skills as you make academic choices and prepare for your career? Make a list of information you need to make solid career choices. Identify where you can obtain this information and how credible these information sources are. Write a short plan that outlines how you'll use this information and that commits you to activities in this academic year that can improve your career readiness.

---

expansion," for example, they indicate a growth strategy. It's a common and popular business strategy. And although there is a tendency to equate growth with effectiveness, organizations can get caught in an "expansion trap" where growth outruns the capacity to manage it.

Organizations pursue growth strategies in a variety of ways. One approach is **concentration**—expanding in the same business area. McDonald's, Dollar General, Auto Zone, and others pursue growth strategies by adding locations while still concentrating on their primary businesses. And as their domestic markets become saturated, some aggressively expand around the world to find new customers and push sales growth.

*Growth through **concentration** is within the same business area.*

Another way to grow is through **diversification**—expanding into different business areas. A strategy of *related diversification* pursues growth by acquiring new businesses or entering business areas similar to what one already does. An example is Starbucks' purchase of Evolution Fresh. This acquisition helped Starbucks grow by expanding in-store product lines. A strategy of *unrelated diversification* pursues growth by acquiring businesses or entering business areas that are different from what one already does. India's Tata Group, for example, owns Eight O'Clock Coffee and Tetley Tea as well as Jaguar and Land Rover.

*Growth through **diversification** is by acquisition of or investment in new and different business areas.*

Growth by diversification is sometimes done by **vertical integration** where a business moves upstream farther from customers to acquire suppliers—*backward vertical integration*, or moves downstream closer to customers to acquire distributors—*forward vertical integration*. Examples of backward vertical integration include Apple Computer buying chip manufacturers to give it more privacy and sophistication in developing microprocessors, and Delta Airlines buying an oil refinery to supply part of its aviation fuel needs. Examples of forward vertical integration include Coca-Cola and PepsiCo owning major bottlers that make drinks from their concentrates and distribute their products regionally.[29] Even a trip to the local farmers' market shows forward vertical integration. All those stands of vegetables and fruits are run by farmers moving downstream to distribute their produce directly to customers.

*Growth through **vertical integration** occurs by acquiring upstream suppliers or downstream distributors.*

Retrenchment and Restructuring Strategies

When organizations are in trouble and experiencing problems brought about by a bad economy or too much growth and diversification, the focus shifts toward **retrenchment** and **restructuring**. These are **turnaround strategies** that pursue radical changes—changes in management, ownership, size, operations—to solve problems. At one end of the extreme a firm may be unable to pay its bills. In some cases retrenchment may take the form of **Chapter 11 bankruptcy**, which under U.S. law gives firms protection while they reorganize to restore solvency. In other cases an insolvent firm goes into outright **liquidation**, where business ceases and assets are sold off to pay creditors.

Short of bankruptcy and liquidation, distressed organizations can try other retrenchment strategies to get back on a path toward competitiveness. Restructuring by **downsizing** reduces size, often by drastically reducing the workforce.[30] When you hear about organizations downsizing, however, you should be skeptical of "across-the-board" cuts. Research shows that downsizing is most successful when cutbacks are done selectively and with specific performance objectives. The term *rightsizing* is sometimes used to describe downsizing with a clear strategic focus.[31]

Restructuring by **divestiture** involves selling off parts of the organization to refocus on core competencies, cut costs, and improve operating efficiency. You'll see this strategy followed by organizations that become overdiversified and whose executives have problems managing so much complexity. Did you know, for example, that eBay once bought Skype with high expectations and later sold it to private investors at a loss? To justify the sale eBay's CEO said: "Skype is a strong standalone business, but it does not have synergies with our e-commerce and online payments business."[32] In other words, the Skype purchase was a costly and bad idea.

> **Retrenchment, restructuring,** and **turnaround strategies** pursue radical changes to solve problems.
>
> **Chapter 11 bankruptcy** under U.S. law protects a firm from creditors while management reorganizes to restore solvency.
>
> **Liquidation** is where a business closes and sells its assets to pay creditors.
>
> A **downsizing** strategy decreases the size of operations.
>
> **Divestiture** sells off parts of the organization to refocus attention on core business areas.

Global Strategies

A key issue in corporate strategy is how to embrace the global economy and its mix of business risks and opportunities.[33] An easy way to spot differences in global strategies is to notice how products are developed and advertised around the world. A firm pursuing a **globalization strategy** tends to view the world as one large integrated market. It makes most decisions from the corporate headquarters and tries as much as possible to standardize products and advertising for use everywhere. The latest Gillette razors from Procter & Gamble, for example, are likely to be sold and advertised similarly around the world.

Firms using a **multidomestic strategy** try to customize products and advertising as much as possible in order to fit local preferences. McDonald's is a good example. Although you can get your standard fries and Big Mac in most locations, you can have a McVeggie in India, a McArabia Kofta in Saudi Arabia, and a Croque McDo in France.

A third approach is the **transnational strategy**, where a firm tries to operate without a strong national identity and blend seamlessly with the global economy. Resources and management talents are acquired worldwide, while manufacturing and other business functions are located wherever in the world they can be accomplished at the lowest cost. Ford is an example. Its global strategy uses design, manufacturing, and distribution expertise all over the world to build core car platforms using common parts and components. These platforms produce cars like the Focus and Fiesta that are then sold around the world with slight modifications to meet regional tastes.

> A **globalization strategy** adopts standardized products and advertising for use worldwide.
>
> A **multidomestic strategy** customizes products and advertising to best fit local needs.
>
> A **transnational strategy** seeks efficiencies of global operations with attention to local markets.

Cooperative Strategies

It's quite common today to hear about **strategic alliances** where two or more organizations join in a targeted partnership to pursue an area of mutual interest. This is basically a strategy of cooperating for common gains. In an *outsourcing alliance*, one organization contracts to purchase important services, perhaps IT or human resources, from another. In a *supplier alliance*, preferred supplier relationships guarantee a smooth and timely flow of quality supplies among

> In a **strategic alliance**, organizations join in partnership to pursue an area of mutual interest.

partners. In a *distribution alliance*, firms join together as partners to sell and distribute products or services.

One interesting strategic direction is called **co-opetition**, or strategic alliances among competitors.[34] The idea is that organizations can still cooperate even as they compete with one another. The airline industry is a great example. United Airlines and Lufthansa are major international competitors, but they also cooperate as "Star Alliance" partners. The alliance provides customers code-sharing on flights and shared frequent-flyer programs. There's also co-opetition in the auto industry, where the cost of developing new technologies provides the stimulus to cooperate. Daimler cooperates with BMW to co-develop new motors and components for hybrid cars; it cooperates with Nissan to co-develop electric car batteries.[35]

Learning Check

LEARNING OBJECTIVE 10.3

Explain alternative corporate strategies.

Be Sure You Can • describe the BCG Matrix as a strategic portfolio planning tool • list and explain the major types of growth and diversification strategies • list and explain the major types of retrenchment and restructuring strategies • list and give examples of global strategies • define *strategic alliance* and explain cooperation as a business strategy

10.4 Business-Level Strategy Formulation

LEARNING OBJECTIVE 10.4

Explain alternative business-level strategies.

> **Learn More About**
>
> Competitive strategies model • Differentiation strategy • Cost leadership strategy • Focus strategy

Harvard's Michael Porter says that "the company without a strategy is willing to try anything."[36] But with a good strategy in place, he believes a business can achieve superior profitability or above-average returns within its industry. The key question in formulating business-level strategy is: "How can we best compete for customers in our market and with our products or services?"

Competitive Strategies Model

Figure 10.7 shows Porter's model for choosing competitive strategies based on the market scope of products or services, and the source of competitive advantage for the product or service. With respect to *market scope*, the strategic planner asks: "How broad or narrow is the market or target market?" With respect to *source of competitive advantage*, the question is: "Do we seek competitive advantage primarily through low price or through product uniqueness?" Answers to these questions create a matrix of the four business-level strategies listed here and shown in Figure 10.7.

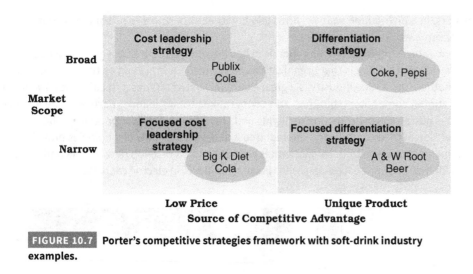

FIGURE 10.7 Porter's competitive strategies framework with soft-drink industry examples.

- *Differentiation*—Make products that are unique and different.
- *Cost leadership*—Produce at lower cost and sell at lower price.
- *Focused differentiation*—Use differentiation and target needs of a special market.
- *Focused cost leadership*—Use cost leadership and target needs of a special market.

Differentiation Strategy

A **differentiation strategy** seeks competitive advantage through uniqueness. This means developing goods and services that are clearly different from the competition. The strategic objective is to attract customers who stay loyal to the firm's products and lose interest in competitors.

Success with a differentiation strategy requires organizational strengths in marketing, research and development, and creativity. An example in the apparel industry is Polo Ralph Lauren, retailer of upscale classic fashions and accessories. In Ralph Lauren's words, "Polo redefined how American style and quality is perceived. Polo has always been about selling quality products by creating worlds and inviting our customers to be part of our dream."[37]

The differentiation strategy examples in Figure 10.7 are Coke and Pepsi from the soft drinks industry. These firms continually battle for customer attention and loyalty. Although part of their differentiation may be actual taste, another part is pure perception. Coke and Pepsi spend enormous amounts on advertising to create beliefs that their products are somehow distinctly different from one another.

> A **differentiation strategy** offers products that are unique and different from the competition.

Cost Leadership Strategy

A **cost leadership strategy** seeks competitive advantage by operating with lower costs than competitors. This allows organizations to make profits selling products or services at low prices their competitors can't profitably match. The objective is to continuously improve operating efficiencies in purchasing, production, distribution, and other organizational systems.

Success with the cost leadership strategy requires tight cost and managerial controls, as well as products or services that are easy to create and distribute. This is what might be called the "Walmart" strategy—a firm takes every possible step to keep costs so low that they can offer customers the lowest prices and still make a reasonable profit. The example in Figure 10.7 is Publix Cola, where because of economies of scale and branding these beverages can be offered at a fraction of the cost of "name brand" alternatives. An example from the financial services industry is the Vanguard Group. It keeps operating costs low to attract customers who want buy mutual funds with low expense ratios and minimum fees.

> A **cost leadership strategy** seeks to operate with low cost so that products can be sold at low prices.

You might be wondering if it's possible to combine cost leadership with differentiation. Porter says, "No." He refers to this combination as a *stuck-in-the-middle strategy* and believes it is rarely successful because differentiation increases costs. "You can compete on price or you can compete on product, but you can't compete on both," marketers tend to say. Porter agrees.

Focus Strategy

A **focus strategy** concentrates on serving a unique market segment better than anyone else.

A **focused differentiation strategy** offers a unique product to a special market segment.

A **focused cost leadership** strategy seeks the lowest costs of operations within a special market segment.

A **focus strategy** concentrates attention on a special market segment in the form of a niche customer group, geographical region, or product/service line. The objective is to serve the needs of the segment better than anyone else. Competitive advantage is achieved by combining focus with either differentiation or cost leadership.[38]

NetJets offers private, secure, and luxury air travel for those who can pay a high fee, such as wealthy media stars and executives. This is a **focused differentiation strategy** because the firm sells a unique product to a special niche market. Also in airlines, carriers such as Ryan Air and Easy Jet in Europe offer heavily discounted fares and "no-frills" flying. This is a **focused cost leadership** strategy because it offers low prices to attract budget travelers. The airlines still make profits by keeping costs low. They fly to regional airports and cut out free services such as bag checks and in-flight snacks.[39]

Figure 10.7 shows both types of focus strategies in the soft drink industry. Specialty drinks such as A&W Root Beer, Dr. Pepper, and Mountain Dew represent the focused differentiation strategy. Each focuses on a special market segment and tries to compete on the basis of product uniqueness. Drinks like Big K Diet Cola represent the focused cost leadership strategy. They also focus on special market segments, but try to compete by keeping operating costs low so that their soda brands can be profitably sold to consumers at low prices.

LEARNING OBJECTIVE 10.4

Explain alternative business-level strategies.

Be Sure You Can • list and explain the four competitive strategies in Porter's model • explain the differences between focused differentiation and focused cost leadership strategies • clarify the roles of both price and cost in a cost leadership strategy • illustrate how Porter's competitive strategies apply to products in a market familiar to you

10.5 Strategy Implementation

LEARNING OBJECTIVE 10.5

Describe the foundations for strategy implementation.

WileyPLUS

See Author Video

> **Learn More About**
> Management practices and systems • Strategic control and corporate governance • Strategic leadership

A discussion of the corporate history on Patagonia, Inc.'s website includes this statement: ". . . we've made many mistakes but we've never lost our way for very long."[40] Not only is the firm being honest in the information it shares with the public, it also is communicating an important point about strategic management—mistakes will be made. Sometimes those mistakes will be in poor strategy selection. Other times they will be failures of implementation caused by poor management practices and systems, failures in control and governance, or inadequate strategic leadership.

Management Practices and Systems

In order to successfully put strategy into action, the entire organization and its resources must be mobilized in support. This involves the complete management process—from planning and controlling through organizing and leading. No matter how well or elegantly conceived, a strategy requires supporting structures and workflows staffed by talented people. The strategy needs leaders who motivate employees so that individuals and teams do their best work. The strategy also needs to be properly monitored and controlled to ensure that the desired results are achieved.

Failures of substance in strategic management show up in poor analysis and bad strategy selection. *Failures of process* reflect poor handling of the ways strategic management is accomplished. A common process failure is the **lack of participation error**. It shows up as a lack of commitment and follow-through by those excluded from the strategic planning process.[41] Another process failure is *goal displacement*. This is the tendency to get so bogged down in details that the planning process becomes an end in itself, rather than a means to an end.

Lack of participation error is a failure to include key persons in strategic planning.

Strategic Control and Corporate Governance

Strategic control makes sure strategies are well implemented and that poor strategies are scrapped or modified.

Top managers exercise **strategic control** by making sure strategies are well implemented and that poor strategies are scrapped or modified quickly to meet performance demands of changing conditions. We expect them to always be "in control"—measuring results, evaluating the success of existing strategies, and taking action to improve things. Yet the financial crisis and recent economic recession showed that strategic control was inadequate at many firms, including the automakers and big banks.

Corporate governance is the system of control and performance monitoring of top management.

When strategic control fails at the level of top management, it is supposed to kick in at the level of **corporate governance**. This is the system of control and monitoring of top management performance exercised by boards of directors in business firms and boards of trustees in nonprofits. Corporate governance is intended to ensure that the strategic management of the organization is successful.[42] But, boards are sometimes too compliant and uncritical in endorsing or confirming what top management is doing. Instead of questioning, criticizing, and requiring change, they condone the status quo. Weak corporate governance doesn't subject top management to rigorous oversight and accountability. The result is organizations that end up doing the wrong things, doing bad things, or just performing poorly.

When governance fails, blame sometimes can be traced back to the composition of the board and expectations for how it operates. Most boards consist of *inside directors* chosen from senior management and *outside directors* chosen from other organizations. In some boards insiders are too powerful, and the CEO may even be the board chairperson. In others the board lacks outside members whose skills match with the organization's strategic challenges. In still others board members may be insufficiently observant or critical because

---

Ethics: Know Right from Wrong | The work is meaningless, no conversation is allowed on the production lines, and bathroom breaks are limited.

Can the Sharing Economy Create Good Jobs?

M4OS Photos/Alamy Stock Photo

The advice is increasingly frequent in everyday conversation. Need a ride? Call Lyft or Uber instead of a taxi. Need a small job done in your home or business? Go online with TaskRabbit and book a "tasker" ready to jump on it. Need someone to watch your dog while you take a long weekend in the city? Let DogVacay match you with a nearby dog sitter. And there's more to come in the "gig" or "sharing"

economy with its boundless opportunities for Web-driven business innovation.

A fast growing number of U.S. workers are active on shared economy platforms. Some are supplementing full-time jobs with extra income, some are covering expenses because they can't find traditional full-time employment, while others are working this way because they like the flexibility. But the naysayers are there. Even though clients seem delighted for the most part, many wonder if this sharing economy is really good for workers.

Most of those driving the cars, doing the tasks, and walking the pets work without the benefits and legal protections that traditional workers enjoy. One columnist argues: "It is a great deal for the owners, but a bad one for workers." Critics say that the sharing economy contributes to income disparity between those holding really good jobs with attractive futures and those doing as-available jobs for low pay and few long-term growth prospects.

What Do You Think?

The sharing economy is here, but what are its implications for large and small employers, career seekers, and society at large? Is this a hot spot for innovation and eventual job creation, or is it another sign that income inequalities are here to stay? How can the sharing economy be turned into a strategic opportunity that benefits employers and workers alike?

they are friends of top management. Current directions to strengthen board oversight and control of management include separating the roles of CEO and board chair, appointing outside directors with relevant expertise, and having board members take on more active leadership roles.[43]

Strategic Leadership

Ford's former CEO Alan Mulally led the company out of recession and back onto a path toward growth. Paul Ingrassia, an auto analyst, called his success "one of the great turnarounds in corporate history" and praised Mulally's efforts "to simplify, relentlessly and systematically, a business that had grown way too complicated and costly to be managed effectively."[44] What Mulally showed at Ford is **strategic leadership**—the capability to inspire people to successfully engage in a process of continuous change, performance enhancement, and implementation of organization strategies.[45]

One of the big lessons learned in studying how businesses perform during economic crisis is that a strategic leader has to maintain strategic control. This means that the CEO and top management should always be in touch with the strategy. They must know how well it is being implemented, whether the strategy is generating success or failure, and if the strategy needs to be modified or changed. The following list identifies other key responsibilities of strategic leadership.[46]

> **Strategic leadership** inspires people to continuously change, refine, and improve strategies and their implementation.

- *A strategic leader has to be the guardian of trade-offs*. It is the leader's job to ensure that the organization's resources are allocated in ways that are consistent with the strategy. This requires the discipline to sort through many competing ideas and alternatives, to stay on course, and not to get sidetracked.
- *A strategic leader needs to create a sense of urgency*. The leader can't allow the organization and its members to grow slow and complacent. Even when doing well, the leader retains focus on getting better and being alert to conditions that require adjustments to the strategy.
- *A strategic leader needs to make sure that everyone understands the strategy*. Unless strategies are understood, the daily tasks and contributions of individuals and teams lose context and purpose. Everyone might work very hard, but without alignment to strategy the impact is dispersed and fails to advance common goals.
- *A strategic leader needs to be a teacher*. It is the leader's job to teach the strategy and make it a "cause." In order for strategy to work, it must become an ever-present commitment throughout the organization. This means that a strategic leader must be a great communicator. Everyone must understand the strategy and how it makes their organization different from others.

Learning Check

LEARNING OBJECTIVE 10.5

Describe the foundations for strategy implementation.

Be Sure You Can • explain how the management process supports strategy implementation • define *corporate governance* • explain why boards of directors sometimes fail in their governance responsibilities • define *strategic control* and *strategic leadership* • list the responsibilities of a strategic leader in today's organizations

Management Learning Review: Get Prepared for Quizzes and Exams

Summary

LEARNING OBJECTIVE 10.1 Discuss the process and importance of strategic management.

- Competitive advantage is achieved by operating in ways that allow an organization to outperform its rivals; a competitive advantage is sustainable when it is difficult for competitors to imitate.

- A strategy is a comprehensive plan that sets long-term direction and guides resource allocation for sustainable competitive advantage.

- Corporate strategy sets direction for an entire organization; business strategy sets direction for a business division or product/service line; functional strategy sets direction for the operational support of business and corporate strategies.

- Strategic management is the process of formulating and implementing strategies that achieve goals in a competitive environment.

For Discussion Can an organization have a good strategy and still fail to achieve competitive advantage?

LEARNING OBJECTIVE 10.2 Identify the essential elements in strategic analysis.

- The strategic management process begins with analysis of mission, clarification of core values, and identification of objectives.

- A SWOT analysis systematically assesses organizational strengths and weaknesses, and environmental opportunities and threats.

- Porter's five forces model analyzes industry attractiveness in terms of competitive rivalry, new entrants, substitute products, and the bargaining powers of suppliers and buyers.

For Discussion Would a monopoly get a perfect score for industry attractiveness in Porter's five forces model?

LEARNING OBJECTIVE 10.3 Explain alternative corporate strategies.

- Growth strategies pursue greater sales and broader markets by concentration that expands in related product or business areas, and diversification that expands in new and different product and business areas.

- Restructuring strategies pursue ways to correct performance problems by such means as liquidation, bankruptcy, downsizing, divestiture, and turnaround.

- Global firms take advantage of international business opportunities through globalization, multidomestic, and transnational strategies.

- Cooperative strategies create strategic alliances with other organizations to achieve mutual gains, including such things as outsourcing alliances, supplier alliances, and even co-opetition among competitors.

- The BCG Matrix is a portfolio planning approach that classifies businesses or product lines as "Stars," "Cash Cows," "Question Marks," or "Dogs" for purposes of strategy formulation.

For Discussion Is it good news or bad news for investors when a firm announces that it is restructuring? Why?

LEARNING OBJECTIVE 10.4 Explain alternative business-level strategies.

- Potential sources of competitive advantage in business-level strategy formulation are found in things like lower costs, better quality, more knowledge, greater speed, and strong financial resources.

- Porter's model of competitive strategy bases the choice of business-level strategies on two major considerations—market scope of product or service, and source of competitive advantage for the product or service.

- A differentiation strategy seeks competitive advantage by offering unique products and services that are clearly different from those of competitors.

- A cost leadership strategy seeks competitive advantage by operating at low costs that allow products and services to be sold to customers at low prices.

- A focus strategy seeks competitive advantage by serving the needs of a special market segment or niche better than anyone else; it can be done as focused differentiation or focused cost leadership.

For Discussion Can a business ever be successful with a combined cost leadership and differentiation strategy?

LEARNING OBJECTIVE 10.5   Describe the foundations for strategy implementation.

- Management practices and systems—including the functions of planning, organizing, leading, and controlling—must be mobilized to support strategy implementation.
- Pitfalls that inhibit strategy implementation include failures of substance—such as poor analysis of the environment; and failures of process—such as lack of participation by key players in the planning process.

- Boards of directors play important roles in control through corporate governance, including monitoring how well top management fulfills strategic management responsibilities.
- Top managers exercise strategic control by making sure strategies are well implemented and are changed if not working.
- Strategic leadership inspires the process of continuous evaluation and improvement of strategies and their implementation.

For Discussion Can strategic leadership by top managers make up for poor corporate governance by board members? Why or why not?

Self-Test 10

Multiple-Choice Questions

1. The most appropriate first question to ask in strategic planning is _____.

   a. "Where do we want to be in the future?"

   b. "How well are we currently doing?"

   c. "How can we get where we want to be?"

   d. "Why aren't we doing better?"

2. The ability of a firm to consistently outperform its rivals is called _____.

   a. vertical integration   c. incrementalism

   b. competitive advantage   d. strategic intent

3. In a complex conglomerate such as General Electric that owns a large number of different businesses, a(n) _____ level strategy sets strategic direction for a strategic business unit.

   a. institutional   c. corporate

   b. business   d. functional

4. The _____ is a predominant value system for an organization as a whole.

   a. strategy   c. core competency

   b. mission   d. corporate culture

5. Cost efficiency and product quality are two examples of _____ objectives of organizations.

   a. official   c. operating

   b. informal   d. institutional

6. An organization that is downsizing by laying off workers to reduce costs is implementing a _____ strategy.

   a. growth   c. restructuring

   b. cost differentiation d. vertical integration

7. When PepsiCo acquired Tropicana, a maker of orange juice, the firm's strategy was growth by _____.

   a. related diversification c. vertical integration

   b. concentration   d. cooperation

8. In Porter's five forces framework, having _____ increases industry attractiveness.

   a. many rivals

   b. many substitute products

   c. low bargaining power of suppliers

   d. few barriers to entry

9. A _____ in the BCG Matrix would have a high market share in a low-growth market, and the correct grand or master strategy is _____.

   a. Dog, growth   c. Question Mark, stability

   b. Cash Cow, stability d. Star, retrenchment

10. Strategic alliances that link together airlines in code sharing and joint marketing agreements are examples of how businesses can use _____ strategies.

   a. divestiture   c. cooperation

   b. growth   d. backward integration

11. The two questions asked by Porter to identify competitive strategies for a business or product line are: 1—What is the market scope? 2—What is the _____?

   a. market share

   b. source of competitive advantage

   c. core competency

   d. industry attractiveness

12. According to Porter's model of competitive strategies, a firm that wants to compete with its rivals in a broad market by selling a very low-priced product would need to successfully implement a _____ strategy.

   a. retrenchment   c. cost leadership

   b. differentiation d. diversification

13. When Coke and Pepsi spend millions on ads trying to convince customers that their products are unique, they are pursuing a _____ strategy.

   a. transnational   c. diversification

   b. concentration   d. differentiation

14. The role of the board of directors as an oversight body that holds top executives accountable for the success of business strategies is called _____.

    a. strategic leadership
    b. corporate governance
    c. logical incrementalism
    d. strategic opportunism

15. An example of a process failure in strategic planning is _____

    a. lack of participation
    b. weak mission statement
    c. bad core values
    d. insufficient financial resources

Short-Response Questions

16. What is the difference between corporate strategy and functional strategy?

17. What would a manager look at in a SWOT analysis?

18. What is the difference between focus and differentiation as competitive strategies?

19. What is strategic leadership?

Essay Question

20. Kim Harris owns and operates a small retail store selling the outdoor clothing of an American manufacturer to a predominately college-student market. Recently, a large department store outside of town has started selling similar but lower-priced clothing manufactured in China, Thailand, and Bangladesh. Kim believes she is starting to lose business to this store. Assume you are part of a student team assigned to do a management class project for Kim. Her question for the team is: "How can I best deal with my strategic management challenges in this situation?" How will you reply?

Career Skills & Competencies: Make Yourself Valuable!

Evaluate Career Situations

What Would You Do?

1. The Mission Statement

You've just been given a great assignment to serve as personal assistant to the company president of a mid-sized firm operating just outside a major U.S. city. It will last for six months and then, if you've done a good job, the expectation is you'll be moved into a fast-track management position. The president comes to you and says: "It's time to revisit the mission statement and our corporate values. Set things up for us." There are about a dozen people on the top management team and the company as a whole employs 700+, all in one location. How will you proceed to get the mission and values of this company updated?

2. Cooperate or Compete, or Both?

A neighborhood business association has this set of members: coffee shop, bookstore, drugstore, dress shop, hardware store, and bicycle shop. The owners of these businesses are interested in how they might cooperate for better success. As a business consultant to the association, what strategic alliances would you propose as ways to join sets of these businesses together for mutual gain?

3. Saving a Bookstore

For some years you've owned a small specialty bookshop in a college town. You sell some textbooks but mainly cater to a broader customer base. The store always has the latest fiction, nonfiction, and children's books in stock. You've recently experienced a steep decline in overall sales, even for those books that would normally be considered bestsellers. You suspect this is because of the growing popularity of e-books and e-readers such as the Amazon Kindle and Barnes & Noble Nook. Some of your friends say it's time to close the store and call it quits because your market is dying. Is it hopeless? Or, can a new business strategy save you?

Reflect on the Self-Assessment

Intuitive Ability

Instructions

Complete this survey as quickly as you can. Be honest with yourself. For each question, select the response that most appeals to you.[47]

1. When working on a project, do you prefer to
   (a) be told what the problem is but be left free to decide how to solve it?
   (b) get very clear instructions for how to go about solving the problem before you start?

2. When working on a project, do you prefer to work with colleagues who are
   (a) realistic?
   (b) imaginative?

3. Do you most admire people who are
   (a) creative?
   (b) careful?

4. Do the friends you choose tend to be
   (a) serious and hard working?
   (b) exciting and often emotional?

5. When you ask a colleague for advice on a problem you have, do you

    (a) seldom or never get upset if he or she questions your basic assumptions?

    (b) often get upset if he or she questions your basic assumptions?

6. When you start your day, do you

    (a) seldom make or follow a specific plan?

    (b) usually first make a plan to follow?

7. When working with numbers, do you find that you

    (a) seldom or never make factual errors?

    (b) often make factual errors?

8. Do you find that you

    (a) seldom daydream during the day and really don't enjoy doing so when you do it?

    (b) frequently daydream during the day and enjoy doing so?

9. When working on a problem, do you

    (a) prefer to follow the instructions or rules that are given to you?

    (b) often enjoy circumventing the instructions or rules that are given to you?

10. When you are trying to put something together, do you prefer to have

    (a) step-by-step written instructions on how to assemble the item?

    (b) a picture of how the item is supposed to look once assembled?

11. Do you find that the person who irritates you *the most* is the one who appears to be

    (a) disorganized?

    (b) organized?

12. When an unexpected crisis comes up that you have to deal with, do you

    (a) feel anxious about the situation?

    (b) feel excited by the challenge of the situation?

Scoring

Total the number of "a" responses selected for questions 1, 3, 5, 6, 11; enter the score here [a = _____]. Total the number of (b) responses for questions 2, 4, 7, 8, 9, 10, 12; enter the score here [b = _____]. Add your (a) and (b) scores and enter the sum here [a + b = _____]. This is your intuitive score. The highest possible intuitive score is 12; the lowest is 0.

Interpretation

In his book *Intuition in Organizations* (Newbury Park, CA: Sage, 1989), pages 10–11, Weston H. Agor states, "Traditional analytical techniques . . . are not as useful as they once were for guiding major decisions. . . . If you hope to be better prepared for tomorrow, then it only seems logical to pay some attention to the use and development of intuitive skills for decision making." Agor developed the preceding survey to help people assess their tendencies to use intuition in decision making. Your score offers a general indication of your strength in this area. It may also suggest a need to further develop your skill and comfort with more intuitive decision-making approaches.

Contribute to the Class Exercise

Strategic Scenarios

Preparation

In today's turbulent economic environment, it is no longer safe to assume that an organization that was highly successful in the past will continue to be so in the near future—or that it will even be in existence. Changing times exact the best from strategic planners. Think about the situations currently facing the following well-known organizations. Think, too, about the futures they may face in competitive markets.

Chipotle	National Public Radio
Apple Computer	*New York Times*
Netflix	Sony
Ann Taylor	Zynga
Domino's Pizza	AT&T
Nordstrom	Federal Express

Instructions

Form into groups. Choose one or more organizations from the list (or as assigned by your instructor) and answer for this organization the following questions:

1. What in the future might seriously threaten the success, perhaps the very existence, of this organization? As a group, develop at least three such *future scenarios*.

2. Estimate the probability (0% to 100%) of each future scenario occurring.

3. Develop a strategy for each scenario that will enable the organization to deal with it successfully.

Thoroughly discuss these questions within the group and arrive at your best possible consensus answers. Be prepared to share and defend your answers in general class discussion.

Manage a Critical Incident

Kickstarting a Friend's Business Idea

You've worked hard, made a fair amount of money, and have a nice stock portfolio. You're also known among your friends as "the guy with the money." As with lottery winners, you've become a bit of a target—some want handouts, some loans, and others just do their share of freeloading. But now one of your friends has come with a business proposal. She's just back from a trip to Southeast Asia and is raving about all the neat fabrics available in local markets in places like Cambodia, Thailand, and Vietnam. She's also a great fan of the TV show *Project Runway*. So, she wants to import fabrics, buy some sewing machines and materials, rent a small storefront, and set up a shop called The Design Place. The basic idea is that a customer can come in, find fabrics, use workspace, and then design and sew their own fashions. She thinks the idea will be a winner, but has come to your for advice and—she hopes—some startup financing.

Questions

What questions will you ask and what will you say to help your friend do a good strategic analysis of her business idea? Without knowing any more than you do now, what do you believe is the real strategic potential of The Design Place? Are there examples of do-it-yourself stores within other product spaces that could serve as guides for your evaluation and help in developing her business proposal?

Collaborate on the Team Project

Contrasting Strategies

Question

How do organizations in the same industry fare when they pursue similar or very different strategies?[48]

Instructions

1. Research recent news reports and analyst summaries for each of the following organizations:

- Southwest Airlines and Delta Airlines
- *New York Times* and *USA Today*
- Under Armour and Lululemon
- National Public Radio and Sirius XM Satellite Radio

- Tesla and General Motors
- Amazon and Alibaba

2. Use this information to write a short description of the strategies that each seems to be following in the quest for success.

3. Compare the strategies for each organizational pair. Identify whether or not, and why, one organization has a strategic advantage in the industry.

4. Choose other pairs of organizations and do similar strategic comparisons for them.

5. Prepare a summary report highlighting (a) the strategy comparisons and (b) suggestions on how organizations in the same industry can choose strategies to best compete with one another.

Analyze the Case Study

Dunkin' Donuts | Betting Dollars on Donuts

Go to **Management Cases for Critical Thinking** at the end of the book to find this case.

Organization Structures

Get There Faster with Objectives

David McNew/Getty Images

"Ask 100 randomly selected Americans, 'What is the biggest problem with American universities?' I would bet the most frequent answer would be, 'they cost too much'."

Richard K. Vedder, Distinguished Professor of Economics Emeritus at Ohio University and author of *Restoring the Promise: Higher Education in America* (2019).

Career Readiness – What to Look for **Inside**

Thought Leadership

Analysis > *Make Data Your Friend* Managers May Overestimate Their Managing Skills

Choices > *Think before You Act* Playing Musical Chairs to Increase Collaboration

Ethics > *Know Right from Wrong* Help! I've Been Flattened into Exhaustion

Insight > *Learn about Yourself* Empowerment Gets More Things Done

Skills Make You Valuable

- **Evaluate** *Career Situations:* What Would You Do?
- **Reflect** *On the Self-Assessment:* Empowering Others
- **Contribute** *To the Class Exercise:* Organizational Metaphors
- **Manage** *A Critical Incident:* Crowdsourcing Evaluations to Cut Management Levels
- **Collaborate** *On the Team Project:* Designing a Network University
- **Analyze** *The Case Study:* NPR: Many Voices Serving Many Needs

---

Chapter Quick Start

Organizing puts people together with resources to help achieve performance goals. Although organizations still make use of traditional structures, new approaches that are more horizontal, team-driven, and collaborative are increasingly common. Trends in organizational design are reshaping structures to best align people and tasks with demands of the new workplace.

LEARNING OBJECTIVES

11.1 Explain organizing as a management function and contrast formal and informal organization structures.

11.2 Identify the strengths and weaknesses of traditional organizational structures.

11.3 Identify the strengths and weaknesses of team, virtual, and network structures.

11.4 Discuss how and why organizational designs are changing in today's workplace.

217

It is much easier to talk about high-performing organizations than to create them. There is no one best way to do things. No one organizational form is the right choice for all environments and markets. And what works well at one moment in time can quickly become outdated or even dysfunctional in the next. This is why you often hear about organizations making changes to their structures in attempts to improve performance.

Management scholar and consultant Henry Mintzberg says that people need to understand how their organizations operate to work well in them.[1] Whenever job assignments and reporting relationships change, whenever an organization grows or shrinks, whenever old ways of doing things are reconfigured, people struggle to fit into new ways of working. They ask questions such as: "Who's in charge?" "How do the parts connect?" "How should processes and people come together?" "Whose ideas have to flow where?" They also worry about the implications of new arrangements for their job security and careers.

11.1 | Organizing as a Management Function

LEARNING OBJECTIVE 11.1

Explain organizing as a management function and contrast formal and informal organization structures.

> **Learn More About**
>
> What is organization structure? • Formal structures • Informal structures and social networks

Organizing arranges, connects, and integrates people and resources to accomplish a common purpose.

Organizing is the process of arranging, connecting, and integrating people and resources to accomplish a goal. Its purpose as one of the basic functions of management is a division of labor and coordination of processes and results to achieve a common purpose.

Figure 11.1 shows the role that organizing plays in the management process. Once plans are created, the manager's task is to ensure they are carried out. Once strategy is set and plans are made, organizing launches implementation and accomplishment by clarifying jobs and working relationships. It identifies who does what, who is in charge of whom, and how different people and parts of the organization relate to and work with one another. All of this can be done in many different ways. The challenge is to choose the best organizational form to fit the firm's strategy and other situational/market demands.

What Is Organization Structure?

Organization structure is a system of tasks, reporting relationships, and communication linkages.

The way in which the parts of an organization are arranged is usually referred to as **organization structure**. It is the system of tasks, workflows, reporting relationships, and communication

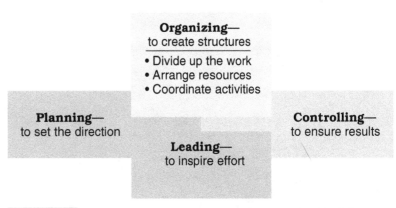

FIGURE 11.1 **Organizing viewed in relationship with the other management functions.**

channels connecting the work and activities of people and groups in a firm. An organization's structure should both allocate tasks through a division of labor and coordinate performance results. A structure that accomplishes both well helps accomplish an organization's strategy.[2] But as stated earlier, the problem for managers is that it is much easier to describe what a good structure does than it is to create one.

Formal Structures

You may know the concept of structure best in the form of an **organization chart**. It diagrams reporting relationships and work positions.[3] A typical organization chart identifies positions, job titles and the lines of authority and communication between them. It shows the **formal structure**, and how the organization is intended to function. But you have to interpret this information with caution. Charts can be useful . . . or confusing and out of date. At best, they provide a snapshot of how an organization is supposed to work in respect to:

- *Division of work*—Positions and titles show work responsibilities.
- *Supervisory relationships*—Lines show who reports to whom.
- *Communication channels*—Lines show formal communication flows.
- *Major subunits*—Positions reporting to a common manager are shown.
- *Levels of management*—Vertical layers of management are shown.

An **organization chart** describes the arrangement of work positions within an organization.

Formal structure is the official structure of the organization.

Informal Structures and Social Networks

Underneath an organization's formal structure is an **informal structure**. This is a "shadow" organization made up of social networks of unofficial, but important, working relationships connecting organizational members.

Look at **Figure 11.2**. No organization can be fully understood without understanding its web of informal networks as well as the formal organizational structure.[4] If the informal structure could be drawn, it would show who talks and interacts with whom, regardless of their formal titles and relationships. The lines of the informal structure cut across levels and move from side to side. They show people interacting through social media, meeting for coffee, joining in exercise groups, and participating in leisure activities—all driven by friendship rather than formal requirements.

A tool known as **social network analysis**, or **sociometrics**, is one way of identifying informal structures and social relationships.[5] This analysis can be done by surveys that ask people to identify others they ask for help most often, with whom they communicate regularly, and

Informal structure is the set of social networks found in unofficial relationships among the members of an organization.

Social network analysis or **sociometrics** identifies the informal structures and their embedded social relationships that are active in an organization.

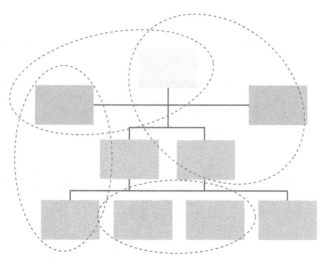

FIGURE 11.2 **Informal structures and the "shadow" organization.**

who give them energy and motivation.[6] It can also be done using data mined from an organization's social media sites, and even with data gathered from special electronic badges worn by employees and that record their interactions.[7] Lines are then drawn to create a social network map or informal structure that shows how a lot of work really gets done and who the "influencers" really are. This information can be used to update the organization chart to reflect how things actually work. It also helps legitimate the informal networks people use in their daily work and identifies talented people whose value as connectors and networkers may otherwise go unnoticed by management.[8]

Informal structures and social networks bring advantages that are essential to organizational success. They allow people to make contacts with others who can help them get things done. They stimulate informal learning as people work and interact throughout the workday. And, they are also sources of emotional support and friendship that satisfy social needs.

Of course, informal structures also have potential disadvantages. They can be susceptible to rumor, carry inaccurate information, breed resistance to change, and even divert work efforts from important objectives. Another problem sometimes found in informal structures is "in" and "out" groups. Those who perceive themselves as "outsiders" may become less engaged in their work and more dissatisfied.

Learning Check

LEARNING OBJECTIVE 11.1

Explain organizing as a management function and contrast formal and informal organization structures.

Be Sure You Can • define *organizing* as a management function • explain the difference between formal and informal structures • discuss the potential advantages and disadvantages of informal structures in organizations

11.2 | Traditional Organization Structures

WileyPLUS

See Author Video

LEARNING OBJECTIVE 11.2

Identify the strengths and weaknesses of traditional organizational structures.

> **Learn More About**
> Functional structures • Divisional structures • Matrix structures

A guiding principle of organizing is that performance should improve when tasks are divided and people are allowed to become experts in specific jobs. But there are different ways to accomplish this division of labor, and each has potential advantages and disadvantages. The traditional alternatives are the functional, divisional, and matrix structures.[9]

Functional Structures

A **functional structure** groups together people with similar skills who perform similar tasks.

In **functional structures**, people with similar skills and who perform similar tasks are grouped together into formal work units. Members of functional departments share technical expertise, interests, and responsibilities. The first example in **Figure 11.3** shows a functional structure you might find in a medium-sized business, with top management arranged by the functions of

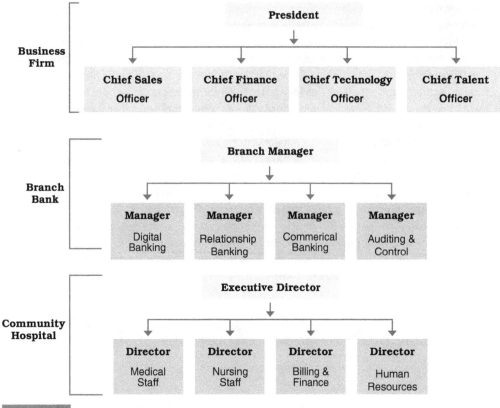

FIGURE 11.3 Functional structures in a business firm, branch bank, and community hospital.

marketing, finance, technology, and human resources. Under this structure, sales tasks are the responsibility of the Chief Sales Officer, data networks and information systems tasks are the responsibility of the Chief Technology Officer, and so on. The figure also shows how functional structures are used in other types of organizations such as banks and hospitals.

Advantages of Functional Structures   The goal of the functional structure is to put together people with the same expertise and help them work well together. If each function does its work properly, the organization as a whole should be successful. These structures work well for organizations with only a few products or services. They also tend to work best in relatively stable environments where problems are predictable and the demands for change and innovation are limited. The major advantages of functional structures include the following:

- Economies of scale with efficient use of resources.
- Task assignments consistent with expertise and training.
- High-quality technical problem solving.
- In-depth training and skill development within functions.
- Clear career paths within functions.

Disadvantages of Functional Structures   One of the major problems with functional structures is the tendency for each department or function to focus primarily on its own concerns, avoid communications with other functions, and neglect "big picture" issues. There is too little cross-functional collaboration as a sense of common purpose gets lost and as self-centered and narrow viewpoints become emphasized.[10] This is shown in **Figure 11.4** as the **functional chimneys** or **functional silos problem**—a lack of communication, coordination, and problem solving across functions. A *Wall Street Journal* reporter describes the problem this way: "How do you get aggressive, fast-talking salespeople to cooperate with reserved, detail-oriented engineers?"[11]

Organizations are supposed to be cooperative systems, but the functional chimneys problem builds invisible walls that hinder collaboration across functions. This happens because the

The **functional chimneys** or **functional silos problem** is a lack of communication, coordination, and problem solving across functions.

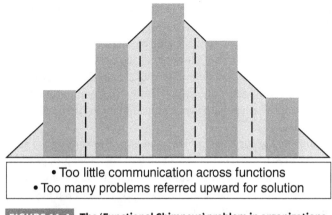

- Too little communication across functions
- Too many problems referred upward for solution

FIGURE 11.4 The 'Functional Chimneys' problem in organizations.

functions become formalized not only on the organization chart, but also in people's mind-sets. Members of various functions end up viewing the function as the center of the organizational world rather than as one among many important parts that need to be working together. This problem tends to get worse as organizations get larger and as the functions get more specialized.

Divisional Structures

A **divisional structure** groups together people working on the same product, in the same area, with similar customers, or on the same processes.

A second organizing alternative is the **divisional structure**. As illustrated in **Figure 11.5**, this structure puts together people who work on the same product or process, serve similar customers, or are located in the same geographical region. The idea is to overcome some of the disadvantages of a functional structure, especially the "functional chimneys" problem. Divisional structures are common in organizations with diverse operations extending across many products, territories, customer segments, and work processes.[12]

A **product structure** groups together people and jobs focused on a single product or service.

Types of Divisional Structures

Product structures group together jobs and activities focused on a single product or service. They clearly link costs, profits, problems, and successes in a market area with a central point of accountability. This prompts managers to be responsive to changing market demands and customer tastes. Procter & Gamble, for example,

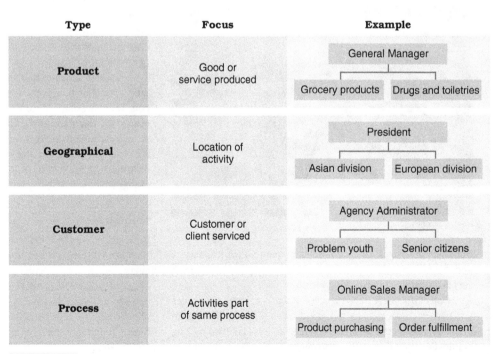

FIGURE 11.5 Divisional structures based on product, geographical, customer, and process.

is organized around six divisions: grooming, health care, beauty care, fabric and home care, baby and feminine care, family care and new ventures.[13]

Geographical structures, sometimes called *area structures*, group jobs and activities being performed in the same location. They are typically used to differentiate products or services in various locations, such as in different parts of a country. They also help global companies focus attention on the unique cultures and requirements of particular regions. Heads of the geographical divisions are typically given responsibility for their own logistics, sales, and other business functions.

A **geographical structure** groups together people and jobs performed in the same location.

Customer structures group together jobs and activities serving the same customers or clients. The goal is to serve the diverse needs of different customer groups. Banks, for example, use them to give separate attention to consumer and commercial loan customers. If you look again at Figure 11.5, you'll see that it also shows a government agency using the customer structure to serve different client populations.

A **customer structure** groups together people and jobs that serve the same customers or clients.

A **process structure** groups together jobs and activities that are part of the same processes. A **work process** is a group of related tasks that collectively creates something of value for customers.[14] An example is order fulfillment by an online retailer, a process that takes an order from point of customer initiation all the way through product delivery.

A **process structure** groups jobs and activities that are part of the same processes.

A **work process** is a group of related tasks that collectively creates a valuable work product.

Advantages and Disadvantages of Divisional Structures
Organizations use divisional structures for a number of reasons, including to avoid the functional chimneys problem and other limitations of functional structures. The potential advantages of divisional structures include:

- More flexibility in responding to environmental changes.
- Improved coordination across functional departments.
- Clear points of responsibility for product or service delivery.
- Expertise focused on specific customers, products, and regions.
- Greater ease in changing size by adding or deleting divisions.

Choices: Think before You Act | Workers within organizations spend roughly 40% to 60% of their interaction time every workday talking with their direct neighbors.

Playing Musical Chairs to Increase Collaboration

Monkey Business Images/Shutterstock.com

Goodbye, private office . . . goodbye, permanent work space . . . and, "hello, stranger!" The childhood game of musical chairs is very likely coming to your workplace!

One of the latest trends in office design is to move employees into new workspaces every few months, as a way to increase communication and collaboration. The regular moves end up putting employees from different departments and work functions into contact with one another. Seating assignments may be planned based on tasks or employees' personalities, or even done randomly. But regardless of the method, the goal is the same: break down functional silos and habits that limit communication across internal boundaries, and put people side-by-side to talk, learn, and be creative together.

Research indicates that workers spend roughly 40% to 60% of their interaction time every workday talking with their direct neighbors. They have only a 5% to 10% chance of interacting with someone even just a few steps away. Ben Waber, CEO of Sociometric Solutions, a consulting firm that works on such issues, says: "If I change the organizational chart and you stay in the same seat, it doesn't have much of an effect. If I keep the organization chart the same but change where you sit, it is going to massively change everything."

Your Take?

Is musical chairs in the office going a step too far? What's your reaction to this approach? Would you enjoy changing desks every month or so or hate it, and why? Can this idea be used in larger organizations, or is the usefulness of the approach really likely to be limited to smaller firms and startups employing a lot of new college graduates? Overall, is this a useful way to break down "functional silos," or is it just a passing fad that will soon lose its appeal? What do you think?

Divisional structures have potential disadvantages as well. They can reduce economies of scale and increase costs through the duplication of resources and efforts across divisions. They can also create unhealthy rivalries as divisions compete for resources and top management attention, emphasizing division needs over broader organizational goals.

Matrix Structures

A **matrix structure** combines the functional and divisional approaches to create permanent cross-functional project teams.

The **matrix structure**, often called the *matrix organization*, combines functional and divisional structures. The goal is to gain the advantages and avoid the disadvantages of each. This is accomplished by creating permanent teams in a matrix that cuts across functions to support specific products, projects, or programs.[15] As shown in **Figure 11.6**, members of a matrix structure simultaneously belong to at least two formal groups—a functional group and a product, program, or project team. They also report to two supervisors—one within the function and the other within the team.

The benefits of matrix structures derive from increased collaboration. Team members work across functional lines to pursue common goals while sharing expertise and information. This structure goes a long way toward eliminating functional chimneys problems and poor cross-functional communication. The potential advantages of matrix structures include:

- Better communication and cooperation across functions.
- Improved decision making; problem solving takes place at the team level where the best information is available.
- Increased flexibility in adding, removing, or changing operations to meet changing demands.
- Better customer service; there is always a program, product, or project manager informed and available to answer questions.
- Better performance accountability through the program, product, or project managers.
- Improved strategic management; top managers are freed from lower-level problem solving to focus on more strategic issues.

As you might expect, matrix structures also have potential disadvantages. The additional team leaders needed to staff a matrix structure result in higher costs. The two-supervisor

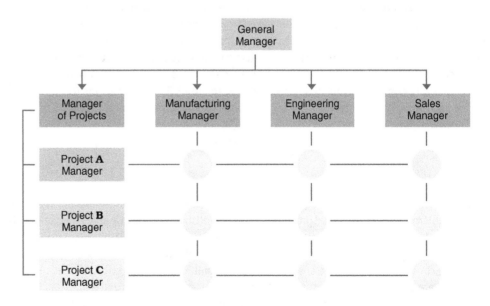

Persons assigned to both projects and functional departments

FIGURE 11.6 **Matrix structure in a small, multiproject business firm.**

system is susceptible to power struggles. Problems and frustrations occur when functional supervisors and team leaders don't coordinate well and end up sending conflicting messages and priorities, or even competing with one another for authority. Matrix teams may develop something called "groupitis," where strong team loyalties cause a loss of focus on larger organizational goals. And, team meetings in the matrix can take lots of time.

Learning Check

LEARNING OBJECTIVE 11.2

Identify the strengths and weaknesses of traditional organizational structures.

Be Sure You Can • explain the differences between functional, divisional, and matrix structures • list advantages and disadvantages of a functional structure, divisional structure, and matrix structure • draw charts to show how each type of traditional structure could be used in organizations familiar to you

11.3 | Team and Network Structures

LEARNING OBJECTIVE 11.3

Identify the strengths and weaknesses of team and network structures.

WileyPLUS

See Author Video

> **Learn More About**
>
> Team structures • Network structures

You will see elements of functional, divisional, and matrix structures in most large organizations, particularly at top levels. They help keep things "organized" and bring a sense of stability to operations. But complexities in today's environments demand flexibility as well.[16] New technologies . . . climate change . . . transforming societies . . . evolving social values . . . information transparency, all these things and more pressure organizations to constantly change everything from strategies to products to workforce composition to systems and practices. So-called **agile organizations** are structured to be fast moving, open to change, and internally connected top to bottom and side to side.[17] The foundations for agility are teams and networks, with technology helping to make connections easy and fast across time and space.

A **agile organization** is structured to be fast moving, open to change, and internally connected top to bottom and side to side.

Team Structures

Organizations with **team structures** make use of both permanent and temporary teams to solve problems, complete special projects, and accomplish day-to-day tasks.[18] Like the matrix structure, the intention of team structures is to break down functional silos, foster horizontal connections, and create faster decision making at the levels where work gets done.

As shown in **Figure 11.7**, many of these teams will be **cross-functional teams** whose members are drawn from different areas of work responsibility.[19] Others will be **project teams** created for a specific assignment and that disband once the task is completed. Still others may be **self-managing teams** whose members share roles and leadership responsibilities while working together to accomplish a common goal.

A **team structure** uses permanent and temporary cross-functional teams to improve lateral relations.

A **cross-functional team** brings together members from different functional departments.

Project teams are convened for a particular task or project and disband once it is completed.

Members of **self-managing teams** share roles and leadership responsibilities while working toward a common goal.

FIGURE 11.7 Team structures empower human talents to create agile organizations.

Advantages and Disadvantages of Team Structures The main advantages of team structures are empowerment and flexibility. Teams boost morale when members experience a greater sense of task involvement and identification, as well as increased enthusiasm for their contributions to the organization. The various forms of teamwork break down functional and interpersonal barriers and bring together diverse talents. Members of teams share knowledge and expertise to deal with problems and opportunities. And, teams improve performance by increasing the speed and quality of decisions. By harnessing the "3T" powers of teams, technology, and temporariness, organizations are even able to create **virtual structures**. They change shapes constantly as teams are called into action wherever and whenever needed, and then rest until needed again.

The complexities of teams and teamwork create potential disadvantages as well. Team structures can create conflicting loyalties for members with both team and functional assignments. They also include issues of time management and group process. By their very nature, teams spend a lot of time in meetings. Whether meetings are face-to-face or virtual, not all meeting time is productive. The quality of outcomes depends on how well tasks, relationships, and team dynamics are managed.

Network Structures

Think "networks" the next time you request an Uber or Lyft, or book on Airbnb. They are part of the sharing economy we are getting so used to. And, they also use **network structures** that operate with a central core of full-time employees surrounded by "networks" of outside contractors and partners supplying essential services.[20] Because the central core is relatively small and surrounding networks can be expanded or contracted as needed, this structure lowers costs and improves speed in dealing with changing environments.[21] The central core keeps things stable, while the network connections promote agility.

Instead of doing everything for itself with full-time employees, a network structure contracts out as much work as possible. This is done through **strategic alliances** which are cooperative agreements with partners. Some are *outsourcing strategic alliances* to purchase services such as accounting or product distribution, or to hire labor from independent contractors on the employment side. Others are *supplier strategic alliances* that guarantee a smooth and timely flow of quality supplies.

Network structures aren't limited to large and high-tech settings such as Uber and Airbnb. You'll find them in universities, for example, where services such as residences, food service, and even student recruiting is done by contractors.[22] They are also helpful for entrepreneurs

A **virtual structure** uses 3T powers of teams, technology, and temporariness to change shapes and act whereever and whenever needed.

A **network structure** uses information technologies to link with networks of outside suppliers and service contractors.

A **strategic alliance** is a cooperation agreement with another organization to jointly pursue activities of mutual interest.

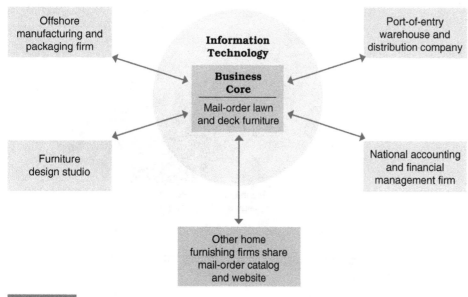

FIGURE 11.8 **A network structure for a Web-based retail business.**

wanting to start businesses. Look at the small business example in **Figure 11.8**, which shows how a network structure might work for a company selling lawn and deck furniture online and through a catalog.

In this example, merchandise is designed on contract with a self-employed furniture designer. It is manufactured and packaged by subcontractors located around the world—wherever materials are found at the lowest cost and best quality. Stock is distributed from a contract warehouse—ensuring quality storage and on-time expert shipping. Accounting and website maintenance are handled by outside firms with better technical expertise than the merchandiser could afford to employ on a full-time basis. A quarterly catalog is even produced in cooperation with two other firms that sell different home furnishings with a related price appeal.

Advantages and Disadvantages of Network Structures   Network structures are lean and fast. They help organizations stay cost-competitive by reducing overhead and increasing operating efficiency. They can quickly adjust to changing markets. But, they have potential disadvantages as well. The more complex the networks, the harder they are to control and coordinate. If one part of the network breaks down, the entire system can fail. Loss of control over contracted activities and personnel is a continuing worry for ride- sharing and home-sharing firms, for example. Network structures may also experience a lack of loyalty among contractors that are used infrequently rather than on a long-term basis. Outsourcing also can be risky, especially when breakdowns occur in critical activities such as finance, logistics, and human resource management.[23]

Learning Check

LEARNING OBJECTIVE 11.3

Identify the strengths and weaknesses of team, virtual, and network structures.

Be Sure You Can • describe how organizations can be structured to harness the power of teams • explain how a virtual structure works • illustrate how a network structure operates with speed and efficiency • discuss the potential advantages and disadvantages of network structures

WileyPLUS

See Author Video

11.4 Organizational Designs

LEARNING OBJECTIVE 11.4

Discuss how and why organizational designs are changing in today's workplace.

> **Learn More About**
> Mechanistic and organic organizational designs • Trends in organizational designs

Organizational design is the process of creating structures that accomplish mission and objectives.

Organizational design is the process of choosing and implementing structures to accomplish an organization's mission and objectives.[24] Because every organization faces its own unique challenges and opportunities, no one design can be applied in all circumstances or at all points an the organization. The best design is one that achieves a good match between structure and situational contingencies—including task, technology, environment, and people.[25] The choices among design alternatives are broadly framed in the distinction between mechanistic or bureaucratic designs at one extreme, and organic or adaptive designs at the other end.

Mechanistic and Organic Organizational Designs

A **bureaucracy** emphasizes formal authority, order, fairness, and efficiency.

The classic **bureaucracy** is described by Max Weber as being based on logic, order, and the legitimate use of formal authority.[26] It is a vertical structure, and its distinguishing features include a clear-cut division of labor, strict hierarchy of authority, formal rules and procedures, and promotion based on competency. And according to Weber, it should be orderly, fair, and highly efficient.[27]

Unfortunately, the bureaucracies we know are often associated with "red tape." Instead of being orderly and fair, they seem cumbersome and impersonal.[28] Rather than view all bureaucratic structures as inevitably flawed, however, management theory asks two contingency questions. When is bureaucracy a good choice for an organization? When it isn't, what alternatives are available?

Analysis: Make Data Your Friend | "It doesn't matter what industry you're in. People have blind spots about where they are weak."

Managers May Overestimate Their Managing Skills

Karen Moskowitz/The Image Bank/Getty Images

A survey by Development Dimensions International, Inc., found that managers were overestimating their management skills. "It doesn't matter what industry you're in. People have blind spots about where they are weak," says DDI vice president Scott Erker. Consider these results from a sample of 1,100 first-year managers:

- 72% never question their ability to lead others.
- 58% claim planning and organizing skills as strengths.
- 53% say they are strong in decision making.
- 32% claim proficiency in delegating.
- Skills needing improvement were delegating, gaining commitment, and coaching.

Your Thoughts?

Would you, like the managers in this survey, overestimate your strengths in management skills? What might explain managers' tendencies toward overconfidence? What would you identify as being among the skills on which you most need improvement? What might account for the fact that 72% of managers never question their ability to lead others?

Pioneering research concludes that two very different organizational forms can be successful, depending on the firm's external environment.[29] A more bureaucratic form, called "mechanistic," thrives in stable environments but has problems in uncertain and rapidly changing ones. In dynamic environments a much less bureaucratic form, called "organic," performs best. **Figure 11.9** shows the mechanistic and organic approaches as opposite extremes on a continuum of organizational design alternatives.

Organizations with more **mechanistic designs** are highly bureaucratic. As shown in the figure, they are vertical structures that typically operate with centralized authority, many rules and procedures, a precise division of labor, narrow spans of control, and formal coordination. They can be described as "tight" structures of the traditional pyramid form.[30] Such mechanistic designs work best for organizations doing routine tasks in stable environments.

Organizations with more **organic designs** are able to change forms in dynamic and uncertain environments in order to adapt quickly to changing times. The figure depicts them as agile, horizontal structures with decentralized authority, fewer rules and procedures, shared tasks, wide spans of control, and emphasizing personal means of coordination.[31]

A **mechanistic design** is centralized, with many rules and procedures, a clear-cut division of labor, narrow spans of control, and formal coordination.

An **organic design** is decentralized, with fewer rules and procedures, open divisions of labor, wide spans of control, and more personal coordination.

Trends in Organizational Designs

The complexity, uncertainty, and change inherent in today's environment are prompting more organizations to shift toward horizontal structures and agile organic designs. We see this in the matrix, team, virtual, and network structures discussed previously. And more generally, a number of trends are evident as structures and practices are adjusted to add teams, fit new technologies, and deal with challenging conditions.

More Delegation and Empowerment
All managers must decide what work they should do themselves and what should be left for others. At issue here is **delegation**—entrusting work to others by giving them the right to make decisions and take action. Unfortunately, many managers and team leaders don't do enough delegation and end up overloaded with work that could be done by others. And one of the reasons is **self-enhancement bias**. This is the tendency to see yourself as more capable, intelligent, and ethical than others. Self-enhancement bias makes it hard to "let go" and give others a chance to work independently without close supervision.[32]

Delegation is the process of distributing and entrusting work to others.

Self-enhancement bias is the tendency to view oneself as more capable, intelligent, and ethical than others.

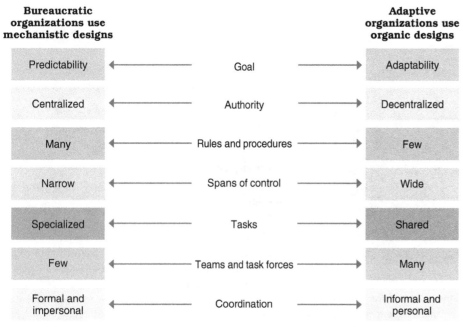

FIGURE 11.9 Organizational design alternatives: from bureaucratic to adaptive organizations.

The **authority-and-responsibility principle** is that authority should equal responsibility when work is delegated.

When it comes to delegating, a classical principle of organization warns managers to make sure the person being delegated to has sufficient authority to perform. The **authority-and-responsibility principle** states that authority should equal responsibility when work is delegated by a supervisor to a subordinate. When done well, the process of delegation involves these three steps:

- *Step 1*—The manager assigns responsibility by carefully explaining the work or duties someone else is expected to do. This responsibility is an expectation for the other person to perform assigned tasks.

- *Step 2*—The manager grants authority to act. Along with the assigned task, the right to take necessary actions (for example, to spend money, direct the work of others, or use resources) is given to the other person.

- *Step 3*—The manager creates accountability. By accepting an assignment, the person takes on a direct obligation to the manager to complete the job as agreed.

Empowerment allows others to make decisions and exercise discretion in their work.

Delegation that is done well leads to empowerment, meaning that workers are allowed to make decisions and use discretion in their jobs. You can think of it as freedom to act. Empowerment builds performance potential by allowing individuals freedom to use their talents, contribute ideas, and do their jobs in the best possible ways. And because empowerment creates a sense of ownership, it also increases commitment to follow through on decisions and work hard to accomplish goals.

Trend: Managers are delegating more. They are finding ways to empower people at all organizational levels to make more decisions that affect themselves and their work.

Insight: Learn about Yourself | Do you have a problem "letting go," or letting others do their share?

Empowerment Gets More Things Done

It takes a lot of trust to be comfortable with **empowerment**—letting others make decisions and exercise discretion in their work. But if you aren't willing and able to empower others, you may try to do too much on your own and end up accomplishing too little.

The fundamental, underlying reason for organizations is synergy—bringing together the contributions of many people to achieve something that is much greater than any individual could accomplish alone. Empowerment enables synergy to flourish. It means collaborating with others to accomplish firm objectives—allowing others to do things that you might be good at doing yourself. Many managers fail to empower others, and the result is their organizations often underperform.

How often do you get stressed out by group projects in your classes, feeling like you're doing all the work? Do you have a problem "letting go," or letting others do their share of group assignments? The reason may be the fear of losing control. People with control anxiety often end up trying to do too much. This unfortunately raises the risks of missed deadlines and poor performance.

If the prior description fits you, your assumptions probably align with those in the upper left box in the Empowerment Quick Test. Alternatively, you could be in the lower right box and perhaps find that you work smarter and better while also making others happier.

Get To Know Yourself Better

Are you someone who easily and comfortably empowers others? Or do you suffer from control anxiety, with little or no willingness to delegate? The next time you are in a study or work group,

EMPOWERMENT QUICK TEST

In a team situation, which square best describes your beliefs and behaviors?

It's faster to do things myself than explain how to do them to others

Some things are just too important not to do yourself

?

People make mistakes, but they also learn from them

Many people are ready to take on more work, but are too shy to volunteer

be a self-observer. The question is: How well do you handle empowerment? Write a short narrative that accurately describes your behavior to someone who wasn't present. Focus on both your tendencies to empower others and how you respond when others empower you. Compare that narrative with the results from the chapter Self-Assessment—Empowering Others. Is there a match?

Tall Structure
(narrow span of control)

Flat Structure
(wide span of control)

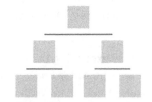 

FIGURE 11.10 **Contrasting spans of control in tall and flat organization structures.**

Fewer Levels of Management

A typical organization chart shows the **chain of command**, or the line of authority that vertically links each position with successively higher levels of management. The number of persons reporting directly to a manager is called the **span of control**.

When organizations get bigger they tend to add levels of management to the chain of command. These **tall structures** tend to have narrow spans of control as shown in **Figure 11.10**. Because tall organizations have more managers, they are more costly. They also tend to be less efficient, less flexible, and less customer-sensitive. Wider spans of control are found in **flat structures** with fewer levels of management. This reduces overhead costs and improves agility. It can also be good for workers who gain empowerment and independence because of reduced supervision.[33]

Trend: Organizations are cutting unnecessary levels of management and shifting to wider spans of control. Managers are taking responsibility for larger teams whose members operate with less supervision.

Decentralization with Centralization

Should most decisions be made at the top levels of an organization, or should they be dispersed by extensive delegation across all levels? The former approach is referred to as **centralization**; the latter is called **decentralization**. And the decision to operate one way or another is a strategic choice.

At Rovio, the Finnish company making *Angry Birds*, one person used to be in charge of game development—centralization. But as the firm grew this wasn't working anymore. In response, a decision was made to create smaller "tribes" and give each "their own profit and loss sheet, their own management, their own targets."[34] In other words, Rovio shifted from centralization to decentralization.

A closer look at the Rovio story would likely show that the centralization and decentralization issue isn't an either/or choice. A game maker is already a high-tech setting. It should be able to operate with greater decentralization without giving up centralized control.[35] High-speed information systems allow top managers to easily stay informed about day-to-day performance matters throughout an organization. With this information so readily available, they can be confident in allowing more decentralized decision making. If something goes wrong, say in one of Rovio's tribes, information systems should sound an alarm that triggers almost immediate corrective actions.

Trend: Delegation, empowerment, and horizontal structures are contributing to more decentralization in organizations; at the same time, advances in information technology help top managers maintain centralized control.

Reduced Use of Staff

When it comes to coordination and control in organizations, the issue of line–staff relationships is critical. People in **staff positions** provide expert advice and guidance to line personnel. In a large retail chain, for example, line managers in each store typically make daily operating decisions regarding direct merchandise sales. But, staff specialists at the corporate or regional levels often provide direction and support so that all

The **chain of command** links all employees with successively higher levels of authority.

Span of control is the number of subordinates directly reporting to a manager.

Tall structures have narrow spans of control and many hierarchical levels.

Flat structures have wide spans of control and few hierarchical levels.

Centralization is the concentration of authority for most decisions at the top level of an organization.

Decentralization is the dispersion of authority to make decisions throughout all organization levels.

Staff positions provide technical expertise for other parts of the organization.

Help! I've Been Flattened into Exhaustion

Tom Grill/Photographer's Choice RF/Getty Images

Dear Stress Doctor:

My boss came up with the great idea of laying off some managers, assigning more workers to those of us who haven't been laid off, and calling us "coaches" instead of supervisors. She says this is all part of a new management approach to operate with a flatter structure and more empowerment.

For me this means a lot more work coordinating the activities of 17 operators instead of the 6 that I previously supervised. I can't get everything cleaned up on my desk most days, and I end up taking a lot of work home.

As my organization "restructures" and cuts back staff, it puts a greater burden on the rest of us. We get exhausted, and our families get short-changed and angry. I even feel guilty now taking time to watch my daughter play soccer on Saturday mornings. Sure, there's some decent pay involved, but that doesn't make up for the heavy price in terms of lost family time.

But you know what? My boss doesn't get it. I never hear her ask: "Camille, are you working too much? Don't you think it's time to get back on a reasonable schedule?" No! What I often hear instead is "Look at Andy; he handles our new management model really well, and he's a real go-getter. I don't think he's been out of here one night this week before 8 pm."

What am I going to do, just keep it up until everything falls apart one day? Is a flatter structure with fewer managers always best? Am I missing something here with the whole "new management"?

Sincerely,
Overworked in Cincinnati

What Do You Think?

Is it ethical to restructure, cut management levels, and expect remaining managers to do more work? Or is it simply the case that managers used to the "old" ways of doing things need extra training and care while learning "new" management approaches? What about this person's boss—is she on track with her management skills? Aren't managers supposed to help people understand their jobs, set priorities, and fulfill them, while still maintaining a reasonable work–life balance?

---

the stores operate with the same credit, purchasing, employment, marketing, and advertising procedures.

Problems in line–staff distinctions can and do come up, and organizations sometimes find that staff size grows to the point where its costs outweigh its benefits. This is why cutbacks in staff positions are common during downsizing and other turnaround efforts. There is no one best solution to the problem of how to divide work between line and staff responsibilities. What is best for any organization is a cost-effective staff component that satisfies, but doesn't overreact to, needs for specialized technical assistance to line operations. But overall, the trend toward reduced use of staff across all industries is increasing.

Trend: Organizations are lowering costs and increasing efficiency by employing fewer staff personnel and using smaller staff units.

Learning Check

LEARNING OBJECTIVE 11.4

Discuss how and why organizational designs are changing in today's workplace.

Be Sure You Can • define *organizational design* • describe the characteristics of mechanistic and organic designs • explain when the mechanistic design and the organic design work best • describe trends in levels of management, delegation and empowerment, decentralization and centralization, and use of staff

Management Learning Review: Get Prepared for Quizzes and Exams

Summary

LEARNING OBJECTIVE 11.1 Explain organizing as a management function and contrast formal and informal organization structures.

- Organizing is the process of arranging people and resources to work toward a common goal.
- Organizing decisions divide up the work that needs to be done, allocate people and resources to do it, and coordinate results to achieve productivity.
- Structure is the system of tasks, reporting relationships, and communication that links people and positions within an organization.
- The formal structure, such as that in an organization chart, describes how an organization is supposed to work.
- The informal structure of an organization consists of the informal relationships that develop among members.

For Discussion If organization charts are imperfect, why bother with them?

LEARNING OBJECTIVE 11.2 Identify the strengths and weaknesses of traditional organizational structures.

- In functional structures, people with similar skills who perform similar activities are grouped together under a common manager.
- In divisional structures, people who work on a similar product, work in the same geographical region, serve the same customers, or participate in the same work process are grouped together under common managers.
- A matrix structure combines the functional and divisional approaches to create permanent cross-functional project teams.

For Discussion Why use functional structures if they are prone to functional chimneys problems?

LEARNING OBJECTIVE 11.3 Identify the strengths and weaknesses of team, virtual, and network structures.

- Team structures use cross-functional teams and task forces to improve lateral relations and problem solving at all levels.
- Virtual organizations use information technology to mobilize a shifting mix of strategic alliances to accomplish tasks and projects.
- Network structures use contracted services and strategic alliances to support a core organizational center.
- Agile structures combine team and network structures with the advantages of technology to accomplish tasks and projects.

For Discussion What problems could reduce the effectiveness of team-oriented organization structures?

LEARNING OBJECTIVE 11.4 Discuss how and why organizational designs are changing in today's workplace.

- Contingency in organizational design basically involves finding designs that best fit situational features.
- Mechanistic designs are bureaucratic and vertical, performing best for routine and predictable tasks.
- Organic designs are adaptive and horizontal, performing best in conditions requiring change and flexibility.
- Key organizing trends include fewer levels of management, more delegation and empowerment, decentralization with centralization, and fewer staff positions.

For Discussion Which of the organizing trends is most likely to change in the future, and why?

Self-Test 11

Multiple-Choice Questions

1. The main purpose of organizing as a management function is to _____.

   a. make sure that results match plans
   b. arrange people and resources to accomplish work
   c. create enthusiasm for the work to be done
   d. match strategies with operational plans

2. _____ is the system of tasks, reporting relationships, and communication that links together the various parts of an organization.

   a. Structure
   b. Staff
   c. Decentralization
   d. Differentiation

3. Rumors and resistance to change are potential disadvantages often associated with _____ .

   a. virtual organizations

   b. informal structures

   c. delegation

   d. specialized staff

4. An organization chart showing vice presidents of marketing, finance, manufacturing, and purchasing all reporting to the president is depicting a _____ structure.

   a. functional

   b. matrix

   c. network

   d. product

5. The functional chimneys problem occurs when people in different functions _____ .

   a. fail to communicate with one another

   b. try to help each other work with customers

   c. spend too much time coordinating decisions

   d. focus on products rather than functions

6. A manufacturing business with a functional structure has recently developed three new product lines. The president of the company might consider shifting to a(n) _____ structure to gain a stronger focus on each product.

   a. virtual

   b. informal

   c. divisional

   d. network

7. _____ structure tries to combine the best elements of the functional and divisional forms.

   a. Virtual

   b. Boundaryless

   c. Team

   d. Matrix

8. The system of dual reporting relationships—to both a functional and project manager—is characteristics of a _____ structure.

   a. functional

   b. matrix

   c. network

   d. product

9. Better lower-level teamwork and more top-level strategic management are among the expected advantages of a _____ structure.

   a. divisional

   b. matrix

   c. geographical

   d. product

10. "Tall" organizations tend to have long chains of command and _____ spans of control.

   a. wide

   b. narrow

   c. informal

   d. centralized

11. A student volunteers to gather information on a company for a group case analysis project. The other members of the group agree and tell her to go ahead and choose the information sources. In terms of delegation, this group is giving the student _____ to fulfill the agreed-upon task.

   a. responsibility

   b. accountability

   c. authority

   d. decentralization

12. The current trend in the use of staff in organizations is to _____.

   a. give staff personnel more authority over operations

   b. reduce the number of staff personnel

   c. remove all staff from the organization

   d. combine all staff functions in one department

13. The bureaucratic organization described by Max Weber is similar to the _____ organization described by Burns and Stalker.

   a. adaptive

   b. mechanistic

   c. organic

   d. adhocracy

14. Which type of organization design best fits an uncertain and changing environment?

   a. mechanistic

   b. bureaucratic

   c. organic

   d. traditional

15. An organization that employs just a few "core" or essential full-time employees and outsources a lot of the remaining work show signs of using a _____ structure.

   a. functional

   b. network

   c. matrix

   d. mechanistic

Short-Response Questions

16. What symptoms might indicate that a functional structure is causing problems for the organization?

17. Explain by example the concept of a network organization structure.

18. Explain the practical significance of this statement: "Organizational design should be done in contingency fashion."

19. Describe two trends in organizational design and explain their importance to managers.

Essay Question

20. Faisal Sham supervises a group of seven project engineers. His unit is experiencing a heavy workload, as the demand for different versions of one of his firm's computer components is growing. Faisal finds that he doesn't have time to follow up on all design details for each version of the product. Until now he has tried to do this all by himself. Two of the engineers have shown an interest in helping him coordinate work on the various designs. As a consultant, how would you advise Faisal in terms of delegating work to them?

Career Skills & Competencies: Make Yourself Valuable!

Evaluate Career Situations

What Would You Do?

1. The New Branch Manager

As the newly promoted manager of a branch bank, you will be leading a team of 22 people. Most members have worked together for a number of years. How can you discover the informal structure or "shadow organization" of the branch and your team? Once you understand them, how will you try to use informal structures to advantage while establishing yourself as an effective manager in this situation?

2. Advisor to the Business School

The typical university business school is organized on a functional basis, with department heads in accounting, finance, information systems, management, and marketing all reporting to a dean. You are on your alma mater's advisory board, and the dean is asking for advice. What suggestions might you give for redesigning this structure to increase communication and collaboration across departments, as well as improve curriculum integration for students in all areas of study?

3. Entrepreneur's Dilemma

As the owner of a small computer repair and services business, you would like to allow employees more flexibility in their work schedules. But you also need consistent coverage to handle drop-in customers as well as at-home service calls. There are also times when customers need what they consider to be "emergency" help outside of normal 8 a.m. to 5 p.m. office times. You've got a meeting with employees scheduled for next week. Your goal is to come out of the meeting with a good plan to deal with this staffing dilemma. How can you achieve this goal?

Reflect on the Self-Assessment

Empowering Others

Instructions

Think of times when you have been in charge of a group in a work or student situation. Complete the following questionnaire by recording how you feel about each statement according to this scale:[36]

1	2	3	4	5
Strongly disagree	Disagree	Neutral	Agree	Strongly agree

When in charge of a team, I find that:

1. Most of the time other people are too inexperienced to do things, so I prefer to do them myself.
2. It often takes more time to explain things to others than to just do them myself.
3. Mistakes made by others are costly, so I don't assign much work to them.
4. Some things simply should not be delegated to others.
5. I often get quicker action by doing a job myself.
6. Many people are good only at very specific tasks, so they can't be assigned additional responsibilities.
7. Many people are too busy to take on additional work.
8. Most people just aren't ready to handle additional responsibilities.
9. In my position, I should be entitled to make my own decisions.

Scoring

Total your responses to get an overall score. Possible scores range from 9 to 45.

Interpretation

The lower your score, the more willing you appear to be to delegate to others. Willingness to delegate is an important managerial characteristic. It is how you, as a manager, can empower others and give them opportunities to assume responsibility and exercise self-control in their work. With the growing importance of horizontal organizations and empowerment, your willingness to delegate is worth thinking about seriously.

Contribute to the Class Exercise

Organizational Metaphors

Instructions

Form into groups as assigned by the instructor and do the following:

1. Think about organizations and how they work.

2. Select one of the following sets of organizational metaphors.

   a. human brain—spiderweb

   b. rock band—chamber music ensemble

   c. cup of coffee—beehive

   d. cement mixer—star galaxy

   e. about the fifth date in an increasingly serious relationship—a couple celebrating their 25th wedding anniversary

3. Brainstorm how each metaphor in your set can be used to explain how organizations work.

4. Brainstorm how each metaphor is similar to and different from the other in this explanation.

5. Draw pictures or create a short skit to illustrate the contrasts between your two metaphors of an organization.

6. Present your metaphorical views of organizations to the class.

7. Be prepared to explain what can be learned from your metaphors and engage in class discussion.

Manage a Critical Incident

Crowdsourcing Evaluations to Cut Management Levels

Performance reviews in your firm have always been completed by managers and then discussed with workers. But you've been reading about 360° reviews that include feedback from peers and others working with or for the person being evaluated. You're also aware that new technology makes it easy to conduct evaluations online and even to make them happen in almost real time, on a project-by-project basis, without a manager leading the process. As soon as a task is completed by an individual or team, a 360° review can be done online and the feedback immediately used for future performance improvement. You'd like to start crowdsourcing evaluations at your firm in order to save costs by cutting management levels, and also to improve the flow and timeliness of performance feedback. Before going further, you sit down to make a list of the pros and cons of the idea.

Questions

What's on your list of pros and cons, and why? You next decide to make another list of resources and support from key persons that would be needed to implement the practice. What's on this second list and why?

Collaborate on the Team Project

Designing a Network University

Instructions

In your assigned team, do the following.

1. Discuss the concept of the network organization structure as described in the textbook.

2. Create a network organization structure for your college or university. Identify the "core staffing" and what will be outsourced. Identify how outsourcing will be managed.

3. Draw a diagram depicting the various elements in your "Network U."

4. Identify why "Network U" will be able to meet two major goals: (a) create high levels of student learning, and (b) operate with cost efficiency.

5. Present and justify your design for "Network U" to the class.

Analyze the Case Study

NPR | Many Voices Serving Many Needs

Go to *Management Cases for Critical Thinking* at the end of the book to find this case.

CHAPTER 12

Organizational Culture and Change

Get There Faster with Values

Katharine Andriotis/Alamy Stock Photo

"I love the fact that while I'm at work, I don't feel like I'm working. Most of my colleagues are having fun doing what they do every day, which makes for an extremely happy work atmosphere."

Costco employee review on Comparably.com

Career Readiness – What to Look for Inside

Thought Leadership

Analysis > *Make Data Your Friend*
Organization Cultures Face Emerging Work–Life Trends

Choices > *Think before You Act*
Saying "OK" to Chest Bumps

Ethics > *Know Right from Wrong*
Hidden Agendas in Organizational Change

Insight > *Learn about Yourself*
Get Comfortable with Tolerance for Ambiguity

Skills Make You Valuable

- **Evaluate** *Career Situations:*
  What Would You Do?
- **Reflect** *On the Self-Assessment:*
  Change Leadership IQ
- **Contribute** *To the Class Exercise:*
  Force-Field Analysis
- **Manage** *A Critical Incident:*
  Proposal for Open Office Design and Hotdesking
- **Collaborate** *On the Team Project:*
  Organizational Culture Walk
- **Analyze** *The Case Study:*
  Gamification: Finding Legitimacy in the New Corporate Culture

Chapter Quick Start

Every organization has a "culture" that reflects its personality. These cultures influence members' attitudes, behaviors, commitments, and performance accomplishments. They also influence customer loyalty and public image. One of the most important career decisions we make is to choose an employer that offers a good "fit" between its culture and our preferences. Part of that fit relates to how the culture handles change and the ways managers act, or not, as change leaders.

LEARNING OBJECTIVES

12.1 Explain organizational culture and its influence on behavior in organizations.

12.2 Describe subcultures and diversity in multicultural organizations.

12.3 Identify alternative change strategies and types of resistance to change found in organizations.

237

"Culture" is a word we hear a lot these days as we become more aware of diversity in everyday living. And when it comes to the world at large, cultural differences between people and nations are often in the news. However, there's another type of culture that can be just as important: the cultures of organizations. Just as nations, ethnic and religious groups, nations, and families have cultures, organizations do too. These cultures distinguish organizations from one another and give members a sense of collective identity. The "fit" between the individual and an organization's culture is very important. The right fit is good for both employers and job holders, and finding the right fit in your work and membership organizations is a real career issue.

"Change" is another hot-button word we also face in our lives and at work. Just as people are being asked to adapt and be ever more flexible, organizations are too. Managers are expected to support change initiatives launched from higher levels, and they also are expected to be change leaders in their own teams and work units. Some organizational cultures push change, while others resist it. We act the same ways. And now is a good time to check your readiness to master challenges of change in your career and personal life.

12.1 | Organizational Cultures

LEARNING OBJECTIVE 12.1

Explain organizational culture and its influence on behavior in organizations.

WileyPLUS

See Author Video

> **Learn More About**
>
> Understanding organizational cultures • Observable culture of organizations • Values and the core culture of organizations

Organizational culture is the system of shared beliefs and values that guides behavior in organizations.

Think of the stores where you shop; the restaurants that you patronize; the place where you work. What is the "vibe" like? Do you notice, for example, that atmospheres in the stores of major retailers like Anthropologie, Gap, Hollister, and Banana Republic seem to fit their brands and customer identities?[1] Are you envious when someone says "It's just like a family at my work" or "We have fun while we're working" or "The whole place just pulls together to get the job done"? They are talking in very positive ways about **organizational culture**. Sometimes called the *corporate culture*, this is the system of shared beliefs and values that shapes and guides the behavior of an organization's members.[2]

You can think of organizational culture as the personality or atmosphere of the organization. It's what you see and hear when walking around an organization as a visitor, a customer, or an employee. Look carefully, check the climate, and listen to the conversations. Whenever someone speaks of "the way we do things here," they are providing insight into the organization's culture. These cultures create unique identities that differentiate one organization from the next. And, they have a strong impact on how an organization performs and on the quality of work life for its members.[3]

Understanding Organizational Cultures

Zappos CEO Tony Hsieh has built a fun, creative, and customer-centered culture. He says: "The original idea was to add a little fun," and then everyone joined in the idea that "We can do it better." Now the notion of an unhappy Zappos customer is almost unthinkable. "They may only call once in their life," says Hsieh, "but that is our chance to wow them."[4] Amazon.com CEO Jeff Bezos liked Zappos so much he bought the company. The Girl Scouts are among a number of organizations that send executives to study Zappos' culture and bring back ideas for improving their own. Hsieh's advice is that if you "get the culture right, most of the other stuff, like brand and the customer service, will just happen."[5]

Types of Organizational Cultures

It takes a keen eye to be able to identify and understand an organization's culture. But such understanding can be a real asset to job seekers. No one wants to end up in a situation with a bad person–culture fit. You can get a good read on an organization's culture by asking and answering questions like the following.[6]

How tight or loose is the structure? • Do most decisions reflect change or the status quo? • What outcomes or results are most highly valued? • How widespread is empowerment and worker involvement? • What is the competitive style, internal and external? • What value is placed on people, as customers and employees? • Is teamwork a way of life in this organization?

One of the popular descriptions of organizational cultures is shown in **Figure 12.1**. Based on a model called the competing values framework, it identifies four different culture types.[7] *Hierarchical cultures* emphasize tradition and clear roles. *Rational cultures* emphasize process and slow change. *Entrepreneurial cultures* emphasize creativity and competition. *Team cultures* emphasize collaboration and trust. How do these organization culture options sound to you? Are you prepared to identify the cultures in organizations you interview with and, perhaps, even rule out those with a potentially poor person–culture fit?

Strong Organizational Cultures

Although culture isn't the only determinant of what happens in organizations, it counts a lot. The organizational culture helps set and communicate values, shape attitudes, reinforce beliefs, direct behavior, and establish performance expectations.[8] And importantly, an organization's culture sets a moral tone that guides—or not—ethical behavior.

In **strong organizational cultures**, the culture is clear, well defined, and widely shared by members. When the strong culture is positive, it acts as a performance asset by bonding together the organization and the talents of members. It discourages dysfunctional and unethical behaviors and encourages helpful and ethical ones. It keeps the vision clear for all to rally around.[9] But when the strong culture is negative, its power is equally strong in the other direction.

Changing General Motor's strong and negative organizational culture was a major priority for Mary Barra when she became GM's CEO. She claimed that GM's historical culture of cost containment and avoidance of responsibility encouraged covering up rather than addressing problems. She criticized the "GM Nod" where people would nod in agreement but take no action. She also criticized the "GM Salute" where crossed arms indicated that "responsibility belongs to someone else, not me."[10]

Strong and positive organizational cultures should be the goal, but they don't happen by accident. They are created by leaders who communicate and model the right tone. And they are reinforced through **socialization**, the process through which new members learn the culture

Strong organizational cultures are clear, well defined, and widely shared among members.

Socialization is the process through which new members learn the culture of an organization.

Team Culture	Hierarchical Culture
• Authority shared, distributed • Teams and teamwork rule • Collaboration, trust valued • Emphasis on mutual support	• Authority runs the system • Traditions, clear roles • Rules, hierarchy valued • Emphasis on predictability
Entrepreneurial Culture	**Rational Culture**
• Authority goes with ideas • Flexibility and creativity rule • Change and growth valued • Emphasis on entrepreneurship	• Authority serves the goals • Efficiency, productivity rule • Planning, process valued • Emphasis on modest change

FIGURE 12.1 **Four culture types found in organizations.**

and the values of the organization.[11] Socialization often begins in an anticipatory way with education, such as when business students learn the importance of professional appearance, integrity, and interpersonal skills. It continues with an employer's onboarding orientation and training programs. Disney's highly regarded strong culture, for example, is supported by major investments in socializing and training new hires. Founder Walt Disney is quoted as saying: "You can dream, create, design and build the most wonderful place in the world, but it requires people to make the dream a reality."[12]

Observable Culture of Organizations

Organizational culture is usually described from the perspective of the two levels shown in **Figure 12.2**. Like an iceberg, there is an observable component—the part that stands out above the surface and is visible to the discerning eye, and a core component—the part that lies below the surface and is harder to see.[13]

The **observable culture** is expressed in the ways that people dress at work, how they arrange their offices, how they speak to and behave toward one another, the nature of their conversations, and how they talk about and treat customers and clients. Test this out the next time you go to a store, restaurant, or service establishment. How do people look, act, and behave? How do they interact with one another? How do they treat customers? What's the tone and content of their conversations? Are they enjoying themselves? When you answer such questions, you are starting to identify the organization's observable culture.

The observable culture is also found in the stories, heroes, rituals, and symbols that are part of daily organizational life. It's in spontaneous celebrations of work accomplishments or personal milestones such as a co-worker's birthday. In workplaces like Apple, Disney, and Zappos, it's in stories told about the founders and the firm's startup history. At colleges and universities it includes the pageantry of graduation and honors ceremonies. In sports teams it's evident in the pregame rally, sideline pep talk, and all the "thumping

The **observable culture** is visible in the way members behave, and in the stories, heroes, rituals, and symbols that are part of daily organizational life.

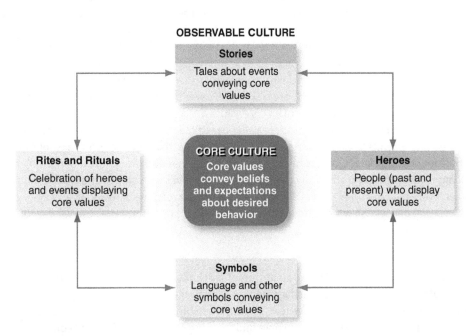

FIGURE 12.2 Levels of organizational culture—surface level observable culture and deep level core culture.

and bumping" that takes place after a good play. When you are trying to understand the observable culture of an organization, look for the following indicators.[14]

- *Heroes*—the people singled out for special attention and whose accomplishments are recognized with praise and admiration; they include founders and role models.
- *Ceremonies, rites, and rituals*—the ceremonies and meetings, planned and spontaneous, that celebrate important events and accomplishments.
- *Legends and stories*—oral histories and tales, told and retold among members, about dramatic incidents in the life of the organization.
- *Metaphors and symbols*—the special use of language and other nonverbal expressions that communicate important themes and values of the organization.

Values and the Core Culture of Organizations

The **core culture** exists at a deep level in organizations and consists of **core values** or underlying assumptions and beliefs that shape and guide people's behaviors. You know core values, so to speak, when you experience them. This may be when you are trying to claim lost luggage at an airline counter and are treated really well, or when returning a product to a retail store and are greeted with a smile and "no questions asked." Values set in the core culture are a strong influence on how such transactions play out. And when customer experiences aren't positive, the culprit may well be weak or just plain bad core values. The same holds true for the presence of unethical and disrespectful behaviors.

The **core culture** consists of the core values, or underlying assumptions and beliefs that shape and guide people's behaviors in an organization.

Core values are beliefs and values shared by organization members.

Ethical and Value-Based Management
How would you react if you found out senior executives in your organization talked up values such as honesty and ethical behavior, but then acted very differently—tolerating sexual harassment, bullying people, altering financial reports, or spending company funds on personal pleasures? Most likely you'd be upset, and justifiably so. It's important not to be fooled by values statements alone when trying to understand an organization's core culture. It's easy to write a set of core values, post them on the Web, and talk about them. It's a lot harder to live up to them every day.

If core values are to have any positive effect, everyone in the organization—from top to bottom—must reflect these values in their day-to-day actions. It's in this context that managers and team leaders have a special responsibility to "walk the talk" in order to make the expressed values real. The term **value-based management** describes managers who actively help to develop, communicate, and enact core values every day.

Value-based management actively develops, communicates, and enacts shared values.

Although you might tend to associate value-based management with top executives, the responsibility extends to all managers and team leaders. Like the organization as a whole, every work team or group has its own a culture. The nature of this culture and its influence on team outcomes has a lot to do with how the team leader behaves as a values champion and role model. Every manager—regardless of level—always has the responsibility to act as a **symbolic leader**, someone whose words and actions consistently communicate the core values[15] of the team and organization.

A **symbolic leader** is someone whose words and actions consistently communicate core values.

Workplace Spirituality
The notion of **workplace spirituality** is sometimes discussed along with value-based management. Although the first tendency might be to associate "spirituality" with religion, the term is used more broadly in management. It describes an organizational culture that helps people find meaning and a sense of shared community in their work. The core value underlying workplace spirituality is respect for human beings. The

Workplace spirituality creates meaning and shared community among organizational members.

Choices: Think before You Act | Researchers link rituals with increased employee involvement and a higher sense of connection among team members.

Saying "OK" to Chest Bumps

Media Bakery13/Shutterstock.com

Bring a bit of ritual to the office culture and increase performance. At least that's the wisdom being followed by some forward-thinking organizations. When was the last time you shared a chest bump with a co-worker? In many workplaces people are afraid to even try, given the concerns about sexual harassment and unwanted physical contact. But at others, the organization culture welcomes such practices.

Rituals are in at Salo LLC, a Minneapolis human resource management company. A ringing gong signals a deal that has been closed. You might even see a couple of employees doing a chest bump to celebrate a success. What's it all about? Answer: harnessing the power of organizational culture as a performance booster.

Researchers note that many of us follow rituals before doing things—like the major league baseball player who tightens and re-tightens his batting gloves before each pitch. Some consider rituals confidence boosters. When rituals move into the office, they are linked with increased employee involvement and a higher sense of connection among team members. Of course, newcomers may have to be treated with extra care. At Salo, for example, new marketing manager Maureen Sullivan was surprised to see the chest bumping. But she learned to accept it, saying: "Alrighty, that's what we do here. We just really get into it."

Your Take?

Is this taking organizational culture a step too far? Would you be comfortable in an office environment where things like chest bumps were part of the daily ritual? Do you find such activities a source of potential confidence, camaraderie, and engagement? Or, are they a real turnoff? If you were a team leader, would you try to take advantage of rituals to boost morale and performance? Are practices like these good for only certain types of work settings and personalities?

guiding principle is that people are enriched when they are engaged in meaningful work and feel personally connected with others inside and outside of the organization.[16]

A culture of workplace spirituality will have a strong ethical foundation, value human dignity, respect diversity, and focus on linking jobs with real contributions to society. Anyone who works in a culture of workplace spirituality should derive pleasure from knowing that what is being accomplished is personally meaningful, created through community, and valued by others. Anyone who leads a culture of workplace spirituality values people by emphasizing meaningful purpose, trust and respect, honesty and openness, personal growth and developments, worker-friendly practices, and ethics and social responsibility.[17]

Learning Check

LEARNING OBJECTIVE 12.1

Explain organizational culture and its influence on behavior in organizations.

Be Sure You Can • define *organizational culture* and explain the importance of strong cultures to organizations • define and explain the onboarding process of *socialization* • distinguish between the observable and core cultures • explain how value-based management helps build strong culture organizations • describe how workplace spirituality is reflected in an organization's culture

| 12.2 | # Multicultural Organizations and Diversity

LEARNING OBJECTIVE 12.2

Describe subcultures and diversity in multicultural organizations.

> **Learn More About**
>
> Multicultural organizations • Organizational subcultures • Power, diversity, and organizational subcultures

U.S. laws make it illegal to discriminate in hiring and employment decisions based on race, religion, national origin, ethnicity, able-bodiedness, or sex. Those who believe they have been a victim of discrimination can appeal to the U.S. Equal Employment Opportunity Commission. But, did you know that workers who are gay, lesbian, transgender, or bisexual aren't covered by current laws? The proposed Employment Non-Discrimination Act (ENDA) is intended to close this gap by adding gender identity and sexual orientation to the list of anti-discrimination protections. As of this writing, ENDA has yet to be voted into law.[18]

Multicultural Organizations

In the book *Beyond Race and Gender*, consultant R. Roosevelt Thomas, Jr., points out that the way people are treated at work—with respect and inclusion, or with disrespect and exclusion—is a direct reflection of the organization's culture and leadership.[19] We use the term **multiculturalism** to describe inclusiveness, pluralism, and respect for diversity in the workplace. The core values of a truly **multicultural organization** communicate support for multiculturalism and empower the full diversity of all members. Common characteristics of multicultural organizations include:[20]

Multiculturalism in organizations involves inclusiveness, pluralism, and respect for diversity.

A **multicultural organization** has core values that respect diversity and support multiculturalism.

- *Pluralism*—Members of both minority cultures and majority cultures are influential in setting key values and policies.
- *Structural integration*—Minority-culture members are well represented in jobs at all levels and in all functional responsibilities.
- *Informal network integration*—Various forms of mentoring and support groups assist in the career development of minority-culture members.
- *Absence of prejudice and discrimination*—A variety of training and task-force activities address the need to eliminate culture-group biases.
- *Minimum intergroup conflict*—Diversity does not lead to destructive conflicts between members of majority and minority cultures.

Commitment to multiculturalism is more than a moral issue. Research notes that organizations with inclusive cultures gain performance advantages because their workforces offer a wide mix of talents and perspectives.[21] The *Gallup Management Journal* reports that a racially and ethnically inclusive workplace is good for morale. Workers who feel included say they are likely to stay with their employers and recommend them to others.[22] Catalyst studies find that firms with at least three female board members financially outperform those with no women on the board. Evidence also shows that the presence of women on boards is good for innovation, governance, and research and development.[23] But Thomas Kochan and colleagues at MIT advise that the *presence* of diversity alone does not guarantee these types of positive outcomes. The performance advantages of multiculturalism and inclusion emerge only when *respect* for diversity is firmly embedded in the organizational culture.[24]

Organizational Subcultures

Organizational subcultures or **co-cultures** consist of members who share similar beliefs and values based on their work, personal characteristics, shared experiences, or social identities.

Ethnocentrism is the belief that one's membership group and subculture or co-culture is superior to all others.

Generational subcultures form among persons who work together and share similar ages, such as millennials and baby boomers.

Organizations—like societies at large—contain a mixture of **organizational subcultures** or **co-cultures**. They exist within the larger organizational culture and consist of members with similar values and beliefs based on their work responsibilities, personal characteristics, shared experiences, and social identities. Subcultures form around in-group similarities that can be personally comforting. But they also emphasize out-group differences and can make it hard to create a truly multicultural organization. As it does in everyday life, **ethnocentrism**—the belief that one's subculture or co-culture is superior to all others, can creep into organizations and negatively affect the way people relate to and work with one another.

Age differences create **generational subcultures** in organizations.[25] The mix of generations in a workforce now spans from post–World War II baby boomers to Millenials and Generation Z.[26] What are the implications? Harris and Conference Board polls report that younger workers tend to be more dissatisfied than older workers.[27] Studies also describe younger workers as having short time orientations, giving high priority to work–life balance, and expecting to hold several different jobs and work for different employers throughout of their career.[28] Just imagine the possible conflicts when recent college graduates work for and report to senior managers who grew up with quite different life experiences and values. And how about the reverse, when older workers end up on teams headed by much younger leaders?

Gender subcultures form among persons who share gender identities and display common patterns of behavior.

The **double-bind dilemma** is where female leaders get criticized when they act consistent with female subculture stereotypes and when they act consistent with male subculture stereotypes.

Members of **gender subcultures** share identities and tend to display common patterns of behavior. The effects can be exclusionary and detrimental to multiculturism goals. When men work together, for example, conversations in an "alpha male" or "bro" subgroup culture may emphasize sports metaphors, games, and stories focused on winning and losing.[29] This subculture may even involve what one corporate sociologist calls "heavy sexualized talk."[30] Where does this leave someone who is uncomfortable with such an environment? And what about women that suffer a **double-bind dilemma** in leadership roles? This occurs when they get criticized as being "too soft" when they act consistent with female stereotypes, but also get criticized as being "too hard" when acting consistent with male stereotypes. In other words, female leaders may be "damned if they do, and damned if they don't," and may find it hard to get credit for effective leadership.[31]

Analysis: Make Data Your Friend | 74% of working adults say they don't have enough time for their children.

Organization Cultures Face Emerging Work–Life Trends

Ariel Skelley/Getty Images

If you have any doubts regarding the importance of work–life issues and their implications for organizational cultures and management practices, consider these facts:

- 78% of American couples are dual-wage earners.
- 63% believe they don't have enough time for their spouses or partners.
- 74% believe they don't have enough time for their children.
- 35% are spending time caring for elderly relatives.
- Both baby boomers (87%) and millennials (89%) rate flexible work as important.
- Both baby boomers (63%) and millennials (69%) want opportunities to work remotely at least part of the time.

Your Thoughts?

What organizational culture issues are raised by these facts? What should employers do to best respond to the situation described here? What about you? Are you prepared to succeed in a work culture that doesn't respect these facts? Or, are you preparing right now to always find and be attractive to employers who do?

The many possible subcultures in organizations also include **occupational and functional subcultures** that form around shared professions and skills.[32] People from different occupations and functions can have difficulty understanding and working well with one another. Employees in a business may overidentify as "systems people" or "marketing people" or "finance people." They may spend most of their time with each other, develop a shared "jargon" or common technical language, and view their roles in the organization as more important than those of the other functions. It's easy under such conditions for teamwork and cooperation across the occupational or functional boundaries to suffer.

Occupational and functional subcultures form among persons who share the same skills and work responsibilities.

Ethnic subcultures and **national subcultures** enter the workplace as people share the same ethnicity or nationality. What happens when co-workers hear a group of software engineers that share a language—say Mandarin or Hindi—speaking it together? We love fashion and are used to all different manners of dress, but how do we react when three women in head scarves and ankle-length skirts walk into the office coffee room while chatting back and forth? We emphasize the importance of understanding and respecting cross-cultural differences when traveling internationally. Can't the same attention help us better deal with diversity among ethnic and national subcultures at home and in the workplace?

Ethnic subcultures or **national subcultures** form among people who work together and have roots in the same ethnic community or nationality.

Power, Diversity, and Organizational Subcultures

The term "diversity" basically means the presence of differences. These differences in organizations may or may not be distributed equally among subcultures and in the power structures. What happens when one subculture, for example white males, is in the "majority" and holds most of the power, while others are among the less powerful "minorities"? What happens when those in the majority feel their traditional dominance threatened as others gain positions, stature, and power?

Glass Ceilings and the Leaking Pipeline
Even though demographics and hiring practices are changing, there is still likely to be more workforce diversity at lower and middle levels of organizations than at the top. Look at **Figure 12.3**. It depicts the **glass ceiling** as an invisible barrier that limits the advancement of or equal pay for women and minorities. What are the implications for women and minority members seeking to advance and prosper in an organization where the majority culture consists almost exclusively of white males? How easy is it for women, people of color, and other minority members to advance when promotions are controlled by decision makers from an alternative and dominant culture?

The **glass ceiling** is an invisible barrier to advancement by women and minorities in organizations.

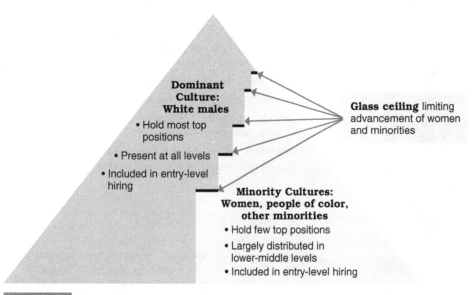

FIGURE 12.3 Glass ceilings as barriers to women and minority cultures in traditional organizations and career opportunities.

If women hold over 50% of management jobs, why do they still hold proportionally fewer CEO positions and board seats in large firms? Why are persons of color underrepresented as well? A McKinsey report finds 68% of senior management jobs being held by white men, 19% by white women, 9% by men of color, and 4% by women of color. Among new hires, only 79 women are promoted to manager for every 100 men that get promoted. In a report summarizing these data, McKinsey concludes: "Progress on gender equality at work has stalled."[33] Again, the question is "Why?"

One reason why more women haven't gotten to the top is that they often hit plateaus or "fall off the cliff" at earlier career stages. The leaking pipeline problem occurs when otherwise qualified and high-performing females and minorities drop out of upward-tracking career paths. And, their reasons for doing so aren't always based on personal goals on the one hand or outright prejudice or discrimination at the other. The forces of diversity bias in organizational cultures can be subtle and insidious as they make it hard for women and minority members to achieve and advance.[34]

The **leaking pipeline problem** occurs when otherwise qualified and high-performing women and minorities drop out of upward career paths.

Diversity Bias

Prejudicial behavior can be driven by an **unconscious bias** or **implicit bias** that people don't realize they have but that still influences their behavior.[35] This embedded bias shows up in how we treat others in conversations, who we form friendships with, and who we recruit, hire, and promote for our teams. The low percentages of women and minorities in top management and on corporate boards, for example, may be due less to blatant discrimination and more due to the unconscious bias of white males giving preferences to others who are "like" themselves. When unconscious bias is pointed out, furthermore, we are often surprised because the bias displayed differs markedly from our self-concepts.

Unconscious bias or **implicit bias** is an embedded prejudice that people don't recognize they have but that still influences their behavior toward others.

Prejudicial behavior can also be driven by **structural bias** in the form of organizational or team norms and practices that discourage or inhibit the advancement of women and minorities.[36] Team expectations that "no one goes home until the job is done," for example, may sound good from a performance perspective. But, they also send signals that hurt caregivers and single parents who rely on fixed schedules to balance work and family responsibilities. Another structural bias is a lack role models and mentors that can support women and minorities and advocate for their career progress.

Structural bias exists as organizational norms and practices that discourage or inhibit the advancement of women and minorities.

Harassment and Discrimination

Subculture challenges faced by minority and female employees can range from misunderstandings and a lack of sensitivity due to unconscious or structural bias on the one hand to overt harassment and discrimination on the other. **Microaggressions** occur as disrespectful, demeaning, and hurtful sexist and racist behaviors. These can be unintentional - like a mistaken assumption - or intentional - like a nasty comment. The result is mistreatment and harm to members of less powerful subcultures, including women, people of color, lesbians, gays, bisexuals, transgender persons, and queer people.[37]

Microaggressions are disrespectful, demeaning, and hurtful sexism and racism behaviors.

Sexual harassment in employment has gained visibility with the help of the #MeToo movement. Some 30% of women report being sexually harassed at work and the figure rises to 55% for women in senior management positions.[38] Data from the U.S. Equal Employment Opportunity Commission (EEOC) show that sex discrimination is a factor in approximately 30% of bias suits filed by workers.[39] The EEOC also reports an increase in pregnancy-related discrimination complaints.[40]

Discrimination in hiring is a real concern. One study distributed fake résumés to recruiters. The résumés documented equal credentials but different family details. Results showed that men with children were the most hirable—being viewed as responsible, while women with children were the least hirable—being viewed as likely to sacrifice work for family responsibilities.[41] A review of 25 years of research on hiring bias showed a stable pattern of white male job applicants getting one-third more interview invites when compared to African-Americans.[42]

Pay discrimination is another issue. A senior executive in the computer industry reported her surprise at finding out that the top performer in her work group, an African American male, was paid 25% less than everyone else. This wasn't because his pay had been cut to that level, she said. It was because his pay increases had always trailed those given to his white co-workers. The differences added up significantly over time, but no one noticed or stepped forward to make the appropriate adjustment.[43]

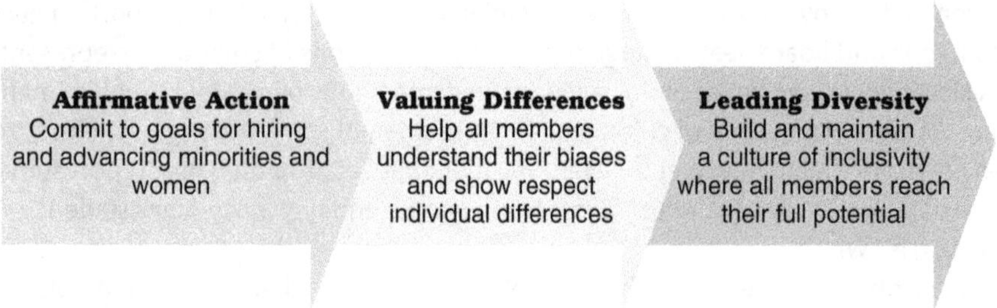

Affirmative Action	Valuing Differences	Leading Diversity
Commit to goals for hiring and advancing minorities and women	Help all members understand their biases and show respect individual differences	Build and maintain a culture of inclusivity where all members reach their full potential

FIGURE 12.4 Continuum of leadership approaches to diversity.

People respond to harassment and discrimination in different ways. Some challenge the system by filing complaints or taking legal actions. Some quit to pursue employment elsewhere or start their own businesses. Still others may try to quietly "fit in" and "go with the flow." They resort to **biculturalism** and try to display majority culture characteristics that seem necessary to blend in and succeed in the work environment. For example, gay and lesbian employees may hide their sexual orientation from co-workers out of fear of prejudice or discrimination. Transgender persons may adopt an expected identity rather than present to coworkers in their accepted one. These last two examples show people placing themselves in **glass closets**—self-imposed personas that hide one's sexual orientation and gender identity from others at work.[44]

> **Biculturalism** is when minority members display characteristics of majority cultures in order to succeed.

> The **glass closet** is a self-imposed persona adopted by LGBTQ persons in order to hide their sexual orientation and gender identities from others.

Multiculturalism and Diversity Leadership

"Glass ceilings" . . . "leaking pipelines" . . . "biculturalism" . . . "glass closets" . . . wouldn't it be nice if we didn't have to talk about such things? Wouldn't it be nice if everyone could experience the benefits of multiculturalism in the workplace? There should be no doubt that all workers—minority and majority alike—want similar things—respect for their talents and identities, and to be in a work setting that allows them to achieve their full potential. But meeting these aspirations requires an inclusive organizational culture and the best in multicultural and diversity leadership.

Figure 12.4 is based on ideas on diversity leadership set forth by R. Roosevelt Thomas.[45] It shows a continuum of management approaches to diversity. The first is *affirmative action*. Here, leaders commit their organizations to specific goals for hiring and advancing minority and female employees. The second is *valuing diversity*. Here, leaders commit their organizations to education, training, and messaging that help employees better understand their biases—conscious and unconscious—and respect individual differences.

Thomas pushes us to further embrace the third approach—**leading diversity**. Diversity leaders fully commit their organizations to values of inclusivity and respect for all, hold members accountable for living up to these values, and model the values daily in their own behaviors. Diversity leaders embrace multiculturism. They invest in training and support efforts to identify and remove unconscious biases. They seek out and eliminate structural biases and replace them with policies and procedures that are supportive of women and minorities. Finally, they value diversity as not just a goal but as a mission-driven strategic imperative.

> **Leading diversity** is a leadership approach that creates an organizational culture that respects diversity and supports multiculturalism.

Learning Check

LEARNING OBJECTIVE 12.2

Describe subcultures and diversity in multicultural organizations.

Be Sure You Can • define *multiculturalism* and explain the concept of a multicultural organization • identify common organizational subcultures • discuss glass ceilings, the leaking pipeline problem, and glass closets • describe unconscious bias and structural bias • explain the challenges of truly leading diversity in organizations diversity

WileyPLUS

See Author Video

12.3 Organizational Change

LEARNING OBJECTIVE 12.3

Identify alternative change strategies and types of resistance to change found in organizations.

> **Learn More About**
>
> Models of change leadership • Transformational and incremental change • Phases of planned change • Change strategies • Resistance to change

What if an organization's culture is flawed, and condones bad behaviors like bullying and sexual harassment? What if it doesn't encourage high performance? What if subcultures clash and adjustments must be made? What if diversity isn't valued on a team or in an organization? Simply put, what can managers and leaders do when an organization's or a team's culture needs to be changed? We use the word "change" so often that culture changes like these may seem easy, almost routine. But that's not always the case.[46] Former British Airways CEO Sir Rod Eddington once said that "Altering an airline's culture is like trying to perform an engine change in flight."[47]

Models of Change Leadership

A **change leader** takes initiative in trying to change the behavior of another person or within a social system.

A **change leader** is someone who takes initiative to change existing patterns of behavior of a person or within a social system. These are managers who act as *change agents* and make things happen, even when inertia has made systems and people reluctant to embrace new ways of doing things. Managers who are strong change leaders are alert to cultures, situations, and people needing change, recognize good ideas and opportunities, and ready and able to support the implementation of new ideas in actual practice.

Every manager and team leader should ideally act as a change leader. But the reality is that most of us have tendencies to stay with the status quo, accepting things as they are and not wanting to change. **Figure 12.5** contrasts a true "change leader" with a "status quo manager." Whereas the status quo manager is backward-looking, reactive, and comfortable with habit, the change leader is forward-looking, proactive, supportive of new ideas, and comfortable with criticism.

In **top-down change**, the change initiatives come from senior management.

Top-Down Change **Top-down change** is where senior managers initiate changes with the goal of improving organizational performance. Although it sounds straightforward that "what the boss wants the boss will get," research suggests otherwise. As many as 70% of large-scale change efforts in American firms actually fail.[48] The most common reason for failure is

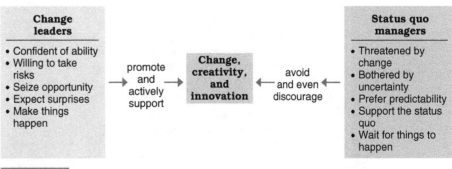

FIGURE 12.5 Change leaders versus status quo managers.

poor implementation. The change is initiated but never completed because it isn't supported at lower levels. Change programs have little chance of success without the support of those who must implement them. And, that support is most likely to come when those who do the implementation are involved in the change planning process. When change is driven from the top without lower-level inputs and participation, it can easily fail.

Bottom-Up Change

A major risk as organizations grow in size is that good ideas get lost in the labyrinth. **Bottom-up change** taps into ideas initiated from lower organizational levels and lets them percolate upward. One way managers can unlock the potential for bottom-up change is by holding "diagonal slice meetings" that bring together employees from across functions and levels. They are asked for ideas about what might be wrong and what changes might be made to improve things. Another way is to build an organizational culture that values empowerment and encourages everyone regardless of rank or position to use their job knowledge and common sense to improve things.

In **bottom-up change**, change initiatives come from all levels in the organization.

Transformational and Incremental Change

Changes initiated at the top levels of an organization are likely to be large-scale and strategic repositioning changes focused on big issues that affect the organization as a whole. Lower-level changes most often deal with adjustments in structures, systems, technologies, products, and people to support strategic positioning. Both types are important in the organizational change pyramid shown in **Figure 12.6**.[49]

Transformational change is radical or frame-breaking change that results in a major and comprehensive redirection of the organization.[50] It is led from the top and creates fundamental shifts in strategy, culture, structures, and even the organization's underlying sense of purpose or mission. As you might expect, transformational change is intense, highly stressful, complex, and difficult to achieve. Popular advice to would-be leaders of transformational changes includes these guidelines:[51]

Transformational change results in a major and comprehensive redirection of the organization.

- Establish a sense of urgency for change.
- Form a powerful coalition to lead the change.
- Create and communicate a change vision.
- Empower others to move change forward.
- Celebrate short-term wins, and recognize those who help.
- Build on success; align people and systems with new ways.
- Stay with it; keep the message consistent; champion the vision.

FIGURE 12.6 **The organizational change pyramid.**

Incremental change bends and adjusts existing ways to improve performance.

Incremental change is modest, frame-bending change. It basically bends or nudges current systems and practices to better align them with emerging problems and opportunities. The intent isn't to break and remake the system, but rather to move it forward through continuous improvements. Common incremental changes in organizations involve the evolution of products, processes, technologies, and work systems. They keep organizational processes and structures tuned up—like the engine in an automobile—in between transformations—when the old vehicle is replaced with a new one.

Phases of Planned Change

Good insights for leading change are found in a simple but helpful model developed many years ago by the psychologist Kurt Lewin. He recommended that planned change be viewed as a process with three phases. Phase 1 is *unfreezing*—preparing a system for change. Phase 2 is *changing*—making actual changes in the system. Phase 3 is *refreezing*—stabilizing the system after change.[52] In today's fast-paced organizational environments, we can add another phase to Lewin's model called *improvising*—making adjustments as needed while change is taking place.[53]

Unfreezing is the phase during which a situation is prepared for change.

Unfreezing Planned change has a better chance for success when people are ready for it and open to doing things differently. **Unfreezing** is the phase in which the change agent prepares a situation for change by developing felt needs for change among those affected by a change initiative. The goal is to get people to view change as a way to solve a real problem or pursue a meaningful opportunity. Common errors at the unfreezing stage are not creating a sense of urgency for change and neglecting to build a coalition of influential persons who support it.

Ethics: Know Right from Wrong | Some managers use deception to avoid losing power while giving the appearance of sharing power.

Hidden Agendas in Organizational Change

Thomas Barwick/DigitalVision/Getty Images

Sharing power is a popular choice when implementing a change strategy. It means allowing others to have a decision-making role and to be involved throughout the change process. This approach can generate a lot of good ideas and helps establish all-important "buy-in" to support the proposed change. But, suppose the ideas offered and the ensuing conversations move in a direction that top management thinks is wrong? What happens then?

Some managers are afraid of losing influence while sharing power during organizational change. So, they resort to hidden agendas. They handpick key members to be on their change teams. They also ask them to take prominent roles in discussions and support only the "right" ideas. The goal is to make sure that change heads in the predetermined "preferred" direction while still giving everyone involved a sense of being included and empowered. It's a very political way of appearing to share power—enjoying the image-related benefits of inclusiveness, but still maintaining dominance.

What Do You Think?

Although this situation happens frequently in organizations, does that make it right? What are the ethical issues involved? When is such an approach more or less likely to be ethical? As a manager, would you handpick the leaders of a change effort in order to get your way—even if that meant that alternative points of view were likely to be excluded from the process? What if your boss selected you to represent your department on a task force just because you agreed with his or her favored approach? If you knew that most of your co-workers disagreed, would you do what your boss wanted you to do or would you try to represent the wishes of the majority of your co-workers? What are the potential risks associated with your choice?

Some call unfreezing the "burning bridge" phase of change, suggesting that in order to get people to jump off a bridge, you might just have to set it on fire. Managers simulate the burning bridge by engaging people with facts and information that communicate the need for change—environmental pressures, declining performance, and examples of benchmarks or alternative approaches. The goal is to help people to break old habits and recognize new ways of thinking about or doing things.

Changing   **Figure 12.7** shows that unfreezing is followed by the changing phase, where actual changes are made in such organizational targets as tasks, people, culture, technology, and structures. Lewin believes that many change agents commit the error of entering the changing phase prematurely. They are too quick to change things and end up creating harmful resistance. In this sense the change process is like building a house; you need to put a good foundation in place before you begin framing the rooms. With a poor foundation, the house will likely fall at some point. Similarly, if you try to implement change before people are prepared and feel a need for it, your attempt is more likely to fail.

Changing is the phase where a planned change actually takes place.

Refreezing   The goal of refreezing in Lewin's model is to stabilize the change. Refreezing is accomplished by linking change with appropriate rewards, positive reinforcement, and resource support. It is important in this phase to evaluate results, provide feedback to those involved, and make any required modifications to the original change that either undershot or overshot evolving contingencies.

Refreezing is the phase at which change is stabilized.

When refreezing is done poorly, changes are too easily forgotten or abandoned with the passage of time. The most common error at the refreezing stage is declaring victory too soon and withdrawing support before the change has really become a fixed aspect of normal routines. In today's dynamic environment there may also not be a lot of time for refreezing before change becomes necessary again. We end up preparing for more change even before the present one is fully implemented.

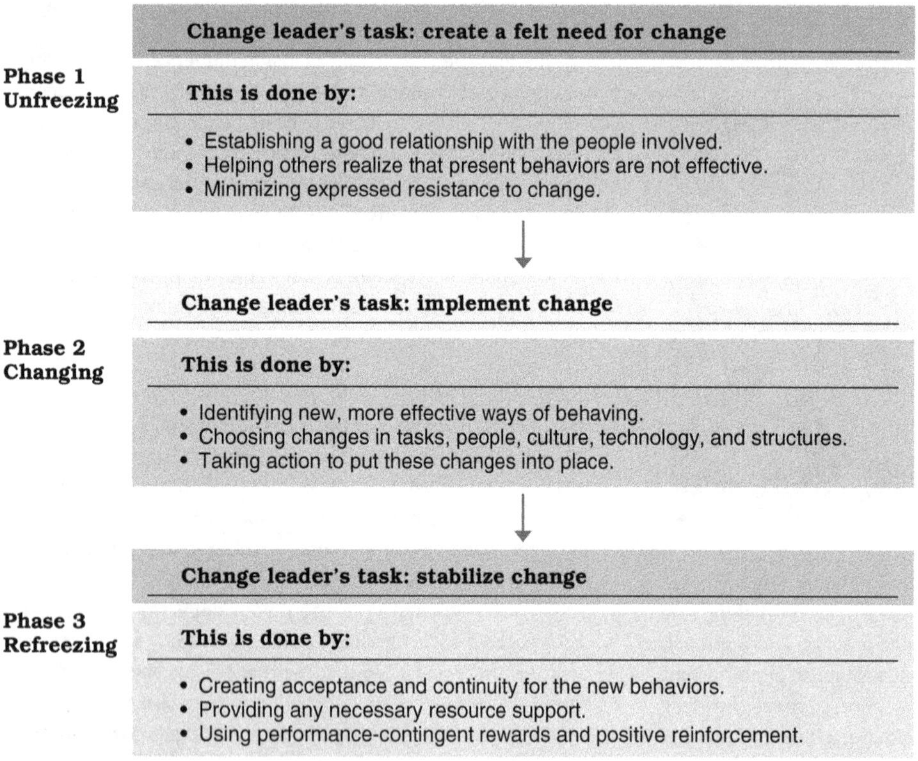

Phase 1 Unfreezing	**Change leader's task: create a felt need for change** **This is done by:** • Establishing a good relationship with the people involved. • Helping others realize that present behaviors are not effective. • Minimizing expressed resistance to change.

↓

Phase 2 Changing	**Change leader's task: implement change** **This is done by:** • Identifying new, more effective ways of behaving. • Choosing changes in tasks, people, culture, technology, and structures. • Taking action to put these changes into place.

↓

Phase 3 Refreezing	**Change leader's task: stabilize change** **This is done by:** • Creating acceptance and continuity for the new behaviors. • Providing any necessary resource support. • Using performance-contingent rewards and positive reinforcement.

FIGURE 12.7   **Lewin's three phases of planned organizational change.**

Improvising

Improvisational change makes continual adjustments as changes are being implemented.

Although Lewin's model depicts change as a linear, three-step process, the reality is that change is dynamic and complex. Managers must not only understand the phases of planned change, they must be prepared to deal with them simultaneously. They should also be willing and able to engage in the process of **improvisational change** where adjustments are continually made as aspects of the change initiative are implemented.[54]

Consider the case of bringing new technology into an organization or work unit. A technology that is attractive in theory may appear complicated in practice to new potential users. The full extent of its benefits or inadequacies may not become known until it is actually tried out. A change leader can succeed in such situations by continually gathering feedback on how the change is progressing, and then improvising to revise and customize the new technology to best meet users' needs and address their concerns about the complexity of the new system.

Change Strategies

Strategy is a major issue when managers actually try to move people and systems toward change. **Figure 12.8** summarizes three change strategies —force-coercion, rational persuasion, and shared power.[55] Managers, as change agents and change leaders, must understand each strategy and its limitatioins.

Force-Coercion Strategies

A **force-coercion strategy** pursues change through formal authority and/or the use of rewards or punishments.

A **force-coercion strategy** uses formal authority plus rewards and punishments to push people to get behind a change. A change agent using force-coercion believes that people are motivated by self-interest and by the potential for personal gains or losses.[56] In *direct forcing*, change agents "order" or "command" that change take place. In *political maneuvering*, they work indirectly to gain advantage over others and make them change. This involves bargaining, obtaining control of important resources, forming alliances, or granting small favors.

Although force-coercion seems quick and easy, most people go along only out of fear of punishment or hope for reward. The likely outcome is temporary compliance that lasts only as long as the rewards and punishments persist. Force-coercion may be most useful as an unfreezing strategy to break old patterns and encourages willingness to try new approaches.

Rational Persuasion Strategies

A **rational persuasion strategy** pursues change through empirical data and rational argument.

Change agents using a **rational persuasion strategy** try to bring about change through persuasion backed by special knowledge, empirical

Change Strategy	Power Bases	Managerial Behavior	Likely Results
Force–Coercion Using formal authority to create change by decree and position power	Legitimacy Rewards Punishments	*Direct forcing* and unilateral action *Political maneuvering* and indirect action	Faster, but low commitment and only temporary compliance
Rational Persuasion Creating change through rational persuasion and empirical argument	Expertise	*Informational efforts* using credible knowledge, demonstrated facts, and logical argument	
Shared power Developing support for change through personal values and commitments	Reference	*Participative efforts* to share power and involve others in planning and implementing change	Slower, but high commitment and longer-term internalization

FIGURE 12.8 Alternative change strategies and their leadership implications.

data, and rational arguments. Change agents following this strategy believe that people are guided by reason. Once the value of a specific course of action is demonstrated by information and relevant facts, it is assumed that a rational person will accept it. This is a good strategy for both unfreezing and refreezing a change situation; It is likely to result in longer-lasting and more internalized change than force-coercion.

To succeed with the rational persuasion strategy, a manager must convince others that making a change will leave them better off than they were before the change. This persuasive power can come directly from the change agent if she has personal credibility as an "expert." It can also be gained by bringing in consultants and other outside experts, or earned through credible demonstration projects and benchmarks in success stories.

Shared Power Strategies
A **shared power strategy** uses participation and involvement to identify values, assumptions, and goals from which support for change naturally emerges. Sometimes called a *normative–reeducative strategy*, this approach is empowerment based and highly collaborative. Power is shared as the change agent works together with others to develop consensus to support change. This strategy is often slow and time consuming, but the power sharing is likely to result in longer-lasting, internalized change.

The great "power" of sharing power in the change process lies with unlocking the creativity, experience, and energies of people within the system. Some managers hesitate to engage this strategy for fear of losing control or of having to compromise on important organizational goals. But Harvard scholar Teresa M. Amabile points out that they should have the confidence to share power regarding means and processes, if not overall goals. "People will be more creative," she says, "if you give them freedom to decide how to climb particular mountains. You needn't let them choose which mountains to climb."[57]

A **shared power strategy** pursues change by participation in assessing change needs, values, and goals.

Resistance to Change

When people resist change, they are most often defending something important to them that now appears to be threatened by impending change. Look at the list in **Figure 12.9**. How often have you felt such things and how did you react when being asked to make changes in your life or work?

A change leader can achieve a lot by listening to resistance and then using this information to improve the change process and even modify the change itself.[58] Instead of viewing resistance as something to be "overcome," it is better viewed as feedback. The presence of resistance usually means that something can be done to achieve a better "fit" among the planned change, the situation, and the people involved. Feedback in the form of resistance—if listened to—can provide lots of clues on what's causing problems with a planned change effort and

---

- *Fear of the unknown*—not understanding what is happening or what comes next.
- *Disrupted habits*—feeling upset to see the end of the old ways of doing things.
- *Loss of confidence*—feeling incapable of performing well under the new ways of doing things.
- *Loss of control*—feeling that things are being done "to" you rather than "by" or "with" you.
- *Poor timing*—feeling overwhelmed by the situation or that things are moving too fast.
- *Work overload*—not having the physical or emotional energy to commit to the change.
- *Loss of face*—feeling inadequate or humiliated because the "old" ways weren't "good" ways.
- *Lack of purpose*—not seeing a reason for the change and/or not understanding its benefits.

FIGURE 12.9   **Common reasons why people resist change.**

what might be done to improve things. In fact, one of the easiest ways to track progress is by monitoring these resistance to change checkpoints.[59]

1. *Check benefits*—Do the people involved see a clear advantage in making the change? Everyone should know "what is in it for me" or "what is in it for our group or the organization as a whole."

2. *Check compatibility*—Is the change perceived as breaking comfort levels? It's best to keep the change as close as possible to the existing values and ways of doing things. Minimizing the scope of change helps to keep it more acceptable and less threatening.

3. *Check simplicity*—How complex is the change? It's best to keep the change as easy as possible to understand and to use. People should have access to training and assistance to make the transition to new ways as easy as possible.

4. *Check triability*—Are things moving too fast? People tend to do better when they can try the change little by little, making adjustments as they go. Don't rush the change, and be sure to adjust the timing to best coincide with work schedules and cycles of high/low workloads.

There are other positive ways to deal with resistance to change.[60] *Education and communication* uses discussions, presentations, and demonstrations to educate everyone beforehand about a change. *Participation and involvement* allows others to contribute ideas and help design and implement the change. *Facilitation and support* provides encouragement and training, engages active listening to problems and complaints, and seeks ways to reduce

---

Get Comfortable with Your Tolerance for Ambiguity

The next time you are driving somewhere and following a familiar route only to encounter a "detour" sign, test your **tolerance for ambiguity**. Is the detour just a minor inconvenience? Do you go forward without any further thought? Or is it a big deal, perhaps causing you anxiety and anger? Do you show a tendency to resist change in your normal routines? Change creates anxiety and breaks us from past habits and conditions. Uncertainty puts many things out of our immediate control. Depending on your tolerance for ambiguity, you may be more or less comfortable dealing with these realities.

Which alternatives in the Tolerance for Ambiguity Double Check best describe you? What are the insights for your tolerance for ambiguity? It takes personal flexibility and a lot of confidence to cope well with unpredictability, whether it's in a college course or in a work situation. Some people struggle with the unfamiliar. They prefer structure, security, and clear directions. They get comfortable with fixed patterns in life and can be afraid of anything "new."

Have we been talking about you? Or are you willing and able to work with less structure? Do you enjoy flexibility, setting your own goals, and making decisions? Are you excited by the prospect of change and new—as yet undefined—opportunities? It's important to find a good fit between your personal preferences for ambiguity and the pace and nature of change in the career field and organizations where you ultimately choose to work. To achieve this fit, you have to understand your own tolerance for ambiguity and how you are likely to react in change situations.

An instructor who gives precise assignments and accepts no deviations *or* one who gives open-ended assignments and lets students suggest alternatives?

In a typical course, do you prefer...

An instructor who keeps modifying the course syllabus using student feedback *or* one who gives out a detailed syllabus and sticks to it?

Tolerance for Ambiguity Double Check

Get To Know Yourself Better

Write a short narrative describing your "ideal" employer in terms of organization culture, management styles, and frequency of major changes. Add a comment that explains how this ideal organization fits your personality, including insights from self-assessments completed in other chapters. What does this say about how you may have to change and adapt in order to fulfill your career aspirations?

performance pressures. *Negotiation and agreement* provides incentives to gain support from those who are actively resisting or ready to resist change initiatives.

Two other approaches for managing resistance are common, but they are also risky in terms of negative side effects. *Manipulation and co-optation* seeks to covertly influence others by selectively providing information and structuring events in favor of the desired change. *Explicit and implicit coercion* forces people to accept change by threatening undesirable consequences for noncompliance with what is being asked in the change process.

Learning Check

LEARNING OBJECTIVE 12.3

Identify alternative change strategies and types of resistance to change found in organizations.

Be Sure You Can • define *change leader* and *change agent* • discuss pros and cons of top-down change and bottom-up change • differentiate incremental and transformational change • describe Lewin's three phases of planned change • discuss improvising as an approach to planned change • discuss pros and cons of the force-coercion, rational persuasion, and shared power change strategies • list several reasons why people resist change • describe strategies for dealing with resistance to change

Management Learning Review: Get Prepared for Quizzes and Exams

Summary

LEARNING OBJECTIVE 12.1   Explain organizational culture and its influence on behavior in organizations.

- Organizational culture is an internal environment that establishes a personality for the organization and influences the behavior of members.
- The observable culture is found in the rites, rituals, stories, heroes, and symbols of the organization; the core culture consists of the core values and fundamental beliefs on which the organization is based.
- In organizations with strong cultures, members behave with shared understandings and act with commitment to core values.
- Key dimensions of organizational culture include hierarchical culture, dependable culture, enterprising culture, and social culture.
- Among trends in managing organizational cultures, value-based management and workplace spirituality are popular directions and considerations.

For Discussion Which of the various dimensions of organizational culture are most important to you as an employee?

LEARNING OBJECTIVE 12.2   Describe subcultures and diversity in multicultural organizations.

- Multicultural organizations operate with internal cultures that value pluralism, respect diversity, and build strength from an environment of inclusion.
- Organizations have many subcultures, including those based on occupational, functional, ethnic, age, and gender differences.
- Challenges faced by members of minority subcultures in organizations include sexual harassment, pay discrimination, job discrimination, and the glass ceiling effect.
- Managing diversity is the process of developing an inclusive work environment that allows everyone to reach their full potential.

For Discussion What can the leader of a small team do to reduce diversity prejudice being expressed by one team member?

LEARNING OBJECTIVE 12.3 Identify alternative change strategies and types of resistance to change found in organizations.

- Change leaders are change agents who take initiative to change the behavior of people and organizational systems.
- Organizational change can proceed with a top-down emphasis, with a bottom-up emphasis, or a combination of both.
- Incremental change makes continuing adjustments to existing ways and practices; transformational change makes radical changes in organizational directions.

- Lewin's three phases of planned change are unfreezing—preparing a system for change; changing—making a change; and refreezing—stabilizing the system. To this can be added a fourth—improvising as needed.
- Change agents should understand the force-coercion, rational persuasion, and shared power change strategies.
- People resist change for a variety of reasons, including fear of the unknown and force of habit.
- Good change agents deal with resistance in a variety of ways, including education, participation, support, and facilitation.

For Discussion Can a change leader ever be satisfied that the refreezing stage of planned change has been accomplished in today's dynamic environments?

Self-Test 12

Multiple-Choice Questions

1. Pluralism and the absence of discrimination and prejudice in policies and practices are two important hallmarks of _____.
   a. the glass ceiling effect
   b. a multicultural organization
   c. quality circles
   d. affirmative action

2. When members of minority cultures feel that they have to behave in ways similar to the majority culture, this is called _____.
   a. biculturalism
   b. symbolic leadership
   c. the glass ceiling effect
   d. inclusivity

3. Engineers, scientists, and information systems specialists are likely to become part of separate _____ subcultures in an organization.
   a. ethnic
   b. generational
   c. functional
   d. occupational

4. Stories told about an organization's past accomplishments and heroes such as company founders are all part of what is called the _____ culture.
   a. observable
   b. underground
   c. functional
   d. core

5. Honesty, social responsibility, and customer service are examples of _____ that can become foundations for an organization's core culture.
   a. rites and rituals
   b. values
   c. subsystems
   d. ideas

6. Which leadership approach is most consistent with an organizational culture that values the full utilization of all diverse talents of all the organization's human resources?
   a. Managing diversity
   b. Affirmative action
   c. Status quo
   d. Rational persuasion

7. When members of a dominant subculture, such as white males, make it hard for members of minority subcultures, such as women, to advance to higher level positions in the organization, this is called the _____ effect.
   a. dominator
   b. glass ceiling
   c. brick wall
   d. end-of-line

8. An executive pursuing transformational change would give highest priority to which one of these change targets?
   a. an out-of-date policy
   b. the organizational culture
   c. a new information system
   d. job designs in a customer service department

9. _____ change results in a major change of direction for an organization, while _____ change makes small adjustments to current ways of doing things.
   a. Frame-breaking; radical
   b. Frame-bending; incremental
   c. Transformational; frame-breaking
   d. Transformational; incremental

10. The presence or absence of a felt need for change is a key issue in the _____ phase of the planned change process.
    a. improvising
    b. evaluating
    c. unfreezing
    d. refreezing

11. When a manager listens to users, makes adaptations, and continuously tweaks and changes a new MIS as it is being implemented, the approach to technological change can be described as _____.

a. top-down

b. improvisational

c. organization development

d. frame breaking

12. A manager using a force-coercion strategy will rely on _____ to bring about change.

a. expertise

b. benchmarking

c. formal authority

d. information

13. The most participative of the planned change strategies is _____.

a. force-coercion

b. rational persuasion

c. shared power

d. command and control

14. True internalization and commitment to a planned change is most likely to occur when a manager uses a(n) _____ change strategy.

a. education and communication

b. rational persuasion

c. manipulation and co-optation

d. shared power

15. Trying to covertly influence others, offering only selective information, and structuring events in favor of the desired change is a way of dealing with resistance by _____.

a. participation

b. manipulation and co-optation

c. force-coercion

d. facilitation

Short-Response Questions

16. What core values might be found in high-performance organizational cultures?

17. Why is it important for managers to understand subcultures in organizations?

18. What are the three phases of change described by Lewin, and what are their implications for change leadership?

19. What are the major differences in potential outcomes of using the force-coercion, rational persuasion, and shared power strategies of planned change?

Essay Question

20. Two businesswomen, former college roommates, are discussing their jobs and careers over lunch. You overhear one saying to the other: "I work for a large corporation, while you own a small retail business. In my company there is a strong corporate culture and everyone feels its influence. In fact, we are always expected to act in ways that support the culture and serve as role models for others to do so as well. This includes a commitment to diversity and multiculturalism. Because of the small size of your firm, things like corporate culture, diversity, and multiculturalism are less important to worry about." Do you agree or disagree with this statement? Why?

Career Skills & Competencies: Make Yourself Valuable!

Evaluate Career Situations

What Would You Do?

1. Two Job Offers

You will soon have to choose between two really nice job offers. They are in the same industry, but you wonder which employer would be the "best fit." You have a sense that their "cultures" are quite different. Fortunately, you've been invited back to spend a full day at each before making your decision. One of your friends suggests that doing a balance-sheet assessment of cultural pluses and minuses for each employer could be helpful. What aspects of organizational culture would you identify as important to your job choice? Given the items on your list, what can you look for or do in the coming visits to discover the real organizational cultures pluses and minuses for each item?

2. Team Culture Nightmare

The promotion to team manager puts you right where you want to be in terms of career advancement. Even though you've had to move to a new location, it's a great opportunity . . . if you can do well as team leader. That's the problem. Now that you're in the job, you realize that the culture of the team is really bad. Some of the ways you've heard members describe it to one another are "toxic," "dog-eat-dog," "watch your back," and "keep your head down." Realizing that culture change takes time but that's it's also necessary in this situation, what can you do right away as the new team leader to set the team on course for a positive change to its culture?

3. Tough Situation

Times are tough at your organization, and, as the director of human resources, you have a problem. The company's senior executives have decided that 10% of the payroll has to be cut immediately. Instead of laying off about 30 people, you would like to have everyone cut back their work hours by 10%. This way the payroll would be cut but everyone would get to keep their jobs. But you've heard that this idea isn't popular with all of the workers. Some are already grumbling that it's a "bad idea" and the company is just looking for excuses "to cut wages." How can you best handle this situation as a change leader?

Reflect on the Self-Assessment

Change Leadership IQ

Instructions

Indicate whether each of the following statements is true (T) or false (F).[61]

T F 1. People invariably resist change.

T F 2. One of the most important responsibilities of any change effort is that the leader clearly describes the expected future state.

T F 3. Communicating what will remain the same after change is as important as communicating what will be different.

T F 4. Planning for change should be done by a small, knowledgeable group, and then that group should communicate its plan to others.

T F 5. Managing resistance to change is more difficult than managing apathy about change.

T F 6. Complaints about a change effort are often a sign of change progress.

T F 7. Leaders find it more difficult to change organizational goals than to change the ways of reaching those goals.

T F 8. Successful change efforts typically involve changing reward systems to support change.

T F 9. Involving more members of an organization in planning a change increases commitment to making the change successful.

T F 10. Successful organizational change requires certain significant and dramatic steps or "leaps," rather than moderate or "incremental" ones.

Scoring

Questions 2, 3, 6, 8, 9, 10 are true; the rest are false. Tally the number of correct items to indicate the extent to which your change management assumptions are consistent with findings from the discipline.

Contribute to the Class Exercise

Force-Field Analysis

Instructions

1. Form into your class discussion groups and review this model of **force-field analysis**—the consideration of forces driving in support of a planned change and forces resisting the change.

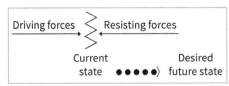

2. Use force-field analysis and make lists of driving and resisting forces for one of the following situations:

a. *"Home Schooling" at College Level.* Things are changing in colleges and universities as budget declines create pressures for a rethinking of educational programming. Home schooling has grown popular at primary and secondary levels. Why can't it work for college as well, at least for the first two years? At least one vice president at the local university is in favor of making a proposal to move her campus to a 3rd/4th-year-only status and have years 1 and 2 go fully online. She wonders what she should prepare for when sharing her ideas with the rest of the executive team.

b. *Scheduling Dilemma.* A new owner has just taken over a small walk-in-and-buy-by-the-slice pizza shop in a college town. There are presently eight employees, three of whom are full-time and five of whom are part-time. The shop is open seven days a week from 10:30 a.m. to midnight. The new owner believes there is a market niche available for late-night pizza and would like to stay open each night until 4 a.m. She wants to make the change as soon as possible.

c. *Instructor's Choice.* A situation assigned by the instructor.

3. Choose the three driving forces that are most significant for the proposed change. For each force, develop ideas on how it could be further increased or mobilized in support of the change.

4. Choose the three resisting forces that are most significant for the proposed change. For each force, develop ideas on how it could be reduced or turned into a driving force.

5. Be prepared to participate in a class discussion led by your instructor.

Manage a Critical Incident

Proposal for Open Office Design and Hotdesking

You are just starting to work with an architect on designs for a new office space for your fast-growing tech startup. She proposes a design that does away with private offices, includes two or three personal cubicles with flexible dividers, and provides lots of flexible open spaces for casual and arranged meetings. She also proposes a shift to "hotdesking" for the sales representatives because they spend a lot of time away from the office. This means that they will not have permanent space and will instead "sign up" to use temporary cubicle desks when they come into the office. You really like the total design concept because it supports collaboration and teamwork while also saving space and facilities costs as the firm grows. But, you're worried about possible resistance from employees who are used to having private offices and their own desks. You sit down to write a list of "pros" and "cons" for the architect's proposal. You also make some notes on how to engage the staff with these ideas in order to head off any problems.

Questions

What's on your list and what's in your notes? What kind of change leadership approach do you think will be most likely to work with this group and situation?

Collaborate on the Team Project

Organizational Culture Walk

Question

What organizational cultures do we encounter and deal with every day, and what are their implications for employees, customers, and organizational performance?

Instructions

1. In your team, make two lists. List A should identify the things that represent the core cultures of organizations. List B should identify the things that represent the observable cultures of organizations. For each item on the two lists, identify one or more indicators that you might use to describe this aspect of the culture for an actual organization.

2. Take an *organizational culture walk* through a major shopping area of your local community. Choose at least three business establishments. Visit each as customers. As you approach, put your "organizational culture senses" to work. Start gathering data on your lists A and B. Keep gathering it while you are at the business and right through your departure. Take good notes, and gather your thoughts together after leaving. Do this for each of the three organizations you choose.

3. Analyze and compare your data to identify the major cultural attributes of the three organizations and how they influence customers and organizational performance.

4. Use your results to make some general observations and report on the relationship between organizational cultures and performance as well as among organizational cultures, employee motivation, and customer satisfaction.

Analyze the Case Study

Gamification | Finding Legitimacy in the New Corporate Culture

Go to **Management Cases for Critical Thinking** at the back of the book to find this case.

CHAPTER 13

Human Resource Management

Nurturing Turns Potential into Performance

Chris Ryan/OJO Images/Getty Images

Pew Research reports that 50% of working fathers and 56% of working mothers have "very" or "somewhat" difficult times balancing work and family . . . 50% of working fathers and 23% of working mothers feel they "spend too little time with kids."

Chapter Quick Start

As a manager or team leader it's all about talent—the talent that you hire, nurture, develop, and support to accomplish goals. It's the same with you. Talent is a great personal asset that holds the key to your future. But it needs constant attention and investment for you to stay marketable and successful. This chapter discusses how human resource management, or HRM, locates, cultivates, and sustains talent in organizations. As you read, don't forget the personal career applications.

LEARNING OBJECTIVES

13.1 Explain the human resource management process and its legal framework.

13.2 Describe how managers help organizations attract a quality workforce.

13.3 Discuss how managers help organizations develop a quality workforce.

13.4 Summarize how managers help organizations maintain a quality workforce.

260

Career Readiness – What to Look for Inside

Thought Leadership

Analysis > *Make Data Your Friend* Costs of Ignoring Internal Job Candidates

Choices > *Think before You Act* Teammates Know You, But Should They Pay You?

Ethics > *Know Right from Wrong* Personality Test? Drug Test? Social Media Test?

Insight > *Learn about Yourself* Conscientiousness Is a Career Booster

Skills Make You Valuable

- **Evaluate** *Career Situations:* What Would You Do?
- **Reflect** *On the Self-Assessment:* Performance Assessment Assumptions
- **Contribute** *To the Class Exercise:* Upward Appraisal
- **Manage** *A Critical Incident:* Athletic Director's Dilemma
- **Collaborate** *On the Team Project:* Future of Labor Unions
- **Analyze** *The Case Study:* RealRecruit: Protecting Student Athletes

The key to managing people in ways that lead to profit, productivity, innovation, and real organizational learning ultimately lies in how you think about your organization and its people. . . . When you look at your people, do you see costs to be reduced? . . . Or, when you look at your people do you see intelligent, motivated, trustworthy individuals—the most critical and valuable strategic assets your organization can have?

With these words from his book *The Human Equation: Building Profits by Putting People First*, Jeffrey Pfeffer challenges managers to invest in people and their talents.[1] Organizations investing more in people outperform those that don't. High-performing organizations thrive on strong foundations of **human capital**—the economic value of people with job-relevant knowledge, skills, abilities, experience, ideas, energies, and commitments. The best employers put people first, and they reap the benefits of doing so.

> **Human capital** is the economic value of people with job-relevant knowledge, skills, abilities, ideas, energies, and commitments.

13.1 | Human Resource Management

LEARNING OBJECTIVE 13.1

Explain the human resource management process and its legal framework.

WileyPLUS

See Author Video

> **Learn More About**
>
> Human resource management process • Strategic human resource management • Legal environment of human resource management

A marketing manager at IDEO, a Palo Alto–based consulting design firm, once said: "If you hire the right people . . . if you've got the right fit . . . then everything will take care of itself."[2] This is what **human resource management**, or HRM, does—attracting, developing, and maintaining a talented and energetic workforce. Organizations that can't do this well have very little chance of being competitive in the long term.

> **Human resource management** is a process of attracting, developing, and maintaining a talented workforce.

Human Resource Management Process

The purpose of human resource management is to support organizational performance by aligning people and their talents with organizational strategies and objectives. All managers and team leaders are responsible for making sure that highly capable and enthusiastic people are in the right positions and working with the support they need to be successful. The process of HRM involves three main tasks.

1. *Attracting a quality workforce*—talent acquisition through human resource planning, employee recruitment, and employee selection.

2. *Developing a quality workforce*—talent development through employee onboarding and orientation, training and development, and performance management.

3. *Maintaining a quality workforce*—talent retention through career development, work–life balance, compensation and benefits, retention and turnover, and labor–management relations.

A key concept in human resource management is "fit"—individual/job fit and individual/organization fit. **Person–job fit** is the extent to which an individual's knowledge, skills, experiences, and personal characteristics match well with work requirements.[3] **Person–organization fit** is the extent to which an individual's values, interests, and behavior match well with the culture of the organization.[4] It's best for the organization and the individual when both fits are strong and positive.

> **Person–job fit** is the extent to which an individual's knowledge, skills, experiences and personal characteristics are consistent with the requirements of their work.
>
> **Person–organization fit** is the extent to which an individual's values, interests, and behavior are consistent with the culture of the organization.

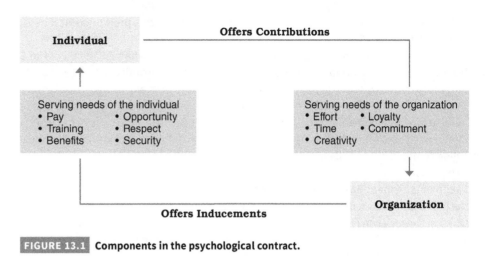

Components in the psychological contract.

Strategic Human Resource Management

Google's parent company, Alphabet, has a Vice President for People Operations. Netflix has a Chief Talent Officer. Lyft has a Vice President of Talent & Inclusion. These job titles signify that people are highly valued and that HRM is considered "strategic" at these new economy companies. Think of **strategic human resource management** as a process of valuing and mobilizing human capital to best implement organizational strategies.[5]

Success with strategic human resource management begins with having an **employee value proposition** that creates a positive person–organization fit. EVPs accomplish this by offering packages of opportunities and rewards—such as pay, benefits, good jobs, and advancement possibilities—that make diverse and talented people want to join, work hard, and stay loyal to an organization.

Employee value propositions are **psychological contracts** that summarize mutually beneficial exchanges of values between individuals and organizations.[6] As shown in **Figure 13.1**, the value offered by the individual—what the employer gets in the psychological contract—includes effort, loyalty, commitment, creativity, and skills. The value offered by the employer—what the employee gets—includes pay, benefits, meaningful work, flexible schedules, and personal development opportunities.

A positive exchange of values creates a healthy psychological contract and any imbalance can cause problems. From the individual's side, a perceived lack of inducements may cause dissatisfaction, loss of motivation, poor performance, and turnover. From the employer's side, a perceived lack of contributions may reduce confidence in the employee, limit rewards given, and derail career advancement.

Legal Environment of Human Resource Management

Evolving societal norms continue to change how businesses approach a number of core human resource management (HRM) practices. More attention than ever is being paid to fairness in hiring. Hire a relative? Promote a friend? Fire an enemy? Not anymore. Managers and employers can't simply do whatever they want when it comes to human resource management practices. Everything has to be done within the framework of government laws and regulations about employment practices.

Laws Protecting Against Discrimination
If valuing people is at the heart of human resource management, **job discrimination** is its enemy. This happens when organizations don't hire or promote someone for reasons unrelated to their performance potential. Think of this the next time you or someone else wonders: "Why didn't I get invited for a job

Strategic human resource management mobilizes human capital to implement organizational strategies.

Employee value propositions are packages of opportunities and rewards that make diverse and talented people want to belong to and work hard for the organization.

Psychological contracts summarize mutually beneficial exchanges of values between individuals and organizations.

Job discrimination occurs when someone is denied a job or work assignment for reasons that are not job relevant.

interview? Is it because my first name is Omar?" "Why didn't I get that promotion? Is it because I'm obviously pregnant?"

The cornerstone of U.S. laws protecting against job discrimination is Title VII of the Civil Rights Act of 1964, amended by the Equal Employment Opportunity Act of 1972 and the Equal Employment Opportunity Act (EEOA) of 1991. These acts encourage **equal employment opportunity** (EEO), the right to employment without regard to sex, race, color, ethnicity, national origin, able-bodiedness, or religion. It is illegal under Title VII to consider any of these factors in decisions related to hiring, promoting, compensating, terminating, or in any way changing someone's terms of employment.

> **Equal employment opportunity** is the requirement that employment decisions be made without regard to sex, race, color, ethnicity, national origin, able-bodiedness, or religion.

The intent of equal employment opportunity is to ensure the rights of all persons to gain and keep employment based only on their ability to do the job and their performance once on the job. This right is federally enforced by the Equal Employment Opportunity Commission (EEOC). This agency can file civil lawsuits against organizations that fail to provide timely resolution of charges of discrimination lodged against them. The laws generally apply to all public and private organizations with 15 or more employees.

Organizations that contract with the federal government are expected to show **affirmative action** by having plans that ensure equal employment opportunity for "qualified minorities, persons with disabilities, women, and covered veterans."[7] When the pros and cons of affirmative action are debated, criticism tends to focus on the use of group membership-such as female or minority status as a criterion in employment decisions.[8] Members of majority populations sometimes raise claims of *reverse discrimination* if they believe preferential treatment given to women and minorities interferes with their employment rights.

> **Affirmative action** is an effort to give preference in employment to women and minority group members who have traditionally been underrepresented.

As a general rule, legal protections for equal employment opportunity do not restrict an employer's right to establish **bona fide occupational qualifications** (BFOQs). These are criteria that can be justified as a reasonable necessity for the normal operation of a business and are clearly related to the capacity to perform a job. BFOQs based on race and color are not allowed under any circumstances. Those based on sex, religion, age, able-bodiedness, and national origin are possible, but organizations must take great care to support these requirements.[9] Examples of an age-based BFOQ include mandatory retirement for pilots and bus drivers based on public safety concerns.

> **Bona fide occupational qualifications** are employment criteria justified by the capacity to perform a job.

Employment Biases and Controversies

Question: "I was interviewing for a sales job and the manager asked me what child care arrangements I had made. Was this his question legal?"

Answer by labor attorney: "This is a perfect example of what not to ask a job applicant and could be considered direct evidence of gender bias against women based on negative stereotypes."

As **Figure 13.2** shows, the legal protections against employment discrimination are extensive. But the example just given also shows that we must be realistic. Laws help to fight discrimination, but they can't guarantee that it won't happen. Laws are complex and changing, and legal interpretations evolve over time. Grey areas, open issues, and controversies remain.

Gender discrimination or **sex discrimination** based on a person's physical sex is illegal under Title VII. But the lines are less clear in respect to **gender identity discrimination** and **sexual orientation discrimination** that result in job biases against lesbian, gay, bisexual, and transgendered persons. Title VII doesn't include explicit protections for LGBTQ workers. The Employment Non-Discrimination Act of 2013 (ENDA) provide these protections, but it is still pending government approval.[10] In the meantime, the EEOC is interpreting the sex discrimination component of Title VII as "forbidding any employment discrimination based on gender identity or sexual orientation." Examples of claims addressed under this interpretation by the EEOC include:[11]

> **Sex discrimination** or **gender discrimination** is employment bias toward a job seeker or job holder based on the person's physical sex.
>
> **Gender identity discrimination** or **sexual orientation discrimination** is employment bias toward job seekers or job holders who are lesbian, gay, bisexual, or transgendered persons.

- Failing to hire an applicant because she is a transgender woman.

- Firing an employee because he is planning or has made a gender transition.

- Denying an employee equal access to a restroom corresponding to the employee's gender identity.
- Harassing an employee because of his or her sexual orientation.
- Refusing to promote someone because they are gay or straight.

Sexual harassment is behavior of a sexual nature that affects a person's employment situation.

The #MeToo movement has brought increased awareness that **sexual harassment** in conduct or in language use remains an important workplace concern. The EEOC defines it as behavior of a sexual nature that creates a hostile work environment, interferes with a person's ability to do a job, or impedes a person's promotion potential.[12] *Quid pro quo sexual harassment* is where job decisions are based on whether an employee submits to or rejects sexual advances. *Hostile work environment sexual harassment* occurs when any unwelcome form of sexual conduct creates an intimidating, hostile, or offensive work setting.[13]

Pay discrimination occurs when men and women are paid differently for doing the same work.

The Equal Pay Act of 1963 prohibits **pay discrimination** that compensates men and women differently for doing the same work. So when Lilly Ledbetter was about to retire from Goodyear and realized that male coworkers were being paid more, she sued. She initially lost the case because the Supreme Court said she had waited too long to file the claim. She was smiling though when the Lilly Ledbetter Fair Pay Act became the very first bill signed by President Barack Obama. It expanded workers' rights to sue employers on equal pay issues. When he signed the act, the president said, "Making our economy work means making sure it works for everybody."[14]

Comparable worth holds that persons performing jobs of similar importance should be paid at comparable levels.

Another issue regarding gender disparities in pay involves **comparable worth**, that persons performing jobs of similar importance should be paid at comparable levels. Why should a long-distance truck driver, for example, be paid more than an elementary school teacher? Does it make any difference that truck driving is a traditionally male occupation and teaching is a traditionally female occupation? Advocates of comparable worth argue that historical disparities across occupations can result from gender bias. They would like to have the issue legally resolved.

Equal Pay Act of 1963	Requires equal pay for men and women performing equal work in an organization.
Title VII of the Civil Rights Act of 1964 (as amended)	Prohibits discrimination in employment based on race, color, religion, sex, or national origin.
Age Discrimination in Employment Act of 1967	Prohibits discrimination against persons over 40; restricts mandatory retirement.
Occupational Health and Safety Act of 1970	Establishes mandatory health and safety standards in workplaces.
Pregnancy Discrimination Act of 1978	Prohibits employment discrimination against pregnant workers.
Americans with Disabilities Act of 1990	Prohibits discrimination against a qualified individual on the basis of disability.
Civil Rights Act of 1991	Reaffirms Title VII of the 1964 Civil Rights Act; reinstates burden of proof by employer, and allows for punitive and compensatory damages.
Family and Medical Leave Act of 1993	Allows employees up to 12 weeks of unpaid leave with job guarantees for childbirth, adoption, or family illness.

FIGURE 13.2 **Sample of U.S. laws against employment discrimination.**

Ethics: Know Right from Wrong | Since when is someone's Facebook profile meant to be an online résumé?

Personality Test? Drug Test? Social Media Test?

MLouisphotography/Alamy Stock Photo

It used to be that preparing for a job interview meant being ready to answer questions about your education, work experience, interests, and activities. Now there's another question to prepare for: What's your Instagram user name and password?

Believe it or not, it's true. Don't be surprised if an interviewer asks for access to your social media pages. They don't want just a quick glance at the public profile; they want access to the private profile, too. It's time to get worried when the recruiter says, "Please friend me."

"It's akin to requiring someone's house keys," says a law professor. One job candidate turned over a password because "I needed the job to feed my family. I had to." Another refused the interviewer's request and withdrew her application. She didn't want to work for an employer that would even ask to view her private Web pages.

A survey by Microsoft Research found 70% of recruiters saying that they had rejected applicants based on information they found online. Although a social media profile can be a treasure chest of information for recruiters and employers, it is less clear whether it is ethical to tap this resource to measure candidates' character and make employment decisions. Since when is an Instagram feed meant to be an online résumé?

Sometimes recruiters make negative hiring decisions after finding relatively mild forms of questionable behavior such as using poor grammar, posting negative comments about prior employers, or uploading drinking pictures. This may be information or pictures that the individual has little control over. What happens if a "friend" posts a picture of someone from a party from years ago, or if inaccurate or untrue information is posted as a joke among friends?

What Do You Think?

What are the ethical issues involved with regard to recruiters asking for access to personal Facebook—or other online social network—pages? Should it be held against applicants if they refuse? Is it okay for managers to search online sites to check up on what employees are doing outside of work? Should what someone does outside of work cost them their job? On the other hand, shouldn't individuals who knowingly post online information understand that it may end up in the hands of their employers? Where do the lines of responsibility fall?

How about **pregnancy discrimination**? It's against the law, but pregnancy bias complaints filed with the EEOC are common. And research paints a bleak picture. One study had actors play roles of being visibly pregnant and nonpregnant while applying for jobs as corporate attorneys and college professors. Results showed that interviewers were more negative toward the "pregnant" females, even making comments such as "She'll try to get out of doing work" and "She would be too moody."[15]

Age discrimination is also against the law. But the EEOC reports an increased number of age bias complaints. Federal laws protect employees aged 40 and older, and the number of workers in this age group is increasing with the "graying" of the American workforce. The possibility of age discrimination exists whenever an older worker is laid off or loses his or her job. But as one attorney points out, "There's always the fine line between discrimination and a legitimate business decision."[16] About 20% of age discrimination suits result in some financial settlement in favor of the person filing the claim. However, this doesn't always include getting the job back.

Our new economy has given rise to a growing number of people engaged in **alternative employment**. This means that they work on call in temporary or part-time jobs, hire themselves out with temporary staffing agencies, or freelance as **independent contractors** for a changing mix of employers. Organizations are using alternative employment to reduce costs, avoid long-term commitments, and increase staffing flexibility. An NPR/Marist poll found that more than half of those in alternative employment don't receive benefits such as health insurance, retirement plans, sick pay, and holiday leave.[17] Many, called **permatemps**, are employed in a temporary

Pregnancy discrimination penalizes female job holder or job applicant for being pregnant.

Age discrimination penalizes a job holder or job applicant for being aged 40 and older.

People in **alternative employment** work in temporary on-call or part-time jobs or as freelance independent contractors.

Independent contractors are hired as needed and are not part of the organization's permanent workforce.

Permatemps are workers that are employed in a temporary status for an extended period of time.

status for an extended period of time. Critics say this trend is creating a new class of "disposable workers" who are caught in "a race to the bottom" and labor in a system where "when they're used up it's on to the next one."[18]

Employee privacy or **workplace privacy** is the right to privacy while at work.

Issues relating to **employee privacy** or **workplace privacy**, the right to privacy both on and off the job, are sensitive, debatable, and timely.[19] Technology makes it easy for employer practices to become invasive, and even cross legal and ethical lines. The best advice is to assume you have no privacy at work and act accordingly. But what about rights to privacy outside of work? While vacationing in Europe, a Florida teacher posted to her "private setting" Facebook pages photos that showed her holding alcoholic beverages. After they came to the attention of school administrators, she was asked to resign. She did so, but later filed a lawsuit arguing that her resignation was forced. Would you believe she lost the case in court?[20] The number of such lawsuits is growing. Just how they are resolved should help clear up what is and what is not against the law in respect to social media use and employee rights to privacy.

Learning Check

LEARNING OBJECTIVE 13.1

Explain the human resource management process and its legal framework.

Be Sure You Can • describe the human resource management process • explain what makes HRM "strategic" • define *discrimination, equal employment opportunity, affirmative action*, and *bona fide occupational qualification* • identify major laws that protect against discrimination in employment • discuss legal issues of sexual harassment, comparable worth, independent contractors, and workplace privacy

---

13.2 | Attracting a Quality Workforce

WileyPLUS

See Author Video

LEARNING OBJECTIVE 13.2

Describe how managers help organizations attract a quality workforce.

> **Learn More About**
> Human resource planning • Recruitment process • Selection techniques

The first responsibility of human resource management is talent acquisition. Its goal is to attract a high-quality workforce with the talents needed for the organization to meet its performance goals. An advertisement once run by Motorola put it this way: "Productivity is learning how to hire the person who is right for the job." To attract the right people, an organization must know exactly what it is looking for in terms of the jobs to be done and the talents needed to do them well. It must create employee value propositions that make the organization stand out as a preferred employer. And, it must have the HRM systems in place to excel at employee recruitment and selection.

Human Resource Planning

Human resource planning analyzes staffing needs and identifies actions to fill those needs.

Human resource planning is the process of analyzing an organization's staffing needs and determining how to fill them. As shown in **Figure 13.3**, human resource planning begins with assessing staffing needs and the current workforce, and deciding what additions,

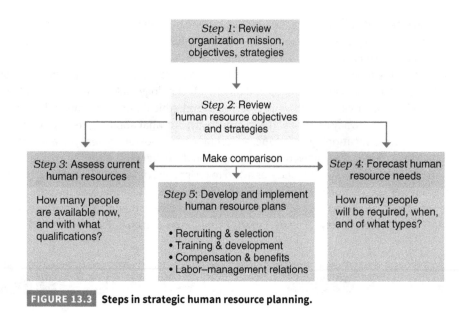

FIGURE 13.3 **Steps in strategic human resource planning.**

replacements, and upgrades are necessary. The process involves **job analysis**—the systematic evaluation of job facets to determine what is done when, where, how, why, and by whom.[21] This information is used to write or update **job descriptions** that describe specific job duties and responsibilities. The information in a job analysis is used to create **job specifications** that identify the qualifications—such as education, prior experience, and skills—needed for a given job.

A **job analysis** studies exactly what is done in a job, and why.

A **job description** details the duties and responsibilities of a job holder.

Job specifications list the qualifications required of a job holder.

Recruitment Process

Recruitment is a set of activities designed to attract a talented pool of job applicants. It typically involves advertising a job vacancy, making contact with potential candidates, and screening them to create a pool of applicants potentially meeting the organization's staffing needs. This process today increasingly involves social media where employers not only advertise jobs, but also engage with actual and potential applicants to explore their interests, experiences, and talents. If you want to get hired at Zappos, for example, the front door is Zappos Insiders.[22] The interface allows potential employees to link with existing ones, showcase their personalities and talents, and learn what's going on at the firm. When a job vacancy opens, those with good reputations on Zappos Insiders get the first calls.

Recruitment is a set of activities designed to attract a talented pool of job applicants.

Recruitment is becoming more candidate-centric. In an economy where talent is at a premium, employers are focused on learning about candidates' needs and expectations while creating a positive recruiting experience. Research finds that two-thirds of job candidates are likely to reject an offer if they've had a bad recruiting experience.[23] And, more than 70% of them go on to share their bad experiences with others. When queried about suggestions for improvement, job seekers suggest providing candidates with all relevant information, using technology to improve communication, streamlining the application process, and optimizing the application process for mobile devices.[24]

External and Internal Recruitment
Most recruiting that takes place on college campuses and through social media connections is **external recruitment** in which job candidates are sought from outside the hiring organization. External recruits are found through company websites and social media, virtual job fairs, specialized recruiting sites such as Monster and CareerBuilder, employment agencies and headhunters, university placement centers, personal contacts, and employee referrals. Through **social recruiting**, employers browse social media sites like LinkedIn, Facebook, Reddit, and Twitter, looking for people whose online

External recruitment seeks job applicants from outside the organization.

Social recruiting is where employers browse social media sites looking for prospective job candidates.

Internal recruitment seeks job applicants from inside the organization.

profiles show things like leadership, special skills, and connections that make them attractive as prospective job candidates.

Internal recruitment seeks job applicants from within the organization. Most organizations have a procedure for announcing vacancies through electronic postings and in-house social media sites. They also rely on managers and team leaders to recommend internal candidates for advancement. The college internship is a form of internal recruitment that is an increasingly important pathway to employment. It provides an experience-based opportunity for both employer and candidate to consider one another for long-term commitments. Many employers view hiring interns as a preferred pathway for talent acquisition.

There are advantages and disadvantages to both external and internal recruitment. External recruitment brings in outside applicants with fresh perspectives, expertise, and work experience. But extra effort is needed to get reliable information about outside candidates. A major downside is that a hiring decision might turn out bad because either not enough information was gathered about the applicant, or because what was discovered turned out to be inaccurate.

Internal recruitment is usually quicker and focuses on employees with well-known performance records. A history of internal recruitment builds workforce loyalty and motivation, and helps to improve retention of high-quality employees. But internal recruiting also has downsides. Limiting job searches to internal talent pools increases the risk that the best candidate may not be chosen. A valuable opportunity to bring in outside expertise and viewpoints also may be lost at the very moment when new insights, skills, and creativity are most needed by the organization.

Analysis: Make Data Your Friend | "Highly qualified and motivated job candidates are ignored while companies focus on recruiting less enthusiastic ones."

Costs of Ignoring Internal Job Candidates

Beau Lark/Corbis/Getty Images

- Why is it that just 28% of hiring managers consider hiring from within as an important source of job candidates?
- Why is it that less than a third of employers required that job vacancies be posted for review by internal candidates before looking outside?
- Why is it that employers ranked recruiting from the outside higher than recruiting "highly skilled talent"?

These are among the questions raised in a *Wall Street Journal* article discussing hiring mistakes and how to avoid them. The gist of the article is that there is some allure—albeit perhaps false, to

recruiting "outsiders" and overlooking "insiders." This is true even though hiring the insider might save costs, tap valuable talents, and send positive signals that insiders who work hard and do well can look forward to advancement. The articles goes on to say: "Highly qualified and motivated job candidates are ignored while companies focus on recruiting less enthusiastic ones."

It turns out that active insiders—ones looking for job advancement with their current employer—tend to want different things than passive outsiders who have to be convinced it's time to leave their current job and move to a new employer. Consider these findings from a LinkedIn study of the goals for inside and outside job candidates.

- *Advancement opportunities*—insiders (31%) . . . outsiders (43%)
- *More challenging work*—insiders (26%) . . . outsiders (21%)
- *Better fit with skill set*—insiders (25%) . . . outsiders (21%)
- *Better compensation and benefits*—insiders (30%) . . . outsiders (43%)

Your Thoughts?

Can you see value in recruiters looking inside as well as outside when filling job vacancies? Can you also see why employers might assume that you do better bringing in someone new from the outside than by promoting from within? What do the survey results suggest about the costs and benefits of inside and external recruiting? If you are an insider interested in advancement, what might you do to stay visible and attractive when job opportunities arise?

Realistic Job Previews   In what may be called **traditional recruitment**, the emphasis is on selling the job and organization to applicants. The focus is on communicating the most positive features of the position, perhaps to the point where negatives are downplayed or even concealed. This may create unrealistic expectations leading to turnover when new hires become disillusioned and quit. The individual suffers a career disruption; the employer suffers lost productivity and the added costs of having to recruit again.

The alternative to traditional recruitment is a **realistic job preview** that provides candidates with all pertinent information about the job and organization without distortion, and before the job is accepted.[25] Rather than seeking to "sell" applicants on the positive features of the job or organization, realistic job previews are open and balanced. Both favorable and unfavorable aspects of work are covered.

A realistic preview helps to avoid costly mismatches. For those who do take the job, knowing both the good and the bad ahead of time builds realistic expectations that better prepare them for the inevitable ups and downs of a new position. The expected benefits of realistic recruiting practices include higher levels of early job satisfaction, greater trust in the organization, and less inclination to quit prematurely.

Traditional recruitment focuses on selling the job and organization to applicants.

Realistic job previews provide job candidates with all pertinent information about a job and an organization, both positive and negative.

Selection Techniques

Once a a pool of job candidates exists, the next step is to determine whom to hire. This process of **selection** involves gathering and assessing information about job candidates and making a hiring decision.

Selection is choosing individuals to hire from a pool of qualified job applicants.

Insight: Learn about Yourself | Conscientiousness is often at the top of recruiters' "must-have" lists.

Conscientiousness Is a Career Booster

Conscientiousness is the degree to which an individual is achievement-oriented, careful, hard-working, organized, persevering, responsible, and thorough. People who are low on conscientiousness tend to be laid back, less goal-oriented, less driven by success, and less self-disciplined. They are also often procrastinators.

Many employers tend to hire for attitude and train for skill. They try to identify future top performers by focusing on key personality characteristics that are likely to predict job success. Conscientiousness is often at the top of recruiters' "must-have" lists. Their search for clues about an individual job candidate's potential covers things like those shown in the box.

Are you someone whom others would describe as efficient, prompt, systematic, thorough, careful, practical, neat, and steady? If you can check off each of these attributes as a positive personal characteristic that accurately describes you then you're on the right path when it comes to conscientiousness. This is a good path to be on. Conscientiousness often is associated with job success. Remember too that conscientiousness is easy to monitor. Its presence or absence will always be evident in the way you approach work and how you follow through with the tasks and challenges you face.

Conscientiousness is a personality characteristic that is positively related to work performance across a wide range of jobs. How about you? Can your credentials meet a recruiter's conscientiousness challenge? Why or why not?

How to Show Recruiters You Are Conscientious

- Professional Résumé—Presenting a carefully proofed, well-designed, and organized resume shows that you value a high-quality product and attend to details.

- Interview Preparation—Doing research beforehand and being well informed shows conscientiousness.

- Self-Presentation—First impressions count; conscientiousness shows up in dressing appropriately and acting professionally in with regard to manners and engagement.

- Career Plans—Being able to thoughtfully discuss career and personal plans shows you are goal-oriented and conscientious.

Get To Know Yourself Better

Just how conscientious are you, not only in work and school situations but in your everyday life? Take the conscientiousness test in the box. Ask: "How would others rate me on these same characteristics?" Ask also: "Should I just accept where I am in terms of conscientiousness, or are there things I can do to change my behavior in ways that can make me more conscientious in the future?" Put your thoughts about whether conscientiousness is one of your personal traits down on paper. Share it with someone who knows you well and ask whether they agree, or not. Honest feedback can be important to your professional development.

Reliability means that a selection device repeatedly gives consistent results.

Validity means that scores on a selection device have a demonstrated correlation with future job performance.

Reliability and Validity

The selection process involves measurement and prediction, and the reliability and validity of techniques used are very important. **Reliability** means that the selection technique is consistent in generating the same results time after time. A personality test, for example, is reliable if the same individual receives a similar score when taking the test on two separate occasions. **Validity** means that there is a clear relationship between what the selection device is measuring and eventual job performance. A skills assessment is valid, for example, if there is clear evidence that once on the job individuals with high scores outperform those with low scores.

Interview Ins and Outs

Very few individuals are hired for managerial and professional positions without at least one screening interview. They are used to evaluate applicants on technical skills and experience, communication skills and personal impression, and potential person–organization culture fit. Employers use the traditional face-to-face interview, the telephone interview, and the virtual or online video interview at various points in the selection process. The likelihood is that success in a telephone or online virtual interview will determine whether or not a candidate gets to the face-to-face and on-site interview stage.

Google is famous for asking questions like: "A man pushed his car to a hotel and lost his fortune. What happened?" Whole Foods might ask: "What's your perfect last meal?" Expedia might ask: "If you could go camping anywhere, where would you put your tent?"[26] These types of interview questions are designed less for testing "right" answers and more for finding out how well a candidate might fit with the organizational culture. But you have to be prepared for standard questions as well: "What are your strengths and weaknesses?" "Where do you see yourself in five years?" "What can you offer us that someone else cannot?" "What value can you put on the table your very first day on the job?" [27]

Behavioral interviews ask job applicants about past behaviors.

Situational interviews ask job applicants how they would react in specific situations.

The predictive validity of interviews increases as the amount of structure increases.[28] **Behavioral interviews** ask job candidates about their past behavior, focusing specifically on actions likely to be important in the work environment. An example is: "Describe how you have resolved a conflict with a co-worker or team mate." **Situational interviews** ask applicants how they would react when confronted with specific work situations they would be likely to experience on the job. For example: "How would you as team leader handle two team members who do not get along with one another?"[29]

An assessment center examines how job candidates handle simulated work situations.

In **work sampling**, applicants are evaluated while performing actual work tasks.

A **job audition** is a "trial hire" where job candidates are given short-term employment contracts to demonstrate their performance capabilities.

Employment Tests

Employment tests of various types are often used to identify a candidate's intelligence, aptitudes, personality, interests, and ethics. The validity of employment testing improves the more directly it relates to the actual work to be done. One approach is the **assessment center**. It allows recruiters to evaluate a candidate's job potential by observing performance in experiential activities that simulate daily work. A related approach is **work sampling** which has candidates work on actual job tasks while observers grade their performance. Something called a **job audition** is also becoming more popular. Think of it as a "trial hire" where job candidates are given short-term employment contracts—say four to six weeks—to demonstrate their performance capabilities. When the contract is up, the employer decides whether to offer a full-time job. This gives the candidate a chance to show what they can do, while giving the employer a chance to reduce the risk of making a hiring mistake.

Learning Check

LEARNING OBJECTIVE 13.2

Describe how managers help organizations attract a quality workforce.

Be Sure You Can • explain the difference between external recruitment and internal recruitment • discuss the value of realistic job previews to employers and to job candidates • differentiate reliability and validity as two criteria of selection tools • discuss the pros and cons of job interviews and employment tests

| 13.3 | # Developing a Quality Workforce |

LEARNING OBJECTIVE 13.3

WileyPLUS

See Author Video

Discuss how managers help organizations develop a quality workforce.

> **Learn More About**
>
> Onboarding and socialization • Training and development • Performance management and coaching • Performance assessement approaches

The second responsibility of human resource management is talent development. This process of developing a quality workforce begins when new hires are brought on board with care so their first experiences are positive. When people join an organization they have to "learn the ropes" and become familiar with "the way things are done." The best employers don't leave all of this to chance. They arrange entry experiences to guide this learning process. They also invest in talent development by offering lots of training and well-chosen job experiences so that everyone keeps keep their abilities and skills at the highest possible levels.

Onboarding and Socialization

The first formal experience newcomers have often begins with some form of **orientation**. This is an event designed to initially welcome new employees, complete necessary paperwork, and familiarize them with their jobs, co-workers, and key policies and practices of the organization. Orientation is ideally part of a broader and longer-term process of **onboarding**. It's purpose is to build engagement with the organization and its culture, people, opportunities, and performance expectations. When done well, onboarding communicates mission and teamwork expectations in a positive and, ideally, motivating way. Picture new hires at the Disney World Resort learning during onboarding that everyone, regardless of their specific job title is a "cast member" who is there along with all others "to make the customer happy."

Socialization is a process through which onboarding works. It's how new members learn and adapt to the ways and expectations of the organization.[30] Importantly, it's success often determines how well a new hire is going to fit in and perform. A technique used by Neil Blumenthal, co-founder of the online eyewear retailer Warby Parker, is to "provide realistic short-term goals to establish quick wins, which will get the employee into a rhythm where he or she is motivated."[31]

When things go well in onboarding, socialization sets the right foundations for high performance, job satisfaction, and work enthusiasm. When onboarding is weak or neglected, however, newcomers end up getting socialized by chance, most often while interacting with co-workers.[32] Even though learning from experienced workers can be helpful, it can also turn out just the opposite. Who among us hasn't worked with someone that was unhappy and disgruntled, and didn't hesitate to tell us—and anyone else who might listen—all about it?

Orientation initially familiarizes new employees with their jobs, co-workers, and key policies and practices of the organization.

Onboarding is a longer-term process of engaging new hires with the organization's mission, culture, people, opportunities, and performance expectations.

Socialization is a process of learning and adapting to the organizational culture.

Training and Development

Training is a set of activities that helps people acquire and improve job-related skills. This applies both to initial training and to skill upgrading to meet changing job requirements. Organizations that value their human resources invest in extensive training and development programs so employees have the capabilities to perform well and manage their personal lives.[33]

On-the-job training takes place on the job. A common approach is **job rotation**, which allows people to spend time working in different jobs or departments or even geographical locations, expanding the range of their job capabilities.[34] Another approach is **coaching**,

Training provides learning opportunities to acquire and improve job-related skills.

In **job rotation**, people switch tasks to learn multiple jobs.

Coaching occurs as an experienced employee offers performance advice to a less experienced co-worker.

Mentoring assigns new hires and early-career employees as protégés to more senior employees.

In **reverse mentoring**, younger employees mentor seniors to improve their technology skills.

Management development is training to improve knowledge and skills in the management process.

A **performance management system** sets standards, assesses results, and plans for performance improvements.

Performance assessment or **performance review** is the process of formally evaluating performance and providing feedback to a job holder.

Performance coaching provides frequent and developmental feedback for how a worker can improve job performance.

where an experienced person provides performance advice to a newcomer or less experienced co-worker. **Mentoring** is a form of coaching in which early-career employees are formally assigned as protégés to senior, veteran job holders. The mentoring relationship gives new employees regular access to advice on developing skills and getting better informed about the organization. Some organizations, including Mastercard and Cisco, are also using **reverse mentoring** where younger employees mentor seniors to improve their technology skills. At Capgemini Consulting, global practice leader Didier Bonnet says "the main aim is to raise the digital IQ of business leaders in the firms."[35]

Off-the-job training is accomplished outside the work setting. It provides an opportunity to enhance job-critical skills and develop skills that might be needed before a promotion or transfer. An example is **management development**—formal training to improve knowledge and skill in the fundamentals of management. New managers just starting out often benefit from training that emphasizes team leadership and communication. Middle managers may benefit from training on multifunctional viewpoints or techniques for motivating employees. Top managers may benefit from advanced management training on decision-making and negotiation skills, as well as to expand their awareness of corporate strategy and direction.

Performance Management and Coaching

An important part of human resource management is the design and implementation of **performance management system**. This system ensures that performance standards and objectives are set, that performance is regularly assessed, and that steps are taken to improve future performance through coaching and constructive feedback.

Performance assessment or **performance review**, also called *performance appraisal* and *performance evaluation*, is the process of formally assessing employees' work accomplishments and providing feedback. This serves both evaluation and development purposes.[36] The *evaluation purpose* focuses on past performance and measures results against standards. Performance is documented for the record and for the purpose of allocating rewards such as financial incentives and bonuses. The *development purpose* focuses on future performance. Performance goals and obstacles are identified, along with areas where training or supervisory support may be needed. The manager acts in a counseling role and gives attention to job holders' developmental needs.

It's no secret that the process of performance assessment is often criticized. One of the reasons is that reviews aren't frequent enough and often viewed an "annual" ritual. Another is that they focus too much on performance evaluation and too little on development and performance improvement.[37] Use of ongoing **performance coaching** helps minimize these problems. It provides employees with frequent and developmental feedback as more of an ongoing dialogue than a formal, scheduled event. The coaching helps clarify performance expectations and prevent small problems from getting out of control. It also increases trust and improves the quality of supervisor–subordinate relationships.

Technology now facilitates frequent, almost real-time, performance assessment and coaching. At Lyft, for example, special software scans employee calendars for scheduled meetings and then queries attendees for feedback on one another's performance.[38] There is also a trend toward eliminating formal performance reviews altogether and replacing them with more frequent and informal "check-ins" between employees and supervisors. PricewaterhouseCoopers employees can request performance feedback "snapshots" at any time from their managers.[39]

Performance Assessment Approaches

The performance assessment process is fraught with potential miscues and problems, including open disagreements and debates. Giving and receiving performance feedback can be uncomfortable, emotional, and even anger inducing events. It is important to choose well among alternative performance assessment methods, and to make sure that they are as reliable and valid as possible given the circumstances.[40] Remember, a *reliable assessment* yields the same result over time or for different raters while a *valid assessment* measures only factors directly relevant to job performance.

Trait-Based Performance Assessment

Trait-based approaches are designed to measure the extent employees have characteristics or traits considered important in the job. For example, trait-based measures assess characteristics such as dependability, initiative, conscientiousness, and leadership. One of the oldest and most widely used performance appraisal methods is a **graphic rating scale**. It is a checklist for rating individuals on traits or performance characteristics such as quality of work, job attitude, and punctuality. Although this approach is quick and easy, it tends to be very subjective and, as a result, also tends to have poor reliability and validity.

A **graphic rating scale** uses a checklist of traits or characteristics to evaluate performance.

Behavior-Based Performance Assessment

Behavior-based approaches evaluate employees on specific actions that are important parts of the job. The **behaviorally anchored rating scale**, or BARS, describes actual behaviors for various levels of performance in a job. In the case of the customer-service representative illustrated in **Figure 13.4**, "extremely poor" performance is clearly defined as rude or disrespectful treatment of customers.

A **behaviorally anchored rating scale** uses specific descriptions of actual behaviors to rate various levels of performance.

The BARS is more reliable and valid than the graphic rating scale because it anchors performance to specific descriptions of work behavior. Behavior-based appraisals also are more consistent with the developmental purpose of performance appraisal because they provide specific feedback to employees for areas in need of improvement. But one problem is that a BARS evaluation may be influenced by **recency bias**. This is the tendency to focus on recent behaviors rather than on behavior throughout the evaluation period.

Recency bias overemphasizes the most recent behaviors when evaluating individuals' performance.

The **critical-incident technique** is a behavior-based approach that can diminish recency bias. With this technique an inventory is kept of employees' effective and ineffective job behaviors. Using the case of the customer-service representative, a critical-incidents log might contain the following entries: Positive example—"Took extraordinary care of a customer who had purchased a defective product from a company store in another city"; negative example—"Acted rudely in dismissing the complaint of a customer who felt that a sale item was erroneously advertised." Such a written record can be discussed in specific terms with the employee and used for both evaluative and developmental purposes.

The **critical-incident technique** keeps a log of employees' effective and ineffective job behaviors.

Results-Based Performance Assessment

Rather than employees' traits or specific behaviors, results-based assessments focus on actual performance accomplishments. This sounds ideal, but in some jobs the outcomes that are the easiest to measure aren't necessarily the most important. Results-based measures may ignore the impact of circumstances beyond the employee's control, such as inadequate technology or poor performance by another member of their team. And when people are evaluated only on goal attainment, and

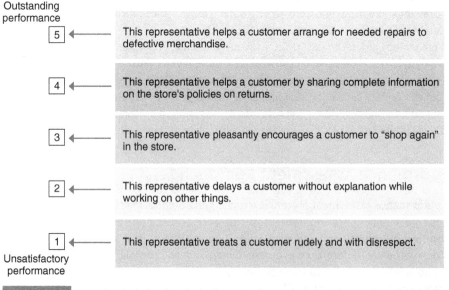

Outstanding performance

5 — This representative helps a customer arrange for needed repairs to defective merchandise.

4 — This representative helps a customer by sharing complete information on the store's policies on returns.

3 — This representative pleasantly encourages a customer to "shop again" in the store.

2 — This representative delays a customer without explanation while working on other things.

1 — This representative treats a customer rudely and with disrespect.

Unsatisfactory performance

FIGURE 13.4 **Sample of a behaviorally anchored rating scale for performance appraisal.**

especially when goals are set impossibly high, they may adopt unethical approaches to accomplish the goals.[41]

Leniency is the tendency to give a higher performance rating than deserved.

A **multiperson comparison** compares one person's accomplishments with those of others.

A common error in results-based performance appraisal is **leniency**—the tendency to rate employees more favorably than they deserve in order to avoid the unpleasant task of giving negative feedback.[42] This risk may be reduced by using **multiperson comparisons** that compare one person's accomplishments with those of others. In *rank ordering*, all employees are arranged in order of performance. The best performers go at the top of the list, while the worst performers go at the bottom; no ties are allowed. In a *forced distribution*, each employee is placed into a frequency distribution, which requires that a certain percentage of employees fall into specific performance classifications, such as the top 10%, the next 40%, the next 40%, and the bottom 10%.

360-degree appraisals include superiors, subordinates, peers, and even customers in the appraisal process.

360-Degree Feedback

It is increasingly popular to include more than one's immediate boss in the performance assessment process.[43] In **360-degree appraisals**, feedback is gathered from multiple sources to provide a more comprehensive evaluation. They typically include inputs not only from an employee's immediate supervisor, but also from higher ups, peers, teammates, subordinates, and customers—all of whom have a stake in the job holder's performance. Most 360-degree appraisals also include a self-evaluation. When feedback from all of these sources is assessed and shared, the results can provide a useful summary of an individual's strengths, weaknesses, and development needs.[44]

Learning Check

LEARNING OBJECTIVE 13.3

Discuss how managers help organizations develop a quality workforce.

Be Sure You Can • define *orientation* and *socialization* and describe their importance to organizations • give examples of on-the-job and off-the-job training • explain the benefits of performance coaching discuss strengths and weaknesses of trait-based, behavior-based, and results-based performance assessments • explain how 360-degree appraisals work

13.4 | Maintaining a Quality Workforce

WileyPLUS

See Author Video

LEARNING OBJECTIVE 13.4

Summarize how managers help organizations maintain a quality workforce.

> **Learn More About**
>
> Flexibility and work–life balance • Compensation and benefits • Retention and turnover • Labor–management relations

The third responsibility in human resource management is talent retention. "Hiring good people is tough . . . keeping them can be even tougher" states an article in the *Harvard Business Review*.[45] The point is that it isn't enough to hire and train workers to meet an organization's immediate needs. They must also be successfully nurtured, supported, and retained. A Society for Human Resource Management survey of employers shows that popular tools for maintaining a quality workforce include flexible work schedules and personal time off, competitive salaries, and good benefits—especially health insurance and retirement plans.[46]

Flexibility and Work–Life Balance

Today's increasingly fast-paced, complex, and multifaceted lifestyles have contributed to increased concerns about **work–life balance**—how people balance demands of their careers with their personal and family needs.[47] Not surprisingly, the "family friendliness" of an employer is now frequently used as a screening criterion by job candidates. It is also used in "best employer" rankings in publications such as *Working Mother*, *Fortune*, and *Forbes,* and online sources such as LinkedIn and Glassdoor.

Work–life balance is enhanced when workers have flexibility in scheduling work hours, work location, vacations, and personal time off. Flexibility allows people to more easily balance their personal lives and work responsibilities. Research shows that workers who have flexibility, at least with regard to when they begin and end their workday, are less likely to leave their jobs.[48] Some employers improve flexibility by helping workers handle family matters through initiatives such as on-site day care and elder care, and offering concierge services for miscellaneous needs such as dry cleaning and getting a haircut. Others have moved into innovative programs like short-term work sabbaticals to help motivate and retain their best performers.[49] A few even offer limitless vacation time, allowing (and trusting), employees to take as much vacation time as they want, whenever they want.

> **Work–life balance** involves balancing career demands with personal and family needs.

Compensation and Benefits

It may be that no other work issue receives as much attention as pay. A market-competitive salary or hourly wage helps in hiring the right people. The way pay increases are subsequently handled can have a significant impact on employees' job attitudes, motivation, and performance, and it can also influence whether they look for another job elsewhere.

Benefits also play a very important part in attracting and retaining employees. How many times does a graduating college student hear "Be sure to get a job with benefits!"?[50] An attractive and recent benefit offered by some progressive employers is assistance with paying off student loans. Options range from giving monthly stipends to help offset loan payments to matching loan payments with 401k contributions so that no time is lost building retirement assets.[51] Could this be a benefit you might ask for in a job negotiation?

Merit Pay Systems

The trend in compensation today is largely toward "pay-for-performance."[52] If you are part of a **merit pay** system, your pay increases are based at least in part on how well you perform. The idea is that a good merit raise is a positive signal to high performers; no merit raise or a low merit raise sends a negative signal to low performers. Because pay is contingent on performance, both groups are expected to work harder in the future.

Although they make sense in theory, merit systems have their problems. One survey reported by the *Wall Street Journal* found that only 23% of employees understood their companies' reward systems.[53] Concerns about merit pay systems include: Who assesses performance? What happens if the employee doesn't agree with the assessment? Is the system fair and equitable to everyone involved? Is there enough money to make the merit increases meaningful?

> **Merit pay** awards pay increases in proportion to performance contributions.

Bonuses and Profit-Sharing Plans

How would you like to someday receive a letter like this one, once sent to two top executives by Amazon.com's chairman Jeff Bezos? "In recognition and appreciation of your contributions," his letter read, "Amazon.com will pay you a special bonus in the amount of $1,000,000."[54] **Bonus pay** plans provide one-time or lump-sum payments to employees who meet specific performance targets or make some other extraordinary contribution, such as an idea for a work improvement. These pay plans have been most common at the executive level, but many companies now use them more extensively across all levels. At Applebee's, for example, "Applebucks" are small cash bonuses given to reward employee performance and increase loyalty.

In contrast to straight bonuses, **profit-sharing** plans give employees a proportion of the net profits earned by the organization during a performance period. **Gain-sharing** plans extend the profit-sharing concept by allowing groups of employees to share in any savings or

> **Bonus pay** plans provide one-time payments based on performance accomplishments.
>
> **Profit-sharing** plans distribute to employees a proportion of net profits earned by the organization.
>
> **Gain-sharing** plans allow employees to share in cost savings or productivity gains realized by their efforts.

Choices: Think before You Act | Fifteen members of a work team are asked to distribute a pool of 1,200 stock options as annual bonuses to one another

Teammates Know You, But Should They Pay You?

Helder Almeida/Shutterstock.com

Traditionally, managers or team leaders made final pay raise decisions. But times may be changing in an increasingly crowdsourcing world. Your pay may now be decided by your teammates, not your boss.

Picture this. Fifteen members of a work team log into to an online exchange run by their employer. Their task is to distribute a pool of 1,200 stock options as an annual bonus to their teammates. The only rule is that they can't give any to themselves. Each person's final bonus options are the sum of what other team members give them. When the exchange closes each individual gets notified of their bonus awards and the distribution of bonuses awarded in the team—no names attached.

The example is real. It comes from a San Francisco start-up called Coffee & Power. The pay practice was initiated by entrepreneur and co-founder Philip Rosedale. The idea is that because teammates know one another best, they also know who deserves to be recognized at bonus time.

Those in favor of the practice might say that by giving the bonus decision to the team, it empowers members who get to invest in and reward one another for their performance and contributions. One Coffee & Power employee says the approach "lets me reward people that management may not always recognize." *Those against the practice might say* it's a bit like having students give each other grades on a team project. There's too much room for results to be manipulated according to friendships and perceived "need." Too often, performance falls by the wayside as an award criterion in favor of less relevant, nonperformance factors.

Your Take?

At this point, you've surely done peer evaluations in teams and perhaps even assigned grades to team members. What's your take on the Coffee & Power approach to bonuses? Does this use of technology really dig down to the level of truly rewarding individual contributions to team performance? Or, is it a practice that potentially introduces more problems than it is worth?

"gains" realized when their efforts or ideas result in measurable cost reductions or productivity increases. As incentive systems, profit-sharing plans, gain-sharing plans, and bonus plans have the advantage of helping to ensure that individual employees work hard by linking their pay to the performance of the organization as a whole.

Stock Ownership and Stock Options Some employers provide employees with ways to accumulate stock in their companies and thus develop a sense of ownership. The idea is that stock ownership will motivate employees to work hard so that the company becomes and stays successful. **Employee stock ownership plans**, or ESOPs, help employees purchase stock in their employing companies, sometimes at special discounted rates. For example, almost 95% of employees are stock owners at Anson Industries, a Chicago construction firm.[55] An administrative assistant says it has made a difference in her job performance: "You have a different attitude . . . everyone here has the same attitude because it's our money." Of course, there are downside risks of ESOPs. When a company's market value falls, so too does the value of employee-owned stock.

Another approach is to grant employees **stock options** linked to their performance or as part of their hiring packages. Stock options give owners rights to buy shares of stock at a future date at a fixed price. Employees gain financially if the stock price rises above the option price, but the stock options lose value if the stock price drops. The logic is that option holders will work hard so that the company performs well and they can reap financial benefits. The Hay Group, a global human resource management consulting firm, reports that the most admired U.S. companies are those that offer stock options to a greater proportion of their workforces.[56]

Employee stock ownership plans (ESOPs) help employees purchase stock in their employing companies.

Stock options give the right to purchase shares at a fixed price in the future.

Benefits

Employee benefits packages include nonmonetary forms of compensation that are intended to improve the work and personal lives of employees. Some benefits are required by law, such as contributions to Social Security, unemployment insurance, and workers' compensation insurance. Many organizations offer additional benefits that include health insurance, retirement plans, pay for time not worked—such as personal days and vacations, sick leave, and maternity and paternity leave. But, the majority of U.S. workers don't have access to these discretionary benefits. Although the Family and Medical Leave Act (FMLA) requires employers to offer unpaid leaves for medical and family problems, President Barack Obama once told a Summit on Working Families: "There is only one country in the world that does not offer paid maternity leave, and that is us."[57] And when it comes to the "working sick" problem, some 40 million Americans lack paid sick leave benefits.[58]

The ever-rising costs of benefits, particularly medical insurance and retirement, are a major concern for employers. Many are attempting to gain control over health care expenses by shifting more of the insurance costs to employees and by restricting choices among health care providers. They also are encouraging healthy lifestyles as a way to decrease health insurance claims.

Flexible benefits programs are increasingly common. These plans allow employees to choose a set of benefits within a certain dollar amount. The trend also is toward more **family-friendly benefits** that help employees balance work and non-work responsibilities. These include child care, elder care, flexible schedules, parental leave, and part-time employment options. Increasingly common as well are **employee assistance programs** that help employees deal with personal problems including stress, counseling on alcohol and substance abuse, referrals for domestic violence and sexual abuse, and family and marital counseling.

> **Employee benefits** are nonmonetary forms of compensation such as health insurance and retirement plans.

> **Flexible benefits** programs allow employees to choose from a range of benefit options.

> **Family-friendly benefits** help employees achieve better work–life balance.

> **Employee assistance programs** help employees cope with personal stresses and problems.

Retention and Turnover

Retirement is one of those experiences that can increase employees' fears and apprehensions as it approaches. Many organizations offer special counseling and other forms of support for retiring employees, including advice on company benefits, financial management, estate planning, and use of leisure time. Increasingly on the radar at many firms are **early retirement incentive programs**. These give workers financial incentives to retire early. The potential benefits for employers include the opportunity to lower payroll costs by reducing positions, replacing higher-wage workers with less expensive newer hires, and creating openings that can be used to hire workers with different, more current, skills and talents.

The most extreme replacement decisions involve **termination**, which is involuntary and permanent dismissal. In some cases termination is based on performance problems or violations of policy. In other cases the employees involved may be performing well, but may be terminated as part of strategic restructuring through workforce reduction. In all cases, terminations should be handled fairly, according to organizational policies and in compliance with all relevant federal and state statues.

Many employment relationships are governed by the **employment-at-will** doctrine. This principle assumes that employers can terminate employees at any time for any reason. Likewise, employees may quit their job at any time for any reason. In other cases, the principle of **wrongful discharge** gives workers legal protections against discriminatory firings, and employers must have bona-fide job-related cause to terminate the employee. In situations where workers belong to unions, terminations also are potentially subject to labor contract rules and specifications

> **Early retirement incentive programs** offer workers financial incentives to retire early.

> **Termination** is the involuntary dismissal of an employee.

> **Employment-at-will** means that employees can be terminated at any time for any reason.

> **Wrongful discharge** is a doctrine giving workers legal protections against discriminatory firings.

Labor–Management Relations

Labor unions are organizations to which workers belong and that deal with employers on workers' behalf.[59] They are found in many industrial and business occupations, as well as among public-sector employees including teachers, police officers, firefighters, and government workers. Unions have historically played an important role in American society. Although

> A **labor union** is an organization that deals with employers on the workers' collective behalf.

they often are associated with wage and benefit issues, workers also join unions because of things like poor relationships with supervisors, favoritism or lack of respect by supervisors, little or no influence with employers, and failure of employers to provide a mechanism for grievance and dispute resolution.[60]

The National Labor Relations Act of 1935 (known as the Wagner Act) protects employees by recognizing their right to join unions and engage in union activities. It is enforced by the National Labor Relations Board (NLRB). The Taft-Hartley Act of 1947 protects employers from unfair labor practices by unions and allows workers to decertify unions. And, the Civil Service Reform Act of 1978 clarifies the right of government employees to join and to be represented by labor unions.

Although union membership has been on the decline in the United States, dropping from 20.1% in 1983 to just 10.5% in 2018, unions have historically had a significant impact on the lives of the majority of American citizens. Notable accomplishments attributed to unions include (1) the "weekend," which emerged from the Fair Labor Standards Act of 1938, a federal standard for a shorter workweek and leisure time; (2) an end to child labor, which had been normative in the United States until 1938 with the first passage of federal legislation regulating child labor; (3) employer-based health care, which emerged in the 1950s; and (4) the Family Medical Leave Act, which provides for job-protected leave for employees to care for infants or a family member with an illness.[61]

Notwithstanding the downward membership trend, unions remain an important force in the workplace.[62] They serve as a collective "voice" for their members and act as bargaining agents to negotiate **labor contracts** with employers. These contracts specify the rights and obligations of employees and management with respect to wages, work hours, work rules, seniority, hiring, grievances, and other conditions of employment. They are developed through **collective bargaining**, the process through which labor and management representatives negotiate, administer, and interpret labor contracts. It typically involves face-to-face meetings between labor and management representatives. During this time, a variety of demands, proposals, and counterproposals are exchanged. Several rounds of bargaining may be required before a contract is reached or a dispute over a contract issue is resolved.

As you might expect, the collective bargaining process is time-consuming and expensive, and it can lead to problems. One of the areas where unions and employers can find themselves in conflict during collective bargaining relates to so-called **two-tier wage systems**. They pay new hires less than more senior workers already doing the same jobs. Agreeing to a two-tier system isn't likely to be the preference of union negotiators. But, management representatives are likely to argue that it helps manage costs, keeps the firm profitable, and retains jobs that would otherwise be lost. When negotiations break down and labor–management relations take on an adversarial character, the conflict can be prolonged and extremely costly for both sides. This happens primarily when labor and management view each other as "win–lose" adversaries. In these situations the collective bargaining becomes more of a battle than a constructive dialogue. The ideal process, by contrast, is characterized by a mutual "win–win" approach with a focus on achieving benefits to labor in terms of fair treatment and to management in terms of workforce quality.

A **labor contract** is a formal agreement between a union and an employer about the terms of work for union members.

Collective bargaining is the process of negotiating, administering, and interpreting a labor contract.

Two-tier wage systems pay new hires less than more senior workers already doing the same jobs.

Learning Check

LEARNING OBJECTIVE 13.4

Summarize how managers help organizations maintain a quality workforce.

Be Sure You Can • define *work–life balance* • explain why compensation and benefits are important elements in human resource management • explain potential benefits and problems for merit pay plans • differentiate among bonuses, profit sharing, and stock options • define *flexible benefits plans* and discuss their advantages • define *labor union* and *collective bargaining*

Management Learning Review: Get Prepared for Quizzes and Exams

Summary

LEARNING OBJECTIVE 13.1 Explain the human resource management process and its legal framework.

- The human resource management process involves attracting, developing, and maintaining a quality workforce.
- Human resource management becomes strategic when it is integrated into the organization's strategic management process.
- Employees have legal protections against employment discrimination; equal employment opportunity requires that employment and advancement decisions be made without discrimination.
- Current legal issues in human resource management include sexual harassment, comparable worth, rights of independent contractors, and employee privacy.

For Discussion What gaps in legal protections against employment discrimination still exist?

LEARNING OBJECTIVE 13.2 Describe how managers help organizations attract a quality workforce.

- Human resource planning analyzes staffing needs and identifies actions to fill these needs over time.
- Recruitment is the process of attracting qualified job candidates to fill positions.
- Realistic job previews provide candidates with both positive and negative information about the job and organization.
- Selection involves gathering and assessing information about job candidates and making decisions about whom to hire.
- The selection process often involves screening applicants for qualifications, interviewing applicants, administering employment tests, and doing preemployment checks.

For Discussion Is it realistic to expect that when interviewing with a potential employer you will get a "realistic" job preview?

LEARNING OBJECTIVE 13.3 Discuss how managers help organizations develop a quality workforce.

- Orientation is the process of formally introducing new employees to their jobs, performance expectations, and the organization.
- On-the-job training includes job rotation, coaching, modeling, and mentoring; off-the-job training includes approaches like management development programs.
- Performance appraisal serves both evaluation and development purposes.
- Common performance appraisal methods focus on evaluating employees' traits, behaviors, or performance achievements.

For Discussion What are the potential downsides to using 360-degree feedback in the performance review process?

LEARNING OBJECTIVE 13.4 Summarize how managers help organizations maintain a quality workforce.

- Complex demands of job and family responsibilities have made work–life balance programs increasingly important in human resource management.
- Compensation and benefits packages must be attractive so that an organization stays competitive in labor markets.
- Merit pay plans link compensation and performance; bonuses, profit sharing, and stock options are also forms of incentive compensation.
- Retention decisions in human resource management involve promotions, retirements, and/or terminations.
- The collective bargaining process and labor–management relations are carefully governed by law.

For Discussion What creative options can employers offer to attract and retain motivated lower-wage employees?

Self-Test 13

Multiple-Choice Questions

1. Human resource management is the process of _____, developing, and maintaining a high-quality workforce.
    a. attracting
    b. compensating
    c. appraising
    d. training

2. _____ programs are designed to ensure equal employment opportunities for persons historically underrepresented in the workforce.
    a. Realistic recruiting
    b. External recruiting
    c. Affirmative action
    d. Employee assistance

3. The Age Discrimination in Employment Act prohibits discrimination against persons _____.

    a. 40 years and older

    b. 50 years and older

    c. 65 years and older

    d. of any age

4. _____ is the idea that jobs that are similar in terms of their importance to the organization should be compensated at the same level.

    a. Affirmative action

    b. Realistic pay

    c. Merit pay

    d. Comparable worth

5. A _____ is a criterion that can be legally justified for use in screening candidates for employment.

    a. job description

    b. bona fide occupational qualification

    c. job specification

    d. BARS

6. The first step in strategic human resource management is to _____.

    a. forecast human resource needs

    b. forecast labor supplies

    c. assess the existing workforce

    d. review organizational mission, objectives, and strategies

7. In human resource planning, a(n) _____ is used to determine exactly what is done in an existing job.

    a. critical-incident technique

    b. assessment center

    c. job analysis

    d. multiperson comparison

8. If an employment test yields different results over time when taken by the same person, it lacks _____; if it bears no relation to actual job performance, it lacks _____.

    a. equity, reliability

    b. specificity, equity

    c. realism, idealism

    d. reliability, validity

9. Which phrase is most consistent with a recruiter offering a job candidate a realistic job preview?

    a. "There are just no downsides to this job."

    b. "No organization is as good as this one."

    c. "There just aren't any negatives."

    d. "Let me tell you what you might not like once you start work."

10. Socialization of newcomers occurs during the _____ step of the staffing process.

    a. recruiting

    b. orientation

    c. selecting

    d. training

11. The _____ purpose of performance appraisal is being addressed when a manager describes training options that might help an employee improve future performance.

    a. development

    b. evaluation

    c. judgment

    d. legal

12. When a team leader is required to rate 10% of team members as "superior," 80% as "good," and 10% as "unacceptable" for their performance on a project, this is an example of the _____ approach to performance appraisal.

    a. graphic

    b. forced distribution

    c. behaviorally anchored rating scale

    d. realistic

13. An employee with domestic problems due to substance abuse would be pleased to learn that his employer had a(n) _____ plan to help on such matters.

    a. employee assistance

    b. cafeteria benefits

    c. comparable worth

    d. collective bargaining

14. Whereas bonus plans pay employees for special accomplishments, gain-sharing plans reward them for _____.

    a. helping to increase social responsibility

    b. regular attendance

    c. positive work attitudes

    d. contributing to cost reductions

15. In labor–management relations, the process of negotiating, administering, and interpreting a labor contract is known as _____.

    a. arbitration

    b. mediation

    c. reconciliation

    d. collective bargaining

Short-Response Questions

16. What are the different advantages of internal and external recruitment?

17. Why is orientation an important part of the human resource management process?

18. Why is a BARS potentially superior to a graphic rating scale for use in performance appraisals?

19. How does mentoring work as a form of on-the-job training?

Essay Question

20. Sy Smith is not doing well in his job. The problems began to appear shortly after Sy's job was changed from a manual to computer-based operation. He has tried hard but is just not doing well in learning to use the computer; as a result, he is having difficulty meeting performance expectations. As a 55-year-old employee with over

30 years with the company, Sy is both popular and influential among his work peers. Along with his performance problems, you have also noticed that Sy seems to be developing a more negative attitude toward his job. As Sy's manager, what options would you consider in terms of dealing with the issue of his retention in the job and in the company? What would you do, and why?

Career Skills & Competencies: Make Yourself Valuable!

Evaluate Career Situations

What Would You Do?

1. Tattoos in the Office

A co-worker has come to you with a problem. He has tattoo "sleeves" on both arms that extend to the wrists. Even in a long-sleeved shirt they are difficult to cover. He's upset because he learned that someone else got the promotion he had been hoping for. Everyone respects his high performance, diligence, and loyalty to the company. But it's also common knowledge that the boss "doesn't like tattoos." What advice can you give to your colleague about handling the current situation regarding the lost promotion? What advice, if any, can you offer about having both a career and tattoos?

2. Bad Appraisal System

As the new head of retail merchandising at a local department store, you are disappointed to find that the sales associates are evaluated on a graphic rating scale that uses a simple list of traits to gauge their performance. You believe that better alternatives are available, ones that will not only meet the employer's needs but also be helpful to the sales associates themselves. After raising this issue with your boss, she says "Fine, I hear you. Give me a good proposal and I'll take it to the store manager for approval." What will you propose, and how will you justify it as being good for both the sales associates and the boss?

3. The Union Wants In

There's a drive to organize the faculty of your institution and have them represented by a union. The student leaders on campus are holding a forum to gather opinions on the pros and cons of a unionized faculty. Because you represent a popular student organization in your college, you are asked to participate in the forum. You are expected to speak for about three minutes in front of the other student leaders. So, are you for or against faculty unionization? What will you say at the forum, and why?

Reflect on the Self-Assessment

Performance Assessment Assumptions

Instructions

In each of the following pairs, check the statement that best reflects your assumptions about performance assessment and appraisal.[61]

Performance assessment is:

1. (a) a formal process that should be done annually.
   (b) an informal process that should be done continuously.
2. (a) a process best planned for the person being assessed.
   (b) a process best planned with the person being assessed.
3. (a) done as an organizational requirement.
   (b) done regardless of organizational requirements.
4. (a) a time for team leaders to evaluate performance of team members.
   (b) a time for team members to evaluate their team leaders.
5. (a) a time to clarify performance standards for a worker.
   (b) a time to clarify a worker's career needs.
6. (a) a time to confront poor performance.
   (b) a time to express appreciation.
7. (a) an opportunity to improve direction and control.
   (b) an opportunity to increase enthusiasm and commitment.
8. (a) only as good as the organization's procedures for it.
   (b) only as good as the manager's coaching skills.

Scoring

There is no formal scoring for this assessment, but if you look carefully and think through your answers there may be a pattern worth thinking more about.

Interpretation

The "a" responses represent a more traditional approach to performance appraisal that emphasizes its evaluation function. This role largely puts the supervisor in the role of documenting a subordinate's performance for control and administrative purposes. The "b" responses represent more emphasis on the counseling or development role. Here, the supervisor is concerned with helping the subordinate perform better and learn how he or she might be of help.

Contribute to the Class Exercise

Upward Appraisal

Instructions

Form into work groups as assigned by the instructor. After the instructor leaves the room, complete the following tasks.[62]

1. Create a master list of comments, problems, issues, and concerns about the course experience to date that members would like to communicate to the instructor.

2. Select one person from the group to act as the spokesperson who will give your feedback to the instructor when he or she returns to the classroom.

3. The spokespersons should meet to rearrange the room (placement of tables, chairs, etc.) for the feedback session. This arrangement should allow the spokespersons and instructor to communicate in view of the other class members.

4. While spokespersons are meeting, group members should discuss what they expect to observe during the feedback session.

5. The instructor should be invited in; spokespersons should deliver feedback while observers make notes.

6. After the feedback session is complete, the instructor will call on observers for comments, ask the spokespersons for their reactions, and engage the class in general discussion about the exercise and its implications.

Manage a Critical Incident

Athletic Director's Dilemma

You are the athletic director at a large private university with a highly comprehensive, highly competitive intercollegiate athletics program. Every year the football team is ranked in the top 25 and is always in the hunt for an NCAA Division I national championship. The football team captain at your university has just been in your office. He presented you with a petition signed by 70% of the players that requests permission to start the process leading to unionization. The players aren't asking to be paid, but they believe it is in their best interests to have union protection when it comes to their physical well-being, academic progress, and financial affairs. Since you are at a private university, the players are within their rights and can speak with unions such as the National College Players Association about representing them. The next step in the process will be for the players to distribute formal "union cards" for signatures. If at least 30% sign the cards, they could ask the National Labor Relations Board to endorse their request to unionize. This is a complete surprise to you.

Questions

You have to contact the university president, but you want to be well prepared. What notes will you make about on goals, critical issues, possible outcomes, and stakeholders in this situation? What will be on your list of possible recommendations? What will be your preferred course of action, and why?

Collaborate on the Team Project

Future of Labor Unions

Question: What is the future for labor unions in America?

Instructions

1. Perform library research to identify trends in labor union membership in the United States.

2. Analyze the trends to identify industries and settings where unions are gaining and losing strength. Develop possible explanations for your findings.

3. Talk with members of labor unions—friends, family, community members—to gather their viewpoints on the benefits of unions and issues affecting the future of unions in the United States.

4. Talk with managers in different types of organizations to get their views on unions, how they work, and the advantages and disadvantages they present to management.

5. Consider examining data on labor union trends in other countries.

6. Prepare a report that uses the results of your research to answer the project question.

Analyze the Case Study

RealRecruit | Protecting Student Athletes

Go to *Management Cases for Critical Thinking* at the end of the book to find this case.

CHAPTER 14

Leading and Leadership Development

A Leader Lives in Each of Us

LOC Photo/Alamy Stock Photo

"I have a dream," said Dr. Martin Luther King, Jr., and his voice has traveled from the steps of the Lincoln Memorial in Washington, D.C., on August 28, 1963, across generations. Like other visionary leaders, Dr. King communicated shared dreams and inspired others to pursue lofty goals.

Career Readiness – What to Look for **Inside**

Thought Leadership

Analysis > *Make Data Your Friend*
Followers Report Shortcomings of Leaders

Choices > *Think before You Act*
Sometimes "No" May Be Your Best Answer

Ethics > *Know Right from Wrong*
A Step over the Line into Community Service

Insight > *Learn about Yourself*
There's No Substitute for Integrity

Skills Make You Valuable

- **Evaluate** *Career Situations:*
  What Would You Do?
- **Reflect** *On the Self-Assessment:*
  Least-Preferred Co-worker Scale
- **Contribute** *To the Class Exercise:*
  Most Needed Leadership Skills
- **Manage** *A Critical Incident:*
  Playing Favorites as a Team Leader
- **Collaborate** *On the Team Project:*
  Leadership Believe-It-or-Not
- **Analyze** *The Case Study:*
  Zappos: They Do It with Humor

Chapter Quick Start

"Leadership" is one of those words that we hear and use all the time but rarely stop to think much about. In fact, leadership is a complicated process that demands a lot from both leaders and followers. It also requires great situational understanding and personal insight. This review of leadership thinking can help you build career skills and reach your full leadership potential.

LEARNING OBJECTIVES

14.1 Discuss leadership and explain its links to power, vision, and service.

14.2 Describe key leader behaviors that impact leadership effectiveness.

14.3 Identify how situational contingencies influence leadership effectiveness.

14.4 Summarize the challenges of personal leadership development.

"Leadership" is one of the most popular topics in the field of management. The consensus is that leaders become great by bringing out the best in the people who follow them. As the late Grace Hopper, management expert and the first female admiral in the United States Navy, once said: "You manage things; you lead people."[1] Leadership scholar and consultant Barry Posner believes, "The present moment is the domain of managers. The future is the domain of leaders."[2] Consultant and author Tom Peters claims the leader is "rarely—possibly never?—the best performer."[3] All seem to agree that leaders thrive through and from the successes of others.

Although the leadership advice is clear, the task of leading isn't easy. Managers and team leaders face challenging responsibilities. Resources can be scarce and performance expectations are always high. Time frames for getting things done can be short, while problems are complex, ambiguous, and multidimensional.[4] It takes self-awareness and hard work to be a great leader. There are many challenges to be mastered on the way to successful leadership at work and in our communities. This chapter offers an opportunity to find out more about the leader in you.

14.1 | The Nature of Leadership

WileyPLUS

See Author Video

LEARNING OBJECTIVE 14.1

Discuss leadership and its links to power, vision, and service.

> **Learn More About**
>
> Leadership and power • Leadership and vision • Leadership and service • Leadership and followers

Leadership is the process of inspiring others to work hard to accomplish important tasks.

It helps to think of **leadership** as inspiring others to work hard to accomplish important tasks.[5] As shown in **Figure 14.1**, it also is one of the four basic functions of management. *Planning* sets the direction and objectives; *organizing* brings together resources to turn plans into action; *leading* builds commitments and enthusiasm for people to apply their talents to help accomplish plans; and *controlling* helps to ensure that plans turn out right.

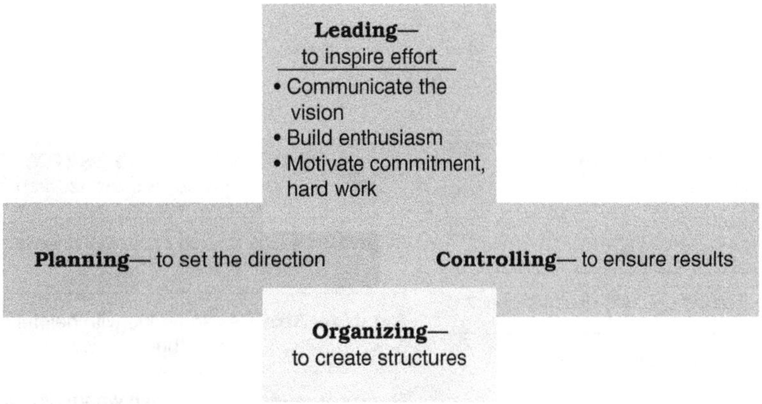

Leading—
to inspire effort
• Communicate the vision
• Build enthusiasm
• Motivate commitment, hard work

Planning— to set the direction

Controlling— to ensure results

Organizing—
to create structures

FIGURE 14.1 Leading viewed in context with the other management functions.

Leadership and Power

Leadership success begins with the ways we use power to influence others. Harvard professor Rosabeth Moss Kanter once called *power* "America's last great dirty word."[6] She was concerned that people, including managers, are uncomfortable with the concept of power. They don't realize how critical it is for leadership.

Power is the ability to get others to get something done, or to make things happen the way you want. The "positive" face of power is that it is the foundation of effective leadership. This means using power not to influence others for the sake of personal satisfaction, but for the good of the group or organization.[7]

Theoretically, anyone in a managerial position—team leader, department head, supervisor—has power, but how well it is used varies from person to person. Leaders gain power both from their position and from their personal qualities.[8] You can remember this as an equation: Managerial Power = Position Power + Personal Power. As shown in **Figure 14.2**, the three bases of position power are rewards, coercion and legitimacy. The three bases of personal power are expertise, relationships, and reference.

> **Power** is the ability to get others to do something you want done or to make things happen the way you want.

Position Power

Position Power Position power comes from the things managers and leaders can offer others—rewards, punishments, and authority. **Reward power** is the ability to influence through rewards. It is being able to offer something of value—a positive outcome—as a way to influence others. This involves incentives such as pay raises, bonuses, promotions, special assignments, and verbal or written compliments. In mobilizing reward power, a manager says, in effect: "If you do what I ask, I'll reward you." As you might expect, this works as long as people want the reward and the leader makes it available. But take the reward or its value away, and the power is quickly lost.

> **Reward power** is the capacity to offer something of value as a means of influencing other people.

Coercive power is the ability to influence through punishment. It is the ability to punish or withhold positive outcomes in order to influence others. A manager may coerce using threats, verbal reprimands, pay penalties, and possible termination. In mobilizing coercive power, a manager says, in effect: "If you don't do what I want, I'll punish you." How would you feel if you were threatened in these ways? If you're like most people, you'll resent the threat and the person making it. You might do what you're told or at least go through the motions. But you're unlikely to continue once the threat is gone. And, lingering feelings of resentment are likely to influence your motivation, how you feel about your job, and your relationships with your manager and the organization.

> **Coercive power** is the capacity to punish or withhold positive outcomes as a means of influencing other people.

Legitimate power is the ability to influence using authority. It is the right to make decisions because of organizational position or status. In using legitimate power, a manager says, in effect: "I am the boss and so you need to do what I say." When your instructor assigns homework, exams, and team projects, you typically do what you're asked to do. Why? You do it because the request is legitimate in the context of the course. But if the instructor moves outside course boundaries and tells you to attend a community event, for example, legitimacy is lost and you are much less likely to go.

> **Legitimate power** is the capacity to influence others by virtue of formal authority, or the rights of office.

Power of the POSITION: *Based on things managers can offer to others.*	**Power of the PERSON:** *Based on how managers are viewed by others.*
Rewards—"If you do what I ask, I'll give you a reward."	**Expertise**—as a source of special knowledge and information.
Coercion—"If you don't do what I ask, I'll punish you."	**Relationships**—as someone with helpful connections with other people.
Legitimacy—"Because I'm the boss, you *must* do as I ask."	**Reference**—as a person with whom others like to identify.

FIGURE 14.2 Sources of position and personal power and how they work.

Personal Power   Although useful, position power alone isn't enough. It's very often personal power that comes from expertise, relationships, and reference that makes the difference between success and failure in a leadership situation, and even in your career.

Expert power is the ability to influence others through special skills, expertise, knowledge, and reputation. When a manager uses expert power, the implied message is one of credibility: "You should do what I want because of what I know and what I have accomplished." This expertise is part of our **human capital**, the ability to things done based on what we know and can do. It can be earned from credentials, by experience, and, perhaps most importantly, through achievements. But expert power has to be protected by staying credible and not pretending to have expertise that isn't really there. Although some people, such as medical doctors and attorneys, are granted at least temporary expertise due to credentials, they can quickly lose it through mistakes and bad behavior. Most of us acquire expertise one step at a time. Gaining it, in fact, may be among of your biggest early career challenges.

Relationship power is the ability to influence others through access to connections and networks.[9] This includes being in the center of information flows and being a well-liked and reliable partner in social networks. When a manager uses relationship power, the implied message is: "I have good access to other people so I can get things done." This power is part of **social capital**, the ability to get things done based on who you know.

Reference power is the ability to influence others through identification, because of others' admiration and desire for positive identification with you. Reference power comes from charisma and interpersonal attractiveness. When a manager uses this power, the implied message is: "You should do what I want to maintain a positive, self-defined relationship with me." Reference power can be developed and maintained through good interpersonal relationships that encourage others' admiration and respect. Remember, it is a lot easier to get others to do what you want when they like you than when they don't.

> **Expert power** is the ability to influence others' because of specialized knowledge.
>
> **Human capital** is the ability to get things done based on what we know and can do.
>
> **Relationship power** is the ability to influence others through access to connections and networks.
>
> **Social capital** is the ability to get things done because of who you know.
>
> **Reference power** is the capacity to influence other people because of their desire to identify personally with you.

Analysis: Make Data Your Friend | Only 37% of workers in a Harris survey believe leaders display "integrity and morality."

Followers Report Shortcomings of Leaders

Andersen Ross Photography Inc/DigitalVision/Getty Images

Harris Interactive periodically conducts surveys of workers' attitudes toward their jobs and employers. The results for "leaders" and "top managers" reveal some surprising shortcomings:

- 37% believe their top managers display integrity and morality.
- 39% believe leaders most often act in the best interest of the organization.
- 22% see leaders as ready to admit mistakes.
- 46% believe their organizations give them freedom to do their jobs.
- 25% of women and 16% of men believe their organizations pick the best people for leadership.
- 33% of managers are perceived by followers as "strong leaders."

Your Thoughts?

How do the leaders you have had experience with stack up? Which ones rate as strong or weak, or as moral or immoral? How would you describe your best leader and his or her impact on you? What makes the greatest difference in the ways leaders are viewed by followers?

Leadership and Vision

"Great leaders," it is said, "get extraordinary things done in organizations by inspiring and motivating others toward a common purpose."[10] Their power is enhanced by communicating a compelling **vision**—a hoped-for future that can improve things in the work team or in the organization as a whole. But simply sharing a vision isn't enough. Great leaders—exceptional leaders—are able to transform their vision into real accomplishments.

The term **visionary leadership** describes leaders who offer a clear and compelling sense of the future, and an understanding of the actions needed to get there successfully.[11] This means not only having a clear vision, but also communicating the vision and motivating and inspiring people to work hard in its pursuit. Think of it this way. Visionary leadership gives meaning to people's work; it makes what they do seem worthwhile and valuable. Noted educational leader Lorraine Monroe says: "The job of a good leader is to articulate a vision that others are inspired to follow."[12] Her views match those of the late John Wooden, member of the college basketball hall of fame and coach of 10 NCAA Division I men's national championship teams at UCLA. Wooden once said: "Effective leadership means having a lot of people working toward a common goal. And if you can achieve that with no one caring who gets the credit, you're going to accomplish a lot."[13]

Vision is a clear sense of the future.

Visionary leadership brings to the situation a clear sense of the future and an understanding of how to get there.

Leadership and Service

Institutions function better when the idea, the dream, is to the fore, and the person, the leader, is seen as servant to the dream.
                    —Robert Greenleaf of the Greenleaf Center for Servant Leadership[14]

The real leader is a servant of the people she leads. A really great boss is not afraid to hire smart people. You want people who are smart about things you are not smart about.
                    —Lorraine Monroe of the Monroe Leadership Institute[15]

When thinking about leadership, power, and vision, it is important to remember the critical importance of personal integrity. The concept of "service" is central to integrity, and leaders who have integrity act as "servants of the organization."[16] More and more you'll hear about **servant leadership** that is based on serving others and helping them fully use their talents so that organizations benefit society.[17] Ask this question: Who is most important—the leader or the followers? For those who believe in servant leadership, the correct answer is clear—the followers. A servant leader is "other-centered" and not "self-centered."

When servant leaders shift focus away from themselves and toward others, what happens? The answer is **empowerment**, allowing others to gain and use power in their work. Servant leaders realize that power is not a "zero-sum" quantity. They reject the idea that in order for someone to gain power, another has to give it up.[18] They empower others by providing them with information, responsibility, authority, and trust to make decisions and act independently. They also expect that people who are empowered will work hard to help the organization accomplish its mission.

Servant leadership is follower-centered and committed to helping others in their work.

Empowerment allowing others to gain and use power in their work.

Leadership and Followers

Leaders depend on followers to achieve important goals and objectives. So, what roles do followers play in leadership? How do followers influence leadership success and failure? Do follower perceptions and expectations of effective leadership vary? These are the kinds of questions leaders and followers should be asking.

Followership is the act of joining with a leader to accomplish tasks and goals.

If leadership is inspiring others, **followership** is joining with a leader to accomplish important objectives.[19] The work of scholar Mary Uhl-Bien and others strongly suggests that the emphasis should be on the word "joining." They view leadership as something that is "co-produced" and "shared" by leaders and followers, rather than a result of a leader's actions alone. They criticize tendencies—sometimes referred to as the *romance of leadership* and the *subordination of followership*—that give leaders too much credit for accomplishments while ignoring contributions of followers.[20]

Research on followership focuses on the perceptions of both leaders and followers. Some followers, for example, are comfortable being told what to do and take little responsibility for shared leadership. Other followers see themselves as partners with responsibility to make real leadership contributions. They are unhappy in top-down leadership situations but act energized and motivated in shared leadership ones.[21]

Learning Check

LEARNING OBJECTIVE 14.1

Discuss leadership and explain its links to power, vision, and service.

Be Sure You Can • define *power* • illustrate three types of position power and discuss how managers use each • illustrate three types of personal power and discuss how managers use each • define *vision* • explain the concept of visionary leadership • explain the notion and benefits of servant leadership • define *empowerment* and *followership* • explain the "romance of leadership" and "subordination of followership"

14.2   Leadership Traits and Behaviors

WileyPLUS

See Author Video

LEARNING OBJECTIVE 14.2

Describe key leader behaviors that impact leadership effectiveness.

> **Learn More About**
> Leadership traits • Leadership behaviors • Classic leadership styles

Societies have recognized for centuries that while some people do really well as leaders, others do not. The question is: "Why?" Historically, the answer has been sought by studying leader traits, behaviors, and situational contingencies. Although they differ in how leadership effectiveness is explained, each approach offers useful insights on leadership development.

Leadership Traits

Question—"What personal traits and characteristics are associated with leadership success?"

An early direction in leadership thinking involved the search for universal traits or distinguishing personal characteristics separating effective from ineffective leaders.[22] Research cautions against relying on physical characteristics as indicators of leadership potential or success. However, followers do tend to admire leaders who are honest, competent, forward looking, inspiring, and credible.[23] A comprehensive review by Shelley Kirkpatrick and Edwin Locke identifies these personal traits of many successful leaders:[24]

- *Drive*—Successful leaders have high energy, display initiative, and are tenacious.
- *Self-confidence*—Successful leaders trust themselves and have confidence in their abilities.
- *Creativity*—Successful leaders are creative and original in their thinking.
- *Cognitive ability*—Successful leaders have the intelligence to integrate and interpret information.
- *Job-relevant knowledge*—Successful leaders know their industry and its technical foundations.
- *Motivation*—Successful leaders enjoy influencing others to achieve shared goals.
- *Flexibility*—Successful leaders adapt to fit the needs of followers and the demands of situations.
- *Honesty and integrity*—Successful leaders are trustworthy, honest, predictable, and dependable.

Leadership Behaviors

Question—"How is leadership success affected by leader interactions with followers?"

In addition to studying traits, researchers also investigated how leaders behave when dealing with followers.[25] If the most effective behaviors could be identified, they reasoned, then it would be possible to train leaders to become skilled at using them. Suggestions from a stream of research that began in the 1940s, spearheaded by studies at The Ohio State University and the University of Michigan, focused attention on two dimensions of leadership behavior - concern for the task and concern for the people doing the work.[26]

- *A leader high in concern for task*—plans and defines the work to be done, assigns task responsibilities, sets clear work standards, urges task completion, and monitors results.
- *A leader high in concern for people*—acts with warmth and supports followers, maintains good social relations with them, respects their feelings, is sensitive to their needs, and shows trust in them.

The results of leader behavior research at first suggested that followers of people-oriented leaders would be the most productive and satisfied.[27] However, researchers eventually moved toward the high-high position that effective leaders were high in concern for both people and task.[28] This type of leader focuses on task accomplishments while also sharing decisions with team members, empowering them, encouraging participation, and supporting teamwork.

Classic Leadership Styles

Question—"How do various leadership styles show concerns for task and people?"

Leader behavior research made it easy to identify different **leadership styles**—recurring patterns of leader behavior based on concerns for task and people. When people talk about their leaders, even today, their vocabulary often describes the classic leadership styles shown in **Figure 14.3**.[29]

A leader identified with an **autocratic style** emphasizes task over people, retains authority and information, and acts in a unilateral, command-and-control fashion. A leader with a **human relations style** does just the opposite and emphasizes people over task. A leader with a **laissez-faire style** shows little concern for task, lets the group make decisions, and acts with a "do the best you can and don't bother me" attitude. A leader with a **democratic style**,

Leadership style is a recurring pattern of behaviors exhibited by a leader.

An **autocratic** leader acts in a command-and-control fashion.

A **human relations** leader emphasizes people over task.

A **laissez-faire** leader has a "do the best you can and don't bother me" attitude.

A **democratic** leader emphasizes both tasks and people.

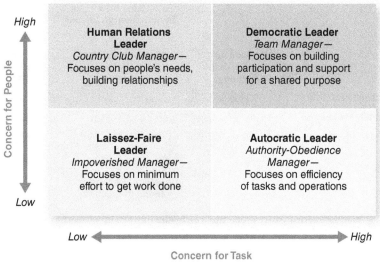

FIGURE 14.3 Classic leadership styles combining concerns for task and concerns for people.

the "high-high" team manager, is committed to both task and people. This leader tries to get things done while sharing information, encouraging participation in decision making, and helping others develop their skills.

Learning Check

LEARNING OBJECTIVE 14.2

Describe key leader behaviors that impact leadership effectiveness.

Be Sure You Can • contrast the trait and leader-behavior approaches to leadership research • identify five personal traits of successful leaders • illustrate leader behaviors consistent with a high concern for task • illustrate leader behaviors consistent with a high concern for people • describe behaviors associated with four classic leadership styles

14.3 | Contingency Approaches to Leadership

WileyPLUS

See Author Video

LEARNING OBJECTIVE 14.3

Identify how situational contingencies influence leadership effectiveness.

Learn More About

Fiedler's contingency model • Hersey-Blanchard situational leadership model • House's path–goal leadership theory • Leader-member exchange theory • Leader-participation model

Over time, scholars became increasingly uncomfortable with both the trait and behavior approaches. They concluded that no one set of traits or behaviors or styles works best all of

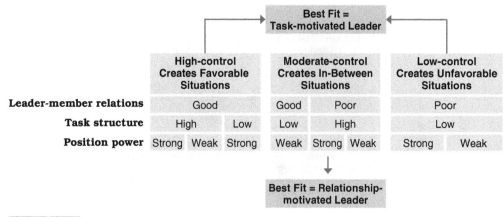

FIGURE 14.4 Fiedler's contingency predictions on leadership effectiveness based on the best style–situation fit.

the time. Instead they developed contingency approaches to help explain the conditions for leadership success in different situations.

Fiedler's Contingency Model

Question—"Which leadership styles work best in different types of situations?"

One of the first contingency leadership models was developed by Fred Fiedler. He proposed that good leadership depends on a match or fit between a person's leadership style and situational demands.[30] Fiedler viewed leadership style as part of personality and difficult to change. Thus, he believed that the key to success is to match leaders with situations where they will fit best. This requires leaders to understand both their personal styles and the situational implications of these styles.[31]

Fiedler measures leadership style using the **least-preferred co-worker scale**, known as the LPC scale. Found as the end-of-chapter self-assessment, it describes tendencies to behave either as a *task-motivated leader* (low LPC score) or *relationship-motivated leader* (high LPC score).

Fiedler describes leadership situations according to the amount of control the leader has. The most favorable situations give the leader a lot of control due to good leader-member relations, high task structure, and strong position power. The least favorable situations are ones with low control due to poor leader-member relations, low task structure, and weak position power.

Figure 14.4 summarizes Fiedler's research showing that no one leadership style is effective all the time. Instead, leadership success depends on having a good style and situational match. The task-motivated style is most successful when the situation is very favorable or unfavorable to the leader. The relationship-oriented style is most successful for in-between situations.

The **least-preferred co-worker scale**, LPC, is used in Fiedler's contingency model to measure leadership style.

Hersey-Blanchard Situational Leadership Model

Question—"How should leaders adjust their leadership styles according to the task readiness of followers?"

The Hersey-Blanchard situational leadership model suggests that successful leaders change behaviors and adjust their styles to fit the abilities and confidence of followers as they perform required tasks. Their model pairs follower task readiness or task maturity with the following four leadership styles.[32]

- *Participating*—emphasizing shared ideas and participative decisions on task directions; a low-task, high-relationship style.
- *Delegating*—allowing the group to take responsibility for task decisions; a low-task, low-relationship style.

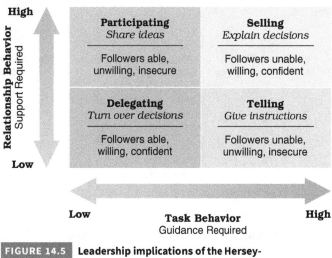

FIGURE 14.5 Leadership implications of the Hersey-Blanchard situational leadership model.

- *Selling*—explaining task directions in a supportive and persuasive way; a high-task, high-relationship style.
- *Telling*—giving specific task directions and closely supervising work; a high-task, low-relationship style.

Figure 14.5 shows that the delegating style works best in high-readiness situations with capable, willing, and confident followers. The telling style works best at the other extreme of low readiness, where followers are unable, unwilling, or insecure. The participating style is recommended for low-to-moderate-readiness followers—able but unwilling, or insecure. Finally, the selling style is most effective for moderate-to-high-readiness followers—unable, but willing or confident.

Hersey and Blanchard also believe that leadership styles should be adjusted as the task readiness of followers changes over time. If the correct styles are used in lower-readiness situations, followers will "mature" and grow in ability, willingness, and confidence. In return, leaders can become less directive and more participative.[33]

House's Path–Goal Leadership Theory

Question—"How can leaders use alternative leadership styles to add value in different types of situations?"

The path–goal theory advanced by Robert House seeks a good fit between leadership style and situation.[34] Importantly, House believed that successful leaders "add value" to situations by moving back and forth among the following leadership styles.

- *Directive leadership*—lets followers know what is expected; gives directions; schedules work; sets and maintains performance standards.
- *Supportive leadership*—does things to make work pleasant; treats team members as equals; acts friendly and approachable; shows concern for the well-beings of others.
- *Achievement-oriented leadership*—sets challenging goals; expects high performance; emphasizes continuous improvement.
- *Participative leadership*—involves team members in decision making; consults with them and asks for suggestions; uses these suggestions when making decisions.

Successful leaders in House's model contribute something that is missing or needs strengthening in a situation, and by avoiding doing things that are already taken care of. When jobs are unclear, for example, it's time for *directive leadership* that clarifies task objectives and expected rewards. When workers lack confidence, *supportive leadership* focuses on existing skills and offers extra assistance. When tasks lack sufficient challenge, *achievement-oriented leadership* helps by setting stretch goals and raising performance aspirations. When motivation is poor, *participative leadership* identifies individual needs and identify valued rewards.[35]

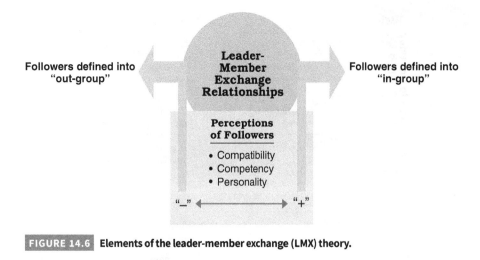

FIGURE 14.6   Elements of the leader-member exchange (LMX) theory.

Path–goal theory also recognizes something called **substitutes for leadership**.[36] These are aspects of the people and work setting that reduce the need for active leader involvement. When substitutes are present, leaders should concentrate on doing other more value-added things. Possible substitutes for leadership include:

- follower characteristics such as ability, experience, and independence
- task characteristics such as the presence of established routines the availability of feedback
- organizational characteristics such as clear plans and precise rules and procedures.

Substitutes for leadership are factors in the work setting that direct work efforts without the involvement of a leader.

Leader-Member Exchange Theory

Question—"How do in-group and out-group dynamics influence leader–follower relationships?"

You may have noticed the tendency for leaders to develop "special" relationships with some team members. This may even get to the point where not everyone is treated the same. Such behavior is central to leader-member exchange, or LMX theory as it is often called.[37]

Described in **Figure 14.6**, LMX theory recognizes that followers fall into "in-groups" and "out-groups." And, your group can make a big difference in your experience with the leader.[38] In-group members – the "favorites" – have special and trusted high-exchange relationships with leaders and often get special rewards, assignments, privileges, and access to information. Out-group members the "also rans" – have a low-quality exchange relationships and may be marginalized, ignored, and receive fewer benefits than in-group members. As you might expect, the most satisfied and loyal followers are the in-group members.[39]

Leader-Participation Model

Question—"How should leaders make decisions in different types of problem situations?"

The Vroom-Jago leader-participation model views successful leaders as choosing the right decision-making methods for various problem situations.[40] An **authority decision** is made by the leader and then communicated to the team. A **consultative decision** is made by the leader after gathering information from members either individually or as a group. A **group or team decision** is made by the team either on its own or with the leader's participation as a contributing member.[41]

Figure 14.7 shows that authority decisions work best when leaders have the information and expertise needed to solve problems and are confident acting alone. They also work best when followers are likely to accept and implement the leader's decisions, and when there is little or no time available for group discussion. Consultative and group decisions work best when the leader lacks information or the expertise needed to solve a problem. They also work best when the problem is unclear, follower acceptance is necessary for implementation, and adequate time is available.

An **authority decision** is made by the leader and then communicated to the group.

A **consultative decision** is made by a leader after receiving information, advice, or opinions from group members.

A **group or team decision** is made by team members.

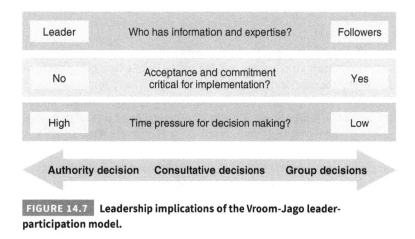

FIGURE 14.7 Leadership implications of the Vroom-Jago leader-participation model.

The participation involved in both the consultative and group decisions offers special benefits.[42] It helps improve decision quality by bringing more information to bear on the problem. It helps improve decision acceptance as participants gain understanding and commitment. And, it contributes to leadership development by allowing others to gain problem-solving experience. Of course, participative decision making is time consuming and leaders don't always have time to involve group members. When problems must be resolved immediately, an authority decision may be the only option.[43]

Learning Check

LEARNING OBJECTIVE 14.3

Identify how situational contingencies influence leadership effectiveness.

Be Sure You Can • contrast the leader-behavior and contingency leadership approaches • explain Fiedler's contingency model • identify the four leadership styles in the Hersey-Blanchard situational model • explain House's path–goal theory • define *substitutes for leadership* • explain LMX theory • contrast the authority, consultative, and group decisions in the Vroom-Jago model

14.4 Personal Leadership Development

WileyPLUS

See Author Video

LEARNING OBJECTIVE 14.4

Summarize the challenges of personal leadership development.

> **Learn More About**
>
> Charismatic and transformational leadership • Emotional intelligence and leadership • Gender and leadership • Moral leadership • Drucker's "good old-fashioned" leadership

There is no one answer to the question of what makes a particular person an effective leader. And, there is always room to grow. Personal leadership development is best viewed as a career readiness commitment, one that you should approach with confidence. But success in personal leadership development has to be earned. It requires self-awareness and continuous learning as you move from one leadership experience to the next.

Charismatic and Transformational Leadership

It is popular to talk about "superleaders" whose vision and strong personality have an extraordinary impact.[44] Dr. Martin Luther King, Jr.'s famous "I Have a Dream" speech, delivered in August 1963 on the Washington Mall, is a good example. Some call people like King **charismatic leaders** because of their ability to inspire others in exceptional ways. We used to think charisma was limited to only a few lucky people. It's now considered one of several personal qualities—including honesty, credibility, and competence—that can be developed with foresight and practice.

A **charismatic leader** inspires followers in extraordinary ways.

Leadership scholars James MacGregor Burns and Bernard Bass link charismatic qualities like enthusiasm and inspiration with **transformational leadership**.[45] Transformational leaders use their personalities, character, and insight to inspire followers. These leaders get others so excited about their jobs and organizational goals that their followers strive for extraordinary performance. Indeed, the easiest way to spot a truly transformational leader is through his or her followers. They are likely to be enthusiastic about the leader, loyal, devoted to his or her ideas, and willing to work exceptionally hard to achieve the leader's vision.

Transformational leadership is inspirational and arouses extraordinary effort and performance.

The pathway to transformational leadership starts with the willingness to bring real emotion to the leader–follower relationship. It involves being a positive role model who acts with integrity and lives up to the trust of others. It requires having both a compelling vision of the future and the ability to communicate that vision to influence others to work hard together to achieve it. Transformational leaders excel because of their strong sense of high aspiration, confidence, and contagious enthusiasm.

Emotional Intelligence and Leadership

The role of personality in transformational leadership relates to another area of inquiry in leadership development—**emotional intelligence**. Popularized by the work of Daniel Goleman, emotional intelligence, or EI for short, is the ability to understand emotions in yourself and others and use this understanding to navigate social relationships.[46] "Great leaders move us," say Goleman and his colleagues: "Great leadership works through emotions."[47]

Emotional intelligence is the ability to manage our emotions in social relationships.

Not only is EI a key leadership asset, it is one that we can each develop.[48] Consider the emotional intelligence competencies in **Figure 14.8**.[49] A leader strong in emotional intelligence has *self-awareness*. This is the ability to understand one's own moods and emotions, and to understand their impact on one's own work and on others' work. Emotionally intelligent leaders are good at *self-management*, or self-regulation. This is the ability to think before acting and to control otherwise disruptive impulses. Emotional intelligence involves *motivation and persistence* in being willing to work hard for reasons other than money and status. Emotionally intelligent leaders also

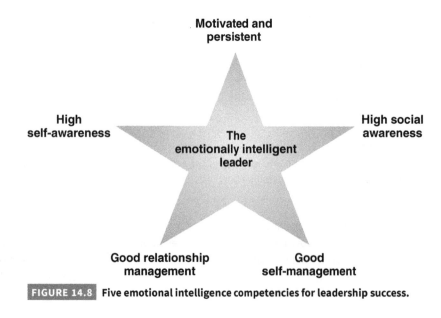

FIGURE 14.8   **Five emotional intelligence competencies for leadership success.**

have *social awareness*, or empathy. They can understand others' emotions and relate to them more effectively. Emotionally intelligent leaders are good at *relationship management*, and can establish rapport with others to build social capital through relationships and informal social networks.

Gender and Leadership

When Sara Levinson was president of NFL Properties, Inc., she asked the all-male members of her NFL management team this question: "Is my leadership style different from a man's?" "Yes," they replied, noting that the very fact that she was asking the question was evidence of the difference. They said her leadership style emphasized communication as well as gathering ideas and opinions from others. When Levinson probed further by asking "Is this a distinctly 'female' trait?," the men said they thought it was.[50]

Are there gender differences in leadership? In pondering this question, three points deserve highlighting. First, research largely supports the **gender similarities hypothesis**. That is, males and females are very similar in terms of psychological properties.[51] Second, research leaves no doubt that both women and men can be equally effective as leaders.[52] Third, research shows that men and women are sometimes perceived as using different styles and arriving at leadership success from different angles.[53]

When men and women are viewed differently as leaders, the perceptions tend to fit traditional stereotypes.[54] Men may be expected to act as task-oriented, "take-charge" leaders who are directive and assertive in traditional command-and-control ways. Women may be expected to act as "take-care" leaders who behave in supportive and nurturing ways. These stereotyped expectations can create a **leadership double bind**, where a woman gets criticized for displaying stereotypically male leadership characteristics and also gets criticized for showing female ones. She can't win when either breaking or conforming to stereotyped female leadership expectations.[55]

In contrast to the double bind scenario, studies report favorable perceptions of female leaders. They have been rated by peers, subordinates, and supervisors as being more participative than male leaders. They have also been described and as good at motivating others, high in emotional

> The **gender similarities hypothesis** holds that males and females have similar psychological properties.

> In the **leadership double bind**, women get criticized for displaying stereotypical male leadership characteristics and also for displaying stereotypical female leadership characteristics.

Choices: Think before You Act | Sooner or later someone in "authority" is going to ask us to do something that seems odd or incorrect, or just plain suspicious.

Sometimes "No" May Be Your Best Answer

RF/Radius Images/Media Bakery

McDonald's Restaurant—A telephone caller claiming to be a police officer and having "corporate" on the line, directs the assistant store manager to take a female employee into the back room and interrogate her while he is on the line. The assistant manager does so for over three hours and follows "Officer Scott's" instructions to the point where the 18-year-old employee is naked and doing jumping jacks.

The hoax was discovered only when the assistant manager called her boss to check out the story. The caller was later arrested and found to have tried similar tricks at over 70 McDonald's restaurants.

Managers are supposed to make decisions, and employees are supposed to follow their lead. Although that is certainly the conventional wisdom, sometimes saying "Yes" to an authority figure isn't the correct thing to do. There may be times when it's best to disobey. Sooner or later someone in "authority" is going to ask for something that seems odd or incorrect or just plain suspicious. If what's asked is wrong, but you still comply with the request, you'll share the blame. Blind followership can't be excused with the claim: "I was just following orders." But, who's prepared for the unexpected?

Your Take?

If obedience isn't always the right choice, how can you know when it's time to disobey? Should students get more training on both spotting bad directives and learning how to say "No"? Do management courses have enough to say about tendencies to obey, how to double-check decisions to make sure obedience to a manager's request is justified, and even about the price of disobedience? Is it possible to educate and train students to be "principled" followers who don't always follow orders and sometimes question them?

intelligence, and skilled at persuading, fostering communication, listening, mentoring, and supporting high-quality work.[56] In research using 360-degree assessments, female managers were rated more highly than male managers in all but one area of leadership—visioning. The possible explanation was that because women are less directive as leaders, they aren't perceived as visionaries.[57]

The pattern of positive leader behaviors sometimes attributed to women is called **interactive leadership**.[58] Interactive leaders are democratic, participative, connecting, and inclusive. They approach problems and decisions through collaboration and teamwork, show respect for others, and use connections to share power and information. They build good interpersonal relations through communication and involvement and have the confidence to seek consensus.[59] They also tend to get things done more through personal power and good interpersonal relationships than through command-and-control use of position power.[60] Harvard scholar Rosabeth Moss Kanter says that "Women get high ratings on exactly those skills required to succeed in the global information age, where teamwork and partnering are so important."[61]

One of the risks in any discussion of gender and leadership is falling prey to stereotypes that place individual men and women into leadership boxes in which they don't necessarily belong.[62] Perhaps it would be most appropriate to set gender issues aside, accept the gender similarities hypothesis, and focus instead on the notion of interactive leadership. An interactive leader is likely to be a very good fit with the needs of today's organizations and their members. There also is no reason why men and women can't adopt this style equally well.[63]

Interactive leaders are strong communicators and act in democratic and participative ways with followers.

Moral Leadership

Our society expects organizations to be run with **moral leadership**. This is leadership with ethical standards that clearly meet the test of being "good" and "correct."[64] Strength in moral leadership begins with personal integrity, a concept fundamental to transformational leadership.

Moral leadership is always "good" and "right" by ethical standards.

Ethics: Know Right from Wrong | The boss expects you to spend part of your workday on one of her community fundraising activities.

A Step over the Line into Community Service

OJO Images Ltd/Alamy Stock Photo

What if your company's CEO is active in a local community group? It sounds great and she gets a lot of press for philanthropy and leadership in the local Red Cross, homeless shelter, food bank,

and more. The company's reputation for social responsibility also gains from her outreach efforts. But, first thing this morning she appeared in your office and asked you to spend a good part of the workweek helping organize a fundraising event for a local charity. Caught off guard, you've given her a weak "okay."

Now that you've had time to think about it, you're not sure you should do it. After all, you've already got a lot of work on your desk, there's no direct connection between the charity and the firm's business, and the charity isn't one you personally support.

Helping your boss with this request will obviously be good for her. You'll also probably benefit from increased goodwill in your relationship with her. However, the organization could actually end up being worse off as your regular work slips behind schedule, affecting not only you but client activities that depend on you. Sure, you're getting paid to do what she asks—but who benefits?

What Do You Think?

Is it ethical to help your manager in the situation just described? Are you doing a disservice to the organization's other stakeholders if you go along with this request? Is it acceptable for a manager or team leader or top executive to ask others to help them with tasks and activities that are not directly tied to work? Just where would you draw the line on requests like these?

Leaders show **integrity** by acting with honesty, credibility, and consistency in putting values into action.

People who lead with **integrity** act in an honest, credible, and consistent way to put their values into action. A leader with integrity earns the trust of followers. When followers believe leaders are trustworthy, they try to live up to their leader's expectations.

If moral leadership is the goal, why don't we see more of it? Are you surprised that a *Business Week* survey found that just 14% of top executives at large U.S. firms rated "having strong ethical values" as a top leadership characteristic?[65] How about a Harris poll that found only 37% of U.S. adults viewing their top managers as acting with "integrity and morality"?[66] One of the risks in living up to the expectations of moral leadership is **moral overconfidence**, an overly positive view of one's strength of character.[67] Leaders with moral overconfidence may act unethically without realizing it or while using inappropriate rationalizations to justify their behavior. When you hear or think "I'm a good person, so I can't be wrong," this might signal moral overconfidence.[68]

Moral overconfidence is an overly positive view of one's strength of character.

Authentic leadership activates positive psychological states to achieve self-awareness and positive self-regulation.

The concept of servant leadership fits with the concept of a moral leader. So does the notion of **authentic leadership**, described as acting with a high level of self-awareness and a clear understanding of personal values.[69] Authentic leaders act consistent with personal values, are honest, and avoid self-deception. They are respected as genuine by followers and can have a positive influence on them.[70] The values and actions of authentic leaders create a positive ethical climate in their organizations.[71]

Drucker's "Good Old-Fashioned" Leadership

The late and widely respected consultant Peter Drucker offers a time-tested and very pragmatic view of leadership. His many books and articles remind us that leadership effectiveness must have strong foundations, something he refers to as the "good old-fashioned" hard work of a successful leader.[72]

Drucker believed that the basic building block for success as a leader is *defining and establishing a sense of mission*. A good leader sets the goals, priorities, and standards. And, a good leader keeps them always clear and visible. As Drucker put it, "The leader's first task is to be the trumpet that sounds a clear sound."[73] Drucker also highlighted the importance of

---

Insight: Learn about Yourself | Our personal character gets revealed by how we treat those with no power.

There's No Substitute for Integrity

Whether you call it ethical leadership or moral leadership, the lesson is the same: Respect flows toward leaders who behave with **integrity**. If you have integrity, you'll be honest, credible, and consistent in all that you do. This seems obvious. "This is what we have been taught since we were kids," you might say.

So, why are there so many well-publicized examples of leaders who act without integrity? Where, so to speak, does integrity go when some people find themselves in positions of leadership? CEO coach Kenny Moore says that our personal character gets "revealed by how we treat those with no power." Look closely at how people in leadership positions treat everyday workers—servers, technicians, custodians, and clerks, for example. Moore says that the ways we deal with people who are powerless "brings out our real dispositions."

The "integrity line" in the figure marks the difference between where we should and should not be. Below the line are leaders who lie, blame others for personal mistakes, want others to fail, and take credit for others' ideas. They're conceited and selfish. Above the integrity line are honest, consistent, humble, and selfless leaders. Some call such leaders "servants" of the organization and its members.

Get To Know Yourself Better

Why is it that in the news and in everyday experience we so often end up wondering where leadership integrity has gone? Ask: How often have I worked for someone who behaved below the "integrity line"? How did I feel about it, and what did I do? Write a set of notes on your behavior in situations where your own leadership integrity could be questioned. What are some of the lessons available from this experience? Who are your leadership exemplars, the ones you most admire and would like to emulate? At this point in your life, who is the real leader in you?

accepting leadership as a responsibility rather than a rank. He pointed out that good leaders surround themselves with talented people, aren't afraid to develop strong and capable followers, don't blame others when things go wrong, and accept the adage that has become a hallmark of leadership—"The buck stops here."

Finally, Drucker also stressed the *importance of earning and keeping the trust of others*. The key is the leader's personal integrity, the point on which the chapter began. Followers of good leaders trust in their leadership. They believe the leader means what he or she says, and know that his or her actions are consistent with what is said. "Effective leadership is not based on being clever," says Drucker, "it is based primarily on being consistent."[74]

Learning Check

LEARNING OBJECTIVE 14.4

Summarize the challenges of personal leadership development.

Be Sure You Can • define *transformational leadership* • explain how emotional intelligence contributes to leadership success • discuss research insights on the relationship between gender and leadership • define *interactive leadership* • discuss integrity as a foundation for moral leadership • list Drucker's essentials of good old-fashioned leadership

Management Learning Review: Get Prepared for Quizzes and Exams

Summary

LEARNING OBJECTIVE 14.1   Discuss leadership and explain its links to power, vision, and service.

- Leadership is the process of inspiring others to work hard to accomplish important tasks.
- The ability to communicate a vision—a clear sense of the future—is essential for effective leadership.
- Power is the ability to get others to do what you want them to do through leadership.
- Sources of position power include rewards, coercion, and legitimacy or formal authority; sources of personal power include expertise, referent, and information and networking power.
- Servant leadership is follower-centered and focused on empowering others and helping them to fully utilize their talents.
- Followership is the act of joining with a leader to accomplish tasks and goals.
- There is a tendency to give credit to leaders—the romance of leadership, and overlook the contributions of followers—the subordination of followership.

For Discussion   When is a leader justified in using coercive power?

LEARNING OBJECTIVE 14.2   Describe key leader behaviors that impact leadership effectiveness.

- Traits that seem to have a positive impact on leadership include drive, integrity, and self-confidence.
- Research on leader behaviors has focused on alternative leadership styles based on concerns for tasks and concerns for people.
- One suggestion of leader-behavior researchers is that effective leaders are team based and participative, showing both high task and people concerns.

For Discussion   Are any personal traits indispensable "must haves" for success in leadership?

LEARNING OBJECTIVE 14.3   Identify how situational contingencies influence leadership effectiveness.

- Contingency leadership approaches point out that no one leadership style always works best; the best style is one that properly matches the demands of each unique situation.

- Fiedler's contingency model matches leadership styles with situational differences in task structure, position power, and leader-member relations.
- The Hersey-Blanchard situational model recommends using task-oriented and people-oriented behaviors, depending on the "maturity" levels of followers.
- House's path–goal theory points out that leaders add value to situations by using supportive, directive, achievement-oriented, or participative styles.
- The Vroom-Jago leader-participation model advises leaders to choose decision-making methods—individual, consultative, group—that best fit the problems to be solved.

For Discussion What are the career development implications of Fiedler's contingency model of leadership?

LEARNING OBJECTIVE 14.4 Summarize the challenges of personal leadership development.

- Transformational leaders use charisma and emotion to inspire others toward extraordinary efforts and performance excellence.
- Emotional intelligence—the ability to manage our relationships and ourselves effectively—is an important leadership capability.
- The interactive leadership style emphasizes communication, involvement, and interpersonal respect.
- Managers are expected to be moral leaders who communicate high ethical standards and show personal integrity in all dealings with other people.

For Discussion Is transformational leadership always moral leadership?

Self-Test 14

Multiple-Choice Questions

1. Someone with a clear sense of the future and the actions needed to get there is considered a _____ leader.
   a. task-oriented
   b. people-oriented
   c. transactional
   d. visionary

2. Leader power = _____ power + _____ power.
   a. reward, punishment
   b. reward, expert
   c. legitimate, position
   d. position, personal

3. A manager who says "Because I am the boss, you must do what I ask" is relying on _____ power.
   a. reward
   b. legitimate
   c. expert
   d. referent

4. When a leader assumes that others will do as she asks because they want to positively identify with her, she is relying on _____ power to influence their behavior.
   a. expert
   b. referent
   c. legitimate
   d. reward

5. The personal traits now considered important for managerial success include _____.
   a. self-confidence
   b. gender
   c. age
   d. height

6. In the leader-behavior approaches to leadership, someone who does a very good job of planning work, setting standards, and monitoring results would be considered a(n) _____ leader.
   a. task-oriented
   b. control-oriented
   c. achievement-oriented
   d. employee-centered

7. When leader behavior researchers concluded that "high-high" was the pathway to leadership success, what were they referring to?
   a. high initiating structure and high integrity
   b. high concern for task and high concern for people
   c. high emotional intelligence and high charisma
   d. high job stress and high task goals

8. A leader whose actions indicate an attitude of "do as you want, and don't bother me" would be described as having a(n) _____ leadership style.
   a. autocratic
   b. country club
   c. democratic
   d. laissez-faire

9. In Fiedler's contingency model, both highly favorable and highly unfavorable leadership situations are best dealt with by a _____ leader.
   a. task-motivated
   b. laissez-faire
   c. participative
   d. relationship-motivated

10. _____ leadership model suggests that leadership style is strongly anchored in personality and therefore hard to change.
    a. Trait
    b. Fiedler's
    c. Transformational
    d. Path–goal

11. House's _____ theory of leadership says that successful leaders find ways to add value to leadership situations.

   a. trait
   b. path–goal
   c. transformational
   d. life-cycle

12. A leader who _____ would be described as achievement-oriented in the path–goal theory.

   a. sets challenging goals for others
   b. works hard to achieve high performance
   c. gives directions and monitors results
   d. builds commitment through participation

13. The critical contingency variable in the Hersey-Blanchard situational model of leadership is _____.

   a. followers' maturity
   b. LPC
   c. task structure
   d. LMX

14. Vision, charisma, integrity, and symbolism are all on the list of attributes typically associated with _____ leaders.

   a. contingency
   b. informal
   c. transformational
   d. transactional

15. The interactive leadership style, sometimes associated with women, is characterized by _____.

   a. inclusion and information sharing
   b. use of rewards and punishments
   c. command and control
   d. emphasis on position power

Short-Response Questions

16. Why does a person need both position power and personal power to achieve long-term managerial effectiveness?

17. What is the major insight of the Vroom-Jago leader-participation model?

18. What are the three variables that Fiedler's contingency model uses to diagnose the favorability of leadership situations, and what does each mean?

19. How does Peter Drucker's view of "good old-fashioned leadership" differ from the popular concept of transformational leadership?

Essay Question

20. When Marcel Henry took over as leader of a new product development team, he was both excited and apprehensive. "I wonder," he said to himself on the first day in his new assignment, "if I can meet the challenges of leadership." Later that day, Marcel shared this concern with you during a coffee break. Based on the insights offered in this chapter, how would you describe the implications of current thinking on transformational leadership and moral leadership for his personal leadership development?

Career Skills & Competencies: Make Yourself Valuable!

Evaluate Career Situations

What Would You Do?

1. Autocratic Boss

Some might say it was bad luck. Others will tell you it's life and you'd better get used to it. You've just gotten a new team leader, and within the first week it was clear to everyone that she is as "autocratic" as can be. The previous leader was very "democratic," and so is the higher-level manager, with whom you've always had a good working relationship. Is there anything you and your co-workers can do to remedy this situation without causing anyone, including the new boss, to lose their jobs?

2. New to the Team

You've just been hired as a visual effects artist by a top movie studio. The team you are joining has already been together for about two months. There's obviously an in-group when it comes to team leader and team member relationships. This job is important to you; the movie is going to be great résumé material. But you're worried about the leadership dynamics and your role as a newcomer to the team. What can you do to get on board as soon as possible, work well with the team leader, and be valued by other team members?

3. Out of Comfort Zone

Okay, it's important to be "interactive" in leadership. By personality, though, you tend to be a bit withdrawn. If you could do things by yourself, that's the way you would approach your work. That's your comfort zone. Yet you are talented and ambitious. Career growth in your field requires taking on management responsibilities. So, here you are agreeing to take over as a team leader in your first upward career move. Can you succeed by leading within your comfort zone? If not, what can you do to "stretch" your capabilities into new leadership territories?

Reflect on the Self-Assessment

Least-Preferred Co-Worker Scale

Instructions

Think of all the different people with whom you have ever worked—in jobs, in social clubs, in student projects, or other areas of your life. Next think of the one person with whom you could work least well—that is, the person with whom you had the most difficulty getting a job done. This is the one person—a peer, boss, or subordinate—with whom you would least want to work. Describe this person by circling numbers at the appropriate points on each of the following pairs of bipolar adjectives. Work fast. There are no right or wrong answers.[75]

Pleasant	8	7	6	5	4	3	2	1	Unpleasant
Friendly	8	7	6	5	4	3	2	1	Unfriendly
Rejecting	1	2	3	4	5	6	7	8	Accepting
Tense	1	2	3	4	5	6	7	8	Relaxed
Distant	1	2	3	4	5	6	7	8	Close
Cold	1	2	3	4	5	6	7	8	Warm
Supportive	8	7	6	5	4	3	2	1	Hostile
Boring	1	2	3	4	5	6	7	8	Interesting
Quarrelsome	1	2	3	4	5	6	7	8	Harmonious
Gloomy	1	2	3	4	5	6	7	8	Cheerful

Open	8	7	6	5	4	3	2	1	Guarded
Backbiting	1	2	3	4	5	6	7	8	Loyal
Untrustworthy	1	2	3	4	5	6	7	8	Trustworthy
Considerate	8	7	6	5	4	3	2	1	Inconsiderate
Nasty	1	2	3	4	5	6	7	8	Nice
Agreeable	8	7	6	5	4	3	2	1	Disagreeable
Insincere	1	2	3	4	5	6	7	8	Sincere
Kind	8	7	6	5	4	3	2	1	Unkind

Self-Assessment Scoring

Compute your "least-preferred co-worker" (LPC) score by totaling all the numbers you circled; enter that score here [LPC _____].

Interpretation

The LPC scale is used by Fred Fiedler to identify a person's dominant leadership style. He believes that this style is a relatively fixed part of our personality and is therefore difficult to change. Thus, he suggests the key to leadership success is finding (or creating) good "matches" between style and situation. If your score is 73 or above, Fiedler considers you a "relationship-motivated" leader. If your score is 64 or below, he considers you a "task-motivated" leader. If your score is between 65 and 72, Fiedler leaves it up to you to determine which leadership style is most like yours.

Contribute to the Class Exercise

Most Needed Leadership Skills

Instructions

1. Work individually to make a list of the leadership skills you believe you need to develop further in order to be ready for success in your next full-time job.
2. Share your list with teammates, discuss the rationale for your choices, and listen to what they have to say about the list of skills.
3. Prepare a master list of the five leadership skills that your team believes are most important for further development.
4. For each skill on the team list prepare a justification that describes what the skill involves, why it is important to leadership success, and why it is still a candidate for further skills development among your teammates.
5. Present your leadership skills development list along with justifications to the whole class for discussion.

Manage a Critical Incident

Playing Favorites as a Team Leader

One of your colleagues just returned from a leadership training session at which the instructor presented the LMX, or leader-member exchange, theory. Listening to her talk about the training prompted thoughts about your own leader behaviors, and you came to a somewhat startling conclusion: You may be playing "favorites." In fact, the last person you recommended for promotion was a good friend and a member of your biweekly poker night club. Of course he was competent and is doing a good job in the new position. But as you think more about it, there were also two others on the team who may well have been equally good choices. Did you give them a fair chance when preparing your promotion recommendation, or did you short-change them in favor of your friend?

Questions

Well, it's a new day for the team, and basically the start of the rest of your leadership career. What can you do as a team leader to make sure that tendencies toward favoritism don't disadvantage some members? What warning signs can you watch for to spot when and if you are playing favorites?

309

Collaborate on the Team Project

Leadership Believe-It-or-Not

You would think leaders would spend lots of time talking with the people who make products and deliver services, trying to understand problems and asking for advice. But *Business Week* reports a survey showing that quite the opposite is true. Persons with a high school education or less are asked for advice by only 24% of their bosses; for those with a college degree, the number jumps to 54%.

Question

What stories do your friends, acquaintances, family members, and you tell about their bosses that are truly hard to believe?

Instructions

1. Listen to others and ask others to talk about the leaders they have had in the past or currently do have. What strange-but-true stories are they telling?

2. Create a journal that can be shared with class members that summarizes, role-plays, or otherwise communicates the real-life experiences of people whose bosses sometimes behave in ways that are hard to believe.

3. For each of the situations in your report, try to explain the boss's behaviors.

4. For each of the situations, assume that you observed or heard about it as the boss's supervisor. Describe how you would "coach" or "counsel" the boss to turn the situation into a "learning moment" for positive leadership development.

Analyze the Case Study

Zappos | They Do It with Humor

Go to *Management Cases for Critical Thinking* at the end of the book to find this case.

CHAPTER 15

Individual Behavior

There's Beauty in Individual Differences

PEOPLE AND TECHNOLOGY by VISION/Alamy Stock Photo

You don't have to take a selfie to gain more self-awareness. What does your smartphone, tablet, or notebook screen say about your personality?

Chapter Quick Start

When people work, play, and live together they experience lots of ups and downs. There can be relationship and communication miscues, as well as bonds of friendship that fill life with pleasure. This natural ebb and flow reflects individual differences in perceptions, personalities, attitudes, moods, and emotions. Those who understand and respect differences will be more successful than those who are self-centered and insensitive.

LEARNING OBJECTIVES

15.1 Summarize perceptual tendencies and distortions that influence behavior.

15.2 Explain common personality differences and their behavioral implications.

15.3 Discuss the components of attitudes and the importance of job satisfaction.

15.4 Illustrate how emotions, moods, and stress influence individual behavior.

Career Readiness – What to Look for Inside

Thought Leadership

Analysis > *Make Data Your Friend* Paying a High Price for Incivility at Work

Choices > *Think before You Act* Curbing Bias in Hiring Decisions

Ethics > *Know Right from Wrong* My Team Leader is a Workaholic

Insight > *Learn about Yourself* Keep Ambition on Your Side

Skills Make You Valuable

- **Evaluate** *Career Situations:* What Would You Do?
- **Reflect** *On the Self-Assessment:* Self-Monitoring
- **Contribute** *To the Class Exercise:* Job Satisfaction Preferences
- **Manage** *A Critical Incident:* Facing Up to Attributions
- **Collaborate** *On the Team Project:* Difficult Personalities
- **Analyze** *The Case Study:* Panera Bread: Growing a Company with Personality

304

In his books *Leadership Is an Art* and *Leadership Jazz*, Max DePree, former chairperson of the publicly traded furniture manufacturer Herman Miller, Inc., talks about a millwright who worked for his father. When the man died, DePree's father, wishing to express his sympathy to the family, went to their home. There he listened as the widow read some beautiful poems which, to his father's surprise, the millwright had written. DePree says that he and his father often wondered, "Was the man a poet who did millwright's work, or a millwright who wrote poetry?" He summarized the lesson this way: "It is fundamental that leaders endorse a concept of persons," meaning you have to care enough to find and respect the whole person behind the face.[1]

Contrast DePree's story with that of Karen Nussbaum, founder of the national membership organization 9to5. After an incident in her job as a secretary at Harvard University, she dedicated her career "to putting working women's issues on the public agenda."[2] "One day I was sitting at my desk at lunchtime, when most of the professors were out," she says. "A student walked into the office, looked me dead in the eye and said, 'Isn't anyone here?'"[3] Nussbaum pledged to "remake the system so that it does not produce these individuals." Among the action priorities of 9to5 are family-supporting jobs, paid sick leave, equal pay for female employees, and elimination of discriminatory hiring based on gender or sexual orientation.[4]

When people are treated with disrespect at work, as reflected in Nussbaum's story, they may respond with low performance, poor customer service, absenteeism, and antisocial behavior. When they work in supportive settings, positive behavior is much more likely—including higher work performance, less withdrawal and dysfunction, and helpful citizenship behavior. Perceptions, personalities, attitudes, emotions, and moods all have an effect on how we treat one another. And in the workplace, the following types of behaviors are at issue.

- *Performance behaviors*—task performance, customer service, productivity
- *Withdrawal behaviors*—absenteeism, turnover, job disengagement
- *Citizenship behaviors*—helping, volunteering, job engagement
- *Dysfunctional behaviors*—antisocial behavior, intentional wrongdoing

15.1 | Perception

LEARNING OBJECTIVE 15.1

Summarize perceptual tendencies and distortions that influence behavior.

WileyPLUS

See Author Video

> **Learn More About**
>
> Perception and attribution • Perception tendencies and distortions • Perception and impression management

Perception is the process through which people receive and interpret external information from the environment. It affects the impressions we form of ourselves, other people, and our daily experiences. You can think of perception as a filter through which information passes into our consciousness and affects how we think about the world. Because perceptions are influenced by cultural background, values, and other personal and situational circumstances, people can and do perceive the exact same people, events, situations or circumstances in very different ways. Importantly, we most often behave in accordance with our perceptions.[5]

Perception is the process through which people receive, organize, and interpret information from the environment.

Perception and Attribution

What happens when you perceive that someone else in a job or student team isn't performing up to the expectations of the team or their supervisor/instructor? How do you personally

FIGURE 15.1 Contrasts between fundamental attribution error and self-serving bias.

Attribution is the process of explaining events.

explain this situation? Given your explanation, how do you react? These questions involve **attribution**, which is the process of developing explanations for events.

Attribution theory describes how people try to explain their own behavior and the behavior of other people. **Figure 15.1** contrasts two errors we commit when making attributions.[6] The **fundamental attribution error** occurs when someone's performance problems are blamed more on internal failures of the individual than on external factors relating to the environment. In the case of late or poor-quality work, for example, a team leader might blame a team member's lack of job skills or laziness. In response, the leader may try to resolve the problem through rewards, punishments, or even replacement. Because the fundamental attribution error neglects other possible explanations, such as unrealistic time pressures, bad technology, or poor training, opportunities to address these factors and improve performance can be easily missed.

Fundamental attribution error overestimates internal factors and underestimates external factors driving individual behavior.

Self-serving bias explains personal success by internal causes and personal failures by external causes.

Attribution theory also recognizes tendencies toward **self-serving bias**. This happens when individuals blame their personal failures or problems on external causes, while attributing successes to internal causes. You might call this the "It's not my fault!" error when something goes wrong and the "It was me, I did it!" error when things go right. Think of the self-serving bias the next time your favorite sports team loses a close game—"It was bad officiating!" or when your team wins a close one—"It was great coaching and playmaking!" Self-serving bias creates a false sense of confidence and causes reluctance to consider possibilities for change and development. It is an obstacle to learning from both victories and defeats.

Perception Tendencies and Distortions

A variety of perception tendencies and distortions influence the way we communicate with and behave toward one another. Inappropriate use of stereotypes, halo effects, selective perception, and projections can cause us to lose sight of important individual differences.

A **stereotype** occurs when attributes commonly associated with a group are assigned to an individual.

Stereotypes
A **stereotype** occurs when someone is identified with a particular group or category, and then oversimplified attributes associated with that group or category are used to describe the individual, to make assumptions about how the individual will behave or the kinds of things the individual is likely to think or assume. We all use stereotypes, and they aren't always negative or ill-intended. But stereotypes based on individual differences such as gender, age, race, religion, able-bodiedness, national origin, or sexual orientation can, and unfortunately do, bias our perceptions of other people.[7] And because perceptions influence behavior, we may behave toward people in incorrect and disrespectful ways.

The problem with making decisions under the influence of stereotypes is that each individual is just that—an individual, and not a generic archetype. Why, for example, do females get a smaller proportion of international assignments at U.S. companies than their male counterparts?[8] A Catalyst study blames gender stereotypes and perceptions that women lack the abilities or willingness to work abroad effectively.[9]

A **halo effect** occurs when one attribute is used to develop an overall impression of a person or situation.

Halo Effects
A **halo effect** occurs when one personal attribute is used to develop an overall impression of a person or of a situation. When meeting someone new, for example, the halo effect may cause one trait, such as a pleasant smile or a firm handshake, to trigger an overall positive perception. A unique hairstyle or style of clothes, by contrast, may trigger a generalized negative impression. Halo effect errors show up during performance evaluations. One factor, such as punctuality or pleasant personality, may become the "halo" for a positive

Choices: Think before You Act | "... if you have several pair of shoes available, you're much more likely to be able to compare different attributes of the shoes."

Curbing Bias in Hiring Decisions

Jon Feingersh/Jon Feingersh Photography/Superstock

Study Harvard scholars Iris Bohnet, Alexandra van Geen, and Max H. Bazerman asked 100 participants to act as candidates for a new job. They performed a variety of "math and verbal tasks" chosen by the researchers because of the common gender stereotype that "females are believed to be worse at math tasks and better at verbal tasks than males." Another 554 study participants then acted as evaluators to select candidates from this set of 100 for a second round of testing. They were given test results and gender for each candidate. Some evaluators were asked to evaluate the candidates one at a time while others directly compared male and female candidates.

Findings Gender stereotypes influenced the one-by-one evaluations, with female candidates more often chosen for further verbal testing and male candidates for further math testing. When male and female candidates were evaluated together, however, gender stereotypes largely disappeared.

Conclusion One way to curb bias in hiring decisions is to make sure evaluators compare candidates directly rather than one-by-one. Bohnet and colleagues point out: "If you look at one pair of shoes, it's hard to evaluate the quality of those shoes. You will be much more likely to go with stereotypes or heuristics or rules of thumb about shoes. But if you have several pair of shoes available, you're much more likely to be able to compare different attributes of the shoes."

Your Take?

Does this research put its finger on a simple way to remove gender bias from human resource decisions? Is it time to stop assessing candidates one at a time and instead compare them to one another directly?

overall performance assessment, even though an accurate evaluation of the full set of available performance facts would not have led to the same result.

Selective Perception
Selective perception is the tendency to single out aspects of an individual or situation that reinforce existing beliefs, values, or needs.[10] Information that makes us feel uncomfortable tends to get screened out, while information that makes us feel comfortable is allowed in. What this means in organizations is that people from different departments or functions—such as marketing and information systems—see organizational events from their own point of view but don't recognize the validity of others' point of view. One way to reduce or avoid selective perception is to be sure to gather inputs and opinions from people with divergent points of view.

Selective perception is the tendency to define problems from one's own point of view.

Projection
Projection involves assignment of personal attributes to others. A classic projection error is to assume that other people share our needs, desires, and values. For example, suppose you enjoy a lot of responsibility and challenge in your work. Suppose, also, that you are the newly appointed head of a team whose jobs you see as dull and routine. You might move quickly to redesign jobs so that members take on more responsibilities and perform more challenging tasks. But this may not be a good decision. Instead of designing jobs to best fit the team members' needs, you might just have spent a lot of time and effort designing their jobs to fit with your own needs. The members may have been satisfied doing jobs that seem routine to you. Projection errors can be controlled through self-awareness and trying to see things from others' points of view.

Projection is the assignment of personal attributes to other individuals.

Perception and Impression Management

Richard Branson, founder of the Virgin Group, is one of the richest executives in the world.[11] He's also known for informality and being a casual dresser. One of his early successes was launching Virgin Airlines as a competitor to British Airways (BA). The former head of BA, Lord

King, said: "If Richard Branson had worn a shirt and tie instead of a goatee and jumper, I would not have underestimated him."[12] This anecdote reveals how much impressions - intentional and unintentional - can influence our experiences with others.

Scholars discuss **impression management** as the systematic attempt to influence how others perceive us.[13] It's a matter of routine in everyday life and easy to take charge of. Impression management exists in the ways we dress, talk, act, surround ourselves with friends and acquaintances, and adorn with objects such as smartphones, jewelry, and cars. All this conveys what we perceive to be a desirable image to others. When done in a career context, impression management can help us develop relationships with influential people, advance in jobs and careers, and create pathways to group memberships, social invitations, and special assignments.

Some basic impression management tactics for career development are worth remembering. Dress in ways that convey positive appeal—for example, know when to "dress up" and when to "dress down." Use words to engage other people in ways that generate positive feelings toward you. Make eye contact and smile during conversations to create a personal bond. Pay attention to what is being said and avoid distractions. Display high energy and enthusiasm to suggest lots of work commitment and initiative.[14]

> **Impression management** is the systematic attempt to influence how others perceive us.

Learning Check

LEARNING OBJECTIVE 15.1

Summarize perceptual tendencies and distortions that influence behavior.

Be Sure You Can • define *perception* • explain fundamental attribution error and self-serving bias • define *stereotype, halo effect, selective perception*, and *projection* and illustrate how each can adversely affect work behavior • explain impression management

15.2 Personality

WileyPLUS

See Author Video

LEARNING OBJECTIVE 15.2

Explain common personality differences and their behavioral implications.

> **Learn More About**
>
> Big Five personality dimensions • Myers-Briggs Type Indicator • Technology personality • Personal conception and emotional adjustment traits

How often do you complain about someone's "bad personality," tell a friend how much you like someone because of their "nice personality," or worry that co-workers will mistake your "quiet shyness" for a lack of competency? These personality-driven impressions of other people emerge at work as frequently as they do in our everyday lives. Perhaps you have been part of conversations like these: "I can't give him that job; with a personality like that there's no way he can work with customers." "Put Erika on the project—her personality is perfect for the intensity that we expect from the team." "Cynthia should present our proposal—she's got an outgoing personality."

The term **personality** describes a set of enduring characteristics that makes us unique as individuals. No one can doubt that an individual's personality can influence how she or he behaves and how that behavior is seen by others. The implications of personality extend from how we face problems and pursue tasks, to how we handle relationships with everyone from family to friends to co-workers.

> **Personality** is the profile of characteristics making a person unique from others.

Big Five Personality Dimensions

Although there are many different personality traits, some of the most widely recognized are a short list of five that are especially significant in the workplace. Known as the *Big Five*,[15] these personality dimensions are:

1. **Extraversion**—the degree to which someone is outgoing, sociable, and assertive. An extravert is comfortable and confident in interpersonal relationships; an introvert is more withdrawn and reserved.

2. **Agreeableness**—the degree to which someone is good-natured, cooperative, and trusting. An agreeable person gets along well with others; a disagreeable person is a source of conflict and discomfort for others.

3. **Conscientiousness**—the degree to which someone is responsible, dependable, and careful. A conscientious person focuses on what can be accomplished and meets commitments; a person who lacks conscientiousness is careless, often trying to do too much and failing, or doing little.

4. **Emotional stability**—the degree to which someone is relaxed, secure, and generally unworried. A person who is emotionally stable is calm and confident; a person lacking in emotional stability is anxious, nervous, and tense.

5. **Openness to experience**—the degree to which someone is curious, open to new ideas, and imaginative. An open person is broad-minded, receptive to new things, and comfortable with change; a person who lacks openness is narrow-minded, has few interests, and is resistant to change.

> **Extraversion** is being outgoing, sociable, and assertive.
>
> **Agreeableness** is being good-natured, cooperative, and trusting.
>
> **Conscientiousness** is being responsible, dependable, and careful.
>
> **Emotional stability** is being relaxed, secure, and unworried.
>
> **Openness to experience** is being curious, receptive to new ideas, and imaginative.

A considerable body of evidence links the Big Five personality dimensions with a range of individual attitudes and behaviors. For example, conscientiousness is a good predictor of job performance for most occupations. Extraversion often is associated with success in management and sales.[16] Indications are that extraverts tend to be happier than introverts in their lives overall, that conscientious people tend to be less risky, and that those more open to experience are more creative.[17]

Ethics: Know Right from Wrong | "Come to the office a bit early, say 7:30 a.m., she's already there. Do a bit extra and leave at 6 p.m., she's still hard at work."

My Team Leader Is a Workaholic

Monkey Business Images/Shutterstock.com

Dear Management Coach:

I'm stuck. My new team leader is an absolute workaholic. I mean she's great in terms of personality, support, and task direction—all things a great team leader is supposed to be. But the killer is that she works all the time; I don't know if she ever sleeps. Come to the office a bit early, say 7:30 a.m., she's already there. Do a bit extra and leave at 6 p.m., she's still hard at work.

I'm worried about the hidden expectations that go along with this behavior. Is she modeling behavior she expects me to adopt? Is she subtly saying: "If I can do it, you can, too!"

I'm ready to work hard and put in extra hours as needed. However, I have a personal life and lots of other responsibilities. I need this job and I like the work. I'm starting to get stressed. I'm worried about my performance review that is due in about two months.

Should I confront my team leader about these concerns, or just let it go for now?

Your Decision?

What are the ethics here? When a manger works extra long hours, does this put inappropriate pressure on others to do the same? Should a manager who behaves this way "come clean" and tell everyone up-front either that they are expected to work this way also or that it's a personal choice and not expected of them?

When team members see someone—leader or teammate, working this way—do they have an ethical responsibility to double-check that the behavior pattern isn't a signal of personal problems that need attention?

You can easily spot the Big Five personality traits in people with whom you work, study, and socialize. But don't forget that these traits also apply to you. Others form impressions of your personality, and respond to it, just as you do with theirs. Managers often use personality judgments to make job assignments, build teams, and otherwise engage in the daily give-and-take of work in an organization.

Myers-Briggs Type Indicator

The Myers-Briggs Type Indicator is a popular approach to personality assessment. It "types" personalities based on a questionnaire that probes into how people act or feel in various situations. Called the *MBTI* for short, it was developed by Katherine Briggs and her daughter Isabel Briggs-Myers from foundations set forth in the work of psychologist Carl Jung.[18]

Jung's model of personality differences included three main distinctions. The first is how people differ in the ways in which they relate to others—by extraversion (outgoing and sociable) or introversion (shy and quiet). The second is how they differ in the ways they gather information—by sensation (emphasizing details, facts, and routine) or by intuition (looking for the "big picture" and being willing to deal with various possibilities). The third is how they differ in evaluating information—by thinking (using reason and analysis) or by feeling (responding to others' feelings and desires). Briggs and Briggs-Myers added a fourth dimension describing how people differ in relating to the outside world—judging (prefering order and control) or perceiving (acting with flexibility and spontaneity). The four MBTI dimensions can be summarized as follows.

- *Extraverted vs. introverted (E or I)*—social interaction: whether a person tends toward being outgoing and sociable or shy and quiet.
- *Sensing vs. intuitive (S or N)*—gathering data: whether a person tends to focus on details or on the big picture in dealing with problems.
- *Thinking vs. feeling (T or F)*—decision making: whether a person tends to rely on logic or emotions in dealing with problems.
- *Judging vs. perceiving (J or P)*—work style: whether a person prefers order and control or acts with flexibility and spontaneity.

A sample of Myers-Briggs types found in work settings is shown in **Figure 15.2**. These kinds of personality classifications have made the Myers-Briggs a popular management tool.[19] Employers and trainers like it because people can be taught to understand their own personalities and learn how to work with others having different ones. Scholars, however, debate the merits of the MBTI and critics suggest that ease of use has earned it an appeal that outweighs its scientific foundations.[20]

ESTJ (extraverted, sensing, thinking, judging)—decisive, logical, and quick to dig in; common among managers.

ENTJ (extraverted, intuitive, thinking, judging)—analytical, strategic, quick to take charge; common for leaders.

ISJF (introverted, sensing, judging, feeling)—conscientious, considerate, and helpful; common among team players.

INTJ (introverted, intuitive, thinking, judging)—insightful, free thinking, determined; common for visionaries.

FIGURE 15.2 **Sample Myers-Briggs personality types.**

Technology Personality

Recent thinking suggests that personality differences extend to the ways people interact with technology. Someone's **technology personality** is reflected in the frequency of technology and social media use as well as the ways it is used.[21] The following seven technology personality types have been identified by researchers. Why not pause and use this list to check your technology personality and consider its implications for your work and social relationships?

1. *Always On*—early adopters who use technology to create content, actively engage others, and make connections with people they'd like to know, not merely the people they know already.

2. *Live Wires*—very connected, use technology to stay in touch with family and friends, own smartphones and tablets.

3. *Social Skimmers*—highly connected, use social media sites, have substantial online networks and connect with family and friends using mobile technology; primarily use technology to gather information rather than to engage others.

4. *Broadcasters*—less connected, selectively use technology to tell others what they're doing, are less likely to be active on social media, and tend not to text.

5. *Toe Dippers*—low connectivity, use technology to converse, own desktops and laptops, with less than 25% owning a smart phone; most likely to prefer person-to-person contact with others.

6. *Bystanders*—relatively unconnected, mostly own only desktops; use technology primarily to keep up with the news and less frequently to connect with family and friends.

7. *Never-Minders*—relative outliers, who do not use cell phones, texting, or social media, are apprehensive about technology use, and see technology as isolating.

> **Technology personality** reflects levels of social media use and how media are used to connect to others.

Personal Conception and Emotional Adjustment Traits

In addition to the Big Five dimensions, the Myers-Briggs, and the more recent possibility of a technology personality, psychologists have studied a wide range of other personality traits. As shown in **Figure 15.3**, some traits with relevance to work include the personal conception traits of locus of control, authoritarianism, Machiavellianism, and self-monitoring, as well as the emotional adjustment trait of Type A orientation.[22] In general, you can think of a *personal*

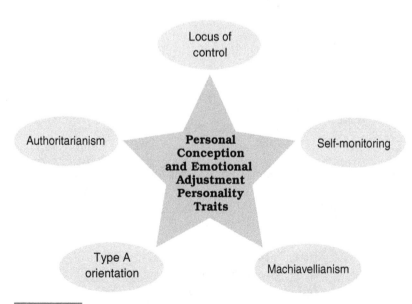

FIGURE 15.3 **Personal conception and emotional adjustment personality traits that influence human behavior at work.**

conception trait as describing how personality influences how people tend relate to the environment, while an *emotional adjustment trait* describes how they handle stress and uncomfortable situations.

Locus of control is the extent to which one believes that what happens is within one's control.

Locus of Control
Scholars have long had a strong interest in **locus of control**, recognizing that some people believe they are in control of their destiny, while others believe that what happens to them is beyond their control.[23] "Internals" are self-confident and accept responsibility for their own actions and the outcomes they lead to. "Externals" are more likely to blame others and outside forces for what happens to them. Research suggests that internals tend to be more satisfied and less alienated from their work when compared to externals.

Authoritarianism is the degree to which a person tends to defer to authority.

Authoritarianism
Authoritarianism is the degree to which a person yields to authority and accepts interpersonal status differences.[24] Someone with an authoritarian personality tends to behave in a rigid, control-oriented way as a leader. This same person is likely to behave in a subservient way and to comply with rules as a follower. The tendency of people with an authoritarian personality to obey rules and follow procedures can cause problems if they follow orders to the point of acting unethically or illegally.

Machiavellianism describes the extent to which someone is emotionally detached and manipulative.

Machiavellianism
In his sixteenth-century book *The Prince*, Niccolo Machiavelli gained lasting fame for giving his prince advice on how to use power to achieve personal goals.[25] The personality trait of **Machiavellianism** describes someone who is emotionally detached and manipulative in his or her use of power.[26] A person with a "high-Mach" personality is exploitative and unconcerned about others, often acting with the assumption that the end (i.e., goal) justifies the means (i.e., how the goal is accomplished). A person with a "low-Mach" personality, by contrast, is deferential in allowing others to exert power over him or her, and does not seek to manipulate others.

Self-monitoring is the degree to which someone is able to adjust behavior in response to external factors.

Self-Monitoring
Self-monitoring reflects the degree individuals are able to adjust and modify their behavior in response to the immediate situation and to external factors.[27] A person high in self-monitoring tends to be a learner, comfortable with feedback, and is both

---

Insight: Learn about Yourself | Individuals blinded by ambition can end up sacrificing substance for superficiality, and even sacrificing right for wrong.

Keep Ambition on Your Side

When it comes to understanding people's behavior, their attitudes, and their professional interactions with others, one of the most important distinctions can be their level of **ambition**, which is the desire to succeed, accomplish things, and achieve high goals. Ambition shows up in personality as a sense of competitiveness and the urge to get better or to be the best at something.

We tend to think of ambition as a positive individual quality to be admired and developed. Scholar and consultant Ram Charan calls it a "personal differentiator" that separates "people who perform from those who don't." But, there's also a potential downside. Charan points out that individuals blinded by ambition can end up sacrificing substance for superficiality, and even sacrificing right for wrong.

Overly ambitious people may exaggerate their accomplishments to themselves and others. They also may try to do too much and end up accomplishing less than they would otherwise have accomplished. Ambitious people who lack integrity can also get trapped by corruption and misbehavior driven by ambition.

Personal Traits Associated with High Performers

- Ambition—to achieve
- Drive—to solve
- Tenacity—to persevere
- Confidence—to act
- Openness—to experience
- Realism—to accept
- Learning—to grow
- Integrity—to fulfill

Get To Know Yourself Better

Review the "personal differentiators" in the small box above. How do you score? Can you say that your career ambition is backed with a sufficient set of personal traits and skills to make success a real possibility? Ask others to comment on the ambition you display as you go about your daily activities. Write a short synopsis of two situations—one in which you showed ambition and one in which you did not.

willing and able to change. Because high self-monitors are flexible in changing behavior from one situation to the next, it may be hard to get a clear read on exactly where they stand on any particular issue. A person low in self-monitoring, by contrast, is predictable and tends to act in a consistent way regardless of circumstances or a particular situation.

Type A Personality   A person with **Type A personality** is high in achievement orientation, impatience, and perfectionism. One of the key aspects of the Type A personality is the tendency for Type A individuals to bring stress on themselves, even in situations that others are likely to find relatively stress-free. When was the last time you did a self-check? Are you prone to personality-driven stress? Can you spot it in others? Watch for the following patterns of behavior associated with Type A personalities.[28]

> A **Type A personality** is a person oriented toward extreme achievement, impatience, and perfectionism.

- Always moving, walking, and eating rapidly
- Acting impatient, hurrying others, being put off by waiting
- Doing, or trying to do, several things at once
- Feeling guilty when relaxing
- Hurrying or interrupting others when they speak

Learning Check

LEARNING OBJECTIVE 15.2

Explain common personality differences and their behavioral implications.

Be Sure You Can • list the Big Five personality traits and give work-related examples of each • list and explain the four dimensions used to assess personality in the MBTI • explain and illustrate different technology personality types • list five personal conception and emotional adjustment personality traits and give work-related examples for each

---

15.3 Attitudes

LEARNING OBJECTIVE 15.3

Discuss the components of attitudes and the importance of job satisfaction.

WileyPLUS

See Author Video

> **Learn More About**
>
> What is an attitude? • What is job satisfaction? • Job satisfaction trends • Job satisfaction outcomes

When Challis M. Lowe was executive vice president at Ryder System, she was one of only two African American women among the five highest-paid executives in over 400 U.S. companies.[29] She rose to the executive VP level after a 25-year career that included several changes of employers and lots of stressors—working-mother guilt, a failed marriage, gender bias on the job, race-based barriers, and an MBA degree earned part-time. Through it all, she said: "I've never let being scared stop me from doing something. Just because you haven't done it before doesn't mean you shouldn't try." That, simply put, is a "can-do" attitude!

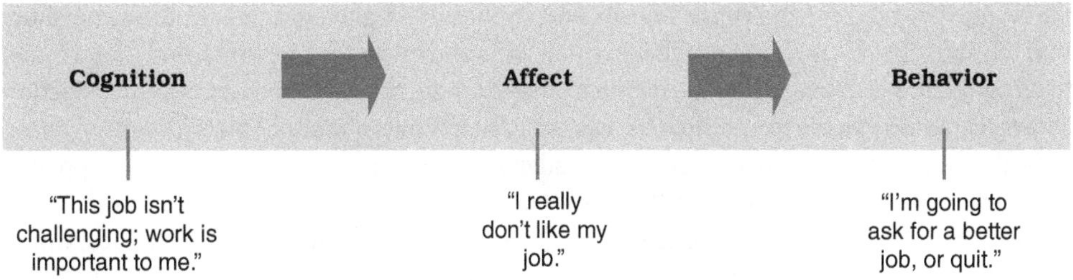

FIGURE 15.4 Cognitive, affective, and behavioral components of attitudes.

What Is an Attitude?

An **attitude** is a predisposition to act in a certain way.

Attitudes are predispositions to act in a certain way toward people and events.[30] In order to fully understand attitudes it helps to recognize the three components shown in **Figure 15.4**. First, the *cognitive component* reflects beliefs or opinions. You might believe, for example, that your management course is very interesting. Second, the *affective or emotional component* of an attitude reflects a specific feeling. For example, you might feel very good about being a management major. Third, the *behavioral component* of an attitude reflects an intention to behave in a way that is consistent with the belief and feeling. Using the same example again, you might say to yourself: "I am going to work hard for an A in all of my courses."

The intentions reflected in an attitude may or may not be confirmed through actual behavior. Despite having a positive attitude and good intentions in your management courses, for example, demands on your time from family, friends, or leisure activities can keep you from studying and preparing for your classes. You might end up not working hard enough to get an A, and fail to live up to your original intentions to get a good grade in the course.

Cognitive dissonance is discomfort felt when attitude and behavior are inconsistent.

The psychological concept of **cognitive dissonance** describes the discomfort felt when one's attitude and behavior are inconsistent with one another.[31] This discomfort often results in coping behaviors. For example, our poor performing student may change his or her attitude to fit their behavior by saying "Oh, I really don't like management that much anyway." The student could also change their future behavior to fit the attitude by dropping out of intramural sports to gain extra study time. A third approach is to rationalize and force the attitude and behavior into compatibility by thinking "Management is an okay major, but I'm gaining great leadership experience in my extracurricular activities."

What Is Job Satisfaction?

People hold attitudes about many aspects of their experiences at work—supervisors, co-workers, tasks, policies, goals, pay, and promotion opportunities, among many others. One of the most often discussed work attitudes is **job satisfaction**, which is whether employees feel positively or negatively about various aspects of work.[32] The following facets of job satisfaction are commonly discussed and measured:

Job satisfaction is the degree to which an individual feels positive or negative about a job.

- *Work itself*—Does the job offer responsibility, interest, challenge?
- *Quality of supervision*—Are task help and social support available?
- *Co-workers*—How much harmony, respect, and friendliness is there?
- *Opportunities*—Are there avenues for promotion, learning, and growth?
- *Pay*—Is compensation, actual and perceived, fair and substantial?
- *Work conditions*—Do conditions offer comfort, safety, support?
- *Security*—Is the job and employment secure?

Job Satisfaction Trends

If you watch the news or get news from the Internet, you'll regularly find reports on employees' job satisfaction. You'll also find reports on lots of job satisfaction studies from the academic literature. The results from these sources and studies don't always agree. But they do show that job satisfaction tends to be higher in small firms and lower in large firms, and that it tends to be correlated with overall life satisfaction.[33] Interestingly, the general trend in job satisfaction shows a gradual decline over time. The least satisfying things about people's jobs often relate to feeling underpaid, not having good career advancement opportunities, and being trapped in the current job. In respect to things that create job satisfaction, a global study finds that pay is less important than opportunities to do interesting work, recognition for performance, work–life balance, chances for advancement, and job security.[34]

Job Satisfaction Outcomes

The best managers and team leaders help others achieve not just high levels of work performance, but also high job satisfaction. You should agree that everyone deserves satisfying work experiences. But beyond its moral quality-of-work-life appeals, does job satisfaction really make a difference in how people behave and perform on the job?

Job Satisfaction and Withdrawal Behaviors

There is a strong relationship between job satisfaction and the **withdrawal behaviors** of absenteeism and turnover. With regard to *absenteeism*, workers who are more satisfied with their jobs are absent less than workers who are dissatisfied with their jobs. With regard to *turnover*, satisfied workers also are more likely to stay in their positions while dissatisfied workers are more likely to quit.[35]

Withdrawal behaviors occur as temporary absenteeism and actual job turnover.

Both absenteeism and turnover are costly in terms of the recruitment and training needed to replace workers, as well as in the productivity lost while new workers are learning how to perform up to expectations.[36] The results from one study revealed that changing retention rates up or down results in magnified changes to corporate earnings. It also warns that declining employee loyalty has a negative impact on corporate performance.[37]

Job Satisfaction and Engagement

There is a relationship between job satisfaction and **engagement**—feeling a sense of purpose, personal growth, belonging, and connection with one's job and employer.[38] High engagement shows up as a willingness to help

Engagement feeling is a positive and connected with one's job and the organization.

Analysis: Make Data Your Friend | Managers don't have a good handle on the real costs incurred when employees are rude and disrespectful toward one another.

Paying a High Price for Incivility at Work

Westend61/Getty Images

Look for losses in the bottom line when rudeness rules the workplace. Most managers say they are against incivility and try to stop it whenever they can. But it's also the case that

managers don't have a good handle on the real costs incurred when employees are rude and disrespectful toward one another. When researchers asked 800 workers from different industries about how they responded when exposed to incivility at work, results showed:

- 48% decreased work effort
- 47% cut back time spent at work
- 80% lost work time due to worry
- 63% performed less well
- 78% were less committed to the organization
- 25% took frustration out on customers

Your Thoughts?

How about it, have you been on the receiving end of incivility? Is incivility taking a toll on the teams and organizations in your life? Is improved civility a hidden pathway to higher performance in our workplaces? How can such improvements be achieved? Are you, for one, ready to put your best foot forward?

others, always trying to do something extra to improve work performance, and feeling and speaking positively about the organization.

Periodic surveys by the Gallup organization find that about 22–34% of American workers self report as being highly engaged in their work. While this figure is disturbingly low on the average, it rises to almost 70% in high performing organizations.[39] Things that count most toward employee engagement are workers believing that they have the opportunity to do their best every day, that their opinions count, that fellow workers are committed to quality, and that there is a connection between their work and the organization's mission.[40]

The flip side of engagement is *disengagement*. Gallup surveys find that 13–20% of workers consider themselves "actively disengaged" from their work.[41] This shows up as low commitment, lack of loyalty, increased absenteeism, and high turnover. It can even result in disruptive and harmful work behaviors.

Employee engagement is connected with two other attitudes that also influence work behavior. **Job involvement** is the extent an employee feels dedicated to a job. Someone with high job involvement psychologically identifies with her or his job and would be expected to work hard at it. **Organizational commitment** reflects the degree of loyalty an employee feels toward the organization. Individuals with high organizational commitment take pride in viewing themselves as an organization member. Researchers find that strong *emotional commitment* to the organization—based on values and interests of others—has as much as four times more positive influence on performance than *rational commitment*—which is based primarily on pay and self-interest.[42]

Job Satisfaction and Organizational Citizenship

Have you ever wondered about those people who are always willing to "go beyond the call of duty" or "go the extra mile" in their work?[43] Such actions represent **organizational citizenship behavior**, OCB, and also are linked with job satisfaction.[44] A good organizational citizen does things that, although not formally required, help advance co-workers' performance, the team, and the organization as a whole. Examples of OCBs include a service representative who goes to extraordinary lengths to take care of a customer, a team member who is always willing to take on extra tasks, or an employee who always volunteers to stay late with no extra pay just to make sure a key assignment gets done right.

Poor organizational citizenship shows up as antisocial and counterproductive behavior that disrupts work processes, relationships, teamwork, satisfaction, and performance.[45] Two of its common forms are incivility and bullying.[46] **Incivility** is antisocial behavior that shows up as individual or group displays of disrespect, social exclusion, and language that is hurtful to others. **Bullying** is antisocial behavior that is intentionally aggressive, intimidating, demeaning, and/or abusive. Both incivility and bullying involve recurring behaviors, making them clearly different from what might be considered just one-time "bad" behaviors.

Job Satisfaction and Performance

We know that job satisfaction influences withdrawal, engagement, and citizenship behaviors. But does it influence performance? The data are, as you might expect, complicated.[47] Three contrasting arguments on the satisfaction and performance relationship are shown in **Figure 15.5**. Can you make a case for each argument based on your personal experiences?

There is a modest link between job satisfaction and objective or quantifiable performance.[48] But it is important to stress the word *modest* when describing this relationship. We shouldn't rush to conclude that making employees happy or increasing their job satisfaction is a foolproof way to improve their job performance. The reality is that some employees will tend to like their jobs, be very satisfied, and still will not perform very well. That is just part of the complexity around individual differences and job performance.

There also is a link between high levels of work performance and job satisfaction. High-performing employees are likely to feel satisfied with their work. Here again, caution is called for; not everyone is likely to fit the model. Some employees may get their jobs done effectively and efficiently, meet high performance expectations, but still not feel satisfied with their job. Given

Job involvement is the extent to which an individual feels dedicated to a job.

Organizational commitment is the loyalty an individual feels toward the organization.

Organizational citizenship behavior is a willingness to "go beyond the call of duty" or "go the extra mile" in one's work.

Incivility is antisocial behavior in the forms of disrespectful acts, social exclusion, and use of hurtful language.

Bullying is antisocial behavior that is intentionally aggressive, intimidating, demeaning, and/or abusive.

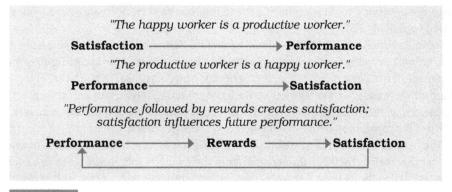

FIGURE 15.5 **Contrasting arguments on the satisfaction and performance relationship.**

that job satisfaction is a good predictor of absenteeism and turnover, having highly productive but unhappy workers is a warning signal. Unless changes are made to increase job satisfaction, productive employees may eventually choose to leave.

Finally, job satisfaction and job performance most likely have a reciprocal influence on one another, with performance influencing satisfaction which then influences future performance. But this is most likely to hold only under certain conditions, particularly those related to rewards. While job performance followed by valued rewards perceived as fair tends to create job satisfaction, any sense of unfairness may have an opposite effect.

Learning Check

LEARNING OBJECTIVE 15.3

Discuss the components of attitudes and the importance of job satisfaction.

Be Sure You Can • define *attitude* and list the three components of an attitude • define *job satisfaction* and list its components • explain the potential consequences of high and low job satisfaction • define *employee engagement, job involvement, organizational commitment*, and *organizational citizenship behavior* • explain three arguments in the job satisfaction and performance relationship

15.4   Emotions, Moods, and Stress

LEARNING OBJECTIVE 15.4

Illustrate how emotions, moods, and stress influence individual behavior.

WileyPLUS

See Author Video

> **Learn More About**
>
> Emotions • Moods • Stress and strain

Situation: When the Boeing 787 Dreamliner was falling behind schedule, Boeing's head of Asia-Pacific sales, John Wojick, held a meeting with the chief sales officer. After a "heated" discussion over delivery dates and customer promises, Wojick "stormed" out and said "Quite frankly we were failing at meeting our commitment to customers." An observer described Wojick as having "an understated manner" and an underlying "fiery temper."[49]

Looking at this incident we might say that Wojick was emotional about the fact that his customers weren't being well served. His temper flared in the meeting and his anger got the better of him. Whether that was good or bad for Boeing's customers . . . for him . . . and for his boss is an open question. For a time at least, both he and his boss probably ended up in bad moods because of their stressful confrontation.

Emotions

An **emotion** is a strong feeling directed toward someone or something. For example, you might feel positive emotion or elation when an instructor congratulates you on a good class presentation, or you might feel negative emotion or anger when an instructor criticizes you in front of the class. In both cases the object of your emotion is the instructor, but how you respond to the aroused emotion is likely to differ—perhaps breaking into a smile with the compliment or making a nasty side comment after the criticism.

Emotional intelligence is an important human skill for managers and an essential leadership capability. Daniel Goleman defines "EI" as the ability to understand emotions in ourselves and in others, and to use this understanding to manage relationships effectively.[50] His point is that we perform at our best when we are good at recognizing and dealing with emotions. Emotional intelligence helps us to avoid letting our emotions "get the better of us." Emotional intelligence also allows individuals to show restraint when the emotions of others would otherwise get the better of them.[51]

To get better at emotional intelligence you should recognize the nature of emotions. They are linked with specific causes. They tend to be brief or episodic. They have specific effects on attitudes and behaviors. And, they might turn into moods.

Moods

Whereas emotions tend to be short term and clearly targeted, **moods** are more generalized feelings or states of mind with hard-define causes that may persist for a longer period of time.[52] Everyone seems to have occasional moods, and we each know the full range of possibilities they represent. How often do you wake up in the morning and feel excited, refreshed, and happy? In contrast, how often do you wake up feeling low, depressed, and generally unhappy? What are the consequences of these different moods for your behavior with friends and family, and your performance at work or at school?

Positive and negative moods can spill over and become "contagious". Such **mood contagion** can easily influence co-workers and teammates, as well as family and friends.[53] And when it comes to moods in the workplace, research suggests it pays to be positive.[54] Followers of leaders who display more positive moods, for example, report being more attracted to their leaders and rate them more favorably.[55]

When you consider moods and mood contagion at work, there's an impression management lesson. If a team leader goes to a meeting in a good mood and gets described as "cheerful," "charming," "humorous," "friendly," and "candid," she or he may be viewed as being on the upswing. But if the leader is in a bad mood and comes away perceived as "prickly," "impatient," "remote," "tough," "acrimonious," or even "ruthless," she or he may be more likely to be perceived as being on a downhill slide.[56]

Stress and Strain

Closely aligned with emotions and moods is **stress**, the tension caused by extraordinary demands, constraints, or opportunities.[57] It is a powerful life force, but also one that isn't always negative. Remember the analogy of a violin. When a violin string is too loose, the sound produced is weak and raspy. When the string is too tight, the sound gets shrill and the string

An **emotion** is a strong feeling directed toward someone or something.

Emotional intelligence is the ability to understand emotions in ourselves and others, and to manage relationships effectively.

Moods are generalized positive and negative feelings or states of mind.

Mood contagion is the spillover of one's positive or negative moods to others.

Stress is a state of tension caused by extraordinary demands, constraints, or opportunities.

might even snap. But when the tension on the string is just right, the sound can be extraordinarily beautiful.

Stressors

Stressors are the experiences and events that cause tensions in our lives. Whether they come from work or non-work situations, from personality, or from trauma, stressors influence our attitudes, emotions and moods, behavior, job performance, and even health.[58] Importantly, stressors from one space—work or non-work—can spill over to affect other areas of one's life.

Having the Type A personality discussed earlier is an example of a personal or self-imposed stressor. In life situations stressors include family events (e.g., the birth of a new child, marriage, divorce, moving), economics (e.g., a sudden loss of extra income), and personal affairs (e.g., a preoccupation with a bad relationship). At work, stressors arise as long hours of work, excessive e-mails, unrealistic deadlines, difficult supervisors or co-workers, unwelcome or unfamiliar work, and unrelenting change. They also include excessively high or low task demands, role conflicts or ambiguities, poor interpersonal relations, and career progress that is too slow or too fast. Two troublesome work stress syndromes are *set up to fail*—facing performance expectations that are impossible to reach, and *mistaken identity*—being given jobs that don't match one's talents.[59]

> A **stressor** is anything that causes tension.

Constructive Stress and Destructive Strain

At times we experience **constructive stress**, sometimes called **eustress**, that is energizing and performance enhancing.[60] It encourages greater effort, stimulates creativity, and increases perseverance. Individuals with a Type A personality, for example, are likely to work long hours and are less likely to be satisfied with poor performance. Challenging task demands move them toward ever-higher levels of task accomplishment. Even non-work stressors, such as new family responsibilities, may cause them to work harder in anticipation of greater financial rewards.

> **Constructive stress** or **eustress** is a positive stress outcome that can increase effort, stimulate creativity, and encourage diligence in one's work.

All too often it seems, we also experience **destructive stress** or **strain** that has a dysfunctional or negative impact on our physical well-being, mental health, and behavior.[61] **Figure 15.6** shows that workers experiencing destructive stress may react with turnover, absenteeism, errors, accidents, dissatisfaction, and reduced performance. A common outcome is **job burnout**, feelings of physical and mental exhaustion that can be personally incapacitating. A less common but very troubling outcome is **workplace rage**, aggressive behavior toward co-workers and the work setting in general. Although this rage is often episodic and moderate, such when someone loses his or her temper, it can also explode into acts of violence and personal tragedy.[62]

> **Destructive stress** or **strain** is a negative stress outcome that impairs the performance and well-being of an individual.
>
> **Job burnout** is a feeling of physical and mental exhaustion from work stress.
>
> **Workplace rage** is showing aggressive behavior toward co-workers or the work setting.

Stress and Strain Management

The best stress management strategy is to prevent stresses and strains from becoming excessive in the first place. If we know we're a Type A personality, we need to own it and take steps to control its impact on our behavior. And if we recognize someone else is a Type A, we should help them do the same. Managers and team

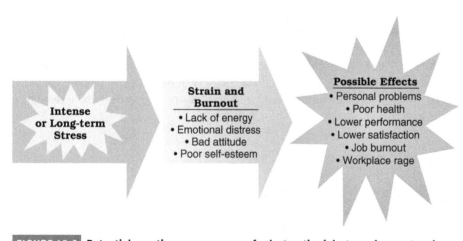

FIGURE 15.6 Potential negative consequences of a destructive job stress–burnout cycle.

leaders can take steps to help others who are showing stress symptoms. Things such as temporary changes in work schedules, negotiated roles, goals discussions, reduced performance expectations, extended deadlines, and even reminders to take time off can all help.

Ultimately, there is no substitute in stress management for taking care of ourselves. This means making a commitment to **personal wellness**, taking responsibility for our own physical and mental health. It means getting rest, exercise, finding and taking pride in yourself, and eating well. It means no smoking and no alcohol or substance abuse. And, it means a life-long commitment to a healthy lifestyle that helps you deal with the inevitable stresses of work and personal life.

Personal wellness is the pursuit of one's full potential through a personal health-promotion program.

Learning Check

LEARNING OBJECTIVE 15.4

Illustrate how emotions, moods, and stress influence individual behavior.

Be Sure You Can • define *emotion, mood,* and *stress* • explain how emotions and moods influence behavior • identify the common stressors found in work and in personal life • differentiate constructive stress and destructive strain • define *job burnout* and *workplace rage* • discuss personal wellness as a stress management strategy

Management Learning Review: Get Prepared for Quizzes and Exams

Summary

LEARNING OBJECTIVE 15.1 Summarize perceptual tendencies and distortions that influence behavior.

- Perception acts as a filter through which people receive and process information from the environment.
- Because people perceive things differently, they may interpret and respond to situations differently.
- A healthy psychological contract occurs with perceived balance between work contributions, such as time and effort, and inducements received, such as pay and respect.
- Fundamental attribution error occurs when we blame others for performance problems while excluding possible external causes; self-serving bias occurs when we take personal credit for successes and blame failures on external factors.
- Stereotypes, projection, halo effects, and selective perception can distort perceptions and result in errors as people relate with one another.

For Discussion Are there times when self-serving bias is actually helpful?

LEARNING OBJECTIVE 15.2 Explain common personality differences and their behavioral implications.

- Personality is a set of traits and characteristics that cause people to behave in unique ways.
- The personality factors included in the Big Five model are extraversion, agreeableness, conscientiousness, emotional stability, and openness to experience.
- The Myers-Briggs Type Indicator profiles personalities in respect to tendencies toward extraversion–introversion, sensing–intuitive, thinking–feeling, and judging–perceiving.
- Additional personality dimensions of work significance include the personal conception traits of locus of control, authoritarianism, Machiavellianism, and behavioral self-monitoring, as well as the emotional adjustment trait of Type A orientation, and technology personality.

For Discussion What dimension would you add to make the "Big Five" the "Big Six" personality model?

LEARNING OBJECTIVE 15.3   Discuss the components of attitudes and the importance of job satisfaction.

- An attitude is a predisposition to respond in a certain way to people and things.
- Cognitive dissonance occurs when a person's attitude and behavior are inconsistent.
- Job satisfaction is an important work attitude that reflects a person's evaluation of the job, co-workers, and other aspects of the work setting.
- Job satisfaction influences work attendance and turnover and is related to other attitudes, such as job involvement and organizational commitment.
- Three possible explanations for the job satisfaction-to-performance relationship: satisfaction causes performance, performance causes satisfaction, and rewards cause both performance and satisfaction.

For Discussion What should a manager do with an employee who has high job satisfaction but relatively low performance?

LEARNING OBJECTIVE 15.4   Illustrate how emotions, moods, and stress influence individual behavior.

- Emotions are strong feelings that are directed at someone or something; they influence behavior, often with intensity and for short periods of time.
- Moods are generalized positive or negative states of mind that can persistently influence one's behavior.
- Stress is a state of tension experienced by individuals facing extraordinary demands, constraints, or opportunities.
- Stress can be constructive in the form of eustress or destructive as strain; a moderate level of strain typically has a positive impact on performance.
- Strain can be managed through both prevention and coping strategies, including a commitment to personal wellness.

For Discussion Is a Type A personality required for managerial success?

Self-Test 15

Multiple-Choice Questions

1. In the psychological contract, job security is a(n) _____, whereas loyalty is a(n) _____.
   - a. satisfier factor, hygiene factor
   - b. intrinsic reward, extrinsic reward
   - c. inducement, contribution
   - d. attitude, personality trait

2. Self-serving bias is a form of attribution error that involves _____.
   - a. blaming yourself for problems caused by others
   - b. blaming the environment for problems you caused
   - c. poor emotional intelligence
   - d. authoritarianism

3. If a new team leader changes job designs for persons on her work team mainly "because I would prefer to work the new way rather than the old," the chances are that she is committing a perceptual error known as _____.
   - a. the halo effect
   - b. a stereotype
   - c. selective perception
   - d. projection

4. If a manager allows one characteristic of a person, say a pleasant personality, to bias performance ratings of that individual overall, the manager is committing a perceptual distortion known as _____.
   - a. the halo effect
   - b. a stereotype
   - c. selective perception
   - d. projection

5. Use of special dress, manners, gestures, and vocabulary words when meeting a prospective employer in a job interview are all examples of how people use _____ in daily life.
   - a. projection
   - b. selective perception
   - c. impression management
   - d. self-serving bias

6. A person with a(n) _____ personality would most likely act unemotionally and manipulatively when trying to influence others to achieve personal goals.
   - a. extraverted
   - b. sensation-thinking
   - c. self-monitoring
   - d. Machiavellian

7. When a person believes that he or she has little influence over things that happen in life, this indicates a(n) _____ personality.
   - a. low emotional stability
   - b. external locus of control
   - c. high self-monitoring
   - d. intuitive-thinker

8. Among the Big Five personality traits, _____ indicates someone who is responsible, dependable, and careful with respect to tasks.
   - a. authoritarianism
   - b. agreeableness
   - c. conscientiousness
   - d. emotional stability

9. The _____ component of an attitude is what indicates a person's belief about something, whereas the _____ component indicates a specific positive or negative feeling about it.

    a. cognitive, affective

    b. emotional, affective

    c. cognitive, attributional

    d. behavioral, attributional

10. The term used to describe the discomfort someone feels when his or her behavior is inconsistent with an expressed attitude is _____.

    a. alienation

    b. cognitive dissonance

    c. job dissatisfaction

    d. person–job imbalance

11. Job satisfaction is known from research to be a good predictor of _____.

    a. job performance

    b. job burnout

    c. conscientiousness

    d. absenteeism

12. A person who is always willing to volunteer for extra work or to help someone else with his or her work is acting consistent with strong _____.

    a. job performance

    b. self-serving bias

    c. emotional intelligence

    d. organizational citizenship

13. Which statement about the job satisfaction–job performance relationship is most likely based on research?

    a. A happy worker will be a productive worker.

    b. A productive worker will be a happy worker.

    c. A productive worker well rewarded for performance will be a happy worker.

    d. There is no link between being happy and being productive in a job.

14. A(n) _____ represents a rather intense but short-lived feeling about a person or a situation, whereas a(n) _____ describes a more generalized positive or negative state of mind.

    a. stressor, role ambiguity

    b. external locus of control, internal locus of control

    c. self-serving bias, halo effect

    d. emotion, mood

15. Through _____, the stress people experience in their personal lives can create problems for them at work while the stress experienced at work can create problems for their personal lives.

    a. eustress

    b. self-monitoring

    c. spillover effects

    d. selective perception

Short-Response Questions

16. What is a healthy psychological contract?

17. What is the difference between self-serving bias and fundamental attribution error?

18. Which three of the Big Five personality traits do you believe most affect how well people work together in organizations, and why?

19. Why is it important for a manager to understand the Type A personality?

Essay Question

20. When Scott Tweedy picked up a magazine article on how to manage health care workers, he was pleased to find some advice. Scott was concerned about poor or mediocre performance on the part of several respiratory therapists in his clinic. The author of the article said that the "best way to improve performance is to make your workers happy." Scott was glad to have read this article and made a pledge to himself to start doing a much better job of making his employees happy. But should Scott follow this advice? What do we know about the relationship between job satisfaction and performance, and how do we apply this knowledge to the performance problems Scott has observed at his clinic?

Career Skills & Competencies: Make Yourself Valuable!

Evaluate Career Situations

What Would You Do?

1. Putting Down Seniors

While standing on line at the office coffee machine, you overhear the person in front of you saying this to his friend: "I'm really tired of having to deal with the old-timers in here. It's time for them to call it quits. There's no way they can keep up the pace and handle all the new technology we're getting these days." You can listen and forget, or you can listen and act. What would you do or say here, and why? What does this comment suggest regarding age-based attributions of technology personality?

2. Compulsive Co-worker

You've noticed that one of your co-workers is always rushing, always uptight, and constantly criticizing herself while on the job. She never takes breaks when the rest of you do, and even at lunch it's hard to get her to stay and just talk for a while. Your guess is that she's fighting stressors from some sources other than work and the job itself. How can you help her out? What might you say?

3. Bad Mood in the Office

Your department head has just told you that some of your teammates have complained to him that you have been in a really bad mood lately. They like you and point out that this isn't characteristic of you at all. But they also think your persistent bad mood is rubbing off on others in this situation. What can you do? Is there anything your supervisors or co-workers might do to help you get out of your funk?

Reflect on the Self-Assessment

Self-Monitoring

Instructions

Indicate your agreement with the following statements by circling the value that aligns with your belief. For example, if you believe that a statement is always false, circle the 0 next to that statement.[63]

5 = Certainly, always true
4 = Generally true
3 = Somewhat true, but with exceptions
2 = Somewhat false, but with exceptions
1 = Generally false
0 = Certainly, always false

1. In social situations, I have the ability to alter my behavior if I feel that something else is called for.   5 4 3 2 1 0

2. I am often able to read people's true emotions correctly through their eyes.   5 4 3 2 1 0

3. I have the ability to control the way I come across to people, depending on the impression I wish to give them.   5 4 3 2 1 0

4. In conversations, I am sensitive to even the slightest change in the facial expression of the person I'm conversing with.   5 4 3 2 1 0

5. My powers of intuition are quite good when it comes to understanding others' emotions and motives.   5 4 3 2 1 0

6. I can usually tell when others consider a joke in bad taste, even though they may laugh convincingly.   5 4 3 2 1 0

7. When I feel that the image I am portraying isn't working, I can readily change it to something that does.   5 4 3 2 1 0

8. I can usually tell when I've said something inappropriate by reading the listener's eyes.   5 4 3 2 1 0

9. I have trouble changing my behavior to suit different people and different situations.   5 4 3 2 1 0

10. I have found that I can adjust my behavior to meet the requirements of any situation I find myself in.   5 4 3 2 1 0

11. If someone is lying to me, I usually know it at once from that person's manner of expression.   5 4 3 2 1 0

12. Even when it might be to my advantage, I have difficulty putting up a good front.   5 4 3 2 1 0

13. Once I know what the situation calls for, it is easy for me to regulate my actions accordingly.   5 4 3 2 1 0

Scoring

Add the circled numbers except for 9 and 12. These are reverse-scored and you should add them into your total using these conversions: 5 = 0, 4 = 1, 3 = 2, 2 = 3, 1 = 4, 0 = 5. High self-monitoring is indicated by scores above 53.

Interpretation

This instrument offers an indication of your awareness of how you are being perceived by others and their reactions to your behavior in social situations. Persons with a high self-monitoring score tend to be quite aware of their public persona—the impression that they are leaving others with. They can use their ability to self-monitor to create a favorable social impression. Their behavior tends to change to match the demands of the situation. Persons with a low self-monitoring score, by contrast, are less aware of the impact that their words, actions, and expressions are having on others. They tend to maintain a fairly consistent self-presentation style and manner, regardless of their audience or the circumstances.

Contribute to the Class Exercise

Job Satisfaction Preferences

Preparation

Rank the following items for how important (1 = least important to 9 = most important) they are to your future job satisfaction.[64]

My job will be satisfying when it—

a. is respected by other people.

b. encourages continued development of knowledge and skills.

c. provides job security.

d. provides a feeling of accomplishment.

e. provides the opportunity to earn a high income.

f. is intellectually stimulating.

g. rewards good performance with recognition.

h. provides comfortable working conditions.

i. permits advancement to high administrative responsibility.

Instructions

Form into groups as designated by your instructor. The group should be split by gender into two subgroups—one composed of men and one composed of women. Each group should first rank the items on their own. Then, the men should develop a consensus ranking of the items as they think women ranked them, and the women should do a consensus ranking of the items as they think men ranked them. The two subgroups should then get back together to share and discuss their respective rankings, paying special attention to reasons for the rankings attributed to the opposite gender group. A spokesperson for the men and for the women in each group should share their subgroup's rankings and highlights of the total group discussion with the class.

Optional Instructions

Form into groups consisting entirely of men or women. Each group should meet and decide which of the work values members of the opposite sex will rank first. Do this again for the work value ranked last. The reasons should be discussed, along with the reasons why each of the other values probably was not ranked first or last. A spokesperson for each group should share group results with the rest of the class.

Manage a Critical Incident

Facing Up to Attributions

You are the senior section manager for a medium-sized manufacturing firm producing high-tech digital devices. You've worked with this company for eight years and supervise teams of materials engineers. As senior manager, you manage these teams, keep them working together effectively, and find ways to cut costs and increase profits. Because of recent government regulations, your manufacturing processes have undergone substantial changes. The firm has had to hire outside consultants to help with the manufacturing transition. The consultants have been tasked with training the engineers on the new protocol and evaluating their performance, which has declined substantially since the transition. Although historically the engineers have been very productive and received high performance evaluations, this last quarter the majority received poor evaluations and has been formally reprimanded by upper management. You have also been reprimanded for the reduced performance. The consultants have attributed the performance declines to poor leadership and poor motivation. You know that neither the leadership these teams are given nor their motivation has changed.

Questions

What role might fundamental attribution errors and self-serving bias be playing here? What are the potential consequences of these poor performance evaluations and formal reprimands, and what can you do to offset any negatives? How might you explain the declining performance of the engineers, and what might you do to stop these declines?

Collaborate on the Team Project

Difficult Personalities

Question

What personalities cause the most problems when people work together in teams, and what can be done to best deal with them?

Instructions

1. Do a survey of friends, family, co-workers, and even the public at large to get answers to these questions:

    a. When you work in a team, what personalities do you have the most difficulty dealing with?

    b. How do these personalities affect you, and how do they affect the team as a whole?

    c. In your experience, for each of the "difficult personalities" that you have described, what have you found to be the best way of dealing with them?

    d. How would you describe your personality, and are there any circumstances or situations in which you believe others could consider your personality "difficult" to deal with?

    e. Do you engage in any self-management when it comes to your personality and how it fits when you are part of a team?

2. Gather the results of your survey, organize them for analysis, and then analyze them to see what patterns and insights your study has uncovered.

3. Prepare a report to share your study with the rest of your class.

Analyze the Case Study

Panera Bread | Growing a Company with Personality

Go to *Management Cases for Critical Thinking* at the end of the book to find this case.

CHAPTER 16

Motivation Theory and Practice

Respect Unlocks Human Potential

Peter Barritt/Alamy Stock Photo

"If you hear a voice within you say 'you cannot paint,' then by all means paint, and that voice will be silenced."

Vincent van Gogh

Career Readiness – What to Look for Inside

Thought Leadership

Analysis > *Make Data Your Friend*
One in Five Americans Already Working from Home

Choices > *Think before You Act*
To Pay or Not to Pay More Than Minimum Wage

Ethics > *Know Right from Wrong*
Information Goldmine Creates Equity Dilemma

Insight > *Learn about Yourself*
The Personal Side of Engagement

Skills Make You Valuable

- **Evaluate** *Career Situations:*
  What Would You Do?
- **Reflect** *On the Self-Assessment:*
  Student Engagement Survey
- **Contribute** *To the Class Exercise:*
  Why We Work
- **Manage** *A Critical Incident:*
  Great Worker Won't Take Vacation
- **Collaborate** *On the Team Project:*
  CEO Pay . . . Too High, or Just Right?
- **Analyze** *The Case Study:*
  Salesforce: Instant Praise, Instant Criticism

Chapter Quick Start

There are times when each of us lacks motivation to persevere and get things done. There are other times when we are so "psyched" it's hard to stop what we're doing. These contrasting situations have intrigued and perplexed generations of social scientists. Even though there's more work to do, we've learned a lot about the conditions under which people—ourselves and others—can be highly motivated to work hard.

LEARNING OBJECTIVES

16.1 Explain how individual needs motivate behavior.

16.2 Contrast how expectancy, equity, goal-setting, and self-efficacy motivate behavior.

16.3 Discuss the motivational implications of reinforcement principles and strategies.

16.4 Summarize the motivational implications of job designs and work schedules.

325

Did you know that J. K. Rowling's first Harry Potter book was rejected by 12 publishers; that the Beatles' "sound" cost them a deal with Decca Records; that Walt Disney lost a newspaper job because he supposedly "lacked imagination," and even though Van Gogh only sold one painting in his lifetime, he painted over 2,000 and created masterpieces of Western art.[1] Thank goodness they didn't give up. Their "motivation" to stay engaged, hard working, and confident in their work paid off abundantly—for them and for the millions who have enjoyed the fruits of their labors.

Did you also know that almost a quarter of global workers surveyed by Gallup say they are actively "disengaged" from their work on any given day . . . that 25% of American employers believe their workers have low morale . . . that up to 40% of workers say that they have trouble staying motivated?[2] Don't you wonder why some people work enthusiastically, persevere in the face of difficulty, and often exceed the requirements of their job? Why do others hold back, quit at the first negative feedback, and do the minimum needed to avoid reprimand or termination? Our society, with its institutions facing complex challenges, deserves better. What can be done to ensure that every person, at every task, in every job, on every workday achieves the best possible performance?[3]

16.1   Individual Needs and Motivation

WileyPLUS

See Author Video

LEARNING OBJECTIVE 16.1

Explain how individual needs motivate behavior.

> **Learn More About**
> Hierarchy of needs theory • ERG theory • Two-factor theory • Acquired needs theory

Motivation accounts for the level, direction, and persistence of effort expended at work.

The term **motivation** describes forces within individuals that account for the level, direction, and persistence of effort they expend at work. A highly motivated person works hard at a job while an unmotivated person does not. The challenge for team leaders and managers is to create conditions where people feel consistently inspired to work hard.

Insight: Learn about Yourself | Are you enthusiastic or lethargic, diligent or lazy, willing to do more than expected or willing to do only what is expected?

The Personal Side of Engagement

Think of **engagement** as personal initiative and the willingness to "go the extra mile" at work. Differences in job engagement show up many ways. Is someone enthusiastic or lethargic, diligent or lazy, willing to do more when a team or co-worker is in need, or only willing to do the minimum expected?

The Conference Board defines engagement as "a heightened emotional connection" with the organization that influences an employee to "exert greater discretionary effort in his or her work." Its surveys show that high engagement generates positive outcomes like lower turnover, higher productivity, and better customer service.

There is a great deal of variation both in employees' work engagement and in students' school engagement. Consider your experiences as a customer. When you're disappointed, perhaps with how a banking transaction or a flight delay is handled, ask: Would a high level of employee engagement generate better customer service in such situations? How about engagement by your teammates in your management course? What do you see and

what would you predict for the career futures of your classmates based on their engagement as students?

> **Indicators of High Engagement**
> - Looks for problems and tries to fix them.
> - Does more than the minimum required.
> - Starts early, stays late, does the "extras."
> - Helps others who are overwhelmed.
> - Looks for and makes improvements.
> - Thinks ahead and plans for the future.

Get To Know Yourself Better

Ask: "How engaged am I in projects at school and at work? Ask also: "What could my instructor do to help increase my engagement? By the same token, what could I do?" Write a summary of your answers. Discuss their implications for both (a) your remaining time as a student, and (b) your future career and your future actions in the workplace.

Most discussions of motivation begin with the concept of individual **needs**—unfulfilled physiological or psychological desires. Although the following theories discuss a slightly different set of needs, all agree that needs create tensions that lead individuals to act in ways to help meet their needs. They advise managers to help people satisfy important needs through their work, and try to eliminate obstacles that block the satisfaction of needs.

> A **need** is an unfulfilled physiological or psychological desire.

Hierarchy of Needs Theory

Abraham Maslow's theory of human needs is an important foundation in the history of management thought. The **lower-order needs** in his hierarchy include physiological, safety, and social concerns, while **higher-order needs** include esteem and self-actualization concerns.[4] Lower-order needs focus on physical and social well-being; higher-order needs focus on psychological development and growth.

Maslow used two principles to describe how these needs affect behavior. The **deficit principle** provides that a satisfied need no longer motivates behavior. People try to satisfy deprived needs—that is, needs for which there is a "deficit." The **progression principle** states that the need at one level does not become activated until the next-lower-level need is already satisfied. People are expected to advance step by step up the hierarchy to satisfy their needs. The progression principle ends at self-actualization. According to the theory, the need to self-actualize can never be met fully. In fact, the more the need for self-actualization is satisfied, the stronger it is theorized to grow.

Figure 16.1 illustrates how managers can use Maslow's ideas to help meet employees' needs. Notice that higher-order self-actualization needs are served by opportunities like creative and challenging work and job autonomy; esteem needs are served by respect, responsibility, praise, and recognition. The satisfaction of lower-order social, safety, and physiological needs depends on positive interactions with others, compensation and benefits, and reasonable working conditions.

> **Lower-order needs** are physiological, safety, and social needs in Maslow's hierarchy.
>
> **Higher-order needs** are esteem and self-actualization needs in Maslow's hierarchy.
>
> The **deficit principle** states that a satisfied need does not motivate behavior.
>
> The **progression principle** states that a need isn't activated until the next lower-level need is satisfied.

ERG Theory

One extension of Maslow's work is the ERG theory proposed by Clayton Alderfer.[5] It collapses Maslow's five needs categories into three. **Existence needs** are desires for physiological and material well-being. **Relatedness needs** are desires for satisfying interpersonal relationships. **Growth needs** are desires for continued psychological growth and development.

> **Existence needs** are desires for physical well-being.
>
> **Relatedness needs** are desires for good interpersonal relationships.
>
> **Growth needs** are desires for personal growth and development.

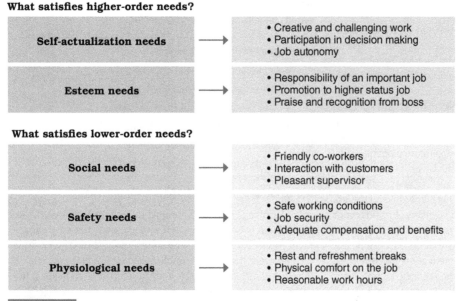

FIGURE 16.1 Opportunities for satisfaction in Maslow's hierarchy of human needs.

Existence and relatedness needs are similar to Maslow's lower order needs, while growth needs are essentially the higher-order needs in Maslow's hierarchy. Beyond that, the dynamics of ERG theory differ somewhat from Maslow's hierarchy of needs. It doesn't include the progression principle. Instead, various needs can influence behavior at any given time. ERG theory also replaces the deficit principle with the **frustration-regression principle**. It holds that an already satisfied need can become reactivated and influence behavior when a higher-level need cannot be satisfied. Someone frustrated by limited opportunities for growth by promotion, for example, might refocus attention on getting better work schedules, working conditions, and pay and benefits to further fulfill their existence needs.

The **frustration-regression principle** states that an already satisfied need can become reactivated when a higher-level need is blocked.

Two-Factor Theory

Frederick Herzberg developed the two-factor theory of motivation from a pattern discovered in almost 4,000 interviews.[6] When asked what they disliked about their jobs, respondents talked mostly about issues related to the work itself. Herzberg called these **satisfier factors**, or motivator factors. When asked what they liked, respondents talked more about issues related to the work environment. Herzberg called these **hygiene factors**. As shown in **Figure 16.2**, Herzberg argued that these factors affect people in different ways.

A **satisfier factor** is found in job content, such as challenging and exciting work, recognition, responsibility, advancement opportunities, or personal growth.

A **hygiene factor** is found in the job context, such as working conditions, interpersonal relations, organizational policies, and compensation.

Two-factor theory links hygiene factors with job dissatisfaction. Job dissatisfaction goes up as hygiene quality goes down. Hygiene factors are found in the job context—the environment in which the work takes place—and include working conditions, interpersonal relations, organizational policies and administration, and compensation. Herzberg believed that improving these factors, by remodeling work spaces or adding a quality cafeteria, can reduce job dissatisfaction. But, he warned that such hygiene improvements will not increase job satisfaction and motivation.

Satisfier factors are found in the job content—the nature of the work itself—and include job challenge, recognition for work well done, a sense of responsibility, the opportunity for advancement, and feelings of personal growth. Herzberg believed that high content jobs rich with satisfier factors are the keys to motivation.

Scholars criticize the science underlying Herzberg's research as being method-bound and difficult to replicate.[7] But, the two-factor theory does remind us that all jobs have two important aspects: *job content*—what people do in terms of job tasks—and *job context*—the work setting in which they do it. Herzberg's advice to managers also makes good sense: (1) Correct poor job context to eliminate job dissatisfaction; (2) build satisfier factors into job content to maximize job satisfaction.

Acquired Needs Theory

David McClelland and his colleagues developed yet another approach to study human needs. They began by asking people to view pictures and write stories about what they saw.[8]

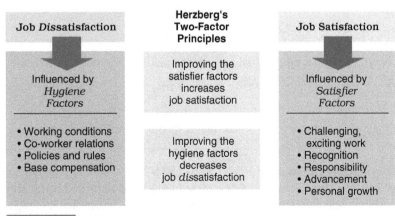

FIGURE 16.2 **Elements in Herzberg's two-factor theory.**

These stories were content-analyzed for themes that display the strengths of three needs—achievement, power, and affiliation.

Need for achievement is the desire to do something better or more efficiently, to solve problems, or to master complex tasks. People with a high need for achievement like to put their competencies to work; they take moderate risks in competitive situations, and are willing to work alone. High-need achievers' work preferences include individual responsibility for results, achievable but challenging goals, and performance feedback.

Need for power is the desire to control people, to influence their behavior, or to be responsible for them. People with a high need for power enjoy being in control of situations and recognized for this responsibility. Importantly, though, McClelland identifies two forms of the power need. The *need for personal power* is exploitative and involves manipulation for personal gratification. This type of power need does not lead to management success. The *need for social power* involves the use of power in socially responsible ways to achieve group or organizational objectives rather than personal gains. This need for social power is essential to effective managerial leadership.

Need for affiliation is the desire to establish and maintain friendly and warm relations with others. People with a high need for affiliation seek companionship, social approval, and satisfying relationships. They tend to like jobs that involve working with others and offer opportunities for social approval. This is consistent with managerial work. But, McClelland suggests that managers must be careful that high needs for affiliation don't interfere with decision making. There are times when managers and leaders must act in ways that others disagree with. If the need for affiliation limits the ability to make tough decisions, managerial effectiveness gets lost. In McClelland's view, successful executives are likely to have a high need for social power that is greater than an otherwise strong need for affiliation.

> **Need for achievement** is the desire to do something better, to solve problems, or to master complex tasks.

> **Need for power** is the desire to control, influence, or be responsible for other people.

> **Need for affiliation** is the desire to establish and maintain good relations with people.

Learning Check

LEARNING OBJECTIVE 16.1

Explain how individual needs motivate behavior.

Be Sure You Can • define *motivation* and *needs* • describe work practices that satisfy higher-order and lower-order needs in Maslow's hierarchy • contrast Maslow's hierarchy with ERG theory • describe work practices that influence hygiene factors and satisfier factors in Herzberg's two-factor theory • explain McClelland's needs for achievement, power, and affiliation • describe work conditions that satisfy people with a high need for achievement

16.2 Process Theories of Motivation

LEARNING OBJECTIVE 16.2

Contrast how expectancy, equity, goal-setting, and self-efficacy motivate behavior.

WileyPLUS

See Author Video

> **Learn More About**
>
> Equity theory • Expectancy theory • Goal-setting theory • Self-efficacy theory

Have you ever received an exam or project grade and felt good about it, only to be discouraged when you hear someone who didn't work as hard got the same or a better grade? Have you ever lost motivation when the goal set by your boss or instructor seems so high that you don't see any chance of succeeding? Most of us have had these types of experiences, perhaps

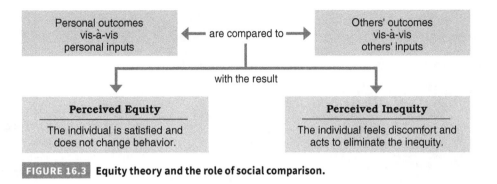

FIGURE 16.3 **Equity theory and the role of social comparison.**

fairly often. They raise the question of exactly what influences decisions to work hard or not in various situations. The equity, expectancy, and goal-setting theories of motivation offer possible answers.

Equity Theory

One of the best known motivation theories is the equity theory brought to us through the work of J. Stacy Adams.[9] It is based on the idea that we all want to be treated fairly in comparison to others. The theory suggests that feeling unfairly treated—whether we receive too little or too much when compared to someone else—makes us uncomfortable. When this happens, we're motivated to eliminate the discomfort and restore a sense of perceived equity to the situation.

Figure 16.3 shows how the equity dynamic works. Perceived inequities occur when people feel that the outcomes they receive for their contributions are unfair in comparison to the outcomes received by others. Equity comparisons at work are especially common whenever rewards are allocated. Things like pay raises, preferred job assignments, work privileges, and even office space or new technology are prime triggers for equity comparisons.

According to equity theory, someone who perceives that she or he is being treated unfairly will be motivated to act in ways that reduce the perceived inequity. There are two basic types of inequity. **Over-reward inequity** is when individuals perceive that they are receiving more than what is fair. Attempts to restore perceived equity in such cases may involve increasing the quantity or quality of work, taking on more difficult assignments, or advocating for others to be compensated more fairly. In **under-reward inequity**, by contrast, the perception is of receiving less than what is deserved in comparison to someone else. Adams predicted that people try to deal with such perceived negative inequity in the following ways.[10]

- Modifying their work inputs by putting less effort into their jobs—"If that's all I'm going to get, I'm going to do a lot less."
- Changing the rewards received by asking for better treatment—"Next stop, the boss's office; I should get what I deserve."
- Altering the inputs or outcomes of their referent—"Bob either needs to work as hard as the rest of us or else he shouldn't get the same bonus that we get."
- Reexamining the person to whom you compare yourself to make things seem better— "Well, if I look at Marissa's situation, I'm still doing pretty well."
- Changing the situation by leaving the job—"No way I'm going to stick around here if this is the way you get treated."

Although there are no clear answers available in equity theory, there are some good insights. The theory reminds us that rewards perceived as equitable should positively affect satisfaction and performance, and those perceived as inequitable may create dissatisfaction and cause performance problems. Probably the best advice is to anticipate equity comparisons whenever rewards are being allocated. It is also important to recognize that people may compare themselves not only with co-workers, but also with others elsewhere in the organization

In **over-reward inequity** (positive inequity) an individual perceives that rewards are more than what is fair.

In **under-reward inequity** (negative inequity) an individual perceives that rewards are less than what is fair.

Ethics: **Know Right from Wrong** | "Why don't I pass this information along anonymously so that everyone knows what's going on?"

Information Goldmine Creates Equity Dilemma

Image Source/Getty Images

A worker opens the top of the office photocopier and finds a document someone has left behind. It's a list of performance evaluations, pay, and bonuses for 80 co-workers. She reads the document, and finds something very surprising. Someone she considers a "nonstarter" is getting paid more than others regarded as "super workers." New hires are also being brought in at much higher pay and bonuses than those of current staff. To make

matters worse, she's in the middle of the list and not near the top, where she would have expected to be. The fact is she makes a lot less money than many others.

Looking at the data, she begins to question why she is spending extra hours working evenings and weekends at home, trying to do a really great job for the firm. She wonders to herself: "Should I pass this information around anonymously so that everyone knows what's going on? Or should I quit and find another employer who fully values me for my talents and hard work?"

In the end she decided to quit, saying: "I just couldn't stand the inequity." She also decided not to distribute the information to others in the office because "it would make them depressed, like it made me depressed."

What Do You Think?

What would you do in this situation? You're going to be concerned and perhaps upset. Would you hit "print," make about 80 copies, and put them in everyone's mailboxes—or even just leave them stacked in a couple of convenient locations? That would get the information out into the gossip chains pretty quickly. But is this ethical? If you don't send out the information, on the other hand, is it ethical to let other workers go about their days with inaccurate assumptions about the firm's pay practices? By quitting and not sharing the information, did this worker commit an ethics mistake?

and even with people employed elsewhere. Finally, we need to remember that people behave according to their perceptions. If someone perceives inequity in a work situation, it's real to them. It is likely to affect their behavior even though the manager or team leader sees things the same way.

Expectancy Theory

Victor Vroom's expectancy theory of motivation asks the question: What determines people's willingness to work hard at organizational-critical tasks?[11] The answer is that motivation depends on the relationships between three expectancy factors depicted in **Figure 16.4** and described here:

- **Expectancy**—a person's belief that working hard will result in achieving a desired level of task performance (this is sometimes called effort-performance expectancy).

- **Instrumentality**—a person's belief that successful performance will be followed by rewards and other work-related outcomes (this is sometimes called performance-outcome expectancy).

- **Valence**—the value a person assigns to the possible rewards and other work-related outcomes.

In expectancy theory, motivation (M), expectancy (E), instrumentality (I), and valence (V) are related to one another in a multiplicative fashion: $M = E \times I \times V$. In other words, motivation is determined by expectancy times instrumentality times valence. Mathematically, a zero at any location on the right side of the equation (that is, for E, I, or V) will result in zero motivation. What this means in practice is that all three factors must be high and positive for motivation to also be high.[12]

Expectancy theory reminds managers and team leaders that people answer the question "Why should I work hard today?" in different ways. Every person has unique needs, preferences,

Expectancy is a person's belief that working hard will result in high task performance.

Instrumentality is a person's belief that various outcomes will occur as a result of task performance.

Valence is the value a person assigns to work-related outcomes.

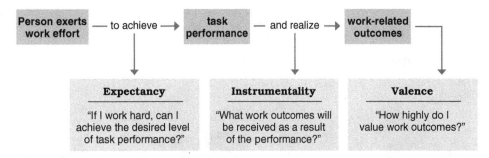

FIGURE 16.4 **Elements in the expectancy theory of motivation.**

and concerns at work. Knowing this, the goal is to build work environments that respect individual differences so that expectancies, instrumentalities, and valences all support motivation.

To maximize expectancy, people must believe in their abilities. They must believe that if they try, they can perform. This is an issue of perceived competency. Managers can build positive expectancies by selecting workers with the right abilities for the jobs to be done, providing them with the best training and development, and supporting them with resources so that the jobs can be accomplished. *To maximize instrumentality, people must see the link between high performance and work outcomes.* This is an issue of rewards for accomplishments. Managers can create positive instrumentalities by clarifying the possible rewards for high performance and then allocating these rewards fairly and on a performance-contingent basis. *To maximize positive valence, people must value the outcomes associated with high performance.* This is an issue of individual differences. Managers can use the content theories to help understand which needs are important to different individuals. Steps can then be taken to link these needs with outcomes having positive valences and that can be earned through high performance.

Goal-Setting Theory

The basic premise of Edwin Locke's goal-setting theory is that task goals can be highly motivating if they are properly set and well managed.[13] Goals give people direction in their work. They clarify the performance expectations in supervisory relationships, between co-workers, and across organizational subunits. They establish a frame of reference for task feedback. Goals also set a foundation for behavioral self-management.

The motivational benefits of goal setting occur when managers and team leaders work with others to set the right goals in the right ways. The list below identifies ways to make goal setting work for you.

- *Set specific goals:* They lead to higher performance than do more generally stated ones, such as "do your best."
- *Set challenging goals:* When viewed as realistic and attainable, more difficult goals lead to higher performance than do easy goals.
- *Build goal acceptance and commitment:* People work harder for goals they accept and believe in; they resist goals forced on them.
- *Clarify goal priorities:* Make sure that expectations are clear as to which goals should be accomplished first, and why.
- *Provide feedback on goal accomplishment:* Make sure that people know how well they are doing with respect to goal accomplishment.
- *Reward goal accomplishment:* Don't let positive accomplishments pass unnoticed; reward people for doing what they set out to do.

Goal Setting and Participation
Participation goes a long way toward unlocking the motivational power of task goals. When managers and team members participate in goal setting and performance review, members are likely to be more motivated. Participation increases

Choices: Think before You Act | "Our decision to invest in front-line employees will directly support our business, and is one that we expect to deliver a return many times over."

To Pay or Not to Pay More Than Minimum Wage

iStock.com/CandyBoxImages

More and more Americans are finding themselves in hourly paid jobs, and many—perhaps most—don't pay very well. The U.S. minimum wage is set by the Fair Labor Standards Act, and the rate since 2009 has been $7.25 per hour for non-tipped employees. Many states now set higher minimums, with the highest being $12 per hour in Washington. While Congress debates raising the federal minimum wage, New York City has already raised its minimum to $15 and Seattle has raised its to $16.

It's tempting for employers to view wages strictly as costs of production and to try and minimize these costs. The less you can pay for labor, the argument goes, the higher the "bottom line." But that's not necessarily true. Whole Foods Markets was founded with the belief that paying more than the minimum builds a stronger and more committed workforce. Co-founder John Mackey describes "conscious capitalism" where business operates as a balancing act among owners/shareholders, customers, and employees as key stakeholders. One way of achieving this balance is paying employees more than either the law or market conditions require.

Your Take?

How about it? Should employers wait for federal or state governments to raise the minimum wage, or should they act on their own to pay more than the required minimum no matter what it may be? Are Gap and Whole Foods onto something that more employers might learn—pay better and get more loyalty and higher performance? Or, are these firms just interesting specialty cases that make good news but probably wouldn't apply in most other settings?

---

understanding of task goals, increases acceptance and commitment to them, and creates more readiness to receive feedback related to goal accomplishment.

It isn't always possible to allow participation when selecting which goals need to be pursued. But it is helpful to allow participation in deciding how best to pursue them. It's also true that the constraints of time and other factors may not allow for participation. But Locke's research suggests that workers respond positively to externally imposed goals if supervisors assigning them are trusted, and if workers believe they will be adequately supported in their attempts to achieve them.

Goal-Setting Downsides

It is important to remember that poorly set and managed goals can have a downside that actually turns the motivation to accomplish them into performance negatives rather than positives.[14] An example is the scandal over patient waiting times in U.S. Veterans Affairs hospitals and clinics. More than 120,000 veterans failed to get care and at least 23 died while waiting for treatment.[15] A VA audit criticized the negative effects of unrealistic goals that were "simply not attainable." The audit found that pressures to meet unattainable goals in order to receive pay bonuses motivated some schedulers to "engage in inappropriate practices in order to make waiting times appear more favorable."[16] Lawmakers claimed the VA had an "outlandish bonus culture" and that the fabricated records were motivated by a "quest for monetary gain."[17]

Research finds that goal-setting downsides are more likely when goals are unrealistically high, when individuals are expected to meet high goals over and over again, and when people striving to meet high goals aren't given the support they need to accomplish them.[18] Scholars Gary Latham and Gerard Seijts conclude that: "It is foolish and even immoral for organizations to assign employees stretch goals without equipping them with the resources to succeed—and still punish them when they fail to reach those goals. This lack of guidance often leads to stress, burnout, and in some instances, unethical behavior."[19]

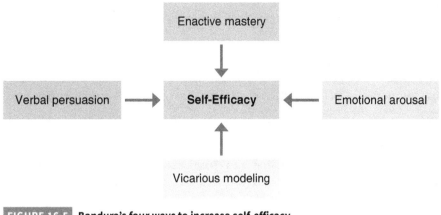

FIGURE 16.5 **Bandura's four ways to increase self-efficacy.**

Self-Efficacy Theory

Self-efficacy is a person's belief that she or he is capable of performing a task.

Based on the work of psychologist Albert Bandura, **self-efficacy** is a person's belief that she or he is capable of performing a specific task.[20] You can think of self-efficacy as confidence, competence, and ability. From a manager's perspective, anything done to boost employees' feelings of self-efficacy is likely to pay off with increased motivation.

Mahatma Gandhi once said: "If I have the belief that I can do it, I shall surely acquire the capacity to do it, even if I may not have it at the beginning."[21] This is the essence of self-efficacy theory. When people believe themselves to be capable, they will set higher goals, be more motivated to work hard at these goals, and persist longer in the face of any obstacles in their way. The *Wall Street Journal* has called this "the unshakable belief some people have that they have what it takes to succeed."[22]

There are clears links between Bandura's self-efficacy theory, elements of Vroom's expectancy theory, and Locke's goal-setting theory. With respect to Vroom, a person with higher self-efficacy will have greater expectancy that he or she can achieve a high level of task performance. With respect to Locke, a person with higher self-efficacy should be more willing to set challenging performance goals. In terms of expectancy and goal setting, managers who help create feelings of self-efficacy in others should boost their motivation.

Figure 16.5 shows four ways that Bandura believes we can increase self-efficacy.[23] First is *enactive mastery*—when a person gains confidence through positive experience. The greater your initial success and the more experience you have with a task, the more confident you become at doing it. Second is *vicarious modeling*—learning by observing others. When someone else is good at a task and we observe how they do it, we gain confidence to do it ourselves. Third is *verbal persuasion*—when someone tells us that we can or encourages us to perform a task. Hearing others praise our efforts and link those efforts with successes can be very motivational. Fourth is *emotional arousal*—when we are highly stimulated or energized to perform well in a situation. A good analogy for arousal is how athletes get "psyched up" and highly motivated to compete.

Learning Check

LEARNING OBJECTIVE 16.2

Contrast how expectancy, equity, goal-setting, and self-efficacy motivate behavior.

Be Sure You Can • explain the role of social comparison in Adams's equity theory • describe how people with felt negative inequity behave • define *expectancy, instrumentality*, and *valence* • explain Vroom's expectancy theory equation: $M = E \times I \times V$ • explain Locke's goal-setting theory • define *self-efficacy* and explain four ways to increase it

| 16.3 | # Reinforcement Theory |

WileyPLUS

See Author Video

LEARNING OBJECTIVE 16.3

Discuss the motivational implications of reinforcement principles and strategies.

> **Learn More About**
>
> The law of effect • Reinforcement strategies • Positive reinforcement • Punishment

The needs and process theories of motivation try to explain why people do things in terms of satisfying needs, resolving felt inequities, evaluating expectancies, and pursuing task goals. Reinforcement theory, by contrast, views human behavior as determined by its environmental consequences. Instead of looking within the individual to explain what drives motivation, this perspective focuses on the external environment and its consequences.

The Law of Effect

The basic premise of reinforcement theory is what E. L. Thorndike called the **law of effect**. It states: Behavior that results in a pleasant outcome is likely to be repeated; behavior that results in an unpleasant outcome is not likely to be repeated.[24] This law underlies the concept of **operant conditioning**, which was popularized by psychologist B. F. Skinner as the process of applying the law of effect to control behavior by manipulating its consequences.[25] You may think of operant conditioning as learning by reinforcement. When applied in management, its goal is to use reinforcement principles to systematically reinforce desirable work behavior and discourage undesirable work behavior.[26]

The **law of effect** states that behavior followed by pleasant consequences is likely to be repeated; behavior followed by unpleasant consequences is not.

Operant conditioning is the control of behavior by manipulating its consequences.

Reinforcement Strategies

Figure 16.6 shows four strategies of reinforcement—positive reinforcement, negative reinforcement, punishment, and extinction. The figure uses a quality example to illustrate how these strategies can be used to influence work behavior. Note that both positive and negative reinforcement strategies strengthen desired work behavior when it occurs; punishment and extinction strategies weaken or eliminate undesirable behaviors.

Positive reinforcement strengthens or increases the frequency of desirable behavior. It does so by making a pleasant consequence contingent on its occurrence. *Example:* A manager

Positive reinforcement strengthens behavior by making a desirable consequence contingent on its occurrence.

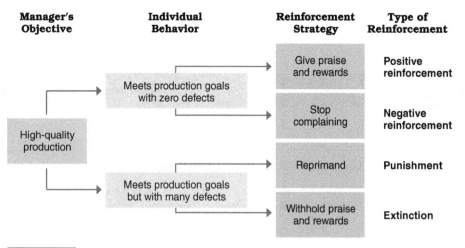

FIGURE 16.6 **Four reinforcement strategies: Case of total quality management.**

Negative reinforcement strengthens behavior by making the avoidance of an undesirable consequence contingent on its occurrence.

Punishment discourages behavior by making an unpleasant consequence contingent on its occurrence.

Extinction discourages behavior by making the removal of a desirable consequence contingent on its occurrence.

compliments an employee on his or her creativity in making a helpful comment during a staff meeting. **Negative reinforcement** also strengthens or increases the frequency of desirable behavior, but it does so by making the avoidance of an unpleasant consequence contingent on its occurrence. *Example:* A manager who has been nagging a worker every day about tardiness stops nagging when the individual shows up on time for work.

Punishment decreases the frequency of an undesirable behavior—or eliminates it entirely. It does so by making an unpleasant consequence contingent on its occurrence. *Example:* A manager issues a written reprimand to an employee whose careless work is creating quality problems. **Extinction** also decreases the frequency of or eliminates an undesirable behavior, but does so by making the removal of a pleasant consequence contingent on its occurrence. *Example:* A manager observes that a disruptive employee is receiving social approval from co-workers who laugh at his jokes during staff meetings; the manager counsels co-workers to ignore the jokes and stop providing approval of this behavior.

Positive Reinforcement

Positive reinforcement deserves special attention. It should be part of any manager's motivational toolkit. Sir Richard Branson, founder of Virgin Group, is a believer. "For the people who work for you or with you, you must lavish praise on them at all times," he says. "If a flower is watered, it flourishes. If not it shrivels up and dies." Besides, he adds, "It is much more fun looking for the best in people."[27] David Novak, former CEO of Yum! Brands, Inc., is also a believer. He claims that one of his most important tasks as CEO was "to get people fired up" and that "you can never underestimate the power of telling someone he's doing a good job." Novak advocates celebrating "first downs and not just touchdowns," which means publicly recognizing and rewarding small wins that keep everyone motivated for the long haul.[28]

The **law of contingent reinforcement** is that a reward should only be given when a desired behavior occurs.

The **law of immediate reinforcement** is that a reward should be given as soon as possible after a desired behavior occurs.

The power of positive reinforcement is governed by two important laws.[29] First is the **law of contingent reinforcement**. It states that for a reward to have maximum reinforcing value, it must be delivered only if the desired behavior is exhibited. Second is the **law of immediate reinforcement**. It states that the more immediate the delivery of a reward after the occurrence of a desirable behavior, the greater the reinforcing value of the reward. These laws are described in the following guidelines for positive reinforcement.

- Clearly identify desired work behaviors.
- Maintain a diverse inventory of rewards.
- Inform everyone what must be done to get rewards.
- Recognize individual differences when allocating rewards.
- Follow the laws of immediate and contingent reinforcement.

Shaping creates desired behavior by the positive reinforcement of successive approximations to it.

Continuous reinforcement rewards each time a desired behavior occurs.

Intermittent reinforcement rewards behavior only periodically.

An important application of positive reinforcement is **shaping**, the creation of a new behavior by the positive reinforcement of successive approximations to it.[30] **Continuous reinforcement** administers a reward each time a desired—or approximated—behavior occurs. **Intermittent reinforcement** rewards behavior only periodically. Continuous reinforcement tends to work best to encourage desired behaviors through shaping, while intermittent reinforcement works best to maintain it.

Punishment

As a reinforcement strategy, punishment is used to eliminate undesirable behavior by making an unpleasant consequence contingent on its occurrence. For example, a manager may punish an employee by issuing a verbal reprimand, suspending the employee, or fining the employee.

Just as with positive reinforcement, punishment can be done poorly or it can be done well. But because punishment can have a harmful effect on relationships, it should be used sparingly. The following guidelines offer advice on how best to handle punishment as a reinforcement strategy.

- Tell the person what is being done wrong.
- Tell the person what is being done right.
- Focus on the undesirable behavior, not on personal characteristics.
- Make sure the punishment matches the behavior so that it is neither too harsh nor too lenient.
- Administer the punishment in private.
- Follow the laws of immediate and contingent reinforcement.

Learning Check

LEARNING OBJECTIVE 16.3

Discuss the motivational implications of reinforcement principles and strategies.

Be Sure You Can • explain the law of effect and operant conditioning • illustrate how positive reinforcement, negative reinforcement, punishment, and extinction influence work behavior • explain the reinforcement technique of shaping • describe how managers can use the laws of immediate and contingent reinforcement • list guidelines for positive reinforcement and punishment

16.4 | Motivation and Job Design

LEARNING OBJECTIVE 16.4

Summarize the motivational implications of job designs.

WileyPLUS

See Author Video

> **Learn More About**
>
> Job simplification • Job enlargement • Job enrichment • Alternative work schedules
> • Alternative employment contracts

One place where motivation theories can have a significant impact is **job design**, the process of arranging job tasks and the conditions of work. Building jobs so that satisfaction and performance go hand in hand is in many ways an exercise in generating "fit" between job tasks and context on the one hand, and people's needs, capabilities, and interests on the other.[31] The basic alternatives are to make jobs smaller, make jobs bigger, change work schedules, and change employment contracts.

Job design is arranging job tasks and the conditions of work.

Job Simplification

Job simplification makes jobs smaller by standardizing work procedures and placing people in well-defined and highly specialized tasks.[32] Simplified jobs, such as those in classic automobile assembly lines, limited menu restaurants such as McDonalds, and call center phone solicitation, are narrow in *job scope*—the number and variety of different tasks a person performs.

The logic of job simplification is straightforward. Because these jobs don't require complex skills, workers should be more easily and quickly trained, less difficult to supervise, and easily replaced if they leave. Because tasks are well defined, workers should become more efficient by performing them over and over again. But, things don't always work out as planned.[33] Routine, structured, and repetitive tasks can cause problems if workers become bored and

Job simplification employs people in clearly defined and specialized tasks with narrow job scope.

alienated. Productivity can decline when unhappy workers do poor work. Costs can increase when low job satisfaction leads to more absenteeism and turnover.

With the fast developing technologies of today, an increasingly common way to eliminate problems with job simplification is **automation**, the total mechanization of a job. One example is in manufacturing, where robots are being used to perform tasks previously done by humans. A second is evident each time you use an ATM, a technology that is basically an automated replacement for a human teller.

Another way to deal with job simplification problems is to make jobs bigger by increasing *breadth*—the extent to which multiple tasks are included in the job. This can be done by **job rotation** that gives workers more variety by periodically shifting them between jobs. It can also be done by **job enlargement** that increases variety by combining into one job two or more tasks that were previously assigned to separate workers.

Job Enrichment

Frederick Herzberg, whose two-factor theory of motivation was discussed earlier, not only questions the motivational value of job simplification, he also is critical of job enlargement and rotation. "Why," he asks, "should a worker become motivated when one or more meaningless tasks are added to previously existing ones, or when work assignments are rotated among equally meaningless tasks?" By contrast, he says: "If you want people to do a good job, give them a good job to do."[34] Herzberg believes this is best done through **job enrichment** that makes jobs bigger by increasing job content through greater *depth*. This is done by moving into the job more of the managerial duties of planning and controlling previously reserved for a supervisor.

Job enrichment gives people more responsibility and sense of ownership in the ways they carry out their tasks. An example is the job characteristics model developed by Hackman and Oldham and shown in **Figure 16.7**.[35] It identifies *five core job characteristics* whose presence or absence can make jobs bigger or smaller.

1. *Skill variety*—the degree to which a job requires a variety of different activities to carry out the work and involves the use of a number of different skills and talents.

2. *Task identity*—the degree to which the job requires completion of a "whole" and identifiable piece of work, one that involves doing a job from beginning to end with a visible outcome.

3. *Task significance*—the degree to which the job has a substantial impact on the lives or work of other people elsewhere in the organization, or in the external environment.

4. *Autonomy*—the degree to which the job gives the individual freedom, independence, and discretion in scheduling work and in choosing procedures for carrying it out.

5. *Feedback from the job itself*—the degree to which work activities required by the job result in the individual obtaining direct and clear information on his or her job performance.

Automation is the total mechanization of a job.

Job rotation increases task variety by periodically shifting workers between different jobs.

Job enlargement increases task variety by combining into one job two or more tasks previously done by separate workers.

Job enrichment increases job depth by adding work planning and evaluating duties normally performed by the supervisor.

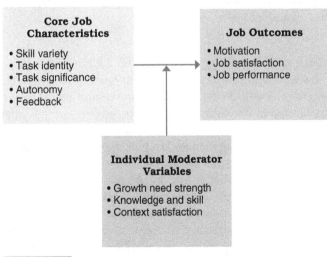

FIGURE 16.7 **Job design essentials using the job characteristics model.**

A job that is high in the five core characteristics is considered enriched. But, an enriched job will not appeal to everyone in the same way. The moderator variables in the figure show that job enrichment works best for those who have strong growth needs, have appropriate job knowledge, skills, and abilities, and that are otherwise satisfied with job context. This match-up creates a good person–job fit that should encourage motivation and satisfaction. When people without these characteristics are placed in enriched jobs, however, a poor person–job fit may decrease satisfaction and performance.

Alternative Work Schedules

"Flexibility" is the key word driving the emergence of a range of alternative ways for people to schedule their work time.[36] Employers are finding that alternative work arrangements help attract and retain motivated workers by offering them flexibility to deal with multiple responsibilities and the complications of work–life balance.

Flexibility in Working Hours
The term **flexible working hours**, also called *flextime*, describes any work schedule that gives employees some choice in allocating their daily work hours. Flexible schedules for starting and ending the workday give employees greater autonomy while meeting their work responsibilities. Some may choose to come into work earlier and leave earlier while still completing a full workday; others may choose to start later and leave later. Flexible scheduling allows employees to handle personal and family needs, as long as they get their work done. Reports indicate that flexible schedules reduce employee stress and diminish job turnover.[37] All top 100 companies in *Working Mother* magazine's list of best employers offer flexible scheduling.

> **Flexible working hours** give employees some choice in daily work hours.

A **compressed workweek** is any work schedule that allows a full-time job to be completed in less than the standard five days of 8-hour shifts. The most common form is the "4–40," that is, accomplishing 40 hours of work in four 10-hour days. A key feature of the 4–40 schedule is that employees receive three consecutive days off from work each week. Many employees are on a four-day schedule at USAA, a diversified financial services company headquartered in San Antonio, Texas, and listed among the 100 best companies to work for in America. Its advantages include improved employee morale, lower overtime costs, less absenteeism, and fewer days lost to sick leave, as well as lower costs of commuting.[38] Potential disadvantages of the compressed workweek include increased fatigue and family adjustment problems for individual employees, as well as scheduling problems for employers.

> A **compressed workweek** allows a full-time job to be completed in less than five days.

Job sharing splits one full-time job between two or more persons. This can be done in a variety of ways, from half day to weekly or monthly sharing arrangements. Organizations benefit by employing talented people who are unable or unwilling to commit to a full-time job. A parent with young children, for example, might be unable to stay away from home for a full workday, but able to work half a day.

> **Job sharing** splits one job between two people.

Telecommuting and Working from Home
It is increasingly popular for people to work by **telecommuting**, also called *work-from-home* or *remote work*. This arrangement allows them to work outside the office for at least a portion of their scheduled work time. Practices associated with telecommuting include *hoteling*, which is when telecommuters come to the home office and use temporary office facilities. Telecommuters sometimes take advantage of *virtual offices* that include everything from carrying an always-present and always-on smart device, to keeping a mobile workspace in an automobile. And, the *co-working center* is a place where telecommuters go to share physical office space outside the home.

> **Telecommuting** involves working from home or from outside the office at least part of the time.

When asked what they like about working remotely, telecommuters report increased productivity, fewer distractions, less time spent commuting to and from work, and the freedom to schedule their own time. On the negative side, they may complain about working too much, experiencing difficulty separating work and personal life, and having less family time.[39] One telecommuter offers this advice: "You have to have self-discipline and pride in what you do, but you also have to have a boss that trusts you enough to get out of the way."[40]

Analysis: Make Data Your Friend | 90% of those working from home say they work harder and longer, but with more work–life balance.

One in Five Americans Already Working from Home

Monkey Business Images/Shutterstock.com

The Society for Human Resource Management reports that the work-from-home option is one of the fastest-growing benefits being offered by employers. The Telework Research Network reports that:

- Employers save about $10,000 per year allowing workers to telecommute at least half time.
- Employees save from $1,600 to $6,800 in commuting costs.
- 47% of workers with telecommuting options say they are "very satisfied" with their jobs.
- 90% of those working from home say they work harder and longer, but with more work–life balance.
- Commuting workers are stuck in traffic for 4.2 billion hours per year while generating 58 million pounds of carbon emissions and burning 2.9 billion gallons of fuel.

Your Thoughts?

Do these data seem consistent or inconsistent with your experiences, and what you hear from family and friends? How important is the telecommuting option for you? How do you explain its motivational impact on workers from different age groups and geographical locations? What are the potential risks to the employer, and are these risks worth taking given potential motivational gains for the workforce?

From the employer's perspective, offering options to telecommute is a way of attracting and retaining talented workers who want more flexibility. But, a lack of face-to-face contact can also detract from the desired work culture by limiting teamwork and collaboration. What do you think? Is telecommuting a motivating cure all for stress and work-family conflicts? Or, is it a culture killer that reduces collaboration and productivity?

Alternative Employment Contracts

Contingency workers are employed on a part-time and temporary basis to supplement a permanent workforce.

Independent contractors are employed in temporary gigs as just-in-time and as-needed workers.

A glaring trend in our new economy is the changing nature of employment contracts. And one of the key directions is the use of more **contingency workers** hired on a temporary or part-time basis.[41] You'll hear them called "temps," "freelancers," and "contract hires." As **independent contractors**, they take gigs and provide just-in-time and as-needed work for employers who want to avoid the cost and responsibilities of hiring full-timers. *Businessweek* says the appeal for employers is that a temporary force is "easy to lay off, no severance; no company funded retirement plan; pay own health insurance; get zero sick days and no vacation."[42]

It's now possible to hire on a part-time basis for every kind of personnel need—from executive support to special expertise in areas like engineering, software development, human resources, and market research. Some worry that temporary employees lack the commitment of permanent workers and may be less productive.[43] But the facts are clear: the use of contingent rather than long-term employment contracts is growing. And, the societal implications are increasingly evident.

Permatemp workers hold part-time and contract jobs without hope for long-term security.

Contingency workers are often paid less than their full-time counterparts. Most do not receive important benefits such as health care, life insurance, pension plans, paid vacations, or even sick days. Many also end up in **permatemp** status where they are stuck in a cycle of part-time and contract work without hope for long-term employment. The results can be personal hardships, stress, and anxiety caused by financial insecurity. As society adjusts to this new era of impermanence in employment contracts, calls for economic justice are on the rise.

Learning Check

LEARNING OBJECTIVE 16.4

Summarize the motivational implications of job designs and work schedules.

Be Sure You Can • illustrate a job designed by simplification, rotation, and enlargement • list five core job characteristics • describe how an enriched job scores on these characteristics • describe advantages of the compressed workweek, flexible work hours, job sharing, and telecommuting • discuss the role of part-time contingency workers in the economy

Management Learning Review: Get Prepared for Quizzes and Exams

Summary

LEARNING OBJECTIVE 16.1 Explain how individual needs motivate behavior.

- Motivation predicts the level, direction, and persistence of effort expended at work; simply put, a highly motivated person works hard.
- Maslow's hierarchy of needs suggests a progression from lower-order physiological, safety, and social needs to higher-order esteem and self-actualization needs.
- Alderfer's ERG theory identifies existence, relatedness, and growth needs.
- Herzberg's two-factor theory describes the importance of both job content and job context to motivation and performance.
- McClelland's acquired needs theory identifies the needs for achievement, affiliation, and power, all of which may influence what a person desires from work.

For Discussion How can team leaders meet the individual needs of members while still treating everyone fairly?

LEARNING OBJECTIVE 16.2 Contrast how expectancy, equity, goal-setting, and self-efficacy motivate behavior.

- Adams's equity theory recognizes that social comparisons take place when rewards are distributed in the workplace.
- People who feel inequitably treated are motivated to act in ways that reduce the sense of inequity; perceived negative inequity may result in someone working less hard in the future.
- The concept of equity sensitivity suggests that not all employees are equally concerned about being treated equitably and that not all employees respond to different types of inequity in the same way.
- Vroom's expectancy theory states that Motivation = Expectancy x Instrumentality x Valence.

- Locke's goal-setting theory emphasizes the motivational power of goals; task goals should be specific rather than ambiguous, difficult but achievable, and set with employees' participation.
- Bandura's self-efficacy theory indicates that when people believe they are capable of performing a task, they experience a sense of confidence and are more highly motivated to work hard at it.

For Discussion What are the most common triggers of felt inequity in the workplace, and what can a manager do about them?

LEARNING OBJECTIVE 16.3 Discuss the motivational implications of reinforcement principles and strategies.

- Reinforcement theory recognizes that human behavior is influenced by its environmental consequences.
- The law of effect states that behavior followed by a pleasant consequence is likely to be repeated; behavior followed by an unpleasant consequence is unlikely to be repeated.
- Reinforcement strategies used by managers include positive reinforcement, negative reinforcement, punishment, and extinction.
- Positive reinforcement works best when applied according to the laws of contingent and immediate reinforcement.

For Discussion Can a manager or a parent rely solely on positive reinforcement strategies?

LEARNING OBJECTIVE 16.4 Summarize the motivational implications of job designs and work schedules.

- Job design is the process of creating or defining jobs by assigning specific work tasks to individuals and groups.
- Job simplification creates narrow and repetitive jobs composed of well-defined tasks with routine operations, such as typical assembly-line jobs.

- Job enlargement allows individuals to perform a broader range of simplified tasks; job rotation allows individuals to shift among different jobs with similar skill levels.
- The job characteristics model of job design analyzes jobs according to skill variety, task identity, task significance, autonomy, and feedback; a job high in these characteristics is considered enriched.
- Alternative work schedules make work hours more convenient and flexible to better fit workers' needs and personal responsibilities; options include the compressed workweek, flexible working hours, job sharing, telecommuting, and part-time work.

For Discussion Should getting an enriched job be reward enough for job holders, or should they also get pay increases?

Self-Test 16

Multiple-Choice Questions

1. Lower-order needs in Maslow's hierarchy match well with _____ needs in ERG theory.

    a. growth

    b. affiliation

    c. existence

    d. achievement

2. When a team member shows strong ego needs in Maslow's hierarchy, the team leader should find that _____ will be motivating to him or her.

    a. alternative work schedules

    b. praise and recognition for job performance

    c. social interactions with other team members

    d. easy performance goals

3. A worker with a high need for _____ power in McClelland's theory tries to use power for the good of the organization.

    a. position

    b. expert

    c. personal

    d. social

4. In Herzberg's two-factor theory, base pay is considered a(n) _____ factor.

    a. valence

    b. satisfier

    c. equity

    d. hygiene

5. Which of the following is a correct match?

    a. McClelland—ERG theory

    b. Skinner—reinforcement theory

    c. Vroom—equity theory

    d. Locke—expectancy theory

6. The expectancy theory of motivation says that motivation = expectancy × _____ × _____.

    a. rewards, valence

    b. instrumentality, valence

    c. equity, instrumentality

    d. engagement, growth

7. When someone has a high and positive "expectancy" in the expectancy theory of motivation, this means that the person _____.

    a. believes he or she can meet performance expectations

    b. highly values the rewards being offered

    c. sees a link between high performance and available rewards

    d. believes that rewards are equitable

8. In the _____ theory of motivation, someone who perceives herself under-rewarded relative to a co-worker might be expected to reduce his or her performance in the future.

    a. ERG

    b. acquired needs

    c. two-factor

    d. equity

9. In goal-setting theory, the goal of "doing a better job" would not be considered a good source of motivation because it fails the test of goal _____.

    a. acceptance

    b. specificity

    c. challenge

    d. commitment

10. The law of _____ states that behavior followed by a positive consequence is likely to be repeated, whereas behavior followed by an undesirable consequence is not likely to be repeated.

    a. reinforcement

    b. contingency

    c. goal setting

    d. effect

11. _____ is a positive reinforcement strategy that rewards successive approximations to a desirable behavior.

    a. Extinction

    b. Negative reinforcement

    c. Shaping

    d. Merit pay

12. B. F. Skinner would argue that "getting a paycheck on Friday" reinforces a person for coming to work on Friday, but it does not reinforce the person for having done an extraordinary job on Tuesday. This is because the Friday paycheck fails the law of _____ reinforcement.

    a. negative

    b. continuous

    c. immediate

    d. intermittent

13. When a job is redesigned to allow a person to do a whole unit of work from beginning to end, it becomes high on which core characteristic?

    a. task identity

    b. task significance

    c. task autonomy

    d. feedback

14. A typical compressed workweek schedule involves 40 hours of work done in _____ days.

    a. 3

    b. 4

    c. 5

    d. a flexible number of

15. A term often used to describe someone who is a long-term but part-time hire is _____ worker.

    a. contingency

    b. virtual

    c. flexible

    d. permatemp

Short-Response Questions

16. What preferences does a person with a high need for achievement bring to the workplace?

17. Why is participation important to goal-setting theory?

18. Where is the common ground in Maslow's, Alderfer's, and McClelland's views of human needs?

19. Why might an employer not want to offer employees the option of a compressed workweek schedule?

Essay Question

20. How can a manager combine the powers of goal setting and positive reinforcement to create a highly motivational work environment for workers with high needs for achievement?

Career Skills & Competencies: Make Yourself Valuable!

Evaluate Career Situations

What Would You Do?

1. Paying the Going Rate

As the owner-manager of a small engineering company, you need to hire a replacement for a recently retired senior employee. The salaries you pay have always been a little below average, but it has never been an issue because you offer excellent benefits and a great work environment. The individual you want to hire has made it clear that she will not accept the job unless the offer is $5,000 more than you'd really like to pay, but it's also the competitive market rate. If you pay her the higher salary you'll risk alienating your current workforce. If you don't, you'll miss out on a great new hire. How can you best handle this dilemma?

2. Across-the-Board Raises

Because of a poor economy your company has not been able to offer pay raises to employees for the past three years. This year the salary budget has been increased by 5%. Your initial thought was to give everyone a 5% raise. Is this a good idea? How should you allocate salary increases in this situation?

3. Job Redesign for Better or for Worse?

As the manager of the university bookstore, you have come up with a plan to give part-time student workers more autonomy and control over their jobs. Your assistant manager believes this is a bad idea. She says that the student workers show no capacity for initiative or responsibility, and just want to do what they're told to do and get their weekly paychecks. She also predicts that both productivity and customer service will suffer under your plan. You think the student workers are bored and disengaged, but otherwise capable. What are you going to do and why?

Reflect on the Self-Assessment

Student Engagement Survey

Instructions

Use the following scale to show the degree to which you agree with the following statements. Write your choices in the margin next to each question.[44]

> 1—No agreement; 2—Weak agreement; 3—Some agreement; 4—Considerable agreement; 5—Very strong agreement

1. I know what is expected of me in this course.

2. I have the resources and support I need to do my coursework correctly.

3. In this course, I have the opportunity to do what I do best all the time.

4. In the last week, I have received recognition or praise for doing good work in this course.

5. My instructor seems to care about me as a person.

6. There is someone in the course who encourages my development.

7. In this course, my opinions seem to count.

8. The mission/purpose of the course makes me feel my area of study is important.

9. Other students in the course are committed to doing quality work.

10. I have a good friend in the course.

11. In the last six class sessions, someone has talked to me about my progress in the course.

12. In this course, I have had opportunities to learn and grow.

Scoring

Score the instrument by adding up all your responses. A score of 0–24 suggests you are "actively disengaged" from the learning experience; a score of 25–47 suggests you are "moderately engaged"; a score of 48–60 indicates you are "actively engaged."

Interpretation

This instrument is a counterpart to a survey used by the Gallup Organization to measure the "engagement" of American workers. The Gallup results are surprising—indicating that up to 19% of U.S. workers are actively disengaged, with the annual lost productivity estimated at some $300 billion per year. One has to wonder: What are the costs of academic disengagement by students?

Contribute to the Class Exercise

Why We Work

Preparation

Read this "ancient story."[45]

In days of old, a wandering youth happened upon a group of men working in a quarry. Stopping by the first man, he said: "What are you doing?" The worker grimaced and groaned as he replied: "I am trying to shape this stone, and it is backbreaking work." Moving to the next man, the youth repeated the question. This man showed little emotion as he answered: "I am shaping a stone for a building." Moving to the third man, our traveler heard him singing as he worked. "What are you doing?" asked the youth. "I am helping to build a cathedral," the man proudly replied.

Instructions

In groups assigned by your instructor:

1. Discuss this short story.

2. Ask and answer the question: "What are the motivation and job design lessons of this ancient story?"

3. Discuss the question: How can managers help employees feel more inspired about what they are doing?

4. Have someone prepared to report and share the group's responses with the class as a whole.

Manage a Critical Incident

Great Worker Won't Take Vacation

Todd is a super hard worker and one of your team's top performers. He's also one of those workers who just won't take a vacation. Oh yes, he takes a day here and there. But each year he leaves as much as two weeks of vacation time on the table. You believe he would benefit from the occasional break, working happier and maybe more productively with some vacation time under his belt. His unwillingness to take time off is also a subject of conversation among his teammates. Their view is that he is starting to make them look and feel bad when they take the vacation time that they earn. Some are starting to act

a bit resentfully toward him, and you recently overheard this comment: "Take a little time off, Todd—for the good of the team, if not for yourself."

Questions

What can you do as the team leader to avoid having Todd's reluctance to take vacation turn into major team morale and working relationships problems? How might you motivate Todd to take more vacation time, without risking his high performance commitment and work ethic? How can you motivate his teammates to accept his behavior and be able to confidently continue with their own work styles?

Collaborate on the Team Activity

CEO Pay . . . Too High, or Just Right?

Question

What is happening in the area of executive compensation, and what do you think about it?

Instructions

1. Check the latest reports on CEO pay. Get the facts and prepare a brief report as if you were writing a short, informative article for *Fortune* magazine. The title of your article should be "Status Report: Where We Stand Today on CEO Pay."

2. Address the equity issue: Are CEOs paid too much, especially relative to the pay of average workers?

3. Address the pay-for-performance issue: Do corporate CEOs get paid for performance or for something else?

4. Gather some data: What do the researchers say? What do the business analysts say? What do the unions say? Find some examples to explain and defend your answers to these questions.

5. Address social responsibility issues: Is it "right" for CEOs to accept pay packages that reward them many times over what workers receive?

6. Take a position: Should a limit be set on CEO pay? If not, why not? If yes, what type of limit should be set? And who should set these limits—the government, company boards of directors, or someone else?

Analyze the Case Study

Salesforce | Instant Praise, Instant Criticism

Go to ***Management Cases for Critical Thinking*** at the end of the book to find this case.

CHAPTER 17

Teams and Teamwork

Two Heads Really Are Better Than One

ullstein bild Dtl./Getty Images

Alone we can do so little; together we can do so much.

- Helen Keller

Career Readiness – What to Look for Inside

Thought Leadership

Analysis > *Make Data Your Friend*
Unproductive Meetings Are Major Time Wasters

Choices > *Think before You Act*
Creating Disharmony to Build a Better Team

Ethics > *Know Right from Wrong*
Social Loafing Is Hurting Team Performance

Insight > *Learn about Yourself*
Don't Short Your Team Contributions

Skills Make You Valuable

- **Evaluate** *Career Situations:*
  What Would You Do?

- **Reflect** *On the Self-Assessment:*
  Team Leader Skills

- **Contribute** *To the Class Exercise:*
  Work Team Dynamics

- **Manage** *A Critical Incident:*
  The Rejected Team Leader

- **Collaborate** *On the Team Project:*
  Superstars on the Team

- **Analyze** *The Case Study:*
  Auto Racing: When the Driver Takes a Back Seat

Chapter Quick Start

Surely you've experienced the highs and the lows of teams and teamwork—as a team member and as a team leader. Teams and teammates can be inspirational and they can also be highly frustrating. People in teams can accomplish great things or end up doing very little. The more we know about teams, teamwork, and our personal tendencies toward team contributions, the better prepared we are to participate in today's team-driven organizations.

LEARNING OBJECTIVES

17.1 Explain the ways teams contribute to organizations.

17.2 Describe current trends in the use of teams in organizations.

17.3 Summarize the key processes through which teams work.

17.4 Discuss the ins and outs of team decision making.

345

"Sticks in a bundle are hard to break"—*Kenyan proverb*

"Never doubt that a small group of thoughtful, determined people can change the world"—*Margaret Mead*, anthropologist

"Pick good people, use small teams and give them great tools so that they are very productive."—*Bill Gates*, businessman and philanthropist

"Gettin' good players is easy. Gettin' 'em to play together is the hard part"—*Casey Stengel*, Hall of Fame Major League baseball manager

From proverbs to societies to sports to business, the operation of teams and teamwork has been a consistent focal point of collective organization and is widely recognized as a critical tool for accomplishing great things.[1] Even so, just the words *group* and *team* elicit both positive and negative reactions from people who have been involved—either as observers or participants—in these collectives. Although it is an embedded idiom in Western culture that "two heads are better than one," we also are warned by an idiom equally embedded in our culture that "too many cooks spoil the broth." A true skeptic of the collective action implied by groups or teams might say: "A camel is a horse put together by a committee."

Teams have a great deal of performance potential but also are extremely complex in how they function. Teams can be a supercharged vehicle to achieve great successes, and they can also be the cause of equally monstrous failures.[2] More than a third of individuals participating in teams report dissatisfaction with teamwork. Less than half of team members report receiving training in team dynamics.[3] Still, many people prefer to work in teams than working alone. What is clear is that there is a great deal of variability in responses to—and the effectiveness of—teams in organizations today.

17.1 | Teams in Organizations

LEARNING OBJECTIVE 17.1

Explain the ways teams contribute to organizations.

> **Learn More About**
>
> Teamwork pros • Teamwork cons • Meetings, meetings, meetings • Organizations as networks of groups

A **team** is a collection of people who regularly interact to pursue common goals.

Teamwork is the process of people actively working together interdependently to accomplish common goals.

A **team** is a relatively small set of people with complementary skills who regularly interact, and work interdependently to achieve shared goals.[4] **Teamwork** is the process of team members working together to accomplish these goals. Managers must be prepared to perform at least the four important teamwork roles shown in **Figure 17.1**. A *team leader* serves as the appointed head of a team or a work unit. A *team member* serves as a contributing part of a project team. A *network facilitator* serves as a peer leader and networking hub for a special task force. A *coach or developer* serves as a team's advisor to improve team processes and performance.

Team leader

Team member

Network facilitator

Coach or Developer

FIGURE 17.1 **Roles managers play in teams and teamwork.**

A fundamental difference between teams and groups is whether members' goals or outcomes require that they work interdependently or independently of one another. The **interdependence** characteristic of teams puts members in positions where they depend on each other to fulfill tasks and carry out their work.[5] Interdependence influences the way team members combine inputs such as ideas and efforts to create outcomes such as a completed task or project.[6] And when team members are interdependent, they tend to share information and communicate more often, as well as act cooperatively and helpfully toward one another.[7]

Interdependence is the extent to which team members depend on one other to complete their work effectively.

Teamwork Pros

Although working effectively with other members can be hard work, the effort is worth it when the team meets anticipated performance expectations.[8] One great benefit of teams is their capacity to accomplish goals and performance expectations far greater than what's possible for individuals alone. This collective performance potential is called **synergy**, the creation of a whole that is greater than the sum of its individual parts.

Synergy is the creation of a whole greater than the sum of its individual parts.

Synergy pools individual talents and efforts to create extraordinary results through collective action. When Jens Voigt, a former Tour de France star, was asked to describe a "perfect cyclist," he instead described this composite of his nine-member team: "We take the time trial legs of Fabian Cancellara, the speed of Stuart O'Grady, the climbing capacity of our leaders, and my attitude." Voigt's point was that the tour is simply too hard for a single rider to win based on individual talents alone.[9]

Team connections can help everyone to do their jobs better—getting help, solving problems, sharing ideas, responding to favors, motivating one another, and avoiding roadblocks. Team relationships can also help satisfy important needs that may be difficult to meet in regular work or personal settings. Just being part of a team that offers positive interpersonal interactions can provide a sense of security, belonging, and emotional support.[10] In sum, it's no secret that teams can be hard work. But it's also true that they're most often worth it. The many benefits of teams include the following.

- Performance gains through synergy
- More resources for problem solving
- Improved creativity and innovation
- Improved decision-making quality
- Greater member commitment to tasks
- Increased member motivation
- Increased need satisfaction of members

Teamwork Cons

We all know that the expected performance gains from teams don't always materialize. Problems with team operations and between members can easily transform their great potential into frustration and failure.[11]

Personality conflicts and work style differences can disrupt how teams function. Unclear tasks, ambiguous agendas, and ill-defined problems and roles can cause teams to work too long on the wrong things. Sometimes members start out motivated and then lose their motivation because teamwork takes too much time and effort away from other tasks, deadlines, and priorities. A lack of success also can hurt members' morale. It's also easy for members to lose motivation when the team is poorly organized and led, or when other members slack off.[12]

Anyone who's had any experience working in teams has encountered **social loafing**. This is the presence of "free-riders" who slack off because responsibility is spread throughout the team and others are present to do the work, picking up the slack.[13] Although social loafing can be very frustrating and can hurt team performance, there are things that leaders or team members can do when others don't do their work. The possibilities include making individual contributions more visible, rewarding individuals for their contributions, making task assignments more interesting, and keeping team sizes small so that free-riders are subject to more intense peer pressure and leader evaluation.[14]

Social loafing is the tendency of some members to avoid responsibility by "free-riding" during group tasks.

Social Loafing Is Hurting Team Performance

George Doyle & Ciaran Griffin/Stockbyte/Getty Images

1. *Psychology study:* A German researcher asked people to pull on a rope as hard as they could. First, individuals pulled alone. Second, they pulled as part of a group. The results from this study showed that people pull harder when working alone than when working as part of a team. Such "social loafing" is the tendency for individuals to reduce their level of effort when working with others.

2. *Faculty office:* A student wants to speak with the instructor about issues with his team's performance on the last project. There were four members, but only two of them did almost all of the work. The other two largely disappeared, showing up only at the last minute to be part of the formal presentation. His point is that the team was disadvantaged because two free-riders were responsible for reduced performance capacity.

3. *Telephone call from the boss:* "John, I really need you to serve on this committee. Will you do it? Let me know tomorrow." In thinking about this, John ponders: I'm overloaded, but I don't want to turn down the boss. I'll accept but let the committee members know about my situation. I'll be active in discussions and try to offer viewpoints and perspectives that are helpful. However, I'll let them know up front that I can't be a leader or volunteer for any extra work.

What Do You Think?

What are the ethical issues involved in team situations when some members sit back and let others do more of the work the entire team is responsible for doing? When you join a team, do all of the team's members have an ethical obligation to do a similar amount of work—why or why not? When it comes to John, does the fact that he intends to be honest with the other committee members make any difference? Isn't he still going to be a social loafer while earning credit from his boss for serving on the committee? Is his approach ethical—or should he simply decline to participate on the committee? What factors would make you more/less comfortable with another member not pulling their weight on the team?

Meetings, Meetings, Meetings

"Meetings are unproductive and inefficient."
"Meetings keep me from completing my own work."
"Meetings come at the expense of deep thinking."

The prior comments come from a survey of senior managers.[15] How do they stack up with your experiences? What do you think when someone says: "Let's have a meeting"? Are you ready and willing to attend? Or are you apprehensive and even irritated to have to set aside time and participate?

Good meetings don't happen by accident. People have to work hard and work together to make meetings productive and rewarding. Face-to-face and virtual meetings are where lots of information is shared, decisions get made, and people gain understanding of the issues and of one another. They're important and necessary. This is why knowing more about teams and teamwork is so useful.

Organizations as Networks of Teams

A **formal team** is an officially recognized collective that is supported by the organization.

Formal teams are officially recognized and supported by the organization. They may be called departments (e.g., market research department), units (e.g., audit unit), groups (e.g., customer service group), or divisions (e.g., office products division). These formal teams create interlocking networks that serve as the foundation of the organization's structure, and managers are key "linking pins" among them. Managers lead formal teams at one level while also serving as members of teams at the next higher level as well as teams formed across functional areas.[16]

An **informal group** is unofficial and emerges spontaneously from relationships and shared interests among members.

Informal groups also are important in all organizations. They emerge from natural or spontaneous relationships. Some informal groups are *interest groups* where members join together to pursue a common cause, such as better working conditions. Some emerge as *friendship groups* that develop for personal reasons, including shared non-work interests and

Unproductive Meetings Are Major Time Wasters

Leontura/E+/Getty Images

A survey of some 38,000 workers around the world links low productivity with bad meetings, poor communication, and unclear goals.

- 69% of meetings attended are considered ineffective.
- 32% of workers complain about team communication.
- 31% complain about unclear objectives and priorities.

Your Thoughts?

Do the results from this survey match your own experiences with team meetings? Given the common complaints about meetings, what can a team leader do to improve them? Think about recent meetings you have attended. In what ways were the best meetings different from the worst meetings? Did your own behavior play a significant role in both of these cases? How do the interactions of team members influence the quality of these meetings? Why?

social connections. Others exist as *support groups*, where members help one another to do their jobs or to cope with problems.

Although informal groups can become forums for airing dissatisfactions and spreading rumors, the social connections they offer also play many positive roles in organizations. Tapping into relationships can help speed workflow and "get things done" in ways not possible within the formal structure. Being part of informal groups can satisfy needs that are otherwise left unmet in one's job, including opportunities for friendship, security, support, and a sense of belongingness.

Learning Check

LEARNING OBJECTIVE 17.1

Explain the ways teams contribute to organizations.

Be Sure You Can • define *team* and *teamwork* • explain why *interdependence* is a key characteristic of teams • identify four roles managers perform in teams • define *synergy* • explain teamwork pros and cons • discuss the implications of social loafing • explain the potential benefits of informal groups

17.2 Trends in the Use of Teams

LEARNING OBJECTIVE 17.2

Describe current trends in the use of teams in organizations.

WileyPLUS

See Author Video

Learn More About

Committees, project teams, and task forces • Cross-functional teams • Self-managing teams • Virtual teams • Team building

The trend is toward greater empowerment in organizations. In practice, one way this shows up is in the expanded use of committees, project teams, task forces, cross-functional teams, self-managing teams, and virtual teams.

Committees, Project Teams, and Task Forces

A **committee** is designated to work on a special task on a continuing basis.

A **committee** brings employees together outside of their daily job duties to work together for a specific purpose. A committee's agenda is typically narrow, focused, and ongoing. Organizations usually have a variety of permanent or standing committees dedicated to a wide variety of issues, such as diversity, quality, and product development. Committees are led by a designated head or chairperson, who is accountable for the committee's performance.

A **project team** or **task force** is convened for a specific purpose and disbands when its task is completed.

Project teams or **task forces** bring people together to work on common problems, but on a temporary basis. The goals and task assignments are specific and completion deadlines are clear. Creativity and innovation may be part of the agenda. Project teams, for example, can be formed to develop a new advertising campaign, redesign an office layout, or streamline a work process.[17]

Cross-Functional Teams

A **cross-functional team** operates with members who come from different functional units of an organization.

The **functional chimneys problem** is a lack of communication across functions.

Many organizations use **cross-functional teams** that pull together members from across different functional units to work on common goals. These teams help reduce the **functional chimneys problem** by eliminating "walls" that can limit communication and cooperation between different departments and functions. Target CEO Gregg Steinhafel, for example, says that his firm uses cross-functional teams from "merchandising, marketing, design, communications, presentation, supply chain and stores" to create and bring new limited-edition fashions to customers.[18]

Self-Managing Teams

Members of a **self-managing work team** have the authority to make decisions about how they share and complete their work.

Traditional work teams consisting of first-level supervisors and their subordinates are increasingly being replaced in a growing number of organizations with **self-managing work teams**. As shown in **Figure 17.2**, members of these teams have a high degree of task interdependence, authority to make decisions about how they work, and collective responsibility for results.[19] The expected advantages are better performance, reduced costs, greater engagement, and higher morale.

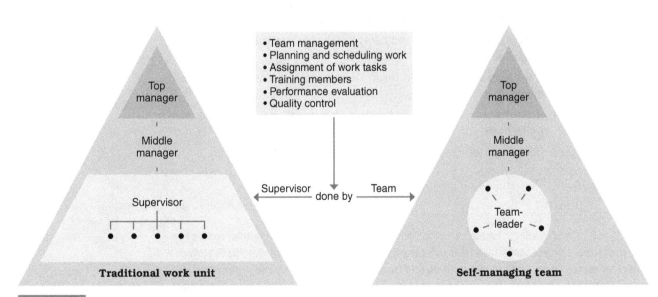

FIGURE 17.2 **Organizational and management implications of self-managing work teams.**

Multitasking is a key feature of all self-managing teams, whose members have the skills to perform several different jobs. Within a team the emphasis is always on participation. Team members share tasks and take responsibility for management functions traditionally performed by supervisors. These "self-management" responsibilities include planning and scheduling work, training members in various tasks, distributing tasks, meeting performance goals, ensuring high quality, and solving day-to-day problems. In some self-managing teams, members have the authority to "hire" and "fire" members.

Virtual Teams

Scene: U.S.-based IT manager needs to meet with team members in Brazil, the Philippines, and Poland. Rather than pay for everyone to fly to a common location, he checks world time zones, sends e-mail and messages to schedule a virtual meeting. Probably working from home, he turns on his tablet to join team members online using any number of virtual meeting platforms.

Members of **virtual teams**, also called *distributed teams*, work together through computer mediation rather than face to face.[20] Their use can save time, lowewer travel costs when members work in different locations, and reduce complications for members working on different time schedules.[21] Virtual teams can also be very efficient because members adhere to time schedules and are less prone to stray off task. Members of virtual teams are also less likely to get sidetracked by interpersonal difficulties. A vice president of human resources at Marriott, for example, once called electronic meetings "the quietest, least stressful, most productive meetings you've ever had."[22]

Virtual teams do have potential disadvantages, ones that need to be addressed through good team leadership. The lack of face-to-face interaction limits the role of emotions and nonverbal cues in communication, and can cause ineffective communication and feelings of depersonalization.[23] "Human beings are social animals for whom building relationships matters a great deal," says one scholar. "Strip away the social side of teamwork and, very quickly, people feel isolated and unsupported."[24] The following guidelines can help keep the possible downsides of virtual teamwork to a minimum.[25]

Members of a **virtual team** work together and solve problems through computer-mediated interactions.

- Select team members high in initiative and capable of self-starting.
- Select members who will join and engage the team with positive attitudes.
- Select members known for working hard to meet team goals.
- Begin with social messaging that allows members to exchange information about each other in order to personalize the process.
- Assign clear goals and roles so that members can focus while working alone and also know what others are doing.
- Gather regular feedback from members about how they think the team is doing and how it might work more effectively.
- Provide regular feedback to team members about team accomplishments.

Team Building

Anyone interested in sports knows only too well that even the most experienced teams run into problems. Long seasons take their tolls, teams have losing streaks, players have slumps, and teammates come and go with injuries and trades. And don't forget the arguments and complaints that cause frictions among team members. When such things happen, the best coaches and managers don't let things go too far. They step in and take actions to restore the teamwork needed for performance success. Work teams face similar challenges and need similar "tune ups."

Team building is a sequence of activities to analyze a team and make changes to improve its performance.

Team building is a sequence of planned activities used to analyze the functioning of a team and to make constructive, systematic changes in how it operates.[26] The process begins with creating awareness that a problem already exists or may develop in the near future. Members then work together to gather data and fully understand the problem, make plans to correct it, implement the plans the team develops, and evaluate results from the plan. This process is repeated as difficulties or new problems are discovered.

There are many ways to gather data for team building, including structured and unstructured interviews, survey questionnaires, and team meetings. Regardless of the method used to understand what's happening, the basic principle of team building remains the same. It is a careful and collaborative assessment of all of the various aspects of the team, ranging from how members work together to the results they achieve.

Team building can be done with consulting assistance or under the direction of a manager. It can also be done in the workplace or take place at outside locations. A popular approach is to bring members together in special outdoor settings where their capacities for teamwork are tested through unusual and physically demanding experiences, such as obstacle courses. There's lots of room for innovation, with options including activities like scavenger hunts, work with charities, cooking schools, building, sculpting, and competitive activities.[27] Says one team-building trainer: "We throw clients into situations to try and bring out the traits of a good team."[28]

Learning Check

LEARNING OBJECTIVE 17.2

Describe current trends in the use of teams in organizations.

Be Sure You Can • differentiate a committee from a task force • explain the benefits of cross-functional teams • discuss potential advantages and disadvantages of virtual teams • list the characteristics of self-managing work teams • explain how self-managing teams are changing organizations • describe the typical steps in team building

17.3 | How Teams Work

WileyPLUS

See Author Video

LEARNING OBJECTIVE 17.3

Summarize the key processes through which teams work.

> **Learn More About**
>
> Team inputs • Stages of team development • Norms and cohesiveness • Task and maintenance roles • Communication networks

An **effective team** achieves high levels of task performance, membership satisfaction, and future viability.

An **effective team** does three things well—performs its tasks, satisfies its members, and remains viable for the future.[29] On the *task performance* side, a team is expected to transform resource inputs (such as ideas, materials, and information) into product outputs (such as a report, decision, service, or commodity). With respect to *member satisfaction*, members should take pleasure from both the team's accomplishments and their contributions toward making these happen. As to *future viability*, the team should have a social fabric and work

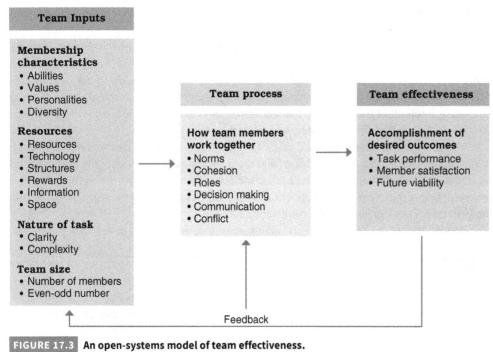

FIGURE 17.3 An open-systems model of team effectiveness.

climate that makes its members willing and able to work well together in the future, again and again as needed.

You sometimes hear top executives saying that team effectiveness comes from having "the right players in the right seats on the same bus, headed in the same direction."[30] The open-systems model in **Figure 17.3** supports this view. It shows that a team's effectiveness is influenced by inputs—"right players in the right seats"—and by process—"on the same bus, headed in the same direction."[31] You can remember the implications of this figure by the following **Team Effectiveness Equation**.[32]

Team effectiveness = Quality of inputs + (Process gains − Process losses)

Team Effectiveness Equation Team effectiveness = Quality of inputs + (Process gains − Process losses).

Team Inputs

Among the important inputs that influence team effectiveness are membership characteristics, resources and setting, nature of the task, and team size.[33] You can think of them as drivers that prepare the team for action. A team with the right inputs has a greater chance of having a positive process and being effective.

Membership Characteristics   The right blend of member characteristics on a team is critical for success. Teams need members with the right abilities, or skill sets, to master and perform tasks well. Teams must also have members whose attitudes, values, and personalities are sufficiently compatible for everyone to work well together. How often, for example, have you read or heard about college sports teams where a lack "chemistry" among talented players leads to subpar team performance? As one of the chapter opening quotes states: "Gettin' good players is easy. Gettin' 'em to play together is the hard part."[34]

Team diversity, in the form of different values, personalities, identities, experiences, demographics, and cultures among members, affects how teams work.[35] It is easier to manage relationships among members of more *homogeneous teams*—teams where members share similar characteristics. It is harder to manage relationships among the members of more *heterogeneous teams*—where members are more dissimilar to one another. As team diversity

Team diversity represents the differences in values, personalities, experiences, demographics, and cultures among members.

Choices: Think before You Act | "There is no 'I' in team!" is a common cry. But basketball superstar Michael Jordan once responded: "There is an 'I' in win."

Creating Disharmony to Build a Better Team

Leon Bennett/Getty Images Sport/Getty Images

"There is no 'I' in team!" is a common cry. But basketball superstar Michael Jordan once responded: "There is an 'I' in win." What's the point here? Jordan is suggesting that someone as expert in task direction as himself shouldn't always be subordinated to the team. Rather, the team's job may be to support his or her talents so that they shine to their brightest potential.

In his book, *There Is an I in Team: What Elite Athletes and Coaches Really Know about High Performance*, Cambridge University scholar Mark de Rond notes that sports metaphors abound in the workplace. We talk about "heavy hitters" and ask teammates to "step up to the plate." The real world of teamwork is dominated by the quest for cooperation, perhaps at the cost of needed friction. And that, according to de Rond, is a potential performance problem. "When teams work well," de Rond says, "it is because, not in spite, of individual differences."

Those in favor of de Rond's views are likely to argue that even if superstars bring a bit of conflict to the team, the result may well be added creativity and a performance boost. Instead of trying to make everyone happy, perhaps it's time for managers and team leaders to accept that disharmony can be functional, adding a needed edge. A bit of team tension may be a price worth paying for high performance. *Those worried about de Rond's views* might say there's a fine line between a superstar's real performance contribution and the collateral damage or negative impact caused by personality and temperament clashes. That line is a hard one to spot and to manage.

Your Take?

Given what we know about teams and your personal experiences with them, should we be finding ways to accommodate superstars on a team . . . or avoid them?

---

increases, so does the complexity of members' interpersonal relationships. But the potential complications of membership diversity also come with special performance opportunities. When heterogeneous teams are well managed, the variety of ideas, perspectives, and experiences can be a valuable problem-solving and performance asset.

Resources and Tasks

Resources and organizational setting also influence how well team members use and pool their talents to accomplish team tasks. Teams function best when members have good information, resources, technology, supportive structures, and rewards. The physical work space also is critical, and many organizations are now architecturally designed to increase collaboration and teamwork.

The nature of the tasks teams are responsible for not only sets standards for the talents needed by members, it also affects how they work together. Clearly defined tasks are easier to deal with. Complex tasks require a lot more in terms of information sharing and coordinated action.[36] The next time you fly, check out the ground crews. You should notice some similarities between them and NASCAR pit crews. There's even a chance that some have been through "Pit Crew U." United is among the organizations sending employees to Pit Instruction & Training in Mooresville, North Carolina. That is where NASCAR racing crews train workers to work intensely and under pressure while meeting goals through teamwork.[37]

Team Size

Team size affects how well members work together, handle disagreements, and make decisions. Having an odd numbers of members, such as in juries, helps prevent "ties" when votes need to be taken. And importantly, the number of potential interactions among team members increases geometrically as teams get bigger. Large team size creates communication and relationship problems for members and leaders. It's also easier for individuals to hide and engage in social loafing in larger teams.

The general conclusions from social science research are that very small teams—four members or fewer—may be dominated by one or two strong members. Six- to eight-member teams are probably best for creative problem solving because their members are better able to form trusting relationships and function more like families. When teams get larger than this, the added size and complexity can be difficult to manage.[38] Amazon.com's founder and CEO Jeff Bezos has a simple rule when it comes to the of product development teams: No team should be larger than two pizzas can feed.[39] Have you ever been on a team that was too large or too small? How did the members interact? And, how well did the team perform?

Stages of Team Development

Although having the right inputs is critical, it doesn't guarantee team effectiveness. **Team process** also plays an important role. This is the way that the members of a team actually work together as they transform inputs into output. Also called *group dynamics*, the process aspects of any group or team include how members develop norms and cohesiveness, share roles, make decisions, communicate, and handle conflicts.[40] Importantly, teams experience different process challenges as they pass through the stages of team development—forming, storming, norming, performing, and adjourning.[41]

> **Team process** is the way team members work together to accomplish tasks.

Forming Stage
The forming stage involves the first entry of individual members into a team. This is a time of initial task orientation and interpersonal testing. When people first come together, they ask questions: "What can or does this team offer me?" "What will I be asked to contribute?" "Can my needs be met while I serve the task needs of the team?"

In the forming stage individuals begin to identify with other members and with the team itself. They are concerned about getting acquainted, establishing relationships, discovering what behavior is acceptable, and learning how others perceive the team's task. This may also be a time when some members rely on others who appear "powerful" or especially "knowledgeable." Prior experience with team members in other situations and personal impressions of organization culture, goals, and practices may affect emerging relationships between members. Difficulties in the forming stage tend to be greater in more culturally and demographically diverse teams.

Storming Stage
Figure 17.4 shows the storming stage as part of a "critical zone" in team development. It is a period of high emotionality and can be hard to pass through successfully. Tensions often emerge over tasks and interpersonal concerns. There may be periods of outright hostility and infighting. Coalitions or cliques may form around personalities or interests. Subgroups may form around faultlines defined by areas of agreement and disagreement. Conflict also may develop as members compete to impose their preferences on other members and to become influential.

Important changes occur in the storming stage as task agendas become clarified and members begin to understand one another's styles. Attention begins to shift toward obstacles

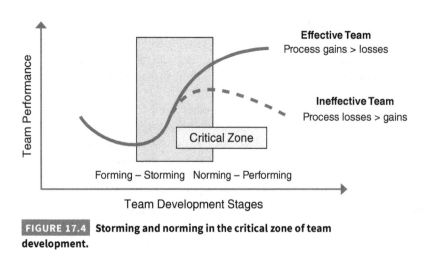

FIGURE 17.4   **Storming and norming in the critical zone of team development.**

that stand in the way of task accomplishment. Efforts are made to find ways to meet team goals while also satisfying members' individual needs. Getting through this zone with success can create long-term gains while failures create long-lasting problems.

Norming Stage

It is in the norming stage that team members begin to cooperate. Shared rules of conduct emerge and the team develops a sense of leadership members start to occupy and fulfill key roles. Interpersonal hostilities start to diminish and harmony is emphasized, but minority viewpoints may still be discouraged.

The norming stage also is part of the critical zone of team development. As members develop initial feelings of closeness, a division of labor, and shared expectations, this helps protect the team from disintegration. In fact, holding the team together may seem more important than accomplishing important tasks.

Performing Stage

Teams in the performing stage are more mature, organized, and well functioning. They score high on the criteria of team maturity shown in **Figure 17.5**.[42] Performing is a stage of integration in which members are able to deal in creative ways with complex tasks and interpersonal conflicts. The team operates with a clear and stable structure, and members are motivated by team goals. The primary challenges in the performing stage are to continue to refine how the team operates and to build relationships that keep everyone working well together as an integrated unit.

Adjourning Stage

The final stage of team development is adjourning, when team members prepare to achieve closure and disband. Temporary committees, task forces, and project teams should disband with a sense that important goals have been accomplished. This can be an emotional period after team members have worked together intensely for a period of time. Adjourning is a time when it is important to acknowledge everyone's contributions, praise them, and celebrate the team's success. A team ideally disbands with everyone feeling they would like to work together again in the future.

Norms and Cohesiveness

A **team norm** is a behavioral expectation, rule, or standard to be followed by team members.

A **team norm** is a behavioral expectation of team members.[43] It is a "rule" or "standard" that guides behavior. Typical norms relate to things like helpfulness, participation, timeliness, work quality, creativity, and innovation. A team's performance norm is critical, as it defines the level

	Very poor			Very good	
1. Trust among members	1	2	3	4	5
2. Feedback mechanisms	1	2	3	4	5
3. Open communications	1	2	3	4	5
4. Approach to decisions	1	2	3	4	5
5. Leadership sharing	1	2	3	4	5
6. Acceptance of goals	1	2	3	4	5
7. Valuing diversity	1	2	3	4	5
8. Member cohesiveness	1	2	3	4	5
9. Support for each other	1	2	3	4	5
10. Performance norms	1	2	3	4	5

FIGURE 17.5 Criteria for assessing the maturity of a team.

of work effort and performance that members are expected to contribute. Work groups and teams with positive performance norms are more successful accomplishing task objectives than teams with negative performance norms.

Managing Team Norms   Team leaders should help and encourage members to develop positive norms. During the forming and storming stages of development, norms relating to expected attendance and levels of commitment are important. By the time the performing stage is reached, norms relating to adaptability and change become relevant. Here are some things leaders can do to help their teams build positive norms:[44]

- Act as a positive role model.
- Reinforce desired behaviors with rewards.
- Control results by performance reviews and regular feedback.
- Train and orient new members to adopt desired behaviors.
- Recruit and select new members who exhibit desired behaviors.
- Hold regular meetings to discuss progress and ways of improving.
- Use team decision-making methods to reach agreement.

There is growing research interest in the extent to which members of teams display virtuousness and share a commitment to moral behavior. **Team virtuousness** is described as the extent to which members adopt norms that encourage shared commitments to moral behavior. Scholars highlight five norms of moral behavior for special attention by team leaders and members alike.[45] *Optimism* expects team members to strive for success even after setbacks. *Forgiveness* expects team members to forgive one another's mistakes and avoid assigning blame. *Trust* expects team members to be courteous and interact in respectful, trusting ways. *Compassion* expects team members to help and support one another and show kindness in difficult times.*Integrity* expects team members to be honest in what they do and say while working together.

> **Team virtuousness** indicates the extent to which members adopt norms that encourage shared commitments to moral behavior.

Managing Team Cohesiveness   Team members vary in their adherence to established group norms. Conformity to norms is largely determined by **team cohesiveness**, the degree to which members are attracted to and motivated to remain part of a team.[46] Members of teams that are highly cohesive value their membership and strive to maintain positive relationships with other members. Because of this, they tend to conform to team norms. In the extreme, violation of a norm on a highly cohesive team can result in a member being expelled or socially ostracized.

> **team cohesiveness** is the degree to which members are attracted to and motivated to remain part of a team.

Figure 17.6 shows the power of cohesiveness. The "best-case" scenario is a team with high cohesiveness and a high performance norm. Strong conformity to norms by members

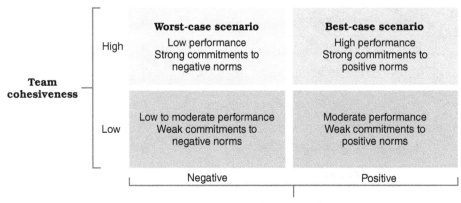

FIGURE 17.6   **How cohesiveness and norms influence team performance.**

of "high-high" teams is likely to have a beneficial effect on team performance. Contrast this with the "worst-case" scenario of high cohesiveness and a low performance norm. Members of "high-low" teams conform to the low performance norm and restrict their work efforts to adhere to the norm.

We've already discussed ways to build positive norms. But, managers and team leaders also must be good at building cohesiveness as well. This can be done in the following ways:

- Create agreement on team goals.
- Reward team rather than individual results.
- Increase membership homogeneity.
- Increase interactions among members.
- Decrease team size.
- Introduce competition with other teams.
- Provide physical isolation from other teams.

Task and Maintenance Roles

A **task activity** is an action taken by a team member that directly contributes to the team's performance purpose.

A **maintenance activity** is an action taken by a team member that supports the emotional life of the team.

Distributed leadership is when all members of a team contribute helpful task and maintenance behaviors.

Research on collectives such as groups and teams identifies two types of roles or activities that are essential if members are to work well together.[47] **Task activities** contribute directly to the team's performance purpose, while **maintenance activities** support the emotional life of the team as an ongoing social system.

Although the team leader or supervisor should give these activities special attention, the responsibility for task and maintenance activities also should be shared and distributed among all team members. Anyone can help lead a team by satisfying these needs. The concept of **distributed leadership** makes every member continually responsible for recognizing when task or maintenance activities are needed, and taking actions to provide them.

Leading through task activities involves making an effort to define and solve problems, and to advance work activities toward performance results. Without the relevant task activities such as initiating agendas, sharing information, and others shown in **Figure 17.7**, teams have difficulty accomplishing their objectives. *Leading through maintenance activities*, by contrast, helps strengthen the team as a social system. When maintenance activities such as gatekeeping, encouraging others, and reducing tensions are performed, good interpersonal and working relationships are achieved, increasing the probability that the team will stay together over the longer term.

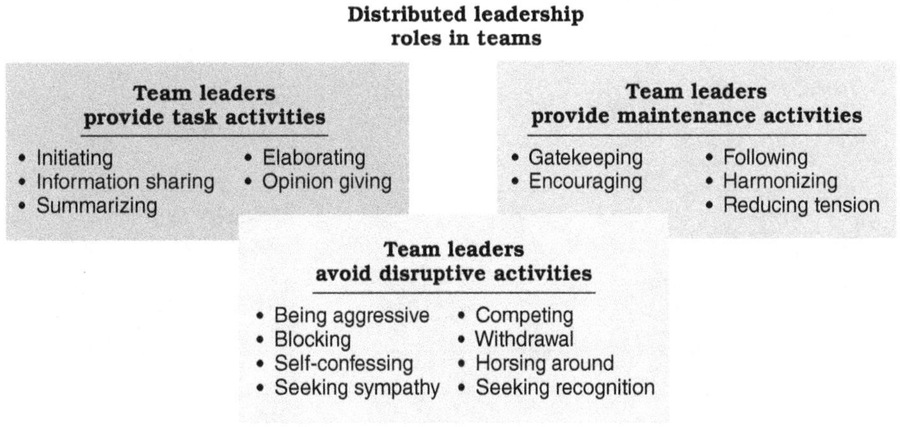

**Distributed leadership
roles in teams**

**Team leaders
provide task activities**

- Initiating
- Information sharing
- Summarizing
- Elaborating
- Opinion giving

**Team leaders
provide maintenance activities**

- Gatekeeping
- Encouraging
- Following
- Harmonizing
- Reducing tension

**Team leaders
avoid disruptive activities**

- Being aggressive
- Blocking
- Self-confessing
- Seeking sympathy
- Competing
- Withdrawal
- Horsing around
- Seeking recognition

FIGURE 17.7 **Distributed leadership helps teams meet task and maintenance needs.**

Both team task and maintenance activities stand in contrast to **disruptive activities** such as showing incivility toward others, withdrawing from discussions, and fooling around. These and any similar behaviors are self-serving and detract from team effectiveness. Unfortunately, very few teams are immune to dysfunctional behavior. Every team member shares responsibility for minimizing it.

Disruptive activities are self-serving behaviors that interfere with team effectiveness.

Communication Networks

There is considerable research on the team interaction patterns and communication networks shown in **Figure 17.8**.[48] When team members must interact intensively and work closely together on complex tasks, this need is best met by a **decentralized communication network**. Sometimes called the *all-channel or star communication network*, this is where all members communicate directly with one another. At other times team members can work on tasks independently, with the required work divided among them. This creates a **centralized communication network**, sometimes called a *wheel or chain communication structure*. In this pattern of interaction, activities are coordinated and results pooled by a central point of control.

A **decentralized communication network** allows all members to communicate directly with one another.

In a **centralized communication network**, communication flows only between individual members and a hub, or center point.

When teams are composed of subgroups with issue-specific disagreements, such as a over the best way to achieve a goal, the resulting interaction pattern often involves a **restricted communication network**. Here, polarized subgroups may even engage in conflict. Communication between subgroups is limited and biased, with negative consequences for group process and effectiveness.

In a **restricted communication network**, subgroups have limited communication with one another.

The best teams use these communication networks in the right ways and at the right times. Centralized communication networks seem to work better on simple tasks.[49] These tasks lend themselves to more centralized control because they require little creativity, information processing, problem solving, or collaborative effort. The reverse is true for more complex tasks, for which interacting groups perform better. Decentralized communication networks support the more intense interactions and information sharing required

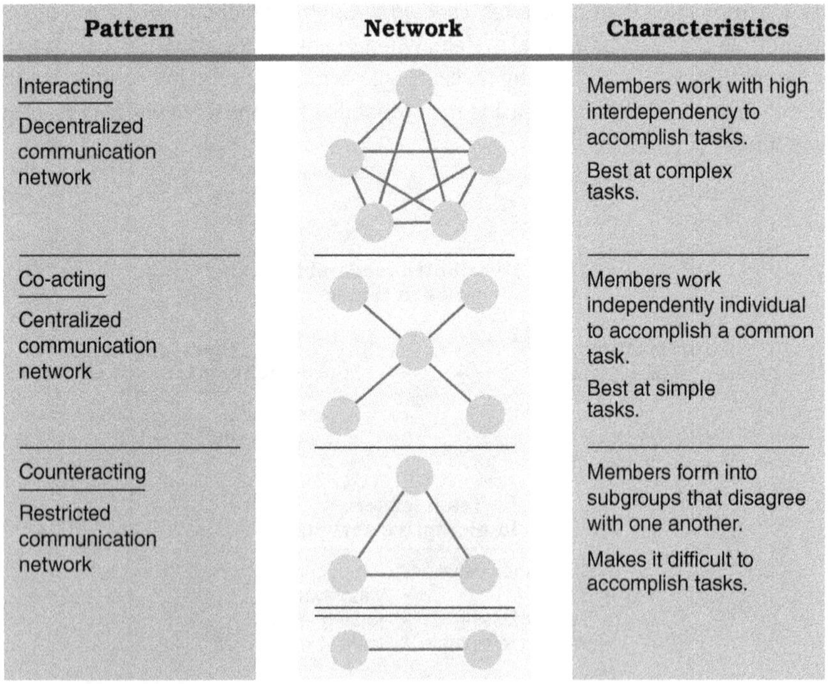

Pattern	Network	Characteristics
Interacting Decentralized communication network		Members work with high interdependency to accomplish tasks. Best at complex tasks.
Co-acting Centralized communication network		Members work independently individual to accomplish a common task. Best at simple tasks.
Counteracting Restricted communication network		Members form into subgroups that disagree with one another. Makes it difficult to accomplish tasks.

FIGURE 17.8 Interaction patterns and communication networks in teams.

to perform complicated tasks. Even conflicting groups can be useful. When teams get complacent, the conflict that emerges can be a source of creativity and critical evaluation. But when these subgroups stop communicating and helping one another, task accomplishment typically suffers.

Learning Check

LEARNING OBJECTIVE 17.3

Summarize the key processes through which teams work.

Be Sure You Can • define team *effectiveness* • identify inputs that influence effectiveness • discuss how membership diversity influences team effectiveness • list five stages of group development • define *group norm* and list ways to build positive group norms • define *cohesiveness* and list ways to increase group cohesion • explain how norms and cohesiveness influence team performance • differentiate between task, maintenance, and disruptive activities • describe the use of decentralized and centralized communication networks

17.4 | Decision Making in Teams

WileyPLUS

See Author Video

LEARNING OBJECTIVE 17.4

Discuss the ins and outs of team decision making.

Learn More About

Ways teams make decisions • Advantages and disadvantages of team decisions • Groupthink

Decision making is the process of making choices among alternative possible courses of action.

Decision making is the process of making choices among alternative courses of action. And, it is one of the most important processes that occurs in teams. The best teams use a variety of decision-making methods as they face different kinds of problems.[50] But as with other aspects of teamwork, decision making can be very challenging.[51] Edgar Schein, a respected scholar and consultant, says all this can be better understood when we recognize that teams use at least six methods to make decisions: lack of response, authority rule, minority rule, majority rule, consensus, and unanimity.[52]

Ways Teams Make Decisions

In *decision by lack of response*, one idea after another is suggested without any discussion taking place. When the team finally accepts an idea, all others have been bypassed by simple lack of response rather than by critical evaluation. The last alternative is chosen by default.

In *decision by authority rule*, the leader, manager, committee head, or other authority figure makes a decision for the team. This can be done with or without discussion and is very time-efficient. Whether the decision ultimately is good or bad, however, depends on whether the authority figure has the necessary information and expertise, and on how well this approach is accepted by other team members.

In *decision by minority rule*, two or three people are able to dominate or "railroad" the team into making a particular decision. This often is done by providing a suggestion and then forcing quick agreement by challenging the team with such statements as "Does anyone object? No? Well, let's go ahead then."

One of the most common things teams do, particularly when signs of disagreement emerge, is to take a vote and arrive at a *decision by majority rule*. Although this is broadly consistent with the democratic political process, it has some problems. The very act of voting can create coalitions as some members become "winners" and others "losers." Those in the minority—the "losers"—may feel left out without having had a fair say. They may be unenthusiastic about implementing the decision of the "majority," and lingering resentments may decrease team effectiveness. Such possibilities are well illustrated in the political arena, where candidates receiving small and controversial victory margins end up struggling against entrenched opposition from the losing party.

Teams often are encouraged to achieve *decision by consensus*. This is where full discussion leads to one alternative being favored by most members, and the other members agree to support it. When consensus is reached, even those who may have opposed the decision know that their views have been heard. Consensus does not require unanimous support, but it does require that members be able to argue, engage in reasonable conflict, and still get along with and respect one another.[53] True consensus occurs only when dissenting members have been able to speak their mind and know they've been heard.[54]

A *decision by unanimity* may be the ideal situation. "Unanimity" means that everyone agrees on what the team will do. This is a logically perfect method, but it also is extremely difficult to achieve in practice. One of the reasons that teams sometimes turn to authority decisions, majority voting, or even minority decisions is the difficulty of managing team processes to achieve consensus or unanimity.

Insight: Learn about Yourself | Sports teams whose members play together the longest win more because the players get to know each other's moves and playing tendencies.

Don't Short Your Team Contributions

Positive **team contributions** are things that members do to help their team succeed at their tasks and help one another enjoy the experience of being on the team.

Scene—Hospital operating room: Scholars notice that heart surgeons have lower death rates for similar procedures performed in hospitals where they do more operations than in hospitals where they do fewer operations.

Why? Researchers say the operations are more likely to be successful because the doctors in the better hospitals spend more time working together with members of their surgical teams. It's not only the surgeon's skills that count; they say "The skills of the team, and of the organization, matter." The ability to practice together increases how effectively the skills of the members of the surgical team can be integrated with one another. Practice increases the potency of team contributions.

Scene—NBA basketball court: Scholars find that basketball teams win more games the longer the players have been together.

Why? Researchers claim it's a "teamwork effect." Sports teams whose members have played together the longest tend to win more games because the players get to know each other's moves and playing tendencies. Players develop a sense, over time, of what their teammates are thinking and where they will be on the court before they get there. Knowledge of other team members increases the benefits of team contributions.

A large part of your career success will depend on how well you work in and lead teams. Take a look at the list of "must have" team skills presented here. Do you have the skills portfolio and personal commitment to make truly valuable team contributions?

"Must Have" Team Skills

- Encouraging and motivating others
- Accepting suggestions
- Listening to different points of view
- Communicating information and ideas
- Persuading others to cooperate
- Resolving and negotiating conflict
- Building consensus
- Fulfilling commitments
- Avoiding disruptive acts and words

Get To Know Yourself Better

Have a serious conversation with others who know and work with you about your performance as a team member and team leader. What do you expect that they'll say? Ask for suggestions on how you could improve your team contributions. Prepare a short presentation to a potential employer describing your team skills. Write a set of notes on how you will describe yourself and what examples you will give to support your potential as a team leader and member.

Advantages and Disadvantages of Team Decisions

When teams take time to make decisions by consensus or unanimity, they gain special advantages over teams relying more on individual or minority decision methods.[55] The process of making a true team decision increases the availability of useful information, knowledge, and expertise. It expands the number of action alternatives that teams examine, and helps to avoid bad decisions that emerge through tunnel vision and the consideration of only one or a few options. Team decisions also increase members' understanding and acceptance. This helps to build commitment to work hard to implement decisions the team has made together.

The potential disadvantages of team decision making trace largely to difficulties with group processes. It can be hard to reach agreement when many people are trying to make a team decision. There may be social pressure to conform and even minority domination, where some members feel forced or "railroaded" into accepting a decision advocated by one vocal individual or small coalition. The time required to make team decisions also can be a real disadvantage. As more people are involved in the dialogue and discussion, decision making takes longer. This added time may be costly, even prohibitively so under certain circumstances.

Groupthink

One of the potential downsides of team decision making is what psychologist Irving Janis called **groupthink**, the tendency for highly cohesive teams to lose their critical evaluative capabilities.[56] Although it may seem counterintuitive, a high level of cohesiveness can be a disadvantage if strong feelings of team loyalty make it hard for members to criticize and evaluate one another's ideas and suggestions objectively.

Members of very cohesive teams may feel so strongly about the group that they won't say or do anything that might harm it. They end up publicly agreeing with actual or suggested courses of action that they have serious private, unspoken doubts or objections about. Teams experiencing groupthink display the following symptoms.

- *Illusions of invulnerability*—Members assume that the team is too good for criticism or is beyond attack.
- *Rationalizing unpleasant and disconfirming data*—Members refuse to accept contradictory data or to thoroughly consider alternatives.
- *Belief in inherent group morality*—Members act as though the group is inherently right and above reproach.
- *Stereotyping competitors as weak, evil, and stupid*—Members refuse to look realistically at other groups.
- *Applying direct pressure to deviants to conform to group wishes*—Members refuse to tolerate anyone who suggests the team may be wrong.
- *Self-censorship by members*—Members refuse to communicate personal concerns to the whole team.
- *Illusions of unanimity*—Members accept consensus prematurely, without testing its completeness.
- *Mind guarding*—Members protect the team from hearing disturbing ideas or outside viewpoints.

Groupthink occurs as the desire to hold the team together and avoid disagreements results in poor decisions. Janis suggests that this played a role in well-known historical disasters such as the lack of preparedness of U.S. naval forces for the Japanese attack on Pearl Harbor, the Bay of Pigs invasion under President Kennedy, the many roads that led to the United States' difficulties in the Vietnam War, and the space shuttle *Challenger* explosion.

Groupthink is a tendency for highly cohesive teams to lose their evaluative capabilities.

When you are leading or are part of a team heading toward groupthink, don't assume there's no way out. After suffering the Bay of Pigs fiasco, for example, President Kennedy approached the Cuban missile crisis quite differently. He purposely did not attend some cabinet discussions and allowed the group to deliberate without him. His absence helped the cabinet members talk more openly and to be less likely to say things that were consistent with his own thinking. When a decision was finally reached, the crisis was successfully resolved.

In addition to having the leader stay absent for some team discussions, Janis has other advice on how to get a team that is moving toward groupthink back on track. You can assign one member to act as a critical evaluator or "devil's advocate" during each meeting. Subgroups can be assigned to work on issues and then share their findings with the team as a whole. Outsiders can be brought in to observe and participate in team meetings and offer their advice and viewpoints on both team processes and tentative decisions. The team can also hold a "second chance" meeting after an initial decision is made to review, change, or even cancel the decision. With actions like these available, there's no reason to let groupthink lead a team down the wrong pathways.

Learning Check

LEARNING OBJECTIVE 17.4

Discuss the ins and outs of team decision making.

Be Sure You Can • illustrate how groups make decisions by authority rule, minority rule, majority rule, consensus, and unanimity • list advantages and disadvantages of group decision making • define *groupthink* and identify its symptoms

Management Learning Review: Get Prepared for Quizzes and Exams

Summary

LEARNING OBJECTIVE 17.1   Explain the ways teams contribute to organizations.

- A team is a collection of people working together interdependently to accomplish a common goal.
- Teams help organizations perform through synergy—the creation of a whole that is greater than the sum of its parts.
- Teams help satisfy important needs for their members by providing sources of job support and social satisfactions.
- Social loafing and other problems can limit the performance of teams.
- Organizations operate as networks of formal and informal teams and groups.

For Discussion Why do people often tolerate social loafers at work?

LEARNING OBJECTIVE 17.2   Describe current trends in the use of teams in organizations.

- Committees and task forces are used to accomplish special tasks and projects.
- Cross-functional teams bring members together from different departments and help improve lateral relations and integration in organizations.
- New developments in information technology are making virtual teams commonplace at work, but virtual teams also pose special management challenges.

- Self-managing teams are changing organizations, as team members perform many tasks previously done by their supervisors.
- Team building engages members in a process of assessment and action planning to improve teamwork and future performance.

For Discussion What are some of the things that virtual teams probably can't do as well as face-to-face teams?

LEARNING OBJECTIVE 17.3 Summarize the key processes through which teams work.

- An effective team achieves high levels of task performance, member satisfaction, and team viability.
- Important team inputs include the organizational setting, nature of the task, size, and membership characteristics.
- A team matures through various stages of development, including forming, storming, norming, performing, and adjourning.
- Norms are the standards or rules of conduct that influence team members' behavior; cohesion is the attractiveness of the team to its members.
- In highly cohesive teams, members tend to conform to norms; the best situation is a team with positive performance norms and high cohesiveness.

- Distributed leadership occurs as members share in meeting a team's task and maintenance needs.
- Effective teams make use of alternative communication structures, such as centralized and decentralized networks, to best complete tasks with distinct communication requirements.

For Discussion What can be done if a team gets trapped in the storming stage of group development?

LEARNING OBJECTIVE 17.4 Discuss the ins and outs of team decision making.

- Teams can make decisions by lack of response, authority rule, minority rule, majority rule, consensus, and unanimity.
- Although group decisions often make more information available for problem solving and generate more understanding and commitment, they are slower than individual decisions and may involve social pressures to conform.
- Groupthink is the tendency for members of highly cohesive teams to lose their critical evaluative capabilities and make poor decisions.

For Discussion Is it possible that groupthink doesn't only occur when groups are highly cohesive, but also when they are pre-cohesive?

Self-Test 17

Multiple-Choice Questions

1. When a group of people is able to achieve more than what its members could by working individually, this is called _____.

   a. social loafing
   b. consensus
   c. viability
   d. synergy

2. One of the recommended strategies for dealing with a group member who engages in social loafing is to _____.

   a. redefine tasks to make individual contributions more visible
   b. ask another member to encourage this person to work harder
   c. give the person extra rewards and hope he or she will feel guilty
   d. just forget about it

3. In an organization operating with self-managing teams, the traditional role of _____ is replaced by the role of team leader.

   a. chief executive officer
   b. first-line supervisor
   c. middle manager
   d. general manager

4. An effective team is defined as one that achieves high levels of task performance, member satisfaction, and _____.

   a. resource efficiency
   b. future viability
   c. consensus
   d. creativity

5. In the open-systems model of teams, the _____ is an important input factor.

   a. communication network
   b. decision-making method
   c. performance norm
   d. set of membership characteristics

6. The team effectiveness equation states the following: Team effectiveness = Quality of inputs + (_____ – Process losses).

   a. Process gains
   b. Leadership impact
   c. Membership ability
   d. Problem complexity

7. A basic rule of team dynamics states that the greater the _____ in a team, the greater the conformity to norms.

   a. membership diversity
   b. cohesiveness
   c. task structure
   d. competition among members

8. Members of a team tend to start to get coordinated and comfortable with one another in the _____ stage of team development.

   a. forming
   b. norming
   c. performing
   d. adjourning

9. One way for a manager to build positive norms within a team is to _____.

   a. act as a positive role model
   b. increase group size
   c. introduce groupthink
   d. isolate the team

10. To increase the cohesiveness of a group, a manager would be best off _____.

    a. starting competition with other groups

    b. increasing the group size

    c. acting as a positive role model

    d. introducing a new member

11. Groupthink is most likely to occur in teams that are _____.

    a. large in size

    b. diverse in membership

    c. high-performing

    d. highly cohesive

12. A team member who does a good job at summarizing discussion, offering new ideas, and clarifying points made by others is providing leadership by contributing _____ activities to the group process.

    a. required   c. disruptive

    b. task   d. maintenance

13. A _____ decision is one in which all members agree on the course of action to be taken.

    a. consensus   c. majority

    b. unanimous   d. nominal

14. A team performing very creative and unstructured tasks is most likely to succeed using _____.

    a. a decentralized communication network

    b. decisions by majority rule

    c. decisions by minority rule

    d. more task than maintenance activities

15. Which of the following approaches can help groups avoid groupthink in situations where there is a very strong leader?

    a. Have the leader stay absent from some team meetings.

    b. Be sure to make decisions by minority rule.

    c. Always vote when disagreements arise.

    d. Remind everyone about the inherent morality of the group.

Short-Response Questions

16. How can a manager improve team effectiveness by modifying inputs?

17. What is the relationship among a team's cohesiveness, performance norms, and performance results?

18. List two symptoms that would alert a manager that a team is suffering from groupthink. What could this manager do to counteract each of these symptoms?

19. What makes a self-managing team different from a traditional work group?

Essay Question

20. Marcos Martinez has just been appointed manager of a production team operating the 11 p.m. to 7 a.m. shift in a large manufacturing firm. An experienced manager, Marcos is pleased that the team members really like and get along well with one another, but they also appear to be restricting their task outputs to the minimum acceptable levels. What could Marcos do to improve things in this situation, and why should he do them?

Career Skills & Competencies: Make Yourself Valuable!

Evaluate Career Situations

What Would You Do?

1. New Task Force

It's time for the first meeting of the task force that you have been assigned to lead. This is a big opportunity, since it's the first time your supervisor has given you this level of responsibility. There are seven members of the task force, all of whom are your peers and co-workers. The task is to develop a proposal for increased use of flexible work schedules and telecommuting in the organization. What will your agenda be for the first meeting, and what opening statement will you make?

2. Declining Performance

You've been concerned for quite some time about a drop in the performance of your work team. Although everyone seems to like one another, the "numbers" in terms of measured daily performance are on the decline. It's time to act. What will you look at, and why, to determine where and how steps might be taken to improve the effectiveness of the work team?

3. Groupthink Possibilities

The members of the executive compensation committee that you are chairing show a high level of cohesiveness. It's obvious that they enjoy being part of the committee and are proud to be on the board of directors. But the committee is about to approve extraordinarily high bonuses for the CEO and five other senior executives. This is occurring at a time when executive pay is getting a lot of criticism from the press, unions, and the public at large. What can you do to make sure groupthink isn't causing this committee to potentially make a bad decision? What clues might you use to determine whether groupthink is having an influence on what is taking place?

Reflect on the Self-Assessment

Team Leader Skills

Instructions

Consider your experience in groups and work teams while completing the following inventory. Rate yourself on each item using the following scale (circle the number that applies).[57]

1 = Almost never   2 = Seldom
3 = Sometimes   4 = Usually
5 = Almost always

Question: "How do I behave in team leadership situations?"

1 2 3 4 5   **1.** Facilitate communications with and among team members between team meetings.

1 2 3 4 5   **2.** Provide feedback/coaching to individual team members on their performance.

1 2 3 4 5   **3.** Encourage creative and "out-of-the-box" thinking.

1 2 3 4 5   **4.** Continue to clarify stakeholder needs/expectations.

1 2 3 4 5   **5.** Keep team members' responsibilities and activities focused within the team's objectives and goals.

1 2 3 4 5   **6.** Organize and run effective and productive team meetings.

1 2 3 4 5   **7.** Demonstrate integrity and personal commitment.

1 2 3 4 5   **8.** Have excellent persuasive and influencing skills.

1 2 3 4 5   **9.** Respect and leverage the team's cross-functional diversity.

1 2 3 4 5   **10.** Recognize and reward individual contributions to team performance.

1 2 3 4 5   **11.** Use the appropriate decision-making style for specific issues.

1 2 3 4 5   **12.** Facilitate and encourage border management with the team's key stakeholders.

1 2 3 4 5   **13.** Ensure that the team meets its commitments.

1 2 3 4 5   **14.** Bring team issues and problems to the team's attention and focus on constructive problem solving.

1 2 3 4 5   **15.** Provide a clear vision and direction for the team.

Self-Assessment Scoring

The inventory measures seven dimensions of team leadership. Add your scores for the items listed next to each dimension below to get an indication of your potential strengths and weaknesses.

1, 9   Building the Team
2, 10   Developing People
3, 11   Team Problem Solving and Decision Making
4, 12   Stakeholder Relations
5, 13   Team Performance
6, 14   Team Process
7, 8, 15   Providing Personal Leadership

Interpretation

The higher your score, the more confident you are on the particular skill and leadership capability. Consider giving this inventory to people who have worked with you in teams and have them rate you. Compare the results to your self-assessment. Also, remember it is doubtful that any one team leader is capable of exhibiting all of the skills listed. More and more, organizations are emphasizing teams that blend a variety of skills, rather than depending on the vision of the single, heroic leader figure. As long as the necessary leadership skills are represented within the membership of the team, it is more likely that the team will be healthy and achieve a high level of performance. Of course, the more skills you bring with you to team leadership situations, the better the team is likely to perform.

Contribute to the Class Exercise

Work Team Dynamics

Preparation

Think about your class work group, a work group you are involved in for another course, or any other group suggested by your instructor. Use this scale to indicate how often each of the following statements accurately reflects your experience in the group.[58]

1. All the time   2. Very often
3. Sometimes   4. Never happens

1. My ideas get a fair hearing.

2. I am encouraged to give innovative ideas and take risks.

3. Diverse opinions within the group are encouraged.

4. I have all the responsibility I want.

5. There is a lot of favoritism shown in the group.

6. Members trust one another to do their assigned work.

7. The group sets high standards of performance excellence.

8. People share and change jobs a lot in the group.

9. You can make mistakes and learn from them in this group.

10. This group has good operating rules.

Instructions

Form teams as assigned by your instructor. Ideally, this will be the group you have just rated. Have all members share their ratings, and then make one overall rating for the team as a whole. Circle the items for which there are the biggest differences of opinion. Discuss those items and try to determine what accounts for these differences. In general, the better a team scores on this instrument, the higher its creative potential. Make a list of the five most important things members believe they can do to help the team perform better. Nominate a spokesperson to summarize your discussion for the class as a whole.

Manage a Critical Incident

The Rejected Team Leader

You have been a team leader at a big-box electronics store for three years, and the team you supervise is great. Everyone is hard working, gets along really well, comes in early, stays late, helps one another, and gets the job done. The members go out together after work and are good friends with each other and with you. A week ago, your team was assigned exclusive responsibility for designing and setting up the upcoming product display for tablets and other mobile devices in an entire section of the store. Crystal—one of your team members—was especially excited about the project. She has been taking online courses at the local technical college and wants to move into advertising design as a career. Because the team works so well together, you had expected the whole process to go smoothly with a bunch of great display formats figured out for you to choose from. But by the end of the week, you'd only gotten one proposal from the team, and it wasn't

very good. You talked to each team member individually. They all stood behind the design the team had submitted. They got mad at you for suggesting that they come up with another design, and wouldn't even listen to you. They wouldn't tell you how they came up with the design, how they figured things out, or share any information with you at all. Even though you are the supervisor, you are also a friend, so it was hard when they reacted in such a hostile way to your feedback—particularly in light of the looming deadline.

Questions

What is happening in this team? These employees know and trust you, but you can't even get them to talk to you about what's happening—why? What can you do to get through the wall they've put around themselves? Why have you been shut out of the team in this way? What does it mean for the project and how you handle the team moving forward?

Collaborate on the Team Project

Superstars on the Team

During a period of reflection following a down cycle for his teams, Sasho Cirovski, head coach of the two-time NCAA Division I University of Maryland men's soccer team, came to a realization. "I was recruiting talent," he said. "I wasn't doing a very good job of recruiting leaders." With a change of strategy, his teams moved back to top-ranked national competition.

Question

What do you do with a "superstar" on your team?

Instructions

1. Everywhere you look—in entertainment, in sports, and in business—a lot of attention goes to the superstars. What is the record of teams and groups with superstars? Do they really outperform the rest?

2. What is the real impact of a superstar's presence on a team or in the workplace? What do they add? What do they cost? Consider the potential cost of having a superstar on a team within the equation: Benefits = Cost − Value. What is the bottom line of having a superstar on the team?

3. Interview the athletic coaches on your campus. Ask them the previous questions about superstars. Compare and contrast their answers. Interview players from various teams, and ask them the same questions.

4. Develop a set of guidelines for creating team effectiveness in a situation where a superstar is present. Be thorough and practical.

Analyze the Case Study

Auto Racing | When the Driver Takes a Back Seat

Go to **Management Cases for Critical Thinking** at the end of the book to find this case.

CHAPTER 18

Communication and Collaboration

Listening is the Key to Understanding

John Lund/Blend Images/Alamy Stock Photo

Kayak.com's former chief technology officer Paul English once placed a two-foot-tall elephant toy, Annabelle, in the conference room. "So often at work," he said, "people have issues that they can't resolve because they won't talk about it."

Chapter Quick Start

A lot of what we accomplish in life and at work depends on our ability to communicate well and collaborate with others. Recruiters look for job candidates with strong communication skills who can achieve positive impact through their writing and presentations, and in teamwork and interpersonal settings. The ability to communicate and collaborate also includes conflict and negotiation situations. How well we handle them can make the difference between success and failure when multiple interests are at play.

LEARNING OBJECTIVES

18.1 Identify the elements in the communication process.

18.2 Describe ways to improve the effectiveness of communication.

18.3 Discuss how conflict can be functional and managed successfully.

18.4 Explain ways to negotiate successfully and avoid negotiation pitfalls.

Career Readiness – What to Look for Inside

Thought Leadership

Analysis > *Make Data Your Friend*
Value of Performance Reviews Gets Increasing Scrutiny

Choices > *Think before You Act*
Tapping into the Science of Persuasion

Ethics > *Know Right from Wrong*
Blogging Is Easy, but Bloggers Should Beware

Insight > *Learn about Yourself*
Collaboration Begins with Communication and Networking

Skills Make You Valuable

- **Evaluate** *Career Situations:*
  What Would You Do?

- **Reflect** *On the Self-Assessment:*
  Conflict Management Strategies

- **Contribute** *To the Class Exercise:*
  Feedback Sensitivities

- **Manage** *A Critical Incident:*
  Headphones on in the Office

- **Collaborate** *On the Team Project:*
  How Words Count

- **Analyze** *The Case Study:*
  Snapchat: Snap the Story of the Moment

368

Whether you work at the top of an organization—building support for strategies and goals, or in teams at other levels—interacting with others to accomplish goals, your career toolkit must include the ability to achieve positive impact through communication and collaboration. You need **social capital**, the capacity to attract support and help from others to get things done. Whereas intellectual capital comes from what you know, social capital comes from the people you know and how well you relate to them. And, it's all about communication, connections, and relationships.

Social capital is a capacity to get things done with the support and help of others.

18.1 | The Communication Process

LEARNING OBJECTIVE 18.1

Identify the elements in the communication process.

WileyPLUS

See Author Video

> **Learn More About**
>
> Effective communication • Persuasion and credibility in communication • Communication barriers • Cross-cultural communication

Figure 18.1 describes **communication** as an interpersonal process of sending and receiving symbols with messages attached to them. This can be understood as a series of questions: "Who?" (*sender*) "says what?" (*message*) "in what ways?" (*channel*) "to whom?" (*receiver*) "with what result?" (*meaning*). It is through this process that people build and use social capital, exchange and share information, lead and inspire followers, and influence one another's attitudes, behaviors, and understanding.

Communication is the process of sending and receiving symbols with meanings attached.

Communication is the means for connecting with people to network, build relationships, and collaborate. It's also the glue that binds together the four functions of planning, organizing, leading, and controlling.[1] *Planning* is accomplished and plans are shared through the communication of information. *Organizing* identifies and structures communication links among people and positions. *Leading* uses communication to achieve positive influence over organization members and stakeholders. *Controlling* relies on communication to process information to measure performance results.

Effective Communication

Most of us think we're good at communicating. However, this confidence can be a significant problem in the communication process: We take our abilities for granted and end up disappointed when things go wrong. Getting things to "go right" requires alertness to issues of "effectiveness" and "efficiency" in the ways we communicate. **Effective communication** occurs when the sender's message is fully understood by the receiver. **Efficient communication** occurs at minimum cost in terms of resources expended. It's great when our communications are both effective and efficient. But, trade offs between the two are common.

In **effective communication** the intended meaning is fully understood by the receiver.

Efficient communication occurs at minimum cost.

An efficient communication may not be effective. We are often too busy or too lazy to invest enough time to make sure that communication is effective. Instead, we shoot for efficiency.

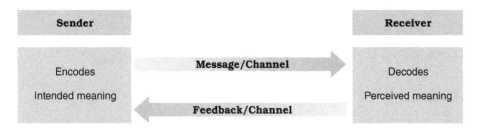

FIGURE 18.1 **The interactive two-way process of interpersonal communication.**

Picture your instructor taking the time to communicate individually with each student about this chapter. It would be virtually impossible and very costly in terms of the instructor's time. This is why managers, co-workers, and even family members often communicate with voice mail, texts, and e-mails rather than visiting face to face. These choices are efficient but not always effective ways of communicating. Although an e-mail sent to several people on a distribution list may save the sender's time, not all receivers might interpret the message in the same way.

By the same token, an effective communication may not be efficient. If a team leader visits each team member individually to explain new procedures, this may guarantee that everyone truly understands the change. But, it also requires a lot of the leader's time. And rightly or wrongly, saving time may be our top priority.

Persuasion and Credibility in Communication

Persuasive communication presents a message in a manner that causes the other person to support it.

Credible communication earns trust, respect, and integrity in the eyes of others.

Communication is not only about sharing information or being "heard." It's about the intent of one party to influence or motivate the other. **Persuasive communication** results in a recipient agreeing with or supporting the message.[2] Managers, for example, get things done by drawing on social capital in their relationships with peers, teammates, co-workers, and supervisors. Their success often comes about more through convincing than by order giving. Scholar and consultant Jay Conger says that without credibility there is little chance that persuasion can be successful.[3] He describes **credible communication** based on trust, respect, and integrity in the eyes of others.

Credibility is gained through expertise, when you are knowledgeable about an issue or have a successful track record dealing with similar issues. In a hiring situation where you are trying to persuade team members to select candidate A rather than B, for example, you must be able to defend your reasons. And, it will always be better if your past recommendations turned out to be good for the team.

Credibility is also gained through relationships, when you work well and get along with the people to be persuaded. In a hiring situation where you want to persuade your boss to provide a special bonus package to attract top job candidates, for example, having a good relationship with your boss can add credibility to your request. This is social capital again: It is always easier to get someone to do what you want if that person likes you.

Communication Barriers

Noise is anything that interferes with the effectiveness of communication.

Scene: A Japanese executive used an interpreter when meeting with representatives of the firm's American joint venture partner. *Result:* About 20% of his intended meaning was lost in the exchange between himself and the interpreter, while another 20% was lost between the interpreter and the Americans.[4]

Noise, as shown in **Figure 18.2**, is anything that interferes with the effectiveness of the communication process. And, this isn't just a cross-cultural issue. Do you recognize its

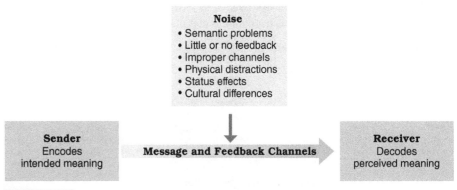

FIGURE 18.2 Downsides of noise, shown as anything that interferes with the effectiveness of the communication process.

everyday potential, perhaps in conversations across generational cultures? Common sources of noise include information filtering, poor choice of channels, poor written or oral expression, failure to recognize nonverbal signals, and physical distractions.

Information Filtering

"Criticize my boss? I don't have the right to." "I'd get fired." "It's her company, not mine." These comments display tendencies toward **information filtering**—the intentional distortion of information to make it appear favorable to the recipient. Management author and consultant Tom Peters calls it "Management Enemy Number 1." He even goes so far as to say that "once you become a boss you will never hear the unadulterated truth again."[5]

The problem with information filtering is that someone tells the boss only what they think he or she wants to hear. It's a reluctance "to speak truth to power." Whether the reason is career protection, fear of retribution for bringing bad news, unwillingness to identify personal mistakes, or just a general desire to please, the end result is the same. The higher level receives biased and inaccurate information from below and ends up making bad decisions.

> **Information filtering** is the intentional distortion of information to make it appear more favorable to the recipient.

Poor Choice of Channels

A **communication channel** is the pathway or medium through which a message is conveyed from sender to receiver. **Figure 18.3** shows how communication channels vary in richness from low and impersonal at the one extreme to high and personal at the other. Good communicators choose the right channel or combination of channels to accomplish their intended purpose.[6]

Written channels—paper or electronic—are most acceptable for simple messages that are easy to convey, and for those that need to go quickly to a lot of people. They also are useful when it is important to document information or directives. But, it's important to remember that these messages are largely impersonal and one-way interactions with only limited opportunity for feedback from recipients.

Spoken channels—face-to-face or electronic—work best for complex and difficult messages and where immediate feedback to the sender is valuable. They are more personal and more likely to be perceived by the receiver as supportive or inspirational.

> A **communication channel** is the pathway through which a message moves from sender to receiver.

Poor Written or Oral Expression

Communication will only be effective when the sender expresses the message in a clearly understood way. Words must be well chosen and used properly, something we often fail to do. Consider the following "bafflegab" found among some executive communications.[7]

A business report said: "Consumer elements are continuing to stress the fundamental necessity of a stabilization of the price structure at a lower level than exists at the present time."

Translation: Consumers keep saying that prices must go down and stay down.

A manager said: "Substantial economies were affected in this division by increasing the time interval between distributions of data-eliciting forms to business entities."

Translation: The division saved money by sending out fewer questionnaires.

A university president said: "We have strived to be as transparent as possible about the strategic alliance plans within the confines of our . . . closed negotiations."

Translation: The negotiations were confidential.

Low Richness • Impersonal • One-way • Fast	Posts, e-bulletins, blogs	Memos, letters, reports	E-mail, voice-mail, texts	Telephone calls, chats	Face-to-face meetings, virtual conferencing	High Richness • Personal • Two-way • Slow

Richness of Communication Channel

 FIGURE 18.3 **Richness of alternative communication channels.**

Nonverbal communication takes place through gestures and body language.

Failure to Recognize Nonverbal Signals

Nonverbal communication takes place through gestures, facial expressions, body posture, eye contact, and the use of interpersonal space. Research shows that the majority of a face-to-face message's impact comes through nonverbal communication.[8] A lack of gestures and other nonverbal signals is one of the weaknesses of voice mail, texts, and e-mails. It's hard for things like emoticons to make up for their absence.

A **mixed message** results when words communicate one message while actions, body language, or appearance communicate something else.

Think of how nonverbal signals play out in your own communications.[9] Sometimes our body language "talks" even as we maintain silence. And when we do speak, our body may "say" different things than our words convey. This is called a **mixed message**—where words communicate one message while actions and body language communicate something else. Watch how people behave in a meeting. A person who feels under attack may move back in a chair or lean away from the presumed antagonist, even while expressing verbal agreement. All of this may be done unconsciously, but the mixed message will be picked up by those tuned in to nonverbal signals.

Overloads and Distractions

Overloads and distractions caused by the availability and abundance of electronic communications can make it hard to communicate well. E-mails, messages, and chats pretty much follow us wherever we go 24/7. They coexist simultaneously on our computer screens and smart devices, and they compete with one another, social media, and video streams for our attention. Our effectiveness in attending to this ever-present and shifting mix of electronic communications is often compromised by the size and stress of overwhelming demands. Even a scheduled meeting may be compromised by overloads and distractions in the form of telephone interruptions, texts, e-mails, drop-in visitors, and lack of privacy.

Choices: Think before You Act | Researchers found that tip giving increased when servers gave customers a piece of candy when presenting the bill.

Tapping into the Science of Persuasion

Rana Faure/Fancy - Vacation Homes - These young couples, families, and solo travelers /Corbis/Getty Images

Scene 1. Hoteliers want to wash fewer towels. So how do they get their customers to reuse more of them? The science of persuading suggests that it's best to identify the request with a social norm. Researchers found that guests reused 33% more towels when left a message card that said "75% of customers who stay in this room reuse their towels."

Lesson: Want to persuade? Identify with the social norm.

Scene 2. Restaurant servers want to maximize tips. How can they get more customers to leave bigger tips? The science of persuading suggests that it's best to create a sense of reciprocity in the server–customer relationship. Researchers found that tip giving increased when servers gave customers a piece of candy when presenting the bill.

Lesson: Want to persuade? Create a sense of reciprocity.

Your Take?

Can these lessons be turned into advice for leaders? Leadership is complicated in any setting. But, it ultimately requires success at influencing other people. Do a self-check of your success in leadership situations: To what extent is "persuasion" part of your leadership skill portfolio? How about the leaders you work with: Do they pass or fail as masters of the science of persuasion? If persuasion is so important, should we spend more time learning and practicing how to do it really well?

Consider the following exchange between George and his manager.[10]

> Okay, George, let's hear your problem [phone rings, manager answers it and promises caller to deliver a report "just as soon as I can get it done"]. Uh, now, where were we—oh, you're having a problem with your technician. She's . . . [manager's assistant brings in some papers that need his immediate signature] . . . you say she's overstressed lately, wants to leave. I tell you what, George, why don't you [phone beeps a reminder, boss looks and realizes he has a lunch meeting] . . . uh, take a stab at handling it yourself. I've got to go now [starts texting].

This manager was not effective in communicating with George, even if he really wanted to. But errors like these can be easily avoided by anyone sincerely interested in communicating face to face with someone. At a minimum, adequate time should be set aside and arrangements made for privacy. The likelihood of interruptions should be anticipated and discipline should be exercised so that attention stays focused on the visitor rather than on devices.

Cross-Cultural Communication

Communicating across cultures requires lots of sensitivity, awareness, and the ability to quickly learn local rights and wrongs. The most difficult situation is when you don't speak the local language, or when one or both of the people trying to communicate are weak in a shared second language. Advertising messages are notorious for getting lost in translation. An old Pepsi ad in Chinese was intended to say "The Pepsi Generation," but it came out as "Pepsi will bring your ancestors back from the dead." A similar KFC ad that was intended to say "finger lickin' good" came out as "eat your fingers off."[11]

Ethnocentrism is a major enemy of effective cross-cultural communication. This is the tendency to consider one's own culture superior to other cultures. It hurts communication in at least three major ways. First, it may lead to poor listening. Second, it may cause someone to address or speak with others in ways that alienate them. Third, it may lead to the use of inappropriate stereotypes.[12]

You can spot ethnocentrism in conversations as arrogance in tone, manners, gestures, and use of words. It also shows up as unintentional failures to respect cultural differences in non-verbal communication.[13] The American "thumbs-up" sign is an insult in Ghana and Australia; signaling "OK" with thumb and forefinger circled together is not okay in parts of Europe. Waving "hello" with an open palm is an insult in West Africa, suggesting the other person has five fathers.[14] Success in communicating and collaborating cross cultures requires a commitment to **cultural etiquette**, the use of appropriate manners, language, and behaviors when interacting with persons from other cultures.

Ethnocentrism is the tendency to consider one's culture superior to any and all others.

Cultural etiquette is the use of appropriate manners, language, and behaviors when interacting with persons from other cultures.

Learning Check

LEARNING OBJECTIVE 18.1

Identify the elements in the communication process.

Be Sure You Can • describe the communication process and identify its key components • differentiate between effective and efficient communication • explain the role of credibility in persuasive communication • list the common sources of noise that limit effective communication • explain how mixed messages interfere with communication • explain how ethnocentrism affects cross-cultural communication

---

WileyPLUS

See Author Video

18.2 | Improving Collaboration through Communication

LEARNING OBJECTIVE 18.2

Describe ways to improve the effectiveness of communication.

> **Learn More About**
>
> Transparency and openness • Use of electronic media • Active listening • Constructive feedback • Space design

Effective communication is essential as people work together in teams and organizations. The better the communication, the more likely it is that collaboration will be successful. Pathways toward better communication are found in such things as attention to transparency and openness, good use of electronic media, active listening practices, focusing on constructive feedback, and appropriate space design.

Transparency and Openness

At HCL Industries, a large technology outsourcing firm, former CEO and current Senior Advisor Vineet Nayar believes that transparency is essential to encourage a "culture of trust" in the firm. Transparency at HCL means that the firm's financial information is fully posted on the internal website. "We put all the dirty linen on the table," Nayar says. Transparency also means that the

---

Analysis: Make Data Your Friend | Only 3% of HR executives give "A" grades to their firms' performance measurement systems.

Value of Performance Reviews Gets Increasing Scrutiny

iStock.com/enis izgi

Surveys show people aren't always pleased with the way managers in their organizations do performance reviews. Some are so concerned that they suggest dropping them altogether. Check these findings from a survey of human resources executives.

- 30% believe that employees trust their employer's performance measurement system.

- 60% give their performance management systems "C" grades or worse.

- Top concerns are that managers aren't willing to face employees and give constructive feedback, and employees don't have a clear understanding of what differentiates good and bad performance.

- Some employers are doing away with annual performance reviews and replacing them with quarterly reviews focusing on feedback, support, and goals. Others are using apps and software to enable real-time peer reviews after projects and meetings. Still others do compensation reviews annually and then ask managers to hold frequent one-on-one meetings so that everyone is always up to date on their performance and the manager's expectations.

Your Thoughts?

Performance review is often a hot topic. The buzzwords are "merit pay" and "performance accountability." But is it really possible to have a performance measurement system that is respected by managers and workers alike? Do the data reported here fit with your own experiences? What are their implications for management practice? Will we soon see a dramatic increase in the number of employers who shift away from formal annual reviews and replace them with something less formal and more timely?

results of 360-degree feedback reviews for all managers get posted as well, including Nayar's own reviews. When managers present plans to the top management team, Nayar insists that they also get posted so that everyone can read them and offer comments. This ensures that by the time a plan gets approved it's most likely to be a good one. Nayar's intent is for all this transparency to stimulate what he calls a company-wide process of "massive collaborative learning."[15]

Communication transparency involves being honest and open in sharing accurate and complete information about the organization and what's happening in the workplace. A lack of transparency is evident when managers try to hide information and restrict access to it. The benefits of communication transparency start with decision making. When people are well informed, they can be expected to make good decisions that serve the interests of the organization. Transparency also encourages motivation and engagement. When people are trusted with information, they can be expected to feel more loyal, be more engaged, and be more committed to goals and plans.

The term **open book management** describes a form of communication transparency where employees are provided with essential financial information about their companies. This includes being open about pay, something that was once thought best kept secret. Research indicates that millennial workers value pay transparency and are more willling than their seniors to share pay details with others. Knowing how one's pay compares with others has also been found to encourage more effort and higher performance.[16]

Communication transparency involves openly sharing honest and complete information about the organization and workplace affairs.

Open book management is where managers provide employees with essential financial information about their companies.

Use of Electronic Media

Are you part of the Twitter community? Do you post to Facebook, Snapchat, or Instagram? Are you a frequent messenger on WhatsApp, or generally a heavy user of your smart devices? Technology hasn't just changed how we communicate. It has created a social media revolution—one that can be a performance asset or detriment, both personally and in the world of work.[17]

To begin, we may be getting so familiar with writing online shorthand that we use it in the wrong places. Sending a message like "Thnx for the IView! I Wd Lv to Wrk 4 U!! ;)" isn't the follow-up most employers like to receive from job candidates. When Tory Johnson, founder and CEO of Women for Hire, Inc., received a thank-you note by e-mail from an intern candidate, it included "hiya," "thanx," three exclamation points, and two emoticons. She says: "That e-mail just ruined it for me."[18] Textspeak and emoticons may be the norm in social networks, but their use can be viewed as inappropriate in work settings.

Privacy also is a concern in any form of electronic communication.[19] An American Management Association survey of 304 U.S. companies found that 66% monitor Internet connections; 43% store and review computer files and monitor e-mail; 45% monitor telephone time and numbers dialed; and 30% have fired employees for misuse of the Internet.[20] When it comes to Web browsing and using social media at work, the best advice comes down to this: Find out the employer's policy and follow it. Don't ever assume that you have electronic privacy, since chances are the employer is checking or can easily check on you.[21]

Active Listening

Whether trying to communicate electronically or face to face, managers must be very good at listening. When people "talk," they are trying to communicate something. That "something" may or may not be what they are actually saying. **Active listening** is the process of taking action to help someone say exactly what he or she really means or wants to communicate.[22] Useful guidelines for active listening include the following.

Active listening helps the source of a message say what he or she really means.

- *Listen for message content:* Try to hear exactly what content is being conveyed in the message.
- *Listen for feelings:* Try to identify how the source feels about the content in the message.

- *Respond to feelings:* Let the source know that her or his feelings are being recognized.
- *Note all cues:* Be sensitive to nonverbal and verbal messages; be alert for mixed messages.
- *Paraphrase and restate:* State back to the source what you think you are hearing.

Active listening takes work and practice. It involves being sincere and trying to find out the full meaning of what is being expressed. It also involves being disciplined in controlling emotions and withholding premature evaluations or interpretations. Different responses to the following two questions contrast how a "passive" listener and an "active" listener might act in real workplace conversations.[23]

> *Question 1:* "Don't you think employees should be promoted on the basis of seniority?" *Passive listener's response:* "No, I don't!" *Active listener's response:* "Am I sensing you believe they should?"

> *Question 2:* "What does the supervisor expect us to do about these out-of-date computers?" *Passive listener's response:* "Do the best you can, I guess." *Active listener's response:* "You're pretty frustrated with those machines, aren't you?"

Constructive Feedback

Feedback is the process of telling someone else how you feel about something that person did or said.

The process of telling others how you feel about something they did or said, or about the situation in general, is called **feedback**. It occurs in the normal give-and-take of working relationships, and in more formal performance review sessions.

The art of giving feedback is an indispensable skill, particularly for managers who regularly give feedback to other people. When poorly done, feedback can be threatening to the recipient and cause resentment. Properly handled feedback—even performance criticism—can be listened to, accepted, and used to good advantage by the receiver.[24] Consider someone who comes late to meetings. Feedback from the meeting chair might be *evaluative*—"You are unreliable and always late for everything." It might be *interpretive*—"You're coming late to meetings; you might be spreading yourself too thin and have trouble meeting your obligations." It might also be *descriptive*—"You were 30 minutes late for today's meeting and missed a lot of the context for our discussion."[25]

Feedback is most useful and constructive, rather than harmful, when it offers real benefits to the receiver and doesn't just satisfy some personal need of the sender. A supervisor who reprimands a computer programmer for errors, for example, may actually be angry about failing to give clear instructions in the first place. Consider the following tips to become a better giver of constructive feedback.[26]

- Give feedback directly and with real feeling, based on trust between you and the receiver.
- Make sure that feedback is specific rather than general; use good, clear, and preferably recent examples to make your points.
- Give feedback at a time when the receiver seems most willing or able to accept it.
- Make sure the feedback is valid; limit it to issues the receiver can be expected to address.
- Give feedback in small doses; never give more than the receiver can handle at any particular time.

Space Design

Proxemics involves the use of space in communication.

Proxemics is the study of how we use space.[27] And space counts in communication. The distance between people conveys varying intentions in terms of intimacy, openness, and status in interpersonal communications. Even the physical layout of an office or room is a form of nonverbal communication. Think about it. Offices with chairs available for side-by-side seating convey different messages than offices where the manager's chair sits behind a desk while those for visitors sit facing it in front.

Organizations today are being run with the premise that the more people communicate with one another, the more they'll collaborate and the better the organization will perform. There is a push to facilitate connections and conversations by designing work spaces with lots of opportunities for team meetings and casual interaction. Examples would include small office "nests" of six to eight co-workers and "focus rooms" where a few people can huddle up while exchanging ideas, working on a project, or just having a chat.

Learning Check

LEARNING OBJECTIVE 18.2

Describe ways to improve the effectiveness of communication.

Be Sure You Can • explain how transparency and openness improves communication • explain how interactive management and practices like structured meetings can improve upward communication • discuss possible uses of electronic media by managers • define *active listening* and list active listening rules • illustrate the guidelines for constructive feedback • explain how space design influences communication

18.3 | Managing Conflict

LEARNING OBJECTIVE 18.3

Discuss how conflict can be functional and managed successfully.

> **Learn More About**
>
> Functional and dysfunctional conflict • Causes of conflict • Conflict resolution • Conflict management styles • Structural approaches to conflict management

Conflict occurs as disagreements on substantive or emotional issues.[28] These disagreements can be overt and openly expressed, or covert and hidden behind false surface harmony and political intrigue. The ability to deal with conflicts is a critical communication and collaboration skill in teams and organizations. Managers and team leaders become ineffective and lose credibility when they deny or hide from conflicts, or pass conflict situations on for others to handle as the "bad cops."[29]

Substantive conflicts involve disagreements over goals and tasks, allocation of resources, distribution of rewards, policies and procedures, and job assignments. **Emotional conflicts** result from feelings of anger, distrust, dislike, fear, and resentment, as well as personality clashes and relationship problems. Both forms of conflict can cause difficulties. But, they can also stimulate creativity and high performance.

Functional and Dysfunctional Conflict

The inverted "U" curve depicted in **Figure 18.4** shows that moderate levels of conflict can be good for performance. This **functional conflict**, or constructive conflict, moves people

Conflict is a disagreement over issues of substance and/or an emotional antagonism.

Substantive conflict involves disagreements over goals, resources, rewards, policies, procedures, and job assignments.

Emotional conflict results from feelings of anger, distrust, dislike, fear, and resentment, as well as from personality clashes.

Functional conflict is constructive and helps task performance.

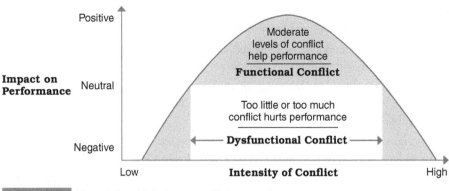

FIGURE 18.4 The relationship between conflict and performance.

toward greater work efforts, cooperation, and creativity. It helps teams achieve their goals and avoid making poor decisions because of groupthink. **Dysfunctional conflict**, or destructive conflict, harms performance, relationships, and individual well-being. It occurs when there is either too much or too little conflict. Too much conflict is distracting and overwhelming. Too little conflict promotes groupthink, complacency, and the loss of a high-performance edge.

Dysfunctional conflict is destructive and hurts task performance.

Causes of Conflict

A number of drivers can cause or set the stage for conflict. *Role ambiguities* in the form of unclear job expectations and other task uncertainties increase the likelihood for people to work at cross-purposes. *Resource scarcities* cause conflict when people have to share or compete for them. *Task interdependencies* breed conflict when people depend on others to perform well in order to perform well themselves.

Competing objectives also are opportunities for conflict. When goals are poorly set or reward systems are poorly designed, individuals and groups may come into conflict by working to one another's disadvantage. Differences in organization structures and in the characteristics of the people staffing them may foster conflict because of incompatible approaches toward work. And, unresolved prior conflicts tend to erupt in later conflicts. Unless a conflict is fully resolved, it may remain latent only to emerge again in the future.

Conflict Resolution

When conflicts do occur, they can be "resolved" in the sense that the causes are corrected, or "suppressed" in that the causes remain but the conflict is controlled. Suppressed conflicts tend to fester and resurface. They postpone issues and problems that may be best addressed immediately, and the suppression itself can be a source of personal stress.[30] True **conflict resolution** eliminates the underlying causes of conflict and reduces the potential for similar conflicts in the future.

Conflict resolution is the removal of the substantive and emotional reasons for a conflict.

Conflict Management Styles

People tend to respond to interpersonal conflict through different combinations of cooperative and assertive behaviors.[31] *Cooperativeness* is the desire to satisfy another party's needs and concerns. *Assertiveness* is the desire to satisfy one's own needs and concerns. There are five interpersonal styles of conflict management that result from combinations of these two tendencies.[32]

- **Avoidance** or *withdrawal*—being uncooperative and unassertive, downplaying disagreement, staying as neutral as possible, withdrawing from the situation.
- **Accommodation** or *smoothing*—being cooperative but unassertive, letting the wishes of others rule, overlooking differences to maintain harmony.
- **Competition** or *authoritative command*—being uncooperative but assertive, working against the wishes of the other party, trying to dominate through skills or force through use of authority.
- **Compromise**—being moderately cooperative and assertive, bargaining for "acceptable" solutions in which each party gains a bit while also giving up something of value.
- **Collaboration** or *problem solving*—being cooperative and assertive, working through differences, solving problems so that everyone gains.

The styles shown in **Figure 18.5** tend to have different outcomes in terms of "wins" and "losses." Avoiding and accommodating often create **lose–lose conflict**.[33] No one achieves their true desires, and the underlying reasons for conflict remain. Although the conflict appears settled or may even disappear temporarily, it tends to recur in the future. Avoidance pretends that conflict doesn't really exist. Everyone withdraws and hopes it will simply go away. Accommodation plays down differences and highlights areas of agreement. Peaceful coexistence is the goal, but the real essence of a conflict may be ignored.

Competing and compromising tend to create **win–lose conflict** where each party strives to gain at the other's expense. Because win–lose methods don't address the root causes of conflict, future similar conflicts are likely to reoccur. In competition, one party wins because superior skill or outright domination allows his or her desires to be forced on the other. An example is authoritative command where a supervisor simply dictates a solution to subordinates. Compromise occurs when trade-offs are made such that each party gives up and gains something. But because each party loses something, this sets the stage for future conflicts.

A collaborating or problem-solving style is a form of **win–win conflict** where issues get resolved to everyone's benefit. Parties recognize that something is wrong and needs attention, and they confront the issues head-on. Win–win outcomes eliminate the underlying causes of the conflict because all matters and concerns are raised and discussed openly. But, this approach also takes more time because it involves information collection and analysis of one another's positions.

> **Avoidance**, or withdrawal, pretends that a conflict doesn't really exist.
>
> **Accommodation**, or smoothing, plays down differences and highlights similarities to reduce conflict.
>
> **Competition**, or authoritative command, uses force, superior skill, or domination to "win" a conflict.
>
> **Compromise** occurs when each party to the conflict gives up something of value to the other.
>
> **Collaboration**, or problem solving, involves working through differences and solving problems so everyone gains.
>
> In **lose–lose conflict** no one achieves their true desires, and the underlying reasons for conflict remain.
>
> In **win–lose conflict** one party achieves its desires, and the other party does not.
>
> In **win–win conflict** the conflict is resolved to everyone's benefit.

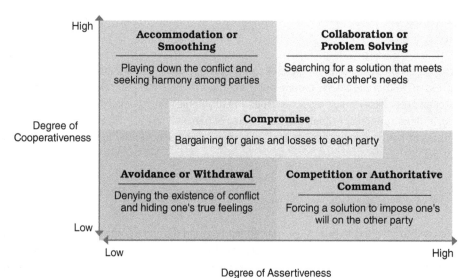

FIGURE 18.5 Alternative conflict management styles.

Structural Approaches to Conflict Management

Not all conflict can be resolved at the interpersonal level. Think about it. Aren't there likely to be times when personalities and emotions are irreconcilable? In such cases a structural approach to conflict management often can help.[34]

When conflict is over resources, the structural solution is to *make more resources available*. Although costly and not always possible, this is a straightforward and common sense approach. When people are stuck in conflict and just can't seem to appreciate one another's points of view, *appealing to higher-level goals* can focus attention on mutually desirable outcomes. In a student team where members are arguing over content choices for a presentation, for example, it might help to remind everyone that the goal is to get an "A".

There are times when it may be necessary to *change the people* by replacing or transfering one or more of the conflicting parties. When the people can't be changed, they might be separated by *altering the physical environment*. It is sometimes possible to rearrange facilities, work space, or workflows to physically separate conflicting parties and decrease opportunities for contact. Organizations also can use *integrating devices* to help manage conflicts between groups. These approaches include assigning people to formal liaison roles, convening special task forces, setting up cross-functional teams, and using a matrix form of organization.

Changing reward systems can help reduce conflicts that arise when people are competing for things like attention and pay. An example is shifting pay bonuses, or even student project grades, to the group level so that individuals benefit based on how well the

---

Blogging Is Easy, but Bloggers Should Beware

Magali Delporte/eyevine/Redux Pictures

It is easy and tempting to set up your own blog, write about your experiences and impressions, and then share your thoughts with others online. So, why not do it?

Catherine Sanderson, a British citizen living and working in Paris, might have asked this question before launching her blog, *Petite Anglaise*. At one point it was so "successful" that she had 3,000 readers. But, the Internet diary included reports on her experiences at work—and her employer wasn't happy when it became public knowledge.

Even though Sanderson was blogging anonymously, her photo was on the site, and the connection was eventually discovered. Noticed, too, was her running commentary about bosses, colleagues, and life at the office. A Christmas party was described in detail, including an executive's "unforgivable *faux pas*." When her blog came to management attention, Sanderson says that she was "dooced"—a term used to describe being fired for what one writes in a blog. She sued for financial damages and confirmation of her rights, on principle, to have a private blog. The court awarded her a year's salary.

What Do You Think?

What are the ethical issues here from both the blogger's and the employer's perspective? What rights do employees have with regard to communicating about their work experiences? Is it ethical for a supervisor to fire an employee any time the employee says something negative about the organization? For example, which is the bigger "crime," to get drunk at the office holiday party or to write a blog that reports that your supervisor got drunk at the office party? What obligations do employees have to their employers even when they are off the clock? In contrast, where does the employer's ability to control employee behaviors outside of work end?

team performs. This reinforces teamwork and reduces tendencies for team members to compete with one another. Lastly, *training in interpersonal skills* helps prepare people to communicate and work effectively in conflict-prone situations. Such "soft" or "people" skills are often at the top of a recruiter's "must have" list. You can't succeed in today's horizontal and team-oriented organizations if you can't work well with other people, even when conflicts and disagreements are inevitable.

Learning Check

LEARNING OBJECTIVE 18.3

Discuss how conflict can be functional and managed successfully.

Be Sure You Can differentiate substantive and emotional conflict • differentiate functional and dysfunctional conflict • explain the common causes of conflict • define *conflict resolution* • explain the conflict management styles of avoidance, accommodation, competition, compromise, and collaboration • discuss lose–lose, win–lose, and win–win conflicts • list the structural approaches to conflict management

18.4 | Managing Negotiation

LEARNING OBJECTIVE 18.4

WileyPLUS

See Author Video

Explain ways to negotiate successfully and avoid negotiation pitfalls.

> **Learn More About**
>
> Negotiation goals and approaches • Gaining agreement • Negotiation pitfalls • Third-party dispute resolution

Situation: Your employer offers you a promotion, but the pay raise being offered is disappointing.

Situation: You have enough money to send one person for training from your department, but two really want to go.

Situation: Your team members are having a "cook-out" on Saturday afternoon and want you to attend, but your husband wants you to go with him to visit his mother in a neighboring town.

Situation: Someone on your sales team has to fly to Texas to meet an important client. You've made the last two trips out of town and don't want to go. Another member of the team hasn't been out of town in a long time and "owes" you a favor.

These are examples of the many work situations that lead to **negotiation**—the process of making joint decisions when the parties involved have different preferences. Stated differently, negotiation is a way of reaching agreement. People negotiate over job assignments, work schedules, work locations, and salaries.[35] Any and all negotiations are ripe for conflict. And, they are a stiff tests of anyone's communication and collaboration skills.[36]

Negotiation is the process of making joint decisions when the parties involved have different preferences.

Negotiation Goals and Approaches

Substance goals in negotiation are concerned with outcomes.

Relationship goals in negotiation are concerned with the ways people work together.

Effective negotiation resolves issues of substance while maintaining a positive process.

Two important goals should be considered in any negotiation. **Substance goals** are concerned with negotiation outcomes. They are tied to content issues. **Relationship goals** are concerned with negotiation processes. They are tied to the ways people work together while negotiating and how they (and any constituencies they represent) will be able to work together again in the future.

Effective negotiation occurs when issues of substance are resolved and working relationships are maintained or even improved. The three criteria of effective negotiation are: (1) *Quality*—negotiating a "wise" agreement that is truly satisfactory to all sides; (2) *Cost*—negotiating efficiently, using a minimum of resources and time; and (3) *Harmony*—negotiating in a way that fosters, rather than inhibits, good relationships.[37]

Gaining Agreements

In distributed negotiation each party stakes win-lose claims on their preferred outcomes.

In principled negotiation each party focuses on understanding the other's positions to create win-win outcomes.

In **distributive negotiation** each party makes win-lose claims for certain preferred outcomes.[38] This emphasis on substance can become self-centered and competitive, with all parties thinking the only way for them to gain is for others to lose. Relationships often get sacrificed as process breaks down in these win–lose situations.

In **principled negotiation**, sometimes called *integrative negotiation*, the orientation is win–win. The goal is to achieve a final agreement based on the merits of each party's claims. No one should lose in a principled negotiation, and positive relationships should be maintained in the process. Four pathways or rules for gaining such integrated agreements are set forth by Roger Fisher and William Ury in their book *Getting to Yes*:[39]

1. Separate the people from the problem.
2. Focus on interests, not on positions.
3. Generate many alternatives before deciding what to do.
4. Insist that results be based on some objective standard.

The attitudinal foundations of principled negotiation involve each party's willingness to trust, share information, and ask reasonable questions. The information foundations involve both parties knowing what is important to them and finding out what is important to the other party. Both come into play during classic two-party labor–management negotiations over a new contract and salary increase.[40]

Look at **Figure 18.6** and consider the situation from the labor union's perspective. The union negotiator has told her management counterpart that the union wants a new wage of $15.00 per hour. This expressed preference is the union's initial offer. However, she also has in mind a minimum reservation point of $13.25 per hour. This is the lowest wage she is willing to accept for the union. Now look at things from the perspective of the management negotiator. His initial offer is $12.75 per hour. But his maximum reservation point, the highest wage he is prepared to eventually offer the union, is $13.75 per hour.

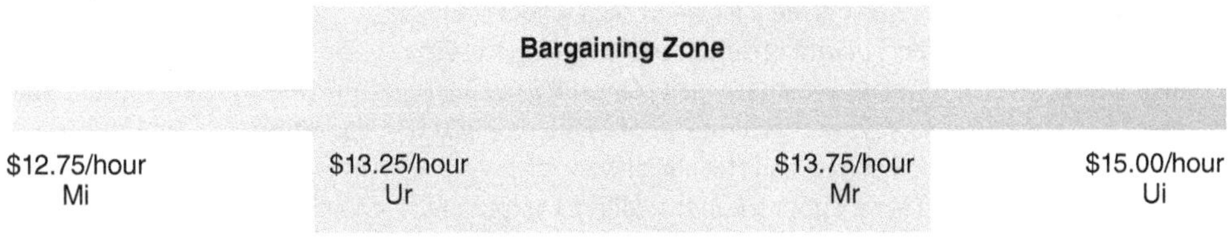

	Bargaining Zone		
$12.75/hour Mi	$13.25/hour Ur	$13.75/hour Mr	$15.00/hour Ui

Mi = Management's initial offer   Mr = Management's maximum reservation point
Ur = Union's minimum reservation point   Ui = Union's initial offer

FIGURE 18.6 The bargaining zone in classic two-party negotiation.

A key task for any negotiator is to discover the other party's reservation point. It is difficult to negotiate effectively until this is known and each party realizes that there is a positive bargaining zone. The **bargaining zone** in a negotiation is defined as the space between one party's minimum reservation point and the other party's maximum reservation point. In our example it lies between $13.25 per hour and $13.75 per hour. This is a "positive" bargaining zone since the reservation points of the two parties overlap. If the union's minimum reservation point was greater than management's maximum reservation point, say $14 per hour, there would be no room for bargaining.

> A **bargaining zone** is the space between one party's minimum reservation point and the other party's maximum reservation point.

Negotiation Pitfalls

The negotiation process is admittedly complex, and negotiators must guard against common pitfalls. The first is the *myth of the "fixed pie."* This involves acting on the distributive win–lose assumption that in order for you to gain, the other person must give something up. This fails to recognize the integrative assumption that the "pie" can sometimes be expanded or utilized to everyone's advantage. A second negotiation error is *nonrational escalation of conflict*. The negotiator gets locked into previously stated "demands" and allows personal needs for "ego" and "saving face" to inflate the perceived importance of satisfying them.

A third negotiating error is *overconfidence and ignoring the other's needs*. The negotiator becomes overconfident, believes his or her position is the only correct one, and fails to consider

---

Insight: Learn about Yourself | Recruiters give communication and networking skills high priority when screening candidates for college internships and first jobs.

Collaboration Begins with Communication and Networking

Recruiters give **communication and networking** skills high priority when screening candidates for college internships and first jobs. They're looking for candidates who can communicate well both orally and in writing, and network well with others for collaboration and teamwork. They also want people who gain social capital through communication and networking so that they can handle conflicts and negotiate successfully. But if you're like many of us, there's work to be done to master these challenges.

The American Management Association found that workers rated their bosses only slightly above average on transforming ideas into words, being credible, listening and asking questions, and giving written and oral presentations. More than three-quarters of university professors rated incoming high school graduates as only "fair" or "poor" in writing clearly, and in spelling and use of grammar. When it comes to decorum or just plain old "good manners," a *BusinessWeek* survey reported that 38% of women complain about "sexual innuendo, wisecracks and taunts" at work.

Social networking is very popular on the college campus and among young professionals, as everyone wants to be linked in. The same skills transfer to the workplace. A good networker acts as a *hub*—connected with others; *gatekeeper*—moving information to and from others; and *pulse-taker*—staying abreast of what is happening.

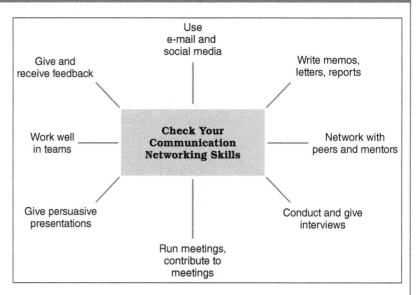

Get to Know Yourself Better

Can you convince a recruiter that you are ready to run effective meetings? . . . write informative reports? . . . deliver persuasive presentations? . . . conduct job interviews? . . . use e-mail and social media well? . . . network well with peers and mentors? . . . keep conflicts constructive and negotiations positive? Where does social capital rank on your own list of personal strengths? Ask friends, co-workers, and family members to rate your communication and networking skills. Turn these ratings into a personal development "To Do" list that you can share with your instructor.

the needs of the other party. The fourth error is *too much "telling" and too little "hearing."* The "telling" error occurs when parties to a negotiation don't really make themselves understood to each other. The "hearing" error occurs when they fail to listen well enough to understand what the other party is saying.[41]

Another potential negotiation pitfall in the age of globalization is *premature cultural comfort*. This occurs when a negotiator is too quick to assume that he or she understands the intentions, positions, and meanings of a negotiator from a different culture. A negotiator from a low-context culture, for example, is used to getting information through direct questions and answers. But this style might lead to difficulties if used with negotiators from a high-context culture. Their tendencies may be to communicate indirectly with nondeclarative language, nonverbal signals, and avoidance of hard-and-fast position statements.[42]

It is important to avoid the *trap of ethical misconduct*. The motivation to negotiate unethically sometimes arises from pure greed and undue emphasis on the profit motive. This may be experienced as a desire to "get just a bit more" or to "get as much as you can" from a negotiation. The motivation to behave unethically also may result from a sense of competition. This is a desire to "win" a negotiation just for the sake of winning it, or because of the misguided belief that someone else must "lose" in order for you to gain.

When unethical behavior occurs in negotiation, the persons involved may try to explain it away with inappropriate rationalizing: "It was really unavoidable." "Oh, it's harmless." "The results justify the means." "It's really quite fair and appropriate."[43] These and other excuses for questionable behavior are morally unacceptable. Their use also runs the risk that any short-run gains will be offset by long-run losses. Unethical negotiators risk being viewed with distrust, disrespect, and dislike, and even risk being targeted for revenge in future negotiations.

Third-Party Dispute Resolution

Even with the best of intentions, it may not always be possible to achieve integrative agreements. When disputes reach a point of impasse, third-party assistance with dispute resolution can be useful. **Mediation** involves a neutral third party who tries to improve communication between negotiating parties and keep them focused on relevant issues. The mediator does not issue a ruling or make a decision, but can take an active role in discussions. This may include making suggestions to move the parties toward agreement.

Arbitration, such as salary arbitration in professional sports, is a stronger form of dispute resolution. It involves a neutral third party, the arbitrator, who acts as a "judge" and issues a binding decision. This usually includes a formal hearing in which the arbitrator listens to both sides and reviews all facets of the case before making a ruling that all parties are required to follow.

Some organizations provide for a process called *alternative dispute resolution*. This approach uses mediation or arbitration, but does so only after direct attempts to negotiate agreements between conflicting parties have failed. A designated **ombudsperson** who listens to complaints and disputes often plays a key role in this process.

> In **mediation** a neutral party tries to help conflicting parties improve communication to resolve their dispute.
>
> In **arbitration** a neutral third party issues a binding decision to resolve a dispute.
>
> An **ombudsperson** is designated by the organization to listen to complaints and disputes in an attempt to resolve them.

Learning Check

LEARNING OBJECTIVE 18.4

Explain ways to negotiate successfully and avoid negotiation pitfalls.

Be Sure You Can • differentiate between distributive and principled negotiation • list four rules of principled negotiation • define *bargaining zone* and use this term to illustrate a labor–management wage negotiation • describe the potential pitfalls in negotiation • differentiate between mediation and arbitration

---

Management Learning Review: Get Prepared for Quizzes and Exams

Summary

LEARNING OBJECTIVE 18.1 Identify the elements in the communication process.

- Communication is the interpersonal process of sending and receiving symbols with messages attached to them.
- Effective communication occurs when the sender and the receiver of a message both interpret it in the same way.
- Efficient communication occurs when the message is sent at low cost for the sender.
- Persuasive communication results in the recipient acting as intended by the sender; credibility earned by expertise and good relationships is essential to persuasive communication.
- Noise is anything that interferes with the effectiveness of communication; common examples are poor utilization of channels, poor written or oral expression, physical distractions, and status effects.

For Discussion When, if ever, is it okay to sacrifice effectiveness in order to gain efficiency in communication?

LEARNING OBJECTIVE 18.2 Describe ways to improve the effectiveness of communication.

- Transparency, in the sense that information conveyed to others is honest, credible, and fully disclosed, is an important way to improve communication in the workplace.
- Interactive management through structured meetings, use of electronic media, and advisory councils can improve upward communication.
- Active listening, through reflecting back and paraphrasing, can help overcome barriers and improve communication.
- Constructive feedback is specific, direct, well-timed, and limited to things the receiver can change.
- Office architecture and space designs can be used to improve communication in organizations.
- Proper choice of channels and use of information technology can improve communication in organizations.
- Greater cross-cultural awareness and sensitivity are important if we are to overcome the negative influences of ethnocentrism on communication.

For Discussion Which of the rules of active listening do people most often break?

LEARNING OBJECTIVE 18.3 Discuss how conflict can be functional and managed successfully.

- Conflict occurs as disagreements over substantive or emotional issues.
- Moderate levels of conflict are functional for performance and creativity; too little or too much conflict becomes dysfunctional.
- Conflict may be managed through structural approaches that involve changing people, goals, resources, or work arrangements.
- Personal conflict management styles include avoidance, accommodation, compromise, competition, and collaboration.
- True conflict resolution involves problem solving through a win–win collaborative approach.

For Discussion When can it be better to avoid conflict rather than to engage in it?

LEARNING OBJECTIVE 18.4 Explain ways to negotiate successfully and avoid negotiation pitfalls.

- Negotiation is the process of making decisions in situations in which participants have different preferences.
- Substance goals concerned with outcomes and relationship goals concerned with processes are both important in successful negotiation.
- Effective negotiation occurs when issues of substance are resolved while the process maintains good working relationships.
- Distributive negotiation emphasizes win–lose outcomes; integrative negotiation emphasizes win–win outcomes.
- Common negotiation pitfalls include the myth of the fixed pie, overconfidence, too much telling and too little hearing, and ethical misconduct.
- Mediation and arbitration are structured approaches to third-party dispute resolution.

For Discussion How can you successfully negotiate with someone who is trapped in the "myth of the fixed pie"?

Self-Test 18

Multiple-Choice Questions

1. When the intended meaning of the sender and the interpreted meaning of the receiver are the same, a communication is _____.
   a. effective
   b. persuasive
   c. selective
   d. efficient

2. The use of paraphrasing and reflecting back what someone else says in communication is characteristic of _____.
   a. mixed messages
   b. active listening
   c. projection
   d. lose–lose conflict

3. Which is the best example of a supervisor making feedback descriptive rather than evaluative?
   a. You are a slacker.
   b. You are not responsible.
   c. You cause me lots of problems.
   d. You have been late to work three days this month.

4. When interacting with an angry co-worker who is complaining about a work problem, a manager skilled at active listening would most likely try to _____.
   a. suggest that the conversation be held at a better time
   b. point out that the conversation would be better held at another location
   c. express displeasure in agreement with the co-worker's complaint
   d. rephrase the co-worker's complaint to encourage him to say more

5. When a manager uses e-mail to send a message that is better delivered face to face, the communication process suffers from _____.
   a. semantic problems
   b. a poor choice of communication channels
   c. physical distractions
   d. information overload

6. If a visitor to a foreign culture makes gestures commonly used at home even after learning that they are offensive to locals, the visitor can be described as _____.
   a. a passive listened
   b. ethnocentric
   c. more efficient than effective
   d. an active listener

7. In order to be consistently persuasive when communicating with others in the workplace, a manager should build credibility by _____.
   a. making sure rewards for compliance are clear
   b. making sure penalties for noncompliance are clear
   c. making sure they know who is the boss
   d. making sure good relationships have been established

8. A manager who understands the importance of proxemics in communication would be likely to _____.
   a. avoid sending mixed messages
   b. arrange work spaces so as to encourage interaction
   c. be very careful in the choice of written and spoken words
   d. make frequent use of e-mail messages to keep people well informed

9. A conflict is most likely to be functional and have a positive impact on performance when it is _____.
   a. based on emotions
   b. resolved by arbitration
   c. caused by resource scarcities
   d. of moderate intensity

10. An appeal to super ordinate goals is an example of a(n) _____ approach to conflict management.
    a. avoidance
    b. structural
    c. dysfunctional
    d. self-serving

11. The conflict management style with the greatest potential for true conflict resolution involves _____.
    a. compromise
    b. competition
    c. smoothing
    d. collaboration

12. When a person is highly cooperative but not very assertive in approaching conflict, the conflict management style is referred to as _____.
    a. avoidance
    b. authoritative
    c. smoothing
    d. collaboration

13. The three criteria of an effective negotiation are quality, cost, and _____.
    a. harmony
    b. timeliness
    c. efficiency
    d. effectiveness

14. In classic two-party negotiation, the difference between one party's minimum reservation point and the other party's maximum reservation point is known as the _____.

 a. critical choice

 b. arena of indifference

 c. myth of the fixed pie

 d. bargaining zone

15. The first rule of thumb for gaining integrative agreements in negotiations is to _____.

 a. separate the people from the problems

 b. focus on positions

 c. deal with a minimum number of alternatives

 d. avoid setting standards for measuring outcomes

Short-Response Questions

16. Briefly describe how a manager would behave as an active listener when communicating with subordinates.

17. Explain the relationship between conflict intensity and performance.

18. How do tendencies toward assertiveness and cooperativeness in conflict management result in win–lose, lose–lose, and win–win outcomes?

19. What is the difference between substance and relationship goals in negotiation?

Essay Question

20. After being promoted to store manager for a new branch of a large department store chain, Kathryn was concerned about communication in the store. Six department heads reported directly to her, and 50 full-time and part-time sales associates reported to them. Given this structure, Kathryn worried about staying informed about all store operations, not just those coming to her attention as the senior manager. What steps might Kathryn take to establish and maintain an effective system of upward communication in this store?

Career Skills & Competencies: Make Yourself Valuable!

Evaluate Career Situations

What Would You Do?

1. Work versus Family

Your boss just sent a text message that he wants you at a meeting starting at 3 p.m. Your daughter is performing in a program at her elementary school at 2:45 p.m., and she expects you to attend. You're out of the office making previously scheduled sales calls that put you close to the school in the early afternoon. The office is all the way across town, and going there will mean you can't get back to the school in time to see your daughter's performance. Do you call your boss, text him, or send him an e-mail? What exactly will you say?

2. Bearer of Bad News

The restaurant you own is hit hard by a bad economy. Customer count is down. So is the average dinner bill. You have a staff of 12, but it's obvious that you have to cut back so that the payroll covers no more than 8. One of the servers has just told you that a regular customer is tweeting that the restaurant is going to close its doors after the weekend. The staff is "buzzing" about the news and customers are asking questions. How do you deal with this situation?

3. Can't Get Along

Two of your co-workers are constantly bickering. They just can't seem to get along, and it's starting to affect the rest of the team—including you. Their bickering seems to have something to do with a difference in wages. One has been there a long time while the other is relatively new. But, the newcomer earns more than the veteran. The other team members think it's time to take the problem to the team leader, and they have asked you to do it. You're willing, but want to give the team leader not just the message but also a suggested plan of action. What will it be?

Reflect on the Self-Assessment

Conflict Management Strategies

Instructions

Think of how you behave in conflict situations in which your wishes differ from those of others. In the space to the left, rate each of the following statements on a scale of "1" = "not at all" to "5" = "very much." *When I have a conflict at work, school, or in my personal life, I do the following:*[44]

1. _____ I give in to the wishes of the other party.

2. _____ I try to realize a middle-of-the-road solution.

3. _____ I push my own point of view.

4. _____ I examine issues until I find a solution that really satisfies me and the other party.

5. _____ I avoid a confrontation about our differences.

6. _____ I concur with the other party.

7. _____ I emphasize that we have to find a compromise solution.

8. _____ I search for gains.

9. _____ I stand for my own and the other's goals.

10. _____ I avoid differences of opinion as much as possible.

11. _____ I try to accommodate the other party.

12. _____ I insist we both give in a little.

13. _____ I fight for a good outcome for myself.

14. _____ I examine ideas from both sides to find a mutually optimal solution.

15. _____ I try to make differences seem less severe.

16. _____ I adapt to the other party's goals and interests.

17. _____ I strive whenever possible toward a 50–50 compromise.

18. _____ I do everything to win.

19. _____ I work out a solution that serves my own as well as other's interests as much as possible.

20. _____ I try to avoid a confrontation with the other person.

Scoring

Total your scores for items as follows.
Yielding tendency: 1 + 6 + 11 + 16 = _____.
Compromising tendency: 2 + 7 + 12 + 17 = _____.
Forcing tendency: 3 + 8 + 13 + 18 = _____.
Problem-solving tendency: 4 + 9 + 14 + 19 = _____.
Avoiding tendency: 5 + 10 + 15 + 20 = _____.

Interpretation

Each of the scores above approximates one of the conflict management styles discussed in the chapter. Look back to Figure 18.5 and make the matchups. Although each style is part of management, only collaboration or problem solving leads to true conflict resolution. You should consider any patterns that may be evident in your scores and think about how to best handle future conflict situations in which you become involved.

Contribute to the Class Exercise

Feedback Sensitivities

Preparation

Indicate the degree of discomfort you would feel in each situation below by circling the appropriate number:[45]

1. High discomfort **2.** Some discomfort **3.** Undecided **4.** Very little discomfort **5.** No discomfort

1 2 3 4 5   1. Telling an employee who is also a friend that she or he must stop coming to work late.

1 2 3 4 5   2. Talking to an employee about his or her performance on the job.

1 2 3 4 5   3. Asking an employee for comments about your rating of her or his performance.

1 2 3 4 5   4. Telling an employee who has problems in dealing with other employees that he or she should do something about it.

1 2 3 4 5   5. Responding to an employee who is upset over your rating of his or her performance.

1 2 3 4 5   6. Responding to an employee's becoming emotional and defensive when you tell her or him about mistakes on the job.

1 2 3 4 5   7. Giving a rating that indicates improvement is needed to an employee who has failed to meet minimum requirements of the job.

1 2 3 4 5   8. Letting a subordinate talk during an appraisal interview.

1 2 3 4 5   9. Having an employee challenge you to justify your evaluation during an appraisal interview.

1 2 3 4 5   10. Recommending that an employee be discharged.

1 2 3 4 5   11. Telling an employee that you are uncomfortable having to judge his or her performance.

1 2 3 4 5   12. Telling an employee that her or his performance can be improved.

1 2 3 4 5   13. Telling an employee that you will not tolerate his or her taking extended coffee breaks.

1 2 3 4 5   14. Telling an employee that you will not tolerate her or his making personal telephone calls on company time.

Instructions

Form three-person teams as assigned by your instructor. Identify the three behaviors with which each person indicates the most discomfort. Then each team member should practice performing these behaviors with another member, while the third member acts as an observer. Be direct, but try to perform the behavior in an appropriate way. Listen to feedback from the observer and try the behaviors again, perhaps with different members of the group practicing each behavior. When finished, discuss the overall exercise.

Manage a Critical Incident

Headphones on in the Office

Sean has just started a new job in your company, where everyone works in an open-plan office. He's just out of college and is happy and getting into his new responsibilities. A music lover, he has been wearing ear buds off and on during the day while working on the computer at his work station. Yesterday an older colleague came over and offered him some advice. "You should take off the headphones in the office," she said, "it's not the way we do things here. People are starting to say that you aren't a team player." Now Sean is relating the incident to you. His point is that headphones today are as common in some offices as they are on the streets. For him it's "just normal to listen to music while he works" and that "it keeps me relaxed so that I work better." But as a newcomer to the company and its corporate culture, Sean is perceived as sending out a nonverbal message when he puts the ear buds in: "Do not disturb!" Sean is looking at you and expecting a reply, probably one that takes his side of this situation.

What do you say, and why? Do you do more than speak with Sean about this situation, and what it might represent in terms of work expectations and the new generation of workers? If so, what will you do and why?

Collaborate on the Team Project

How Words Count

Question

What words do people use in organizations that carry meanings that create unintended consequences for the speaker?

Research Directions

1. Brainstorm with others to make a list of words that you have used or have heard used by people and that cause other persons to react or respond negatively and even with anger toward the person speaking them.

2. For each word on the list, write its "positive" meaning and "negative" meaning.

3. Choose two or three of the words that seem especially significant. Write role-plays that display speakers using each word in the positive sense in conversations and in which the words are interpreted positively by receivers.

4. For these same words, write role-plays that display speakers using each word conversationally with positive intentions but in which they are interpreted negatively by receivers.

5. Explain the factors that influence whether the same words are interpreted positively or negatively by receivers.

6. Draft a report that explains how people in organizations can avoid getting trapped unintentionally in problems caused by poor choice and/or use of words in their conversations.

Analyze the Case Study

Snapchat | Snap the Story of the Moment

Go to *Management Cases for Critical Thinking* at the end of the book to find this case.

Management Cases for Critical Thinking

Management Cases for Critical Thinking

Learn to Master Complex Situations

Ruaridh Stewart/Zuma Press

| Case 1 | Trader Joe's | Keeping a Cool Edge |

The average Trader Joe's location stocks only a small percentage of the products of local supermarkets in a space little larger than a corner store. How did this neighborhood market grow to major status, earn stellar ratings, and become a model of management? Take a walk down the aisles of Trader Joe's and learn how serious attention to fundamentals of management made this chain more than the average Joe.

390

From Corner Store to Foodie Mecca

All across the United States, hundreds of thousands of customers are treasure hunting.[1] Driven by gourmet tastes but hungering for deals, they are led by cheerful guides in Hawaiian shirts who point them to culinary discoveries such as Ahi jerky, ginger granola, and baked jalapeño cheese crunchies. It's just an average day at Trader Joe's, the gourmet, specialty, and natural-foods store.[2]

Foodies, hipsters, and recessionistas alike are attracted to the chain's charming blend of tasty treats and laid-back but enthusiastic customer service. Shopping at Trader Joe's is less a chore than it is immersion into another culture. Crew members and managers wear smiles and are quick to engage in a friendly chat. Chalkboards unabashedly announce slogans such as, "You don't have to join a club, carry a card, or clip coupons to get a good deal."

"When you look at food retailers," says Richard George, professor of food marketing at St. Joseph's University, "there is the low end, the big middle, and then there is the cool edge—that's Trader Joe's."[3] But how does Trader Joe's compare with other stores with an edge, such as Whole Foods? Both source locally and around the world. Each values employees and works to offer the highest quality. However, Trader Joe's has a cozy and intimate atmosphere that its rival lacks.

Trader Joe's limits its stock and sells quality products at low prices—about twice as much per square foot than other supermarkets.[4] But this scarcity benefits Trader Joe's and its customers. According to Swarthmore professor Barry Schwartz, author of *The Paradox of Choice: Why Less Is More*, "Giving people too much choice can result in paralysis . . . [R]esearch shows that the more options you offer, the less likely people are to choose any."[5]

Founder "Trader" Joe Coulombe opened the first Trader Joe's store over 50 years ago in Pasadena, California. Its success led to expansion into a bona-fide chain, as Trader Joe's stores became known as islands of value that replaced run-of-the-mill necessities with exotic, one-of-a-kind foods priced persuasively below those of any reasonable competitor.[6] Coulombe eventually sold the chain to the Albrecht family, German billionaires and owners of Aldi markets in the United States, Europe, and Australia.[7]

Cost Control

Trader Joe's prides itself on its thriftiness and cost-saving measures, proclaiming, "Every penny we save is a penny you save" and "Our CEO doesn't even have a secretary."[8] Its strongest weapon is a deliciously simple approach to stocking stores: (1) search out tasty, unusual foods from all around the world; (2) contract directly with manufacturers; (3) label each product under one of several catchy house brands; and, (4) maintain a small stock, making each product fight for its place on the shelf.

Most Trader Joe's products are sold under a variant of its house brand—dried pasta with the "Trader Giotto's" tag, frozen enchiladas under the "Trader Jose's" label, vitamins under "Trader Darwin's," and so on. But these store brands don't sacrifice quality—readers of *Consumer Reports* give Trader Joe's house brands the highest ratings.[9] The house brand success is no accident. According to Trader Joe's [former] president, Doug Rauch, "the company pursued the strategy to put our destiny in our own hands."[10]

Customer Connection

Ten to 15 new products debut each week at Trader Joe's—and the company maintains a strict "one in, one out" policy. Items that sell poorly or whose cost rises get tossed in favor of new options, something the company calls the "gangway factor."[11] If customers don't like something about a product, out it goes—count spinach and garlic from China among the rejected losers. "Our customers have voiced their concerns about products from this region and we have listened," the company said.[12]

Discontinued items may be brought back if customers complain. "We feel really close to our customers," says Audrey O'Connell, former vice president of marketing for Trader Joe's East. "When we want to know what's on their minds, we don't need to put them in a sterile room with a swinging bulb. We like to think of Trader Joe's as an economic food democracy."[13] In return, customers keep talking and recruit new converts. Word-of-mouth advertising has lowered the corporation's advertising budget to a fraction of that spent by supermarkets.[14]

Trader Joe's culture of product knowledge and customer involvement is carefully cultivated among new hires and current employees. Everyone is encouraged to taste and learn about the products and to engage customers to share what they've experienced. Most shoppers recall instances when helpful crew members took the time to locate or recommend particular items. Job descriptions highlight desired soft skills, such as "ambitious and adventurous, enjoy smiling and have a strong sense of values." They count as much as actual retail experience.[15]

Strength from Within

A responsible, knowledgeable, and friendly "crew" is a natural extension of the firm's promote-from-within philosophy. And crew members earn more than their counterparts at other chain grocers, sometimes by as much as 20%.[16] Starting benefits include medical, dental, and vision insurance; company-paid retirement; paid vacation; and a 10% employee discount.[17] Assistant store managers earn a compensation package averaging $70,000+ a year (including salary and cash bonus) while the store managers' packages average $109,000.[18] Future leaders enroll in training programs such as Trader Joe's University that help develop the loyalty necessary to run stores according to company and customer expectations. The program teaches managers how to get their part-timers to demonstrate the customer-focused attitude shoppers have come to expect.[19]

What does the future hold? Will Trader Joe's allure of cosmopolitan food at provincial prices continue to tempt new consumers? Will management practices continue to attract the talent Trader Joe's needs to maintain its culture and customer focus as the competition heats up?

Case Analysis Questions

1. Discussion In what ways does Trader Joe's demonstrate the importance of each responsibility in the management process—planning, organizing, leading, and controlling?

2. Discussion What lessons does the Trader Joe's story offer to aspiring entrepreneurs who want to get off to a good start in any industry?

3. Problem Solving At the age of 22 and newly graduated from college, Hazel has just accepted a job with Trader Joe's as a shift leader. She'll be supervising four team members who fill part-time jobs in the produce section. Given Trader Joe's casual and nontraditional work environment, what skills will she need, what should she do, and what should she avoid doing in the first few days of work to establish herself as a successful team leader?

4. Further Research Study news reports to find more information on Trader Joe's management and organization practices. Look for comparisons with its competitors and try to identify whether or not Trader Joe's still has the right management approach and business model for continued success. Are there any internal weaknesses in the Trader Joe's management approach or new practices by external competitors, or changing industry forces that might cause future problems?

Nano Calvo/WPics/Redux Pictures

Case 2 Zara International | Fashion at the Speed of Light

In this world of "hot today, gauche tomorrow," no company does fast fashion better than Zara International. Shoppers in a growing number of countries—more than 7,000 stores in 50 countries across 96 different markets—are fans of Zara's knack for bringing the latest styles from sketchbook to clothing rack at lightning speed and reasonable prices.[1]

In Fast Fashion, Moments Matter

Zara's parent company Inditex is known for year-on-year strong sales gains. Low prices and a rapid response to fashion trends have pushed it into the top ranks of global clothing vendors. The chain specializes in lightning-quick turnarounds of the latest designer trends at prices tailored to the young—about $27 an item.[2] Former Louis Vuitton fashion director Daniel Piette described Zara as "possibly the most innovative and devastating retailer in the world."[3]

Inditex shortens the time from order to arrival using a complex system of just-in-time production and inventory management that keeps Zara ahead of the competition. Their distribution centers can have items in European stores within 24 hours of order receipt, and in American and Asian stores in under 48 hours.[4] "They're a fantastic case study in terms of how they manage to get product to their stores so quick," said Stacey Cartwright, former executive vice president and CFO of Burberry Group PLC. "We are mindful of their techniques."[5]

The firm carefully controls design, production, distribution, and retail sales to optimize the flow of goods, without having to share profits with wholesalers or intermediary partners. Customers win with access to new fashions while they're still fresh off the runway.[6] Twice a week Zara's finished garments are shipped to physical distribution centers that all simultaneously distribute products to stores worldwide. These small production batches help the company avoid the risk of oversupply. Because batches always contain new products, Zara's stores perpetually energize their inventories.[7] Most clothing lines are not replenished. Instead they are replaced with new designs to create scarcity value—shoppers cannot be sure that designs in stores one day will be available the next day.

Store managers track sales data with handheld devices. They can reorder hot items in less than an hour. Zara always knows what's selling and what's not. When a look doesn't pan out, designers promptly put together new products. New arrivals are rushed to store sales floors still on the black plastic hangers used in shipping. Shoppers who are in the know recognize these designs as the newest of the new; soon after, any items left over are rotated to Zara's standard wood hangers.[8]

Inside and out, Zara's stores are designed to strengthen the brand. Inditex considers this to be very important because that is where shoppers ultimately decide which fashions make the cut. In a faux shopping street in the basement of the company's headquarters, stylists craft and photograph eye-catching layouts that are e-mailed every two weeks to store managers for replication.[9]

Zara stores sit on some of the glitziest shopping streets—including New York's Fifth Avenue, near the flagship stores of leading international fashion brands—which make its reasonable prices stand out. It's all part of the strategy. "Inditex gives people the most up-to-date fashion at accessible prices, so it is a real alternative to high-end fashion lines," said Luca Solca, Managing Director, Luxury Goods with Sanford C. Bernstein in London. That is good news for Zara as many shoppers trade down from higher priced chains.[10]

A Single Fashion Culture

The Inditex group began in 1963 when Amancio Ortega Gaona, founder and former chairman of Inditex, got his start in textile manufacturing.[11] After a period of growth, he assimilated Zara into a new holding company, Industria de Diseño Textil.[12] Inditex has a tried-and-true strategy for entering new markets: start with a handful of stores and gain a critical mass of customers. Generally, Zara is the first Inditex chain to break ground in new countries, paving the way for the group's other brands, including Pull and Bear, Massimo Dutti, and Bershka.[13]

Inditex farms out much of its garment production to specialist companies, located on the Iberian Peninsula, which it supplies with its own fabrics. Although some pieces and fabrics are purchased in Asia—many of them not dyed or only partly finished—the company manufactures about half of its clothing in its hometown of A Coruña, Spain.[14] Inditex CEO and chairman Pablo Isla believes in cutting expenses wherever and whenever possible. Zara spends just 0.3% of sales on ads, making the 3–4% typically spent by rivals seem excessive in comparison. Isla disdains markdowns and sales as well.[15]

H&M, one of Zara's top competitors, uses a slightly different strategy. Around one-quarter of its stock is made up of fast-fashion items that are designed in-house and farmed out to independent factories. As at Zara, these items move quickly through the stores and are replaced often by fresh designs. But, unlike its rival Zara, H&M also keeps a large inventory of basic, everyday items sourced from inexpensive Asian factories.[16]

Fast Fashion on the Move

Inditex launched its Zara online store in the United States by offering free 2–3 day shipping and free returns in the model of uber-successful e-retailer Zappos.[17] A Zara iPhone app has been downloaded by more prospective clients in the United States than in any other market, according to Isla—more than a million users in just three months. But, when will Inditex's rapid expansion bring undue pressure to its business? The rising number of overseas stores increases

cost and complexity and could strain operations.[18] Is Zara expanding too quickly—opening about 400 stores per year?[19] Will its existing logistics system carry it into another decade of intense growth? Can fast-fashion win the long-term retailing race?

Case Analysis Questions

1. Discussion In what ways are elements of the classical and behavioral management approaches evident in how things are done at Zara International? How can systems concepts and contingency thinking explain the success of some of Zara's distinctive practices?

2. Discussion Zara's logistics system and management practices can handle the current pace of growth, but they will need updating at some point in the future. How could quantitative management approaches and data analytics help Zara executives plan for the next generation of its logistics and management approaches?

3. Problem Solving As a consultant chosen by Zara to assist with the expansion of its U.S. stores, you have been asked to propose how evidence-based management might help the firm smooth its way to success with an American workforce. What areas will you suggest be looked at for evidence-based decision making, and why?

4. Further Research Gather the latest information on competitive trends in the apparel industry, and on Zara's latest actions and innovations. Is the firm continuing to do well? Are other retailers getting just as proficient with the fast-fashion model? Is Zara adapting and innovating in ways needed to stay abreast of both its major competition and the pressures of a changing global economy? Is this firm still providing worthy management benchmarks for other firms to follow?

Dev Chatterjee/Shutterstock.com

Case 3 Warby Parker | Disruption with a Conscience

It was memorable. Four business students at the Wharton School at the University of Pennsylvania, sat together and asked a simple but perplexing question: "Why are glasses so expensive?" The answer, as it turned out, was because the eyewear industry had been dominated by a single company for a generation—Luxottica.

An international conglomerate headquartered in Milan, Italy, Luxottica is the largest eyewear company in world. It owns Sunglass Hut, LensCrafters, Pearle Vision, Target Optical, and Sears Optical. It has 82,000 employees, operates more than 9,000 retail locations, and also owns EyeMed, which is one of the largest vision insurance providers in the United States. Luxottica, although a functionally vertically integrated company, may actually be best known in retail contexts for some of its more famous brands, which include Ray-Ban and Oakley. The company also manufactures eyewear under license for a large number of luxury labels as well, which include Chanel, Prada, Giorgio Armani, Versace, Polo, and Dolce & Gabbana.

For years, Luxottica held an overwhelming, quasi-monopolistic position in the retail eyewear market. This market dominance lead to an artificial inflation in retail eyewear pricing.

And, no competitor was going to upset this balance of power by taking on the heaviest hitter in this industry in an historically conventional way.

Enter the Wharton MBAs. It turns out that their answer to the question of why glasses cost so much would fundamentally disrupt the eyewear industry. Enter the startup called Warby Parker, described as "founded with a rebellious spirit and a lofty objective: to create boutique-quality, classically crafted eyewear at a revolutionary price point." And enter a company with a social conscience. The founder's called their business model "eyewear with a purpose." The intent was to become part of the solution to a worldwide humanitarian problem of more than two billion people needing corrective eyewear but unable to afford them.[1] The Warby Parker commitment was to donate one pair of glasses to someone in need for every pair of glasses sold.

David Gilboa, one of the four cofounders of the now billion-dollar company, had lost his eyeglasses on a backpacking trip in Thailand. Being a graduate student with only a limited budget, he couldn't afford to buy a new pair when the new semester started. He recalls: "When I went to replace them they cost $800 — that's $600 more than my brand new iPhone 3G, a multiprocessing computer. It was nuts."[2] Gilboa quickly enlisted classmates Neil Blumenthal, Andrew Hunt, and Jeffrey Raider in his displeasure. The entrepreneurial result was the founding of Warby Parker.

Gilboa and his team realized that to compete they would have to approach their business in a new way. They couldn't build thousands of stores and hire tens of thousands of employees. But, they could use the Internet to connect directly with customers, source directly from suppliers and cut out the middleman, keep prices low, and keep their key stakeholders in focus. While Luxottica charged high prices for its products, Warby Parker would provide a high quality product at lower—very low—prices. It would do so with a nimble, cost efficient, easy-to-access Internet-based business.

The strategy was good, but not good enough for the four founders. Their startup would be a David competing against a Goliath. It needed a unique identity to distinguish itself and compete successfully against what for all practical purposes was a monopoly in the industry. And, this is where the founders' social consciences stepped in to help. The company became the eyeglass firm that cares, the one that cares enough to help the people around the world who can't access or afford the glasses they need. It brought them to that identity as the company that cares.[3]

Through the Buy a Pair, Give a Pair program, for every pair of eyeglasses that Warby Parker customers buy, the company donates a pair to someone in need of eyewear who doesn't have access, either as a result of cost or because they're located in remote areas where accessibility to eyewear is limited. Since the company's founding, it has donated more than 5 million pairs of eyeglasses to locations throughout the United States and in over 50 countries around the world, with a predominant focus in Africa and Southeast Asia.

Warby Parker is a company that cares—about its customers and about social justice policies designed to help people in need. The company cares enough to ensure that every customer gets the right glasses, at the right price, in a way that's convenient for their lifestyles. It cares enough for its employees to become known throughout the industry as a great place to work.[4] Policies, leadership, and culture make new employees feel welcome, emphasize communication and contact, celebrate successes, and focus on people as learning assets and not just placeholders at a desk. And, Warby Parker cares about humanity and leads with its conscience. From the first day of operations, the company has made donations of new eyewear as a core commitment of its business.[5]

With an innovative model, Warby Parker has successfully tackled the problem of high-priced eyeglasses. It has done so not just through the application of astute business practices, but also with a social conscience. In so doing, it has managed to disrupt the status quo in a previously formidable industry, one pair of glasses at time.

Case Analysis Questions

1. **Discussion**   In what ways can a newer, smaller competitor "punch above its weight" by taking advantage of the Internet? How can the Internet be applied as a tool to help businesses avoid some of the costs associated with doing business following more conventional or "old school" approaches? How do you see the balance of power in industries like the eyewear industry shifting as customers become more comfortable buying eyewear online?

2. **Discussion**   What impact does Warby Parker's decision to donate a pair of eyeglasses for every pair purchased from them have on customers' perceptions of the company? How does Warby Parker's focus on being a great place to work influence how the company is seen in the market?

3. **Problem Solving**   As an operations management consultant, you've been contracted to help a large, traditionally configured clothing company—Marquee Clothes—to become more Internet enabled and competitive in light of customers' shopping habits, attitudes, and expectations. The company has a well-established supply chain infrastructure, currently has more than 50 retail locations, and has been in business for more than 20 years. Over the last several years, with increasing numbers of mall closings, the business has had to shut several of its stores and is seeing much of the foot traffic that traditionally was its bread and butter start to decline as well. Sales have been off the last three quarters, and the 56-year-old owner of the privately held company is concerned that she'll have to close more stores if things don't turn around. She's been convinced by her college-aged daughter that in order to continue to compete, the company is going to have to undergo a makeover and become a twenty-first-century player, with a fully fleshed-out online approach and strategy. What should she do? What are some of the first things that you'd advise? What steps need to be taken to help take Marquee Clothes fully into the twenty-first century.

4. **Further Research**   What's happening now with Warby Parker? What kinds of things is the billion-dollar company doing to stay ahead of other competitors and make headway in the eyewear market? What kinds of steps has Luxottica taken to defend itself against Warby Parker's disruptive tactics?

KaiNedden/laif/Redux Pictures

Case 4 | Patagonia | Leading a Green Revolution

How has Patagonia managed to stay both green and profitable even when the economy is down, consumers are tight for cash, and doing the profitable thing is not necessarily doing the right thing? Are Patagonia's business practices just good for the environment and Patagonia, or are there lessons here others can follow?

Twelve hundred Walmart buyers, a group legendary for their tough-as-nails negotiating tactics, sit in rapt attention in the company's Bentonville, Arkansas, headquarters. They're listening to a small man in a mustard-yellow corduroy sport coat lecture them on the environmental impact of Walmart's purchasing choices.[1] When Patagonia's founder Yvon Chouinard finishes speaking, the buyers leap to their feet and applaud enthusiastically.

Such is the authenticity of Chouinard. Since 1972 he's built the company into one of the most successful outdoor clothing companies in the world, and one that is steadfastly committed to environmental sustainability. Even though the CEO reins were turned over to Rose Marcario several years ago, it's hard to discuss Patagonia without constantly referencing Chouinard. For all practical purposes the two are one. He breathes life into the company and models the outdoorsy athleticism of Patagonia's customers. In turn, Patagonia's business practices reflect Chouinard's values and insistence on minimizing environmental impact, even at the expense of corporate profits.

Taking Risks to Succeed

Patagonia sits at the forefront of a cozy niche: high-quality, performance-oriented outdoor clothes and gear sold at top price points. Derided as *Pradagonia* or *Patagucci* by critics, the brand is aligned with top-shelf labels like North Face and Mountain Hardware. Patagonia clothes are designed for fly fishermen, rock climbers, skiers, and surfers. The clothes are durable, comfortable, sustainably produced, and they are not cheap.

It seems counterintuitive, almost dangerous, to market a $400 raincoat in a down economy. But the first thing you learn about Yvon Chouinard is that he's a risk taker. The second thing you learn is that he's usually right. "Corporations are real weenies," he says. "They are scared to death of everything. My company exists, basically, to take those risks and prove that it's a good business."[2]

And it is a good business. Patagonia succeeds by staying true to Chouinard's vision.[3] "They've become the Rolls-Royce of their product category," says Marshal Cohen, chief industry analyst with market research firm NPD Group. "When people were stepping back, and the industry became copycat, Chouinard didn't sell out, lower prices, and dilute the brand. Sometimes," he says, "the less you do the more provocative and true of a leader you are."[4]

Ideal Corporate Behavior

Chouinard is not shy about espousing the environmentalist ideals intertwined with Patagonia's business model. "It's good business to make a great product, and do it with the least amount of damage to the planet," he says. "If Patagonia wasn't profitable or successful, we'd be an environmental organization."[5]

In many ways, Patagonia is just that—an environmental organization. The company publishes an online library of working documents, the *Footprint Chronicles*, which is intended to help employees to make sustainability decisions in even the most mundane office scenarios. Its mission statement is to "Build the best product, cause no unnecessary harm, use business to inspire and implement solutions to the environmental crisis."

Chouinard has cofounded a number of external environmental organizations, including 1% For the Planet, which secures pledges from companies to donate 1% of annual sales to a worldwide network of environmental causes.[6] The name comes from Patagonia's 30-year practice of contributing 10% of pre-tax profits or 1% of sales—whichever is *greater*—to environmental groups each year. Whatever you do, don't call it a handout. "It's not a charity," Chouinard flatly states. "It's a cost of doing business. We use it to support civil democracy."[7]

Another core value at Patagonia is providing opportunities for motivated volunteers to devote themselves to sustainability causes. Employees can leave their jobs for up to two months to volunteer full-time for the environmental cause of their choice, while continuing to receive full pay and benefits from Patagonia.[8] Every 18 months, the company hosts the Tools for Grassroots Activists Conference, where a handful of participants is invited to engage in leadership training, much of it derived from the advocacy experiences of Patagonia management.[9]

Growing Green

During its early growth phase Patagonia commissioned an external audit of the environmental impact of its manufacturing. Management anticipated bad news about petroleum-derived nylon and polyester. But they were shocked to learn that the production of cotton had a more negative impact on the environment—destructive soil and water pollution, adverse health consequences for fieldworkers, and the consuming of 25% of all toxic pesticides used in agriculture. Chouinard's response was to source organic fibers for all cotton clothing products. Company representatives went directly to organic cotton farmers, ginners, and spinners, seeking pledges from them to increase production, dust off dormant processing equipment, and do whatever it would take to line up enough raw materials to fulfill the company's promise to its customers and the environment. Ever since, all of Patagonia's cotton garments have been spun from organic cotton.

Sustaining Momentum

Now in his 70s, Chouinard continues to seek better ways for Patagonia to do business. "I think entrepreneurs are like juvenile delinquents who say 'This sucks. I'll do it my own way,'" he says. "I'm an innovator because I see things and think I can make it better. So I try it. That's what entrepreneurs do."[10]

One of his innovations is the Common Threads initiative. Designed to minimize the number of Patagonia clothes that wind up in landfills, the program commits the company to making clothes built to last, fix wear-and-tear items for consumers that can be repaired, and collect and recycle worn-out fashions as efficiently and responsibly as possible.[11] Chouinard calls it "our promise that none of our stuff ever ends up in a landfill."[12] Also in terms of cradle to grave manufacturing, he describes "trying to convince zipper companies to make teeth out of polyester or nylon synths, which can be recycled infinitely." The goal is to then be able to "take a jacket and melt the whole thing down back to its original polymer to make more jackets."[13]

Despite his boundless enthusiasm for all things green, Chouinard admits that no process is truly sustainable. "I avoid using that word as much as I can," he says. He pauses for a moment and adds: "I keep at it, because it's the right thing to do."[14]

Case Analysis Questions

1. Discussion How do you think Patagonia executives decide on what products to offer so that the outcomes will be both business practical (think profits) and environmentally friendly (think sustainability)? Take the case of a proposed new hiking boot. What criteria would you use to evaluate it as a new Patagonia product?

2. Discussion Even though he is no longer the CEO, Yvon Chouinard still exerts major influence over Patagonia's business approach. What should he and other Patagonia executives be doing today to make sure that his ideals remain a permanent part of the company's culture after he's no longer active at the company?

3. Problem Solving Picture yourself working for Patagonia. The CEO comes to you and asks for a proposal on a new—"forward looking"—sustainability agenda for the firm. The goal is to drive Patagonia's future, not just celebrate its past. What would you include in this proposed agenda in order to really stretch the firm beyond what it is already doing, and why?

4. Further Research Evaluate the risk that ethics might someday lose out to greed even in a company with the idealism of Patagonia. Look carefully into Patagonia's products and practices and see if you can find any missteps where decisions put profits ahead of the company's publicly stated environmental goals. Can you find evidence for strong governance and leadership that will protect Chouinard's values and legacy far into the future? How about the competition? Just how does Patagonia operate today to ensure that ethics and social responsibility are not displaced as core company values? And finally, how about the competition? Is Patagonia still the best role model, or can you identify other firms that deserve to be studied as well as role models in business and society relationships?

Bloomberg/Getty Images

Case 5 **Harley-Davidson** | Style and Strategy with a Global Reach

Harley-Davidson's American success story began in 1903 when two friends—William Harley and Arthur Davidson—built a motorized bicycle in a machine shop in Milwaukee, Wisconsin.[1] The progeny of that first machine now travel the world—with speed and style. Now the Harley Hog is going electric.

Harley's Roots

When Harley-Davidson was founded it was one of more than 100 firms producing motorcycles in the United States. By the 1950s, it was the only remaining American manufacturer.[2] But in the 1960s, Honda began sales in the United States and Harley had difficulty competing against the Japanese firm's smaller bikes.

The American Machine and Foundry Co. (AMF) bought Harley in 1969 and quickly increased production.[3] However, this rapid expansion led to significant problems with quality, and the better-built Japanese motorcycles began to take over the market.[4] A group of 13 managers bought Harley-Davidson back from AMF in 1981 and began a turn around with the rallying cry "The Eagle Soars Alone." Richard Teerlink, former CEO of Harley, explained: "The solution was to get back to detail. The key was to know the business, know the customer, and pay attention to detail."[5] The goals driving this turn around were increasing quality and improving service to customers and dealers.

Consolidation and Renewal

In 1983, Harley-Davidson asked the International Trade Commission (ITC) for tariff protection on the basis that Japanese manufacturers, including Honda, were stockpiling inventory in the United States and providing unfair competition. The request was granted. Harley was confident enough in 1987 to petition the ITC to have the tariff lifted because the company had improved its ability to compete with foreign imports. Once Harley's image had been restored, the company began to increase production and open new facilties.[6]

The average Harley customer in the 1980s was male, late thirties, with an average household income above $40,000 (approximately $90,000 today). Teerlink said: "Our customers want the sense of adventure that they get on our bikes. . . . Harley-Davidson doesn't sell transportation, we sell transformation. We sell excitement, a way of life."[7] The company created a line of Harley accessories available online, by catalog, or through dealers, all adorned with the Harley-Davidson logo. These jackets, caps, T-shirts, and other items became popular with nonbikers as well. In fact, the clothing and parts had a higher profit margin than the motorcycles; nonbike products made up as much as half of sales at some dealerships.

Global Expansion

Although Harley had been exporting motorcycles ever since it was founded, it was not until the late 1980s that management invested seriously in international markets. Traditionally, the company's ads had been translated word for word into foreign languages. Now, new ads were developed specifically for different markets and Harley rallies were adapted to fit local customs.[8] Harley actively recruited dealers in Europe and Japan, built a large parts warehouse in Germany, and purchased a Japanese distribution company.

Harley's management learned a great deal from these early international activities. Recognizing, for example, that German motorcyclists rode at high speeds—often more than 100 mph—the company began studying ways to give Harleys a smoother ride and emphasizing accessories that would give riders more protection.[9] Its Japanese subsidiary adapted the company's marketing to fit local tastes, even producing shinier and more complete toolkits than those available in the United States. Harley bikes are now symbols of prestige in Japan, and many enthusiasts see themselves as rebels on wheels.[10] The company has also made inroads into the previously elusive Chinese market. It partnered with China's Zongshen Motorcycle Group, which makes more than 4 million small-engine motorcycles each year.[11] Despite China's growing disposable income, the new store has several hurdles ahead of it, including riding restrictions imposed by the government in urban areas.

The Future

The U.S. market still represents almost 75% of Harley's sales.[12] Executives attribute Harley's success to loyal customers and the Harley-Davidson name. "It is a unique brand that is built on personal relationships and deep connections with customers, unmatched riding experiences, and proud history," said Jim Ziemer, Harley's former president and chief executive.[13]

CEO Keith E. Wandell seeks to increase growth by focusing effort and resources on the unique strengths of the Harley-Davidson brand. He also plans to enhance productivity and profitability through continuous improvement. Part of his approach focuses company resources on Harley-Davidson products and experiences, demographic outreach, commitment to core customers, and even more global growth.[14] The latest innovation is the electric Hog, now in prototype and soon on the highways of the world. A Harley spokesperson says: "We anticipate it's going to appeal to a younger, more urban demographic" and that it is part of Harley's commitment to "preserving the riding environment."[15]

Case Analysis Questions

1. **Discussion**   If you were CEO of Harley-Davidson, how would you compare the advantages and disadvantages of using exports, joint ventures, and foreign subsidiaries as ways of expanding international sales?

2. **Discussion**   In America, Harley has shifted the positioning of its products away from simply motorcycles and more toward being status symbols of a particular lifestyle. What are the implications of cultural factors for positioning in other countries that Harley has targeted for growth—ones like Japan, China, France, and Brazil?

3. **Problem Solving**   If you were advising Harley's CEO on business expansion in sub-Saharan Africa, what would you recommend in terms of setting up sales centers and manufacturing sites in countries like South Africa, Kenya, and Zimbabwe? When a new location is targeted, what would you suggest as the proper role for locals to play? Should they run everything, or should there be a mix of locals and expatriates? And if the CEO wants to send expatriates from the United States into some locations, what selection criteria would you recommend, and why?

4. **Further Research**   Is it accurate to say that Harley is still "on top of its game"? How well is the company performing today in both domestic and global markets? Who are its top competitors in other parts of the world, and how well does Harley compete against them? Does the electric Harley have what it takes to fuel the company's next stage of global growth?

Case 6 In-N-Out Burger | Building Them Better

In-N-Out Burger seems like a modest enterprise—only four food items on the menu and little to no advertising. So, how has this West Coast chain achieved near-cult status among regular Joes and foodies alike? For more than 70 years, In-N-Out has wooed customers by providing just the basics—fresh, well-cooked food served quickly in a sparkling clean environment. Its hallmarks are consistency and quality.

Gordon Ramsay is not an easy man to satisfy. The celebrity chef and star of *Hell's Kitchen* is well known for his culinary prowess, perfectionism, and earth-shaking, profanity-strewn tantrums. He is infamous for finding fault with simple and extravagant dishes alike. So it came as a shock to many when Ramsay revealed his affinity for a darling of West Coast fast food. "In-N-Out Burgers [are] extraordinary," Ramsay says, recounting a visit. "I was so bad: I sat in the restaurant, had my double cheeseburger, then minutes later I drove back round and got the same thing again."[1]

Simple Formula for Success

Walk into any In-N-Out Burger location and you'll only find four food items on the menu: Hamburger, Cheeseburger, Double-Double, and French Fries. You can wash those down with a Coke or a milk shake. In addition, there's . . . nothing else. That's the entire menu. Or so In-N-Out would have you think.

Stand next to the ordering counter long enough, and you'll hear customers recite a litany of curious requests. None are on the menu, but sure enough, the cashier rings each one up with a smile: Animal Style (a mustard-cooked patty with extra pickles, extra spread, and grilled onions), Flying Dutchman (two patties, two slices of cheese, no bun or garnish), Protein Style (heavy on the fixings, wrapped in lettuce instead of a bun), or any permutation of patties and cheese slices up to a 4 × 4 (four patties and four slices of cheese barely contained in one bun). It's as if you've gone through the looking glass, and the menu is not what it seems. But the open secret of the secret menu is only part of what keeps customers coming back for more.

In-N-Out's motto is clear: "Give customers the freshest, highest quality foods you can buy and provide them with friendly service in a sparkling clean environment." So is the chain's formula for success: Make only a few food items, consistently make them well, and earn the trust of customers by not deviating from this premise.

All in the Family

Harry Snyder and his wife Esther opened the first In-N-Out Burger in Baldwin Park, California, in 1948. Unlike other carhop-oriented fast-food restaurants of the era, Harry installed a two-way speaker through which drivers could order without leaving their car, creating California's first drive-thru hamburger stand. He brought sons Rich and Guy to work at an early age, where the boys learned their father's insistence on complementing fresh, promptly cooked food with great customer service.

The Snyders' second restaurant opened three years later, and franchising continued slowly until 1976, when Rich took over after his father's death. Although he was only 24 when he became CEO, Rich Snyder expanded In-N-Out into new cities but still retained stringent control. Unlike his dad, who hoped employees would transfer skills learned at In-N-Out to a "better" job, Rich thought: "Why let good people move on when you can use them to help your company grow?"[2] Knowing that his expansion plans would require a pool of talented and loyal store managers, he opened In-N-Out University. Store associates had to please hungry diners, show initiative, and exhibit strong decision-making skills for at least one year before being invited to attend the management training program. Reasoning that the same high-tech tools for performance analysis employed by pro sports teams could also improve his team, Rich videotaped trainees to analyze their performance and produced training films.[3]

Entrepreneurship Under Control

The chain's founding family is fiercely entrepreneurial, and they maintain strict control over the franchisees. Their influence shows everywhere from the sock-hop décor to the secret menu to the treatment of employees as long-term partners rather than as low-cost, disposable resources. They followed their own formula for success instead of chasing, or copying, the competition. They've also avoided the temptations of selling the firm through an IPO. A posting on the firm's website states: "In-N-Out remains privately owned and the Snyder family has no plans to take the company public or franchise any units."[4]

Quality Drives Future Plans

In-N-Out Burger is now led by Guy's daughter Lynsi Lavelle Snyder-Ellingson, who is committed to following the Snyder family's strategy by not changing what already works so well.[5] The firm continues to get rave reviews for making only a handful of items with great attention to quality. Vice President of Planning and Development Carl Van Fleet says: "At In-N-Out Burger, we make all of our hamburger patties ourselves and deliver them fresh to all of our restaurants with our own delivery vehicles. Nothing is ever frozen. Our new restaurant locations are limited by the distance we can travel from our patty making facilities and distribution centers."[6] How did this family-owned burger chain with roadside diner roots inspire such a passionate following?

Case Analysis Questions

1. Discussion Rich Snyder was 24 years old when his father passed away and he assumed leadership of In-N-Out. Was his young age an asset or a liability for leadership of the company? After answering, take a position on this question: Does age really matter in entrepreneurship?

2. Discussion In an era of fusion cuisine and extreme fajitas, is In-N-Out's strategy of offering only four simple food items still on track? How about the firm's approach to employees? Does it give them an edge over the fast-food competition?

3. Problem Solving A would-be entrepreneur walks into your bank and requests financing for a business plan for a sandwich shop modeled after In-N-Out's approach and limited menu. But, all the ingredients would come from local suppliers and growers within a 30-mile radius of town. Is this a winning recipe that deserves financing from your bank? What would you like to see in the business plan before approving the loan?

4. Further Research Imagine you were asked by In-N-Out Burger to research current industry and social trends, and consumer values and tastes. Write an ad campaign that coincides with the current market landscape and still adheres to In-N-Out's core values: quality, consistency, friendliness, and cleanliness. How would your ad appeal to customers in ways that the ads from the big chains—McDonald's, Wendy's, and Burger King—do not? How would you use social media as part of this ad campaign? And, what can you do that would make this ad so attractive that it goes viral on YouTube?

John Crowe/Alamy Stock Photo

| Case 7 | Target | Missing the Bull's Eye

The Target Corporation began its life at the turn of the twentieth century as the Dayton Dry Goods Company. There were no airplanes, plastic, windshield wipers, traffic lights, supermarkets, grocery bags, light switches, or toasters.[1] Things changed over the next 120+ years as the company achieved fantastic—astonishing—growth as its markets and the world at large became increasingly complex.

Target is now the eighth largest retailer in the world.[2] It operates 1,850 stores, located in 1,249 cities, across all 50 states in the United States, with more than 300,000 Target employees, and annual sales in excess of $75 billion dollars.[3] This massive retailing infrastructure is supported by a large network of 37 regional distribution centers, located throughout the United States, that independently employ more than 16,000 team members to service the ongoing inventory requirements of the 1,200+ stores in the chain.[4] Target's direct distribution networks work full-time to keep the retail outlets stocked with more than 80,000 unique SKUs (stock keeping unit).[5]

Target Corporation also maintains a wide range of offices serving different needs for the company. For example, there's the Financial and Retail Services offices in Tempe, Arizona; the Data Science and Engineering Offices in Pittsburgh, Pennsylvania; an Innovation Office in San Francisco, California; and a second office in California, the Silicon Valley Office in Sunnyvale, which is there to serve as "a breeding ground for big ideas and innovation.[6] A lot goes into coordinating this massive enterprise, and the buck stops—or begins, we might say—with the CEO.

Since being hired as the company's top executive, Target's current CEO and Board Chairman, Brian Cornell, has faced some stiff challenges. He works directly with an 11-member executive board and a subsidiary group of 40+ other executives in the operation of the massive organization.[7] There is an endless progression of decisions that the CEO and executive group make that tie all of the moving parts at Target together. And, there are some signs that the way that decisions are being made at the giant retailer may need some re-targeting.

Not long ago Target suffered a massive data breach that led to the loss of the personal data of more than 70 million customers. Shortly thereafter, Target pulled the plug on a massive $5.4 billion failed market expansion into Canada. The failure led to the closure of all its stores north of the border, and was described as "an unmitigated disaster."[8] Target next became embroiled in a controversial transgender restroom policy which led to highly publicized boycotts of its stores.[9] More recently, the company was criticized for misleading advertising of some products being sold as "Made in the USA."[10]

Yes, the world of the twenty-first century is far different from the early days when the Dayton Dry Goods Company was launching itself into the great opportunities of the early 1900s. Target is a massive and complex corporation that faces continuing challenges of growth, competition, and control in a society with changing social values and customer desires. With all of its products, employees, customers, locations, and competitors, how can Target make the decisions it needs in order to continue thrive in the future?

Case Analysis Questions

1. **Discussion**   In what ways does Target's massive infrastructure relate to the complexities of making coherent, competitive decisions? Can a large corporation like Target cope—and thrive—in the information intense environment that it has created? What kinds of solutions might help Target avoid some of the pitfalls that it has experienced most recently?

2. **Discussion**   Target functions using a traditional, top-down structure with a group of C-suite executives led by a CEO. How can an organization with this kind of traditional structure expect to keep all of the moving parts in the company moving in a coordinated way? What kinds of decision-making tools might increase Target's ability to cope with changing market demands?

3. **Problem Solving**   Target has faced a number of very costly issues relating to decision making—how to control and safeguard its customers' private data, whether and in what ways to expand internationally, what kinds of in-store, customer-facing policies make the most sense, defining an ethical and defensible labeling policy, among others. What is clear is that there are issues relating to how information is used and decision making at Target Corporation that could benefit from some reevaluation and restructuring. What kinds of advice might you give to executives at Target for improving decision making at the company? Adopt the role of a business process consultant. How might you help Target to help itself to avoid some of the more controversial decisions that it has made over the last five or six years? Can you think of any data analytics approaches that could be useful? What about decision-making architecture more broadly—how are different kinds of information used in decision making? Who has access to tactical and strategic information? How might Target modify the policies and procedures it has in place for taking raw data, turning it into actionable corporate intelligence, and then effectively leveraging it to execute a tactical initiative?

4. **Further Research**   What is happening at Target Corporation now? What steps has Target taken to avoid the kind of massive data breach that sent its stock price tumbling by almost 50%? How has the company recovered from its massive Canadian expansion failure? What about its transgender restroom policy? What has Target done to improve its image following its "Made-in-the USA" scandal? How is Target coping with the trade war with China?

Laura Hutton/Shutterstock.com

Case 8 | Uber | Riding the Gig Economy

In many ways, the gig economy has begun to revolutionize how people consume products and services. Companies such as Airbnb, for example, provide an online marketplace that connects would-be renters with people seeking accommodations and eliminates the "middleman" in 192 countries worldwide. Companies following a "gig" approach are growing in number and popularity, with more appearing every day. The list is huge and includes—just to name a few—Lyft, which connects drivers with passengers; Turo, which connects rental cars with customers in need of a car; and OpenAirplane, RVshare, Sailo, Boatsetter, Parking Panda, Closet Collective, and Grubhub. We are seeing a revolution in the way the "market" functions . . . or are we?

Uber

Perhaps, currently, the best known of the gig companies making big waves in the press and in the new economy is Uber. And it all started because no one would give them (Uber's founders) a ride. In 2008, Travis Kalanick and Garrett Camp were in Paris and couldn't get a cab. Their experience led to the development of an extremely convenient, relatively safe, and also rather inexpensive app-enabled online driver service. Founded in 2009 and currently operating in 63 countries and 700+ cities, Kalanick and Camp's simple solution—Uber—has become a cultural phenomenon. Uber connects customers in need of a ride with "gig" workers who pick them up. The model is simple and extremely streamlined. Uber provides the market and takes a cut of the proceeds. No cash is exchanged between drivers and passengers. Everything is handled by Uber, whose app-enabled market has changed the way people think about transportation.

Untraditional Financial Models

Following in the path of other well-known new economy companies, Uber has continued to generate eye-popping revenues—estimates put

Uber's revenues in excess of $11 billion in 2018—its balance sheet is startling, but in the wrong way. Although these kinds of sales numbers are astonishing, particularly for a company that is only 10 years old, they have to be understood in light of the company's massive financial losses during the same period. Uber is estimated to have lost nearly $3 billion since its inception (exact figures are difficult to calculate because, as a privately held company, Uber is not required to disclose its financials). It is estimated that Uber spends $1.55 for every dollar in revenue it generates. So, although Uber generates huge annual sales numbers, it also spends a lot of money on drivers' pay, incentives, and bonuses.

What Is Uber Really Doing?

Uber is spending a substantial amount of money on technology. These investments include the recent strategic purchase of Geometric Intelligence—a start-up cofounded by academic researchers focused on making artificial intelligence (AI) systems that can navigate in the real world—perhaps hints at the company's longer-term strategic intent. This intent becomes more apparent when one considers that the company's investments in AI coincide with the fact that Uber is currently running fleets of self-driving cars. These vehicles are operating on the streets of California and in the city of Pittsburgh, Pennsylvania, where Uber is actively and aggressively testing its AI assets on the same city streets on which you and your friends and family drive every day. The city streets have essentially become a laboratory for Uber to road-test the machinery of its long-term vision. Given these kinds of investments, does this long-term vision include human drivers?

What's the Long-Term Vision?

Although some estimates put the number of drivers currently employed by Uber at upward of 150,000, the company's recent investments in AI, navigation technologies, and self-driving cars suggest that this particular gig employer may not be in it for the long term, at least as far as opportunities for human drivers are concerned. What do you think the new CEO of Uber, Dara Khosrowshahi, has in mind for the future of Uber? What role do you think he wants this emerging giant in the mass transit market to play moving forward? Do you think that investments in AI and self-driving cars are a good signal for future human employment with Uber? Why or why not? Is Uber the long-term answer for gig employees?

Case Analysis Questions

1. Discussion   Although many argue that the gig economy has opened up opportunities for individuals to be self-employed in ways that complement their lifestyle, the investments that gig giant Uber is making suggest a different kind of future for the uber-successful taxi substitute. What do think Uber has in mind?

2. Discussion   What are some of the potential applications for fleets of self-driving vehicles? What role might this kind of infrastructure play in towns and cities in the future? How might Uber leverage these kinds of assets to generate a profit? Do you see a way for Uber to be successful while still employing human drivers? How?

3. Problem Solving   You've been hired on by Uber's CEO Dara Khosrowshahi as the Chief Financial Officer and asked to address the issue of huge quarterly losses, despite massive sales revenues. The Uber fleet is not likely to be "self-driving" for at least another five years, and it isn't clear whether the current model will be sustainable until then, particularly given increasing competitive pressures to raise drivers' rates from companies such as Lyft. What steps could you take to address these competing pressures—market pressures to raise rates and the need to generate profits?

4. Further Research   Look into some of the more well-known gig companies currently making headlines in the financial press. Are any of these companies generating a profit? What factors are at work here? How have these profitable companies organized to become profitable? Are any of these companies moving toward models that remove the "human factor"—that mechanize in the way that it looks like Uber could be seeking to mechanize? How are the financial values of some of these gig companies being determined? In light of the huge losses experienced by some gig economies, what factors are likely playing a role in these financial evaluations? Are people speculating on an unknown future?

Rafael Henrique/SOPA ImagesZUMA Press, Inc. / Alamy Stock Photo

Case 9   Electronic Arts | Inside Fantasy Sports

Electronic Arts is the third largest and one of the most profitable players in the video game industry. Exclusive contracts with professional sports teams have enabled it to dominate the sports gaming market. Can EA stay in the pole position as gaming shifts to mobile in a crowded and contentious market?

Founded in 1982 by William "Trip" Hawkins, an early director of strategy and marketing for Apple Computer, EA gained quick distinction for its detail-oriented sports titles compatible with the Nintendo and Sega platforms. Although EA has also received good reviews for its strategy and first-person shooter games, it left its heart on the gridiron, diamond, court, or any other playing field long ago. According to former EA Sports marketing chief Jeffrey Karp, EA wanted to be "a sports company that makes games."

Ad Revenue In, Ad Revenue Out

Word of mouth may still be the most trusted form of advertising, and EA has always depended on fans to spread its gaming gospel. But in a highly competitive—and lucrative—gaming market, EA knows better than to skimp on brand building: it spends two to three times as much to market and advertise a title as it does developing it.[1]

The realism of EA's graphics set it apart from competitors long ago, but the energy and talent used to depict that realism might be wasted if EA games didn't include the one element fans most want to see: their favorite players. However, top athletes aren't cheap, and neither are their virtual depictions. EA spends $100+ million annually to license athletes, players' associations, and teams. It's a complex dance: *FIFA Soccer for iPad*, for example, requires hundreds of different licenses from a total of 22 club leagues, 500 teams, and 15,000 players.[2]

Past Glory

EA's past devotion to sports games has been a winning asset. But a funny thing happened on the way to the bank—over the course of a few short years, the gaming market radically changed. The way games were played in the past is not the way they are played now.

Blame the Wii. Or blame Apple. Or blame Android and social media platforms. Or blame the success of Activision Blizzard's massively successful *World of Warcraft (WoW)* that dominated EA's failed *Star Wars: The Old Republic*, which was intended to compete with *WoW* for gaming dollars. Successive generations of iPhone and iPad improved iOS gaming, and Apple's App Store suddenly became a self-sufficient gaming platform faster than you can say *Angry Birds*. Android apps are keeping the smart device playing field on the move and increasingly popular. Facebook also came into its own as a destination for simple but time-swallowing games. This kind of gaming was worlds away from EA's graphics-intense, true-to-life realism traditions, and it forced the company to do some serious reckoning on its future.[3]

The competition EA faces now is coming on three fronts—one of the growing trends in the gaming industry is free-to-play, console-level quality, for mobile games.[4] Quality and sophistication equivalent of EA's best offerings are now enabled for use on mobile devices. And, it's free. . . . The most dangerous competition that EA may be facing comes from a North Carolina–based competitor, Epic Games, which is the gaming studio responsible for the tremendously successful, free-to-play, *Fortnite*.[5] *Fortnite*'s tremendous success has been attributed to the fact that the console-level quality of this free-to-play game has seamless, cross-platform playability. The experiences that EA offers as a subscription-based pay-to-use service are now being offered for free by the competition. Numerous competitors in this space have emerged. Some of the most prominent include Critical Force,[6] the studio behind the uber-successful *Critical Ops*,[7] Mad Finger Games, whose first-person shooter *Shadow Gun* series have been downloaded tens of millions of times,[8] and Gameloft,[9] with a large stable of high-end graphic, mobile-enabled, free-to-play games, including the highly-successful *Asphalt* franchise.

Playing for Keeps

These competitive clashes have led to management turbulence at EA. Former CEO John Riccitiello stepped down in the face of management failures and tumbling market value.[10] Although historically a leader and an innovator in the gaming space, EA may have become more of a trend follower than a trend setter under his waning days at the top. When arch rival Activism found market success with its game *Call of Duty*, Riccitiello tried to copy their success with similar products. But consumers showed fatigue with first-person shooter military-themed games. EA also failed to remain current with market trends, making a failed foray into online gaming with *SimCity* and not keeping pace with rivals in gaming hardware.[11] Another threat emerged with the announcement that computer code from third-party servers could infiltrate some of the EA gaming platforms.[12] And then unwanted bugs appeared in *Battlefield 4* and the market turned against EA games made for aging console players.[13]

Although still a top player, EA faces substantial challenges from competing game companies, the cost of doing business, legal issues, dissatisfied gamers, and growing free-to-play, mobile-enabled competition. The next great bet by EA is another futuristic shooter game, *Titanfall*. It sounds good, but can EA overcome these threats and continue producing games with franchises that brought the company considerable success in the past? Above all, does EA have its operations under control as it makes plans for the growing big thing—free, high-quality, mobile-enabled games.

Case Analysis Questions

1. Discussion   How can feedforward, concurrent, and feedback controls help Electronic Arts meet its quality goals for video games?

2. Discussion   Which of the control systems and techniques can be most useful to EA's next round of business decisions, and why?

3. Problem Solving   Break the video-game production process down into its various components, a start-to-finish workflow model. Identify for each phase in the process the control standards that could be set so that managers make the process work best overall.

4. Further Research   What is the latest in Electronic Arts' quest to regain its former glory as among the top gaming publishers? How is it doing? What's the quality of its games? Is it positioned for future competitive advantage in an industry moving fast into mobile? Overall, is EA's executive team in control and keeping the company on "top of its game"?

Jessica Rinaldi/Reuters/Newscom

| Case 10 | Dunkin' Donuts | Betting Dollars on Donuts

Once a niche company operating in the northeastern United States, Dunkin' Donuts is opening hundreds of stores and entering new markets. The java giant is also expanding its food and coffee menus to ride the wave of fresh trends and to appeal to a new generation of customers. Can the company keep up with its own rapid growth?

Serving the Caffeinated Masses

There's a lot more to a coffee shop than just change in the tip jar. Some 400 billion cups of coffee are consumed every year, making it the most popular beverage globally. Estimates indicate that more than 150 million Americans drink a total of 465 million cups of coffee a day.[1] With Starbucks driving tastes for upscale coffee, some customers may wonder whether any coffee vendors remember the days when drip coffee came in only two varieties—regular and decaf. But Dunkin' Donuts does, and it's betting dollars to donuts that consumers nationwide will embrace its reputation for value, simplicity, and a superior Boston Kreme donut.

Americans are familiar with the Dunkin' Donuts brand through its more than 8,500 domestic outlets, which have their densest cluster in the Northeast and a growing presence in the rest of the country.[2] But the brand has also managed to carve out an international niche with international shops in 36 countries. Dunkin' shops are not only found in expected markets such as Canada and Brazil, but also in some unexpected locations like Qatar, South Korea, Pakistan, and the Philippines.[3]

Changing Course to Follow Demand

For most of its history, Dunkin' Donuts' primary product focus was implicit in its name: donuts, and coffee in which to dip them. First-time customers acquainted with this simple reputation were often overwhelmed by the wide varieties of donuts stacked end-to-end in neat, mouthwatering rows. But faced with fierce and innovative competition—think Starbucks and local coffee shops—Dunkin' Donuts opted for a time-honored business tradition: follow the leader. The company now offers a competitive variety of espresso-based drinks complemented with a broad number of sugar-free flavorings, including caramel, vanilla, and Mocha Swirl.[4] You can also breakfast on Dunkin's bagel and croissant-based breakfast sandwiches or sausage pancake bites, or have a Big N' Toasted.

Spot on with Partnerships

Dunkin Donuts' history of offering simple and straightforward morning fare has given it the competitive advantage of distinction as *the* anti-Starbucks—earnest and without pretense. Like Craftsman tools and Levi's jeans, the company appeals to unpretentious people who enjoy well-crafted products.

Although Dunkin' Donuts often partners with a select group of grocery retailers—such as Stop & Shop and Walmart—to create a store-within-a-store concept, the company won't set up shop in just any grocery store. "We want to be situated in supermarkets that provide a superior overall customer experience," said John Fassak, vice president of business development. "Of course, we also want to ensure that the supermarket is large enough to allow us to provide the full expression of our brand . . . which includes hot and iced coffee, our line of high-quality espresso beverages, donuts, bagels, muffins, and even our breakfast sandwiches."[5]

But why stop at grocery stores? Taking its cooperation philosophy a step further, Dunkin' Donuts has also entered the lodging market with their first hotel restaurant at the Great Wolf Lodge in Concord, North Carolina—one of North America's largest indoor water parks. Dunkin' Donuts offers a variety of store models to suit any lodging property, including full retail shops, kiosks, and self-serve hot coffee stations perfect for gift shops and general stores, snack bars, and convention registration areas.[6]

You'll also find Dunkin' Donuts packaged coffees for sale on grocery store shelves, just like Starbucks. They accomplished this through a distribution alliance with Procter & Gamble. So, Dunkin' is clearly on the move. Who knows where the brand will pop up next?

Sweet Future or a Cold Cup?

If Dunkin' Donuts can find the sweet spot, by being within most consumers' reach but falling just short of a Big Brother–like omnipresence, the company's strategy of expansion may well be rewarded handsomely. But this strategy is not without its risks. In the quest to appeal to new customers, offering too many original products and placements could dilute the essential brand appeal of coffee and donuts and alienate long-time customers who respect simplicity and authenticity. On the other hand, new customers previously unexposed to Dunkin' Donuts might see it as "yesterday's brand" without the new offerings.

For the time being, Dunkin' Donuts seems determined in its quest for domination of the coffee and breakfast market. Will Dunkin' Donuts strike the *right* balance of products and placement needed to mount a formidable challenge against competitors?

Case Analysis Questions

1. Discussion How does Porter's five forces analysis describe the food industry in which Dunkin' Donuts and Starbucks compete? What are the strategic implications for Dunkin' Donuts?

2. Discussion Could Dunkin' Donuts use strategic alliances to even better advantage than it does now? How could cooperative strategies help it succeed further with its master plan for growth?

3. Problem Solving Until recently, the Starbucks brand was much better known around the world than Dunkin' Donuts. As Dunkin's CEO, what global strategy—globalization, multidomestic, or transnational—would you follow to position Dunkin' as a real challenge to Starbucks in the international markets, and why?

4. Further Research Gather information on industry trends, as well as current developments—domestic and international—affecting Dunkin' Donuts and its competitors. Use this information to build an up-to-date SWOT analysis for Dunkin' Donuts. Based on this analysis, is Dunkin's top leadership doing the right things when it comes to strategic management for sustainable competitive advantage, or not?

ITAR-TASS News Agency/Alamy Stock Photo

Case 11 | National Public Radio | Many Voices Serving Many Needs

When the word "organization" or "company" or "firm" comes up in conversations with your friends and classmates, the focus is most often on large for-profit businesses. Sometimes it's a smaller and local business, or even a franchise operation. The common ground among them, large or small, is actively working to generate profits for owners and shareholders. They do this by selling goods and services with a "bottom line goal"—to generate sales revenues that are greater than costs incurred.

There are other types of organizations that don't always get the attention they deserve. Instead of seeking profits, these "nonprofits" focus on public service and the common good. Think about the American Red Cross, Big Brothers Big Sisters of America, Teach for America, Make-a-Wish Foundation, American Heart Association, United Way, National Audubon Society, Habitat for Humanity, and even nongovernmental organizations like the United Nations.

The underlying mission of a nonprofit organization isn't to generate a financial return for investors. Instead, it is typically to serve some kind of broad public purpose, provide help or services to a particular segment of the population, or to improve the lives of people living in a given community. The revenues that are generated by a nonprofit—if any—or the donations that it collects from community-minded patrons, are used to cover costs while advancing the cause that defines the underlying mission of the organization.

Speaking of donations in support of nonprofits, how often have you tuned in to your local National Public Radio (NPR) affiliate and listened to fund-raising appeals? NPR's stated mission is "to create a more informed public—one challenged and invigorated by a deeper understanding and appreciation of events, ideas, and cultures."[1] But how does NPR approach this goal? How does it survive financially? How does a "national" public radio service link with "local" communities? In answering such questions, you'll find that NPR, like other nonprofits, is just as complex to organize and manage as a for-profit business.

National Public Radio was formally incorporated in 1970 by a group of 90 charter stations for the purpose of providing national news programming.[2] Unlike for-profit corporations which generate returns through the sale of products or services, or commercial broadcasters which sell advertising spots during their programming, NPR's operating budget depends fundamentally on the donations it receives through pledge drives. NPR also receives operating capital from corporate underwriting, state and local government funding, contributions made by institutions of higher education, and allocations made by the Corporation for Public Broadcasting (CPB), which itself is a federally funded media organization.[3]

For-profit media typically operates as a group of television or radio stations that broadcast content provided by the same source. Local affiliates of a parent company are under obligation to broadcast integrated content, which generates branding benefits for the parent company and can create larger markets for the network's content.[4] The parent company distributes its own, exclusive, program content between affiliates,[5] who are responsible for broadcasting it and generating revenues from advertisers.

NPR is linked to local affiliates through a broadcasting syndication.[6] Programming is typically either "live" or "pre-recorded" just prior to the broadcast. This programming is then distributed over the Internet or via satellite feed to local stations who pay for the content. NPR doesn't bind affiliates to an exclusive agreement. Affiliates can broadcast their own slate of programs, which can include NPR content, or other content of their choosing.

NPR collaborates with some 1,000 locally owned and operated member stations. Dispersed across the United States, they distribute content generated by 17 domestic and 17 global news bureaus. It is estimated that NPR content reaches more than 100 million consumers across its radio, smart speaker, social media, apps, and podcast platforms.[7]

What distinguishes the NPR organizational model from the increasingly prevalent consolidation among media corporations[8] is that each member station has autonomy to choose its own slate of programming, its own broadcast schedule, and its own format, to incorporate broadcasting content produced by other radio stations and produce its own content based on the tastes and needs of local consumers.[9] The relationship between local affiliates and NPR is also reciprocal. Local affiliates that generate content based on local stories of interest can funnel this content through the network of regional bureaus. If this content has national appeal, then it is broadcast nationally, which is why local stories are often heard on nationally broadcast programs.

NPR collaborates with local affiliates across the nation, making relevant and timely content available to affiliates, in order to advance the civic goal of helping to create a more informed and educated public. Affiliates participate in this broader goal in many different ways according the specific needs and attributes of the local markets they serve.

Case Analysis Questions

1. **Discussion**   What are the implications of NPR's operating approach in contrast to the that of for-profit media? How might this decision be related to NPRs not-for-profit status? What kinds of issues are likely to play a role in how successful this model is, moving forward, in light of the massive consolidation in the media industry?

2. **Discussion**   How does the structure of NPR relate to questions relating to branding? What about quality control? Would this kind of "organic" organizational structure work in a not-for-profit setting? Why or why not? What other kinds of businesses might benefit from this kind of loose conglomeration? Why, specifically? What about higher education?

3. **Problem Solving**   Draw a diagram that shows what you believe NPR's present organization structure looks like. Be sure to include all possible components in the structure. Consider this structure from the standpoint of an organization design consultant. How could this structure be improved? How can NPR provide even more compelling local and national content without losing its authenticity and independence from major commercial media sponsors?

4. **Further Research**   What is the current state of the media industry today? Look into current trends and patterns orbiting major media organizations. Are there any emerging drawbacks from current approaches being used by major media companies today? What are some of the similarities and differences between the biggest players in the industry? What is the likely future of syndicates like NPR? What are the chances for survival of the "public" or "not for profit" model in light of the growing trends that you've identified? What kinds of changes are organizations such as NPR likely going to have to make to continue to compete?

Ann Hermes/The Christian Science Monitor/Getty Images

Case 12 | Gamification | Finding Legitimacy in the New Corporate Culture

Would you be surprised to see a co-worker playing a video game, and realizing the boss didn't care? Companies are increasingly using video games or "gamification" as a way to enhance productivity and increase creativity and satisfaction in the workplace.

It is more common today to see people playing games at work and being praised—not criticized—for doing it. The new legitimacy of gaming in the corporate world is called "gamification." Games are being used to promote a culture of learning, individualism, and fun, while also focusing attention on the company's bottom-line performance goals.[1]

Enjoyment-Based Economy

Jesse Schell, CEO of Schell Games, says: "We are shifting into an enjoyment-based economy. And who knows more about making enjoyment than game developers?"[2] Gamification is exploding in areas ranging from marketing and politics, to health and fitness, to business and higher education, with analysts predicting that gamification will soon be a multi–billion-dollar industry.[3] The commercial contexts within which gamification continues to grow range from customer engagement, to employee performance to training, to innovation management, to personal development, to sustainability.

Top Firms Are Playing Games

High-profile firms are now riding the gamification band wagon. Many are beginning to use social media–linked games and simulations for recruiting and training. Games are being used to help make a connection with applicants, and to help predict how successful they'll be on the job.

The mega-consumer products company Unilever has developed an entirely digital, user-friendly recruiting process (X). Applicants complete a short form connected to their LinkedIn profile, and from there, spend 20 minutes playing a series of games that provide insight into applicants' personality, communication style, and problem-solving skills. Game results are then used to determine which applicants move to the next phase in the process. Gamification has allowed Unilever to streamline the recruitment process, to efficiently evaluate a much larger number of applicants, and ultimately to make the best selection decisions.

Marriott also uses social media applications to connect employees (and potential employees) through gamification. Marriott uses a Facebook-based game that allows potential employees insight into available career paths in the hospitality industry. The game also is used for training current employees. Siemens also has developed engaging gamification tools for employee training that are designed to help employees better understand their role with the company.

Games serve a growing number of multiple uses. At Khan Academy, a nonprofit educational institution founded by Harvard graduate Salman Khan which reaches approximately 10 million students each month, gamification is a core method for enhancing students' learning experience.[5] An IBM executive says the firm's use of gaming for employees who spend lots of time working from home or traveling is a "way to help colleagues connect and stay engaged." Software Company SAP uses a game that includes "assigning sales leads and environmental challenges that award points for tasks like carpooling," says its chief innovation strategist, Mario Herger.[6]

Games Change Cultures

Gaming interfaces also are changing traditional workplace rules and behavioral norms, or at least realigning them with popular culture. Users believe that gaming helps employees feel more engaged and connected in an online environment that they can enjoy separately from work activities. Gaming can be used in strategic planning to simulate various business scenarios. Reward and competition tactics in games can be applied to boost interest in mundane tasks like data entry and invoicing.

Although some fear that gaming has the potential to breed unhealthy competition and hurt relationships, experts claim it's a great motivator that can increase employees' enthusiasm for their daily

activities and the energy they bring to work. Game-specific problem solving can also enhance critical thinking and analytical abilities, as well as develop desirable personal attributes such as persistence, creativity, and resilience.[7]

But, it's also recognized that gamification has to be well integrated with business needs and objectives. Industry analyst Brian Burke cautions: "To achieve success for companies starting in gamification, the first design point is to motivate players to achieve their goals—and those goals should overlap with the business goals."[8]

To Play or Not to Play

As the gamification trend continues to grow, employees may be asking themselves whether a virtual badge of gaming accomplishment is truly better than a good old-fashioned pat on the back and verbal "job well done" from a manager. Clearly it's no cure-all for all of the issues that can potentially decrease the performance of a team, or an organization. "Adding gamification to the workplace drives performance but it doesn't make up for bad management," says Kris Duggan, co-founder of game-maker Badgeville.[9]

Case Analysis Questions

1. Discussion   What arguments can you make that support the legitimation of gamification in an organization's culture? What examples can you give or create to justify your arguments?

2. Discussion   What arguments can you make against trying to make gamification part of an organization's culture? What examples can you give or create to justify your arguments?

3. Problem Solving   Consider yourself the go-to "idea person" for friends who head two local organizations—a fire department and a public library. Both complain about morale problems and ask you for advice on creating a positive organizational culture. They want to know how your interest in gaming can be used to improve staff morale and performance. What will you suggest and why?

4. Further Research   Review how organizations, including major corporations, nonprofits, and the military, are using gaming. What role is gaming taking on in these settings, and how does its use affect the organizational cultures? What does the evidence suggest—is gamification merely a passing trend, or is it here to stay and may even grow in use in the future?

wavebreakmedia/Shutterstock.com

Case 13 | RealRecruit | Protecting Student Athletes

Along with attention to fair equitable treatment, and the welfare and well-being of employees in organizations,[1] there is an increased focus on how students—and in particular student-athletes—are treated once they matriculate to an institution of higher education.[2] The issue has attracted significant attention in the popular press, from print to television to Internet to live streams and more. Some cases have risen to the level of high profile scandals relating to how members of university staff, athletics teams officials, and members of university administration have treated student athletes.

Among high profile university sexual abuse cases reaching the public eye, the behaviors of players, coaches, athletics trainers, sports medicine practitioners, as well as high-ranking university administrators including presidents and members of boards of trustees have all been brought into question. What can be done to get on top of these situations before they get out of hand and protect student athletes from being damaged through misbehavior in universities?

The ubiquitous availability of sophisticated communications and data transmissions technologies has fundamentally transformed the business landscape in areas including operations management, inventory management, research and development, manufacturing, recruitment, selection, training, marketing/advertising, sales, service, as the tip of the iceberg. Can the same be said of Title IX and collegiate athletics?

Not surprisingly, technologies are fundamentally changing the ways in which student athletes make decisions about what program to matriculate to following acceptance to a college or university. A prime example is RealRecruit. Unless you are a highly recruited, high-profile Division I athlete, then the chances are good that you haven't heard of RealRecruit. But, the company—which makes heavy use of virtual communications technologies—is making real waves in the world of collegiate athletics.

Founded by David Chadwick, a former collegiate basketball player at Rice and Valparaiso,[3] RealRecruit helps universities and athletics departments administrators manage their culture, and head off emergent issues before they become major—potentially catastrophic—issues.[4] RealRecruit's technology platform collects data and information anonymously, from current student athletes. This information is put into a database that the company makes available to university employees and officials, using a format that allows key decision makers to see what's happening in broad strokes on the ground, but doesn't compromise the identity of the key informants. The goal is to provide rich and ideally real-time feedback so that decision makers can stay on top of the situations faced by student athletes.

RealRecruit was started by Chadwick as a class project in school, and was designed to operate as a Yelp-type interface[5] to give prospective scholarship athletes the inside scoop into a given program. The "scoop" was to come directly from current student-athletes, those in the best positions to give real insights into what a given program was like and what it was like to be part of it. The goal was to develop a real-time, public database that athletes being recruited could use to make a more informed decision about where to go.

Chadwick's initial idea changed when he first tested out the system. Once his program went live, he found that what student athletes shared was a lot more serious—reports of sexual assaults, hazing, drugs, sexual abuse, bullying and misconduct by coaches, other students, teammates, and everything in between. With this realization, Chadwick shifted RealRecruit away from his initial vision as public database and toward life as an anonymous channel where officials associated with the Athletics Department could learn about what's going on at their school—directly from the athletes and people involved in their programs.

RealRecruit has grown its client base to include over 70 universities. It has become a channel for administrators and university officials to communicate directly with student-athletes while simultaneously gaining lots of feedback and maintaining students' anonymity. The real-time feedback made possible by the platform gives university officials an opportunity to get ahead of problems before they get out of hand. The availability of this valuable information puts university officials into the driver's seat so they can get ahead of a scandal. It also puts them on the spot, because when something bad happens they're no longer in a position to say—"We didn't know."

RealRecruit also is being used to help schools and athletics departments generate real-time ratings of the members of its athletics employees and staff by the stakeholders most directly knowledgeable of their performance—the student-athletes. This gives schools another layer of feedback that can be used for developmental purposes to improve the performance of these employees. The company is helping colleges and universities improve oversight of employee performance and the treatment of student-athletes, and see what's happening in the Athletics Departments at these institutions.

Case Analysis Questions

1. Discussion In what ways can an anonymous, Internet-enabled database be useful to any organization concerned about not just its performance, but also employee welfare? What are the possible drawbacks associated with a data-driven tool like the one offered by RealRecruit that depends on anonymous feedback and information? What are the pros and cons of having an outside provider play this kind of liaison role between employees and the organization? As a team leader, how might you use an anonymous survey-based approach to improve your relationships with team members? What kinds of questions might you ask?

2. Discussion What impact can the presence of a company like RealRecruit have on the culture and operational activities of big-time athletics departments at universities? Is the feedback it makes available enough to change things? Can RealRecruit really help stem the tide of the kinds of scandals that have been so much in the news lately? How about applications of this technology to students who are not involved in athletics? Why or why not? In what ways might it help them as well?

3. Problem Solving You are the athletic director (AD) at a major Division I university and have direct or indirect responsibility for thousands of individuals. The university recently hired RealRecruit to provide information relating to your athletics program, and to help avoid the kind of scandal that led to the firing of your predecessor. Well, the first reports are in. You've learned that there is illegal sports gambling going on among student athletes, including football and the men's basketball program. This situation can lead to a major, national media–level scandal, and a multi-year NCAA post-season death sentence is also a real possibility. What do you do, and why? Be as specific as possible—build out your plan and timeline for dealing with this situation.

4. Further Research What is happening with RealRecruit? Are there any other up-and-coming players on the horizon in this business space? Is there room for more innovation in this area, something that could be developed by RealRecruit or a competitor? If you were a top university administrator, what would you like to have at your disposal to fend off scandalous events and protect your students—athletes and others?

Noah Berger/Bloomberg/Getty Images

Case 14 Zappos | They Do It with Humor

Zappos.com customers are known for fierce loyalty, and it's easy to see why. CEO Tony Hsieh has built a billion-dollar business by providing happiness to customers and employees. Even fellow businesspeople get happy while seeking to learn more about Zappos's unique blend of humor, compassion, and high-quality customer service. How does Zappos do it?

When Zappos CEO Tony Hsieh was the featured guest on *The Colbert Report*, host Stephen Colbert grilled him about Zappos's phenomenal success and rabid customer loyalty. Hsieh replied that it's Zappos's goal to deliver "WOW" in every shoe or clothing box. Today, the company is consistently ranked highly as one of *Fortune*'s "Best Companies to Work For."[1]

Unusual Leader, Unusual Employer

Zappos.com was launched in 1999 as the brainchild of Hsieh and founder Nick Swinmurn. Within just a few years, the Las Vegas–based firm caught the eye of Amazon's Jeff Bezos. He liked what he saw so much that he bought the firm for Amazon's business stable, pledging not to interfere with Hsieh and Zappos's unique way of doing business.

The blog search engine *Land* called Zappos "the poster child for how to connect with customers online."[2] And under Amazon, Zappos has maintained its focus. The company's relentless pursuit of the ultimate customer experience is the stuff of legend. Zappos offers extremely fast shipping at no cost and will cover the return shipping if you are dissatisfied for any reason at any time. For Hsieh, the Zappos brand is less about a particular type of product and more about providing good customer service. He has said, "We could be in any industry that we can differentiate ourselves through better customer service and better customer experience."[3] He has even ventured that he could see the Zappos name on things as large as airlines or hotels, as long as the service was up to his exacting standards.

A Culture to Thrive In

Zappos's success comes down to the company's culture and the unusual amount of openness Hsieh encourages among employees, vendors, and other businesses. "If we get the culture right," he says, "most of the other

stuff, like the brand and the customer service will just happen. . . . We want the culture to grow stronger and stronger as we grow."

Named "The Smartest Dude in Town" by business magazine *Vegas Inc.*, Hsieh believes employees have to be free to be themselves. That means no call times or scripts for customer service representatives, regular costume parties, and parades and decorations in each department. Customer service reps are given a lot of leeway to make sure every customer is an enthusiastic customer.

Sharing the Fun

Hsieh believes so strongly in the Zappos culture that he's on a mission to share it with anyone who will listen. In a program called Zappos Insights, "Company Evangelists" lead tour groups of 20 around the Las Vegas headquarters. Office cubicles often overflow with kitschy action figures and brightly colored balloons, giving participants a glimpse of a workplace that prizes individuality and fun as much as satisfied customers. Staffers blow horns and ring cowbells to greet participants in the 16 weekly tours, and each department tries to offer a more outlandish welcome than the last. "The original idea was to add a little fun," Hsieh says, but it grew into a friendly competition "as the next aisle said, 'We can do it better.'"[4]

The tours are free, but many visitors actually come for paid one- and two-day seminars that immerse participants in the Zappos culture. Want to learn how to recruit employees who are committed to your company culture? You'll get face time with Zappos HR staff. Yearn to learn what keeps customers coming back? Ask their Customer Loyalty Team. Hungry for a home-cooked meal? The capstone of the two-day boot camp is dinner at Tony Hsieh's house, with ample time to talk customer service with the CEO himself.[5]

Those who want to learn Zappos's secrets without venturing to Las Vegas can subscribe to a members-only community that grants access to video interviews and chats with Zappos management. Ask nicely, and the company will send you a free copy of their *Zappos Family Culture Book*, an annual compilation of every employee's ideas about Zappos's mission and core values. Hsieh has his own tome, too—*Delivering Happiness*.

Zappos's Next Act

So, what comes next? As Zappos grows within the Amazon umbrella, which is constantly growing as well, and as Hsieh devotes more time to community service and his writing and speaking engagements, can the Zappos culture survive growth and a possible leadership transition? Will Zappos continue to remain prosperous and keep its reputation as a great employer? Is Hsieh's unique brand of leadership so built into the firm's practices that Zappos will stay the same even under a new CEO?

Case Analysis Questions

1. Discussion What leadership traits and style does Tony Hsieh demonstrate at Zappos? What aspects of his leadership can you criticize, if any? Is his successful leadership approach transferable to other leaders and other organizations, or is it person and situation specific?

2. Discussion Can you find examples of where House's path–goal theory of leadership can be confirmed or disconfirmed in the Zappos setting? Explain your answer.

3. Problem Solving Tony Hsieh is a big thinker, and Zappos is clearly his baby. But he's also into philanthropy, and community development activities that are taking up more of his time. Perhaps he'll come up with other new business ideas as well. As a leadership coach, what steps would you recommend that he take now to ensure that his leadership style and vision live on at Zappos long after his departure? What can a strong and secure leader like Hsieh do to ensure a positive leadership legacy?

4. Further Research Check the latest on Zappos and Tony Hsieh. How and what are each doing at the present time. Do some research to compare and contrast the leadership style and characteristics of Tony Hsieh with those of his boss at Amazon, Jeff Bezos. How are the leadership styles of the two CEOs alike? In what ways do they differ? For whom would you rather work? Is one better than the other in its situational context?

AP Images/Tom Gannam

Case 15 | Panera Bread | Growing a Company with Personality

Panera Bread is in the business of satisfying customers. With fresh-baked breads, gourmet soups, and efficient service, the franchise has surpassed all expectations for success. But how did a startup food company get so big, so fast?

French Roots, American Staples

What's so exciting about bread and soup? For some people, it conjures up images of bland food that soothes an upset stomach. Others think of the kind of simple gruel offered to jailed prisoners in movies. But for Panera Bread, a company able to successfully spot long-term trends in the food industry, artisan-style bread served with deli sandwiches and soups is a combination proven to please the hungry masses.

Panera's roots go back to 1981, when Louis Kane and Ron Shaich founded Au Bon Pain Company Inc. The chain of French-style bakeries soon became the dominant operator in the bakery/café category on the East Coast. In a 1993 expansion move Au Bon Pain purchased the Saint Louis Bread Company, a Missouri-based chain of about 20 bakery-cafés. It renovated the stores and renamed them Panera Bread, and their sales skyrocketed. In 1999, Panera Bread was spun off as a separate company. Since then, its offerings have grown to include not only a variety of soups and sandwiches, but also soufflés, salads, paninis, breakfast sandwiches, and a variety of pastries and sweets. Most of the menu offerings somehow pay homage to the company name and heritage—bread—and Panera takes great pride that its loaves are handmade and baked fresh daily.[1]

Modern Tastes, Modern Trends

Panera's self-perception as a purveyor of artisan bread well predated the current national trend for fresh bread and the explosion of artisan bakeries throughout metropolitan America.[2] In addition, Panera

proactively responded to unease about trans fats by voluntarily removing them from its menu. "Panera recognized that trans fat was a growing concern to our customers and the medical community; therefore we made it a priority to eliminate it from our menu," said Tom Gumpel, former vice-president of bakery development. Panera menu items are free from trans fats, except for small amounts that occur naturally in dairy and meat products as well as in some condiments.[3]

According to Ron Shaich, former CEO and now executive chairman of the board of Panera, "Real success never comes by simply responding to the day-to-day pressures; in fact, most of that is simply noise. The key to leading an organization is understanding the long-term trends at play and getting the organization ready to respond."[4]

Stay Fresh Personality

Ron Shaich, growing up in Livingston, New Jersey, wasn't focused on being a bread magnate. He wanted to be a public servant, working in government on public policy. As a high school student he even interned for a congressman from his home state. His entrepreneurial spark was ignited during his sophomore year in college at Clark University, when the owner of a local convenience store that didn't cater to students threw him and his friends out. That negative experience lit Shaich's entrepreneurial fire. It was at that point when he had the inspiration for the student government at his college—he was the treasurer—to open a store for students, run by students. The store was a huge success at Clark. He became an impassioned advocate of student governments opening their own stores, speaking on the topic across the country.

Shaich's personal transformation from a government–public service focus to a retailing–market focus emerged from the recognition that a store for the people, run by the people, could be a success. Following college, he matriculated to Harvard business school, where after graduation he went to work for the Original Cookie Company. With a desire to start his own cookie business, he was ultimately able to find a tiny retail location, opening the Cookie Jar in 1980. This first taste of entrepreneurialism ultimately led to a license agreement with Au Bon Pain, and to the story that has become famous with the explosion of Panera Bread Co.[5]

Sticking It Out

All of Panera's attention to monitoring trends paid off handsomely. *BusinessWeek* recognized Panera as one of its "100 Hot Growth Companies." And *Forbes* named it number 4 on its list of "Top 20 Franchises for the Buck." It consistently ranks at the top of Sandleman & Associates' surveys of customer satisfaction.[6] Under Shaich's leadership Panera demonstrated that sticking to company ideals while staying in the lead on industry trends pleased customers time and time again. But can this company continue to navigate the changing dietary trends and concerns about fast food in today's unstable market?

Case Analysis Questions

1. Discussion How might consumers' perception of Panera's menu and atmosphere affect their dining experience and tendencies to return as customers?

2. Discussion Describe how stereotypes about the fast-food industry might positively and negatively affect Panera. Do you think of Panera as a fast-food restaurant, or has the company managed to distinguish itself from this industry segment?

3. Problem Solving What personality characteristics would you expect Panera's founder Ron Shaich to display? How would these characteristics help or hinder him during Panera's early entrepreneurship stage and during its continuing growth stage? As a leadership succession consultant, what would you identify as the three or four most important of Shaich's personal qualities that should be sought after in the next CEO, and why?

4. Further Research   Find data reporting on Panera's recent sales and product initiatives. Find out more about Shaich and how his values and personality affect the company, its mission, and its strategies. Is Panera on the leading edge of its industry, or are other competitors—especially new entrants—starting to nip away at its traditional customers and markets? Does Panera seem to have what it takes to deal with shifting customer values and perceptions of the fast-food industry?

David Paul Morris/Bloomberg/Getty Images

Case 16 | Salesforce | Instant Praise, Instant Criticism

Instead of waiting a year for your annual performance review, how would you like to know where you stand by getting immediate feedback about how you're doing? After all, the once-a-year version might be little more than a boss-administered exercise in unhelpful feedback.

The typical annual review, including past performance, goal setting, pay, and improvement needs can be information overload for many. For goals accomplished today, how valuable and motivating is recognition and feedback six months from now? What if you could get real-time feedback and coaching by asking colleagues, managers, and peers questions such as, "What did you think of my presentation?" or "What can be done better?"

Meaningful Recognition

In today's business environment of rapid speed, employers are beginning to realize the true value of real-time feedback for employee recognition, control, performance, and motivation. When Salesforce bought Rypple, a maker of performance management social software, CEO Mark Benioff said that "the next generation of HCM [human capital management] is not just about a cloud delivery model; it's about a fundamentally better way to recruit, manage, and empower employees in a social world." This approach is nothing new for the customer relationship management (CRM) megafirm. For most of its almost 20 years, Salesforce has used acquisitions to expand the CRM offerings it makes available to clients. In 2016 alone, Salesforce spent almost $4.5 billion acquiring 13 companies.

Leading up to the acquisition, Rypple's top management pitched its software this way: "Performance management has become disconnected from real performance. Today, we move faster. We're more connected. This requires a new approach to performance." Rather than waiting a year to learn what managers think of them, employees using Rypple's

platform send out a quick (50 words or less) pointed question to folks ranging from managers to peers to customers to suppliers. Some call this just-in-time performance improvement. Benioff called it a winner.

Enter Work.com

Rebranded within Salesforce as Work.com, the Rypple product provides a real-time snapshot of employee performance in a single place, on completion of a goal, project, or quarter. Benefits include the ability to give public thanks and solicit feedback in a timely way. A coaching interface allows workers to build coaching networks to spot needed improvements. This helps to resolve problems and issues as they arise rather than after the fact. It also means quicker implementation of needed changes.

Salesforce is always looking to expand the range of client needs it can serve. The CRM innovator has continued to develop strategic partnerships to fast-track its strategic goals. In February 2017, Salesforce announced that it had entered into an "artificial intelligence" partnership with IBM, with the goal of enhancing the range of analytical tools it provides to clients. Artificial intelligence plays a key role in the Salesforce.com model. Said Benioff of the IBM partnership: "AI is accelerating . . . partnering with IBM was a natural given 'how I respect how they have stayed true to customer values.'"

More or Less Motivation?

Some ask if too much feedback becomes a bad thing. Reliance on so much feedback and what other people say can be a detriment to learning the hard way—by making mistakes. Others believe that people are motivated to work hard when their efforts are recognized in a public way. Are you willing to wait a year until your next performance review to get much-needed positive feedback? Or would you like to work in an environment where real-time report cards of your progress are common?

Case Analysis Questions

1. Discussion   Is the annual performance review past its "sell by" date or just in need of some revisions? If real-time reviews are available using software such as Salesforce's Work.com, is there a need for an annual performance review?

2. Discussion   What are some of the potential benefits of having a "real-time" evaluation of your performance? What kinds of things can organizations do differently when employees have this kind of immediate feedback available to them? What about on the flip side? Is there a downside? What are some of the potential drawbacks of giving employees immediate feedback? Can feedback be "too" immediate—that is, close to the situation? Why? In what ways?

3. Problem Solving   You've just taken a new job in human resource management, and the organization's president gave you this high-priority task: Give us a plan that can make performance reviews motivating to employees and bosses alike. "I'm tired," she says, "of hearing everyone complain that annual reviews are demotivating. We need to review performance. Surely there are ways that we can make ours more valuable." As you sit down to think about this assignment, make a few notes on the major issues and things you might recommend. Use insights from motivation theories to justify what's on your list.

4. Further Research   How about the real-time and Web-based approach to performance reviews offered by Salesforce? Do some research and identify the latest developments with it and others like it. Is this online approach to performance assessment the right path to a more motivated workforce? What does the evidence say about benefits? What downsides are users reporting? Overall, what's the current verdict on Work.com and similar products—good for bosses, employers, or employees?

Case 17 | Auto Racing | When the Driver Takes a Back Seat

When you think of auto racing, do you first think of drivers . . . or teamwork? Watch any televised race, and the majority of the camera time is dedicated to the drivers and their cars. But, the driver is simply one member of a larger team that works together to achieve maximum performance. When the driver wins, the team wins as well, and the driver is the first to thank them.

In the world of competitive auto racing, the drivers are the sport's rock stars. They're courted by sponsors, adored by fans, and made the subject of interview after interview by the racing press. While it goes without saying that drivers are absolutely essential to earning a trophy, racing enthusiasts, teammates, and especially drivers will tell you that they can't win the race by themselves—it takes a great team to win a race.

Although three of the major forms of professional auto racing—NASCAR, Formula One, and rally car racing—each use different vehicles, rules, and team structures, teamwork is the common denominator among them. Ray Evernham, former crew chief and team manager for Hendrick Motorsports' DuPont car, describes teamwork this way: "We're all spark plugs. If one doesn't fire just right, we can't win the race. So no matter whether you are the guy that's doing the fabricating or changing tires on Sundays and that's the only job responsibility you have, if you don't do your job then we're not going to win. And no one is more or less important than you."[1]

What are the qualities of successful racing teams? Let's take a look.

NASCAR

NASCAR is the most widely known and watched racing sport in the United States, and the popularity and success of Jeff Gordon has more than a little to do with that. Gordon has the most wins in NASCAR's modern era, has the third-most all-time wins, and has become a spokesperson for the importance of teamwork in NASCAR racing.[2] "My job to communicate is probably the most important thing," Gordon has said. "Because I've got to send a message from the race car and the race track back to the team so that they can make the proper adjustments."

Cars running in NASCAR races hit speeds over 200 miles per hour. But winning or losing can be decided by tenths of a second.[3] Although

it's the driver who gets featured in the winner's circle and in all the advertisements, the difference between crossing the finish line first or losing the race often comes down to the pits, where the efforts of teammates with titles like Car Chief, Fueler, Jackman, Tire Carrier, and Changer have to operate together in just the right way. It's in a crowded pit lane that tires get changed, windshields cleaned, fenders bent back into shape, and spring and balance adjustments fine tuned. Any seconds saved by pit crews are a driver's best friends. Little wonder that racing teams give high priority to hiring the right crew chiefs and building high-performance pit crew teams to maximize their winning chances on race days.

In his analysis of successful NASCAR teams, Robert Williamson notes that an essential characteristic is a team's sense of ownership for all actions—"We won the race, we hit the wall, we had a tire problem, we missed the setup for the track, we nailed that pit stop," rather than noting the success or shortcoming of an individual.[4]

It's impossible for a car to complete a NASCAR race without multiple visits to the pit, and these pit stops are often the best example of teamwork in the sport. Aside from the skill and muscle memory of the pit crew members, other teammates contribute by modifying parts and equipment so they can be changed out in less time. In Sprint Cup racing, NASCAR's highest designation, pit stops can happen in less than twenty seconds![5]

Sprint Cup winner Jimmie Johnson cites the importance of cohesive teamwork even before a car is assembled and tested on the track. "If you really know each other then, you know what each other is looking for, you've built that foundation and belief on the teammates [and] the engineers, you can split those hairs and get it right."[6]

Formula One

The Formula One drivers, team members, and fans have one quality that sets them above all other racing participants: the need for speed. Formula One fields the fastest circuit racing cars in the world, screaming down the track at top speeds as high as 225 miles per hour. Unlike in other racing sports, Formula One teams are required to build their own chassis. Although teams procure specialized engines from specific manufacturers, they are primarily responsible for building their cars from the ground up.

Each formula has its own set of rules that eligible cars must meet (*Formula One* being the fastest of these designations). The McLaren team, one of the most successful in Formula One, and former McLaren engineering director Paddy Lowe understand the importance of teamwork. Speaking on the challenge of incorporating a new component into an existing car, Lowe noted, "You have to factor in the skill of the team to work together in a very short period of time to push in a completely different direction; to understand all the different issues. The reliability, the performance, the skills of the team, all the tools they've created over the years—they all came through to our profit. Everybody moves seamlessly. They know what they've got to do."[7]

Former BMW Motorsport Director Mario Theissen put it simply: "Teamwork is the key to success," he said. "Of course the basis is formed by a competitive technical package, but without a well-integrated, highly motivated team, even the best car will not achieve prolonged success."[8]

Rally Car

Whereas NASCAR and Formula One racers speed around a paved track, rally car racing frequently heads off the circuit and into territory that would make most any NASCAR driver step on the brakes: Finnish rallies feature long, treacherous stretches of ice and snow. The famed French *Méditerranée-le Cap* ran 10,000 miles from the Mediterranean to South Africa. The reputed Baja 1000 Rally ran the length of the Baja California peninsula, largely over deserts without a road in sight.

In rally car racing, drivers race against the clock instead of each other. Races generally consist of several stages that the driver must compete as quickly as possible, and the winning driver completes all stages in the least amount of time.[9]

You could argue that of all racing sports, rally drivers are the most reliant on teamwork to win. Unlike other forms of circuit racing, the driver is not only not racing on a fixed track, but also does not get to see the course before the race begins. Instead, drivers are wholly reliant on a teammate, the navigator, for information on upcoming terrain. Part coach and part copilot, the navigator relies on page notes (detailed information on the sharpness of turns and the steepness of gradients) to keep the driver on course from the passenger seat.[10]

Turkish driver Burcu Çetinkaya had already made a name for herself as a successful snowboarder before deciding to take up rally car racing at the age of twenty-four. She says: "The thing that hooked me about rally driving was working together with a team for a common goal with nature working against you," she said. "I love cars, first of all—I grew up with them and I love every part of them. And I love competition. I have been competing all my life. In a rally, these things come together: nature, competition, teamwork and cars."[11]

One Isn't Enough

Even though they receive the lion's share of the notoriety and adulation, racing drivers are only one member of a larger team, where every team member's performance contributes to the team's success. The best drivers don't let the fame go to their heads. As Jeff Gordon—who knows a thing or two about success—put it, "The only way I can do my job correctly is to be totally clear in my mind and have 100% confidence in every person's job that went into this team so that they can have 100% confidence in what I'm doing as a driver."[12]

Case Analysis Questions

1. Discussion   What formal and informal groups would you expect to find in a complete racing team? What roles could each play in helping the driver toward a winning season?

2. Discussion   Racing teams and their leaders make lots of decisions—from the pressures of race day to the routines of everyday team management. When and in what situations are these decisions made by authority rule, minority rule, majority rule, consensus, or unanimity? How do these decision-making approaches fit certain times and situations but not others? Defend your answer.

3. Problem Solving   Assume you have been retained as a team-building consultant by a famous racing team pit crew whose performance fell badly during the prior season. Design and explain a series of team-building activities you will use to engage team members to strengthen their trust in each other and improve their individual and collective efforts.

4. Further Research   Choose a racing team of interest to you. Research the team, its personnel, and its performance in the most recent racing season. Try to answer this question: What accounts for this team's success or lack of success—driver talent, technology, teamwork, ownership/leadership, or all four? List at least three lessons from your analysis of the racing team that might be valuable and transferable to teams and organizations in any setting.

Case 18   Snapchat | Snap the Story of the Moment

We are in the midst of a constantly shifting technology landscape, and this pace of change is leading to an extremely fluid intersection of culture, communication, social media, and business. There may be no other social media company that so closely captures this intersection as Snapchat, at least for the moment.

It's About the Now

There has always been a generation gap separating how people in distinct generations interact with one another, develop social expectations, talk, dress, think, and act. And, today, there are differences in how each generation uses, thinks, and interacts with technology. Generation X—which is closest in proximity to the millennial generation—did not grow up with the technologies that predominate the current social media landscape.[1] Neither did the baby boomers. In contrast, millennials were born into a world where the Internet was already widespread, and the use of social media was second nature. Although more and more baby boomers and gen-Xers are logging on to Facebook, the popular site has seen a decline in popularity among millennials. (Twitter has also seen a decline among younger users.)[2] Snapchat is different from more "traditional" social media sites because its content—Snaps—is, by definition, transitory. Send a Snap, and it's gone in 10 seconds. Add a Snap to your Story, and it's there for 24 hours. But, either way, the content disappears.[3] Snapchat is all about the "now"—what is happening at this moment.

The Changing Nature of Social Media

Historically, photographs—pictures—have been used, and still continue to be used, in many situations to capture important moments in people's lives. Today, particularly within social media contexts, the use of pictures has changed. This is most especially so with Snapchat, where pictures (and videos) are used to "talk." With the predominantly desktop technologies of a decade ago, pictures were primarily about accumulation of history. People took pictures, saved some to their profile, and gave "friends" the opportunity to comment or "like" the image. Over time, these images became the historic content of people's online identities. The Facebook timeline reflects this idea of historic identity.[3]

Today, we have moved away from static desktop engagement with social media in unprecedented numbers. Ninety-five percent of

Americans today own a mobile phone of some kind, and 77% own a smartphone.[4] This saturation-level ownership has changed how we collectively engage social media. As CEO Evan Spiegel explains, "Now the mobile phone has really empowered this idea of instant expression, which is really showing someone where you are and how you're feeling in the moment."[5] The images Snapchatters send ultimately provide a peek into their identity, which is at the core of social media. The images provide a signal of "who I am right now." Pictures no longer accumulate to tell a story; instead, stories are ones that Snapchatters tell about themselves in real time.

A Cultural Phenomenon—A Visual Revolution?

As of June 2018, there were 191 million active daily users of Snapchat. As of 2019, there were 80 million active daily users in North America alone. Snapchatters send an estimated 3 billion snaps per day every day. This is equivalent to one third of the total number of people on the entire planet. Thirty percent of millennial Internet users in the United States regularly access Snapchat.[6] What these numbers suggest is that Snapchat is more than simply a niche phenomenon. Snapchat—currently trading at approximately $15 per share and having a current market valuation of approximately $13 billion, with revenues in excess of $1 billion in 2018—is being viewed as a trend, not a fad. We are reading fewer books. We are becoming a more visual society. Facebook, video ads, YouTube—more and more people are looking for content delivered via images such as pictures and videos.[7] The way we communicate with each other is changing, and Snapchat is at the forefront of this change, providing a convenient way for people to share the details of their lives in stories with images that last 10 seconds. What does this change in how we communicate mean for business?

Case Analysis Questions

1. Discussion   As a society, we are reading less and watching/viewing more. What implications does this shifting societal trend have for the ways that leaders communicate within their organizations? How managers communicate with employees? How organizations communicate with customers? What are the implications of these trending patterns for how organizations train employees? Motivate employees? Can you be as detailed in video-based communication as you can via written communication? What are some of the benefits of shifting communication patterns? What are some of the potential liabilities?

2. Problem Solving   You've been hired by Snapchat's CEO Evan Spiegel to explain to gen-Xers (your parents) and baby boomers (your grandparents) how to use Snapchat, how to make it part of their everyday lives, and how it could be useful to them at work. How would you describe the way you, personally, use Snapchat? How would you explain how this way of communicating can be applied across generational lines? What kinds of analogies might you use to describe Snapchat? How is it different from/or better than either Facebook or Twitter? Why does Snapchat more effectively capture the way that millennials communicate, and why should this also apply for different generations of potential users? Be as specific as possible.

3. Further Research   Look into the newest social media companies discussed in the business press as potential or likely IPOs over the next year or so. What are the attributes of the companies getting the most "buzz" in the press"? Do you see any common characteristics across these companies? Are there any that stand out? If you had to specify what, precisely, differentiates companies getting the most current buzz, which standout attributes would you choose? Are there more "video-driven" companies out there today? Does Snapchat have an emerging rival? In what ways does Snapchat represent a specific threat to larger rival Facebook? Is Facebook positioned to compete in the "this is me now" space currently dominated by Snapchat? If not, what could Facebook do on the acquisition side to remain competitive moving forward?

Self-Test Answers

Chapter 1

1. d **2.** c **3.** a **4.** b **5.** a **6.** a **7.** c **8.** a **9.** b
10. b **11.** c **12.** a **13.** b **14.** c **15.** c

16. Managers must value people and respect subordinates as mature, responsible, adult human beings. This is part of their ethical and social responsibility as persons to whom others report at work. The work setting should be organized and managed to respect the rights of people and their human dignity. Included among the expectations for ethical behavior would be actions to protect individual privacy, provide freedom from sexual harassment, and offer safe and healthy job conditions. Failure to do so is socially irresponsible. It may also cause productivity losses due to dissatisfaction and poor work commitments.

17. The manager is held accountable by her boss for performance results of her work unit. The manager must answer to her boss for unit performance. By the same token, the manager's subordinates must answer to her for their individual performance. They are accountable to her.

18. If the glass ceiling effect were to operate in a given situation, it would act as a hidden barrier to advancement beyond a certain level. Managers controlling promotions and advancement opportunities in the firm would not give them to African American candidates, regardless of their capabilities. Although the newly hired graduates might advance for a time, sooner or later their upward progress in the firm would be halted by this invisible barrier. Although unstated and perhaps even unrecognized as such by top management, this would be outright discrimination against the African Americans in this firm.

19. Globalization means that the countries and peoples of the world are increasingly interconnected and that business firms increasingly cross national boundaries in acquiring resources, getting work accomplished, and selling their products. This internationalization of work will affect most everyone in the new economy. People will be working with others from different countries, working in other countries, and certainly buying and using products and services produced in whole or in part in other countries. As countries become more interdependent economically, products are sold and resources purchased around the world, and business strategies increasingly target markets in more than one country.

20. One approach to this question is through the framework of essential management skills offered by Katz. At the first level of management, technical skills are important, and I would feel capable in this respect. However, I would expect to learn and refine these skills through my work experiences.

Human skills, the ability to work well with other people, will also be very important. Given the diversity anticipated for this team, I will need good human skills. Included here would be my emotional intelligence, or the ability to understand my emotions and those of others when I am interacting with them. I will also have a leadership responsibility to help others on the team develop and utilize these skills so that the team itself can function effectively.

Finally, I would expect opportunities to develop my conceptual or analytical skills in anticipation of higher-level appointments. In terms of personal development, I should recognize that the conceptual skills will increase in importance relative to the technical skills as I move upward in management responsibility. The fact that the members of the team will be diverse, with some of different demographic and cultural backgrounds from my own, will only increase the importance of my abilities in the human skills area.

It will be a challenge to embrace and value differences to create the best work experience for everyone and to fully value everyone's potential contributions to the audits we will be doing. Conceptually I will need to understand the differences and try to utilize them to solve problems faced by the team, but in human relationships I will need to excel at keeping the team spirit alive and keeping everyone committed to working well together over the life of our projects.

Chapter 2

1. c **2.** b **3.** d **4.** a **5.** a **6.** b **7.** a **8.** c **9.** a
10. a **11.** c **12.** a **13.** d **14.** c **15.** b

16. Theory Y assumes that people are capable of taking responsibility and exercising self-direction and control in their work. The notion of self-fulfilling prophecies is that managers who hold these assumptions will act in ways that encourage workers to display these characteristics, thus confirming and reinforcing the original assumptions. The emphasis on greater participation and involvement in the modern workplace is an example of Theory Y assumptions in practice. Presumably, by valuing participation and involvement, managers will create self-fulfilling prophecies in which workers behave this way in response to being treated with respect. The result is a positive setting where everyone gains.

17. According to the deficit principle, a satisfied need is not a motivator of behavior. The social need will only motivate if it is not present, or in deficit. According to the progression principle, people move step-by-step up Maslow's hierarchy as they strive to satisfy needs. For example, once the social need is satisfied, the esteem need will be activated.

18. Contingency thinking takes an "if–then" approach to situations. It seeks to modify or adapt management approaches to fit the needs of each situation. An example would be to give more customer contact responsibility to workers who want to satisfy social needs at work, while giving more supervisory responsibilities to those who want to satisfy their esteem or ego needs.

19. The external environment is the source of the resources an organization needs to operate. In order to continue to obtain these resources, the organization must be successful in selling its goods and services to customers. If customer feedback is negative, the organization must make adjustments or risk losing the support needed to obtain important resources.

20. A bureaucracy operates with a strict hierarchy of authority, promotion based on competency and performance, formal rules and procedures, and written documentation. Enrique can do all of these things in his store, since the situation is probably quite stable and most work requirements are routine and predictable. However, bureaucracies are quite rigid and may deny employees the opportunity to make decisions on their own. Enrique must be careful to meet the needs of the workers and not to make the mistake—identified by Argyris—of failing to treat them as mature adults. While remaining well organized, the store manager should still be able to help workers meet higher-order esteem and self-fulfillment needs, as well as assume responsibility consistent with McGregor's Theory Y assumptions.

Chapter 3

1. b **2.** a **3.** d **4.** c **5.** c **6.** d **7.** b **8.** a **9.** b **10.** d **11.** c **12.** d **13.** b **14.** d **15.** c

16. The individualism view is that ethical behavior is that which best serves long-term interests. The justice view is that ethical behavior is fair and equitable in its treatment of people.

17. The rationalizations are believing that: (1) The behavior is not really illegal, (2) the behavior is really in everyone's best interests, (3) no one will find out, and (4) the organization will protect you.

18. The socioeconomic view of corporate social responsibility argues that investing in socially responsible behavior is in a firm's long-run best interest. It should be good for profits, it creates a positive public image, it helps avoid government regulation, it meets public expectations, and it is an ethical obligation. In contrast, the classical view of social responsibility is that the only obligation of the firm is to produce profits. This is what should drive executive decision making, and direct expenditures to pursue socially responsible activities are wasteful. The argument is that by pursuing profits the firm will do what society wants most in the long run because, if it doesn't, profits will suffer as customers abandon the firm and its products. The market, in other words, is the arbiter of what society wants.

19. Management scholar Archie Carroll describes the immoral, amoral, and moral manager this way: An immoral manager does bad things on purpose, choosing to behave unethically. The amoral manager does bad things sometimes, but this is not intentional or calculated; it happens because the amoral manager just doesn't incorporate ethics into his or her analysis of the situation. The moral manager, by contrast, always includes ethics as a criterion for evaluating his or her approach to decisions and situations. This manager strives to act ethically and considers ethical behavior a personal goal.

20. The manager could make a decision based on any one of the strategies. As an obstructionist, the manager may assume that Bangladesh needs the business and

that it is a local matter as to who will be employed to make the gloves. As a defensive strategy, the manager may decide to require the supplier to meet the minimum employment requirements under Bangladeshi law. Both of these approaches represent cultural relativism. As an accommodation strategy, the manager may require that the supplier go beyond local laws and meet standards set by equivalent laws in the United States. A proactive strategy would involve the manager in trying to set an example by operating in Bangladesh only with suppliers who not only meet local standards, but also actively support the education of children in the communities in which they operate. These latter two approaches would be examples of universalism.

Chapter 4

1. a **2.** b **3.** b **4.** c **5.** b **6.** d **7.** a **8.** b **9.** c **10.** d **11.** d **12.** a **13.** c **14.** d **15.** b

16. When it comes to organizational stakeholders, the list should always begin with customers and suppliers to establish the output/input players in the value chain. Employees should be included as well as shareholders/investors to identify the interests of the "producers" and the "owners." Given the significance of sustainability, it is important to include society at large and future generations in the stakeholder map; it is also important to include the local communities in which the organization operates. Beyond these basic map components, the stakeholders for any given organization will include a broad mix of people, groups, and organizations from regulators to activist organizations to government agencies, and more.

17. To make "sustainability" part of any goal statement or objective for an organization, the basic definition should reflect the concept of sustainable development. That is, the organization should act in ways that while making use of the environment to produce things of value today the potential for that environment to meet the needs of future generations is also being protected and ideally being enhanced.

18. Product innovations affect what goods and services an organization offers to its customers. Process innovations affect how the organization goes about its daily work in producing goods and services. Business model innovations affect the way the organization makes money and adds value to society.

19. Reverse innovation means finding innovations in alternative settings such as emerging markets and moving them into uses in established markets. An example would be portable and low-cost medical diagnostic equipment developed in markets like India and China and then brought to the United States and sold there.

20. First of all it sounds like a good idea to have a Chief Sustainability Officer, or CSO, in order to focus attention on sustainability goals and also bring some point of accountability at the senior executive level for their accomplishment. In terms of the job description, I would argue that things like this would need to be reflected. First, there should be some acknowledgment of the "triple bottom line" of economic, social, and environmental performance. Second, there should be a clear focus on sustainable development in respect to moving the organization forward in ways that while making use of the environment and its resources, the capacity of the environment to nurture and serve future generations is also being protected. This sets the foundation for further priorities or objectives to be set in the areas of pushing for green management practices that support sustainability in all aspects of an organization's operations. And finally, there should be a responsibility to serve as the "champion" for sustainable innovations that advance the capability of the organization to be sustainable by green products, green processes, and even green business models.

Chapter 5

1. c **2.** c **3.** b **4.** d **5.** a **6.** a **7.** d **8.** c **9.** a **10.** d **11.** d **12.** a **13.** c **14.** c **15.** c

16. The relationship between a global corporation and a host country should be mutually beneficial. Sometimes, however, host countries complain that MNCs take unfair advantage of them and do not include them in the benefits of their international operations. The complaints against MNCs include taking excessive profits out of the host country, hiring the best local labor, not respecting local laws and customs, and dominating the local economy. Engaging in corrupt practices is another important concern.

17. The power-distance dimension of national culture reflects the degree to which members of a society accept status and authority inequalities. Since organizations are hierarchies with power varying from top to bottom, the way power differences are viewed from one setting to the next is an important management issue. Relations between managers and subordinates, or team leaders and team members, will be very different in high-power-distance cultures than in low-power-distance ones. The significance of these differences is most evident in international operations, when a manager from a high-power-distance culture has to perform in a low-power-distance one, or vice versa. In both cases, the cultural differences can cause problems as the manager deals with local workers.

18. A tight culture is one in which clear norms exist for social behavior and members know that deviance from these norms will not be tolerated. There are both norms and a high degree of conformity to those norms. In a loose culture the norms and social expectations are often general and ambiguous. Individuals tend to behave with independence and in recognition that deviation is generally tolerated.

19. For each region of the world you should identify a major economic theme, issue, or element. For example: Europe—the European Union should be discussed for its economic significance to member countries and to outsiders; the Americas—NAFTA should be discussed for its importance to Mexico, the United States, and Canada, and also for implications in political debates within these countries; Asia—the Asia-Pacific Economic Forum should be identified as a platform for growing regional economic cooperation among a very economically powerful group of countries, including China; Africa—the nonracial democracy in South Africa should be cited as an example of growing foreign investor interest in the countries of Africa.

20. Kim must recognize that the cultural differences between the United States and Japan may affect the success of group-oriented work practices such as quality circles and work teams. The United States was the most individualistic culture in Hofstede's study of national cultures; Japan is much more collectivist. Group practices such as the quality circle and teams are natural and consistent with the Japanese culture. When introduced into a more individualistic culture, these same practices might cause difficulties or require some time for workers to get used to them. At the very least, Kim should proceed with caution; discuss ideas for the new practices with the workers before making any changes; and then monitor the changes closely so that adjustments can be made to improve them as the workers gain familiarity with them and have suggestions of their own.

Chapter 6

1. c **2.** a **3.** b **4.** b **5.** b **6.** a **7.** d **8.** a **9.** d **10.** b **11.** a **12.** b **13.** c **14.** c **15.** d

16. Entrepreneurship is rich with diversity. It is an avenue for business entry and career success that is pursued by many women and members of minority groups. Data show that almost 40% of U.S. businesses are owned by women. Many report leaving other employment because they had limited opportunities. For them, entrepreneurship made available the opportunities for career success that they had lacked. Minority-owned businesses are one of the fastest-growing sectors, with the growth rates highest for Hispanic-owned, Asian-owned, and African American–owned businesses, in that order.

17. The three stages in the life cycle of an entrepreneurial firm are birth, breakthrough, and maturity. In the birth stage, the leader is challenged to get customers, establish a market, and find the money needed to keep the business going. In the breakthrough stage, the challenges shift to becoming and staying profitable, and managing growth. In the maturity stage, a leader is more focused on revising/maintaining a good business strategy and more generally managing the firm for continued success, and possibly for more future growth.

18. The limited partnership form of small business ownership consists of a general partner and one or more "limited partners." The general partner(s) play an active role in managing and operating the business; the limited partners do not. All contribute resources of some value to the partnership for the conduct of the business. The advantage of any partnership form is that the partners may share in profits, but their potential for losses is limited by the size of their original investments.

19. A venture capitalist, often a business, makes a living by investing in and taking large ownership interests in fledgling companies, with the goal of large financial gains eventually, when the company is sold. An angel investor is an individual who is willing to make a financial investment in return for some ownership in the new firm.

20. My friend is right—it takes a lot of forethought and planning to prepare the launch of a new business venture. In response to the question of how to ensure that I am really being customer-focused, I would ask and answer for myself the following questions. In all cases I would try to frame my business

model so that the answers are realistic, but still push my business toward a strong customer orientation. The "customer" questions might include: "Who are my potential customers? What market niche am I shooting for? What do the customers in this market really want? How do these customers make purchase decisions? How much will it cost to produce and distribute my product/service to these customers? How much will it cost to attract and retain customers?" After preparing an overall executive summary, which includes a commitment to this customer orientation, I would address the following areas in writing up my initial business plan: a company description—mission, owners, and legal form—as well as an industry analysis, product and services description, marketing description and strategy, staffing model, financial projections with cash flows, and capital needs.

Chapter 7

1. c **2.** b **3.** c **4.** a **5.** a **6.** c **7.** c **8.** b **9.** a **10.** c **11.** b **12.** c **13.** a **14.** b **15.** d

16. An optimizing decision is one that represents the absolute "best" choice of alternatives. It is selected from a set of all known alternatives. A satisficing decision selects the first alternative that offers a "satisfactory" choice, not necessarily the absolute best choice. It is selected from a limited or incomplete set of alternatives.

17. The ethics of a decision can be checked with the "spotlight" question: "How would you feel if your family found out?" "How would you feel if this were published in the local newspaper?" Also, one can test the decision by evaluating it on four criteria: (1) Utility—does it satisfy all stakeholders? (2) Rights—does it respect everyone's rights? (3) Justice—is it consistent with fairness and justice? (4) Caring—does it meet responsibilities for caring?

18. A manager using systematic thinking is going to approach problem solving in a logical and rational way. The tendency will be to proceed in a linear, step-by-step fashion, handling one issue at a time. A manager using intuitive thinking will be more spontaneous and open in problem solving. He or she may jump from one stage in the process to another and deal with many different issues simultaneously.

19. It almost seems contradictory to say that one can prepare for a crisis, but it is possible. The concept of crisis management is used to describe how managers and others prepare for unexpected high-impact events that threaten an organization's health and future. Crisis management involves both anticipating possible crises and preparing teams and plans ahead of time for how to handle them if they do occur. Many organizations today, for example, are developing crisis management plans to deal with terrorism and cyber attacks.

20. This is what I would say in the mentoring situation: continuing developments in information technology are changing the work setting for most employees. An important development for the traditional white-collar worker falls in the area of office automation—the use of computers and related technologies to facilitate everyday office work. In the "electronic office" of today and tomorrow, you should be prepared to work with and take full advantage of the following: smart workstations supported by desktop computers; voice messaging systems, whereby computers take dictation, answer the telephone, and relay messages; database and word processing systems that allow storage, access, and manipulation of data, as well as the preparation of reports; electronic mail systems that send mail and data from computer to computer; electronic bulletin boards for posting messages; and computer conferencing and video-conferencing that allow people to work with one another every day over distance. These are among the capabilities of the new workplace. To function effectively, you must be prepared not only to use these systems to full advantage, but also to stay abreast of new developments as they emerge in the market.

Chapter 8

1. d **2.** a **3.** a **4.** d **5.** b **6.** c **7.** a **8.** d **9.** a **10.** b **11.** a **12.** c **13.** c **14.** d **15.** c

16. The five steps in the formal planning process are: (1) Define your objectives, (2) determine where you stand relative to objectives, (3) develop premises about future conditions, (4) identify and choose among action alternatives to accomplish objectives, and (5) implement action plans and evaluate results.

17. Benchmarking is the use of external standards to help evaluate one's own situation and develop ideas and directions for improvement. The bookstore owner/manager might visit other bookstores in other towns that are known for their success. By observing and studying the operations of those stores and then comparing her store to them, the owner/manager can develop plans for future action.

18. Planning helps improve focus for organizations and for individuals. Essential to the planning process is identifying your objectives and specifying exactly where it is you hope to get in the future. Having a clear sense of direction helps keep us on track by avoiding getting sidetracked on things that might not contribute to accomplishing our objectives. It also helps us to find discipline in stopping periodically to assess how well we are doing. With a clear objective, present progress can be realistically evaluated and efforts refocused on accomplishing the objective.

19. Very often plans fail because the people who make the plans aren't the same ones who must implement them. When people who will be implementing are allowed to participate in the planning process, at least two positive results may happen that help improve implementation: (1) Through involvement they better understand the final plans, and (2) through involvement they become more committed to making those plans work.

20. I would begin the speech by describing the importance of goal alignment as an integrated planning and control approach. I would also clarify that the key elements are objectives and participation. Any objectives should be clear, measurable, and time defined. In addition, these objectives should be set with the full involvement and participation of the employees; they should not be set by the manager and then told to the employees. That understood, I would describe how each business manager should jointly set objectives with each of his or her employees and jointly review progress toward their accomplishment. I would suggest that the employees should work on the required activities while staying in communication with their managers. The managers in turn should provide any needed support or assistance to their employees. This whole process could be formally recycled at least twice per year.

Chapter 9

1. a **2.** b **3.** d **4.** b **5.** b **6.** b **7.** d **8.** b **9.** b **10.** c **11.** a **12.** b **13.** c **14.** c **15.** c

16. The four steps in the control process are: (1) Establish objectives and standards, (2) measure actual performance, (3) compare actual performance with objectives and standards, and (4) take necessary action.

17. Feedforward control involves the careful selection of system inputs to ensure that outcomes are of the desired quality and up

to all performance standards. In the case of a local bookstore, one of the major points of influence over performance and customer satisfaction is the relationship between the customers and the store's employees who serve them. Thus, a good example of feedforward control is exercising great care when the manager hires new employees and then trains them to work according to the store's expectations.

18. Douglas McGregor's concept of Theory Y involves the assumption that people can be trusted to exercise self-control in their work. This is the essence of internal control—people controlling their own work by taking personal responsibility for results. If managers approach work with McGregor's Theory Y assumptions, they will, according to him, promote more self-control—or internal control—by people at work.

19. The four questions to ask when developing a balanced scorecard for inclusion on an executive dashboard are: (1) *Financial Performance*—To improve financially, how should we appear to our shareholders? (2) *Customer Satisfaction*—To achieve our vision, how should we appear to our customers? (3) *Internal Process Improvement*—To satisfy our customers and shareholders, at what internal business processes should we excel? (4) *Innovation and Learning*—To achieve our vision, how will we sustain our ability to change and improve?

20. A very large number of activities are required to complete a new student center building on a college campus. Among them, one might expect the following to be core requirements: (1) land surveys and planning permissions from local government, (2) architect plans developed and approved, (3) major subcontractors hired, (4) site excavation completed, (5) building exterior completed, (6) building interior completed and furnishings installed. Use the figure from the chapter as a guide for developing your CPM/PERT diagram.

Chapter 10

1. a **2.** b **3.** c **4.** d **5.** b **6.** c **7.** a **8.** c **9.** b **10.** c **11.** a **12.** c **13.** d **14.** b **15.** a

16. A corporate strategy sets long-term direction for an enterprise as a whole. Functional strategies set directions so that business functions such as marketing and manufacturing support the overall corporate strategy.

17. A SWOT analysis is useful during strategic planning. It involves the analysis of organizational strengths and weaknesses, and of environmental opportunities and threats.

18. The focus strategy concentrates attention on a special market segment or niche. The differentiation strategy concentrates on building loyalty to a unique product or service.

19. Strategic leadership is the ability to create enthusiasm in people to participate in continuous change, performance enhancement, and the implementation of organizational strategies. The special qualities of the successful strategic leader include the ability to make trade-offs, create a sense of urgency, communicate the strategy, and engage others in continuous learning about the strategy and its performance responsibilities.

20. Porter's competitive strategy model involves the possible use of three alternative strategies: differentiation, cost leadership, and focus. In this situation, the larger department store seems better positioned to follow the cost leadership strategy. This means that Kim may want to consider the other two alternatives.

A differentiation strategy would involve trying to distinguish Kim's products from those of the larger store. This might involve a "Made in America" theme, or an emphasis on leather, canvas, or some other type of clothing material. A focus strategy might specifically target college students and try to respond to their tastes and needs, rather than those of the larger community population. This might involve special orders and other types of individualized services for the college student market.

Chapter 11

1. b **2.** a **3.** b **4.** a **5.** a **6.** c **7.** d **8.** b **9.** b **10.** b **11.** c **12.** b **13.** b **14.** c **15.** b

16. The functional structure is prone to problems of internal coordination. One symptom may be that the different functional areas, such as marketing and manufacturing, are not working well together. This structure also is slow to respond to changing environmental trends and challenges. If the firm finds that its competitors are getting to market faster with new and better products, this is another potential indicator that the functional structure is not supporting operations properly.

17. A network structure often involves one organization "contracting out" aspects of its operations to other organizations that specialize in them. The example used in the text was of a company that contracted out its mailroom services. Through the formation of networks of contracts, the organization

is reduced to a core of essential employees whose expertise is concentrated in the primary business areas. The contracts are monitored and maintained in the network to allow the overall operations of the organization to continue, even though they are not directly accomplished by full-time employees.

18. The term "contingency" is used in management to indicate that management strategies and practices should be tailored to fit the unique needs of specific situations. There is no universal solution that fits all problems and circumstances. Thus, in organizational design, contingency thinking must be used to identify and implement particular organizational points in time. What works well at one point in time may not work well at another, as the environment and other conditions change. For example, the more complex, variable, and uncertain the elements in the environment, the more difficult it is for the organization to operate. This situation calls for a more organic design. In a stable and more certain environment, the mechanistic design is appropriate, because operations are more routine and predictable.

19. Several options for answering this question are described in the chapter.

20. Faisal must first have confidence in the two engineers—he must trust them and respect their capabilities. Second, he must have confidence in himself, trusting his own judgment to give up some work and allow the others to do it. Third, he should follow the rules of effective delegation. These include being very clear on what must be accomplished by each engineer. Their responsibilities should be clearly understood. He must also give them the authority and resources to act in order to fulfill their responsibility, especially in relationship to the other engineers. He must also not forget his own final accountability for the results. He should remain in control and, through communication, make sure that work proceeds as planned.

Chapter 12

1. b **2.** a **3.** d **4.** a **5.** b **6.** a **7.** b **8.** b **9.** d **10.** c **11.** b **12.** c **13.** c **14.** d **15.** b

16. Core values indicate important beliefs that underlie organizational expectations about the behavior and contributions of members. Sample values for high-performance organizations might include expressed commitments to honesty and integrity, innovation, customer service, quality, and respect for people.

17. Subcultures are important in organizations because of the many aspects of diversity found in the workforce today. Although working in the same organization and sharing the same organizational culture, members differ in subculture affiliations based on such aspects as gender, age, sexual orientation, religious and ethnic differences, as well as with respect to occupational and functional affiliations. It is important to understand how subculture differences may influence working relationships. For example, a 40-year-old manager of 20-year-old workers must understand that the values and behaviors of the younger workforce may not be totally consistent with what she believes in, and vice versa.

18. Lewin's three phases of planned change and the relevant change leadership responsibilities are unfreezing—preparing a system for change; changing—moving or creating change in a system; and refreezing—tabilizing and reinforcing change once it has occurred. In addition, we might also talk about an additional or parallel phase of "improvising." This calls for change leadership that is good at gathering feedback, listening to resistance, and making constructive modifications as the change is in progress to smooth its implementation and ensure that what is implemented is a best fit for the circumstances and people involved.

19. Use of force-coercion as a strategy of planned change is limited by the likelihood of compliance being the major outcome. People comply with force only so long as it remains real, visible, and likely, but they have no personal commitment to the behavior. So, when the force goes away, so does the behavior. Also, a manager who relies on forcing people to get changes made is likely to be viewed negatively and suffer from additional negative halo effects in other work with them. Rational persuasion and shared power are likely to have a more long-lasting impact on behavior because employees respond to the change strategy by internalization of the value of the behavior being encouraged. Because of this commitment, the influence on their actions is more likely to be long-lasting rather than temporary as in the case of force-coercion.

20. I disagree with this statement, because a strong organizational or corporate culture can be a positive influence on any organization, large or small. Also, issues of diversity, inclusiveness, and multiculturalism apply as well. In fact, such things as a commitment to pluralism and respect for diversity should be part of the core values and distinguishing features of the culture of every organization. The woman working for the large company is mistaken in thinking that the concepts do not apply to her friend's small business. In fact, the friend—as owner and perhaps founder of the business—should be working hard to establish the values and other elements that will create a strong and continuing culture and respect for diversity. Employees of any organization should have core organizational values to serve as reference points for their attitudes and behavior. The rites and rituals of everyday organizational life also are important ways to recognize positive accomplishments and add meaning to the employment relationship. It may even be that the friend's roles as diversity leader and creator and sponsor of the corporate culture are magnified in the small business setting. As the owner and manager, she is visible every day to all employees. How she acts will have a great impact on any "culture."

Chapter 13

1. a **2.** c **3.** a **4.** d **5.** b **6.** d **7.** c **8.** d **9.** d **10.** b **11.** a **12.** b **13.** a **14.** d **15.** d

16. Internal recruitment deals with job candidates who already know the organization well. It also is a strong motivator because it communicates to everyone the opportunity to advance in the organization through hard work. External recruitment may allow the organization to obtain expertise not available internally. It also brings in employees with new and fresh viewpoints who are not biased by previous experience in the organization.

17. Orientation activities introduce a new employee to the organization and the work environment. This is a time when individuals may develop key attitudes and when performance expectations also will be established. Good orientation communicates positive attitudes and expectations and reinforces the desired organizational culture. It formally introduces the individual to important policies and procedures that everyone is expected to follow.

18. The graphic rating scale simply asks a supervisor to rate an employee on an established set of criteria, such as quantity of work or attitude toward work. This leaves a lot of room for subjectivity and debate. The behaviorally anchored rating scale asks the supervisor to rate the employee on specific behaviors that have been identified as posi-

tively or negatively affecting performance in a given job. This is a more specific appraisal approach and leaves less room for debate and disagreement.

19. Mentoring is when a senior and experienced individual adopts a newcomer or more junior person with the goal of helping him or her develop into a successful worker. The mentor may or may not be the individual's immediate supervisor. The mentor meets with the individual and discusses problems, shares advice, and generally supports the individual's attempts to grow and perform. Mentors also are considered to be very useful for persons newly appointed to management positions.

20. As Sy's supervisor, you face a difficult but perhaps expected human resource management problem. Not only is Sy influential as an informal leader, he also has considerable experience on the job and with the company. Even though he is experiencing performance problems using the new computer system, there is no indication that he doesn't want to work hard and continue to perform for the company. Although retirement is an option, Sy also may be transferred, promoted, or simply terminated. The last response seems unjustified and may cause legal problems. Transferring Sy, with his agreement, to another position could be a positive move; promoting Sy to a supervisory position in which his experience and networks would be useful is another possibility. The key in this situation seems to be moving Sy out so that a computer-literate person can take over the job, while continuing to utilize Sy in a job that better fits his talents. Transfer and/or promotion should be actively considered, both in his and in the company's interest.

Chapter 14

1. d **2.** d **3.** b **4.** b **5.** a **6.** a **7.** b **8.** d **9.** a **10.** b **11.** b **12.** a **13.** a **14.** c **15.** a

16. Position power is based on reward; coercion, or punishment; and legitimacy, or formal authority. Managers, however, need to have more power than that made available to them by the position alone. Thus, they have to develop personal power through expertise, reference, and information and networking. This personal power is essential in helping managers to get things done beyond the scope of their position power alone.

17. The leader-participation model suggests that leadership effectiveness is determined in part by how well managers or leaders handle the many different problem or decision

situations that they face every day. Decisions can be made through individual or authority, consultative, or group-consensus approaches. No one of these decision methods is always the best; each is a good fit for certain types of situations. A good manager or leader is able to use each of these approaches and knows when each is the best approach to use in particular situations.

18. The three variables used in Fiedler's model to diagnose situational favorableness are: (1) position power—how much power the leader has in terms of rewards, punishments, and legitimacy; (2) leader–member relations—the quality of relationships between the leader and followers; and (3) task structure—the degree to which the task is either clear and well defined, or open-ended and more ambiguous.

19. Drucker says that good leaders have more than the "charisma" or "personality" being popularized in the concept of transformational leadership. He reminds us that good leaders work hard to accomplish some basic things in their everyday activities. These include: (1) establishing a clear sense of mission; (2) accepting leadership as a responsibility, not a rank; and (3) earning and keeping the respect of others.

20. In his new position, Marcel must understand that the transactional aspects of leadership are not sufficient to guarantee him long-term leadership effectiveness. He must move beyond the effective use of task-oriented and people-oriented behaviors and demonstrate through his personal qualities the capacity to inspire others. A charismatic leader develops a unique relationship with followers, in which they become enthusiastic, highly loyal, and high achievers. Marcel needs to work very hard to develop positive relationships with the team members. In those relationships he must emphasize high aspirations for performance accomplishments, enthusiasm, ethical behavior, integrity and honesty in all dealings, and a clear vision of the future. By working hard with this agenda and by allowing his personality to positively express itself in the team setting, Marcel should make continuous progress as an effective and a moral leader.

Chapter 15

1. c **2.** b **3.** d **4.** a **5.** c **6.** d **7.** b **8.** c **9.** a **10.** b **11.** d **12.** d **13.** c **14.** d **15.** c

16. A psychological contract is the individual's view of the inducements he or she expects to receive from the organization in return for his or her work contributions. The contract is healthy when the individual perceives that the inducements and contributions are fair and balanced.

17. Self-serving bias is the attribution tendency to blame the environment when things go wrong—"It's not my fault; 'they' caused all this mess." Fundamental attribution error is the tendency to blame others for problems that they have—"It's something wrong with 'you' that's causing the problem."

18. All the Big Five personality traits are relevant to the workplace. Consider the following basic examples. Extraversion suggests whether or not a person will reach out to relate and work well with others. Agreeableness suggests whether a person is open to the ideas of others and willing to go along with group decisions. Conscientiousness suggests whether or not someone can be depended on to meet commitments and perform agreed-on tasks. Emotional stability suggests whether someone will be relaxed and secure, or uptight and tense, in work situations. Openness to experience suggests whether or not someone will be open to new ideas or resistant to change.

19. The Type A personality is typical of people who bring stress on themselves by virtue of personal characteristics. These tend to be compulsive individuals who are uncomfortable waiting for things to happen, who try to do many things at once, and who generally move fast and have difficulty slowing down. Type A personalities can be stressful for both themselves and the people around them. Managers must be aware of Type A personality tendencies in their own behavior and among others with whom they work. Ideally, this awareness will help the manager take precautionary steps to best manage the stress caused by this personality type.

20. Scott needs to be careful. Although there is modest research support for the relationship between job satisfaction and performance, there is no guarantee that simply doing things to make his employees happier at work will cause them to be higher performers. Scott needs to take a broader perspective on this issue and his responsibilities as a manager. He should be interested in job satisfaction for his therapists and do everything he can to help them to experience it. But he should also be performance-oriented and should understand that performance is achieved through a combination of skills, support, and motivation. He should be helping the therapists to achieve and maintain high levels of job competency. He should also work with them to find out what obstacles they are facing and what support they need—

things that perhaps he can deal with on their behalf. All of this relates as well to research that performance can be a source of job satisfaction. Finally, Scott should make sure that the therapists believe they are being properly rewarded for their work, because research shows that rewards have an influence on both job satisfaction and job performance.

Chapter 16

1. c **2.** b **3.** d **4.** d **5.** b **6.** b **7.** a **8.** d **9.** b **10.** d **11.** c **12.** c **13.** a **14.** b **15.** d

16. People high in need for achievement will prefer work settings and jobs in which they have (1) challenging but achievable goals, (2) individual responsibility, and (3) performance feedback.

17. Participation is important to goal-setting theory because, in general, people tend to be more committed to the accomplishment of goals they have helped set. When people participate in the setting of goals, they also understand them better. Participation in goal setting improves goal acceptance and understanding.

18. Maslow, McClelland, and Herzberg would likely find common agreement regarding a set of "higher order" needs. For Maslow these are self-actualization and ego; they correspond with Alderfer's growth needs, and with McClelland's needs for achievement and power. Maslow's social needs link up with relatedness needs in Alderfer's theory and the need for affiliation in McClelland's theory. Maslow's safety needs correspond to Alderfer's existence needs. Herzberg's "satisfier-factors" correspond to satisfactions of Maslow's higher needs, Alderfer's growth needs, and McClelland's need for achievement.

19. The compressed workweek or 4–40 schedule offers employees the advantage of a three-day weekend. However, it can cause problems for employers in terms of ensuring that operations are covered adequately during the normal five workdays of the week. Labor unions may resist, and the compressed workweek will entail more complicated work scheduling. In addition, some employees find that the schedule is tiring and can cause family adjustment problems.

20. It has already been pointed out in the answer to question 16 that a person with a high need for achievement likes moderately challenging goals and performance feedback. Participation of both managers and subordinates in goal setting offers an opportunity to choose goals to which the subordinate will respond, and which also will serve the organization. Further, through goal setting managers and individual subordinates can identify performance standards or targets. The manager can positively reinforce progress toward these targets. Such reinforcement can serve as an indicator of progress to someone with a high need for achievement, satisfying their desire for performance feedback.

Chapter 17

1. d **2.** a **3.** b **4.** b **5.** c **6.** a **7.** b **8.** b **9.** a **10.** a **11.** d **12.** b **13.** b **14.** a **15.** a

16. Input factors can have a major impact on group effectiveness. In order to best prepare a group to perform effectively, a manager should make sure that the right people are put in the group (maximize available talents and abilities), that these people are capable of working well together (membership characteristics should promote good relationships), that the tasks are clear, and that the group has the resources and environment needed to perform up to expectations.

17. A group's performance can be analyzed according to the interaction between cohesiveness and performance norms. In a highly cohesive group, members tend to conform to group norms. Thus, when the performance norm is positive and cohesion is high, we can expect everyone to work hard to support the norm—high performance is likely. By the same token, high cohesion and a low performance norm will yield the opposite result—low performance is likely. With other combinations of norms and cohesion, the performance results will be more mixed.

18. The textbook lists several symptoms of groupthink, along with various strategies for avoiding groupthink. For example, a group whose members censor themselves from contributing "contrary" or "different" opinions and/or whose members keep talking about outsiders as "weak" or the "enemy" may be suffering from groupthink. This may be avoided or corrected, for example, by asking someone to be the "devil's advocate" for a meeting, and by inviting in an outside observer to help gather different viewpoints.

19. In a traditional work group, the manager or supervisor directs the group. In a self-managing team, the members of the team provide self-direction. They plan, organize, and evaluate their work, share tasks, and help one another develop skills; they may even make hiring decisions. A true self-managing team does not need the traditional "boss" or supervisor, because the team as a whole takes on traditional supervisory responsibilities.

20. Marcos is faced with a highly cohesive group whose members conform to a negative or low-performance norm. This is a difficult situation that is ideally resolved by changing the performance norm. In order to gain the group's commitment to a high-performance norm, Marcos should act as a positive role model for the norm. He must communicate the norm to the group clearly and positively and should not assume that everyone knows what he expects of them. He may also talk to the informal leader and gain his or her commitment to the norm. He might carefully reward high-performance behaviors within the group and may introduce new members with high-performance records and commitments. He might also hold group meetings in which performance standards and expectations are discussed, with an emphasis on committing to new high-performance directions. If his attempts to introduce a high-performance norm fail, Marcos may have to take steps to reduce group cohesiveness so that individual members can pursue higher-performance results without feeling bound by group pressures to restrict their performance.

Chapter 18

1. a **2.** b **3.** d **4.** d **5.** b **6.** b **7.** d **8.** b **9.** d **10.** b **11.** d **12.** c **13.** a **14.** d **15.** a

16. The manager's goal in active listening is to help the subordinate say what he or she really means. To do this, the manager should carefully listen for the content of what is being said, paraphrase or reflect back what the person appears to be saying, remain sensitive to nonverbal cues and feelings, and not be evaluative.

17. The relationship between conflict intensity and performance can be pictured as an inverted "U" curve. It shows that performance increases as conflict intensity increases from low to moderate levels. Conflict of moderate intensity creates the zone of constructive conflict, where its impact on performance is most positive. As conflict intensity moves into extreme levels, performance tends to decrease. This is the zone of destructive conflict. When conflict is too low, performance also may suffer.

18. Win–lose outcomes are likely when conflict is managed through high-assertiveness and low-cooperativeness styles. In this situation of competition, conflict is resolved by one person or group dominating another. Lose–lose outcomes occur when conflict is managed through avoidance (where nothing is resolved), and possibly when it is managed through compromise (where each party gives up something to the other). Win–win outcomes are associated mainly with problem solving and collaboration in conflict management, which result from high assertiveness and high cooperativeness.

19. In a negotiation, both substance and relationship goals are important. Substance goals relate to the content of the negotiation. A substance goal, for example, may relate to the final salary agreement between a job candidate and a prospective employer. Relationship goals relate to the quality of the interpersonal relationships among the negotiating parties. Relationship goals are important, because the negotiating parties most likely have to work together in the future. For example, if relationships are poor after a labor–management negotiation, the likelihood is that future problems will occur.

20. Kathryn can do a number of things to establish and maintain a system of upward communication for her department store branch. To begin, she should, as much as possible, try to establish a highly interactive style of management based on credibility and trust. Credibility is earned by building personal power through expertise and reference. In regard to credibility, she might set the tone for the department managers by practicing transparency and sharing information through open-book management. Once this pattern is established, trust will build between her and other store employees, and she should find that she learns a lot from interacting directly with them. Kathryn also should set up a formal communication structure, such as bimonthly store meetings, where she communicates store goals, results, and other issues to the staff and listens to them in return. An e-mail system where Kathryn and her staff can send messages would also be beneficial.

CPSIA information can be obtained
at www.ICGtesting.com
Printed in the USA
BVHW060812090223
657881BV00004B/6